ENVIRONMENTAL POLICY
IN THE 1990s

ENVIRONMENTAL POLICY IN THE 1990s

REFORM OR REACTION?

Third Edition

Edited by

Norman J. Vig
Carleton College

Michael E. Kraft
University of Wisconsin-Green Bay

A Division of Congressional Quarterly Inc.
Washington, D.C.

For
Nora, Jess, and Ted
Steve and Dave

Cover design: Paula Anderson

Third Printing

Library of Congress Cataloging-in-Publication Data

Environmental policy in the 1990s : reform or reaction? / edited by
  Norman J. Vig., Michael E. Kraft. -- 3rd ed.
    xvi, 416p.   : 24 cm.
    Includes bibliographical references and index.
    ISBN 1-56802-242-5. -- ISBN 1-56802-165-8 (pbk.)
    1. Environmental policy--United States.   2. United States-
  -Politics and government--1989–   I. Vig, Norman J.   II. Kraft,
  Michael E.
  GE180.E586   1997
  363.7'056'0973--DC20

                                                                      96-9490

Contents

I. Environmental Policy and Politics in Transition

II. Federal Institutions and Policy Change

III. Public Policy Dilemmas

IV. Toward Global Environmental Policies

V. Conclusion

Tables, Figures, and Boxes

Tables

Figures

Boxes

Preface

As the twenty-first century approaches, environmental policy is being challenged as never before. New demands worldwide for dealing with the risks of climate change, threats to biological diversity, and similar issues will force governments everywhere to seriously rethink policy strategies and find new ways to reconcile environmental and economic goals. Within the United States, a conservative Republican Congress elected in 1994 brought a markedly higher level of criticism of environmental programs and the agencies that implement them. The budget cuts imposed by Congress will hamper achievement of program goals that range from reducing public health risks from air and water pollution and toxic chemicals to protecting threatened ecosystems. They will also compel the Environmental Protection Agency (EPA), the Interior Department, and other agencies to adopt new approaches and to set program priorities in light of their limited resources and escalating demands for environmental protection. Similarly, states and communities will have to take greater responsibility for dealing with local and regional environmental problems, and the private sector will assume additional obligations of its own. As much as the debate over the environment has shifted in important ways in the 1990s, however, government and politics will continue to play crucial roles in shaping our environmental future.

When the first environmental decade was launched more than twenty-five years ago, protecting our air, water, and other natural resources seemed a relatively simple proposition. The polluters and exploiters of nature would be brought to heel by tough laws requiring them to clean up or get out of business within five or ten years. The sense of urgency that swept Congress in 1970 as it passed the Clean Air Act with scarcely a dissenting voice reflected the rise of one of the most dramatic popular movements in American history. Since then, despite ebbs and flows, the tide of public opinion favoring greater environmental protection has entered the mainstream of political life. But preserving the life-support systems of the planet now appears a far larger and more daunting task than anyone imagined a quarter-century ago.

Events in the 1990s have demonstrated the new demands and difficulties for environmentalism. In 1992 the largest international diplomatic conference ever held was convened in Río de Janeiro, Brazil, to address an enormous range of global environmental issues. That same year, Bill Clinton's election as president promised a renewed commitment to environmental protection in the United States. Yet the president was largely unsuccessful in implementing his agenda, and the new Republican Congress proposed major revisions to most of our national environmental legislation.

Translating symbolic commitments into effective action is no easy task. The making of public policy often resembles an awkward dance between idealistic ends and deficient means. The history of environmental protection is no exception. Implementing the major legislation of the 1970s on air and water pollution, hazardous waste, and preservation of public lands and other resources proved to be difficult and frustrating. Although genuine progress was made, few deadlines were met and results have fallen considerably short of expectations. At the same time, environmental protection has turned out to be a moving target. What appeared to be a relatively straightforward job of controlling a few key pollutants by mandating corrective technologies at the "end of the pipe" has become a far larger and more difficult task that may require fundamental changes in human behavior.

By the end of the 1970s it was evident that many of the most serious environmental problems had their origins in the massive use and careless disposal of industrial chemicals whose cumulative health and environmental effects were largely unknown. These second-generation problems required cleanup of thousands of abandoned dumps, leaking toxic waste sites, and military bases and production facilities under Superfund and other programs. By the end of the decade, these programs were plagued by growing controversy over the slow pace and escalating costs of cleanups. But by then a third generation of even more challenging ecological issues captured public attention: global climate change, deterioration of the ozone layer, tropical deforestation, extinction of species, and ocean and coastal pollution. The agenda for the twenty-first century is already crowded with issues that will take the greatest human ingenuity to resolve.

This book seeks to explain the most important developments in environmental policy and politics since the 1960s and to analyze the central issues that face us in the current decade. Like the first and second editions, it focuses on the underlying trends, institutional shortcomings, and policy dilemmas that all policy actors face in attempting to resolve environmental controversies. This edition contains four new chapters, and all other chapters have been revised and updated. We have also attempted to place the Clinton administration and the congressional agenda in the context of the ongoing debate over the cost and effectiveness of past environmental policies. As such, the book has broad relevance for the environmental community and all concerned with the difficulties and complexities of finding solutions to our worsening environmental conditions.

Part I provides a retrospective view of policy development as well as a framework for analyzing policy change in the United States. Chapter 1 serves as an introduction to the book by outlining the basic issues in U.S. environmental policy over the past two and a half decades, the development of institutional capabilities for addressing them, and the successes and failures in implementing policies. The evolving role of the states in implementing federal policies and developing their own innovative approaches is considered in a new analysis by Barry G. Rabe in chapter 2. The states' capabilities have become a more urgent question as Congress seeks to devolve responsibilities from Washington. In chapter 3 Christopher J. Bosso examines public opinion trends and the emergence of new grassroots environmental movements and countermovements. One of his most important conclusions is that environmental groups in the 1990s are becoming more fragmented, decentralized, and diversified in their concerns and modes of action. Part I concludes with a perceptive essay by Robert C. Paehlke that discusses the core values of environmentalism and proposes a variety of ways in which environmental ethics can be incorporated into environmental, social, and economic policies.

Part II analyzes the role of federal institutions in environmental policymaking. Chapter 5, by Norman J. Vig, discusses the role of recent presidents as environmental actors, focusing on the varying approaches of the Reagan, Bush, and Clinton administrations. In chapter 6 Michael E. Kraft examines the causes and consequences of policy gridlock in Congress, especially in light of the new Republican agenda. Walter A. Rosenbaum takes a hard and critical look in chapter 7 at the nation's chief environmental institution, the EPA, discussing a range of proposals for redefining its mission and functions. Chapter 8, by Lettie McSpadden, then explores the evolving role of the federal courts in interpreting environmental laws, reviewing administrative decisionmaking, and ultimately resolving many environmental disputes. McSpadden discusses several new legal trends such as the growing controversy over private property rights and legislative "takings."

Some of the broader dilemmas in environmental policy formulation and implementation are examined in Part III. The first two chapters focus on approaches that are increasingly being advocated to improve the efficiency and effectiveness of environmental regulation. Economist A. Myrick Freeman III discusses the potential for more rational economic decisionmaking, including the use of cost-benefit analysis, in chapter 9. He also asks how market incentives such as pollution taxes and tradable discharge permits could be introduced to achieve better results at less cost. Chapter 10, by Richard N.L. Andrews, takes up a parallel set of questions regarding scientific risk assessment: How well can environmental risks be measured given the technical obstacles and human judgments involved? And should comparative risk assessment be used to set environmental priorities? The last two chapters in Part III consider broader social responsibilities that are increasingly recognized as central to environmental health and progress. In chapter 11 Evan J. Ringquist analyzes the emergence of the environmental justice movement in response to growing awareness of racial and social inequities in the distribution of environmental burdens. He presents new empirical evidence regarding these inequities and discusses potential remedies. Chapter 12 switches the spotlight to evolving business practices. Daniel Press and Daniel A. Mazmanian examine claims for a "greening of business" and find considerable evidence of new trends toward voluntary pollution prevention and reduction.

Part IV shifts our attention to international environmental issues and institutions. Chapter 13, by Marvin S. Soroos, sets the stage by exploring the development of global environmental diplomacy and institution building over the past twenty-five years. He focuses on the 1992 U.N. Conference on Environment and Development and prospects for implementing its goals. In chapter 14 Regina S. Axelrod analyzes the success of the European Union as perhaps the most advanced model for international environmental cooperation. Richard J. Tobin, in chapter 15, examines the plight of nations at the other end of the development spectrum that are struggling with an even more formidable array of threats brought about by rapid population growth and resource exploitation. The last chapter in Part IV, by David Vogel, discusses the potential impacts of new international trade agreements such as the North American Free Trade Agreement (NAFTA) and the General Agreement on Tariffs and Trade (GATT) on national policies for resource preservation and environmental protection.

The final chapter, by the editors, draws on the contributions to the book and on other current research to define an agenda of major environmental issues and new policymaking approaches that are the focus of contention in the closing years of the century. We make some reference to recent initiatives of the Clinton administration and its nemesis in Congress in offering some suggestions for a more constructive policy dialogue in the future.

We thank the contributing authors for their generosity, cooperative spirit, and patience in response to our seemingly ruthless editorial requests. It is a pleasure to work with such a conscientious and punctual group of scholars. Special thanks are also due to Brenda Carter, Nancy Lammers, Kris Stoever, Talia Greenberg, and the rest of the staff at CQ for their customarily splendid editorial work. We also gratefully acknowledge support from the Department of Political Science and the Environmental and Technology Studies Program at Carleton College and the Department of Public and Environmental Affairs at the University of Wisconsin–Green Bay. Finally, we thank our students at Carleton and UW–Green Bay for forcing us to rethink our assumptions about what really matters. As always, any remaining errors and omissions are our own responsibility.

Norman J. Vig
Michael E. Kraft

Contributors

Richard N. L. ("Pete") Andrews is professor of environmental policy in the Department of Environmental Sciences and Engineering and in the Curriculum in Public Policy Analysis, University of North Carolina, Chapel Hill. Formerly chairman of graduate programs in natural resource and environmental policy at UNC and the University of Michigan, Professor Andrews is the author of *Environmental Policy and Administrative Change* (1976) and of numerous journal articles on environmental policy, impact and risk assessment, and benefit-cost analysis. He served on the EPA Science Advisory Board panel that wrote the 1990 *Reducing Risk* report and on the recent National Academy of Public Administration panel that recommended major reforms for the EPA.

Regina S. Axelrod is chairperson of the Department of Political Science at Adelphi University. She has published books and articles dealing with energy and environmental issues in the United States and Europe. Her recent research has focused on energy policy and issues related to subsidiarity in the European Union. She has also lectured at Charles University, Prague, and at the University of Budapest on a Soros Foundation grant.

Christopher J. Bosso is associate professor of political science and department chair at Northeastern University, where he specializes in American politics and public policy. He is the author of *Pesticides and Politics: The Life Cycle of a Public Issue* (1987), winner of the 1988 Policy Studies Organization award for the best book in policy studies. He also has written on the intersection of environmental values and American democratic institutions, on trends within the environmental community, and on public policymaking dynamics generally.

A. Myrick Freeman III is William D. Shipman Professor of Economics at Bowdoin College. He has also held appointments as senior fellow at Resources for the Future, visiting college professor at the University of Washington, and Robert M. La Follette Visiting Distinguished Professor at the University of Wisconsin–Madison. He is the author of *The Measurement of Environmental and Resource Values: Theory and Methods* (1993) and *Air and Water Pollution Control: A Benefit-Cost Assessment* (1982). Professor Freeman is currently a member of the Science Advisory Board of the U.S. Environmental Protection Agency.

Michael E. Kraft is professor of political science and public affairs and Herbert Fisk Johnson Professor of Environmental Studies at the University of Wisconsin, Green Bay. He has held appointments as Robert M. La Follette Visiting Distinguished Professor at the University of Wisconsin-Madison and visiting distinguished professor at Oberlin College. Among other works, he is author of *Environmental Policy and Politics* (1996) and coeditor of *Public Reactions to Nuclear Waste* (1993) as well as *Environmental Policy in the 1980s* (1984) and *Technology and Politics* (1988)—both with Norman J. Vig.

Lettie McSpadden teaches public law and public policy in the Department of Political Science at Northern Illinois University. She is the author of *One Environment under Law* (1976), *The Environmental Decade in Court* (1982), and *U.S. Energy and Environmental Groups* (1990). Professor McSpadden has written numerous articles and book chapters on air and water pollution, natural resources conservation, and other environmental issues. Her special interest is on how federal courts oversee administrative discretion in environmental policy.

Daniel A. Mazmanian is dean of the School of Natural Resources and Environment at the University of Michigan. He served as director of the Center for Politics and Economics at the Claremont Graduate School from 1986 to 1996. Professor Mazmanian has written numerous articles and books, including *Third Parties in Presidential Elections* (1974), *Can Organizations Change? Environmental Protection, Citizen Participation, and the Corps of Engineers* (with Jeanne Nienaber, 1979), *Implementation and Public Policy* (1983, 1989), and *Beyond Superfailure: America's Toxics Policy for the 1990s* (with David Morell, 1992).

Robert C. Paehlke is professor of political studies and environmental and resource studies at Trent University, Peterborough, Ontario. He is the author of *Environmentalism and the Future of Progressive Politics* (1989), coeditor of *Managing Leviathan: Environmental Politics and the Administrative State* (1990), and editor of *Conservation and Environmentalism: An Encyclopedia* (1995). He is a founding editor of the Canadian journal *Alternatives: Perspectives on Society, Technology and Environment*.

Daniel Press is assistant professor of environmental studies at the University of California, Santa Cruz, where he teaches environmental politics and policy. Professor Press is the author of *Democratic Dilemmas in the Age of Ecology* (1994) and is currently studying local open-space preservation in California.

Barry G. Rabe is associate professor of health politics at the University of Michigan School of Public Health. He has written, among other works, *Beyond Nimby: Hazardous Waste Siting in Canada and the United States* (1994) and *Fragmentation and Integration in State Environmental Management*

(1986) and is coauthor of *When Federalism Works* (1986). Professor Rabe's research on NIMBY (not in my backyard) politics received the 1995 J. E. Hodgetts Award from the Institute of Public Administration of Canada. His current research examines the politics of environmental regulatory integration in the Great Lakes Basin and pollution prevention in Canada and the United States.

Evan J. Ringquist is assistant professor of political science at Florida State University, where he teaches courses on environmental and energy policy as well as American government and public policy. Professor Ringquist has written, among other works, *Environmental Protection at the State Level: Politics and Progress in Controlling Pollution* (1993) and is completing a new book on environmental justice, entitled *Green Justice for All? The Influence of Race and Class in Environmental Protection.*

Walter A. Rosenbaum is professor of political science at the University of Florida, Gainesville, where he specializes in environmental and energy policy. During the academic year 1990–1991, he served as a senior analyst in the EPA's Office of the Assistant Administrator for Policy, Planning and Evaluation. Among his many published works are *Environmental Politics and Policy*, 3d ed. (1995), and *Energy, Politics, and Public Policy* (1987).

Marvin S. Soroos is professor and head of the Department of Political Science and Public Administration at North Carolina State University, where he teaches courses in global environmental law and policy. He is the author of *Beyond Sovereignty: The Challenge of Global Sovereignty* (1986), a coauthor of *The Environment in the Global Arena: Actors, Values, Politics, and Futures* (1985), and coeditor of *The Global Predicament: Ecological Perspectives on World Order* (1979). Professor Soroos has also chaired the Environmental Studies Section of the International Studies Association.

Richard J. Tobin is director of environmental programs at the Institute for International Research in Arlington, Virginia, and a policy analyst with the Environmental and Natural Resources Policy and Training Project of the U.S. Agency for International Development (USAID). This project provides technical assistance related to environmental policy in developing countries. His book, *The Expendable Future: U.S. Politics and the Protection of Biological Diversity*, received the Policy Studies Organization's Outstanding Book Award in 1991.

Norman J. Vig is the Winifred and Atherton Bean Professor of Science, Technology, and Society and director of the Environmental and Technology Studies Program at Carleton College. He has written extensively on science and technology policy and is coeditor of several books, including *Environmental Policy in the 1980s* and *Technology and Politics* (both with Michael Kraft).

David Vogel is professor of business and public policy at the Haas School of Business at the University of California, Berkeley. He has written extensively on business-government relations and government regulation in the United States, the European Union, and Japan. Professor Vogel is the author of *National Styles of Regulation: Environmental Policy in Great Britain and the United States* (1986) and *Trading Up: Consumer and Environmental Regulation in a Global Economy* (1995).

PART I. ENVIRONMENTAL POLICY AND POLITICS IN TRANSITION

1

Environmental Policy from the 1970s to the 1990s: An Overview

Michael E. Kraft and Norman J. Vig

Environmental issues soared to a prominent place on the political agenda in the United States and other industrial nations in the early 1990s. The new visibility was encouraging, even if it could not be taken as a clear sign of public consensus on either the severity of ecological and health risks or public policies needed to deal with them. Intense public concern over environmental problems was manifest in opinion surveys conducted domestically and internationally.[1] Policymakers around the world pledged to deal with a range of important environmental challenges, from global climate change and protection of biological diversity to air and water pollution. For instance, delegates to the 1992 United Nations Conference on Environment and Development (the Earth summit), held in Río de Janeiro, approved Agenda 21, an ambitious plan for redirecting the world's economics toward environmental sustainability. In the United States, the Environmental Protection Agency (EPA) sought new ways to improve implementation of the policies under its jurisdiction through "reinvention" of environmental regulation and use of "common sense" approaches.[2]

Despite these promising initiatives, sharp conflict over environmental policy goals, as well as over the means used to achieve them, was equally evident by the mid 1990s. This was especially so in the United States following the watershed 1994 congressional elections. The Republican party took control of both the House and Senate for the first time in forty years, and the party's conservative manifesto, the "Contract with America," promised to greatly reduce the scope of governmental activities. Environmental regulation became one of the prime targets of the GOP "revolution" on Capitol Hill. Nearly every major environmental statute and agency became the object of "reform" proposals that were often intended to undercut long-established and popular programs.[3]

The only other time in the past twenty-five years that environmental policies were attacked so directly was in the early 1980s during Ronald Reagan's presidency. Reagan's actions followed an "environmental decade" (the 1970s), during which the United States and other industrial nations adopted an impressive array of environmental and resource policies, created new institutions such as the EPA to manage programs, and greatly increased spending for them.[4] Under the Reagan administration, these programs were significantly curtailed and deep cuts exacted in the budgets of the EPA and other agencies. That strategy ultimately failed as Congress, the courts, and the American public resisted efforts to weaken or reverse environmental policy.[5] In the early to mid 1990s, many of the same critiques of environmental policy were advanced once again. This time it was the Congress itself that sought to pull the nation back from its previous environmental policies and it was the Clinton White House that rose to their defense.

The precise way in which Congress, and the states, will revise environmental policies over the next few years remains unclear. The outcomes will depend on how environmental issues are defined by the various policy actors, the role of the media in covering the disputes, the state of the economy, the relative influence of opposing interest groups, and political leadership at all levels of government. One thing is certain, however. Political conflict over the environment is not going to vanish any time soon. It will likely increase as the United States and other nations struggle to define precisely how they will respond to the latest generation of environmental problems.

Another conclusion is inescapable. Deep cuts in federal agency budgets in 1996 and the heightened antienvironmental rhetoric and political backlash—in the states as well as in Congress—plainly indicate that environmental policy is at an important crossroads. Future achievements are critically dependent on understanding the new antienvironmental movements within and outside of government, improving our knowledge of the diversity of environmental risks we face, and devising effective policy actions that are broadly acceptable to the American public.

The rest of the 1990s will not be an exact replay of either the 1970s or the 1980s. We can expect to see much continuity in environmental policies for the remainder of the decade and into the early twenty-first century. We should also expect continued evaluation of existing policies and institutions and actions to change them. Some proposals will represent genuine efforts to reform environmental programs by improving their effectiveness and efficiency. Others will be less constructive reactions that are designed to reduce policy commitments made over the past three decades or more. All proposals require careful assessment, however, to determine their likely effects on governmental programs and, ultimately, on the achievement of important ecological, natural resource, and public health goals.

In this chapter we examine the continuities and changes in environmental politics and policy over almost three decades and speculate on their implications for the rest of the 1990s and early twenty-first century. We review the policymaking process in the United States and we assess the performance of government institutions and political leadership. Special attention is given to the major programs adopted in the 1970s, their achievements to date, their costs, and the need for policy reforms and priority setting in light of increasingly constrained budgetary resources. Many of the broad questions explored in this introduction are addressed more fully in the chapters that follow.

The Role of Government and Politics

The greater political salience of environmental protection efforts in the 1990s underscores the important role government plays in devising solutions to the nation's and the world's mounting environmental ills. Global climate change, population growth, the spread of toxic and hazardous chemicals, loss of biological diversity, and air and water pollution each requires diverse actions by individuals and institutions at all levels of society and in both the public and private sectors. These range from scientific research and technological innovation to improved environmental education and significant changes in corporate and consumer behavior. As political scientists, we believe government has an indispensable role to play in environmental protection and improvement. The essays in this volume thus focus on environmental policies and the governmental institutions and political processes that affect them. Our goal is to illuminate that role and to suggest needed changes and strategies for achieving them.

The government plays a preeminent role in this policy area because most environmental threats represent public or collective goods problems. They cannot be solved through purely private actions. Certainly individuals and nongovernmental organizations can do much to protect environmental quality. This is well demonstrated by the impressive growth of grassroots groups at the local and regional level over the past decade and significant efforts by industry to prevent pollution (see chaps. 3 and 12).

Yet such efforts are often insufficient by themselves without the backing of public policy—for example, laws mandating control of toxic chemicals that are backed by the authority of government. The justification for governmental intervention lies partly in the inherent limits of the market system and the nature of human behavior. Self-interested individuals and a free economic marketplace guided mainly by a concern for short-term profits tend to create spillover effects, or "externalities," such as pollution. Collective action is needed to correct such market failures. In addition, the scope and urgency of environmental problems typically exceed the capacity of private markets and individual efforts to deal with them effectively. For these reasons, the United States and other nations have relied on governmental policies—at local, state, national, and international levels—to address those problems.

Adopting public policies does not imply, of course, that voluntary and cooperative actions by citizens in their communities cannot be the primary vehicle of change in many instances. Nor does it suggest that governments should not consider a full range of policy approaches—including market-based incentives and public information campaigns—to supplement or even replace conventional regulatory policies where needed. In an era of profound skepticism about governmental performance and deep citizen distrust of the political process, it is imperative to consider alternative ways of dealing with public problems. The guiding principle should be to rely on those approaches that work best—those that bring about the desired improvements in environmental quality, reduce health and ecological risks to a minimum, and help to integrate and balance environmental and economic goals.

Political Institutions and Public Policy

Public policy is a course of governmental action or inaction in response to social problems. It is expressed in goals articulated by political leaders; in formal statutes, rules, and regulations; and in the practices of administrative agencies and courts charged with implementing or overseeing programs. Policy states an intent to achieve certain goals and objectives through a conscious choice of means, usually within some specified period. In a constitutional democracy like the United States, policymaking is distinctive in several respects: it must take place through constitutional processes, it requires the sanction of law, and it is binding on all members of society. Normally, the process is open to public scrutiny and debate, although secrecy may be justified in matters involving national security and diplomatic relations.

The constitutional requirements for policymaking were established more than two hundred years ago, and they remain much the same today. The U.S. political system is based on a division of authority among three branches of government and between the federal government and the states. Originally intended to limit government power and to protect individual liberty, this division of power may impede the ability of government to adopt timely and coherent environmental policy. Dedication to principles of federalism means that environmental policy responsibilities are distributed among the federal government, the fifty states, and thousands of local governments (see chap. 2).

Responsibility for the environment is divided within the branches of the federal government as well, most notably in the U.S. Congress, with power shared between the House and Senate, and jurisdiction over environmental policies scattered among dozens of committees and subcommittees (see table 1-1). One recent study, for example, found that thirteen committees and thirty-one subcommittees in Congress had some jurisdiction over EPA activities.[6] The executive branch is also institutionally fragmented, with at least some responsibility for the environment and natural resources located in eleven cabinet departments and in the EPA, the Nuclear Regulatory Commission, and other agencies (see fig. 1-1). Although most environmental policies are concentrated in the EPA and in the Interior and Agriculture Departments, the Departments of Energy (DOE) and State are increasingly important actors as well. Finally, the more than one hundred federal trial and appellate courts play key roles in interpreting environmental legislation and adjudicating disputes over administrative and regulatory actions (see chap. 8).

Table 1-1   Major Congressional Committees with Environmental Responsibilities

Committee	Environmental Policy Jurisdiction
House	
Agriculture	agriculture in general, soil conservation, groundwater, forestry and private forest reserves, pesticides and food safety
Appropriations[a]	appropriations for all programs
Commerce (formerly Energy and Commerce)	air pollution; national energy policy in general; exploration, production, pricing, and regulation of energy sources; nuclear energy and nuclear waste; energy conservation; safe drinking water; Superfund and hazardous waste disposal; toxic substances control; noise control
Resources (formerly Natural Resources)	public lands and natural resources in general; national parks, forests, and wilderness areas; irrigation and reclamation; mines and mining; energy and nuclear waste disposal; oceanography, fisheries, international fishing agreements, and coastal zone management; wildlife, marine mammals, and endangered species
Transportation and Infrastructure (formerly Public Works and Transportation)	water pollution, flood control; rivers and harbors; pollution of navigable waters; dams and hydroelectric power; transportation; Superfund and hazardous wastes
Science (formerly Science, Space and Technology)	environmental research and development; energy research and development; research in national laboratories; global climate change; NASA, NOAA, and National Science Foundation
Senate	
Agriculture, Nutrition and Forestry	agriculture in general; soil conservation and groundwater; forestry and private forest reserves; pesticides and food safety; global change
Appropriations[a]	appropriations for all programs
Commerce, Science and Transportation	coastal zone management; inland waterways and marine fisheries; oceans, weather, and atmospheric activities; Outer Continental Shelf lands; technology research and development; surface transportation; global change
Energy and Natural Resources	energy policy in general; conservation research and development; oil and gas production and distribution; nuclear waste policy; mining; national parks and recreation areas; wilderness; wild and scenic rivers; public lands and forests; global change

(Continued on next page)

Table 1-1   *(Continued)*

Committee	Environmental Policy Jurisdiction
Environment and Public Works	environmental policy and research in general; air, water, and noise pollution; safe drinking water; environmental aspects of Outer Continental Shelf and ocean dumping; toxic substances other than pesticides; Superfund and hazardous wastes; solid waste disposal and recycling; nuclear waste policy; fisheries and wildlife; flood control and dams; improvements of rivers and harbors; water resources; global change

Source: Compiled from descriptions of committee jurisdictions reported in Congressional Quarterly Inc., *Players, Politics, and Turf of the 104th Congress* (Washington, D.C.: Congressional Quarterly Inc., March 25, 1995).

[a] Both the House and Senate Appropriations Committees have Interior subcommittees that handle all Interior Department agencies as well as the Forest Service. In both houses a subcommittee on VA, HUD, and Independent Agencies is responsible for EPA appropriations. The Energy Department, Army Corps of Engineers, and Nuclear Regulatory Commission fall under the jurisdiction of the subcommittees on Energy and Water Development. Tax policy affects many environmental, energy, and natural resources policies, and is governed by the Senate Finance Committee and the House Ways and Means Committee.

The implications of this constitutional arrangement were evident in the 1980s as Congress and the courts checked and balanced the Reagan administration's efforts to reverse the environmental policies of the previous decade. They were equally clear in the mid 1990s when the Clinton administration vigorously opposed efforts in Congress to cut back on environmental programs. More generally, divided authority produces slow and incremental alterations in policy, typically after broad consultation and agreement among diverse interests both within and outside of government. Such political interaction and accommodation of interests enhance the overall legitimacy of the resulting public policies. Over time, however, the cumulative effect has been disjointed policies that fall short of ecological or holistic principles of policy design.

Nonetheless, when issues are highly visible, the public is supportive, and political leaders act cohesively, the American political system has proved flexible enough to permit substantial policy innovations.[7] As we shall see, this was the case in the early to mid 1970s, when Congress enacted major changes in U.S. environmental policy, and in the mid 1980s, when Congress overrode objections of the Reagan administration and greatly strengthened policies on hazardous waste and water quality, among others. Passage of the monumental Clean Air Act Amendments of 1990 was a more recent example of the same alignment of forces. With bipartisan support, Congress adopted the act by a margin of 401 to 25 in the House and 89 to 10 in the Senate.

Figure 1-1 Executive Branch Agencies with Environmental Responsibilities

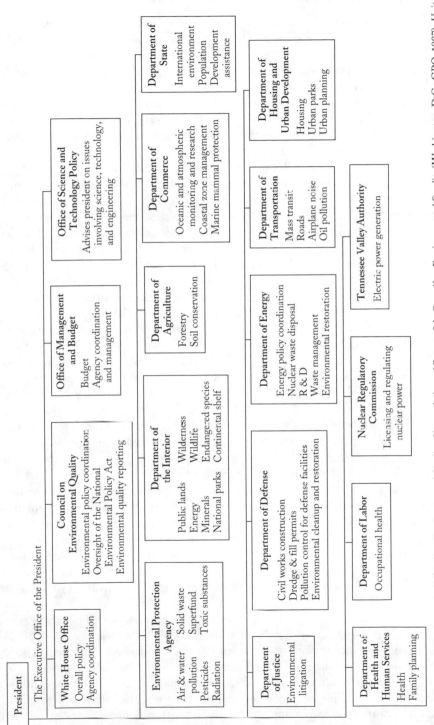

Sources: Council on Environmental Quality, *Environmental Quality: Sixteenth Annual Report of the Council on Environmental Quality* (Washington, D.C.: GPO, 1987), *United States Government Manual 1993/94* (GPO, 1993), and authors.

Policy Processes: Agendas, Streams, and Cycles

Several models are available for analyzing how issues get on the political agenda and move through the policy processes of government. These
theoretical frameworks help us to understand both long-term policy trends
and short-term cycles of progressive action and political reaction. One set of
essential questions concerns *agenda setting:* how do new problems emerge as
political issues that demand the government's attention, if they do achieve
such recognition? For example, why did the federal government initiate controls on industrial pollution in the 1960s and early 1970s but do little about
national energy issues until well into the 1970s?

There are some hurdles to overcome in an issue's rise to prominence: it
must first gain societal recognition as a problem, often in response to demographic, technological, or other social changes; then get on the docket of
governmental institutions, usually through the exercise of organized group
pressure; and finally it must receive enough attention by governmental actors
to reach the stage of decisional or policy action.[8] An issue is not likely to
reach this latter stage unless conditions are ripe (for example, a "triggering
event" that focuses public opinion sharply, as occurred with the Exxon *Valdez*
oil spill in 1989). One model analyzes agenda setting according to the convergence of three "streams" that can be said to flow through the political
system at any time: (1) evidence of the existence of problems, (2) available
policies to deal with them, and (3) the political climate or willingness to act.
Although largely independent of one another, these problem, policy, and
political streams can be brought together at critical times when "policy entrepreneurs" are able to take advantage of the moment and make the case for
policy action.[9]

Once an issue is on the agenda, it must pass through several more stages
in the policy process. These stages are often referred to as the *policy cycle.*
Although terminology varies, most students of public policy delineate at
least five stages of policy development beyond *agenda setting*: these are (1)
policy formulation (the actual design and drafting of policy goals and strategies for achieving them—which may involve extensive use of environmental
science and policy analysis), (2) *policy legitimation* (mobilization of political
support and formal enactment by law or other means), (3) *policy implementation* (provision of institutional resources and detailed administration of
policy), (4) *policy evaluation* (measurement of results in relation to goals and
costs), and (5) *policy change,* including termination (modification of goals or
means).[10]

The policy cycle model is useful because it emphasizes all phases of policymaking. For example, how well a law is implemented is as important as
the goals and motivations of those who drafted and enacted the legislation.
The concept also suggests the continuous nature of the policy process. No
policy decision or solution is "final" because changing conditions, new information, and shifting opinions will require policy reevaluation and revision.
Other short-term forces and events, such as presidential or congressional

elections or environmental accidents, can also profoundly affect the course of policy over its life-cycle. Thus, policy at any given time is shaped by the interaction of long-term social, economic, technological, and political forces and short-term fluctuations in the political climate. All of these factors are manifest in the development of environmental policy.

The Development of Environmental Policy from the 1970s to the 1990s

As implied in the policy cycle model, the history of environmental policy in the United States is not one of continuous improvement in human relations with the natural environment. Rather, it is one of fits and starts, with significant discontinuities, particularly since the late 1960s. It can be understood, to borrow from the concept of agenda setting, as the product of the convergence or divergence of two political currents, one that is deep and long term and the other shallow and short term.

Social Values and Environmental Policy Commitments

The deep political current consists of fundamental changes in American values that began after World War II, changes that accelerated as the nation shifted from an industrial to a postindustrial (or postmaterialist) society. Preoccupation with the economy (and national security) has gradually given way to a new set of concerns that includes quality-of-life issues like the environment.[11] These changes suggest that in the coming decades ecological issues will replace, or be integrated with, many traditional political, economic, and social issues, both domestically and internationally. This integration was evident at the 1992 Earth summit and its concern about sustainable development. It is also championed in *Our Common Future*, an influential report by the World Commission on Environment and Development that helped to shape the Earth summit's agenda.[12] Historian Samuel Hays describes these changes as a social evolutionary process affecting all segments of American society. Political scientist Robert Paehlke, the author of chapter 4 in this volume, characterizes environmentalism as a new ideology with the potential to alter conventional political alignments.[13] These long-term social forces are setting a new direction for the political agenda.

The shallow political current consists of shorter-term political and economic forces—elections, economic cycles, and energy supply shocks—that may alter the salience of environmental issues. These short-term developments may either reinforce or weaken the long-term trends in society that support environmental protection. For example, in the early 1970s the deep and shallow currents converged to produce an enormous outpouring of federal environmental legislation. Yet later in the decade energy shortages and high inflation rates led the Carter administration to pull back from some of its environmental commitments. The election of Ronald Reagan in 1980 shifted the environmental policy agenda sharply to the right for much of the

1980s. The two currents converged once again in the early 1990s at the beginning of the Clinton administration; however, the 1994 congressional elections blunted that particular convergence (see chap. 6). It is too early to tell whether the 1994 elections will result in a new era in environmental protection policies.

Thus the interaction of these two currents helps to explain the fluctuations in environmental policy commitments from one year, or decade, to the next. Over time, however, one can see the continuity of strong public support for environmental protection, expanding government authority, and increasingly effective policy implementation—even if scarce resources and sometimes poor agency management limit success. The near-term discontinuities, such as the antienvironmental actions of the 104th Congress, capture our attention, yet they can be misleading. The longer-term transitions and transformations in American values and environmental behavior arguably are more important. We focus here on the major changes from 1970 to 1996. We discuss the future agenda for environmental politics and policy in the conclusion of the book.

Policies Prior to 1970

Until about 1970 the federal government played a sharply limited role in environmental policymaking—public land management being a major exception. For nearly a century Congress had set aside portions of the public domain for preservation as national parks, forests, grazing lands, recreation areas, and wildlife refuges. The "multiple use" and "sustained yield" doctrines that grew out of the conservation movement at the turn of the century ensured that this national trust would contribute to economic growth under the stewardship of the Interior and Agriculture Departments. Steady progress was also made, however, in managing the lands in the public interest and protecting them from development.[14] After several years of debate, Congress passed the Wilderness Act of 1964 to preserve some of the remaining forest lands in pristine condition, "untrammeled by man's presence." At the same time it approved the Land and Water Conservation Fund Act of 1964 to fund federal purchases of land for conservation purposes.

During the mid 1960s the United States also began a major effort to reduce world population growth in developing nations through financial aid for foreign population programs, chiefly family planning and population research. President Lyndon B. Johnson and congressional sponsors of the programs tied them explicitly to a concern for "growing scarcity in world resources."[15]

Despite this longtime concern for resource conservation and land management, federal environmental policy was only slowly extended to control of industrial pollution and human waste. Air and water pollution were long considered a strictly local matter, and they were not high on the national agenda until the early 1970s. In a very early federal action the Refuse Act of 1899 required individuals who wanted to dump refuse into navigable waters to obtain a permit from the Army Corps of Engineers; however, the corps largely ignored the pollution aspects of the act.[16] After World War II policies to control the most obvious forms of pollution were gradually developed at the local, state, and federal levels. With passage of the Water Pollution Control Act of 1948, the federal government began assisting local authorities in building sewage treatment plants, and it initiated a limited program for air pollution research in 1955. Following the Clean Air Act of 1963 and amendments to the water pollution law, Washington began prodding the states to set pollution abatement standards and to formulate implementation plans based on federal guidelines.[17]

Agenda Setting for the 1970s

The first Earth Day was April 22, 1970. Nationwide "teach-ins" about environmental problems demonstrated ecology's new place on the nation's social and political agendas. With an increasingly affluent and well-educated society placing new emphasis on the quality of life, concern for environmental protection grew apace and was evident across all groups in the population, if not necessarily to the same degree.[18] The effect was a broadly based public demand for more vigorous and comprehensive federal action to prevent environmental degradation. In an almost unprecedented fashion a new environmental policy agenda rapidly emerged. Policymakers viewed the newly visible environmental issues as politically attractive and they eagerly supported tough new measures, even when their full impacts and costs were unknown. As a result, laws were quickly enacted and implemented throughout the 1970s, but with a growing concern over their costs and effects on the economy and an increasing realization that administrative agencies at all levels of government often lacked the resources and the capacity to assume their new responsibilities.

Congress set the stage for the spurt in policy innovation at the end of 1969 when it passed the National Environmental Policy Act (NEPA). The act declared that

> it is the continuing policy of the Federal Government, in cooperation with State and local governments, and other concerned public and private organizations, to use all practicable means and measures, including financial and technical assistance, in a manner calculated to foster and promote the general welfare, to create and maintain conditions under which man and nature can exist in productive harmony, and fulfill the social, economic, and other requirements of present and future generations of Americans.[19]

The law required detailed environmental impact statements for all major federal actions and established the Council on Environmental Quality (CEQ) to advise the president and Congress on environmental matters. President Richard Nixon then seized the initiative by signing NEPA as his first official act of 1970 and proclaiming the 1970s as the "environmental decade." In February 1970 he sent a special message to Congress calling for a new law to control air pollution. The race was on as the White House and congressional leaders vied for environmentalists' support.

Policy Escalation in the 1970s

By the spring of 1970 rising public concern about the environment galvanized the Ninety-first Congress to action. Sen. Edmund Muskie (D-Maine), then the leading Democratic hopeful for the presidential nomination in 1972, emerged as the dominant policy entrepreneur for environmental protection issues. As chair of the Senate Public Works Committee, he formulated proposals that went well beyond those favored by the president. Following a process of policy escalation, both houses of Congress approved the stronger measures and set the tone for environmental policymaking for much of the 1970s. Congress had frequently played a more dominant role than the president in initiating environmental policies, and that pattern continued in the 1970s, particularly because the Democratic party controlled Congress during the Nixon and Ford presidencies. Although support for environmental protection was bipartisan, Democrats provided more leadership on the issue in Congress and were more likely to vote for strong environmental policy provisions than were Republicans.[20]

The increase in new federal legislation in the next decade was truly remarkable, especially since, as we noted above, policymaking in American politics is normally incremental. Appendix 1 lists the major environmental policies enacted between 1969 and 1996. They are arranged by presidential administration primarily to show a pattern of significant policy development throughout the period, not to attribute chief responsibility for the various bills to the particular presidents. These landmark measures covered air and water pollution control (the latter enacted in 1972 over a presidential veto), pesticide regulation, endangered species protection, control of hazardous and toxic chemicals, ocean and coastline protection, better stewardship of public lands, requirements for restoration of strip-mined lands, the setting aside of more than 100 million acres of Alaskan wilderness for varying degrees of protection, and the creation of a "Superfund" (in the Comprehensive Environmental Response, Compensation, and Liability Act, or CERCLA) for cleaning up toxic waste sites.

There were other signs of commitment to environmental policy goals as Congress and a succession of presidential administrations through Jimmy Carter's cooperated on conservation issues. For example, the area designated as national wilderness (excluding Alaska) more than doubled, from 10 million acres in 1970 to more than 23 million acres in 1980. Seventy-five units, totaling some 2.5 million acres, were added to the National Park Service in the same period. The National Wildlife Refuge System grew similarly. Throughout the 1970s the Land and Water Conservation Fund, financed primarily through royalties from offshore oil and gas leasing, was used to purchase additional private land for park development, wildlife refuges, and national forests.

The government's enthusiasm for environmental and conservation policy did not extend to all issues on the environmentalists' agenda. Two noteworthy cases are population policy and energy policy. The Commission on Population Growth and the American Future recommended in 1972 that the nation should "welcome and plan for a stabilized population," but its advice was ignored. Birth rates in the United States were declining and the population issue was politically controversial. Despite occasional reports that highlighted the role of population growth, such as the *Global 2000 Report to the President* in 1980, the issue remained more or less dormant over the next two decades.[21]

For energy issues the dominant pattern was not neglect but policy gridlock. Here the connection to environmental policy was clearer to policymakers than it had been on population growth. Indeed, opposition to antipollution programs as well as land preservation came primarily from conflicting demands for energy production in the aftermath of the Arab oil embargo in 1973. The Nixon, Ford, and Carter administrations all attempted to formulate national policies for achieving "energy independence" by increasing energy supplies, with President Carter's efforts by far the most sustained and comprehensive. President Carter also emphasized conservation and environmental safeguards. For the most part, however, their efforts were unsuccessful. No consensus on national energy policy emerged among the public or in Congress, and presidential leadership was insufficient to overcome these political constraints, although a National Energy Policy Act, a bill of limited scope, was enacted in 1992.[22]

Congress maintained its strong commitment to environmental policy throughout the 1970s, even as the salience of these issues for the public seemed to wane. For example, it strengthened the Clean Air Act of 1970 and the Clean Water Act of 1972 through amendments approved in 1977. Yet concerns over the impact of environmental regulation on the economy and specific objections to implementation of the new laws, particularly the Clean Air Act, began creating a backlash of sorts by the end of the Carter administration.

Political Reaction in the 1980s: The Reagan and Bush Administrations

The Reagan presidency brought to the federal government a very different environmental policy agenda (see chap. 5). Virtually all environmental protection and resource policies enacted during the 1970s were reevaluated in light of the president's desire to reduce the scope of government regulation, shift responsibilities to the states, and rely more on the private sector. Confidence in the efficacy of "environmental deregulation" was predicated on the questionable assumption that enforcement of environmental laws had a major adverse impact on the economy.[23] Whatever the merits of President Reagan's new policy agenda, it was put into effect through a risky strategy that relied on ideologically committed presidential appointees to the EPA and the Agriculture, Interior, and Energy Departments, and on sharp cutbacks in budgets for environmental programs.

Congress initially cooperated with President Reagan, particularly in approving budget cuts, but it soon reverted to its accustomed defense of existing environmental policy, frequently criticizing the president's management of the EPA and the Interior Department under Anne Gorsuch Burford and James Watt, respectively; both Burford and Watt were forced to resign by the end of 1983. Among Congress's most notable achievements of the 1980s were its strengthening of the Resource Conservation and Recovery Act (1984), the Superfund Amendments and Reauthorization Act (SARA) (1986), the Safe Drinking Water Act (1986), and the Clean Water Act (1987) (see app. 1). It was less successful in overcoming policy gridlock on acid rain legislation, the Clean Air Act, and the nation's pesticides law. Only in the late 1980s did energy policy issues reappear on the congressional agenda, as concern mounted over the threat of global climate change. The same pattern of policy neglect and rediscovery characterized many other international environmental issues.

As we will show, budget cuts and loss of capacity in environmental institutions took a serious toll in the 1980s. Yet even the determined efforts of a popular president could not halt the advance of environmental policy. Public support for environmental improvement, the driving force for policy development in the 1970s, increased markedly during the Reagan presidency and represented a stunning rejection of the president's agenda by the American public.[24]

Paradoxically, Reagan actually strengthened environmental forces in the nation. Through his lax enforcement of pollution laws and prodevelopment resource policies, he created political issues around which national and grassroots environmental groups could organize. They appealed successfully to a public that was increasingly disturbed by the health and environmental risks of industrial society and by threats to ecological stability. As a result, membership in environmental organizations soared and a new grassroots activism developed, creating further political incentives for environmental activism at all levels of government (see chap. 3).

By the fall of 1989 there was little mistaking congressional enthusiasm for continuing the advance of environmental policy into the 1990s. Especially in his first two years, President George Bush was eager as well to adopt a more positive environmental policy agenda than his predecessor. Bush's White House, however, was deeply divided on the issue for both ideological and economic reasons. The EPA under Bush's appointee, William K. Reilly, fought continuously with the president's conservative advisers in the White House over the pace and stringency of environmental regulations. By 1992 Bush had lost much of the support of environmentalists he had courted in 1989 and 1990 (see chap. 5).

The Greening of the White House? The Clinton Administration

Environmental issues received considerable attention during the 1992 presidential election campaign. George Bush, running for reelection, criticized environmentalists as extremists who were putting Americans out of work. The Democratic candidate, Bill Clinton, took a far more supportive stance on the environment, symbolized by his selection of Sen. Al Gore (D-Tenn.) as his running mate. The leading environmentalist in the U.S. Congress, Senator Gore was also author of the best-selling *Earth in the Balance,* in which he argued for making the "rescue of the environment the central organizing principle for civilization."[25]

Much to the disappointment of environmentalists, Bill Clinton exerted little visible leadership on the environment during his first two years in office. However, he and Vice President Al Gore quietly pushed an extensive agenda of environmental policy reform as part of their broader effort to "reinvent government," making it more efficient and responsive to public concerns. Clinton was also generally praised for his environmental appointments, most notably Bruce Babbitt as secretary of the interior. Clinton reversed many of the Reagan and Bush era executive actions that were widely criticized by environmentalists, and he favored increased spending on environmental programs, alternative energy and conservation research, and international population policy. Yet Clinton displeased environmentalists as often as he gratified them, particularly with his support for the North American Free Trade Agreement and for signing a "timber salvaging" measure in 1995 that shielded timber companies from having to comply with environmental laws in their logging operations in federal forests (an action Clinton later called a "mistake"). He earned more praise from environmental groups when he began speaking out frequently and forcefully against antienvironmental policy decisions by the 104th Congress (see chap. 5).

Institutional Development and Policy Implementation

Aside from the enactment of landmark environmental policies in the 1970s and 1980s, some important institutional developments greatly affected implementation of those policies. A brief review of the most important is instructive, especially in the context of recent budget cuts that diminish institutional capacity to act on environmental problems.

Institutionalizing Environmental Protection in the 1970s

The most notable institutional development in the 1970s was the establishment of the EPA by President Richard M. Nixon in December 1970. Created as an independent agency that would report directly to the president, it brought together environmental responsibilities that had previously been scattered among dozens of offices and programs. Under its first administrator, William Ruckelshaus, the agency's legislative mandate grew rapidly as a consequence of the policy process summarized earlier, and it acquired many new programs, offices, and staffs. The EPA's operating budget (the funds available to implement its programs) grew from about $500 million in 1973 to $1.3 billion in 1980; full-time employees increased from 8,200 to

10,600, with two-thirds of them in the agency's ten regional offices and other facilities outside of Washington, D.C. Even with its expanded budget and staff, the nation's leading environmental agency found it increasingly difficult by 1980 to meet new program obligations with available resources.

During the 1970s virtually every federal agency was forced to develop some capabilities for environmental analysis under NEPA, which required that environmental impact statements (EISs) be prepared for all "major federal actions significantly affecting the quality of the human environment." Detailed requirements for the statements were set out by the Council on Environmental Quality and enforced in the courts. Provisions for public hearings and citizen participation allowed environmental and community groups to challenge administrative decisions, often by filing legal suits questioning the adequacy of the impact statements. In response to these potential objections, agencies changed their project designs—sometimes dramatically. Even the Army Corps of Engineers, which had often been castigated by environmentalists, learned to adapt.[26] Although the EIS process was roundly criticized (indeed, it was revised in 1979 to focus more sharply on crucial issues), most studies show that it forced greater environmental awareness and more careful planning in many agencies; moreover, such success led to extension of this kind of impact analysis to other policy areas.[27]

Established natural resource agencies, such as Agriculture's Forest Service and Interior's Bureau of Land Management, generally made the transition to better environmental analysis and planning more easily. Long-standing doctrines of multiple use and strong professional norms of land management were gradually adapted to serve new environmental goals and interests. Wilderness preservation, never a dominant purpose of these agencies, came to be accepted as part of their mission.

Both in their compliance with new environmental laws and in their adjustment to democratic norms of open decisionmaking and citizen participation in the 1970s, some agencies and departments lagged seriously behind others. Perhaps the most striking case is the Department of Energy, which for years had neglected changing standards and demands with respect to environmental protection, safety, and health. The price the nation pays for such environmental neglect and mismanagement can be seen in the enormous cost of cleaning up the department's seventeen principal weapons plants and laboratories—more than $200 billion over the next thirty years.[28]

Successive administrations also gave modest support to the development of international environmental institutions. The United States played an active role in convening the U.N. Conference on the Human Environment held in Stockholm, Sweden, in June 1972. This conference, attended by delegations from 113 countries and 400 other organizations, addressed for the first time the environmental problems of developing nations. The result was the creation of the U.N. Environment Programme (UNEP), headquartered in Nairobi, Kenya. Although it disagreed with some of UNEP's initiatives, the United States provided the largest share (36 percent) of its budget between 1972 and 1980 (see chap. 13).[29]

Environmental Relief and Reform in the 1980s

By the time President Reagan assumed office in 1981, the effort to improve environmental quality at federal and state levels had been institutionalized, though not without a good many problems that required both statutory change and administrative reform. Implementation often lagged years behind schedule because much of the legislation of the 1970s overestimated the speed with which new technologies could be developed and applied. The laws also underestimated compliance costs and the difficulty of writing standards for hundreds of major industries. As regulated industries sought to block implementation and environmental organizations tried to speed it up, frequent legal challenges compounded the backlog. Other delays were caused by personnel and budgetary shortages, scientific and technical uncertainties, and the need for extensive consultation with other federal agencies, Congress, and state governments. [30]

As a result of these difficulties, an extensive agenda for reforming environmental policies and improving administrative capabilities emerged by 1980. It was, however, largely unaddressed by the Reagan administration, which was more concerned with providing short term regulatory relief to industry. [31] The president's neglect of policy reform was exacerbated by his reliance on an administrative strategy that J. Clarence Davies described as "designed largely to reverse the institutionalization process" begun in the 1970s. This was accomplished through sharp budgetary reductions, weakening of the authority of experienced professionals in environmental agencies, and elimination or restructuring of many offices, particularly at the EPA. [32] Staff morale and EPA credibility suffered under the leadership of Anne Burford, although both improved to some extent under administrators William Ruckelshaus and Lee Thomas in the Reagan administration and William Reilly in the Bush administration. Nevertheless, the damage done to administrative capacity in the early 1980s was considerable and long lasting. At the end of the Reagan presidency in January 1989, environmentalists still complained that there was no policy leadership at the EPA and that little had been done to "restore the momentum of environmental protection." [33]

They also criticized President Reagan for failing to pursue regulatory reform, saying he "blew the chance to streamline regulations and use marketplace incentives in an honest way to speed up environmental progress, lower regulatory costs, and foster economic growth." Business groups remained dissatisfied with what they believed was still an unnecessarily expensive and rigid system of federal environmental regulation. And even conservative critics expressed disappointment with what the Heritage Foundation termed a "squandered" opportunity to reform environmental protection laws and reduce their cost. [34] Many of the same reform issues, such as risk-based priority setting and use of market incentives to supplement regulation, continue to be widely discussed in the 1990s, and they emerged as major issues in the 103d and 104th Congresses, from 1993 to 1996 (see chaps. 6, 7, 9, and 10).

Institutional Capacity: Environmental Agency Budgets and Policy Implementation

As we try to assess the degree to which environmental quality might improve as a result of present laws and to consider the ability of government to meet the ecological challenges of the late 1990s and early twenty-first century, there is little that is more important than budgets. Although spending more public money does not guarantee policy success, drastic cuts can severely undermine established programs. It is apparent that the massive cuts in environmental funding during the early 1980s had long-term negative effects on the government's ability to implement environmental policies. Equally sharp budget cuts proposed by Congress in 1995 and 1996 may well exact a similar toll over the next decade. The numbers merit a brief review.

In constant dollars (that is, adjusting for inflation), the total authorized by the federal government for natural resource and environmental programs actually declined slightly (2.7 percent) between 1980 and 1994 (see app. 2). The declines were much steeper in some areas, particularly pollution control, where spending fell by 21 percent for the same period; the budget had fallen by a far larger amount before recovering somewhat under the Bush and Clinton administrations. Nonetheless, it is surprising to see that the federal government was actually authorizing considerably *less* for pollution control in 1994 than it had fourteen years earlier.

Overall spending on environmental programs did increase between the early 1970s and the mid 1990s. Yet the same period saw the enactment of virtually all the major environmental laws. Thus, despite some rise in spending over the past twenty-five years, funding often fell short of what was needed to implement these policies and to achieve the environmental quality goals they embodied.

These constraints can be seen in the budgets and staffs of selected environmental and natural resource agencies (see apps. 3 and 4). For example, in constant dollars, the EPA's operating budget in FY 1994 was less than 15 percent higher than it was in FY 1975, despite the important new responsibilities given to the agency by Congress over this period. The picture would be far bleaker if President Bush had not increased that budget by more than 50 percent and the EPA's staff by about 22 percent during his four years in the White House. Even with these increases, the staff in 1995 (excluding Superfund employees) was only slightly larger than it had been in the last year of the Carter administration in 1980.

The picture is more mixed for the natural resource agencies. The Bureau of Land Management, the Army Corps of Engineers, the Office of Surface Mining, and the Forest Service all suffered stagnant or declining budgets (in constant dollars) during the 1980s and early 1990s (see app. 3). In contrast, the Fish and Wildlife Service and the National Park Service enjoyed budget increases during the 1980s and early 1990s. There is little question that limited budgets and staff have severely affected the ability of many agencies to implement environmental policy over the past two decades.

They are likely to be equally significant constraints over the next decade as well. For instance, the EPA announced in early 1996 that congressionally imposed budget cuts already forced the agency to cancel hundreds of enforcement inspections at factories, water treatment plants, and other polluting facilities and to suspend cleanup work at Superfund sites across the nation. The agency warned Congress that further budget reductions would curtail other agency enforcement actions.[35]

Improvement in Environmental Quality and Its Cost

It is difficult, both conceptually and empirically, to measure the success or failure of environmental policies.[36] Yet one of the most important tests of any public policy is whether it achieves its stated objectives. For environmental policy, we should ask if air and water quality are improving, hazardous waste sites are being cleaned up, and wilderness areas are adequately protected. There is no simple way to answer those questions, and it is important to understand why that is so even if some limited responses are possible.

Measuring Environmental Conditions and Trends

Environmental policies entail long-term commitments to broad social values and goals that are not easily quantified. Short-term and highly visible costs are easier to measure than long-term, diffuse, and intangible benefits, and these differences often lead to intense debates over the value of environmental programs.

Variable and often unreliable monitoring of environmental conditions and inconsistent collection of data over time also make it difficult to assess environmental trends. The time period selected for a given analysis can seriously affect the results, and many scholars discount some data collected prior to the mid 1970s as unreliable. To improve monitoring, data collection, and analysis, some have proposed a new and independent Bureau of Environmental Statistics to supplement such activities now handled by the EPA and the Council on Environmental Quality, as well as other federal agencies.[37]

Despite these limitations on measuring environmental conditions and trends, it is nevertheless useful to review selected indicators of environmental quality. They tell us at least something about what we have achieved or failed to achieve after more than twenty-five years of national environmental protection policy.

Air Quality. Perhaps the best data on changes in the environment can be found for air quality, even if disagreement exists over which measures and time periods are most appropriate. The EPA reports that between 1970 and 1994, total emissions of the six principal air pollutants decreased by some 24 percent even while the nation's population, gross domestic product (GDP), and total vehicle miles traveled all increased significantly. Vehicle miles traveled more than doubled, the GDP rose by 90 percent, and the population grew by 27 percent. Looking at the most recent period where data are firmer, between 1985 and 1994, the nation experienced an 86 percent reduction in ambient levels of lead, 28 percent for carbon monoxide, 25 percent for sulfur dioxide, 20 percent for fine particulates, 12 percent for ozone, and 9 percent for nitrogen dioxide. Toxic air emissions from sources such as oil refineries, dry cleaning facilities, and chemical plants are beginning to decrease as new federal regulations on air toxics take effect. The same is true for production and release of ozone-depleting chlorofluorocarbons (CFCs), which began moving downward by the end of 1994, largely as a consequence of actions taken under the Montréal protocol.[38]

Despite these impressive gains in air quality, in 1994 some 62 million people lived in counties that failed to meet at least one of the national air quality standards for the six major pollutants covered by the Clean Air Act. More than 50 million people resided in counties where pollution levels in 1994 exceeded federal standards for ozone, the chief ingredient of urban smog. Such figures vary from year to year, reflecting changing economic activity and weather patterns. For example, in 1988, a hotter and drier year, 112 million Americans lived in counties that did not meet the ozone standard.[39]

One of most significant remaining problems is toxic or hazardous air pollutants, which have been associated with cancer, respiratory diseases, and other chronic and acute illnesses. The EPA had been extremely slow to regulate these pollutants, and it set federal standards for only seven of them by mid 1989. Public and congressional concern over toxic emissions led Congress to mandate more aggressive action in the 1986 Superfund amendments (SARA). That law required manufacturers of more than three hundred different chemicals (later doubled by the EPA) to report annually to the agency and the states in which they operate the amounts of those substances released to the air, water, or land. The EPA's Toxics Release Inventory (TRI) indicated that in 1989 some 22,000 companies released 5.7 billion pounds of hazardous substances to the environment, including 2.4 billion pounds of toxic chemicals emitted into the air. By 1993 emitted air toxics had declined to 1.2 billion pounds, significantly lower but still substantial.[40] These figures tell only part of the story, however, because not all sources of air toxics participate in the TRI program. In the 1990 Clean Air Act Amendments Congress stiffened regulation of toxic air pollutants, so the downward trend in air toxics should continue.

Water Quality. The nation's water quality also has improved since passage of the Clean Water Act of 1972, although more slowly and more unevenly than air quality. Monitoring data are less adequate for water quality than for air quality. For example, the best evidence for the present state of water quality can be found in the EPA's biennial National Water Quality Inventory, which compiles data reported by each state. But in 1994 the states surveyed only 17 percent of rivers and streams and only 42 percent of lakes, ponds, and reservoirs.

Based on those inventories, for the nation as a whole, 36 percent of rivers and streams were found to be impaired to some degree (14 percent severely and 22 percent moderately), as were 37 percent of lakes, ponds, and reservoirs (9 percent severely and 28 percent moderately). Such a classification means they were not meeting or fully meeting the national minimum water quality criteria for "designated beneficial uses" such as swimming, fishing, drinking-water supply, and support of aquatic wildlife. Those numbers show some improvement over previous years, yet they also indicate that many problems remain. The same survey found that 37 percent of the nation's estuaries were impaired, as were fully 97 percent of Great Lakes nearshore waters (including 63 percent that were severely impaired).[41] Prevention of further degradation of water quality in the face of a growing population and strong economic growth could be considered an important achievement. At the same time it clearly falls short of the goals of federal clean water acts.

Most of the huge financial investment in clean water since 1972 (more than $500 billion in public and private sector funds) has been expended on conventional "point" sources of water pollutants (where a particular source is identifiable), and most industries and municipalities have greatly reduced their discharges consistent with the intent of the Clean Water Act. Increasing emphasis on toxic pollutants and nonpoint sources such as agricultural runoff (the regulation of which is required by the Clean Water Act Amendments of 1987) is likely in the future. To date little progress has been made in halting groundwater contamination despite passage of the Safe Drinking Water Act of 1974 and the Resource Conservation and Recovery Act (RCRA) of 1976 and their later amendments. In 1995 EPA reported that groundwater is of good quality overall, but that "many local areas have experienced significant contamination." With some 51 percent of the nation's population relying on groundwater for drinking water, far more remains to be done. Indeed, the Natural Resources Defense Council released a study in 1995 that concluded some 53 million Americans drank water that violated EPA standards under the Clean Water Act; it estimated that nearly 1,000 deaths a year and at least 400,000 cases of waterborne illness may be attributed to contaminated water. It used the findings to urge Congress not to soften the Clean Water Act.[42]

Toxic and Hazardous Wastes. Progress in dealing with hazardous wastes and other toxic chemicals has been the least satisfactory of all pollution control programs. Implementation of the major laws has been extraordinarily slow due to the extent and complexity of the problems, scientific uncertainty, litigation by industry, public fear of siting treatment and storage facilities nearby, budgetary limitations, and poor management and lax enforcement by the EPA. As a result, gains have been quite modest to date judged by the most common measures. By 1995 only about 350 sites had been fully cleaned up out of more than 1,300 on the Superfund National Priorities List (NPL). However, remediation was actively under way at more than 90 percent of the NPL sites. Before budget cuts in 1995 sharply reduced Superfund cleanup activity, approximately 65 to 70 sites were being cleaned up each year.[43]

These limited achievements come at a high price. The EPA in recent years has spent about $30 million per NPL site remediated, with unclear and disputed benefits. Realistic estimates for cleanup of the tens of thousands of hazardous waste sites nationwide range from $484 billion to more than $1 trillion, with the job expected to take three to five decades to complete.[44]

The EPA has also set a sluggish pace in the related area of testing toxic chemicals. For example, under a 1972 law mandating control of pesticides and herbicides, only a handful of chemicals used to manufacture the fifty thousand pesticides in use in the United States has received full testing or retesting. The inadequate progress is especially worrisome in light of new evidence that some of those chemicals may disrupt human immune and reproductive systems and cause neurotoxic disorders.[45]

The track record over the past fifteen years on these programs clearly suggests the need for reevaluation of federal policy. Congress partially addressed that need in its revision of the Superfund program in 1986. It was at work on further revisions in 1993 and 1994, though partisan politics prevented enactment of compromise legislation that had won widespread support from all parties. The 104th Congress took up the challenge once again (see chap. 6).

Natural Resources. Comparable indicators of environmental progress can be found for natural resource use. The National Park System grew from about 26 million acres in 1960 to over 80 million acres by 1993, and the number of units in the system nearly *doubled.* Similarly, since adoption of the 1964 Wilderness Act, Congress has set aside 95 million acres of wilderness through the National Wilderness Preservation System. Since 1968 it has designated 151 Wild and Scenic Rivers with more than ten thousand protected miles. By 1993 the National Forest System consisted of 187 million acres, of which more than 32 million acres were protected as wilderness. The Fish and Wildlife Service manages almost 90 million acres in nearly five hundred units of the National Wildlife Refuge System—triple the land area of 1970.[46]

Other trends in natural resources are much less encouraging. During the 1970s and 1980s, the United States lost an estimated 290,000 acres a year of marshes, swamps, and other ecologically important wetlands to development, although this was well below the estimated 458,000 acres a year lost from the mid 1950s to the mid 1970s. The rate of loss seems to have slowed even more over the past decade, yet it is still unacceptably high, particularly in light of the valuable ecological functions of wetlands.[47]

Protection of biological diversity through the Endangered Species Act (ESA) also has produced only moderate success. As of 1994, twenty-one years after passage of the act, only about nine hundred species had been listed as endangered or threatened, although over the past decade the government has added about fifty new species each year to the list. Scores of critical habitats have been designated, and a number of recovery plans have been put into effect, yet only a few endangered species have fully recovered. Still, the Fish and Wildlife Service reports that more than 41 percent of listed species are stable or improving.

Insufficient budgets and staffs greatly slow the process of listing and recovery, as does conflict over property rights near affected habitats. Due largely to financial constraints, the Fish and Wildlife Service failed to protect hundreds of species even where substantial evidence existed to document threats to their existence. Some 3,500 species are currently candidates for inclusion on the list, but at the current pace of review, it would take decades to resolve their status. Moreover, development of recovery plans to protect all of those species would vastly exceed the annual budget of the agency.[48] The Interior Department's National Biological Service has been engaged in an inventory of the nation's biological diversity, and the department is beginning to emphasize an ecosystem management approach to protection of biodiversity. The future of these programs depends, however, on congressional willingness to reauthorize the much-criticized ESA. In 1995 Congress imposed a moratorium on the listing of new endangered species until it could decide what to do about the act. Achieving consensus on renewal of the ESA proved difficult. Yet Congress decided to end the moratorium in May 1996.

Assessing Environmental Progress

As the data reviewed above suggest, the nation made impressive gains between 1970 and 1996 in controlling many conventional pollutants and in expanding parks, wilderness areas, and other protected public lands. Despite some setbacks in the 1980s, progress on environmental quality continues, even if it is highly uneven. In the future, however, further advances will be more difficult, costly, and controversial. This is largely because the easy problems have already been addressed, and at this point marginal gains in air and water quality will cost more per unit of improvement than in the past (see chap. 9). Moreover, second-generation environmental threats such as toxic chemicals, hazardous wastes, and nuclear wastes are proving to be even more difficult than regulating "bulk" air and water pollutants in the 1970s. In these cases substantial progress may not be evident for years to come, and it will be expensive.

The same is true for the third generation of ecological problems, such as global climate change and protection of biodiversity. Solutions require an unprecedented degree of cooperation among nations and substantial improvement in institutional capacity for research, data collection, and analysis as well as policy development and implementation. Hence, success is likely to come slowly as national and international commitments to environmental protection grow and capabilities improve. Some long-standing problems, such as rapid population growth, will continue to be addressed primarily within nation states, even though the staggering effects on natural resources and environmental quality are felt worldwide. In mid 1995 the Earth's population of 5.7 billion was increasing at an estimated 1.5 percent (or nearly 90 million people) per year, with continued growth expected for another hundred years or more (see chap. 15).

The Costs and Benefits of Environmental Protection

The costs and benefits of environmental protection have been vigorously debated over the past decade. Critics argue that the kinds of improvements cited above are often not worth the considerable costs, particularly if they believe regulations adversely affect economic growth and employment or unduly restrict technological development. Environmentalists and other policy supporters point, however, to the improvements in public health, the protection of "priceless" natural amenities such as wilderness areas and clean lakes, and the preservation of biological diversity. They remain convinced that these benefits are well worth the investment of governmental and private funds. They also question assertions about adverse economic impacts of such policies, for which evidence is slim.[49] Some business leaders agree, and the evidence can be found in their determination to promote greening of their enterprises both for the economic gains they anticipate and to appeal to an environmentally concerned public (see chap. 12).

Skepticism about environmental policies led to several attempts in the 1980s and early 1990s under Presidents Reagan and Bush to impose regulatory oversight by the White House. It was hoped that costs could be limited by subjecting proposed regulations to cost-benefit analysis (see chaps. 5 and 9). The imposition of these controls, particularly by Bush's White House Council on Competitiveness under Vice President Dan Quayle, sharpened debate over the costs and benefits of environmental policies. The council had become a "back door" for business interests seeking to overturn what they saw as excessively costly environmental and other regulations. In January 1993 President Clinton abolished the council by executive order two days after taking office. Clinton signed a new executive order calling for economic impact studies of proposed regulations that were to inform decisionmaking, and especially to make it more cost effective and reasonable. The benefits of regulation would have to justify the costs though not necessarily outweigh them as required under the Reagan-Bush executive order.

The impetus for these kinds of centralized control efforts, and the intensity of the conflict over them, can be seen in the amount of money now spent on environmental protection by the federal government—as well as by state and local governments and the private sector. In 1994 the federal government was spending about $22 billion per year for all environmental and natural resource programs as calculated in the official budget category for these programs; that amounts to slightly less than 1.5 percent of the total federal budget of $1.5 trillion in FY 1994. According to the Clinton administration, the amount rises to about $35 billion (or 2.3 percent of the budget) if related categories are included. These totals are only a small part, however, of the country's annual investment in environmental protection. The EPA estimated in 1994 that the nation's overall spending on the environmental programs that the agency administers was about $140 billion per year, or about 2.2 percent of the GDP. By one calculation, private industry bears about 57 percent of that amount, local governments 24 percent, the federal government 15 percent, and state governments 4 percent.[50]

The benefits of environmental programs are more difficult to calculate and are often omitted entirely from reports on the costs or burdens of environmental policies. Should one measure only public health benefits of pollution control? What about esthetic values? Or the value of conserving ecosystems—water, soil, forests, wetlands—or of preventing disastrous climate change? These kinds of questions have led to a broad reexamination of the way in which nations account for the value of natural resources (see chap. 17).

Making rough comparisons of the benefits and costs of environmental policies, one could fairly conclude that many programs can be justified through standard economic analysis. That is, they produce measurable benefits that exceed the costs. This was true of the original Clean Air Act as it is for efforts to phase out the chloroflourocarbons (CFCs) that destroy the Earth's protective ozone layer. Energy conservation also makes good economic sense given the costs and environmental impacts of new power plants. Some environmental programs, such as thorough cleanup of all hazardous waste sites, however, are so expensive that they would be far more difficult to justify on economic grounds alone (see chap. 9).[51]

Debates over the costs and benefits of environmental policies will continue over the next few years, but with several new twists. Government spending on natural resources and the environment, which rose sharply in the 1970s, is unlikely to increase much in the 1990s for several reasons: persistent concern about federal budgetary deficits and a determination by Congress and the White House to balance the budget; widespread resistance to raising taxes; competing budgetary priorities, particularly from federal entitlement programs; and ideological opposition to regulatory programs by powerful interest groups and elected officials.

The burden of raising additional funds for environmental programs may be shouldered by the states, but some of them are more able and willing to do so than others (see chap. 2). These new conditions mean that more of the additional cost of environmental protection will be borne by the private sector: by industry and, eventually, by the consumer. Another implication is that the federal government as well as the states will have to seek innovative policies that promise improvements in environmental quality without adding substantially to their budgets. A third conclusion is that some form of risk-based priority setting is essential if environmental regulation is to make economic as well as environmental sense. This argument was advanced regularly by EPA administrator William K. Reilly in the early 1990s as well as by his successor, Carol Browner, and it is widely endorsed by students of environmental policy (see chaps. 7 and 10).[52]

Recent policy developments reflect these concerns—for example, the passage of the Pollution Prevention Act of 1990, which puts a premium on preventing, rather than cleaning up, pollution. Industry is already actively seeking ways to reduce the generation of waste, spurred on by sharply rising costs for hazardous waste disposal brought on by new federal standards under RCRA (see chap. 12).[53] A parallel development among environmental groups, particularly the Nature Conservancy, is a successful venture into private purchase of ecologically important land for preservation. Private efforts to save endangered lands have recently been extended to financially strapped developing nations in so-called debt-for-nature swaps.

At another level the question of whether environmental programs are "worth it" must be answered with another question: what are the costs of inaction? In some cases the risks to the environment and to society's well-being are so great that it would be imprudent to delay development of public policy. This is particularly so when modest measures taken at an early enough date might forestall the enormous costs of remedial efforts in the future, whether paid for by governments or the private sector. That was clearly the lesson of environmental contamination at DOE nuclear weapons facilities, as noted above. It is also apparent that such a precautionary policy response is called for in the cases of global climate change and deterioration of the ozone layer, where there is the potential for significant impacts on the environment, human health, and the economy. Much the same argument could be made for preserving biological diversity, investing in family planning programs, and responding to other compelling global environmental problems likely to be high on the agenda in the 1990s.

Conclusion

Over the past two decades, public concern and support for environmental protection have risen significantly, spurring the development of an expansive array of new policies that substantially increased the government's responsibilities for the environment and natural resources, both domestically and internationally.

The implementation of these policies, however, has been far more difficult and controversial than their supporters ever imagined. Moreover, the policies have not been entirely successful, particularly when measured by tangible improvements in environmental quality. Given the country's persistent and severe budgetary constraints, further progress requires that the nation search for more efficient and effective ways to achieve these goals, including the use of alternatives to conventional "command and control" regulation. Despite these qualifications, the record of the past two decades demonstrates convincingly that the U.S. government is able to produce significant environmental gains through public policies. Unquestionably, the environment would be worse today if the policies of the 1970s and 1980s had not been in place.

Emerging environmental threats on the national and international agenda are even more formidable than the first generation of problems addressed by government in the 1970s and the second generation that dominated political debate in the 1980s. Responding to them will require creative new efforts to improve the performance of government and other social institutions, and effective leadership to design appropriate strategies both within government and in society itself. We discuss this new policy agenda in chapter 17.

Government is an important player in the environmental arena, but it cannot pursue forceful initiatives unless the public supports such action. Ultimately, society's values will fuel the government's response to a rapidly changing world environment that, in all probability, will involve severe economic and social dislocations over the next two decades.

Notes

1. See the survey data reviewed in chap. 3. On global opinions as of 1992, see Riley E. Dunlap, George H. Gallup Jr., and Alec M. Gallup, "Of Global Concern: Results of the Health of the Planet Survey," *Environment* 35, no. 9 (1993): 7-15, 33-40.
2. Press briefing by Katie McGinty and others (Washington, D.C.: The White House, April 21, 1994), and a press briefing by Dr. Elaine Kamarck, Carol Browner, and others (Washington, D.C.: The White House, March 16, 1995). For an overview of recent criticisms of the EPA, recommended reforms, and actions taken over the past few years, see the National Academy of Public Administration's study, *Setting Priorities, Getting Results: A New Direction for EPA* (Washington, D.C.: NAPA, April 1995). A popular account of regulatory excess that drew enormous attention in Washington, D.C., in 1995 is Philip K. Howard, *The Death of Common Sense: How Law Is Suffocating America* (New York: Random House, 1994). See also chaps. 7 and 10 in this volume.
3. Bob Benenson, "GOP Sets the 104th Congress on New Regulatory Course," *Congressional Quarterly Weekly Report,* June 17, 1995, 1693-1705. See also four reports by the Natural Resource Defense Council: "Breach of Faith: How the Contract's Fine Print Undermines America's Environmental Success" (Washington, D.C.: NRDC, February 1995); "Stealth Attack: Gutting Environmental Protection through the Budget Process" (Washington, D.C.: NRDC, July 1995); "Selling Our Heritage: Congressional Plans for America's Public Lands" (Washington, D.C.: NRDC, July 1995); and "The Year of Living Dangerously: Congress and the Environment in 1995" (Washington, D.C.: NRDC, December 1995).
4. See Walter A. Rosenbaum, *Environmental Politics and Policy,* 3d ed. (Washington, D.C.: CQ Press, 1995); J. Clarence Davies III and Barbara S. Davies, *The Politics of Pollution,* 2d ed. (Indianapolis: Bobbs-Merrill, 1975); and Michael E. Kraft, *Environmental Policy and Politics: Toward the Twenty-first Century* (New York: HarperCollins, 1996).
5. Norman J. Vig and Michael E. Kraft, eds., *Environmental Policy in the 1980s: Reagan's New Agenda* (Washington, D.C.: CQ Press, 1984).
6. NAPA, *Setting Priorities,* 124-125.
7. John W. Kingdon, *Agendas, Alternatives, and Public Policies,* 2d ed. (New York: HarperCollins, 1995).
8. Roger W. Cobb and Charles D. Elder, *Participation in American Politics: The Dynamics of Agenda-Building* (Boston: Allyn and Bacon, 1972).
9. Kingdon, *Agendas.*
10. For a more thorough discussion of how the policy cycle model applies to environmental issues, see Kraft, *Environmental Policy and Politics.* The general model is reviewed in James E. Anderson, *Public Policymaking: An Introduction,* 2d ed. (Boston: Houghton Mifflin, 1994).
11. Ronald Inglehart, *The Silent Revolution: Changing Values and Political Styles among Western Publics* (Princeton, N.J.: Princeton University Press, 1977).
12. World Commission on Environment and Development, *Our Common Future* (New York: Oxford University Press, 1987).
13. Samuel P. Hays, *Beauty, Health, and Permanence: Environmental Politics in the United States, 1955-1985* (New York: Cambridge University Press, 1987); and Robert C. Paehlke, *Environmentalism and the Future of Progressive Politics* (New Haven, Conn.:

Yale University Press, 1989). For a comprehensive review of public opinion surveys on the environment and the evolution of the environmental movement, see Riley E. Dunlap and Angela G. Mertig, eds., *American Environmentalism: The U.S. Environmental Movement, 1970–1990* (Philadelphia: Taylor and Francis, 1992).

14. Paul J. Culhane, *Public Lands Politics: Interest Group Influence on the Forest Service and the Bureau of Land Management* (Baltimore: The Johns Hopkins University Press, 1981), esp. chap. 1.

15. Michael E. Kraft, "Population Policy," in *Encyclopedia of Policy Studies,* 2d ed., ed. Stuart S. Nagel (New York: Marcel Dekker, 1993).

16. Davies and Davies, *Politics of Pollution.*

17. Evan J. Ringquist, *Environmental Protection at the State Level: Politics and Progress in Controlling Pollution* (Armonk, N. Y.: M. E. Sharpe, 1993), chap. 2; and Davies and Davies, *Politics of Pollution,* chap. 2. A much fuller history of the origins and development of environmental policy than is provided here can be found in Michael J. Lacey, ed., *Government and Environmental Politics: Essays on Historical Developments since World War Two* (Baltimore: The Johns Hopkins University Press, 1989).

18. Hays, *Beauty, Health, and Permanence.* See also Riley E. Dunlap, "Public Opinion and Environmental Policy," in *Environmental Politics and Policy: Theories and Evidence,* 2d ed., ed. James P. Lester (Durham: Duke University Press, 1995); and Robert Cameron Mitchell, "Public Opinion and Environmental Politics in the 1970s and 1980s," in *Environmental Policy in the 1980s,* ed. Vig and Kraft.

19. Public Law 91-90 (42 USC 4321-4347), sec. 101. See Lynton K. Caldwell, *Science and the National Environmental Policy Act: Redirecting Policy through Procedural Reform* (Tuscaloosa: University of Alabama Press, 1982).

20. Michael E. Kraft, "Congress and Environmental Policy," and Sheldon Kamieniecki, "Political Parties and Environmental Policy," in *Environmental Politics and Policy,* 2d ed., ed. Lester.

21. Kraft, "Population Policy"; Council on Environmental Quality and Department of State, *The Global 2000 Report to the President,* vol. 1 (Washington, D.C.: GPO, 1980).

22. James Everett Katz, *Congress and National Energy Policy* (New Brunswick, N.J.: Transaction, 1984). For a discussion of the politics surrounding passage of the 1992 act and an outline of the provisions, see Kraft, *Environmental Politics and Policy,* chap. 5.

23. See, for example, Edwin H. Clark II, "Reaganomics and the Environment: An Evaluation," in *Environmental Policy in the 1980s,* ed. Vig and Kraft.

24. See Riley E. Dunlap, "Public Opinion on the Environment in the Reagan Era," *Environment* 29 (July-August 1987): 6-11, 32-37; and Mitchell, "Public Opinion and Environmental Politics."

25. Keith Schneider, "For Clinton and Gore, Contradictions in Balancing Jobs and Conservation," *New York Times,* October 13, 1992, A12; and Al Gore, *Earth in the Balance: Ecology and the Human Spirit* (Boston: Houghton Mifflin, 1992), 269.

26. Daniel A. Mazmanian and Jeanne Nienaber, *Can Organizations Change? Environmental Protection, Citizen Participation, and the Corps of Engineers* (Washington, D.C.: Brookings, 1979).

27. Richard N. L. Andrews, *Environmental Policy and Administrative Change: Implementation of the National Environmental Policy Act* (Lexington, Mass.: Lexington, 1976); Caldwell, *Science and the National Environmental Policy Act.;* and Robert V. Bartlett, *Policy through Impact Assessment: Institutionalized Analysis as a Policy Strategy* (New York: Greenwood, 1989).

28. Michael E. Kraft, "Searching for Policy Success: Reinventing the Politics of Site Remediation," *Environmental Professional* 16 (September 1994): 245-253; and Milton E. Russell, William Colglazier, and Bruce E. Tonn, "The U.S. Hazardous Waste Legacy," *Environment* 34 (1992): 12-15, 34-39.

29. John McCormick, *Reclaiming Paradise: The Global Environmental Movement* (Bloomington: Indiana University Press, 1989), 110. McCormick provides a useful overview of international developments during this period.

30. Alfred A. Marcus, *Promise and Performance: Choosing and Implementing Environmental Policy* (Westport, Conn.: Greenwood, 1980); Lettie McSpadden Wenner, *The Environmental Decade in Court* (Bloomington: Indiana University Press, 1982); R. Shep Melnick, *Regulation and the Courts: The Case of the Clean Air Act* (Washington, D.C.: Brookings, 1983); and Marc K. Landy, Marc J. Roberts, and Stephen R. Thomas, *The Environmental Protection Agency: Asking the Wrong Questions*, 2d ed. (New York: Oxford University Press, 1994).

31. George C. Eads and Michael Fix, *Relief or Reform? Reagan's Regulatory Dilemma* (Washington, D.C.: Urban Institute Press, 1984).

32. J. Clarence Davies III, "Environmental Institutions and the Reagan Administration," and Richard N. L. Andrews, "Deregulation: The Failure at EPA," in *Environmental Policy in the 1980s*, ed. Vig and Kraft.

33. See Philip Shabecoff, "Reagan and Environment: To Many a Stalemate," *New York Times*, January 2, 1989, 1, 8.

34. Ibid., 8.

35. John H. Cushman Jr., "E.P.A. Is Canceling Pollution Testing Across the Nation," *New York Times*, November 25, 1995, 1, 8; and Cushman, "Program to Clean Toxic Waste Sites Is Left in Turmoil," *New York Times*, January 15, 1996, 1, A9.

36. Kraft, *Environmental Policy and Politics*, chap. 6; Robert V. Bartlett, "Evaluating Environmental Policy," in *Environmental Policy in the 1990s*, 2d ed., ed. Vig and Kraft; Evan J. Ringquist, "Evaluating Environmental Policy Outcomes," in *Environmental Politics and Policy*, 2d ed., ed. Lester; and Gerrit Knaap, T. John Kim, and John Fitipaldi, eds., *Environmental Program Evaluation* (Champaign: University of Illinois Press, 1996).

37. See Paul R. Portney, "Needed: A Bureau of Environmental Statistics," *Resources* 90 (Winter 1988): 12-15; and Clifford S. Russell, "Monitoring and Enforcement," in *Public Policies for Environmental Protection*, ed. Portney. The best single source of trend data on environmental quality can be found in the CEQ, *Environmental Quality: Twenty-fourth Annual Report* (Washington, D.C.: Council on Environmental Quality, 1995).

38. Environmental Protection Agency, "Air Quality Trends" (Research Triangle Park, N.C.: Office of Air Quality Planning and Standards, September 1995); and Richard A. Kerr, "Ozone-Destroying Chlorine Tops Out," *Science* 271 (January 5, 1996): 32. The EPA document is a summary of the more extensive annual *National Air Quality and Emissions Trend Report*. For a broader discussion of air quality trends and policies, see Paul R. Portney, "Air Pollution Policy," in *Public Policies for Environmental Protection*, ed. Portney; and Gary C. Bryner, *Blue Skies, Green Politics: The Clean Air Act of 1990*, 2d ed. (Washington, D.C.: CQ Press, 1996).

39. EPA, "Air Quality Trends," and CEQ, *Environmental Quality*, 15.

40. Ibid., 12-13.

41. Environmental Protection Agency, "National Water Quality Inventory 1994 Report to Congress: Executive Summary" (Washington, D.C.: Office of Water, December 1995). See also Debra S. Knopman and Richard A. Smith, "Twenty Years of the Clean Water Act," *Environment* 35 (January-February 1993): 17-20, 34-41; and CEQ, *Environmental Quality*, chap. 2.

42. EPA, "National Water Quality," 30; and Erik Olsen and Diane Cameron, "The Dirty Little Secret about Our Drinking Water" (Washington, D.C.: NRDC, February 1995).

43. CEQ, *Environmental Quality*, 293-294. For a more positive assessment than usually found, see Charles De Saillan, "In Praise of Superfund," *Environment* 35 (October 1993): 42-44. For critical overviews of the Superfund program, see Daniel Mazmanian and David Morell, *Beyond Superfailure: America's Toxics Policy for the 1990s* (Boulder: Westview, 1992); and John A. Hird, *Superfund: The Political Economy of Risk* (Baltimore: The Johns Hopkins University Press, 1994).

44. Russell, Colglazier, and Tonn, "U.S. Hazardous Waste Legacy," and Kraft, "Searching for Policy Success."

45. Theo Colborn, Dianne Dumanoski, and John Peterson Myers, *Our Stolen Future* (New York: NAL/Dutton, 1996).

46. CEQ, *Environmental Quality*, chap. 5 and 473-474.

47. EPA, "National Water Quality," 28-29; and CEQ, *Environmental Quality*, chap 3.

48. CEQ, *Environmental Quality*, chap. 6; see also Richard J. Tobin, *The Expendable Future: U. S. Politics and the Protection of Biological Diversity* (Durham: Duke University Press, 1990); and Steven Lewis Yaffee, *The Wisdom of the Spotted Owl: Policy Lessons for a New Century* (Washington, D.C.: Island Press, 1994).

49. See, e.g., Portney, *Public Policies for Environmental Protection*, and Tom Tietenberg, *Environmental Economics and Policy* (New York: HarperCollins, 1994). Estimates of economic impacts show a wide variance, depending on the methods and models used, and on the economic indicators selected, but generally they are small. A number of studies indicate that at the state level environmental protection and economic prosperity go hand in hand. See Stephen M. Meyer, *Environmentalism and Economic Prosperity* (Cambridge: MIT Press, forthcoming). The same is true at the international level; see, for example, Roger H. Bezdek, "Environment and Economy: What's the Bottom Line," *Environment* 35 (September 1993): 7-11, 25-32; and Michael E. Porter and Claas van der Linde, "Green and Competitive: Ending the Stalemate," *Harvard Business Review* (September-October 1995): 120-134.

50. See the budget tables in appendixes 2 and 3. The Clinton administration's estimate of overall spending on the environment is reported in NRDC, "Stealth Attack." The Commerce Department's estimates of total national spending on pollution abatement and control are lower than the EPA's. Commerce reports a total of $102 billion for 1992 (current dollars). See CEQ, *Environmental Quality*, 390. For the estimates of who pays for these amounts, see Paul Portney and Katherine N. Probst, "Cleaning Up Superfund," *Resources* 114 (Winter 1994): 2-5.

51. Portney, *Public Policies for Environmental Protection.*

52. See NAPA, *Setting Priorities;* and J. Clarence Davies, ed., *Comparing Environmental Risks: Tools for Setting Governmental Priorities* (Washington, D.C.: Resources for the Future, 1996).

53. See Joel S. Hirschhorn and Kirsten U. Oldenburg, *Prosperity without Pollution: The Prevention Strategy for Industry and Consumers* (New York: Van Nostrand Reinhold, 1991).

2

Power to the States:
The Promise and Pitfalls of Decentralization

Barry G. Rabe

The problem which all federalized nations have to solve is how to secure an efficient central government and preserve national unity, while allowing free scope for the diversities, and free play to the . . . members of the federation. It is . . . to keep the centrifugal and centripetal forces in equilibrium, so that neither the planet States shall fly off into space, nor the sun of the Central government draw them into its consuming fires.

—Lord James Bryce
The American Commonwealth

A quarter-century ago the conventional wisdom on federalism viewed "the planet States" as sufficiently lethargic to require a powerful "Central government" in many areas of environmental policy. States were widely derided as mired in corruption, hostile to innovation, and unable to take a serious role in environmental policy out of fear of alienating key economic constituencies. In more recent years, the tables have turned—so much so that the conventional wisdom now berates an overheated federal government that squelches state creativity and capability to tailor environmental policies to local realities. The decentralization mantra of the 1990s calls for the extended transfer of environmental policy resources and regulatory authority from Washington, D.C., to states and localities. Such a transfer would pose a potentially formidable test of the thesis that more localized units know best.

What accounts for this sea-change in our understanding of the role of states in environmental policy? How have they evolved in recent decades and what sorts of functions do they assume most comfortably and effectively? Despite state resurgence, are there areas in which states fall short? If so, should they defer authority to their federal counterparts? Looking ahead, should regulatory authority devolve to the states, or are there better ways to sort out national and state responsibilities?

This chapter will address these questions, relying heavily on evidence of state performance in environmental policy. This will involve both an overview of state evolution and a set of brief case studies that explore state strengths and limitations. These state-specific accounts will be interwoven with assessments of the federal government's role, for good or ill, in the development of state environmental policy.

The States as "New Heroes" of American Federalism

Political scientists and policy analysts are generally most adept at analyzing institutional foibles and policy failures. Indeed, much of the literature on environmental policy follows this pattern, with criticisms becoming particularly voluminous and potent when directed toward federal efforts in this area. By contrast, states have received much more generous treatment. Many influential books on state government and federalism, in addition to journals, think tanks, and professional associations, portray states as highly dynamic and effective. Environmental policy is often depicted as a prime example of this general pattern of state effectiveness. Some analysts go so far as to characterize states as the "new heroes" of American federalism, having long since eclipsed a doddering federal government. According to this line of argument, states are consistently at the cutting edge of policy innovation, eager to find creative solutions to environmental problems. When the states fall short, an overzealous federal partner is often said to be at fault.

Such commentary has considerable empirical support. The vast majority of state governments have undergone fundamental changes since the first Earth Day in 1970. Many have drafted new constitutions and gained access to unprecedented revenues through expanded taxing powers. Substantial amounts of federal transfer dollars have further swelled state coffers, allowing them to pursue policy commitments that would previously have been unthinkable. In turn, state bureaucracies have expanded and become more professionalized, as have the staffs serving governors and legislatures.[1] This activity has been further stimulated by increasingly competitive two-party systems in many regions, intensifying pressure on elected officials to deliver desired services. Expanded use of direct democracy provisions, such as the initiative and referendum, and increasing activism by state courts have further contributed to this new era. Studies of this resurgent "statehouse democracy" show that policymaking at the state level has proven highly responsive to dominant public opinion within each state.[2] On the whole, citizens are thought to be a good deal more satisfied with the package of public services and regulations dispensed from their state capitals than with those from Washington.

This transformed state role is evident in virtually every area of environmental policy. States collectively spent more than $10 billion on environmental and related natural resource concerns in FY 1991, with only about 20 percent of that funding coming from federal grant programs. The Council of State Governments has estimated that about 70 percent of all significant environmental legislation enacted by states has little or nothing to do with federal policy.[3] Many areas of environmental policy are clearly dominated by states, including most areas of waste management, groundwater protection, and coastal zone management. And even in those areas of policy that bear a firm federal imprint, such as air pollution control and pesticides regulation, states have considerable opportunity to oversee implementation and move beyond federal standards if they so choose. Political scientist DeWitt John speaks for a wide range of policy analysts in noting that "states are willing to spend their own dollars and enact their own policies, without being forced by the federal government to do so. Virtually all states have taken some steps to go beyond federally imposed requirements, and some have taken the lead in several areas." [4]

That growing commitment is further reflected in the institutional arrangements established by states to address environmental problems. Many states have long since moved beyond their traditional placement of environmental programs in public health departments in favor of comprehensive agencies that gather most environmental responsibilities under a single organizational umbrella. Arizona, New Mexico, Oklahoma, Tennessee, Utah, and Virginia have followed this pattern over the past few years, leaving only Colorado, Hawaii, Idaho, Kansas, Montana, and North Dakota adhering to the historic form. [5]

These agencies have sweeping, cross-programmatic responsibilities and have continually grown in staff and complexity over the past decade. Ironically, many mirror the organizational framework of the much-maligned U.S. Environmental Protection Agency (EPA), dividing regulatory activity by environmental media of air, land, and water and thereby increasing the likelihood of shifting environmental contamination back and forth across medium boundaries. Despite this fragmentation, such institutions do provide states with a firm institutional foundation for addressing a wide array of environmental concerns.

This expanded state commitment to environmental policy may be accelerated not only by the broader factors introduced above but also by features somewhat unique to this policy area. First, a growing number of scholars contend that broad public support for environmental protection provides much impetus for bottom-up policy development. Such "civic environmentalism" stimulates numerous state and local stakeholders to take creative collective action independent of federal intervention. [6] In turn, game-theoretic analyses of efforts to protect "common-pool resources" such as river basins side decisively with local or regional approaches to resource protection as opposed to top-down controls. Many such analyses go so far as to argue that any central government intervention in such settings is often unnecessary at best and downright destructive at worst. [7]

Second, the proliferation of environmental policy professionals, representing industry, advocacy groups, and particularly state agencies, has created a sizable base of talent and ideas for policy innovation. Contrary to conventional depictions of agency officials as shackled by elected "principals," an alternative view finds considerable policy entrepreneurship in state and local policymaking circles. This pattern is especially evident in environmental policy, where numerous areas of specialization place a premium on expert opinion. [8]

Third, environmental policy in many states is further stimulated by direct democracy, facilitating initiatives, referendums, and recall of elected officials not allowed at the federal level. Twenty-four states and Washington, D.C., have some form of direct democracy, representing well over half the U.S. population. Moreover, a number of states are currently considering the addition of such provisions, and thousands of localities employ some direct democracy form of their own. This policy tool has been used to consider an array of state environmental policy options, including nuclear plant closure, mandatory deposits on beverage containers, recycling programs, support for waste facility siting proposals, mandatory disclosure of commercial product toxicity, public land acquisition, state agency reconfiguration, and multi-million-dollar bond issues for a host of environmental purposes. Use of this tool has grown at an exponential rate in recent decades, particularly in environmental policy, and numerous policies first launched in a single state through direct democracy have become models for other states.[9]

The Cutting Edge of Policy: Cases of State Innovation

The convergence of these various political forces has served to unleash substantial new environmental policy at the state level. Scholars have attempted to analyze some of this activity through various ranking schemes that determine which states are most innovative. They consistently conclude that certain states tend to take the lead in most areas of policy innovation, followed by an often uneven pattern of innovation diffusion across state and regional boundaries. Somewhat related studies attempt to examine which economic and political factors are most likely to influence the rigor of state policy or the level of resources devoted to it.[10] An important but less-examined question concerns recent developments in state environmental policy and whether or not they constitute a marked improvement over conventional approaches. Evidence from select states suggests that a number of state innovations offer worthy alternatives to prevailing approaches. Indeed, many of these innovations were direct responses to shortcomings in existing regulatory design. A series of brief case studies offers some indication of the breadth and potential effectiveness of state innovation.

Pollution Prevention

One of the greatest challenges facing U.S. environmental policy is the need to shift from a pollution control mode to one of prevention. Historically speaking, both federal and state policies have performed poorly in the prevention area, but growing evidence suggests that some states are pursuing prevention in an increasingly systematic and effective way. All fifty states now have at least one formal pollution prevention program, with the oldest and most common of these involving technical assistance to industries and networking services that link potential collaborators. A smaller but growing set of state programs, however, is redefining pollution prevention in larger terms, cutting across conventional programmatic boundaries with a series of mandates and incentives for pursuit of prevention opportunities. States such as Massachusetts, Minnesota, New Jersey, New York, and Wisconsin have been particularly innovative in this area.

Among these, Minnesota may now have the most multifaceted program to date. The state dramatically increased its traditional technical assistance efforts in 1990 with passage of the Minnesota Toxic Pollution Prevention Act. This legislation calls on approximately three hundred and fifty Minnesota firms to submit annual toxic pollution prevention plans. These plans must outline each firm's current use and release of a long list of toxic pollutants and establish formal goals for their reduction or elimination over a specified period of time. Firms have considerable latitude in determining how to attain these goals, contrary to the technology-forcing character of much federal regulation. But they must meet state-established reduction timetables and pay fees on releases. Overall releases of these substances have begun to drop markedly in recent years. In addition, a related Minnesota program achieved a 52 percent drop in releases of seventeen of the most toxic substances found in industrial waste during its first four years of operation.

In both these instances, firms often relied not on expensive technological solutions but on equipment modification; substitution of less-dangerous chemicals; manufacturing-process adjustments; and improved training, housekeeping, and equipment maintenance. Minnesota officials have supplemented these efforts with ongoing training and conferences, awards for pollution prevention excellence, and grants to local governments. In addition, the state created an Interagency Pollution Prevention Advisory Team with representatives of twenty agencies to implement an aggressive gubernatorial executive order to pursue pollution prevention opportunities in all state-sponsored activities.

Regulatory Integration

Both federal and state environmental protection efforts have long been suspect owing to their reliance on medium-based strategies to control pollution. This approach is unsatisfactory not only because it reacts to pollution after it is created but also because it tends to shift pollutants to the medium least regulated at a given moment. Few states showed much awareness of this problem, much less addressed it, prior to the mid 1980s.[11] But there is growing evidence that some states are beginning to look systematically at various regulatory areas—such as permitting, monitoring, inspection, and enforcement—to find more integrative ways to approach environmental problems, thereby minimizing pollutant transfer across medium boundaries.

Permitting may be the regulatory tool most in need of integration. Permits are used to limit specific pollutant releases into individual environmental media but often target narrow concerns without any consideration of possible impact on other programs or media. Many states have attempted to streamline their administration of permit programs, although these have generally served to accelerate the process of permit issuance rather than explore integration prospects. More recently, states such as New Jersey and Minnesota have taken particularly bold steps toward integration. New Jersey, for example, is using data from its Minnesota-like pollution prevention planning requirements to attempt to transform its approach to permitting. Eighteen manufacturing facilities around the state have been selected for a project whereby each of their disparate permits are eliminated in favor of a single document that outlines a unified environmental protection strategy. As in the Minnesota prevention case, firms are given considerable flexibility in determining how to reach state-established emissions reduction goals. They are nevertheless expected to achieve significant environmental improvements and refrain from cross-media transfers.

In the first case completed under this program, state officials found a major pharmaceutical firm mired in a typical maze of permits administered by different officials with distinct program orientations at separate times. In all, the facility had 897 separate permits for air quality alone, in concert with dozens of additional permits for other areas such as water quality and solid and hazardous waste management. Upon review of the entire facility through integrated inspection and permit review, state officials discovered numerous instances of inadvertent cross-media transfer and pollution prevention opportunities waiting to be seized. They compressed all permits into a single document with individual chapters for each of the thirty-one separate parts of the facility. This comprehensive permit establishes significant emissions-reduction goals for the facility. The firm is pleased with the process and has been followed by numerous others eager to volunteer, environmental advocacy groups have registered support, and the governor participated in the permit signing ceremony and heralded the event as a model for regulatory innovation.[12] Four additional cases in New Jersey have subsequently been completed with comparable outcomes.

Such integrative activity is not confined to permitting, as select states are reviewing other cornerstones of the traditional regulatory process. Idaho, Massachusetts, and Minnesota have taken particularly prominent roles in reworking inspection and enforcement efforts to better consider cross-media concerns. In turn, states such as California, Maine, Massachusetts, New Jersey, and Wisconsin have pursued reorganizational options that might better foster integration—and prevention—strategies. These range from wholesale reorganization of agencies into divisions that merge single-medium programs (as in Massachusetts) to issue-specific efforts to pull together officials from diverse programs to secure a unified focus on a particular problem (as in Wisconsin).

Economic Incentives

Economic analysts of environmental policy have long lamented the U.S. system's penchant for command-and-control rules and regulations. They would prefer to see a more economically sensitive set of policies, such as fees on emissions and incentives to reward good environmental performance. Neither federal nor state governments have escaped such critical scrutiny, although a number of states have attempted to respond in recent years. In all, the states have enacted more than two hundred and fifty measures that can be characterized as "green taxes," including environmentally related charges and tax incentives.[13] Many states have become increasingly reliant on emission or waste fees, to provide both an economic disincentive to pollute and a source of funds for program management. A growing number of states are also revising their tax policies for environmental purposes. For example, Iowa exempts all pollution-control equipment purchased for use in the state from taxation, while Louisiana exempts such equipment from the state sales tax. Other states, such as New Jersey and Oregon, offer a series of tax credits for purchase of recycling equipment or capital investments necessary to facilitate recycling or reuse of a particular product. At the same time, states are also considering ways to adjust pricing of commercial goods to encourage use of recycled products, such as an Ohio proposal to create a price preference of up to 10 percent for purchases of high-grade recycled paper rather than virgin paper.

Perhaps the most visible economic incentive programs involve refundable taxes on beverage containers. Ten states, covering 30 percent of the population, have such programs in place. Particular provisions of these programs vary somewhat, although most operate with limited direct involvement by state officials. Deposits are passed along a system that includes consumers, container redemption facilities such as grocery stores, and firms that actually reuse or recycle the containers.

Michigan's program is widely regarded as among the most successful of these state efforts and, like a number of others, is a product of direct democracy. Nearly two-thirds of Michigan voters endorsed a ballot proposal for the deposit program in 1976, despite the fact that forces opposing the program outspent proponents by a ten-to-one margin during the campaign. All subsequent polling has indicated continuing high levels of public support for the program, and it clearly influenced comparable action in a few other states in the years immediately following enactment. The state's program is alone in placing a dime deposit on containers—double the more conventional nickel—which may contribute to its unusually high compliance rate. Whereas most states achieve a return rate of 79 to 83 percent, Michigan has consistently reached a rate of 95 percent or higher. Various studies have concluded that the program has contributed to significant declines in litter and the volumes of solid waste requiring disposal, as well as generated energy savings and reduction in injuries from container-caused lacerations. Some controversy has emerged over whether deposits from unclaimed containers should be given to distributors or revert to the state. In addition, some contend that container deposit programs reduce the economic viability of curbside recycling programs as they remove relatively lucrative items from their portion of the recycling stream. Nonetheless, these concerns are generally regarded as minor and unlikely to block the continued implementation of this popular program.[14]

The diffusion of this innovation to other states has not been as extensive as might be expected, in large part due to strong opposition from beverage manufacturers and distributors in states where proposals have been advanced. But while no additional states have imposed deposit requirements on beverages since 1983, a growing number of them are using this method to promote recycling of such items as lead-acid batteries, motor oil, pesticide containers, and appliances. In turn, Florida has eschewed the Michigan deposit strategy but has imposed a two-cent advance-disposal fee on containers that are not recycled at a rate of at least 50 percent.[15]

One particularly effective spin-off of this approach involves efforts by Oregon, Minnesota, Virginia, and Wisconsin to address the problem of used tires. The proliferation of such tires, due to the growth in number of automobiles in use and miles driven as well as the glacial pace of used tire decomposition, has led to serious environmental problems in many regions of the nation. Tire piles are notorious breeding grounds for insects and have been shown to facilitate the spread of diseases such as encephalitis; some piles have caught fire, leading to significant release of unrestricted toxic air emissions.

Oregon pioneered the use of economic incentives for waste tires with legislation enacted in 1987 intended to address a substantial backlog of used tires and to facilitate reuse of the approximately 2 million tires removed from active use in the state each year. The state banned disposal of whole waste tires unless recycling proved unworkable and established a $1 fee on retail sale of new tires for use in a waste tire-recycling account. This account was intended to provide partial reimbursement to firms that made use of waste tires. It provided a penny per pound of material used (reaching $20 per ton) for new products such as doormats, benches, buoys, and artificial reefs and also set aside funds to clean up existing tire piles. The program proved so successful, it began to phase out in 1991 and was closed entirely in 1993. Tire piles have disappeared in Oregon, and markets have now emerged to handle the ongoing supply of used tires without the reimbursement subsidies. In the event the problem recurs, the state has kept $1.5 million from the fund as a contingency and retains legislative authority to reactivate its efforts.[16] It continues to operate a permitting program that oversees collection, transport, and storage of waste tires.

Emissions Trading

A somewhat more exotic form of economic-based regulation involves the creation of a regionally based market whereby allowances to pollute can be purchased and swapped. California has been experimenting with such mechanisms for nearly two decades. In 1994 the state's South Coast Air Quality Management District sought to expand on these efforts through the creation of a regional market for trading permits to achieve substantial reductions in nitrogen oxide and sulfur dioxide emissions. Its RECLAIM program (Regional Clean Air Incentives Market) determines the overall level of allowable emissions in the region and enables different firms to trade pollution allowances, with the intent of "affording sources maximum flexibility in deciding how best to control those pollutants and stimulating innovation and technological advances."[17] The role of government in this process shifts markedly from its conventional one. Rather than assure that every significant emissions source is using mandated technology in the proper way, the district instead examines overall regional trends through continuous emissions monitoring and guards against any abuses in the market trading system. There is already discussion of extending this approach to other major air pollutants, including volatile organic compounds.

Disclosure Mandates

California has also played a prominent role in developing policy that places essential information concerning potential risk posed by chemicals directly in the hands of the citizenry. As in the Michigan deposit program, California's Safe Drinking Water and Toxic Enforcement Act of 1986 was a direct democracy measure passed with overwhelming voter support. Better known as Proposition 65, this legislation supplements existing right-to-know programs through mandatory disclosure of exposure to chemicals known by the state to cause cancer or reproductive toxicity. The state must update this list annually, and firms may not "knowingly and intentionally" expose any person to listed chemicals without providing "clear and reasonable warning." Exemptions from the list require evidence that exposure will pose "no significant risk."

California's warning list now contains approximately five hundred chemicals, including pharmaceutical products and others with an array of commercial uses. More than two hundred and fifty numeric standards have been established to set a clear line for implementing the "no significant risk" provisions. Whereas such standards are imposed at a halting pace at the federal level, this legislation gives companies an incentive to move apace with risk assessment in order to establish clear guidelines on what substances require warning procedures. To assure compliance, the legislation imposes stiff penalties for violations and allows "any person in the public interest" to bring suit against violations sixty days after notice. There are stiff penalties for violations, 25 percent of which can be used as "bounty" rewards for individuals who successfully bring suit. A 1992 report by a Proposition 65 review panel concluded that "by federal standards, Proposition 65 has resulted in 100 years of progress in the areas of hazard identification, risk assessment, and exposure assessment." Industry evaluations are less enthusiastic, although many leaders confirm the burden has not been as onerous as anticipated. Interestingly, no other state has followed California's path in this area to date, although others have experimented with various forms of environmental information disclosure to the public.[18]

State Limits

Such a promising set of innovations would seem to augur well for the states' involvement in environmental policy. Any such enthusiasm must be tempered, however, with an enduring concern over how evenly that innovative vigor extends over the entire nation. One of the long-standing rationales for giving the federal government so much authority in environmental policy is that states face inherent limitations in environmental policy. Rather than a consistent, across-the-board pattern of dynamism, we shall see a more uneven pattern of performance than the current conventional wisdom might antici-pate. This imbalance becomes particularly evident when environmental problems are not confined to the boundaries of a specific state. Many environ-mental issues are by definition transboundary, raising enduring questions of interstate and interregional equity in allocating responsibility for the burden of environmental protection.

Uneven State Performance

Many of the efforts to rank states according to their environmental regulatory rigor, institutional capacity, or general innovativeness tend to resemble schemes to evaluate the relative strengths of collegiate basketball and football teams. Some of these are done with great methodological sophistication, whereas others simply poll a set of observers. Both tend to reach similar conclusions and draw particular attention to whatever teams receive the highest rankings. A similar phenomenon applies in environmen-tal policy rankings, with the same subset of states reaching the top rungs year after year. By contrast, a significant number of states consistently tend to fall much further down the list, raising questions as to their overall regulatory capacity and commitment. As political scientist William Lowry has noted, "not all states are responding appropriately to policy needs within their borders. . . . If matching between need and response were always high and weak programs existed only where pollution was low, this would not be a problem. However, this is not the case."[19] Interestingly, given all the hoopla surrounding the newfound dynamism of states in environmental policy, and public policy more generally, there has been remarkably little analysis of the performance of those states that not only fail to crack "top ten" rankings but also consistently lag below the median.

What we do know about such states should surely give one pause over the extent to which state dynamism is truly cross-cutting. Despite consider-able economic growth in formerly poor regions, such as the Southeast, substantial variation endures among state governments in their rates of public expenditure, with no demonstrable change in the amount of interstate expenditure variation over the past quarter-century.[20] Similar fiscal patterns are evident in environmental and natural resource spending. State expendi-tures in fiscal year 1991 ranged from more than $65 per capita in nine states to less than $25 per capita in fifteen others. Similar variation is evident when viewing such spending as a percentage of total state expenditures or in dollars per manufacturer, and it has remained relatively stable over time.[21] Cost of living differences among states account for only a small portion of this variation in state expenditure levels. In turn, efforts to classify states by other measures reveal similarly discordant patterns. A number of states, such as Colorado, North Carolina, and Utah, prohibit their environmental agencies from exceeding any federal regulatory standards, whereas some others tend to view federal standards as establishing minimum levels that they frequently elect to exceed.

While some states are unveiling exciting new programs, there is growing reason to worry about how effectively states in general handle core functions either delegated to them under federal programs or left exclusively to their oversight. Studies of water quality program implementation undertaken by the U.S. General Accounting Office and the Natural Resources Defense Council in the 1990s have found enormous variation in the methods used by states to determine water quality and the frequency with which they undertake enforcement actions when violations are discovered.[22] States also employ highly variable water quality standards in areas such as sewage contamination, groundwater protection, nonpoint water pollution, wetland preservation, fish advisories, and beach closures. Inconsistencies abound in reporting accuracy, suggesting that national assessments of water quality trends that rely on data from state reports may be highly suspect. Moreover, many major water bodies receive remarkably minimal monitoring attention of any sort from state authorities. States such as Alabama and Texas, for example, conduct no regular monitoring of their extensive marine beaches, yet report consistently that all estuaries and coastal waters meet the swimmability goals of the Clean Water Act. Ironically, large percentages of these same waters have been closed for fishing over extended periods due to high levels of bacteriological pollution. Insufficient drinking-water monitoring by state and local officials has led to a number of disease outbreaks in recent years, perhaps most notably the 1993 Milwaukee-area contamination of drinking water by livestock runoff that caused an estimated 370,000 citizens to become ill with cryptosporidiosis, a gastrointestinal illness.[23]

Comparable problems have emerged in state enforcement of air quality and waste management programs, where officially reported numbers on regulatory actions, emission levels, waste disposal capacity, and waste reduction levels are of similarly questionable utility.[24] Despite efforts in some states to integrate and streamline permitting, many states have extensive backlogs in the permit programs they operate and thereby have no real indication of facility compliance with various regulatory standards. According to a 1993 EPA study, more than half of all water pollution permits have expired, reaching rates of up to 94 percent in Virginia and 93 percent in New Mexico.[25]

Enduring Federal Dependency

More sweeping assertions of state resurgence are further undermined by the penchant of many states to cling to organizational design and program priorities set in Washington, D.C. Some states, including those described above, have indicated that it is possible to pursue far-reaching agency reorganization and other integrative policies without significant opposition—or grant reduction—from the federal government. But the vast majority of states continues to adhere to a medium-based, pollution control framework for agency organization, contributing to the enduring programmatic fragmentation common among state programs and departments. Although a growing number of state officials speak favorably and knowledgeably about shifting toward integrative approaches, many remain hard-pressed to give any concrete illustration of how their states have begun to move in that direction.

In fact, a good deal of the most innovative state-level activity has been at least partially stimulated—and underwritten—through federal grants. Although a number of states have developed fee systems to cover a growing portion of their costs, many states rely heavily on federal grants to fund pollution prevention activities. In the early 1990s more than one-third of all state pollution prevention expenditures came from federal sources, with some states completely reliant on federal dollars for their prevention efforts.[26] Similarly, states have continued to be recipients of other important sources of federal support, including grants and technical assistance for twenty-six state comparative risk assessment and reduction projects.[27] On the whole, states receive approximately 20 percent of their total program funding from federal grants, although a number of states rely on Washington for as much as 30 to 40 percent of their total funding. Those states most reliant on federal dollars tend, predictably, to be those least likely to rank among the most innovative and effective states.

Furthermore, for all the opprobrium heaped on the federal government in environmental policy, Washington has provided states with at least four other forms of valuable assistance, some of which has directly contributed to the resurgence and innovation of state environmental policy. First, federal development of a Toxics Release Inventory, modeled in 1986 after a program initially attempted in New Jersey, has emerged as a vital component of many of the most promising pollution prevention and cross-media integration initiatives. This program has generated unprecedented information concerning toxic releases and provided states an essential data source for exploring alternative regulatory approaches. Current pollution prevention programs in states such as New Jersey, Minnesota, New York, and elsewhere would be unthinkable without such an annual data source. Second, states remain almost totally dependent on the federal government for the essential insights gained through research and development. Each year the federal government outspends the states in environmental research and development by more than twenty to one, and states have shown little indication of wanting to pick up this burden in search of research programs tailored to their particular technological and informational needs.

Third, the most successful efforts to coordinate environmental protection on a multistate, regional basis have received a great deal of federal input and support. A series of initiatives in the Chesapeake Bay and Great Lakes

Basin has received much acclaim for tackling difficult issues and forging regional partnerships; federal participation—through grants, technical assistance, coordination, and efforts to unify regional standards—has proven useful in both cases.[28] By contrast, other major bioregions, including the Puget Sound, Gulf of Mexico, Columbia River system, and Mississippi Basin, have lacked comparable federal participation and have generally not experienced creative interstate partnerships.[29] Their experience contradicts the popular thesis that regional coordination improves when central authority is minimal or nonexistent.

Fourth, the hamhandedness of regulatory actions by EPA headquarters is legendary, but the federal role in overseeing state-level program implementation looks a good deal more constructive when examining the role played by the agency's ten regional offices. Most state-level interaction with the EPA involves such regional offices, which employ approximately two-thirds of the total EPA workforce. Relations between state and regional officials are generally more cordial and purposeful than those between state and central EPA officials, although only a handful of scholars have begun to explore them in any depth.[30] In fact, regional offices have played a central role in many of the most promising state-level innovations, including those in Minnesota and New Jersey discussed above. Their involvement may include formal advocacy on behalf of the state with central headquarters, direct collaboration on meshing state initiatives with federal requirements, and special grant support or technical assistance.

The Interstate Environmental Balance-of-Trade

States may not only remain dependent on the federal government, but they may also be structurally ill-equipped to handle a large range of environmental concerns. In particular, states may be very reluctant to invest significant energies to tackle those problems that literally might migrate to another state in the absence of intervention. The days of state agencies captured securely in the hip pockets of major industries are probably long gone, but state regulatory dynamism does appear to diminish when faced with such cross-boundary issues.

The state imperative of economic development clearly contributes to this phenomenon. As states increasingly devise development strategies that resemble the industrial policies of western European nations, a range of scholars have concluded they are far more deeply committed to strategies that promote "investment" or "development" than those that involve social service provision or public health promotion.[31] Environmental protection can be eminently compatible with economic development goals, promoting overall quality of life and general environmental attractiveness that entices private investment. In many states, major industries such as tourism have played an active role in seeking strong environmental programs designed to maintain natural assets, thereby assuring a continuous flow of tourists. Even in New Jersey, widely known as an industrial and chemical behemoth, tourism is the state's fourth-largest industry, and it has lobbied assiduously to secure state support for environmental protection likely to benefit popular natural areas. On the whole, the limited formal linkage between environmental protection and economic development remains evident in the very tenuous, slow development of state "sustainable development" programs. But the linkage is increasingly evident and influential in certain environmental areas.[32] Such convergence clearly sustains support for many state environmental programs.

But much of what a state might undertake in environmental policy may largely serve to benefit other states or regions, thereby reducing an individual state's incentive to take meaningful action. In fact, there are many instances in which states continue to pursue a "we make it, you take it" strategy. As political scientist William Gormley Jr. has noted, there are cases in which "states can readily export their problems to other states," resulting in potentially serious environmental "balance of trade" problems.[33] In such situations, states may be inclined to export environmental contaminants to other states while enjoying any economic benefits to be derived from the activity that generated the contamination.

Such cross-boundary transfer takes many forms, and may be particularly prevalent in those environmental policy areas where long-distance migration of pollutants is most likely. Air quality policy has long fit this pattern. States such as Ohio and Pennsylvania, for example, have depended heavily on burning massive quantities of high-sulfur coal to meet energy demands. Prevailing winds invariably transfer pollutants from this activity to other regions, particularly New England, leading to serious concern over acid deposition. In turn, states around the nation have relied heavily on so-called dispersion enhancement to improve local air quality. Average industrial stack height in the United States soared from 243 feet in 1960 to 730 feet in 1980.[34] Although this resulted in significant air quality improvement in many areas near elevated stacks, it generally served to disperse air pollution problems elsewhere. It has also contributed to the growing problem of airborne toxics that ultimately pollute water or land in other regions; between 80 to 90 percent of many of the most dangerous toxic substances found in Lake Superior, for example, stem from air deposition, much of which is generated outside of the Great Lakes Basin. Growing interstate conflicts, often becoming protracted battles in the federal courts, have emerged in recent decades as states allege they are recipients of such unwanted "imports." Midwestern states such as Illinois, Indiana, Michigan, and Wisconsin and Eastern states such as Connecticut, Delaware, Massachusetts, New Jersey, New York, and Rhode Island, among others, continue to be mired in such disputes.

States have also facilitated cross-boundary movement of their environmental problems by erecting such high standards that contaminants must invariably be shipped elsewhere for disposal. This allows state officials to "claim credit" for taking bold environmental protection steps while enabling them to "avoid blame" for concentrating contaminants anywhere within state boundaries. The disposal of sludge generated by wastewater treatment plants illustrates this pattern, as states have been largely left free to set their own standards. Many states, including those usually ranking atop innovation lists, tend to set the toughest standards. But for many of them, such as New York, criteria are set so high that in-state sludge generators uniformly turn to states with lower standards for disposal. As a result, most of the state's sludge is shipped to facilities in Oklahoma and Texas.

Perhaps nowhere is this type of interstate transfer more evident than in disposal of solid, hazardous, biomedical, and low-level radioactive wastes. Each type of waste features some degree of federal regulatory oversight and legitimate challenges can be made concerning the effectiveness of guiding federal legislation. But in many respects this area has offered a test of decentralization, as states have been given enormous latitude to devise their own systems of waste management and facility siting, either working independently or in concert with other states. In the area of low-level radioactive waste, in fact, federal legislation enacted in 1980 and 1985 was virtually dictated to Congress by the demands of state gubernatorial and legislative associations.[35]

This test of state capacity to take effective collective action has had its triumphs, including some of the efforts to promote waste reduction and prevention discussed above. Moreover, many states have moved to close their most environmentally suspect waste disposal facilities, particularly unlined landfills. Louisiana and New Jersey have closed nearly one thousand solid waste dumps apiece, allowing only the most technically sophisticated firms to stay in business. But many other aspects of waste management policy at the state level have involved a disconcerting pattern of interstate and interregional transfer of waste. Many states, including a number of those usually deemed among the most innovative and committed environmentally, continue to generate massive quantities of waste and have been hugely unsuccessful in siting modern treatment, storage, and disposal facilities. Instead, out-of-state (and region) export has been an increasingly common pattern, with wastes often shipped to facilities opened before concern over hazardous waste and facility siting became widespread. In fact, many of the largest of these facilities are located in states widely derided as least innovative and active on environmental issues, making them the dumping ground for wastes generated in states thought to be more environmentally responsible. At its worst, the system resembles a shell game in which waste is ultimately deposited in the least resistant state or facility at a given moment.

Many states have banded together, forming compacts (for low-level radioactive waste) or associations (for hazardous waste) that hold some promise of devising regional strategies to share the waste management burden. But these have been little more than mechanisms to assure a steady flow of federal grant dollars and to delay the larger question of long-term distributional fairness. A few states—and Canadian provinces—have made some progress in developing comprehensive systems of waste management, although these remain exceptional cases.[36] While planning efforts generally languish, the conflict between states endures, occasionally becoming quite nasty. Former Tennessee governor Ned McWherter, for example, actively opposed further importation of hazardous waste into his state, declaring: "We don't want New York, New Jersey, or Ohio bringing their hazardous waste into Tennessee and taking advantage of little counties...that can't have a big Philadelphia-type-lawyer staff."[37] Tennessee and nearly two-dozen other states responded to the waste import problem in the 1980s by erecting a wide array of barriers to further imports. These ranged from differential regulatory standards and fees, in some cases tripling charges for disposal of out-of-state wastes, to a South Carolina effort to use its militia to turn away low-level radioactive waste shipments heading toward the nation's lone remaining disposal facility, which happened to be located in the Magnolia State.[38] Many of these state barriers have since been ruled unconstitutional by state and federal courts, most commonly because of perceived violation of the interstate commerce clause. As a result, the pattern of export continues unabated. In 1991, for example, North Carolina, which prides itself as a leader in environmental protection, exported more than 90 percent of its hazardous waste requiring management away from its site of generation to twenty-five separate states. In the same year, Ohio discovered it had hosted more than 20 percent of the nation's capacity for hazardous waste incineration. It reacted by seeking new restrictions on use of this capacity.

Waste transfer may constitute an extreme type of intergovernmental environmental problem. Yet it suggests that certain issues may not be best addressed through decentralized units. Policy analysts should be examining policy options for states with an eye to whether burden shifting across state boundaries is likely to be an option. If not, the case for decentralization becomes considerably stronger.

Looking Ahead

Determining the most appropriate role for states to play in environmental policy becomes all the more important given political developments set in motion by the November 1994 elections and the shift to Republican control of both chambers of Congress. Many prominent Republican proposals, including some incorporated into the now-famous "Contract with America," could have considerable impact on states, in many instances transferring to them greater authority for program design, funding, and implementation.

Perhaps the most visible early step taken by the 104th Congress involved passage of a bill, signed into law by President Bill Clinton, that bans any new legislation that imposes new regulatory mandates on states or localities if they lack sufficient federal funding to cover compliance costs. This represents a response to a growing chorus of state and local complaints about so-called unfunded mandates, whereby Congress attempts to give detailed marching orders to states and localities but provides little if any financial support necessary for implementation. Environmental regulations, such as those imposed by federal air, surface water, and drinking-water quality legislation, are frequently cited as among the most burdensome. The mayor of Columbus, Ohio, for example, has estimated that his city will have to provide well over $1 billion to comply with fourteen major environmental mandates between 1991 and 2000, representing an average payment of $856 per Columbus family per year.[39] The new federal legislation received broad acclaim but may have limited actual impact. It is loaded with exclusionary loopholes, does not apply to any mandate already in existence, and can be nullified by any future act of Congress.[40] Similar limitations have been evident in the seventeen states that have either passed legislation or amended their constitutions to limit the ability of states to impose mandates on local governments.[41]

A potentially more significant policy change may involve future cutbacks in federal environmental expenditures. Proposed changes would substantially reduce federal agency capacity to pursue core functions, thereby shifting responsibility for many of these activities to the state level. In turn, proposed reduction of federal transfer payments to states would shrink many of the grant programs that states have continued to depend on for essential environmental protection tasks and many of their most imaginative activities. If the experience of the Reagan era's new federalism is any guide, most states will prove unwilling or unable to generate their own revenues to replace federal program cuts.[42] At the same time, states may be forced to confront major reductions in federal grants at the very moment that their own revenue sources may begin to dwindle. Most states enjoyed generally robust fiscal health in the 1994 and 1995 fiscal years, with overall tax revenues growing at about twice the anticipated rate in 1995. However, given signs that the economy is slowing somewhat, most state fiscal analysts expect that trend will begin to reverse. Moreover, a 1995 study by the National Conference of State Legislators indicates that states intend in coming years to slow spending growth in environmental protection and a few other policy areas, planning instead to increase outlays for such areas as criminal justice and medical care for the poor.[43] Thus, the very point of likely decline of federal transfer dollars may well coincide with stagnation in states' own-source revenues.

This pinch may be particularly evident in a number of states with elected leaders firmly committed to substantial reduction of overall tax burden, state spending, and regulatory activity. These policy shifts, in many states, stem from tremendous Republican gains in governorships and state legislative seats in the 1994 elections. Republicans enjoyed a net gain of twelve governorships, giving them control of these offices in thirty states, and a net gain of eighteen state legislative chambers, providing them with majorities in slightly more than half of all such chambers. In many states, these partisan gains have translated into strong attacks on existing environmental programs. Ironically, those states promoting the most far-reaching reductions of taxation, spending, and regulatory rigor include those historically ranked among the most innovative and fiscally supportive of environmental programs, such as California, Michigan, New Jersey, New York, and

Wisconsin. In Michigan, for example, Republican control of the governorship and both legislative chambers after the November 1994 elections has resulted in a state agency reorganization widely seen as an effort to rein in environmental policy, resignations by many veteran state environmental officials in protest of recent policy shifts, and directives to state environmental agencies to eliminate at least 20 percent of their workforce and total administrative expenditures by 1998. Meanwhile, the state is also giving serious consideration to legislation that would minimize state agency monitoring, inspection, and enforcement powers and has passed a law that shields firms from public disclosure or punishment when they discover they are in violation of state environmental laws. In such cases, there is little indication of a creative effort to make state environmental policy more effective. Instead, the predominant theme appears to be rolling back as much regulatory activity as quickly as possible, with scant consideration of innovative alternative approaches.

The future role of states in environmental policy may be further shaped by three additional developments. First, intensified debate at the federal level over the meaning of the so-called takings clause of the Constitution has been supplemented by a flurry of state legislative proposals that call on state or local governments to compensate landowners for any property value decline that can be attributed to environmental regulation. Such legislation has been introduced in forty-nine states in recent years, with more than 120 such bills introduced in the first six months of 1995 alone.[44] It has already received hearings under direct democracy, as Arizona voters rejected a takings proposal in 1993 and Washington voters followed suit in 1995. If enacted, this legislation could profoundly alter the way states approach environmental policy, particularly in such controversial areas as wetlands and groundwater protection.

Second, the era of term limits is beginning to unfold, alive and well at the state level although blocked for congressional seats by a 1995 U.S. Supreme Court decision. As of 1996 forty-one states had imposed some form of term limits on governors, and twenty states had placed them on legislators. More states are expected to join these ranks, given overwhelming voter support in virtually every setting in which term limits have been proposed in recent years. Individual states impose different restrictions on gubernatorial and legislative terms, but term limits more generally will serve to oust many elected officials who championed the environmental programs that have given states such a dynamic image. It is anyone's guess as to what impact the arrival of cascades of new elected officials, all allowed to stay in office for limited periods, will have on long-term environmental policy.

Third, states continue to follow recent patterns toward divided, joint-party control of state government. Republican successes in the 1994 elections further contributed to this pattern of state-level divided democracy. In 1996 twenty-six states, including many of the most populous, featured formally divided power between Republicans and Democrats. This may explain the increasingly acrimonious policymaking at the state level and could conceivably facilitate gridlocks analogous to those long lamented in Washington. In any event, much environmental policy will have to receive support from both parties in a great many states given their respective hold on at least some portion of state government.

Amid the continued squabbling over the proper role of the federal government vis-à-vis the states in environmental policy in recent decades, there has been remarkably little effort to sort out which functions might best be concentrated in Washington or transferred to state capitals. Some current and retired legislators, including Republicans David Durenberger, Daniel Evans, and Nancy Kassebaum and Democrats Thomas Downey and Charles Robb, have offered useful proposals over the past decade that might allocate such responsibilities more reasonably than at present. These have been supplemented by thoughtful scholarly works by economist Alice Rivlin, vice-chair of the Federal Reserve Board, and political scientists Paul Peterson, Richard Nathan, and David Walker.[45] Interestingly, many of these experts concur that environmental protection policy defies easy designation as warranting extreme centralization or decentralization. Instead, they consistently call for a process of selective decentralization, one leading to an appropriately balanced set of responsibilities across governmental levels. In moving toward a more functional environmental federalism, certain broad design principles might be useful to consider.

A more discerning environmental federalism might begin by concentrating federal regulatory energies on those problems that are clearly national in character. Many air and water pollution problems, for example, are by definition cross-boundary concerns unlikely to be resolved by a series of unilateral state actions. In contrast, problems such as protecting indoor air quality and clean up of abandoned hazardous waste dumps present more geographically confinable challenges; they are perhaps best handled through substantial delegation of authority to states. As a general rule, the federal regulatory presence might intensify as the likelihood of cross-boundary contaminant transfer escalates. Such an initial attempt to sort out functions might be reinforced by federal policy efforts to encourage states or regions to take responsibility for internally generated environmental problems rather than tacitly allow exportation to occur. In the area of waste management, for example, per mile fees on waste shipment might provide a disincentive for long-distance transfer, instead encouraging states and regions to either develop their own capacity or pursue waste reduction options more aggressively. The growing use of economic approaches to environmental policy at both state and federal levels provides numerous models that might be used to encourage states to be more responsible environmental citizens in the federal system.

There are, of course, many areas in which some shared federal and state role remains appropriate, reflecting the inherent complexity of many environmental problems. Effective intergovernmental partnerships may already be well established in certain areas. Even a 1995 National Academy of

Public Administration study that excoriates many aspects of federal environmental policy concedes that the existing partnership between federal and state governments "is basically sound, and major structural changes are not warranted. The system has worked." [46] But even if essentially sound, the partnership could clearly benefit from further maturation. Alongside the sorting-out activities discussed above, both federal and state governments could do much more to promote creative sharing of policy ideas and environmental data. There is remarkably little dissemination of such information across state and regional boundaries and potentially considerable advantage to be gained from increasing such activity. More broadly, the federal government might also explore other ways to encourage states to work cooperatively, especially on common-boundary problems. State capacity to find creative solutions to pressing environmental problems is on the ascendance, as we have seen. But as Lord Bryce concluded many decades ago, cooperation among states does not arise automatically.

Notes

1. Alan Rosenthal, *Governors and Legislatures: Contending Powers* (Washington, D.C.: CQ Press, 1990).
2. Robert S. Erikson, Gerald C. Wright, and John P. McIver, *Statehouse Democracy: Public Opinion and Policy in the American States* (New York: Cambridge University Press, 1993).
3. R. Steven Brown et al., *Resource Guide to State Environmental Management*, 3d ed. (Lexington, Ky.: Council of State Governments, 1993), 4-102.
4. DeWitt John, *Civic Environmentalism: Alternatives to Regulation in States and Communities* (Washington, D.C.: Congressional Quarterly, 1994), 80.
5. Deborah Hitchcock Jessup, *Guide to State Environmental Programs*, 3d ed. (Washington, D.C.: Bureau of National Affairs, 1994).
6. John, *Civic Environmentalism*.
7. Elinor Ostrom, *Governing the Commons: The Evolution of Institutions for Collective Action* (New York: Cambridge University Press, 1990); Elinor Ostrom, Roy Gardner, and James Walker, *Rules, Games, and Common-Pool Resources* (Ann Arbor: University of Michigan Press, 1994).
8. Mark Schneider and Paul Teske with Michael Mintrom, *Public Entrepreneurs: Agents for Change in American Government* (Princeton, N.J.: Princeton University Press, 1995); Dennis O'Grady and Keon S. Chi, "Innovators in State Government," in *The Book of the States, 1994-95* (Lexington, Ky.: Council of State Governments, 1994), 496-507; Barry G. Rabe and Janet B. Zimmerman, "Beyond Environmental Regulatory Fragmentation: Signs of Integration in the Case of the Great Lakes Basin," *Governance* 8 (January 1995): 58-77.
9. Thomas E. Cronin, *Direct Democracy: The Politics of Initiative, Referendum, and Recall* (Cambridge, Mass.: Harvard University Press, 1989).
10. Evan J. Ringquist, *Environmental Protection at the State Level: Politics and Progress in Controlling Pollution* (Armonk, N.Y.: M.E. Sharpe, 1993); James P. Lester, "A New Federalism? Environmental Policy in the States," in *Environmental Policy in the 1990s*, ed. Norman J. Vig and Michael E. Kraft (Washington, D.C.: CQ Press, 1994), 51-68.
11. Barry G. Rabe, *Fragmentation and Integration in State Environmental Management* (Washington D.C: Conservation Foundation, 1986).
12. Barry G. Rabe, "Integrated Environmental Permitting: Experience and Innovation at the State Level," *State and Local Government Review* 27 (Fall 1995), 209-220.

13. J. Andrew Hoerner, "Life and Taxes," *The Amicus Journal* (Summer 1995): 14-17.
14. National Academy of Public Administration, *The Environment Goes to Market: The Implementation of Economic Incentives for Pollution Control* (Washington, D.C.: National Academy of Public Administration, 1994), 138-159.
15. Betsy Fishbein, "Extended Product Responsibility for Consumers and Producers" (Paper prepared for President's Commission on Sustainable Development, January 30, 1995, 4).
16. Interview with Terence Hollins, Oregon Department of Environmental Quality (July 6, 1995).
17. National Academy of Public Administration, *The Environment Goes to Market*, 55.
18. Daniel Mazmanian and David Morell, *Beyond Superfailure: America's Toxics Policy for the 1990s* (Boulder: Westview, 1992), 169-174; "California's Prop 65: Lessons for the National Risk Debate?" *Risk Policy Report* (January 20, 1995): 24-25.
19. William R. Lowry, *The Dimensions of Federalism: State Governments and Pollution Control Policies* (Durham: Duke University Press, 1992), 125.
20. Paul E. Peterson, *The Price of Federalism* (Washington, D.C.: Brookings, 1995), chap. 4.
21. R. Steven Brown, "Emerging Models for Environmental Management," in *The Book of the States, 1994-95* (Lexington, Ky.: Council of State Governments, 1994), 544.
22. U.S. General Accounting Office, "Water Pollution: Greater EPA Leadership Needed to Reduce Nonpoint Source Pollution" (Washington, D.C.: U.S. General Accounting Office, 1990), and U.S. General Accounting Office, "Water Pollution: Stronger Efforts Needed by EPA to Control Toxic Water Pollution" (Washington, D.C.: U.S. General Accounting Office, 1991); Robert W. Adler, Jessica C. Landman, and Diane M. Cameron, *The Clean Water Act 20 Years Later* (Washington, D.C.: Island Press, 1993).
23. Christopher H. Foreman Jr., *Plagues, Products & Politics: Emergent Public Health Hazards and National Policymaking* (Washington, D.C.: Brookings, 1994), 141-142.
24. Ringquist, *Environmental Protection at the State Level;* Mazmanian and Morell, *Beyond Superfailure*, 107-110.
25. "Expired Permits," *Detroit Free Press,* February 20, 1995, 6A.
26. Laura L. Barnes, ed., *The Pollution Prevention Yellow Pages* (Washington, D.C.: National Pollution Prevention Roundtable, 1994); U.S. General Accounting Office, "Pollution Prevention: EPA Should Reexamine the Objectives and Sustainability of State Programs" (Washington, D.C.: U.S. General Accounting Office, 1994).
27. National Academy of Public Administration, *Setting Priorities, Getting Results: A New Direction for EPA* (Washington, D.C.: National Academy of Public Administration, 1995), 140-144; Christopher J. Paterson and Richard N.L. Andrews, "Procedural and Substantive Fairness in Risk Decisions: Comparative Risk Assessment Procedures," *Policy Studies Journal* 23 (Spring 1995): 85-95.
28. Tom Horton and William M. Eichbaum, *Turning the Tide: Saving the Chesapeake Bay* (Washington, D.C.: Island Press, 1991); Theodora Colborn et al., *Great Lakes, Great Legacy?* (Washington, D.C.: World Wildlife Fund, 1990).
29. Adler, Landman, and Cameron, *The Clean Water Act 20 Years Later*, 221-224, 251.
30. Richard J. Tobin, "Environmental Protection and the New Federalism: A Longitudinal Analysis of State Perceptions," *Publius: The Journal of Federalism* 22 (Winter 1992): 93-107; Thomas W. Church and Robert T. Nakamura, *Cleaning Up the Mess: Implementation Strategies in Superfund* (Washington, D.C.: Brookings, 1993).
31. Peterson, *The Price of Federalism*; Peter K. Eisinger, *The Rise of the Entrepreneurial State: States and Local Economic Development Policy in the United States* (Madison: University of Wisconsin Press, 1988); Frank R. Baumgartner and Bryan D. Jones, *Agendas and Instability in American Politics* (Chicago: University of Chicago Press, 1993), chap. 11.
32. Brown, "Emerging Models for Environmental Management," 539-540.
33. William T. Gormley Jr., "Intergovernmental Conflict on Environmental Policy: The Attitudinal Connection," *Western Political Quarterly* 40 (1987): 298-299.
34. Lowry, *The Dimensions of Federalism*, 45.

35. Mary R. English, *Siting Low-Level Radioactive Waste Disposal Facilities* (New York: Quorum, 1992); Richard C. Kearney, "Low-Level Radioactive Waste Management: Environmental Policy, Federalism, and *New York," Publius: The Journal of Federalism* 23 (Summer 1993): 57-73.

36. Barry G. Rabe, *Beyond NIMBY: Hazardous Waste Siting in Canada and the United States* (Washington, D.C.: Brookings, 1994).

37. Bruce J. Parker and John H. Turner, *Federal/State Issues Under RCRA* (Washington, D.C.: National Solid Wastes Management Association, 1990), 14.

38. David H. Feldman, Jean H. Peretz, and Barbara D. Jendrucko, "Policy Gridlock in Waste Management: Balancing Federal and State Concerns," *Policy Studies Journal* 22 (Winter 1994): 589-603.

39. Gregory S. Lashutka, "Risk Policy—A Mayor's Perspective," *Risk Policy Report* (January 20, 1995): 20-21.

40. Timothy J. Conlan, James D. Riggle, and Donna E. Schwartz, "Deregulating Federalism? The Politics of Mandate Reform in the 104th Congress," *Publius: The Journal of Federalism* 25 (Summer 1995): 23-39.

41. Keith Schneider, "Many States Are Limiting the Power to Pass the Bucks," *New York Times,* February 5, 1995.

42. James P. Lester, "New Federalism and Environmental Policy," *Publius: The Journal of Federalism* 16 (Winter 1986): 149-165; Charles E. Davis and James P. Lester, "Decentralizing Federal Environmental Policy," *Western Political Quarterly* 40, no. 2 (1987): 555-565.

43. Peter T. Kilborn, "Economic Growth Leaves States in Best Shape Since Early 80s," *New York Times,* July 16, 1995, 1, 9. Also see Steven D. Gold, ed., *The Fiscal Crisis of the States: Lessons for the Future* (Washington, D.C.: Georgetown University Press, 1995).

44. Kirk Emerson and Charles R. Wise, "Statutory Approaches to Regulatory Takings: State Property Rights Legislation Issues and Implications for Public Administration" (Paper delivered at the annual meeting of the American Political Science Association, Chicago, August 3, 1995).

45. Alice M. Rivlin, *Reviving the American Dream: The Economy, the States, and the Federal Government* (Washington, D.C.: Brookings, 1992); Peterson, *The Price of Federalism.* Also see Thomas J. Anton, *American Federalism and Public Policy: How the System Works* (New York: Random House, 1989).

46. National Academy of Public Administration, *Setting Priorities, Getting Results*, 71.

3

Seizing Back the Day:
The Challenge to Environmental Activism
in the 1990s

Christopher J. Bosso

If the American environmental community at Earth Day 1995 seemed bewildered and directionless, it was for good reason. A new Republican majority in the 104th Congress spearheaded a conservative assault at the foundations of a federal regulatory regime constructed over previous decades. This new majority was bolstered by well-organized "private property rights" and "Wise Use" groups that, with allies in industry, also led campaigns for sweeping changes in state laws. An apparent lack of public concern about environmental issues and a general mood of fiscal retrenchment encouraged these forces to pursue agendas whose audacity stunned even environmentalists who agreed on the need to overhaul existing command-and-control regulatory approaches.[1]

For environmentalists, the 104th Congress was more bad news after two disappointing years under Clinton. Even relatively conservative groups like the National Wildlife Federation were disillusioned by the administration's promotion of the controversial North American Free Trade Agreement (NAFTA) and its failure to get the Democrat-controlled 103d Congress to revise pollution statutes. Environmentalists were also dismayed by the administration's inability to secure reform of the long-detested grazing, mining, and timber policies and to elevate the Environmental Protection Agency (EPA) to cabinet-level status, and, finally, by President Bill Clinton's tendency to "split the difference" with his foes (see chaps. 5 and 6). The 104th Congress made President Clinton look good by way of contrast, but that was small solace to an environmental lobby already reeling from years of sagging memberships, stagnant revenues, internal struggles, and leadership changes.[2]

This chapter assesses the state of American environmentalism at the national level in the 1990s. First, it looks at the context for policy activism by assessing the degree to which citizen attitudes shape laws and regulations. Second, it examines the "property rights" and "Wise Use" forces that helped to shaped the new congressional agenda. Third, it looks at the internal dynamics of contemporary environmental advocacy, in particular asking how the national membership groups fell into such straits. Finally, it speculates on the challenge for environmental advocacy in the United States and even worldwide. If environmentalists are on the right side of history, they can nonetheless lose major battles along the way, and their response to the present crisis may shape the next generation of environmental politics.

Public Opinion: Ambiguous Mandates

The House of Representatives on November 2, 1995, deleted from a FY 1996 appropriations bill a set of riders restricting the EPA's power to regulate in an array of environmental policy realms. The 227-194 majority vote to remove the controversial riders was remarkable first because it included sixty-three Republicans who defied party leaders after ten months of unusual party discipline in support of the Republican "Contract with America." Second, it reversed an unusual 210-210 vote in July that, in effect, reinstated the riders after they were killed just days earlier by a 212-206 vote.[3] The saga of the riders is a good place to start in assessing the murky relationship between public opinion and environmental policy.

The Salience Trap

The Republican agenda in the 104th Congress reflected widespread if somewhat unfocused public demands for leaner and less intrusive government, attitudes that party leaders translated into support for major revisions in federal environmental policies. Citizens also seemed little interested in environmental issues: a January 1995 Gallup poll found that only 1 percent of respondents mentioned the environment as the "most important problem" facing the nation, down dramatically from an already low 11 percent in 1992.[4] Any sense of urgency had also ebbed, with only 35 percent in an April Gallup poll agreeing that "immediate and drastic" measures were needed to preserve the environment, down from 57 percent in early 1991.[5] More telling, especially for Republican strategists, 29 percent of the respondents in a May 1995 Times-Mirror study felt that environmental laws or regulations had struck "about the right balance," up from 17 percent in 1992, while those believing that they had gone "too far" increased from 10 percent to 22 percent. By contrast, those who thought the laws "have not gone far enough" decreased from 63 percent to 43 percent.[6] Armed with such data, one could conclude, as Bowman and Ladd noted, "For most Americans the urgency has been removed, and the battle to protect the environment is being waged satisfactorily."[7] The new Republican majority seemed to have public permission to pursue its agenda.

A year later, however, Republican leaders openly acknowledged that efforts to reshape the nation's pollution laws and to "rein in" the EPA had badly damaged the party's public image and handed Democrats the advantage on environmental issues into the 1996 campaign.[8] What had happened? It appeared that Republicans had fallen into a "salience trap," assuming that low public issue salience as measured by "most important issue" polls equaled weak public support for environmental protection. This kind of error is common because, as Robert Mitchell argues, salience measures are headline-sensitive, which makes them "an untrustworthy guide to how the public will respond to policy changes in apparently non-salient issues."[9] Low issue salience should not be confused with weak support, especially when actions by policymakers revive issue salience. The Reagan administration fell into such a trap in 1981 under remarkably similar political conditions, with its attacks on federal policies and appointment of controversial officials like Interior Secretary James Watt eventually sparking a public backlash that forced the administration into a less openly confrontational stance.[10]

By contrast, establishing a connection between public opinion and public policy is easier under conditions of high issue salience.[11] Environmental issues were far more salient in the late 1980s in the wake of disasters like the core meltdown at the Chernobyl nuclear reactor in the Ukraine. Such public issue concern no doubt prompted George Bush's 1988 campaign promise to be "the environmental president" and in 1990 also helped to break a decade-long impasse on revising the Clean Air Act. But issue salience ebbed in the early 1990s as the public focused on the Persian Gulf War and the recession. Bush thereafter adopted a more deregulatory tack on environmental policy issues, and in 1992 tried to attract anxious voters by labeling Clinton and Gore as environmental extremists. Issue salience dropped lower in 1993-94 in the absence of agenda-setting disasters, perceptions of Clinton administration support for environmental protection, and a vigorous debate over progress on highly symbolic problem areas, such as endangered species like the American bald eagle. Add to this mix strong voter responsiveness to conservatives' antiregulatory rhetoric, and the stage was set for another test of the salience trap.

For one thing, despite the electoral outcome in 1994 ample evidence suggested that citizens still worried about environmental progress. Data in the Times-Mirror study cited earlier can be interpreted to show that 72 percent did not feel that environmental laws and regulations had gone "too far," while a Gallup poll at the same time found that 83 percent of Americans believed the nation needed to take at least "some additional" actions to address environmental problems.[12] Voters may evince theoretical support for less government and may accept some streamlining in bureaucratic rules, but they also wanted to maintain a strong federal role in protecting the environment.

There were, of course, nuances within these general views, reflecting in some cases media coverage of ongoing controversies. For example, the Times-Mirror study found that majorities of 61 percent and 70 percent respectively felt the nation had not done enough to fight air and water pollution, yet fewer (42 percent) felt the same about endangered species or (48 percent) wetlands preservation.[13] These differences reflected not only public satisfaction with successful efforts to save a few highly visible endangered species but also showed the effects of media coverage of land use and preservation battles, like the "jobs versus owls" controversy in the Pacific Northwest that marked much of the 1992 election. Stories invariably pitted a beleaguered small property owner against seemingly ridiculous federal efforts to protect some heretofore unknown species of rat or salamander.[14] These often apocryphal tales, peddled relentlessly to reporters by opponents of federal wetlands policies and the Endangered Species Act, had the desired effect: in the Times-Mirror study, 66 percent of respondents agreed that government should compensate individuals and businesses when laws or regulations lower the market value of their land, suggesting some public support for the kinds of "takings" legislation that passed in the House and in some state legislatures.[15]

Yet even here public views showed great subtlety. Although half the respondents agreed that a "destitute" homeowner should be able to sell an acre of wetlands for home construction, 61 percent would protect an endangered species rather than allow a company to harvest timber on its own land.[16] Public sympathy for the "little guy" against "big government" did not extend automatically to business. Indeed, despite public antipathy about the federal government in the abstract, a January 1995 Gallup poll found that on environmental issues more respondents (46 to 38 percent) still trusted government over private business.[17] Equally intriguing, despite the economic stagnation of the early 1990s, 69 percent of those polled for the Times-Mirror study rejected a stark trade-off between a clean environment and economic development. When forced into a choice, 63 percent still chose environmental protection.[18]

What do these data say to policymakers? First, as Dunlap notes, issue salience may fluctuate, but overall public concern about the environment endures "to the point that support for environmental protection can be regarded as a 'consensual' issue which generates little open opposition."[19] Despite progress on older problems like water pollution, new and more daunting problems like ozone depletion always seem to emerge. Second, despite low issue salience, about a third of Americans in early 1995 still considered themselves "strong" environmentalists,[20] with self-identification particularly high among the young, the college educated, liberals, and Democrats.[21] A sizable core constituency for environmental protection endures regardless of issue salience, and even those who don't consider themselves strong environmentalists are concerned about the health of future generations. Politicians perceived as outright hostile to progress on the environment risk igniting latent concern into active outrage.

But strong general support for environmental protection does not preclude initiatives that can be defended as preserving important values like individual freedom or "traditional ways of life." For one thing, Americans generally are "Lite Greens," wary of making major life-style changes in the name of environmental protection.[22] They might recycle and buy "green goods" in increasing numbers—no small matter in a market economy—but they still resist altering wasteful energy consumption habits, among other things. The swift demise of any kind of "Btu tax" in Clinton's 1993 economic plan suggests some of the limits to easy public support for environmental initiatives. Strong, diffuse support also does not keep citizens from siding with economic interests proclaiming to defend local industries or jobs or, of course, from voting for candidates with dubious environmental records. If, as Dunlap observes, relatively few candidates want to be painted as openly antienvironment, "there is as yet little evidence of a 'green bloc' of single-issue voters comparable to the anti-abortion or anti-gun control blocs."[23]

The environment thus competes with other, often more salient priorities. Absent major disasters or crises, public concern for environmental protection does not translate automatically into support for specific policies. It translates only into opportunities to transform attitudes into action.

Public Opinion and the 104th Congress

The environment as such was not a major national issue in the 1994 elections, but specific environmental disputes did influence some races. In particular, antipathy toward Clinton administration land use policies within relatively narrow constituencies in some western states contributed to the defeat of a dozen or so House Democrats, among them Speaker Tom Foley of Washington. More important to the tenor of debate in the 104th Congress, the losing Democrats in most cases were moderates replaced by robust conservative Republicans like Helen Chenoweth of Idaho, whose hostility to the federal government in general and environmental regulations in particular made the ideological swing in the 1994 elections far greater than the partisan one. The cumulative effect was a new congressional majority (especially in the House) whose environmental agenda was a breathtaking break from the past, whether the issue was compensation for the supposed adverse effects of environmental laws on private property, the devolution of federal responsibility to the states, or simply the desire to deregulate whole swatches of federal policy (see chap. 6). Public opinion seemed permissive about, if not entirely supportive of, this agenda.

By mid 1995 Republicans began to encounter the limits to which public opinion allows major policy redirections in the absence of clear crisis. Public anxiety about the Republican environmental agenda began to crystalize during the summer as environmental groups publicized the more controversial planks in the House agenda. The Clinton White House meanwhile began to see the environment as one area where voters, particularly in eastern and suburban House districts, seemed to oppose the scope and nature of the GOP regime change. Pollsters found that even in conservative Virginia, citizens who supported the general thrust of the Republican agenda made "a clear exception where environmental regulation is involved."[24] Public concern seemed to escalate as the year went on. An NBC/*Wall Street Journal* poll in July reported that 79 percent of respondents wanted environmental laws maintained or strengthened, while a Louis Harris poll in August found that 60 percent opposed reducing the powers of the EPA.[25] Not surprisingly, the president and vice president soon began to wage an open campaign to warn voters of a Republican "stealth attack" on the environment.[26]

For their part, Republican pollsters increasingly cautioned their leaders about a public backlash against the party's environmental agenda. Frank Luntz, whose research provided the symbolic foundations for the

"Contract with America," as early as March 1995 noted that only 29 percent of respondents supported cutbacks in federal environmental regulations.[27] "The public may not like or admire regulations, may not think more are necessary, but puts environmental protection as a higher priority than cutting regulation," Luntz commented later and warned about the danger of rekindling the environment as a public issue.[28] His caution was echoed by pollster Linda DiVall, who observed that Americans "believe that the country has gone a long way in establishing certain basic environmental thresholds, and if there is a sense that these are being repealed too quickly at the sacrifice of some of the real environmental gains, people begin to feel that Republicans are pushing too far."[29]

By January 1996, a year after taking control of Congress for the first time in more than forty years, Republicans openly admitted the truth in these warnings. Party cohesion had splintered over environmental policy issues and by conservative attacks on EPA funding and autonomy, while President Clinton used the State of the Union Address to attack the Republican environmental agenda. Worse, pollster DiVall in January 1996 reported that 55 percent of Republican voters did not trust their own party on the environment and warned that the party faced serious potential losses in 1996 if voters acted on their concerns.[30]

The degree to which public opinion can shape policy will be well tested in the rest of the 104th Congress, not to mention the 1996 elections. Fears of a public backlash will probably limit the extent to which even House conservatives will *openly* attack existing policies and EPA funding; such fears will also force Republicans to moderate both the language and the substance of their environmental agenda. What is more, Republican candidates for Congress and the presidency alike will be forced by energized Democrats to make at least symbolic commitments to continued environmental progress. On the other hand, broad public opinion does not automatically preclude strategically positioned players from making even major policy changes in the relative quiet and safety of congressional committee rooms, using as shields appropriations and budget measures that maximize the capacity of entrenched interests to get their way. Indeed, the more low-visibility budget cuts already made in 1995 over time might well shape EPA regulatory capacity just as profoundly as any of the more visible legislative vehicles.[31]

All things being equal—and in politics they rarely are—the American system tends to favor parochial economic interests over more diffuse national ones. Constituency groups like loggers and ranchers enjoy distinct advantages in a system based on geographical representation which environmentalists can overcome only when they mobilize latent public fears about environmental degradation. This may well happen in 1996, and Democrats certainly hope to ride the environment to victory at the polls. Yet, unless an enraged public produces a new congressional majority, the agendas promoted in the 104th Congress will endure indefinitely. Environmentalists have never really had to contend with a Congress controlled by their ideological foes, but, unless the 1996 elections become a referendum on the environment, they may have to get used to the idea.

The Opposition: "Property Rights" and "Wise Use" Groups

Congressional Republicans may lead the rebellion, but its shock troops are provided by an assortment of often well-organized and well-funded groups rallied loosely around "property rights" and "Wise Use" banners. These groups mobilized the votes that decided a number of congressional races, while generous campaign contributions from industries such as timber and energy companies seeking greater access to federal lands certainly aided any number of sympathetic (and mostly Republican) candidates. Although it is hard to measure the extent to which these groups shaped the environmental agenda of the 104th Congress, there is no doubt that their priorities slipstreamed nicely with GOP efforts to deregulate, defund, and devolve policy away from the federal government.

Property rights groups are spread throughout the nation and chiefly agitate for compensating private property owners whenever governmental actions adversely affect a property's "fair market" value, such as when a wetlands designation precludes commercial development. Some, such as the Chicago-based Environmental Conservation Organization (or ECO), are little more than professional staff operations fronting for real estate or development interests, but others (e.g., the Maryland-based Fairness to Land Owners Coalition) are comprised of small property holders worried about governmental restrictions on the use of their land. The same distinctions hold true for the possibly hundreds of Wise Use groups clustered largely in the West, which generally promote local control over the vast federal lands in the region. Some, like the mining-industry backed People for the West! or the Sahara Club, supported by the off-track vehicle industry, seem little more than industry fronts. Others, however, are the latest progeny of a grassroots conservative populism that long has flourished in the region's remote spaces.[32] All share a staunch belief in "multiple" uses of federal lands for grazing, mining, logging, and recreation and a hostility to what they see as (at best) misconceived attempts by urban and suburban interests to end traditional rural ways of life. Many Wise Users consider themselves real conservationists, lovers of the outdoors who hunt and fish and who oppose locking up public lands from resource use. In some ways their complaints are the newest version of a century-old split between the conservationism of Gifford Pinchot, with its emphasis on the "managed use" of natural resources, and the arguably more absolutist dictates of preservationists in the spirit of John Muir.[33]

Like the environmental community, this self-proclaimed "countermovement" has discernible wings.[34] The "moderates" are often citizens who own property in or near national parks or workers in towns dependent on industries like logging, who in either case worry that government and environmental groups alike have become too powerful and insensitive to their basic economic needs. Property rights activists in particular campaign against what they consider confiscatory policies placing severe restrictions on the use of their land and led efforts in Congress to mandate compensation for "takings" broadly defined.

The more zealous Wise Use activists, especially those in the Rocky Mountain states, hold views that dovetail with conservative populism's strident defense of private property, its deep suspicion of the federal government, and its occasional xenophobia. Many are veterans of the Sagebrush Rebellion of the 1970s that spawned Reagan officials like James Watt and Anne Burford. Others come from the Young Americans for Freedom, the National Rifle Association, and other conservative groups that find few if any constitutional bases for restricting any use of private property. These activists seek to open all federal lands to resource exploitation and campaign against reauthorizing the Endangered Species Act. At the outermost fringes are groups like the John Birch Society, the Reverend Sung Yung Moon's Unification Church, and others in the reactionary anticommunist right who see environmentalism as the newest left-wing threat to American society. Some, such as in the Utah-based National Federal Lands Conference, are said to support or are members of various antifederal "militias" that have sprung up in recent years, and their leaders profess beliefs that, for instance, environmental laws are part of a conspiracy to allow the United Nations to take over the nation. Indeed, fear of such a cabal leads some of these activists to oppose efforts to create a U.S.-Canada Cascades International Park. [35] The latest wrinkle is the "county supremacy" movement, in which county governments in some western states have used novel interpretations of the Tenth Amendment to assert legal control over federal lands. A few states like South Dakota have followed suit. [36] However, an effort to convene a "Conference of the States" to propose a constitutional amendment clarifying state power over federal lands was derailed after extreme right-wingers warned that it might be a ruse to surrender the country to the United Nations. [37]

The overall dimensions of the private property and Wise Use "countermovement" thus are hard to gauge. Its proponents claim tens of thousands of members, but critics counter that the movement has no more than a few hundred hard-core activists backed by an interlocking phalanx of professional organizers and conservative foundations, promoted by allies in industry, libertarian think tanks, and conservative media personalities like Rush Limbaugh. What is more, say critics, these forces have craftily manipulated mainstream media into making the "movement" more than it is. "In terms of media food chain, we've elevated Wise Use to this large alternative movement," notes *New York Times* correspondent Tim Egan, "but really all I see are the same old faces." [38] Wise Users reply that the same could be said about the environmental lobby and claim that theirs is the *true* movement to reclaim the nation from alleged liberal control over government, business, education, and the media.

There is no argument, however, that Wise Use groups have helped to shape the public debate. In recent years they have enjoyed successes in state legislatures, in federal courts populated by Reagan and Bush appointees, and, at least prior to the Clinton administration, within parts of the federal bureaucracy sympathetic to producer interests, such as the Bureau of Land

Management. With the 104th Congress these groups now had prized access to the innermost corridors of power, their clout ultimately extending not from the superiority of their message, nor even the overall size of their memberships, but from the focused political leverage of those who live and vote in communities where the often ill-defined choices between "environment" and "jobs" are made. If Congress in particular responds to the loudest constituency demands, in recent years property rights and Wise Use groups seem to have been the only clear and consistent voices being heard.

As a result, these groups have shown a capacity to stop policy initiatives. In the 103d Congress, Wise Users and their conservative allies in both parties blocked progress on almost all environmental legislation and generally made life miserable for Secretary of the Interior Bruce Babbitt, probably the Wise Users most disliked Clinton cabinet member (next to Attorney General Janet Reno). In the 104th Congress their ties to the new majority gave these groups tremendous clout in setting the public agenda, framing policy debate, crafting the language of legislation, and, of course, shaping the federal budget. To students of Congress, none of this comes as any surprise, but to environmentalists long accustomed to a Democratic Congress the new political landscape was disconcerting.

Outside Washington a well-coordinated campaign has swamped state legislatures with property rights bills, variations of which have become law in twenty-one states (mostly in the West, South, and Southwest). But state legislatures are notoriously easy places for well-organized and well-funded groups to shape public policy. A more telling measure of public support for property rights measures is the success rate of the various "takings" initiatives put on the ballot in several states. Thus far, such referendums have failed by large margins even in states where property rights and Wise Use groups proliferate, defeated by strong grassroots opposition uniting environmentalists and more traditional conservationists, including those who hunt and fish.[39]

The overall record suggests, as David Helvarg argues, that these various groups comprise "a new and militant force on the political Right that has the power to impede and occasionally sidetrack attempts at environmental protection," but which so far has yet to generate broad public support.[40] The more radical Wise Use goals seem unlikely to prevail in an open fight, even in a Congress dominated by conservatives. Even so, the alliance between Wise Users and conservatives is a potent one because it can wield great leverage over legislation and agency budgets, and because it acts as a rallying point for those alienated from major institutions, among them "corporate environmentalism."[41] Regardless of short-term defeats, continued Republican control over Congress gives the Wise Use-conservative alliance the structural and constitutional capacity to shape the nation's environmental agenda into the future. In this regard, at least, the Wise Use backlash represents contemporary environmentalism's greatest challenge, and if Congress remains in Republican hands beyond 1996, the 1994 elections may mark the end of an environmental era that began in the late 1960s.

Table 3-1 Membership Trends among Selected National Groups, 1970–1995

Group	Year Founded	1970	1980	1985	1990	1995
Sierra Club[a]	1892	113,000	181,000	364,000	630,000	570,000
National Audubon Society	1905	148,000	400,000	550,000	600,000	570,000
National Parks and Conservation Assoc.	1919	45,000	31,000	45,000	100,000	450,000
Izaak Walton League	1922	54,000	52,000	47,000	50,000	54,000
Wilderness Society	1935	54,000	45,000	147,000	350,000	310,000
National Wildlife Federation[b]	1936	540,000	818,000	900,000	997,000	1.8 million
Defenders of Wildlife	1947	13,000	50,000	65,000	80,000	118,000
Nature Conservancy	1951	22,000	NA	400,000	600,000	825,000
World Wildlife Fund	1961	NA	NA	130,000	400,000	1.2 million
Environmental Defense Fund	1967	11,000	46,000	50,000	200,000	300,000
Friends of the Earth[c]	1969	6,000	NA	30,000	9,000	35,000
Environmental Action	1970	10,000	20,000	15,000	23,000	10,000
League of Conservation Voters	1970	NA	NA	35,000	55,000	NA
Natural Resources Defense Council	1970	NA	40,000	55,000	150,000	185,000
Greenpeace USA	1971	NA	NA	800,000	2.35 million	1.6 million

Sources: Annual reports; *Public Interest Profiles, 1992–1993* (Washington, D.C.: Foundation for Public Affairs/Congressional Quarterly, 1993); *Encyclopedia of Associations*, various editions (Detroit: Gale Research); *Outside* 19 (March 1994): 65–73; *Buzzworm: The Environmental Journal* 2, (May/June 1990): 65–77; *National Journal*, July 28, 1990, 1828; *Congressional Quarterly Weekly Report*, January 20, 1990, 144; Environmental Protection Section, Congressional Research Service, *Selected Environmental and Related Interest Groups: Summary Guide*, CRS Report 91–295 ENR (March 22, 1991), passim; *National Journal*, January 4, 1992, 30; *Chronicle of Philanthropy* 4 (March 24, 1992): 31.

Note: Figures are rounded and in many cases are best-guess approximations based on conflicting data, definitions, or reporting dates. NA = not available.

[a] Does not include over 100,000 members of the Sierra Club Legal Defense Fund, the technically separate legal arm of the Sierra Club.

[b] Full members only. The Federation also counted affiliated memberships (e.g., schoolchildren) of around 4.4 million in 1995.

[c] Merged in 1990 with the 30,000 member Oceanic Society and the non-member Environmental Policy Institute.

Table 3-2 Operating Budgets of Selected National Groups, 1980–1995

Group	1980	1985	1990	1993	1995
Sierra Club	9.5	22.0	40.0	43.2	35.0
National Audubon Society	10.0	24.0	36.0	43.4	46.0
National Parks and Conservation Assoc.	NA	1.7	6.0	12.0	13.0
Wilderness Society	1.5	6.5	17.7	16.5	14.5
National Wildlife Federation	34.5	46.0	89.5	93.1	97.2
Defenders of Wildlife	NA	3.0	4.3	6.5	6.6
Nature Conservancy	NA	NA	111.3	125.1	141.7
Environmental Defense Fund	1.9	3.3	15.8	21.9	24.6
Friends of the Earth	1.0	1.0	3.4	3.4	3.4
Environmental Action	0.5	0.6	1.1	1.0	1.0
League of Conservation Voters	0.5	1.6	1.4	2.0	4.0
Natural Resources Defense Council	3.5	7.0	16.0	17.0	17.5
Greenpeace USA	NA	24.0	40.0	40.7	26.0

Sources: Annual reports; *Public Interest Profiles, 1992-1993* (Washington, D.C.: Foundation for Public Affairs, Congressional Quarterly, 1993); *Encyclopedia of Associations,* various editions (Detroit: Gale Research); *Outside* 19 (March 1994): 65-73; *Buzzworm: The Environmental Journal* 2 (May/June 1990), 65-77; *National Journal,* July 28, 1990, 1828; *Congressional Quarterly Weekly Report,* January 20, 1990, 144; Environmental Protection Section, Congressional Research Service, *Selected Environmental and Related Interest Groups: Summary Guide,* CRS Report 91-295 ENR (March 22, 1991), passim; *National Journal,* January 4, 1992, 30; *Chronicle of Philanthropy* 4 (March 24, 1992): 31.

Note: In millions of dollars. Figures are rounded and often are approximations based on disparate data, reporting dates, and fiscal years. Figures do not include non-recurring capital expenditures, such as for land. NA = not available.

Environmental Groups: A Lobby or a Movement?

In politics five years is a lifetime, and for environmentalists the contrast between 1990 and 1995 could not have been starker. The organized environmental community in the United States began the 1990s never stronger or more confident. For the major environmental groups, the 1980s meant huge membership increases (see table 3-1) and revenues that often more than tripled (see table 3-2). Small wonder that the massive global observance of Earth Day 1990 seemed to herald a once-fringe movement that had matured into a permanent political force.[42]

Since 1990, however, little seems to have gone right for the national environmental community. For most major groups the decade has seen stagnant memberships and soft revenues—in some cases, real decreases—which in turn forced groups to lay off staff, freeze salaries, and institute stringent cost-cutting measures.[43] The few groups that seemed to thrive tended to be relatively nonthreatening organizations like the Nature Conservancy, which purchases ecologically important land, or those whose missions focus on issues with strong emotional appeal, such as the World Wildlife Fund (pandas) and the National Parks and Conservation Association. Clinton's election did not help matters because environmentalists no longer had a foe in the White House around whom to organize direct-mail campaigns. In fact, for many groups the fiscal picture grew worse in 1993-94, only to brighten somewhat in 1995 as the 104th Congress provided a new rallying point.

These conditions have sparked a level of intramural dispute over organizational goals and tactics unparalleled since the early 1980s, when environmentalists struggled to respond to the Reagan Revolution. The tone of debate sharpened after 1994, and is unlikely to soften even with any rebound in memberships and revenues that might result from public concerns about the 104th Congress. Indeed, in 1995 there was an especially strong whiff of rebellion in the ranks of the major groups, typified by an extraordinarily public dispute over the future direction of the Sierra Club and accented by forced resignations of longtime leaders at both the National Wildlife Federation and National Audubon Society.[44]

For the major national organizations the recurring dilemma is to maintain the resources necessary to remain active "players" in the national policy arena without blunting the zeal that motivates their most committed members. The "corporate environmentalism" tag hung on them by friend and foe has some merit insofar as these professionalized staff organizations rely heavily on direct mail and other marketing tools to maintain the huge memberships and big budgets seen as necessary to play the conventional lobbying game. Yet "success" creates pressures to weigh the budgetary effects of issue stances and tactics, and, to some degree, to stay "respectable" so that middle-class members feel that their dues are spent wisely. Size by itself also creates tendencies toward more centralized decisionmaking, often at the expense of local chapters housing the group's most dedicated activists.[45]

Some of this is old news to groups like Audubon or the Sierra Club, both of which went through similar organizational spasms in the late 1960s and early 1980s, yet in some respects many of these groups seem caught in a struggle for their very souls. This sounds a bit melodramatic, but there is little other way to interpret the forced departure of Jay Hair at the traditionally cautious and even somewhat conservative National Wildlife Federation, or the "retirement" of Peter Berle at the National Audubon Society. Both executives, it must be noted, were selected in the early 1980s precisely to transform relatively decentralized conservation groups into professionalized national environmental lobbies. Both did so, even brilliantly, but in the process alienated many of each organization's most faithful grassroots members. Even more telling was the eyebrow-raising election for board of directors at the Sierra Club. One new director was David Brower, a legendary activist who split bitterly with the Club in the 1960s over similar issues of goals and tactics. Even more telling was the election of David Fore-man, harsh critic of accommodation and cofounder of Earth First!, a grass-roots group that in the late 1980s won a measure of notoriety for its "direct action" tactics against logging companies and federal bureaucrats. [46] By elect-ing two visible critics of mainstream environmentalism, the members of the Sierra Club seemed to be expressing a preference for a more "radical" and less Washington-focused advocacy. Similar views echo throughout the main-stream environmental community.

Rethinking the Green Lobby

This said, the greatest source of tension within the major groups may be the extent to which they should continue to pour resources into their Wash-ington lobbies. Certainly many will—and should—maintain an active pres-ence in the nation's capital if only to avoid ceding strategic ground to their industry and ideological opponents, yet the debate is not so odd if one assesses the disappointing record of the "green lobby" in recent years. Even passage of the 1990 Clean Air Act amendments, hailed by many as a break-through after years of stalemate, to critics was a disappointing example of the limitations inherent in the "inside" strategy. [47] Their sense of futility was only deepened by the failures of the 103d Congress. To many activists the prob-lem was clear: a united green lobby probably can repulse legislative efforts it opposes, but it has had little success in building support for its own reforms or policy ideas. [48]

This sense of futility is all the more telling because the contemporary environmental lobby is well-established, respected, and sophisticated. From extensive use of free and paid media, telephone banks, and direct mail to "fax trees" and World Wide Web sites, environmentalists have copied and even perfected techniques used by virtually every advocacy group, including their property rights and Wise Use foes. As critic Mark Dowie argues, however, this cultivated image of insider clout belies the sobering reality that environmen-talists are seriously outgunned by the battalions of corporate lobbyists, the resources industries pour into their lobbying efforts, and, more bluntly, by the millions of dollars in campaign contributions that flow into Congress from corporate political action committees. [49] Looked at from this perspective, the Washington environmental lobby is an expensive, albeit necessary, bauble.

What is more, for public interest groups seeking to challenge dominant social and economic values, much less corporate power, just being a "respected" member of the national lobbying community comes at an insidious price. Above all, argues Kirkpatrick Sale, it means that the mainstream groups have at least quietly made the commitment to work within the political system, in the process becoming, as Sale says, a "reformist citizens' lobby, pressured on the fringes by more radical groups but for the most part willing to work within the system and reap the victories, and rewards, therein." [50] By doing so these groups succumb to "the inherently conservatizing pressure to play by the 'rules of the game' in the compromise world of Washington, D.C." [51]

This "conservatizing pressure" seemed evident with the passage of NAFTA, which most major groups finally supported despite deep divisions within their own staffs and memberships. Support for NAFTA came especially from organizations like the National Wildlife Federation and Environmental Defense Fund, supporters of free-market philosophies from which in some cases came many of the new administration's political appointees. Many of these groups had opposed NAFTA when Bush occupied the White House, lending credence to charges that support for the treaty ultimately came out of a desire to maintain access to the Clinton White House. Critics in anti-NAFTA groups like Sierra Club, Greenpeace, Friends of the Earth, and in organized labor, also charged that environmentalist support for NAFTA was "purchased" outright by the corporate donations upon which many mainstream groups depend.[52] At the least, as Rep. Marcy Kaptur (D-Ohio) said of pro-NAFTA environmentalists, "I think they got caught between their funders, some of whom are large corporations who are in favor of NAFTA, and their membership, which is very environmentally conscious. I think they caught themselves politically."[53]

For many environmental groups to grow accustomed to, even comfortable with, the compromise world of Washington is a natural result of decades of attention to and reliance on federal policy, especially given the tremendous variability of state government capacities and intentions (see chap. 2). It also was part of a natural tendency for successful movements to spin off lobby groups, law firms, think tanks, and other institutions that together help to give a movement's ideas respectability in the halls of power. But, as Dowie argues, the pitfalls of institution building in Washington became woefully apparent in the 1990s.[54] First, a focus on the federal government exposed environmentalists to the full force of the post-cold war collapse in public faith in the federal establishment. "Big environmentalism" became synonymous with "big government"—remote, professionalized, and arcane. Second, the focus on Washington to some degree came at the expense of grassroots organizing, which critics accuse the major groups of ignoring as they poured attention and resources into their national lobbies. Worse, national leaders often seemed to pursue agendas contrary to the needs of local groups, especially those representing poor and minority residents, a perception that sparked criticism by activists representing the emerging "environmental justice" movement (see chap. 11).[55] Finally, environmentalists convinced of the goodness and popularity of their cause seemed to discount the Wise Use backlash at the local level, leaving many who might otherwise be natural allies—especially working-class voters—to fall in with their Wise Use foes.

Some of these criticisms are fair, though similar debates have erupted within virtually every other movement (e.g., women's rights, disability rights) over the past two decades. Other criticisms seem less warranted because many of the major groups have been far more active at the grassroots than critics like Dowie admit. Besides, despite criticisms the national groups are still environmentalism's flagships, the experienced professional organizations able to go toe-to-toe with entrenched interests, pursue complex lawsuits in the federal courts, provide financial and technical assistance to activists in an array of local, state, and, increasingly, international arenas, and even to stand up against governments. *Somebody* has to play these roles because that is the way the political system works. In this sense the national groups are guilty of being normal Washington lobbies, thereby facing the usual perils of bureaucratic stagnation, staff careerism, routinized issue advocacy, and passive "checkbook memberships."[56] Such organizational pathologies may be bearable for corporate lobbies that, after all, tend to defend the economic status quo, but they can be enervating for activists seeking to change the world.

The War for the Grassroots

Whatever the merits of maintaining their Washington lobbies, environmentalists are faced with the challenge of retaking the initiative on two fronts where property rights and Wise Use groups have succeeded rather brilliantly in recent years. First, groups long reliant on Washington lobbying and relatively passive memberships will probably need to focus more energies and resources on building and mobilizing resilient grassroots constituencies, particularly among those in the working class most vulnerable to the Wise Use siren song.

In this respect the possibilities at the grassroots looks less bleak than recent electoral outcomes suggest. Even as Republicans swept to power in 1994 voters supported eight out of thirteen environmental initiatives on statewide ballots, while voters in Arizona decisively defeated Proposition 300, the first real property rights referendum. The relatively moderate "takings" measure was passed by the state legislature in 1992, but environmentalists led by the regional Sierra Club chapter got the law on to the ballot, out-organized the property rights forces, and effectively framed the debate by calling the law's compensation scheme a "taxpayer's nightmare."[57] In 1995 a coalition that again included environmentalists and labor unions helped to defeat a takings referendum in the state of Washington, home to some of the nation's most ardent Wise Use activists.[58] Environmentalists succeeded in each case because they built broad grassroots alliances that overcame opponents who often were better-funded and more strategically positioned.

Beyond such referendums, the national environmental groups already find themselves spending more time and resources working with state and regional groups to build a grassroots with stronger connections to members of Congress and state legislators. There is also intense pressure within many of the groups—witness the events at the National Wildlife Federation, Audubon Society, and Sierra Club—to reverse years of organizational centralization and devolve more decisionmaking authority and resources to local and state chapters. The irony here is that for many of these groups such a devolution would revive a style of group governance and agenda setting that predated the contemporary, more Washington-centered environmental era.[59] As times change, so must organizations.

The real issue, however, is what a potent new environmental grassroots must look like. Given that the major groups are dominated by middle-class suburban interests, which Wise Use activists have used effectively to recruit alienated working-class voters, any green grassroots worth discussing must include constituencies not traditionally regarded as part of the environmental movement. These constituencies encompass less affluent and often minority residents who live closest to environmental problems and who typically are motivated less by wildlife conservation or wetlands preservation than by concerns about human health.[60] A stronger focus on health may alienate the more biocentric, "deep ecology" activists, but it is inevitable if environmentalists are to strengthen their base (see also chap. 4). As Freudenberg and Steinsapir argue, the link to health creates "the potential for a cross-class movement with a broader agenda, more diverse constituencies, and a more radical critique of contemporary society than that of the national environmental organizations."[61]

Such efforts have intensified in response to the new conservative agenda. A recent development was the creation of Environment Strategies, an organization designed to coordinate public education campaigns on a handful of public health and safety issues.[62] Another is a more vigorous effort to connect environmentalists with advocates for children's health issues, given that children tend to be particularly affected by air and water pollution, pesticides, and other hazards.[63] Such an alliance, organized under the Children's Environmental Health Network, has already united environmentalists with constituency groups whose ideological support for smaller government is tempered by powerful concerns about the impacts of deregulation on children's health. A strong focus on health also may help environmentalists connect with "life-style conservatives" whose opposition to strong federal power is matched by suspicions about the corrosive impacts of corporate activities on their health and their hometowns—views familiar to environmentalists who profess faith in decentralized decisionmaking and small institutions.[64] Divisive issues like abortion and economic growth certainly remain, but the commonalities raise tantalizing possibilities for a new breed of American environmental populism.

The Promise and Pitfalls of Electoral Politics

At this writing activist Ralph Nader has already agreed to stand as the nominee of the U.S. Green Party for president in 1996, thus continuing the effort to create an effective national environmental party. However, although such an approach has some utility for raising public consciousness and for getting issues on the agenda for debate, the lessons of European green parties and the nature of the U.S. electoral system suggest limited payoffs for the independent party route.

The fortunes of European green parties in the 1990s highlight the potential pitfalls for their American cousins. They fared relatively well in the 1980s as principled critics of economic and political orthodoxy but, as an admittedly skeptical Anna Bramwell argues, their fortunes faded in the early 1990s as "established political parties, together with international agencies, took on board those environmental programmes and criticisms that could be incorporated into established, institutionalized forms of political life." [65] In short, in countries with a strong green vote the major parties eventually co-opted the most popular green ideas, often leaving more purist Greens to promote less palatable "fringe" goals. Green parties have made a bit of a rebound in recent years but, like any relatively small party, their clout within European systems depends far more on their ability to wield political leverage in situations of narrow parliamentary majorities rather than their capacity to forge governing majorities in their own right.

American Greens, for their part, already face an electoral system that makes it almost impossible for them to win national office and a system of governance that fractures parties even as it creates great incentives to form interest groups. [66] Whatever their problems, the major American environmental groups already act as the nation's quasi-green parties, playing the kind of policy formation roles typical of green parties in the strong-party European systems. [67] Even so, an American Green party is hardly doomed to irrelevance because individual candidates might win local elections, maybe even the odd House seat, and, as Bill Clinton no doubt worries, a candidate like Nader might certainly pull in enough votes to affect the outcome in states like California. Most important, the history of American third parties suggests that a Green party can influence issue debate and encourage people to use environmental issues as voting cues. It may be unable to forge the coalitions necessary to win statewide or national office, but it can help to define the ideas that become part of the nation's public discourse.

Putting a Green party option aside, mainstream environmentalists are left with two practical ways to fight their foes in the electoral arena. One is to join more openly with other social and economic groups to rebuild the Democratic party, which of the two major parties today offers more ecologically sensitive candidates and national party platforms. The nature of coalitional politics in the American party system makes it likely that environmental values always will be balanced against other, sometimes more immediate, social and economic concerns, but the nature of the Democratic party coalition makes it likely that environmental values will at least enjoy a major place at the table. The libertarian strain of conservatism that currently dominates the national Republican party and the agenda-setting role played by private property and Wise Use forces within the party are particularly hostile to mainstream environmentalism's goals, so environmentalists intent on playing party politics seem to have little practical choice.

Yet joining openly with the Democratic party involves more political risk than most mainstream groups are willing to take, particularly if Republicans retain control over Congress and regain the White House in 1996. For one thing, being another faction within the Democratic party might force environmentalists to pull their punches for the sake of party unity or to publicly support a Democratic president who many feel isn't entirely on their side. Environmental groups were criticized for doing exactly this during Clinton's first two years, not the least during the bitter fight over NAFTA. Earth First!'s David Foreman, a former Goldwater Republican himself, argues that conservationists—he avoids the "E" label—should abandon Clinton in 1996 if he fails to stand up to Congress on major wildlife and public lands issues. Above all, says Foreman, "when conservation groups engage in electoral politics, they should be single-issue proponents" not tied to any one party.[68]

Most mainstream environmental groups seem to adhere to this view for a variety of reasons, including reluctance to alienate members, so they are expanding efforts to rouse constituent pressure on environmentally suspect candidates and officeholders of both parties. In August 1995, for example, the Sierra Club ran radio ads attacking the environmental positions of more than a dozen House freshmen who won in 1994 with less that 55 percent of the vote.[69] One target—and a good case study of how such a grassroots-level electoral strategy works—was Rep. Susan Kelly (R-N.Y.), a first-term House member from the Hudson River Valley who campaigned as a moderate and an environmentalist but who initially went along with party leaders to support items in the "Contract with America." By the summer Kelly was swamped by a coordinated effort that generated reams of faxes and letters to local papers, pickets at her district office, and public criticisms by former allies in the local environmental community. By the fall, Kelly's voting pattern changed noticeably as a result of these efforts and because worried Republican leaders started to allow members to deviate from the party line if local needs so dictated.[70] Party loyalty rarely withstands constituent pressure, a lesson of the American system of governance that environmentalists are eager to exploit as the 1996 elections loom.

Environmentalists cannot hope to match the campaign donations of their corporate foes. However, they—like labor unions, the Christian Coalition, or the National Rifle Association—have both sophisticated national operations and faithful grassroots activists that together can keep the heat on legislators and, when the time comes, get out the vote. If members of Congress were as sensitive to a politically potent green grassroots as they were to senior citizens on Social Security, it may not matter to most environmentalists which party is in control.

Defining the New Societal Paradigm

The second great challenge facing the environmental community—the global environmental community, for that matter—is to seize from their foes the agenda for action and the very definition of the issues under debate. If anybody needed a reminder, the outcome of the 1994 election emphasized that, in the words of E. E. Schattschneider, "the definition of the alternatives is the supreme instrument of power."[71] Property rights libertarians and Wise Users, bearing vivid images of rapacious federal "envirocrats" and Range Rover suburbanites, certainly understood the lesson.

In this regard, the federal regulatory regime that dominated national politics since the 1960s is under challenge from all sides, and the struggle today is to define the policy regime of the next generation. Despite everything else environmentalists once contented themselves that their definitions of the issues still mattered. Now they are not so sure, because in some ways the environmental lobby has been outflanked by political forces not tied to the existing regulatory regime. Indeed, for many the environmental lobby itself is identified as part of a federal establishment that has come under sharp attack at the end of the cold war. Fair or not, such perceptions are part and parcel of political life.

How environmentalists can recapture the public agenda and define the issues under debate is for another time and place.[72] Suffice it to say that if they cannot seize the initiative back from their foes, environmentalists risk becoming little more than a coterie of middle-class reformers trying to smooth over the rougher edges of consumer-driven capitalism, not a true movement that redefines social and economic orthodoxy. Some groups, like the law and market-oriented Environmental Defense Fund and the Natural Resources Defense Council, are comfortable in filling their reformist roles, and their talents will be useful in the service of more effective environmental policy. Others, like the Nature Conservancy, will use free-market capitalism to buy and protect endangered ecosystems. They too will perform important roles, but within rules of the game defined by others.

The push for a true redefinition of orthodoxy probably will come from elsewhere, from decentralized membership groups like the Sierra Club, engulfed in another painful process of reinvention, to newer grassroots groups already forming out of the disenchanted splinters of the mainstream. The environmental movement is redefining itself yet again, pushed to do so by those currently on the fringes but given permission to change by those uncertain that the present course is the correct one. If environmentalism during the past twenty years was typified by the legislative and judicial strategies of the major national groups, the future may be defined more by groups like Earth First! and the Mothers of East Los Angeles, neither of which subscribes to the view that protecting the environment is something best left to the professionals, or by cross-national advocacy groups like the Rainforest Action Network. Such groups may not have the shelf life of the major organizations, but their values and their tactics will inevitably influence the future of the mainstream. The "radical" has a way of becoming conventional, as the histories of most of the major environmental groups should attest.

For all environmentalists, the exciting news is that the world itself is undergoing a seismic transition in which the very definition of the reigning social paradigm is up for grabs. With the collapse of Soviet-style communism, which was never ecologically benign, environmentalism now may occupy center stage as the single great nonnationalist critique of capitalism.[73] Defenders of free-market capitalism understand this potential too well and are working hard to discredit any challenge before it emerges. The question is whether environmentalists can seize this opportunity to define the next paradigm, or whether they will end up spending yet another generation trying to nibble away at the margins of orthodoxy.

Notes

1. Gregg Easterbrook, whose book, *A Moment on the Earth: The Coming Age of Environmental Optimism* (New York: Viking, 1995), got a cool reception from many environmentalists, warned that the new Congress threatened the nation's environmental progress. See "Authors Criticize Congress for Directionless Environmental Reform," *BNA Management Briefing, Greenwire,* American Political Network Inc., October 16, 1995.
2. See Christopher J. Bosso, "After the Movement: Environmental Activism in the 1990s," in *Environmental Policy in the 1990s,* 2d ed., ed. Norman J. Vig and Michael E. Kraft (Washington, D.C.: CQ Press, 1993), 31-50; and Bosso, "The Color of Money: Environmental Groups and the Pathologies of Fund Raising," in *Interest Group Politics,* 4th ed., ed. Allan J. Cigler and Burdett A. Loomis (Washington, D.C.: CQ Press, 1995), 101-130.
3. John Cushman Jr., "House Rejects Plan to Restrict the Use of Pollution Laws," *New York Times,* November 11, 1995, 1.
4. Lydia Saad, "Welfare, Federal Deficit Emerge as Public Concerns," *Gallup Poll Monthly* (January 1995): 6-8.
5. David W. Moore, "Public Sense of Urgency about Environment Wanes," *Gallup Poll Monthly* (April 1995): 17-20.
6. The Times-Mirror Magazines National Environmental Forum, *The Environmental Two-Step: Looking Back, Moving Forward* (Washington, D.C.: Roper Starch Worldwide, May 1995), 2.
7. Karlyn H. Bowman and Everett Carll Ladd, *Attitudes toward the Environment* (Washington, D.C.: American Enterprise Institute, 1995), cited in Margaret Kriz, "Drawing a Green Line in the Sand," *National Journal,* August 8, 1995, 2976.
8. John H. Cushman Jr., "GOP: Backing Off from Tough Stand over Environment," *New York Times,* January 26, 1996, 1.
9. Robert C. Mitchell, "Public Opinion and the Green Lobby: Poised for the 1990s?" in *Environmental Policy in the 1990s,* 1st ed., ed. Vig and Kraft (Washington, D.C.: CQ Press, 1990), 84.
10. Ibid., 83.
11. See Anthony Downs, "Up and Down with Ecology: The Issue-Attention Cycle," *Public Interest* 28 (1972): 38-50.
12. Times-Mirror, *Environmental Two-Step,* 2; Moore, "Public Sense of Urgency," 19.
13. Times-Mirror, *Environmental Two-Step,* 50.
14. Keith Schneider, "When the Bad Guy Is Seen as the One in the Green Hat," *New York Times,* February 16, 1992, E3.
15. Times-Mirror, *Environmental Two-Step,* 50-51.
16. Ibid., 50-51.
17. Moore, "Public Sense of Urgency," 18.
18. Times-Mirror, *Environmental Two-Step,* 48.
19. Riley E. Dunlap, "Public Opinion and the Environment (U.S.)," in *Conservation and Environmentalism: An Encyclopedia,* ed. Robert Paehlke (New York: Garland, 1995), 536.
20. Kriz, "Drawing a Green Line," 2976.
21. Moore, "Public Sense of Urgency," 20.
22. Kriz, "Drawing a Green Line," 2976.
23. Riley E. Dunlap, "Public Opinion in the 1980s: Clear Consensus, Ambiguous Commitment," *Environment* 33 (October 1991): 33.
24. John Cushman Jr., "Environment Gets a Push from Clinton," *New York Times,* July 5, 1995, A11.

25. Margaret Kriz, "How Green the Grass Roots?" *National Journal*, September 16, 1995, 2265.
26. Editorial, "House of Environmental Horrors," *New York Times*, August 7, 1995, A12.
27. Kriz, "Drawing a Green Line," 2076
28. Margaret Kriz, "The Green Card," *National Journal*, September 16, 1995, 2262.
29. Cushman, "GOP: Backing Off," 12.
30. Ibid., 1.
31. John R. Cushman Jr., "EPA Is Canceling Pollution Testing across the Nation: Budget Cuts Are Blamed," *New York Times*, November 25, 1995, 1.
32. For a critical analysis of Wise Use, see David Helvarg, *The War against the West* (San Francisco.: Sierra Club Books, 1994).
33. See Samuel P. Hays, *Conservation and the Gospel of Efficiency* (Cambridge, Mass.: Harvard University Press, 1958).
34. Christopher J. Bosso, "Adaptation and Change in the Environmental Movement," in *Interest Group Politics*, 3d ed., ed Allan J. Cigler and Burdett A. Loomis (Washington, D.C.: CQ Press, 1991), 152-176.
35. *National Parks* 69 (January-February 1995): 16.
36. *National Parks* 69 (March-April 1995): 16.
37. "National Yard Sale," *Sierra* 80 (September-October 1995): 29.
38. David Helvarg, "Grassroots for Sale: The Inside Scoop on (un)Wise Use," *Amicus Journal* 16 (Fall 1994): 25.
39. Andrew Branan, "Going against the Greens," *Ripon Forum* 30 (July 1995): 10.
40. Helvarg, "Grassroots for Sale," 24.
41. Brian Tokar, "The 'Wise Use' Backlash: Responding to Militant Anti-Environmentalism," *Ecologist* 25 (July 1995): 150.
42. Robert D. McFadden, "Millions Join Battle for a Beloved Planet," *New York Times*, April 23, 1990, 1.
43. John Lancaster, "War and Recession Taking Toll on National Environmental Organizations," *Washington Post*, February 15, 1991, A3.
44. "Enviro Groups: Money, Management Woes Paralyze Greens," *Greenwire*, American Political Network Inc., July 18, 1995.
45. See Bosso, "Color of Money."
46. "Tough Times, Seasoned Warriors," *Sierra* 80 (March-April 1995): 85. On Brower, see John McPhee, *Encounters with the Archdruid* (New York: Farrar, Straus, Giroux, 1971). On Foreman, see Christopher Manes, *Green Rage: Radical Environmentalism and the Unmaking of Civilization* (Boston: Little, Brown, 1990).
47. Richard E. Cohen, *Washington at Work: Back Rooms and Clean Air*, 2d ed. (Boston: Allyn and Bacon, 1995).
48. Michael McCloskey, "Twenty Years of Change in the Environmental Movement: An Insider's View," in *American Environmentalism: The U.S. Environmental Movement, 1970-1990*, ed. Riley E. Dunlap and Angela G. Mertig (Philadelphia: Taylor and Francis, 1993), 83.
49. Mark Dowie, *Losing Ground: American Environmentalism at the Close of the Twentieth Century* (Cambridge, Mass.: MIT Press, 1995), 192-195.
50. Kirkpatrick Sale, "The U.S. Green Movement Today," *The Nation*, July 19, 1993, 94.
51. Robert C. Mitchell, Angela G. Mertig, and Riley E. Dunlap, "Twenty Years of Environmental Mobilization: Trends among National Environmental Organizations," in *American Environmentalism*, ed. Dunlap and Mertig, 24.
52. See Bosso, "Color of Money," 119-122; Dowie, *Losing Ground*, 184-188.
53. Michelle Ruess and Tom Diemer, "Environmentalists Split on Trade Policy," *Cleveland Plain Dealer*, July 18, 1993, 4A.
54. Dowie, *Losing Ground*, xiii.
55. David Hahn-Baker, "Rocky Roads to Consensus: Traditional Environmentalism Meets Environmental Justice," *Amicus Journal* 16 (Spring 1994): 41-43
56. Michael T. Hayes, "The New Group Universe," *Interest Group Politics*, 2d ed., ed.

Cigler and Loomis, 133-145.

57. Nancy Shute, "The Big November Win: Arizona's 'Takings' Bill Went Down Hard," *Amicus Journal* 165, (Winter 1994): 25.

58. Lois Jacobson, "Land-Rights Battle with Fresh Twists," *National Journal*, October 14, 1995, 2537-2538.

59. Frank Graham Jr., *The Audubon Ark: A History of the National Audubon Society* (New York: Knopf, 1990).

60. See Robert Gottleib, *Forcing the Spring: The Transformation of the American Environmental Movement* (Washington, D.C.: Island Press, 1993).

61. Nicholas Freudenberg and Carol Steinsapir, "Not in Our Backyards: The Grassroots Environmental Movement," *Society and Natural Resources* 4 (1991): 240.

62. Margaret Kriz, "Getting Ready for Round Two," *National Journal*, March 11, 1995, 644.

63. Renee Skelton, "Green Groups and Children's Advocates Are Finding Each Other," *Amicus Journal* 17 (Summer 1995): 34.

64. Margaret Kriz, "The Greening of a Conservative," *National Journal*, June, 6, 1995, 1419.

65. Anna Bramwell, *The Fading of the Greens: The Decline of Environmental Politics in the West* (New Haven, Conn.: Yale University Press, 1994), 203.

66. See R. Kent Weaver and Bert A. Rockman, eds., *Do Institutions Matter? Government Capabilities in the United States and Abroad* (Washington, D.C.: Brookings, 1993).

67. Bramwell, *Fading of the Greens*, 56.

68. David Foreman, "Around the Campfire," *Wild Earth* 5 (Spring 1995): 2.

69. Kriz, "Green Card," 2263.

70. Andrew Revkin, "Back to Her Roots," *New York Times*, October 10, 1995, B1.

71. E.E. Schattschneider, *The Semi-Sovereign People: A Realist's View of Democracy in America* (Hinsdale, Ill.: Dryden, 1960), 68.

72. But see, for example, Christopher J. Bosso, "The Contextual Bases of Problem Definition," in *The Politics of Problem Definition: Shaping the Policy Agenda*, ed. David A. Rochefort and Roger W. Cobb (Lawrence: University Press of Kansas, 1994), 182-203.

73. Bramwell, *Fading of the Greens*, x.

4

Environmental Values and Public Policy

Robert C. Paehlke

A corporation wants to locate in your community but would alter a wetland habitat for its new facility. Should government approve construction in that location? Should the landowner be compensated if it does not?

Epidemiological evidence suggests that releases of a particular chemical would likely induce a small number of cancers per 1 million human exposures. Avoiding future releases will cost millions of dollars. How should this decision be made and by whom (the EPA, state governments, the courts, scientists, and/or corporations)? These questions about the ethical dimensions of environmental politics are very much a part of the contemporary political agenda.

Recently the problems confronting environmental ethics have grown even larger. For example, because the world's climate may be negatively affected by carbon dioxide (CO_2) emissions, many new questions arise. Should we increase the taxes on gasoline in order to encourage more selective automobile use? Should government subsidize fuel-efficient forms of public transportation? The present political climate militates against such interventions, but what alternative approaches would be as effective? What values are more important, what risks more serious? It is vitally important that citizens and decisionmakers learn to think ethically about environmental matters.

This chapter treats environmental politics as an expression of a set of values. It presumes David Easton's definition of politics as the authoritative allocation of values.[1] It sets out the value dimensions of contemporary environmentalism and identifies some of the difficult issues that the wide acceptance of these values urges onto the political agenda.[2] It also develops a framework for integrating these values with other prominent political values. This framework might be called a "triple E" perspective, for environment, economy, and equity.

From the nineteenth century to the middle of the twentieth century, politics centered on the struggles between economic values (capital accumulation, enhanced trade, economic growth) and equity values (wages, working conditions, social welfare, public health, and public education). Although these issues have not been resolved, it might be argued that with the end of the cold war, other issues and tensions are coming to the fore. Two sets of issues are of particular concern to us here—those that arise between environment and economy on the one hand, and environment and equity on the other. Points of mutual support as well as of conflict occur in both cases. There is little doubt, however, that many contemporary political issues can be better understood within this wider framework.

The Principal Dimensions of Contemporary Environmental Values

Historians as well as philosophers have observed that the contemporary environmental movement is based on a transformation of human social values. The historian Samuel Hays noted that new values, rooted in the advances in prosperity and educational levels following World War II, have emerged in virtually all wealthy societies.[3] Others have suggested that these recent value shifts run deeper than those that sustained the earlier conservation movement. The philosopher George Sessions has concluded that the ecological "revolution" is fundamentally religious and philosophical and involves "a radical critique of the basic assumptions of modern Western society."[4] More recently, many analysts have suggested that the churches must take an important role in environmental politics if they wish to remain the leading institution within which values are considered.[5]

Using opinion survey instruments, Ronald Inglehart and other social scientists have measured related shifts in popular attitudes, postulating a "silent revolution" that entails the spread of "postmaterialist" values.[6] Riley Dunlap, Lester Milbrath, and others have identified a "new environmental paradigm."[7] Whatever name one attaches to the change, the environmental movement and the responses to it are the political manifestation of significant turmoil in societal values.

Recently, and in the early 1980s, the forceful assertion of environmental values has provoked a strong reaction from the political right—even from some who would accept relatively "shallow" environmental values. In chapter 1, Kraft and Vig distinguish between "deep" and "shallow" currents of environmentalism. They suggest that environmental values have moved into the mainstream of American political culture but that short-term political currents often conflict with these underlying trends.[8] Such conflict has seldom been more apparent than in the 104th Congress (see chap. 6). This raises the question of which values are central to the environmental movement, how they relate to other values and to policymaking, and whether they are strong enough to withstand present challenges.

But what values constitute the essential core of an environmental perspective? In an earlier work, I set out a list of thirteen central environmental values, and others have developed similar lists to this one:

1. An appreciation of all life forms and a view that the complexities of the ecological web of life are politically salient.
2. A sense of humility regarding the human species in relation to other species and to the global ecosystem.

3. A concern with the quality of human life and health, including an emphasis on the importance of preventive medicine, diet, and exercise to the maintenance and enhancement of human health.
4. A global rather than a nationalist or isolationist view.
5. Some preference for political and/or population decentralization.
6. An extended time horizon—a concern about the long-term future of the world and its life.
7. A sense of urgency regarding the survival of life on Earth, both long-term and short-term.
8. A belief that human societies ought to be reestablished on a more sustainable technical and physical basis. An appreciation that many aspects of our present way of life are fundamentally transitory.
9. A revulsion toward waste in the face of human need (in more extreme forms, this may appear as asceticism).
10. A love of simplicity, although this does not include rejection of technology or "modernity."
11. An esthetic appreciation for season, setting, climate, and natural materials.
12. A measurement of esteem, including self-esteem and social merit, in terms of such nonmaterial values as skill, artistry, effort, or integrity.
13. An attraction to autonomy and self-management in human endeavors and, generally, an inclination to more democratic and participatory political processes and administrative structures.[9]

This list and others like it can be distilled to three core items: (1) the protection of biodiversity, ecological systems, and wilderness; (2) the minimization of negative impacts on human health; and (3) the establishment of sustainable patterns of resource use. These core items are relatively new as significant actors on the stage of political ideas. They are all ideas with an extended history, but were for at least a century swamped by the larger ideological battles of left and right—the struggles over and between economy and equity. In the 1990s a growing response to each of these three core items has come to the fore.

Ecology as a Core Value

The first of the three core environmental values is captured to a large extent in the concept of ecology. All life forms are bound up each with the other in a complex, and frequently little understood, web of life. Fruit bats are essential to the propagation of many tropical trees and numerous other plant species in other climatic zones. Forests, in turn, help to determine the climate of the planet as a whole. The transformation of forest to agriculture in Latin America can dramatically affect migratory songbird populations in North America. The web of life ties all species together inextricably.

Human well-being, and indeed human survival, depends on the success of an almost endless list of plant and animal species, often in ways we barely understand. Our global food reserves would endure for but a matter of months should our food production capabilities suddenly decline. That capability is determined in turn by rainfall and temperature, by the activities of many insect species such as bees, and by microbiological life within the soils of the planet. All of these in turn are affected by both plants and animals. Our well-being is determined by other species in other ways as well, not the least of which is our deep need for contact with, or awareness of the existence of, wild nature. The significant place of wild nature in human history has been captured in an important recent book by Max Oelschlaeger, who writes:

> By abandoning the view that nature is no more than an ecomachine or a stockpile of resources to fuel the human project, preservationists tend not to be bulls in an ecological china shop. They typically reject a strictly economic approach to valuing wilderness, and entertain other considerations such as rarity, species diversity, and even beauty. And by adopting a holistic view, preservationists are attentive to the pervasive linkages and interactions essential to any concept of a wilderness ecosystem. [10]

The deep ecologists, who express biocentric or ecocentric values, go further than this. They see preservationism (as distinct from the mere conservation of "resources") as itself anthropocentric and therefore suspect. In other words, biocentrism and ecocentrism go beyond strict preservationism by questioning "speciesism": the idea that humankind is somehow superior to, and therefore entitled to impose its values on, nature. [11] Deep ecology is a philosophical perspective that sees humans as no higher or lower than other life forms. All life forms are equally valued, and the ecological whole that they comprise cannot and should not be "managed" in the interests of any particular species. [12] Human interference in the natural processes of the living planet should be kept to a minimum. For some, animal rights and vegetarianism follow logically from a deep ecology perspective.

Consider some of the political and policy implications of a deep ecology perspective (or even a strict preservationist perspective). Should we continue to permit the cutting of forests? Forests, after all, from the perspective of other species, are home and indeed the source of life. Should we not, for example, strictly control the number of humans and the character of their transportation within wilderness areas, including national parks? Should we not disallow the testing of toxic substances on animals, and, indeed, all animal experimentation? [13] Should farmers be allowed to fill in hedgerows on their lands given that these provide corridors essential to the local survival of many animal species? What of filling in wetlands for shopping malls? And what of ultimate situations where humans and other species both require use of the same land for survival? The way we understand and value ecology clearly has very important political implications, and each of the questions posed above has gained in political salience in recent years. As Oelschlaeger put it in the preface to his book: "*The Idea of Wilderness* ... is ... subversive, for I have assumed that what the members of a democratic society think ultimately makes a difference."[14] Ideas and values, if widely shared, can establish a new political agenda. They can also provoke a strong political response.

Recent actions in U.S. courts and Congress seem to raise questions about how broadly ecological values are shared. Numerous cases have recently been heard in the courts regarding environmental policy "takings" from property rights (reductions in property value owing to restrictions on the use of that property). Some of these cases regarding interpretation of the provisions of the Fifth Amendment have been heard by the Supreme Court, and hundreds of other cases are in the courts seeking compensation to property owners, for example, for restrictions on the transformation of wetlands or requirements that endangered species be protected.[15] These cases have been supported by leading conservative legal foundations and by a growing property rights movement. The Congress is currently threatening to pass legislation that may provide for compensation when property values are diminished by as little as 20 percent by regulatory actions and for a required offer to buy when agency action results in a property value loss of 50 percent or more.[16]

Health as a Core Value

Health, the second core belief of environmentalism, is widely supported, but nonetheless also at times controversial. The present era is highly health conscious, and many Americans are concerned about their exposure to toxic chemicals. Strong parallels also exist between an increased interest in outdoor recreational activities and public concern regarding wilderness protection. Concerns regarding diet, food additives, and "natural" foods are often linked to environmental concerns regarding pesticides and herbicides. Keeping fit often produces an increased concern for air and water quality. Health is more than the absence of illness, and physical well-being is very hard to separate from environmental well-being.

Nonetheless, the minimization of impacts on human health can also be politically contentious. Here one might consider the opposing views of two noted social scientists. Aaron Wildavsky argues that in a clash between health values and wealth values the latter should be encouraged by public policy. Wealth, in his view, largely determines health.[17] That is, the wealthier the nation, the healthier it is. Wildavsky would thus never expend more public funds on health than the calculable value of the lives saved, or improved, by such expenditures. A contrasting view is put forward by Mark Sagoff. As he sees it, health and environmental protection must sometimes come first, economics second. In Sagoff's words:

> Since the New Deal, environmental law and policy have evolved as a continuous compromise between those who approach the protection of public health, safety, and the environment primarily in ethical terms and those who conceive it primarily in economic terms. The first attitude is moral: It regards hazardous pollution and environmental degradation as

evils society must eliminate if it is to live up to its ideals and aspirations. The second attitude is prudential or practical. It argues that the benefits of social regulation should be balanced more realistically against the costs.[18]

In recent years the views of those who would balance costs and benefits economically have prevailed, both in the executive branch (through President Ronald Reagan's Executive Order 12291) and in the courts (in, for example, the decisions on the exposure standards for benzene and cotton dust). In Sagoff's view this trend has run counter to the historic intent of most environmental health legislation. Sagoff would prefer a balance between economic costs and benefits and an ethical assertion of the right to health protection. In effect, Wildavsky might be asked if additional wealth automatically produces increments of health. His view does not account for the inferior health performance in some very wealthy nations, including the United States. Nor for the enormous health costs of the single-minded (if ineffective) drive for economic growth in eastern Europe and the former Soviet Union.

There is agreement that environmental health is an important societal value. There is disagreement as to how to maximize health outcomes and as to how large a risk we might simply accept as the price of (economic) prosperity. Should we emphasize the avoidance of risks, or should we take chances in the name of increased wealth and assume that health improvements will follow? Wildavsky draws an analogy with a jogger who must run a greater short-term risk of a heart attack while running in order to achieve a lower long-term risk of heart disease. If automobiles, toxic chemicals, or nuclear power advance our economy significantly while adding a small increment to overall health risks, these are risks worth taking. Most environmentalists would disagree, both on moral grounds (the risks are mostly involuntary) and on practical grounds (the risks are large, the economic gains minimal).

The political battle on this issue has been joined in the Congress around bills that would require risk analysis and/or cost-benefit analysis prior to the passage of some or all environmental and health regulations. In this debate Rep. John D. Dingell (D-Mich.) was compelled to ask: "What is the cost-benefit analysis that is going to determine the price of a healthy child?"[19] Science is a part of these procedures, but neither risk assessment, nor cost-benefit analysis, are "pure" or "certain"—the former often requires highly uncertain estimates, the latter requires value assumptions. This is not to say that such procedures do not have a place; it is to say that science cannot decide whether we wish to err on the side of prudence or on the side of cost-effectiveness when human health and human lives are clearly involved (see chaps. 9 and 10).

Sustainability as a Core Value

The third core belief of environmentalism, sustainability, is less frequently debated currently, but may be the most important dimension of environmentalism because it, even more than ecology and health, implies a thoroughgoing transformation of industrial society. As a goal, sustainability requires a radically reduced dependence on nonrenewable resources, a commitment to extract renewable resources no more rapidly than they are restored in nature, and a minimization of all human impacts on natural ecosystems. In sum, sustainability sets the economic opportunities and ecological foundation of future generations on the same ethical level as those of present generations. Those who promote sustainability assume that now is the time to acknowledge how finite and fragile Earth is.

Perhaps the most important aspect of sustainability is the recognition that fossil fuels are not renewable. There is no obvious substitute which can supply comparable amounts of energy at a comparable cost. Nor can humankind continue to extract wood from forests or fish from the seas at present rates; they are not being replenished at those rates. Nor can we continue to burn combustible fuels at present rates lest we significantly alter the global climate, if we have not already done so. Sustainability, then, shifts the focus of societal concern from the present to the future and presumes a fundamental obligation to future generations.

Lester Milbrath, a political scientist, argues that the need to focus public policy on sustainability is an urgent one. Our "entire social system is in jeopardy," he writes, and "we cannot continue on our present trajectory." He argues that "open-minded recognition of the deep systemic nature of our problem would allow a planned gradual transition, with minimal dislocation and pain."[20] Milbrath and many others come to this view in a consideration of human population trends and the long-term potential for food supply and adequate resources, global climate change, and numerous other patterns and trends. Joel Kassiola entitles his inquiry *The Death of Industrial Civilization* and argues that future economic growth is fundamentally limited by ecological and resource constraints.[21] Indeed, there is a widespread sense that the Western standard of living, or anything like it, cannot ultimately be enjoyed by humankind as a whole, nor even indefinitely by those who enjoy it now. Yet human numbers continue to grow, as does the rate at which we extract nonrenewable resources (or remove renewable resources too rapidly for recovery). At the same time, a variety of possible futures are attainable that are both less resource dependent and profoundly comfortable. Advocates of sustainable development are seeking a viable future for postindustrial society.[22]

The fundamental question is how many (and which) people within the wealthy economies are prepared to consider some sacrifice of economic well-being or convenience to help achieve sustainability and other environmental values. To what extent are our economic and environmental values fundamentally in conflict? Kempton, Boster, and Hartley take us part of the way to a better understanding of these tensions. Most Americans, they find, accept many environmental values, but some flinch when it comes to making some specific economic sacrifices to achieve them.[23] However, in this study even a group of sawmill workers, in majority, would allow that life-style changes should sometimes be forced for the sake of the environment. This group would resist fuel taxes and, understandably, job losses—but a strong majority of all participants in the survey would favor, for example, taxing products depending on their environmental effects.

Competing Values and an Environmental Ethic

The three core values of the environmental movement are clearly important, but they must compete with other values (especially those of economy and equity). To complicate matters further, they also sometimes conflict with each other. For example, high-yield, sustainable forests may lack the diversity that would otherwise provide habitats for many animal species. Similarly, even the act of protecting human health, and thereby ensuring that human population will rise, reduces resource sustainability and virtually guarantees the diminution of nonhuman habitat. Such dilemmas do not absolve us of the task of sorting out difficult value questions; indeed politics, as the authoritative allocator of values, requires it. Technical solutions to some environmental problems exist, but they are usually partial solutions that sometimes create their own problems.

There is in the end no avoiding hard questions. An environmental ethic helps us to establish priorities. Acknowledging that all nonhuman species have a right to a wild existence carries implications, as we have seen, for the meaning and character of property rights. Similarly, if all humans are to have a right to a healthy environment, some industries must spend monies that they would prefer to put to other uses. A societal commitment to sustainability—as we will see—suggests that we may all need to adjust many dimensions of our everyday behavior, including what we buy, what we throw away, and which mode of transportation we select in various circumstances.

Environmental values, then, involve much more than just concern for attractive animals and the protection of scenic beauty. The core values of environmentalism, if taken seriously, challenge nothing less than how we organize our society and how we live our lives. These values provoke policy dilemmas and can lead to choices so hard as to be almost impossible to make. Yet we must make them. The following three sections focus on the tough questions in the hope that considering challenging cases will deepen our understanding of the political significance of environmentalism. These cases arise out of each of the three core values of environmentalism: ecology, health, and sustainability. I have also identified one case that arises out of all three simultaneously.

The Ethical Challenge of Ecology

Throughout the developing world humans and other large animals compete for space. In the wealthy nations this competition has largely been resolved in favor of the human species. Lions and bears no longer roam the forests of Europe. Few bison populate the vast prairies of North America; gone, too, are the nonhuman predator populations they once supported. Now much of the wild habitat of the elephant is threatened, and the rhino, and the cheetah, and the tiger, and a long list of other creatures less grand. So too are the tropical rain forests as a whole—as well as the nontropical rain forests of the Pacific Northwest. These are popular issues in part because it was one thing for humankind to appropriate some of the planet, another thing to appropriate nearly all of it. Few would disagree with the assertion that the lives of future humans would be profoundly less rich should we as a species appropriate most of the space required by other species. Yet here is the dilemma: both the animals and humans now need the same land. Who will decide what to do? And how?

Particularly perplexing issues include how best to protect the spotted owl, the tiger, and the elephant. The case of the spotted owl is familiar to most North Americans. Its protection under the U.S. Endangered Species Act blocked the logging of some old-growth forests, its habitat. Intense political conflict erupted in the Pacific Northwest following this decision, conflict that gave further impetus to the property rights movement. Loggers, industry, small businesses, and the local media rallied against both the decision and the owl. In the process, some environmental positions have been widely misunderstood. The owl itself, however deserving of protection, has been seen by environmentalists as but one species under threat. In their view, the ancient forest itself deserves protection. As Patrick Mazza put it, "the spotted owl is a 'canary in a coal mine,' whose troubles signal a warning for the entire old growth ecosystem." [24] The jobs are soon to be lost in any case because little old-growth forest remains. The larger question is, should humankind remove and replace all the forests of the world? The replacement forest may be vastly different ecologically. The issue for most environmentalists is not the economic value of forests, but whether all the world exists simply for our benefit. Jobs that might have existed for a few years more must, in this view, come to an end a few years sooner.

The "spotted owl" dilemma is difficult—very difficult if one's life is directly affected—but it is not nearly so tough as the case of tigers and elephants, both of which require vast wilderness habitats. The land the tiger needs is also coveted by Indian peasants who would hope to grow crops there and nearby. Given the numbers of humans in India, and their present rate of growth, it is only a matter of time before this is literally a matter of human lives versus tiger lives. Additionally, as humans encroach on tiger populations, fatalities are inevitable.

Laura Westra and others provide important ethical arguments to help resolve these enormous moral dilemmas. As she puts it, "just as all individual and group interests need to start with the preservation of their existence, so too all our moral doctrines prescribing appropriate principles for human interaction should be preceded by a principle aimed at preserving life in general, in and through ecosystems." [25] There is no doubt that sometimes, and increasingly, these values will carry a very high price.

In East Africa humans who hunt elephants are now themselves hunted and killed regularly by protection authorities. Something near to a state of war exists. Most African nations are cooperating in seeking an end to trade in ivory worldwide. Other African nations with more stable elephant populations (Zimbabwe, Botswana, and South Africa) issue permits to hunt elephants. This strategy has been partially successful against poaching, and elephant populations appear, for now, to be secure in these countries. [26] But should the existence of elephants in the wild depend on the desire of some humans to kill them? Do not both tigers and elephants have an absolute right to a safe habitat somewhere on the planet?

Most people—if unaffected personally—would answer the last question affirmatively. But the implications may be far more radical than most understand. As George Sessions has stated:

> Population biologists have argued that 1 to 2 billion people living lightly on the planet would be sustainable given the ecological requirements of maintaining carrying capacity for all species. A human population decrease from its present level to that level (by humane needs such as steady low birth rates) would also be good for humans and for the diversity of human cultures, as well as for wild species and ecosystems. [27]

The individual policy dilemmas, however difficult, pale to insignificance if one accepts the profound nature of the challenge posed by this view. Those human numbers may be optimal, but that conclusion hardly provides our species with a means of humanely achieving a significant population reduction. There is no general agreement that such a goal is either feasible or desirable. Some feel, however, that it is possible in the long run, and from this perspective our zoos and parks are seen as arks for a very different planetary future.

The Ethical Challenge of Health

Cost-benefit analysis regarding health matters requires placing a price on human lives, an ethical dilemma if ever there was one. The cost of changing an industrial process is calculated and compared to the additional health costs of continued human exposures at present levels. Environmental exposures of other species are usually ignored. Indeed, calculations are usually for either human occupational exposures or human environmental exposures, but not both. [28] Typically, a small number of human fatalities is set against an estimate by industry of the cost of cleaning up. The costs of nonfatal illnesses are often underestimated or ignored and so too are some nonhealth gains to industry associated with most retooling of industrial processes. Thus, the price assigned to the estimate of human lives lost is a significant part of the overall calculation.

What is important here is seeing that all of the above objections are technical objections. The ethical objection is, simply put, that a human life is beyond price. If a life can be saved, it should be saved. Yet if that were literally true governments might be expected to set speed limits at 10 miles per hour (mph) or to close down all oil refineries and uranium mines. One is drawn back to Sagoff's view that what is appropriate is some compromise, some balancing, between the two approaches to matters of environmental and occupational health. Cost-benefit calculations can be made, but governments should not imagine that they are utterly bound by them. Other factors must be considered. Do technologies exist that would ameliorate or eliminate the problem? How deep are the polluters' pockets relative to the cost of cleaning up? How important to society is the product associated with the imposed risk? Regarding this latter question, consider that it is possible that some human lives may be lost to achieve dandelion-free suburban lawns. Does that make ethical sense even if risking those lives generates millions of dollars in economic activity? In the case of asbestos (a known potent carcinogen), does it not matter if the substance is used in protective garments for fire fighters or for a more trivial purpose? Should we not also ask whether or not substitutes are readily available?

Releases of chemicals into the wider environment raise additional important questions. In particular, one must consider the likely duration of the environmental impact. If a risk will exist in perpetuity, the price is infinite regardless of the value one assigns to any one life. But in practice, we more frequently err in an opposite way. We site toxic chemical dumps, or municipal solid waste containing hazardous chemicals, on clay soils because they delay movement through the ground. But ultimately those chemicals will reach larger bodies of water. Arguably, it makes more sense to bury toxic wastes in sand, but to bury them in an amount and form that will release no more than we can tolerate in nearby aquifers. Otherwise all we are doing is assigning a toxic world to distant future generations. We are unable, it seems, to reason morally beyond our own grandchildren.

The Ethical Challenge of Sustainability

Any number of policy complexities arise from sustainability values as well. In the mid 1970s and again in the early 1980s North Americans were acutely aware of the long-term nonsustainability of fossil fuel supplies. This reality remains, though it has slipped for the present from public consciousness. Acutely in the public mind at present, however, are the limits of future lumber supplies from old-growth sites. So, too, in many locations are acceptable sites for the disposal of municipal solid waste. But lest all the news appears to be bad, feasible options are available in many cases. Building materials can be made from recycled household and industrial wastes, slowing the speed with which we "run out" of both lumber and landfill sites. Even more dramatically, by changing the rules by which electrical utilities and their customers make supply-and-demand decisions, we could save enough electricity to eliminate any need for new coal-burning power plants. This latter assertion perhaps needs a brief elaboration.

Electrical utilities traditionally worried almost exclusively about supply, while demand management was primarily the customer's concern. The more the utility supplied, the more money they made. Utilities also rarely considered for long how durable or expandable their supply sources were; it was assumed that other supply sources could always be found, if necessary. Demand management frequently fell between the cracks as neither builders nor building managers were concerned about electricity bills because they did not pay them—tenants did. Builders avoided the higher capital costs of more efficient lighting and other devices. Many commercial tenants were unconcerned about electrical efficiency because they paid a share of electricity costs related to the square footage they occupied rather than the amount of electricity they actually used. In the late 1980s utilities in several states were ordered by state regulatory agencies to treat efficiency improvement as investments made on behalf of their customers. The savings have been considerable: for the utilities, for their customers, for the economy as a whole, and for the sustainability of energy supplies.[29] Demand reduction has generally proved to be cheaper than new supply; there are, it would seem, some win-win possibilities.

Nonetheless, policy choices remain because some jobs are placed at risk (while others are created) and some firms may suffer significant economic losses (while others gain). Those who supply or build new power plants are hit very hard by these changes. So, too, are some employees of utilities. Achieving greater sustainability may well require significant transformations throughout industrial society, but these transformations can be eased by intelligent public policy and forward-looking private initiatives. Laid-off loggers can work in replanting and stream protection initiatives, and some "greening of business" initiatives strengthen firms and the economy in the long run (see chap. 12).

A final example here provides a clearer appreciation of the importance of this issue and leads to a discussion of integrating environmental, economic, and equity values. Automobiles, their manufacture and repair, and related industries, generate at least 25 percent of the gross national product (GNP) of North America. Related industries include road building, tires, auto parts, and significant proportions of the steel industry, the cement industry, aggregates (sand and gravel) extraction, fast foods, motels, advertising, and so forth. Yet the automobile itself may well be unsustainable—at least in present numbers, traveling current average annual distances. Automobiles consume land, pollute the air, use up the least durable of fossil fuels, contribute to global warming, reduce the habitat of other species, and are a major source of acid precipitation. All three core environmental values are simultaneously offended. It has increasingly been argued in recent years that a sustainable future will see more compact cities that in turn are less dependent on automobile transportation, however fueled.[30] European cities are at present typically twice as compact as North American cities, and citizens of those cities typically use half the transportation fuel of their North American counterparts.[31] Yet Europeans are equally prosperous overall and the cities in question are arguably more pleasant (Paris, London, Amsterdam). In addition, several European cities have very recently carved out core areas from which automobiles are completely excluded. Such efforts are already coming to North America and this trend will accelerate with the next round of fossil fuel price increases.

The principal point here is that environmental values, if taken seriously, could transform the future of industrial societies. The economic, social, and political implications of these changes are important and wide-ranging. Governments will require, then, ways to integrate these new values with the other important values that have always served as at least implicit guides to public policy. Here one might speak of three fundamental value sets: environment, economy, and equity. Below, I consider the relationships between two pairs of value sets: environment/economy and environment/equity. Many such considerations have been implicit within the preceding analysis as well. Economy and equity are so central to politics as a value-integrating process that they deserve additional attention here.

The Environment and the Economy

As Charles Lindblom has observed, contemporary political leaders are held to be responsible for the success or failure of the economy.[32] Accordingly, rising unemployment or falling profits often result in electoral difficulties for incumbents. Increasingly now our political leadership is also seen to be responsible for environmental damage. To the extent that environmental protection and economic growth are in conflict, political leaders are thus held to an impossible mandate. Some would prefer to abandon one set of goals, usually environmental. Others place an emphasis on win-win scenarios, on the possibility of sustainable development. In other words, the perhaps impossible mandate is seen by some to be achievable—the simultaneous maximization of environmental values and economic values is taken to lie somewhere between assumption and hope. But, putting aside equity considerations for the moment, can environment and economy be simultaneously advanced?

On the positive side, some significant economic sectors are highly compatible with environmental protection.[33] Growth in public transport systems results in improved air quality and the more efficient use of land, materials, and energy. Demand-side management by electrical utilities has similarly positive environmental effects, and it can also be a considerable economic stimulus to manufacturers and installers of electrical equipment for heating, cooling, lighting, and electrical motors. Recycling-based manufacturing of paper, building materials, packaging, metal products, and plastic products also enhances environmental quality on a variety of fronts. So, too, of course, do the production, installation, and maintenance of pollution abatement equipment. Similarly, reduced dependence on agricultural chemicals can result in more economically viable farming operations in part because consumers are willing to pay more for organic produce. To the extent that governmental policies allow and/or encourage economic transformations of this sort, economy and environment can improve simultaneously.

In addition, many sectors of a modern economy have only very small, or readily avoidable, effects on the environment. Significant growth in these sectors would have negligible environmental effects. Additional expenditures on education, social services, health care, or the arts and entertainment, for example, add little to the burden borne by the environment. This is an aspect of the debate on the appropriate level of social and other expenditures that has too often been left aside. But other economic sectors also have quite modest net impacts. These include some of the more dynamic sectors of the global economy. Computers, automation, and telecommunications have modest impacts per dollar of value added. In addition, they may make offsetting contributions. Communications can substitute for travel with very significant energy savings and a corresponding pollution reduction. Robots need little lighting or heat and do not add to highway congestion at rush hour. Equity effects aside for the moment, automation has enormous potential for reducing the total energy and materials devoted to manufacturing work spaces. Energy and materials use, much more than GNP, determines total environmental impact.

Some economic sectors, however, would appear irretrievably in conflict with environmental values in the long term—especially ecological and sustainability values. No one would propose eliminating any economic sector by fiat. Yet it is hard to imagine how environmental values will not increasingly come into conflict with the growth goals of some sectors of the contemporary economy. Sectors where clashes are likely include the automobile industry (and thereby other attendant industries), the forest industry, the chemical industry, coal mining and use, the packaging industry, and the construction industry (as regards suburban sprawl). And one should not omit tobacco producers. Often, but not always, such clashes can be resolved relatively painlessly as when less toxic substitutes can be found or new products or processes developed. Even when resolutions are not painless, the burden can be spread and softened through imaginative public policy initiatives.

Comfortable, happy, healthy lives for ourselves and our families are, it would appear, in conflict with exactly those same goals. The automobile that keeps us out of the rain on our way to basketball practice pollutes the air we breathe. The materials used to produce the extra rooms in our home may require the diminution of habitat and perhaps outdoor recreational space. Our dry-cleaned clothes mandate the production and use of hazardous chemicals.[34] The suburban lifestyle we have collectively embraced since the 1940s and 1950s may be environmentally inappropriate for the population levels and energy reserves of the early twenty-first century. The potential value conflicts are clearly very deep and must be resolved both at the many points where polity and economy intersect and in the inner recesses of present and future minds. When we cannot have both economy and environment, which is the more important to us? (And exactly when can we not have both?)

These tensions, both potential and immediate, could be resolved in a number of ways. Even being able to step back and ask questions is, of course, a luxury. In poor nations the choices are more stark: food or nature? economic collapse or forests for tomorrow? a manufacturing sector or clean air? Choice is the ultimate luxury, and North Americans still have choices—so long as we do not just assume that economic values must always prevail, or that politics is a waste of time.

Changes in governmental tax and subsidy regimes could spur rapid adaptations. Many now agree that the extraction of energy and raw materials should no longer be subsidized in any way.[35] Also, some environmentalists urge that automobile transportation no longer be subsidized.[36] Taxation burdens might, in general, be shifted at least in part from work (income tax), property ownership, and gross sales to energy, materials use, land use, and waste disposal. Such structural changes would allow the marketplace to gradually handle the multitude of production and consumption decisions associated with improving sustainability.

Such measures, combined with protection of environmentally sensitive lands and regulations to protect human health, could help to effectively integrate environmental and economic values. Also, through green products, green investment options, environmental audits, and other techniques, the private sector and individual consumers can take significant initiatives irrespective of the government's commitment (see chap. 12).

Even those industries identified above as likely to be in conflict with environmental values could make fundamental breakthroughs in both profitability and improved environmental protection. The electrical utilities are a crucial case in point here: the commitment to demand-side management improved their profits in many cases. Gains may not be achieved by every industry challenged by environmental values, but losses can be minimized or turned around within those firms and sectors that are best able to anticipate change.

The Environment and Equity

The integration of environmental values and economic values has received a lot of consideration in recent years. A good deal of attention has been devoted as well to the great challenges associated with achieving improved North-South equity and environmental protection simultaneously.[37] But political leaders have given less consideration to the linkages between environmental values and improvements in equity within wealthy economies. Such linkages are nonetheless both real and complex. They are so significant that some argue that environmental values are not likely to be politically successful unless and until major environment-equity tensions are at least partly resolved. Important points of value intersection—sometimes conflictual, sometimes mutually supportive—exist as regards gender and environment, class and environment, race and environment, and regional equity and environment.

Gender provides an interesting starting point because a commonality of interests between environmentalists and feminists has been frequently asserted in recent years.[38] Many of the complexities of these debates need not be reiterated here, but three matters are fundamental. The first is human population, the second is the parallel between the domination of women and of nature, and the third is women's distinctive perspective on sustainability.

All three core values of environmentalism would be more easily achieved if the total human population were stabilized or in gradual decline toward an optimal level. This is particularly true for ecology and sustainability values, which in all likelihood are unobtainable unless human population growth is halted. Many of the major objectives of the women's movement are thus essential to environmentalists. Access to family planning services and freedom of choice regarding abortion are obviously important. But perhaps even more important is the fact that there is no stronger determinant of ultimate family size than equal opportunity for women. Environmentalists and the women's movement concur, then, in a fundamental way on issues significant to both.

Second, there are parallels between the domination of women and the domination of nature. These parallels are so strong that they reach into the very structure of our language as in the "rape" of the land, "virgin" forests, and "mother" Earth. Another dimension of the parallel character of male-female and human-nature domination is that in both cases subjectivity is denied. The domination arises out of a self-regarding lack of respect. The habits and attitudes born of one form of domination re-create themselves within the other.

Third, women's distinctive biological (and cultural) role in childbearing and early nurture may well have other environmental implications. Whether or not this distinctiveness has been overstated in the past, bearing children may well incline women to a greater sensitivity to the needs of future generations.

Sustainability issues are seen in perhaps a different light than they are seen by men. So, too, may be the habitat needs of other species. Women have frequently assumed leadership roles within the environmental movement.[39] Overall, there is some potential for cooperation between those advancing gender equity and those seeking environmental protection, and there would appear to be few points of tension.

The linkages between environmental values and class equity values are quite different. Here, tensions have been widespread, particularly over perceived threats to employment opportunities. A sense of threat has been particularly striking in the forest industry, but it has also arisen for workers in the nuclear industry, for coal miners, for ranchers (as regards protection or reintroduction of predators), for highway construction and packaging workers, and for farmers (regarding pesticide use). It exists as well within a variety of polluting industries where the cost of cleanup may appear to threaten competitiveness. It could also exist in the auto industry in the future, though the United Auto Workers' union has had a very long history of positive involvement with conservation and environmental protection.[40]

These tensions are both real and politically significant, but they do not reveal the whole story. As noted above, environmental protection initiatives also generate significant employment opportunities.[41] Renewable energy supply sources are more employment intensive and less environmentally threatening than are energy supply megaprojects. Energy efficiency improvements create jobs in manufacturing, installation, and construction. Recycling is highly labor intensive. Bottle bills, pushed through in ten states by environmental organizations, are net generators of employment. Urban reconfiguration and public transport expenditures create employment, as do pollution abatement and environmental restoration. Overall, the jobs gained may well be more numerous than the jobs put at risk. This does not necessarily help those who lose their jobs, but it could if transitions were accomplished in a more orderly and gradual fashion. Nonetheless, some political tension on the class-environment front is unavoidable.

Environmentalists have become somewhat more thoughtful on such questions in recent years. Some have suggested that the time has or will come when there should be some decoupling of employment and income. Wealthy societies could perhaps afford to replace present transfer payments (social security, unemployment insurance, welfare, food stamps) with a universal social income. Net income would remain the same for most people, but some of it would come from a nonemployer source. The income level for some unemployed persons might rise, but only modestly. The largest difference would be that all adults would receive the income and thus there would be no disincentive to working (as with welfare) and no disincentive to education (as with unemployment insurance). Another problem with the present situation is that almost any risk to employment is seen as unacceptable, regardless of the tragedy attendant on continued employment (as in the cutting of the last of the old-growth forests). In effect, the problem lies in the distribution of work and income and the absence of full employment.[42] This may be the single largest political problem involved with the integration of equity values and environmental values, and it thus deserves a great deal of attention in the future.

Also increasingly important are the linkages between racial equity and environmental protection (see chap. 11 on environmental justice). However, here—as with gender—the interests tend to be parallel, although, as with class, perceptions sometimes diverge. In the 1970s some African American leaders saw environmental protection as likely to divert public funds from social justice needs. Given government's limited domestic budget, this was, and remains, an appropriate concern. But as with the issue of employment (itself, of course, a central concern of all visible minorities), there is another side captured in the new movement for environmental justice. Minorities have historically borne the brunt of occupational hazards, pollution, and waste disposal, including hazardous waste disposal.[43] The realization of this fact has had a very real political effect in recent years, especially in the South. Robert Bullard's book *Dumping in Dixie* carefully portrays the growing environmental awareness among African Americans in their opposition to the disproportionate siting of hazardous waste dumps, incinerators, municipal landfills, plants using heavy metals, and chemical factories in their neighborhoods.[44] More than this, major environmental organizations are paying increasing attention to the environmental issues that affect minorities disproportionately, such as lead poisoning, the hazards faced by farm workers, and the general level of toxic exposures in minority communities.[45] The growing importance of the environmental justice movement in the early 1990s has brought these two important social movements into new forms of cooperation and some prospects for greater mutual respect in the future.[46]

Regionally based environment-equity matters also have a potential for future value conflict. For example, the strong push for recycling may have a negative effect on already depressed resource-producing regions. This is particularly pronounced in isolated regions in Canada, where many communities depend on pulp and paper production to survive. New plants to produce paper products from recycled stock will likely locate in high population areas near to the source of supply. Closure of distant mills will hurt some already economically marginal regions. Conversely, older urban cores in the United States, particularly in the Northeast, are as regionally underadvantaged as any places in North America. They may well benefit from recycling and, as well, from any turn toward more compact urban areas and the corresponding increase in urban core restoration and public transport expenditures.

Thus, on the whole, the prospects for integrating equity and environmental values would seem promising, though neither easy nor simple. What is clear is that adding environment to the traditional political agenda will forever change the face of politics. Multidimensionality is accentuated and accelerated. Not that politics was ever simple. But ideology can no longer be seen in simplistic left-right/liberal-conservative terms. Not only the end of the cold war assures this new reality. Widely held environmental values will enormously diversify each citizen's coherent intellectual options while increasing the variety of possible political coalitions and combinations.

The integration of economy, equity, and environment is and must be primarily a political process, one fraught with ethical dilemmas and disputes. Moreover, these matters cannot be resolved solely on the basis of either facts or expertise. Solutions require a thoughtful collective sense of what kind of society we want. In a democracy, fundamental values are matters each of us must establish for ourselves. Democratic institutions succeed or fail on the basis of their ability to integrate citizen values within effective collective decisions. But more than that, our society itself will not succeed in the long run unless we face up to the difficult issues and choices now before us. That in turn requires that most, if not all, citizens understand environmental, economic, and equity values. It also requires both a widespread tolerance for the values of others and an ongoing prospect for broad participation in the political process.

Notes

1. David Easton, *The Political System* (New York: Knopf, 1953).
2. Evidence of the level of acceptance of environmental values is contained in *Wildlife and the Public Interest* (New York: Praeger, 1989) and in Riley E. Dunlap, "Polls, Pollution and Politics: Public Opinion on the Environment in the Reagan Era," *Environment* 29 (July-August 1987): 6-11, 32-37.
3. Samuel P. Hays, "From Conservation to Environment: Environmental Politics in the United States Since World War Two," *Environmental Review* 6 (Fall 1982): 20.

4. George Sessions, "The Deep Ecology Movement: A Review," *Environmental Review* 11 (Summer 1987): 107.
5. See Max Oelschlaeger, ed., *After Earth Day: Continuing the Conservation Effort* (Denton: University of North Texas Press, 1992), chaps. by Susan Bratton and Oelschlaeger.
6. Ronald Inglehart, *The Silent Revolution: Changing Values and Political Styles among Western Publics* (Princeton, N.J.: Princeton University Press, 1977).
7. Riley E. Dunlap and K. VanLiere, "The New Environmental Paradigm," *Journal of Environmental Education* 9, no. 4 (1978): 10-19; and Lester W. Milbrath, *Environmentalists: Vanguard for a New Society* (Albany: The State University of New York Press, 1984).
8. The movement of environmental values into the mainstream of American political culture is established and assessed in Willett Kempton, James S. Boster, and Jennifer A. Hartley, *Environmental Values in American Culture* (Cambridge, Mass.: MIT Press, 1995).
9. Robert Paehlke, *Environmentalism and the Future of Progressive Politics* (New Haven, Conn.: Yale University Press, 1989), 144-145.
10. Max Oelschlaeger, *The Idea of Wilderness: From Prehistory to the Age of Ecology* (New Haven, Conn.: Yale University Press, 1991), 292.
11. Ibid.
12. See Warwick Fox, *Toward a Transpersonal Ecology* (Boston: Shambhala, 1990); see also Bill Devall and George Sessions, *Deep Ecology: Living as if Nature Mattered* (Salt Lake City: Peregrine Smith Books, 1985) and Arne Naess, *Ecology, Community, and Lifestyle: Outline of an Ecosophy* (Cambridge: Cambridge University Press, 1989).
13. See, for example, Tom Regan, *All That Dwell Therein: Animal Rights and Environmental Ethics* (Berkeley and Los Angeles: University of California Press, 1982), and the extensive work of Peter Singer.
14. Oelschlaeger, *Idea of Wilderness*, ix.
15. Charles A. Wise and Kirk Emerson, "Regulatory Takings: The Emerging Doctrine and Its Implications for Public Administration," *Administration and Society* 26 (1994): 305-336.
16. Bob Benenson, "House Passes Property Rights Bill," *Congressional Quarterly Weekly Report*, March 4, 1995, 680.
17. Aaron Wildavsky, *Searching for Safety* (New Brunswick, N.J.: Transaction, 1988).
18. Mark Sagoff, *The Economy of the Earth* (New York: Cambridge University Press, 1988), 195-196.
19. Quoted at p. 681 in Bob Benenson, "House Easily Passes Bills to Limit Regulations," *Congressional Quarterly Weekly Report*, March 4, 1995, 679-682; see also Margaret Kriz, "Risky Business," *National Journal*, February 18, 1995, 417-421.
20. Lester Milbrath, *Envisioning a Sustainable Society* (Albany: State University of New York Press, 1989), 338.
21. Joel J. Kassiola, *The Death of Industrial Civilization* (Albany: State University of New York Press, 1990).
22. See World Commission on Environment and Development, *Our Common Future* (New York: Oxford University Press, 1987), and the many works that have followed from it.
23. Kempton, Boster, and Hartley, *Environmental Values*, 255-270; see especially responses to questions 23, 37, 42, 92, and 103.
24. Patrick Mazza, "The Spotted Owl as Scapegoat," *Capitalism, Nature, Socialism* (June 1990): 100.
25. Laura Westra, *An Environmental Proposal for Ethics: The Principle of Integrity* (Lanham, Md.: Rowman and Littlefield, 1994), xvii. See also Holmes Rolston III, *Conserving Natural Value* (New York: Columbia University Press, 1994).
26. Michael L. Nieswiadomy, "Economics and Resource Conservation," in Oelschlaeger, *After Earth Day*, 123-124.

27. Ibid., 19.
28. Robert C. Paehlke, "Occupational and Environmental Health Linkages," in *Controlling Chemical Hazards*, ed. Raymond P. Cote and Peter G. Wells (London: Unwin Hyman, 1991), 175-197.
29. See, for example, David Moscovitz, Steven Nadel, and Howard Geller, *Increasing the Efficiency of Electricity Production and Use: Barriers and Strategies* (Washington, D.C.: American Council for an Energy-Efficient Economy, 1991).
30. See, for example, Marcia D. Lowe, "Rethinking Urban Transport," in *State of the World, 1991*, ed. Lester R. Brown (New York: Norton, 1991), 56-73.
31. Peter Newman and Jeffrey Kenworthy, *Cities and Automobile Dependence: An International Sourcebook* (Hants, Eng.: Gower, 1989).
32. Charles E. Lindblom, *Politics and Markets* (New York: Basic Books, 1977).
33. For more information on simultaneous gains noted in this paragraph see, for example, Moscovitz, Nadel, and Geller, *Increasing Efficiency*; and Brown, ed., *State of the World*, 1991 and 1992 (New York: Norton, 1991 and 1992), esp. chaps. 2, 3, and 4 in 1991 and 3, 8, and 9 in 1992.
34. Kirk R. Smith, "Air Pollution: Assessing Total Exposure in the United States," *Environment* 30 (October 1988): 10-15, 33-38.
35. See Jim MacNeill, Pieter Winsemius, and Taizo Yakushiji, *Beyond Interdependence* (New York: Oxford University Press, 1991).
36. Francesca Lyman, "Rethinking Our Transportation Future," *E Magazine* 1 (September-October 1990): 34-41.
37. See, for example, MacNeill, Winsemius, and Yakushiji, *Beyond Interdependence*.
38. Perhaps the best single introductory article is still Karen J. Warren, "Feminism and Ecology: Making Connections," *Environmental Ethics* 9 (1987): 3-20. See also Judith Plant, ed., *Healing the Wounds: The Promise of Ecofeminism* (Toronto: Between the Lines, 1989); I. Diamond and G. Orenstein, eds., *Reweaving the World: The Emergence of Ecofeminism* (San Francisco: Sierra Club Books, 1990); and Janet Biehl, *Finding Our Way: Rethinking Ecofeminist Politics* (Montreal: Black Rose Books, 1991).
39. Carolyn Merchant, "Earth Care: Women and the Environmental Movement," *Environment* 23 (June 1981): 6-13, 38-40.
40. Robert Paehlke, "Environmentalisme et syndicalisme au Canada anglais et aux Etats-Unis," *Sociologie et Sociètès* 13 (April 1981): 161-179.
41. See Paehlke, *Environmentalism and the Future of Progressive Politics*; and Michael Renner, "Creating Sustainable Jobs in Industrial Economies," in *State of the World, 1992*, ed. Brown.
42. For a thorough discussion of work distribution from a leftist perspective, see Stanley Aronowitz and William DiFazio, *The Jobless Future* (Minneapolis: University of Minnesota Press, 1994).
43. James C. Robinson, *Toil and Toxics: Workplace Struggles and Political Strategies for Occupational Health* (Berkeley and Los Angeles: University of California Press, 1991).
44. Robert D. Bullard, *Dumping in Dixie: Race, Class, and Environmental Quality* (Boulder: Westview, 1991); and Charles Lee, *Toxic Waste and Race in the United States* (New York: United Church of Christ Commission for Racial Justice, 1987).
45. See, for example, the extensive treatment of environmental justice issues in *Environmental Action* (January-February 1990): 19-30, and the extensive sources cited therein. In this special issue, Environmental Action, a large environmentalist organization, faces up to the white middle-class past of the environmental movement.
46. The evolving politics of race and environment is discussed in Robert Bullard, ed., *Unequal Protection: Environmental Justice and Communities of Color* (San Francisco: Sierra Club Books, 1994); Robert Gottlieb, *Forcing the Spring: The Transformation of the American Environmental Movement* (Washington, D.C.: Island Press, 1993); and Debra J. Salazar and Lisa A. Moulds, "Toward an Integrated Politics of Social Justice and Environment: African American Leaders in Seattle" (Paper presented to American Society for Environmental History in Las Vegas, Nevada, March 1995).

PART II. FEDERAL INSTITUTIONS AND POLICY CHANGE

5

Presidential Leadership and the Environment: From Reagan to Clinton

Norman J. Vig

Throughout our history, American presidents have used the power of the veto to protect our values as a country. . . . Today, I am vetoing the biggest Medicare and Medicaid cuts in history, deep cuts in education, a rollback in environmental protection, and a tax increase on working families.

—President Bill Clinton
December 6, 1995

With these words, Bill Clinton exercised his constitutional powers to veto the most revolutionary budget enacted by Congress since the New Deal. Among other objections, the president argued that the Republican plan for balancing the budget would drastically undermine public health, environmental protection, and preservation of natural resources for future generations.[1] The Republicans, for their part, claimed that many environmental regulations were unnecessary, and that public health and natural resources could be protected at far less cost to the taxpayer.

In fact, by 1995 the normally muted differences between the two parties on environmental issues had become a deep ideological divide. Under the guise of the "Contract with America," the new Republican majorities in both houses of Congress had launched an effort to revise and defund much of the federal environmental legislation enacted over the previous quarter-century (see chaps. 1 and 6). President Clinton, himself under fire from environmentalists for weak leadership, responded by threatening to veto almost all of the proposed changes if they reached his desk. At this writing, it appears that environmental policy will be an important issue in the 1996 presidential election.[2]

The tension between economic interests and preservation of natural resources has been at the heart of public debate over the environment for the past century and has often pitted one branch of government against another. But since President Theodore Roosevelt proclaimed the Conservation era in the early 1900s, presidents have periodically used the bully pulpit of their office to rally public support for national environmental policies that also contribute to the long-term health of the economy. During the New Deal, Franklin D. Roosevelt put millions of people back to work on conservation and reclamation projects.[3] More recently, presidents have had to deal with a wide array of new issues involving pollution of air, water, and the land and threats to the global environment.

This chapter examines the role of recent presidents in shaping national environmental policies, with particular emphasis on the administrations of Ronald Reagan, George Bush, and Bill Clinton. First we briefly consider the general powers and limitations of the presidency and their relationship to policymaking.

Presidential Powers and Constraints

From a policy cycle perspective, presidents obviously have great potential influence (see chap. 1). First, they have a major role in *agenda setting.* They can raise issues to public attention, define the terms of public debate, and rally public opinion and constituency support through speeches, press conferences, and other media events. Without presidential endorsement, major policy initiatives have rarely been successful. Second, they can take the lead in *policy formulation* by devoting presidential staff and other resources to particular issues, by mobilizing expertise inside and outside of government, and by consulting widely with interest groups and members of Congress in designing and proposing legislation. They can also stop legislation through use of the veto power. Third, presidents use their powers as chief executive to shape *policy implementation.* They make key appointments to all agencies, propose annual operating budgets, issue executive orders, and oversee management and efficiency in the bureaucracy. An increasingly important function is regulatory oversight; that is, how the president influences regulatory policymaking by agencies such as the Environmental Protection Agency (EPA). Finally, presidents have a rapidly growing role in *international leadership,* as environmental issues are increasingly international or global in scope.

At the same time, presidents cannot govern alone; they are only part of a government of "separated powers."[4] They are reliant on Congress to enact legislation and to provide the funding to carry out all activities of government. In recent years federal deficits and demands for spending reduction have become an enormous constraint on all new policymaking. When Congress and the presidency are controlled by different parties, the president may have little control over the policy agenda (see chap. 6). But even when the president's own party has a majority in one or both houses, majority coalitions may be difficult or impossible to build on particular issues. Moreover, congressional committees have substantial powers of legislative initiative, administrative oversight, and investigation that can blunt executive initiatives and embarrass the president. Nearly all major rules and regulations are also challenged in the courts by affected parties, often tying up administrative actions in litigation that goes on for years (see chap. 8). Last but not least, the media scrutinize the president more closely than any other public official and can make or break a president's reputation. Some scholars have argued that these constraints have multiplied and that the era of bold presidential leadership is over.[5]

Whether this is true or not, much depends on the particular circumstances in which a president comes to office and on the skill of each incumbent in exploiting his opportunities. Scholars of the presidency have pointed to several major variables in analyzing presidential performance.

One is the nature of the president's agenda and personal leadership style. Some presidents are "active" in the sense that they vigorously utilize presidential powers to pursue major policy change. Others are more "passive" or pursue only incremental change; they are sometimes called "guardians." Agendas may be "expansive" in the sense of advocating new governmental programs, "contractionary" in seeking to reverse existing policies or reduce the role of government, or "consolidative" if their goal is to preserve or refine past gains.[6] Thus Ronald Reagan entered office as an "active contractionary" president, George Bush as a "passive consolidator," and Bill Clinton as an "active expansive" leader.

Whatever the president's personal agenda, his role also depends on the nature of the Congress he inherits.[7] If a president faces a Congress that is either split (with one party controlling each house, as during 1981 to 1986) or in the hands of the opposition party (as during 1987 to 1992 and 1995 to 1996), he may be forced to limit his policy agenda and choose between a more confrontational or conciliatory style of leadership. President Bush opted for a conciliatory, bipartisan strategy during the 101st Congress (1989-1990), but retreated to a more negative, confrontational stance during the 102d (1991-1992) as the Democratic Congress became more assertive in pursuing its own legislative agenda (Bush exercised the veto twenty-one times in 1992 alone). President Clinton attempted to capitalize on his party's control of the 103d Congress by following a generally partisan but conciliatory legislative strategy, yet he had only limited success as his expansive programs united the Republican opposition and alienated many conservative Democrats. After the 1994 election produced a radically different Congress, Clinton had little choice but to adopt an essentially defensive, confrontational posture.

A third factor is how the president organizes his office and utilizes his executive powers. Some presidents manage the White House much more coherently and effectively than others. Some, like Dwight Eisenhower, Richard Nixon, and Ronald Reagan, have preferred a centralized, hierarchical style of management that concentrates power in a chief of staff and other top assistants; others, like Franklin Roosevelt, John Kennedy, and Bill Clinton, opted for a more open and decentralized "spokes in a wheel" model that encourages competition for the ear of the president from multiple policy sources.[8] Organizational styles seem to reflect the president's own personality and temperament more than any model's inherent advantage, but some staff arrangements prove markedly more successful than others in developing effective political strategies and managing the policy agenda.

A final dimension of presidential leadership concerns public confidence: ultimately presidential power rests on an incumbent's ability to persuade the public that he is on the right course. Some presidents are much better public communicators than others (e.g., Ronald Reagan as compared with Jimmy Carter or George Bush). In part this is a matter of rhetorical skill, but the substance of the message is also important.[9] Some presidents, like Bill Clinton, have been skillful speakers but have had difficulty in defining the message they wish to convey.

With these criteria in mind, we can turn to the records of the last three presidents in defining and shaping environmental policies. It should be emphasized that aside from public land use issues, environmental problems did not become a major federal responsibility until 1970. Riding the wave of the new environmental movement that peaked that year, President Nixon declared an "environmental decade," supported passage of the National Environmental Policy Act and Clean Air Act, and established the Environmental Protection Agency by executive order. Although Nixon later retreated from leadership on environmental issues, subsequent presidents largely cooperated with Congress in enacting a remarkable array of bipartisan environmental legislation in the 1970s (see app. 1).[10]

The Reagan Revolution: Challenge to Environmentalism

The "environmental decade" came to an abrupt halt with the landslide victory of Ronald Reagan in 1980. Although the environment was not a major issue in the election, Reagan was the first president to come to office with an avowedly antienvironmental agenda. Reflecting the Sagebrush Rebellion brewing in the west, as well as long years of public relations work for corporate and conservative causes, Reagan viewed environmental conservation as fundamentally at odds with economic growth and prosperity. He saw environmental regulation as a barrier to "supply side" economics and sought to reverse or weaken many of the policies of the previous decade.[11] Although only partially successful, Reagan's contractionary agenda laid the groundwork for a renewed attack on environmental policy a decade later.

After a period of economic decline and weak leadership, Reagan's landslide victory provided a strong mandate for policy change. With a new Republican majority in the Senate as well, he was able to gain congressional support for the Economic Recovery Act of 1981, which embodied much of his program. The law reduced income taxes by nearly 25 percent and cut spending deeply for environmental and social programs. Despite this initial victory, however, President Reagan faced a Congress that was divided on most issues and did not support his broader environmental agenda. On the contrary, the bipartisan majority that had enacted most of the environmental legislation of the 1970s remained largely intact.

Faced with this situation, Reagan turned to what has been termed an "administrative presidency."[12] Essentially, this involved an attempt to change federal policies by maximizing control of *policy implementation within the executive branch*. That is, rather than trying to rewrite legislation, Reagan attempted to alter its content and effect through control of the bureaucracy.

The administrative strategy initially had four major components: careful screening of all appointees to environmental and other agencies to ensure compliance with Reagan's ideological agenda; tight policy coordination through cabinet councils and White House staff; deep cuts in the budgets of environmental agencies and programs; and an enhanced form of regulatory oversight to eliminate or revise regulations considered too burdensome by industry.

Reagan's appointment of officials who were overtly hostile to the mission of their agencies aroused strong opposition from the environmental community. In particular, his selection of Anne M. Gorsuch (later Burford) to head the Environmental Protection Agency and James G. Watt as secretary of interior provoked controversy from the beginning because both were attorneys who had spent long years litigating against environmental regulation. Both made it clear that they intended to rewrite the rules and procedures of their agencies to accommodate industry and public land users.

In the White House, President Reagan lost no time in changing the policy machinery to accomplish the same goal. He attempted to abolish the Council on Environmental Quality (CEQ), and when that failed because it would require congressional legislation, he drastically cut its staff and ignored its advice. In its place he appointed Vice President George Bush to head a new "Task Force on Regulatory Relief" to review and propose revisions or rescissions of regulations in response to complaints from business. All regulations were also vetted by a staff agency, the Office of Information and Regulatory Affairs (OIRA) in the Office of Management and Budget (see below). To ensure broader policy coordination, Reagan appointed the Cabinet Council on Natural Resources and the Environment under Secretary Watt to oversee the EPA and other agencies. This hierarchical organization was designed to exert maximum policy control from above.

Finally, Reagan's budget cuts had major impacts on the capacity of environmental agencies to implement their growing policy mandates. The EPA lost approximately one-third of its operating budget and one-fifth of its personnel in the early 1980s. The CEQ lost most of its staff and barely continued to function. In the Interior Department and elsewhere, funds were shifted from environmental to development programs.[13]

Perhaps the most controversial aspect of Reagan's pincer movement on environmental policy was his use of enhanced regulatory oversight through OIRA. This shadowy body, which originated in the Carter administration to deal with paperwork reduction, operated behind closed doors without the normal rules of administrative procedure and public accountability. Executive Order 12291 of February 1981 required all agencies to submit "regulatory impact statements" to OIRA; these statements were to include cost-benefit analyses justifying regulatory activity (control was further extended by Executive Order

12498 of 1985, which required agencies to submit regulatory calendars a year in advance to allow more time to scrutinize pending regulations). Using this authority, OIRA held up, reviewed, and rewrote hundreds of EPA and other regulations to reduce their impact on industry. Although regulatory oversight is an accepted and necessary function of the modern presidency, the Reagan White House effort to shape and control all regulatory activity in the interests of political clients raised serious questions of improper administrative procedure and violation of statutory intent.[14]

Not surprisingly, Congress responded by investigating OIRA procedures and other activities of Reagan appointees, especially Burford and Watt. Burford came under heavy attack for confidential dealings with business and political interests that allegedly led to "sweetheart deals" on such matters as Superfund cleanups. After refusing to disclose documents, she was found in contempt of Congress and forced to resign (along with twenty other high EPA officials) in March 1983. James Watt was pilloried in Congress for his efforts to open up virtually all public lands (including wilderness areas) and offshore coastal areas to mining and oil and gas development. In response, Democrats in the House of Representatives attached riders to appropriations bills blocking many of his actions. Watt resigned later in 1983 over some ill-advised remarks he made about the ethnic composition of a commission that had been appointed to investigate his coal-leasing policies, but by that time he had alienated almost everyone in Congress.[15]

Reagan's deregulatory campaign was largely spent by the end of his first term owing to these embarrassments and to widespread public and congressional opposition to weakening environmental protection. Recognizing that his policies had backfired, Reagan took few new initiatives during his second term. His appointees to the EPA and Interior after 1983 were able to defuse some of the political conflict generated by Watt and Burford. EPA administrators (William Ruckelshaus and Lee Thomas) were able to restore some funding and credibility to their agency, though the agency was permanently weakened by the drastic budget and personnel cuts of the early 1980s that made it increasingly difficult to cope with new legislative mandates (see chap. 7).

In other respects the 1980s were years of lost opportunity. In areas such as energy policy the initiatives of the Ford and Carter administrations to promote fuel conservation and renewable energy development were largely abandoned, leading to renewed growth in energy consumption and oil imports after 1986. Opposition from the Reagan administration—as well as from certain key Democratic leaders in Congress, such as Sen. Robert Byrd of West Virginia and Rep. John Dingell of Michigan—blocked revision of the Clean Air Act to deal with acid rain, urban smog, and toxic pollutants throughout the decade. A new range of international environmental issues received only limited attention through 1988. The one exception was the leadership exerted by the United States in negotiating the Montréal protocol (1987) to limit production of chlorofluorocarbons (CFCs) and other ozone-depleting gases (see chap. 13). On other international issues the administration reversed or weakened previous policy commitments; for example, it opposed the Law of the Sea Treaty and cut off funding for U.N. programs to promote family planning and population control.

Reagan clearly lost the battle of public opinion on the environment. His policies had the unintended effect of revitalizing environmental organizations. Membership in such groups increased by leaps and bounds, and polls indicated a steady growth in public concern for the environment that peaked in the late 1980s (see chap. 3). It is not surprising that George Bush decided to distance himself from Reagan's environmental record in the 1988 election.

The Bush Transition

George Bush's presidency returned to a more moderate tradition of Republican leadership, particularly in the first two years. While promising to "stay the course" on Reagan's economic policies, he also pledged a "kinder and gentler" America. Although his domestic policy agenda was the most limited of any recent president, it included action on the environment. Indeed, during the campaign Bush declared himself a "conservationist" in the tradition of Teddy Roosevelt and promised to be an "environmental president." Like President Richard M. Nixon twenty years earlier, he rode a wave of environmental concern during the first half of his term that culminated in passage of a new Clean Air Act. But, also like Nixon, he retreated to a harsher stance on the environment later in his term in the face of economic recession and business pressures; indeed, by 1992 he sounded much more like Ronald Reagan.

In a remarkable speech at Detroit Metropark, near Lake Erie, on August 31, 1988, Bush laid out an ambitious environmental agenda calling for a new Clean Air Act and other reforms. Among other things, Bush committed himself to a program of "no net loss" of wetlands and called for strict enforcement of toxic waste laws. In reference to global warming, Mr. Bush stated: "Those who think we are powerless to do anything about the 'greenhouse effect' are forgetting about the 'White House effect'." "In my first year in office," he said, "I will convene a global conference on the environment at the White House. . . . And we will act."[16]

If Bush surprised almost everyone by seizing the initiative on what most assumed was a strong issue for the Democrats, he impressed environmentalists even more by actively soliciting their advice and by appointing a number of environmental leaders to his administration.[17] William Reilly, the highly respected president of the World Wildlife Fund and the Conservation Foundation, became EPA administrator; and Michael Deland, formerly New England director of the EPA, became chairman of the Council on Environmental Quality. Bush promised to restore CEQ to an influential role, and made it clear that he intended to work closely with the Democratic Congress to pass a new Clean Air Act early in his administration.

Yet Bush's nominees to head the public land and natural resource agencies were not much different from those of the Reagan administration. In particular, his choice of Manuel Lujan Jr., a ten-term retired congressman

(R-N.M.), to serve as secretary of the interior indicated that no major departures would be made in western land policies. The president's top White House advisers were also much more conservative on environmental matters than Reilly and Deland.

President Bush saw himself more as a consolidator and guardian of Republican gains than as a policy innovator; indeed, the precautionary principle of "do no harm" appeared to guide his approach to leadership.[18] He did not attempt to restore the "administrative presidency." Lacking any clear agenda, he saw less need to exert tight control over the bureaucracy. He also had more respect for professional expertise than Reagan and preferred a more pragmatic, collegial style of decisionmaking. Although Bush appointed a strong chief of staff, John Sununu, he preferred to have several top aides work out policy compromises as a "team." On environmental matters, this gave enormous influence to several key White House officials: Sununu, OMB director Richard Darman, science adviser D. Allan Bromley, and chairman of the Council of Economic Advisers Michael Boskin. This quadrumvirate—all former university professors—was to exert an increasingly conservative influence on policy.

President Bush pursued a bipartisan legislative strategy in building a coalition to amend the Clean Air Act. Indeed, he had few other options, as the Democrats had large majorities in both houses of Congress; his party held only 175 seats in the House, the fewest of any twentieth-century president starting his term. At the same time, traditional Republican constituencies in business and industry were certain to oppose major environmental initiatives. Like President Nixon in 1970, he would have to take the lead to overcome this resistance and seek a bipartisan majority for new legislation.

Bush accomplished this in passage of the Clean Air Act of 1990, arguably the single most important legislative achievement of his presidency. His draft bill, sent to Congress on July 21, 1989, had three major goals: to control acid rain by reducing sulfur dioxide (SO_2) emissions from coal-burning power plants by nearly half by the year 2000; to reduce air pollution in some eighty urban areas that still had not met 1977 air quality standards; and to lower emissions of some two hundred airborne toxic chemicals by 75 to 90 percent by 2000. To achieve the acid precipitation goals—to which the White House devoted most of its attention—Bush proposed an innovative approach advocated by environmental economists that relies on marketable pollution allowances rather than "command and control" regulation to achieve emission reductions more efficiently (see chap. 9).

Bush's staff negotiated with Senate Majority Leader George Mitchell (D-Maine) and others behind closed doors for ten weeks in early 1990 to reach a bipartisan Senate compromise on the basic outlines of the bill. Many of the technical details were subsequently filled in by the House Energy and Commerce Committee and by a joint conference committee. But without White House leadership, it is unlikely that the ten-year stalemate on clean air legislation would have been broken. As Richard Cohen concluded, "Ultimately the Clean Air Act showed that presidents matter. Once Bush was elected and decided to keep his vague clean-air campaign promises, the many constraints of divided government disappeared."[19]

The president drew a line against any further commitments in another highly contentious area: what to do about global climate change, especially pressures for the United States to agree to an international convention to stabilize CO_2 emissions. Although Bush had promised to confront "the greenhouse effect" with "the White House effect," it soon became apparent that strong forces within the administration (as well as from energy industries) opposed any policy that would limit fossil fuel production and consumption.

Climate change policy was formally put under control of the Domestic Policy Council committee, chaired by science adviser Allan Bromley. Sununu, Darman, and Boskin were highly skeptical of climate change theories and were primarily concerned with the economic costs of limiting fossil fuel consumption, an area in which little information was available.[20] Other advice, including that from William Reilly, got a hostile reception in the White House.

President Bush, who showed little personal interest in the subject, thus adopted a policy stance on climate change similar to Reagan's policy on acid rain: more research was needed. In the meantime, the administration would follow a "no regrets" approach—actions would be taken against the possibility of global warming only if they could be fully justified on other grounds. For example, production of CFCs, which were considered a potent greenhouse gas as well as an ozone-depleting chemical, could be phased out because of their potential impact on the ozone layer. Thus, while the president substantially increased funding for global climate research and development (to a combined total of more than $1 billion annually) and supported accelerated curtailment of CFCs, he continued to resist all pressures to limit CO_2 emissions.

During the last eighteen months of the Bush administration, Vice President Dan Quayle increasingly entered the spotlight as head of the Council on Competitiveness, an obscure White House body that Bush had appointed in 1989. The "Quayle Council"—which included the secretaries of treasury and commerce, White House counsel C. Boyden Gray, and Sununu, Darman, and Boskin—assumed a role similar to that of Bush's own Task Force on Regulatory Relief in the early Reagan administration (its powers were later justified on the same legal basis, namely Reagan's Executive Order 12291 of 1981). Its function was to invite and respond to industry complaints of excessive regulation, to analyze the costs and benefits of regulation, and to hold up or rewrite any new regulations that were considered unnecessarily burdensome. It operated in secrecy, frequently pressuring the EPA and other agencies to ease regulations. During 1991 the council began to intervene actively in regulatory processes to rewrite environmental rules and regulations.[21]

Among the council's most controversial actions were revisions of the manual for defining wetlands, which would have removed as many as half of the lands designated as wetlands from federal protection; changes in regulations for recycling, mixed-waste incineration, and hazardous waste disposal; weakening of regulations for implementing the new Clean Air Act; and opposition to the global biodiversity treaty. These and other actions led to protests from Congress reminiscent of those during the Reagan presidency that the council was acting illegally by violating both statutory intent and rules for open administrative procedures that had been worked out in the 1980s. There is also evidence that regulatory relief was increasingly tied to campaign contributions as the 1992 elections approached.[22]

Bush carried his regulatory relief policy a step further by declaring a three-month moratorium on new regulations in his 1992 State of the Union address. (He later extended the moratorium through the election.) In fact, the volume of regulation increased at a substantially faster rate during the first three years of the Bush administration than in the Reagan years.[23] No doubt this contributed to Bush's sensitivity on the issue as the election approached. And although the White House held up some of the Quayle Council's proposed orders during the campaign because they were considered too controversial, Bush and Quayle continued to push for reduced regulation.[24]

But it was probably Bush's stance toward the U.N. Conference on Environment and Development in June 1992 that most defined his environmental image. The president threatened to boycott the historic summit until he had ensured that the climate change convention to be signed would contain no binding targets for CO_2 reduction. He further alienated much of world opinion as well as the American environmental community by refusing to sign the biodiversity treaty at the conference, despite efforts by his delegation chief, William Reilly, to seek a last-minute compromise. To add insult to injury, Reilly's cable to the White House was leaked to the press, apparently by a Quayle Council staff member.[25] Thus, despite Bush's other accomplishments in foreign policy, the United States was isolated and embarrassed in international environmental diplomacy (see chap. 13).

In summary, what began as a productive environmental administration deteriorated into defensive disarray in its final year. Many environmentalists who had supported Bush were dismayed by the tenor of his reelection campaign, which became increasingly negative, angry, and harsh. In retrospect, Bush's retreat was an indication of more profound changes to come in American politics.

The Clinton Presidency: Embattled Environmentalism

Environmental issues were clearly overshadowed by the economy and other controversies during the 1992 election. According to one exit poll, only 6 percent of voters considered the environment one of the most important issues, ranking it ninth in importance. However, "green" voters reported that they voted for Clinton over Bush by more than a five to one margin (table 5-1). Clinton and Gore also received endorsements from the

Table 5-1 Issues Voters Care About, 1992

| Issue | All Voters | Voter Preference | | |
		Clinton	Bush	Perot
Economy, jobs	43%	52%	24%	24%
Deficit	21	36	26	38
Health care	19	67	19	14
Family values	15	23	65	11
Taxes	14	26	57	17
Abortion	13	37	55	8
Education	13	60	25	15
Foreign policy	8	9	86	5
Environment	6	73	14	13

Source: Newsweek, special election issue, November-December 1992, 10. Data are from an election day poll of 15,241 voters conducted by Voter Research and Surveys, an association of ABC News, CNN, CBS News, and NBC News. The margin of error is ±1.1 percentage points. Voters were allowed to select more than one issue.

Sierra Club, the League of Conservation Voters, and other environmental organizations.

It is not surprising that the Clinton ticket won most of the support of environmentalists. Vice presidential candidate Al Gore had been regarded as the Senate's leading environmentalist and had published his best-selling book *Earth in the Balance* in early 1992. Gore's environmental credentials were evidently an important factor in his vice presidential nomination because Clinton's environmental record as governor of Arkansas was mediocre at best.[26] Under attack from both the White House and Democratic rival Jerry Brown, Clinton acknowledged his shortcomings in an Earth Day speech in April 1992 but promised strong environmental action as president. The Democratic platform also took a strong environmental stance.[27]

Clinton's campaign promises included pledges to raise the corporate average fuel economy (CAFE) standard for automobiles; to encourage mass transit programs; to increase the use of natural gas and oppose increased reliance on nuclear power; to support renewable energy research and development; to create a new solid waste reduction program and provide other incentives for recycling; to pass a new Clean Water Act with standards for nonpoint sources; to reform the Superfund program; to tighten enforcement of toxic waste laws; to protect ancient forests; to make "no net loss" of wetlands a reality; to preserve the Arctic National Wildlife Refuge as a wilderness area; to emphasize pollution prevention and use of market forces to reward conservation and penalize polluters; to limit U.S. CO_2 emissions to 1990 levels by the year 2000; to negotiate more debt-for-nature swaps to preserve precious lands such as tropical rain forests; and to restore funding to U.N. population programs.[28]

Beyond this impressive list of commitments, Clinton and Gore departed from traditional rhetoric about the relationship between environmental protection and economic growth. They argued that the jobs-versus-environment debate presented a "false choice" because environmental cleanup creates jobs and the future competitiveness of the U.S. economy will depend on developing environmentally clean, energy-efficient technologies. They proposed a variety of investment incentives and infrastructure projects to promote such "green" technologies. Like FDR sixty years earlier, Clinton promised to put people back to work on projects that improve the environment. All of these promises created high expectations among environmentalists.

Clinton entered office with a large reform agenda and a clear desire to be an activist president. He faced several major hurdles from the beginning, however. He had received only 43 percent of the vote, a weak policy mandate at best. His coattails had also been short, resulting in a ten-seat loss in the House of Representatives and no gain in the Senate. Many members of Congress ran well ahead of Clinton in the election, making them wary of dependence on his leadership. Clinton's agenda was also filled with other major policy commitments such as health care reform that would crowd out environmental initiatives at the beginning of his term. Finally, Clinton would be faced with two other constraints that surfaced in Ross Perot's quixotic independent campaign for the presidency in 1992 that would increasingly come to characterize politics for the decade: calls for deep spending cuts to balance the budget, and a mood of public skepticism and negativism about government and politics generally. By 1994 this mood had exploded into a burst of anger at the federal government. As journalist Elizabeth Drew put it, Clinton would be "an activist President in a cynical age."[29]

The Green Administration

President Clinton's early actions indicated that he intended to deliver on his environmental agenda. His appointments to key environmental positions were largely applauded by the environmental community, though there was some grumbling that more members of its ranks were not placed in higher positions.[30] Perhaps most important to them was the fact that Vice President Gore was given the lead responsibility for formulating and coordinating environmental policy. His influence was quickly seen in reorganization of the White House and in Clinton's budget proposals, which contained elements of the new thinking on sustainable development that he and Gore had espoused during the campaign.

One of the administration's first acts was to abolish the Quayle Council on Competitiveness. Plans were subsequently announced to replace the Council on Environmental Quality (CEQ) with a new Office of Environmental Policy (OEP). The new office was to coordinate departmental policies on environmental issues and to ensure integration of environmental considerations into the work of other policy bodies such as the Domestic Policy Council, the National Security Council, and the new National Economic Council. The new OEP director, Kathleen McGinty, and EPA administrator Carol Browner were both former Senate environmental aides of Mr. Gore. Browner was given cabinet status pending enactment of legislation to formally transform the EPA into a cabinet department, and McGinty became a significant presence in the White House.[31]

Other appointments to the cabinet and executive office staffs were largely pro-environment, though they tended to be competent pragmatists rather than radicals.[32] The most notable environmental leader was Bruce Babbitt, the former Arizona governor and president of the League of Conservation Voters, who was appointed secretary of the interior. In contrast to his predecessors in the Reagan and Bush administrations, Babbitt came to office with a strong reform agenda for western public land management.[33] Several environmental activists from such organizations as the Wilderness Society and Audubon Society were also appointed to influential policy positions in his department. On the other hand, environmentalists were disappointed that retiring senator Tim Wirth (D-Colo.) was passed over for secretary of energy in favor of Hazel R. O'Leary, a little-known utility executive from Minnesota. Wirth was, however, appointed undersecretary of state for global affairs, a new position.

Clinton's managerial style, like that of Franklin Roosevelt, favored free-wheeling competition of ideas from many advisers to allow him to deliberate on policy options before making final decisions. This "multiple advocacy" model differs sharply from the more hierarchical organization of the White House under strong chiefs of staff in the Reagan and Bush administrations.[34] Clinton appointed his boyhood friend and fellow Arkansan, Thomas F. "Mack" McLarty III, as his first chief of staff. McLarty, who had no experience in Washington politics, promised to be an "honest broker" rather than an "aggressive gatekeeper" in the White House.[35]

The Frustrated Presidency

Although Clinton entered office with an expansive agenda and great talent and enthusiasm for policymaking, his administration quickly got bogged down in peripheral controversies that undermined confidence in his presidency. Disputes over gays in the military, the Lani Guinier nomination as assistant attorney general, nonpayment of social security taxes for domestic help by attorney general nominees, mishandling of the White House travel office, and the suicide of White House counsel Vincent Foster all derailed the administration during its first six months. Despite considerable success in enacting an economic program and other legislation during his first year in office, congressional blockage of health care reform and "gridlock" on most other initiatives during 1994 proved disastrous for the president. The Republican sweep in the congressional elections appeared to be a repudiation of the Clinton administration as much as of Congress. Overall, Clinton's first two years turned out to be enormously frustrating.[36]

How much of this frustration was preventable will be debated for many years. To some extent the perceived failures of the Clinton presidency were due to larger political forces beyond the president's control—for example, people's rising distemper with political life generally and the trend toward sharp ideological polarization of the two major parties. Clinton's options for working with Congress were clearly limited by this polarization and by the strategy and tactics of the Republican opposition. [37] At the same time, presidential scholars argue that Clinton brought many of his administration's problems on himself.

One line of argument is that Clinton was unable or unwilling to define or communicate his own core beliefs and priorities. Much of the debate about Clinton's "waffling" on issues focused on a combination of uncertain values (is he a "New Democrat" or a "liberal"?) and personality traits that often led to an appearance of indecision and inconsistency. Seeking to please everyone, he has often been "defined by his compromises, not his principles." [38] Another line of criticism focuses on Clinton's sloppy organizational and management skills, leading to poor staff work, bad timing, and other tactical blunders. Chaos in White House lines of authority and responsibility led to several reorganizations and to McLarty's replacement as chief of staff by Leon Panetta in July 1994. [39]

These broader problems are beyond the scope of this chapter, but they bear on some of the Clinton administration's frustrations in pursuing its environmental agenda.

Two events early in the term gave the administration an appearance of environmental policy failure. Interior secretary Babbitt promptly launched a campaign to "revolutionize" western land use policies, including a proposal in Clinton's first budget to raise grazing fees on public lands closer to private market levels (something natural resource economists had advocated for many years). The predictable result was a furious outcry from cattle ranchers and their members of Congress. After meeting with several western Democratic senators, Clinton quickly backed down and removed the grazing fee proposal from the bill. The secretary was left to fight a humiliating losing battle on the issue without presidential support. [40] Much the same thing happened on the "Btu tax." This was a proposal to levy a broad-based tax on the energy content of fuels as a means of promoting energy conservation and raising revenue. Originally included in the president's budget package at the request of Vice President Gore, it was eventually dropped in favor of a much smaller gasoline tax (4.3 cents per gallon) in the face of fierce opposition from members of both parties in Congress. [41]

Clinton's failure to gain support even from his own party on these early initiatives undermined the confidence of environmentalists in the president. The same was true of Clinton's actions on key global issues. Although he signed the biodiversity treaty rejected by President Bush and announced his intentions to achieve the target proposed at the Río summit for stabilizing carbon dioxide emissions by the year 2000, the administration failed to implement either policy. The biodiversity treaty was not brought up for ratification by the Senate in the 103d Congress, and the administration's climate change action plan announced in October 1993 called only for weak voluntary measures, which were soon admitted to be inadequate. Clinton thus failed to restore U.S. leadership in environmental diplomacy, though congressional intransigence was also to blame for defeat of the energy tax and for opposition to new international financial commitments. [42]

The administration's overall legislative record during the 103d Congress (1993-1994) was mixed. Although the president succeeded in getting nearly two-thirds of his major bills passed, some of the most important legislation was blocked by an increasingly hostile opposition—most notably his health care reform. What of environmental legislation? The Clinton record here is much weaker, partly because other priorities kept environmental bills on the back burner for most of the session. Although the administration worked with Congress on proposals to reform the major environmental statutes up for reauthorization—the Clean Water Act, Safe Drinking Water Act, Endangered Species Act, and Superfund—none was enacted. On only one of these policies—revision of the Superfund Act—did the administration come close to brokering a compromise among the contending interests, but this effort was scuttled by the Republicans, who did not want to hand Clinton a victory shortly before the 1994 elections.[43] As a result, the only major piece of environmental legislation that passed the 103d Congress was the California Desert Protection Act, which did squeak through in the waning days of the session, but this was due far more to skillful leadership in the Senate than in the White House.

Clinton took a much more divisive stance on legislation to enact the North American Free Trade Agreement (NAFTA) and new General Agreement on Tariffs and Trade (GATT). During the election campaign he had promised not to support NAFTA unless protections for labor and the environment were added. Environmental groups were deeply divided over the treaty, with most of the larger Washington-based organizations supporting the negotiation of a side agreement on environmental protection, and other groups, such as the Sierra Club and most grassroots organizations, adamantly opposing the treaty (see chaps. 3 and 16). Clinton alienated many environmentalists as well as a majority of congressional Democrats by allying with Republicans to pass NAFTA in 1993 and GATT in 1994.

One of the administration's conspicuous failures was its inability to enact a bill elevating the EPA to cabinet rank. In this case the White House submitted legislation to establish a new Department of Environmental Protection and worked with the relevant committees to move it along. The Senate passed an amended version of the legislation in May 1993, but it stalled in the House as additional amendments were added.[44] The White House eventually concluded that it was better to abandon the bill than to accept a version that would have crippled the EPA's regulatory authority. (Many of the amendments would reappear in more extreme form in the regulatory reform proposals of the new GOP majority in 1995.)

Despite this setback, the administration must be given credit for raising environmental considerations to a higher level of attention in the White House. The Office of Environmental Policy was in contact with the vice president's office, cabinet secretaries, and the other White House staffs on a daily basis. Its director, Kathleen McGinty, played a critical role in chairing policy groups on a wide range of subjects (e.g., on Superfund revision, environmental justice guidelines for agencies, habitat conservation agreements, flood-plain management, and environmental aspects of NAFTA). At the end of 1994, however, it was decided to fold the OEP into the Council for Environmental Quality, which would have been abolished by the EPA cabinet bill but now continued to exist. This arrangement was justified on grounds that the CEQ was being elevated to perform the policy functions of OEP, so there was no longer need for a separate policy office. [45]

The White House also developed a new, more balanced approach to regulatory oversight in the OMB's Office of Information and Regulatory Affairs. Besides abolishing the Quayle Council, Clinton replaced Reagan's executive orders 12291 and 12498 with a new executive order (12866) on regulatory planning and review on September 30, 1993. The order set out the administration's regulatory philosophy as well as new procedures for reviewing individual regulations. In its statement of philosophy, the order declared:

> In deciding whether and how to regulate, agencies should assess all costs and benefits of available regulatory alternatives, including the alternative of not regulating. Costs and benefits shall be understood to include both quantifiable measures (to the fullest extent that these can be usefully estimated) and qualitative measures of costs and benefits that are difficult to quantify, but nevertheless essential to consider. Further, in choosing among alternative regulatory approaches, agencies should select those approaches that maximize net benefits (including potential economic, environmental, public health and safety, and other advantages; distributive impacts; and equity), unless a statute requires another regulatory approach. [46]

This guidance definitely suggests that agencies need to balance a variety of goals and values in justifying regulations, but avoids any narrow economic definition of costs and benefits. Nevertheless, under its director, Sally Katzen, the Clinton OIRA has required the EPA and other agencies to seek greater cost-effectiveness. [47]

President Clinton also issued executive orders requiring consideration of environmental justice (see chap. 11) and mandating pollution prevention and waste reduction throughout the federal government.

In other respects, the Clinton administration's record has also been considerably more innovative and successful than it is given credit for. A more cooperative, conciliatory approach has generally characterized implementation of policies by the Environmental Protection Agency under Carol Browner. Drawing a page from the Reagan and Bush administrations, she has quietly emphasized voluntary agreements with industry to meet or exceed emissions standards through pollution prevention or innovative means of control (see chaps. 7 and 12). More generally, the "reinventing government" initiative chaired by Vice President Gore led to a far-reaching set of "common sense" proposals for reforming the EPA's regulatory procedures to make them more flexible and "user friendly" within the limits of the law. [48]

Despite these and other innovations in environmental policy and administration (see chap. 17), Clinton received little credit from environmentalists during his first two years. The League of Conservation Voters awarded the president only a "C+" for his first year, and Washington-based organizations and grassroots activists alike expressed deep disappointment if not outrage at what they perceived as weak leadership. [49] One reason was simply that the president failed miserably in communicating his environmental policies to the public; indeed, by one count he made only *one* major public speech on the environment (on Earth Day 1993) during his first nineteen months in office (see fig. 5-1). The election of 1994 created an immensely more difficult political environment for him—but also a renewed opportunity for environmental leadership.

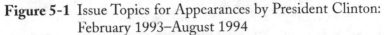

Figure 5-1 Issue Topics for Appearances by President Clinton: February 1993–August 1994

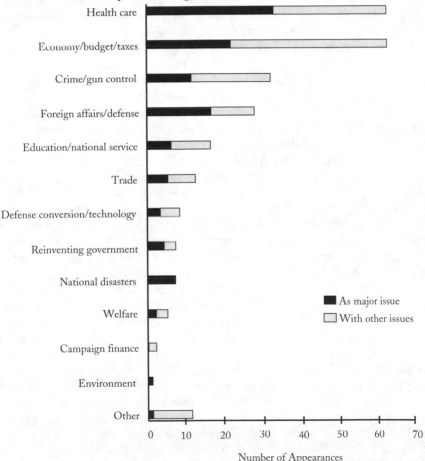

Source: Adapted from Charles O. Jones, "Campaigning to Govern: The Clinton Style," in *The Clinton Presidency: First Appraisals*, ed. Colin Campbell and Bert A. Rockman (Chatham, N.J.: Chatham House, 1995), 32.

The New Congressional Challenge

The 1994 elections gave Republicans control of both houses of Congress and thirty-one governorships. Claiming a mandate for the "Contract with America" that some three hundred GOP candidates for the House of Representatives had pledged to support, the new House Speaker, Newt Gingrich (R-Ga.), vowed "to begin decisively changing the shape of the government." [50]

Although the Contract made no specific reference to the environment, it soon became clear that the Republicans would use its call for smaller government and less regulation to propose deep cuts in virtually all environmental programs; indeed, by early 1995 it was evident that environmental policies and agencies were prime targets of the "revolution." Given Clinton's relative silence and willingness to compromise on environmental matters in his first two years, it is not surprising that antienvironmental forces sensed an opportunity to make dramatic gains. With the help of industry lobbyists, the new congressional leaders unleashed a massive effort to rewrite the environmental legislation of the past quarter-century (see chap. 6).

Clinton could do little to stem the tide during the first "hundred days" of the Republican Congress, and the administration remained virtually silent on environmental issues. [51] At the nadir of his power in April 1995, Clinton was reduced at a press conference to reminding reporters that "the president is relevant here, especially an activist president." [52] However, by the time the House of Representatives passed a drastic revision of the Clean Water Act on May 16, opinion polls suggested that Republican environmental policies might be deeply unpopular with the public (see chap. 3). It was also evident that this and other legislation lacked both sufficient support to pass in the Senate and the two-thirds majority in the House necessary to override a presidential veto. The president and his new pollster, Dick Morris, sensed an opportunity to regain public support by taking a tough stance against the "extremism" of the Republican environmental agenda. [53]

Clinton's newly aggressive stance was signaled on May 30 in a fiery speech in Rock Creek Park in Washington—a place "where Theodore Roosevelt loved to walk"—in which he vowed to veto the "Dirty Water Act" and castigated the Republicans for abandoning long-standing traditions of bipartisan support for the environment. [54] The threat of vetoes was frequently wielded throughout the summer, although Clinton enraged environmentalists by signing an appropriations rescission bill in late July that contained a provision allowing almost unlimited "salvage logging" without regard for environmental restrictions. [55] To mend fences, the president made highly publicized speeches at Baltimore Harbor and in Yellowstone National Park in August. On both occasions he invoked what he called the nation's "common ground," as in this passage from the Yellowstone speech:

> We have a big stake in what you see around here at Yellowstone. It's part of what I call our "common ground," and we should not do anything this

year—anything—to weaken our ability to protect the quality of our land, our water, our food, the diversity of our wildlife, and the sanctity of our national treasures. We can balance the budget without doing any of that. [56]

The president and other members of his administration—especially Interior Secretary Babbitt, who campaigned throughout the country against the Republican proposals—appeared to have been successful by early fall in rallying public opinion against any significant weakening of environmental protection. [57] Indeed, a public backlash contributed to a revolt within House Republican ranks against the "mispositioning" of the party on environmental issues (see chap. 6). [58] After a number of defeats in both houses, the GOP leadership switched to a strategy of burying provisions in riders to appropriation bills and in the budget reconciliation bill. Although most of the riders were stripped from the reconciliation bill before it was vetoed by Clinton, several important provisions (notably one that would open the Arctic National Wildlife Refuge to oil development) were only dropped in the final FY 1996 budget.

Overshadowing these successes, however, was the fact that President Clinton was forced by a temporary shutdown of the federal government in mid November to accept in principle the Republicans' demand for an agreement to balance the budget in seven years. Although he largely won the budget battle of 1996, it will be difficult to maintain discretionary spending for environmental programs in future years.

Conclusion

The record of the last three presidents demonstrates that the White House has had a vital but hardly singular or consistent role in shaping national environmental policies. Most of Ronald Reagan's antienvironmental initiatives were repudiated by Congress, but he indirectly influenced the environmental agenda by intervening in regulatory processes, cutting agency budgets and personnel, delaying new environmental commitments, and challenging the cost and effectiveness of programs established in the 1970s. George Bush attempted to strike a balance between cooperating with Congress (on the Clean Air Act) and holding the line on other new policies, and he restored some of the funding and integrity of regulatory processes lost in the 1980s. However, his administration remained deeply divided internally, and Bush adopted a conservative reelection strategy that dissipated the reform momentum and may have contributed to his defeat. Bill Clinton seemed to adopt a reverse strategy of neglecting environmental commitments during the first half of his term when his party controlled Congress and taking a firm stance only after the opposition gained ascendancy. Despite many positive accomplishments, he has demonstrated that inept management of the presidential office can negate an ambitious reform agenda. Although Clinton has effectively if belatedly utilized the bully pulpit and the veto power to mobilize public support for past environmental goals, he or his successor will have to restore a bipartisan working relationship with Congress to deal with the daunting environmental agenda of the future (see chap. 17).

Notes

1. Remarks by the President in Vetoing the Republican Budget, The Oval Office, December 6, 1995.
2. Margaret Kriz, "The Green Card," *National Journal*, September 16, 1995, 2262-2267; "A Greener White House," *New York Times*, November 26, 1995, E10.
3. See, e.g., Paul R. Cutright, *Theodore Roosevelt: The Making of a Conservationist* (Urbana: University of Illinois Press, 1985); Donald E. Worster, ed., *American Environmentalism: The Formative Period, 1860-1915* (New York: Wiley, 1973); Samuel P. Hays, *Conservation and the Gospel of Efficiency* (Cambridge, Mass.: Harvard University Press, 1959); and Edgar B. Nixon, ed., *Franklin D. Roosevelt and Conservation, 1911-1945*, 2 vols. (Washington, D.C.: GPO, 1957). On the Roosevelts' use of presidential powers, see also Robert A. Shanley, *Presidential Influence and Environmental Policy* (Westport, Conn.: Greenwood, 1992).
4. Charles O. Jones, *The Presidency in a Separated System* (Washington, D.C.: Brookings, 1994), and *Separate but Equal Branches: Congress and the Presidency* (Chatham, N.J.: Chatham House, 1995).
5. Hugh Heclo and Lester M. Salamon, *The Illusion of Presidential Government* (Boulder: Westview, 1981); David K. Nichols, *The Myth of the Modern Presidency* (University Park: Pennsylvania State University Press, 1994).
6. These terms are from Jones, *Presidency in a Separated System*, chap. 5. Jones also adds a "fiscal" agenda orientation to refer to policymaking specifically to deal with the budget deficit. There is a large literature on presidential "leadership styles," including James David Barber's *Presidential Character: Predicting Performance in the White House*, 4th ed. (Englewood Cliffs, N.J.: Prentice-Hall, 1992), which emphasizes psychological traits of presidents; Colin Campbell, *Managing the Presidency: Carter, Reagan, and the Search for Executive Harmony* (Pittsburgh: University of Pittsburgh Press, 1988); and Richard T. Johnson, "Presidential Style," in *Perspectives on the Presidency*, ed. Aaron Wildavsky (Boston: Little, Brown, 1975).
7. See esp. Jones, *Presidency in a Separated System*, chaps. 6-7.
8. A classic work on White House organization is Stephen Hess, *Organizing the Presidency*, 2d ed. (Washington, D.C.: Brookings, 1988). See also John P. Burke, *The Institutional Presidency* (Baltimore: The Johns Hopkins University Press, 1992); and John Hart, *The Presidential Branch: From Washington to Clinton*, 2d ed. (Chatham, N.J.: Chatham House, 1995).
9. See Samuel Kernell, *Going Public: New Strategies for Presidential Leadership* (Washington, D.C.: CQ Press, 1986), and Jeffrey Tulis, *The Rhetorical Presidency* (Princeton, N.J.: Princeton University Press, 1987).
10. See, e.g., Charles O. Jones, *Clean Air* (Pittsburgh: University of Pittsburgh Press, 1975); John C. Whitaker, *Striking a Balance: Environment and Natural Resources Policy in the Nixon-Ford Years* (Washington, D.C.: American Enterprise Institute, 1976); Charles O. Jones, *The Trusteeship Presidency: Jimmy Carter and the United States Congress* (Baton Rouge: Louisiana State University Press, 1988); and Shanley, *Presidential Influence*.
11. On Reagan's background and economic policies, see Lou Cannon, *Reagan* (New York: Putnam's, 1982), esp. chap. 21; and William A. Niskanen, *Reaganomics* (New York: Oxford University Press, 1988). For a more detailed analysis of Reagan's environmental record, see Michael E. Kraft and Norman J. Vig, "Environmental Policy in the Reagan Presidency," *Political Science Quarterly* 99 (Fall 1984): 414-439; and Vig and

Kraft, eds., *Environmental Policy in the 1980s: Reagan's New Agenda* (Washington, D.C.: CQ Press, 1984).

12. Richard P. Nathan, *The Administrative Presidency* (New York: Wiley, 1983). Cf. Robert F. Durant, *The Administrative Presidency Revisited* (Albany: State University of New York Press, 1992), for a somewhat different interpretation.

13. On the impact of the Reagan budget cuts, see esp. Robert V. Bartlett, "The Budgetary Process and Environmental Policy," and J. Clarence Davies, "Environmental Institutions and the Reagan Administration," in *Environmental Policy in the 1980s*, ed. Vig and Kraft.

14. See Barry D. Freedman, *Regulation in the Reagan-Bush Era: The Eruption of Presidential Influence* (Pittsburgh: University of Pittsburgh Press, 1995); Richard A. Harris and Sidney M. Milkis, *The Politics of Regulatory Change: A Tale of Two Agencies* (New York: Oxford University Press, 1989), 100-113, 257-265; and V. Kerry Smith, *Environmental Policy under Reagan's Executive Order: The Role of Cost-Benefit Analysis* (Chapel Hill: University of North Carolina Press, 1984).

15. For a more detailed summary of Watt's policies, see Paul J. Culhane, "Sagebrush Rebels in Office: Jim Watt's Land and Water Policies," in *Environmental Policy in the 1980s*, ed. Vig and Kraft, 293-318; and C. Brant Short, *Ronald Reagan and the Public Lands: America's Conservation Debate* (College Station: Texas A&M University Press, 1989). See also J. Clarence Davies III, "Environmental Institutions and the Reagan Administration," in *Environmental Policy in the 1980s*, ed. Vig and Kraft, 154-157. Burford tells her side of the story in Anne M. Burford (with John Greenya), *Are You Tough Enough?* (New York: McGraw-Hill, 1986).

16. John Holusha, "Bush Pledges Aid for Environment," *New York Times,* September 1, 1988; Bill Peterson, "Bush Vows to Fight Pollution, Install 'Conservation Ethic'," *Washington Post,* September 1, 1988.

17. Philip Shabecoff, "Bush Lends an Ear to Environmentalists," *New York Times,* December 1, 1988, 13.

18. On Bush's decisionmaking style, see Michael Duffy and Dan Goodgame, *Marching in Place* (New York: Simon and Schuster, 1992); Colin Campbell and Bert Rockman, eds., *The Bush Presidency: First Appraisals* (Chatham, N.J.: Chatham House, 1991); and Burt Solomon, "In Bush's Image," *National Journal,* July 7, 1990, 1642-1647.

19. Richard Cohen, *Washington at Work: Back Rooms and Clean Air* (New York: Macmillan, 1992), 175. See also Gary C. Bryner, *Blue Skies, Green Politics: The Clean Air Act of 1990* (Washington, D.C.: CQ Press, 1993).

20. D. Allan Bromley, *The President's Scientists: Reminiscences of a White House Science Adviser* (New Haven, Conn.: Yale University Press, 1994), 149-155. On the role of Sununu and other advisers in the White House, see also Fred Barnes, "Raging Bulls," *New Republic,* March 19, 1990, 11-12; Dan Goodgame, "Big Bad John Sununu," *Time,* May 21, 1990, 21-25; and Leslie H. Gelb, "Sununu v. Scientists," *New York Times,* February 19, 1991, 17.

21. The most detailed analysis of the Quayle Council is Charles Tiefer, *The Semi-Sovereign Presidency* (Boulder: Westview, 1994), chap. 4. See also Kirk Victor, "Quayle's Quiet Coup," *National Journal,* July 6, 1991, 1676-1680; Christine Triano and Nancy Watzman, "Quayle's Hush-Hush Council," *New York Times,* November 20, 1991; Michael Duffy, "Need Friends in High Places?, *Time,* November 4, 1991, 25; Philip J. Hilts, "Quayle Council Debate: Issue of Control," *New York Times,* December 17, 1991; and Bob Woodward and David Broder, "Quayle's Quest: Curb Rules, Leave 'No Fingerprints'," *Washington Post,* January 9, 1992.

22. Tiefer, *Semi-Sovereign Presidency,* 87.

23. John H. Cushman Jr., "Big Growth in Federal Regulation Despite Role of Quayle's Council," *New York Times,* December 24, 1991; Robert D. Hershey Jr., "Regulations March On, Despite a Moratorium," *New York Times,* September 21, 1992.

24. Robert D. Hershey Jr., "White House Sees a Mission to Cut Business Regulation," *New York Times,* March 23, 1992; David E. Rosenbaum, "Bush Is Extending Regula-

tion Freeze with a Fanfare," *New York Times,* April 29, 19; Schneider, "Environment Laws Are Eased by Bush as Election Nears," *New York Times,* May 20, 1992; and Michael Wines, "Bush, in Far West, Sides with Loggers," *New York Times,* September 15, 1992, A25. For a critical analysis of this electoral strategy, see Gregg Easterbrook, "Black Thumbs," *New Republic,* November 6, 1992, 26-27.

25. Keith Schneider, "White House Snubs U.S. Envoy's Plea to Sign Río Treaty," *New York Times,* June 5, 1992; Schneider, "Bush Aide Assails U.S. Preparations for Earth Summit." The press reported that the memo was leaked by the staff of the Quayle Council; Tiefer, *Semi-Sovereign Presidency,* 85.

26. Keith Schneider, "Clinton Relies on Voluntary Guidelines to Protect Environment in Arkansas," *New York Times,* April 4, 1992; Schneider, "Pollution in Arkansas Area May Be Key Campaign Issue," *New York Times,* April 21, 1992; and Michael Weisskopf and David Maraniss, "When Irresistible Force Met Arkansas' Timber Industry," *Washington Post National Weekly Edition,* June 29-July 5, 1992.

27. Gwen Ifill, "Clinton Links Ecology Plans with Jobs," *New York Times,* April 23, 1992. The Democratic and Republican platforms are reprinted in *Congressional Quarterly Weekly Report,* July 18 and August 22, 1992. Ross Perot's position can be found in *United We Stand: How We Can Take Back Our Country* (New York: Hyperion, 1992).

28. From Gov. Bill Clinton and Sen. Al Gore, *Putting People First* (New York: Times Books, 1992), 89-99.

29. Elizabeth Drew, *On the Edge: The Clinton Presidency* (New York: Simon and Schuster, 1994), 420.

30. Margaret Kriz, "Their Turn," *National Journal,* February 13, 1993, 388-391.

31. Ann Devroy, "Clinton Announces Plan to Replace Environmental Council," *Washington Post,* February 9, 1993; Keith Schneider, "The Nominee for E.P.A. Sees Industry's Side Too," *New York Times,* December 17, 1992.

32. Burt Solomon, "Clinton's Gang," *National Journal,* January 16, 1993.

33. Timothy Egan, "Sweeping Reversal of U.S. Land Policy Sought by Clinton," *New York Times,* February 24, 1993; and Margaret Kriz, "Quick Draw," *National Journal,* November 13, 1993, 2711-2716.

34. Bert A. Rockman, "The Leadership Style of George Bush," in *The Bush Presidency: First Appraisals,* ed. Bert Rockman and Colin Campbell (Chatham, N.J.: Chatham House, 1991); Campbell and Rockman, eds., *The Clinton Presidency: First Appraisals* (Chatham, N.J.: Chatham House, 1995); and Fred I. Greenstein, "The Presidential Leadership Style of Bill Clinton: An Early Appraisal," *Political Science Quarterly* 108 (Winter 1993-1994): 589-601.

35. Peter Kerr and Thomas C. Hayes, "Praise for an Arkansan, and Criticism of a Deal," *New York Times,* December 21, 1992. McClarty was replaced as chief of staff on July 17, 1994, by OMB director Leon Panetta. Panetta's deputy, Alice Rivlin, became OMB director and was then appointed to the Federal Reserve.

36. The best early analysis of the Clinton administration is Campbell and Rockman, eds., *Clinton Presidency.* See also Stanley A. Renshon, ed., *The Clinton Presidency: Campaigning, Governing, and the Psychology of Leadership* (Boulder: Westview, 1995); Bob Woodward, *The Agenda: Inside the Clinton White House* (New York: Simon and Schuster, 1994); and Drew, *On the Edge.*

37. Barbara Sinclair, "Trying to Govern Positively in a Negative Era: Clinton and the 103d Congress," in *Clinton Presidency,* ed. Campbell and Rockman, 88-125; and Richard E. Cohen, *Changing Course in Washington: Clinton and the New Congress* (New York: Macmillan, 1994).

38. Quoted in Colin Campbell, "Management in a Sandbox: Why the Clinton White House Failed to Cope with Gridlock," in *Clinton Presidency,* ed. Campbell and Rockman, 65. See also Paul J. Quirk and Joseph Hinchliffe, "Domestic Policy: The Trials of a Centrist Democrat," ibid., 262-289.

39. Drew, *On the Edge,* esp. 240-241, 348-349, 422-424. See also Campbell, "Management in a Sandbox"; Bert Rockman, "Leadership Style and the Clinton Presidency,"

in *Clinton Presidency*, ed. Campbell and Rockman, 352-354; and Greenstein, "Presidential Leadership Style of Bill Clinton."

40. Drew, *On the Edge*, 110; Margaret Kriz, "Turf Wars," *National Journal*, May 22, 1993, 1232-1235; Richard L. Berke, "Clinton Backs Off from Policy Shift on Federal Lands," *New York Times*, March 31, 1993; Keith Schneider, "Clinton the Conservationist Thinks Twice," *New York Times*, April 4, 1993; and James Conaway, "Babbitt in the Woods: the Clinton Environmental Revolution That Wasn't," *Harpers*, December 1993, 52-60.

41. Drew, *On the Edge*, 71-72, 166-173; Cohen, *Changing Course*; and Sinclair, "Trying to Govern Positively in a Negative Era," 105-107. Gore pushed hard for the tax, which passed the House, but was outmaneuvered by Treasury Secretary Lloyd Bentsen and members of the Senate Finance Committee; see Woodward, *Agenda*, 89-92, 218-222.

42. Richard L. Berke, "Clinton Supports Two Major Steps for Environment," *New York Times*, April 22, 1993; and William K. Stevens, "With Energy Tug of War, U.S. Is Missing Its Goals," *New York Times*, November 28, 1995. See also Robert Paarlberg, "Earth in Abeyance: Explaining Weak Leadership in U.S. International Environmental Policy" (Paper presented at the annual meeting of the American Political Science Association, Chicago, September 1995).

43. On the Superfund compromise, see Margaret Kriz, "How the Twain Met," *National Journal*, June 4, 1994, 1291-1295.

44. Laura Michaelis, "Bill Elevating EPA to Cabinet Worries Environmentalists," *Congressional Quarterly Weekly Report*, March 27, 1993, 746; Catalina Camia, "Senate OKs Elevation of EPA; Hurdles Await in the House," ibid., May 8, 1993, 1140-1142.

45. Interview with Kathleen McGinty, Washington, D.C., June 10, 1995.

46. Executive Order 12866—Regulatory Planning and Review, *Federal Register*, vol. 58, no. 190, October 4, 1993.

47. Office of Information and Regulatory Affairs, "The First Year of Executive Order No. 12866" (n.d.); and Sally Katzen, interview with the author, Washington, D.C., July 28, 1995.

48. President Bill Clinton and Vice President Al Gore, "Reinventing Environmental Regulation," White House, March 16, 1995, reprinted in Al Gore, *Common-Sense Government Works Better and Costs Less* (New York: Random House, 1995), app. D.

49. See, e.g., Tom Wicker, "Waiting for an Environmental President," *Audubon* (September-October 1994): 49ff.; "How Green Is the White House?," *E Magazine*, March 1994, 36; and *National Journal*, February 13, 1993, 404.

50. "Taking Speaker's Mantle, Gingrich Vows 'Profound Transformation'," *Congressional Quarterly Weekly Report*, December 10, 1994, 3522.

51. Keith Schneider, "As Earth Day Turns 25, Life Gets Complicated," *New York Times*, April 16, 1995, E6.

52. Quoted in *Newsweek*, December 25, 1995, 50.

53. For a summary of the Republican agenda and responses to it, see "GOP Sets the 104th Congress on New Regulatory Course," *Congressional Quarterly Weekly Report*, June 17, 1995, 1693-1701; "The GOP's War on Nature," *New York Times*, May 31, 1995, A14; and Kriz, "Green Card."

54. Ann Devroy, "Veto Vowed for Clean Water Rewrite," *Washington Post*, May 31, 1995; "Clinton Vows to Veto Clean Water Rewrite," Minneapolis *Star Tribune*, May 31, 1995. Vice President Gore had planned to give the speech, but on the advice of Morris, the president "took the speech for himself." *Greenwire*, June 5, 1995.

55. Clinton vetoed an earlier version of the rescission bill on June 7 and gained restoration of some environmental funding, but the revised legislation signed on July 27, 1995, rescinded $16.4 billion of previously approved spending, including $1.3 billion from the EPA's budget. A congressional rider to the bill, which environmentalists fiercely opposed, was later ruled by a federal judge to allow logging of large areas of old-growth forests in Oregon and Washington while suspending most environmental regulations through 1996. Clinton later claimed, to the incredulity of observers, that

he did not fully understand this section of the bill when he signed it, despite the warnings of environmentalists. See Timothy Egan, "Recriminations as Northwest Loggers Return," *New York Times,* December 5, 1995.

56. Todd S. Purdum, "Clinton and Old Faithful Let Off Steam," *New York Times*, August 26, 1995.

57. "It's Not Just Owls Anymore," *Newsweek,* September 4, 1995, 23. Babbitt made more than one hundred speeches attacking the Republican agenda; see, e.g., "Springtime for Polluters," *Washington Post,* October 22, 1995, C2.

58. John E. Cushman Jr., "Moderates Soften G.O.P. Agenda on Environment," *New York Times,* October 24, 1995; Allan Freedman, "Republicans Concede Missteps in Effort to Rewrite Rules," *Congressional Quarterly Weekly Report,* December 2, 1995, 3645-3647; Freedman, "Republicans Strive to Gain Environmental Advantage," *Congressional Quarterly Weekly Report,* May 18, 1996, 1384-1386.

6

Environmental Policy in Congress:
Revolution, Reform, or Gridlock?

Michael E. Kraft

The American people sent us a message in November, loud and clear: Tame this regulatory beast! . . . Our constituents want us to break the Feds' stranglehold on our economy and to get them out of decisions that are best left to the individual.

—Thomas J. Bliley (R-Va.)
Chair, House Commerce Committee, 1995

What this [regulatory reform bill] does is undermine every single environmental and public health standard in the country.

—Carol Browner
EPA administrator, 1995

The 1994 elections marked a turning point in congressional action on the environment. For nearly three decades the U.S. Congress, our most representative national political institution, enacted—and over time strengthened—a remarkable array of environmental policies (see app. 1). In doing so, members of Congress within both political parties recognized and responded to rising public concern about environmental degradation. For the same reasons they stoutly defended those policies during the 1980s when they were assailed by Ronald Reagan's White House.[1] The 104th Congress elected in November 1994 brought a strikingly different posture on the environment to Capitol Hill as the new Republican majority promised to mount a revolution against the very same policies. The contrast is evident in two statements above by Rep. Thomas Bliley (R-Va.) and Environmental Protection Agency (EPA) administrator Carol Browner over the much-disputed legislative proposals to reform federal regulation.

With the conservative, antigovernment "Contract with America" as the cornerstone of their legislative agenda, the Republicans in Congress fought intensely to reign in what they viewed as regulatory bureaucracies run amok. Environmental agencies such as the EPA were prime targets of their efforts to reduce the costs and burdens of regulation.[2] The Clinton administration and most congressional Democrats were equally intent on blocking what they characterized as attempts to roll back twenty-five years of progress in protecting public health and the environment. The short-term effect was

119

environmental policy gridlock. Neither radical changes nor moderate reforms could be approved. Thus, existing policies—with their many acknowledged flaws—continued in force. The longer-term impacts are less clear and will depend on how a multiplicity of policy and budgetary conflicts are eventually resolved over the next several years. The stakes are high, and the fierce battles between the forces of revolution and reform in Congress are certain to shape U.S. environmental policy for years to come.

In this chapter I examine some of the most significant policy efforts of the 104th Congress and compare them with the way previous Congresses have dealt with environmental issues. I give special attention to the distinctive roles Congress plays in the policymaking process and to the phenomenon of environmental gridlock. I suggest as well a basis for assessing congressional actions. Responding effectively to environmental problems at home and internationally depends on the extent to which members of Congress are able and willing to accurately assess the problems, carefully evaluate the success of current programs, and design new policies and approaches that promise to reduce serious risks to human and ecological health. Measured against these criteria, the 104th Congress does not fare too well. Other recent Congresses do only marginally better.

Congress and Environmental Policy

Under the U.S. Constitution, Congress shares responsibility with the president for federal policymaking on the environment. Congress is given chief responsibility for enacting public policies and for appropriating the funds necessary to implement them. Presidents generally have greater opportunities to set the political agenda and even to provide leadership on policy formulation and legitimation. Yet, historically, it has been Congress rather than the White House that has led the way on environmental policies, usually with broad bipartisan agreement.[3]

The way in which Congress exercises its formidable powers depends on several key conditions, including whether the president's party also dominates Congress and by what margins. Divided government, which has been common in recent decades, necessitates coalition building and policy compromise if anything is to be accomplished. Yet whether Congress is willing to work cooperatively with the White House depends on its judgments about the president's legitimacy and competency as measured in part by his standing in the polls, his leadership abilities, and his talents as an administrator.[4]

Congressional actions reflect that institution's dualistic nature. It is an assembly of politicians who represent politically disparate districts and states as well as a national lawmaking body. Local electoral pressures, including the need to raise large sums of money for reelection campaigns, induce members to respond to interests and concerns often quite distinct from those affecting presidential actions. They also contribute to a short-term and narrow view of environmental policy issues rather than to the long-term and broad perspective advocated by environmental scientists and policy analysts. As a result, members of Congress are likely to be more concerned with local and regional economic impacts of environmental and resource policies than with their ultimate benefits to the nation as a whole.

A major effect of these institutional characteristics is that action on environmental policies is rarely easy. Sometimes it is impossible. The public may thus see a Congress that appears to do little about environmental problems, a perception that reinforces its already critical view of that institution. Press coverage of Congress also tends to be negative, and the media do a poor job of building public understanding of complex legislative processes. The result is a public belief that Congress is, as two political scientists put it, "slothful, slow, conflict-ridden, immobilized, and inactive."[5] In addition, presidents often castigate Congress for failing to act on their proposals, as President George Bush did in railing against "the gridlocked Democratic Congress."

Most of these criticisms miss the mark. The "do-nothing Congress" is in fact a deeply divided Congress. The fundamental political reality is that all too often it can find no way to reconcile diverse and conflicting interests and form a policy consensus. Still, in 1990 Congress approved a far-reaching extension of the Clean Air Act, the nation's most demanding environmental statute.[6] That and similar decisions suggest the need to review briefly the way in which Congress has dealt with environmental issues over the past twenty-five years. Of special interest are the reasons why the outcome is sometimes gridlock and sometimes progress in advancing environmental and natural resource policies. Such a review should also provide a useful context in which to examine and assess the actions of the 104th Congress.

The Causes and Consequences of Environmental Gridlock

Policy gridlock refers to an inability to resolve conflicts in a policymaking body such as Congress, which results in governmental inaction in the face of important public problems. There is no consensus on *what* to do and therefore no movement in any direction. Present policies, or slight revisions of them, continue until agreement on change is reached.

Why Gridlock Occurs

One of the major reasons for environmental policy deadlock in Congress is the constitutionally mandated separation of powers among policymaking institutions—with multiple opportunities to check and balance each other. This structural arrangement is designed to frustrate the whims of temporary majorities and to make change difficult. Closely allied with this dispersal of power is the increase over the past several decades in the political independence of members. The electoral incentives have created a highly individualistic Congress in which representatives and senators vigorously pursue their narrow district, state, or regional interests regardless of the preferences of party leaders.[7]

Although divided authority and these institutional biases contribute significantly to policy gridlock, they are not the only causes. At least five other factors are important as well.

One of these is the complexity and intractability of environmental problems, compounded by scientific uncertainty over their scope, causes, and implications. The more complex the issue and the less the consensus among scientists on causes and solutions, the more likely gridlock is to occur. Where scientific consensus reigns, Congress is less likely to impede policy action.

Another cause of policy stalemate is insufficient public consensus. The more the public agrees on basic policy directions, the easier it is for Congress to act. That should be good news for environmental policy because polls have long indicated widespread public support for environmental protection (see chap. 3). Yet the public's understanding of environmental issues is quite limited, and its views sometimes inconsistent—in part because environmental issues are rarely that salient for most people. Absent a clear public voice, members cannot easily respond to their concern for the environment.

A third explanation is the power of organized interests. Such groups willingly enter the political vacuum created by an inattentive and disengaged public. They also have increased their presence in Washington, D.C., markedly over the past two decades in what observers have termed an "advocacy explosion"—a sharp rise in the number of groups, the scope of their activities, and the intensity of their efforts. Business groups have become especially well represented and generally have greater resources than environmental organizations.[8] Yet the more interest groups disagree (and are well positioned to act on their beliefs), the greater the probability of gridlock.

A fourth explanation for environmental gridlock concerns the perceptions that citizens and policymakers alike have of short-term costs and long-term benefits. Action on problems such as climate change or protection of biological diversity—with highly visible short-term costs and uncertain long-term benefits—is difficult without compelling scientific evidence of the risks to human or ecological health or to economic well-being.

A final reason for gridlock is the absence of effective political leadership. Scholars have argued for years that presidential leadership was one of the most assured ways to overcome the institutional fragmentation of American government and, conversely, that weak presidents would fare poorly even with a Congress of their own party.[9] Similarly, effective leadership within Congress at either the committee level or among party leaders may help to forge the majorities needed for enacting legislation, as evident in the House in 1995 under Speaker Newt Gingrich (R-Ga.) and his principal deputy, Majority Leader Dick Armey (R-Texas).

In summary, it is apparent there is no single reason for environmental stalemate, and no simple solution to it. This kind of policy paralysis reflects the structure of the political system, the nature of environmental problems, public opinion, the power of organized interests, and the difficulties political leaders face in the prevailing political climate in trying to build majority coalitions. The increasingly partisan, polarized, and caustic debates that substitute for deliberation in the contemporary Congress compound the challenges of environmental policymaking. So too do public cynicism toward politics and the lack of a broadly based vision for our collective environmental future. Overcoming gridlock requires dealing with all of these factors.

Gridlock's Effects

Generally the term "gridlock" has a negative connotation in the press and among the American public. It is seen as something to be ended quickly or avoided in the first place. Yet gridlock may be considered a positive political outcome, depending on one's appraisal of the consequences. Environmentalists might argue, for example, that when government cannot act on a pressing problem that creates adverse impacts on human health or the environment, the effects are clearly negative. Under these circumstances they naturally see gridlock as something to be overcome. However, if disagreement and immobility allow the continuation of policies that would otherwise be weakened, environmentalists would welcome the outcome. At least they have the satisfaction of seeing the present policies left intact. In contrast, business interests concerned about the imposing costs and burdens of current environmental policies would likely judge the impacts differently. So too would policy analysts convinced that present policies are inefficient and in need of reform. They would see such stalemate as a lost opportunity to improve the effectiveness of those policies.[10]

Disagreement over the effects of environmental gridlock also reflects two competing expectations for the policy process. One emphasizes prompt and "rational" problem solving—with political conflict over policy goals and means seen as largely irrelevant. The other stresses representation of diverse interests and resolution of conflicts through the political processes of policy legitimation.

From the first perspective, gridlock needlessly, even dangerously, blocks sound policy proposals. Dire consequences are foreseen unless decisive action is taken swiftly. These views can be found in the environmental community as well as among the ideological conservatives well represented in Congress.[11] From the second perspective, widespread consultation with affected interests is seen as crucial to secure their approval and to help ensure successful implementation. Such policy legitimation may take additional time, but it also allows improvement in our knowledge of environmental and health risks, the assembly of credible data on the costs and benefits of action, and a fuller analysis of policy alternatives—all of which might enhance our ability to choose the most appropriate solutions.

These general observations about environmental policymaking and gridlock in Congress can be appreciated only by revisiting specific actions Congress took on environmental policy from the 1970s through the early 1990s. Chapter 1 provided an overview of policy evolution during this period. Here I turn to the patterns of congressional efforts to grapple with environmental challenges prior to the election of the 104th Congress in 1994.

From the "Environmental Decade" to
Deadlock in the 1980s and 1990s

The 1970s offer examples of both successful and unsuccessful environmental policymaking. The record for this "environmental decade" is nevertheless remarkable, particularly in comparison with most of the 1980s. The National Environmental Policy Act, Clean Air Act, Clean Water Act, Endangered Species Act, and Resource Conservation and Recovery Act, among others, were all signed into law in the 1970s. That outcome demonstrates that despite the much-discussed infirmities of the U.S. political system, major environmental policies can be approved in fairly short order under the right conditions. Some of those conditions are reviewed in chapter 1. They included rising public concern over environmental threats, the growth in membership and political clout of environmental groups, and an expansion of the "scope of conflict" that allowed challenges to "subgovernments" (alliances of congressional committees, agencies, and interest groups) that once dominated policy areas such as pesticide use, public lands, nuclear power, and water projects.[12]

Environmental Gridlock Emerges

The pattern of the 1970s did not last. Congress's enthusiasm for environmental policy gradually gave way to apprehension about its impact on the economy, and policy stalemate became the norm in the early 1980s. The shift had more to do with politics and ideology than economics. Ronald Reagan's election as president in 1980 altered the political climate. For the first time since 1955, the Republicans also captured the Senate, giving conservatives in both parties the opportunity to bar environmental policy proposals and to roll back some policies already in existence. The economic recession of 1980-1982 and the high cost of energy also shaped Reagan's decision to subordinate the environment to economic recovery.

These alterations in the political environment threw Congress into a defensive posture. It was forced to *react* to the Reagan administration's radical policy actions. Rather than proposing new programs or expanding old ones, Congress focused its resources on oversight and criticism of the administration's policies. Bipartisan agreement became more difficult. Thus for most of Reagan's first term, political conditions were ripe for protracted conflict between the president and Congress.

As environmental issues became more complex, less salient to the public, and more contentious, there were also fewer incentives for policy leadership on Capitol Hill. Members were increasingly cross-pressured by environmental and industry groups, partisanship on these issues increased, and Congress and President Reagan battled over budget and program priorities.[13] As we will see, conditions in the 104th Congress were remarkably similar, but with the congressional and presidential roles reversed. The Clinton White House defended environmental programs against a hostile Congress.

The cumulative effect of these developments in the 1980s was that Congress was unable to agree on new environmental policy directions. Members kept programs alive through continuing appropriations and short-term extensions of the existing acts, but they could not formally reauthorize them. During the Ninety-seventh Congress, eight comprehensive environmental programs were due for reauthorization; only two were enacted. Although it renewed the Toxic Substances Control Act and the Endangered Species Act in 1982, Congress deferred action on programs for clean air, clean water, pesticide regulation, noise control, safe drinking water, and hazardous waste control.

Gridlock Eases: 1984 to 1990

The legislative logjam began breaking up in late 1983, as President Reagan's environmental agenda was repudiated by the American public. These developments altered what John Kingdon has called the "politics stream."[14] Environmental groups took advantage of the favorable political mood to push ahead on their deferred policy agenda. The new pattern was evident in 1984 when, after several years of deliberation, Congress approved major amendments to the 1976 Resource Conservation and Recovery Act that strengthened the program and set tight new deadlines for EPA rule-making on control of hazardous chemical wastes.

Although the Republicans still controlled the Senate, the Ninety-ninth Congress (1985-1986) compiled a record dramatically at odds with the deferral politics of the Ninety-seventh and Ninety-eighth Congresses. In 1986 the Safe Drinking Water Act was strengthened and expanded, and Congress approved the Superfund Amendments and Reauthorization Act (SARA) and added a separate Title III, the Emergency Planning and Community Right-to-Know Act (EPCRA). EPCRA was an entirely new program mandating nationwide reporting requirements for toxic and hazardous chemicals produced, used, or stored in communities, as well as state and local emergency planning for accidental releases.[15] By 1987 Congress reauthorized the Clean Water Act over a presidential veto. In early 1987 the Sierra Club congratulated Congress for its "solid record on environmental quality and public lands issues." It added that "bipartisan majorities supported the improvement of key laws despite resistance from President Reagan."[16]

The Democrats regained control of the Senate following the 1986 election, and the newly elected members of both the House and Senate were a more environmentally oriented group. Yet despite what was by any measure a highly productive record, several major environmental policy measures failed not only in the Ninety-ninth Congress but in the One Hundredth Congress (1987-1989) as well. These included renewal of the Clean Air Act, the Federal Insecticide, Fungicide, and Rodenticide Act (FIFRA)—the nation's key pesticide control act—and new legislation on acid rain and energy use.

The disappointment in this limited progress was captured in one analyst's assessment: "Congress stayed largely stalemated on a range of old environmental and energy problems in 1988, even while a generation of new ones clamored for attention."[17] Much the same could be said for the 101st and 102d Congresses (1989-1993) during the Bush administration.

Yet Congress and the president were able to agree on enactment of the monumental Clean Air Act Amendments of 1990 and on the Energy Policy Act of 1992, an important if modest advancement in promoting energy conservation and a restructuring of the electric utility industry to promote greater competition and efficiency. Success on the Clean Air Act was particularly important because for thirteen years it symbolized Congress's inability to reauthorize controversial environmental programs. Congress was able to approve the 1990 act for several reasons: improved scientific research and reports of worsening ozone in urban areas—which helped to reduce opposition by key interest groups such as the Chemical Manufacturers Association—and a realization by members that the American public would tolerate no further delays in dealing with air quality problems. President George Bush also vowed to "break the gridlock" and support renewal of the act, and Sen. George Mitchell (D-Maine), newly elected as Senate majority leader, was equally determined to enact a clean air bill.[18]

The 103d Congress: Gridlock Returns

Unfortunately, enactment of the 1990 Clean Air Act was no signal that a new era of cooperative and bipartisan policymaking on the environment was about to begin. Nor was the election of Bill Clinton and Al Gore in 1992, even though the Democrats then controlled both houses of Congress. Most of the major environmental laws were once again up for renewal. Yet despite an emerging consensus on legislative reforms in reauthorizing the Clean Water Act, Safe Drinking Water Act, Superfund, and FIFRA, among others, in the end the 103d Congress remained far too divided to act.

Coalitions of environmental groups and business interests clashed regularly on all of these measures, and neither congressional leaders nor the Clinton White House was successful in resolving the conflicts. The administration came close with the much criticized Superfund program. It brought all parties together through its National Commission on the Superfund (also known as the Keystone Commission), and by the end of 1994 there appeared to be agreement on needed reforms. Much the same was true for the Safe Drinking Water Act, where a broad array of interest groups came close to reaching consensus on the act's renewal.

Yet environmentalists refused to compromise on several key issues and instead tried to mobilize the public, arguing that "two decades of environmental progress are in danger of being rolled back." Other policy actors were also adamant in their demands. Even state and local governments began to lose patience with the EPA. In a major shift from their previous position, they became openly critical of the burdens and costs of "unfunded mandates" imposed on them by the EPA under federal statutes such as the Safe Drinking Water Act.[19]

In this political context, of special importance was an apparent decision by the Clinton White House to give environmental policy a relatively low priority (see chap. 5). The president and his staff were preoccupied with other issues such as health care reform, and they did not push environmental issues as much as they might have. The same can be said for the Democratic leadership in Congress. The Democrats held only a slim margin, especially in the Senate, and they could not easily assemble a majority for controversial environmental measures. With weak leadership in the White House as well as in Congress, a divided membership, and conflicting pressures from interest groups, renewal of the major environmental laws was likely to be difficult at best.

The search for consensus on environmental policy became even more elusive as the 1994 election neared. Republicans increasingly believed they would do well in November, and partisan politics helped to scuttle whatever hopes remained for action in 1994. Like the environmentalists, the Republicans, their conservative Democratic allies in these battles, and business leaders thought they could strike a more favorable compromise in the next Congress. In the end, the only major environmental policy on which lawmakers could agree was the California Desert Protection Act, establishing new wilderness areas in that state. All the other proposals for reforming federal environmental laws would have to be revisited in the 104th Congress beginning in 1995.

The 104th Congress Takes Charge: A Mandate for Revolution?

Few analysts had predicted the extraordinary outcomes of the 1994 midterm elections, even after one of the most expensive, negative, and anti-Washington campaigns in modern times. Republicans captured both houses of Congress, adding fifty-two seats in the House to their previous total and eight seats in the Senate. Moreover, they won twenty-one of twenty-five open seats and defeated thirty-four Democratic incumbents while suffering *not one* loss of a Republican incumbent. The election produced a 55-45 initial majority in the Senate, and a 230-204 majority in the House (there is one Independent member). These margins were later widened slightly when several conservative Democrats switched parties, yet they remained small by historical standards. This was also a Congress of newcomers; a majority of the House Republicans were serving their first or second terms. Only thirty-eight of the seventy-three Republican freshmen in that body reported ever holding elective office, and only twenty-seven of them had previous legislative experience.[20]

The surprising Republican electoral sweep nationwide owed much to voter disenchantment with the political status quo (especially in Congress), unhappiness with the Clinton administration, and pervasive economic uncertainty despite a strong economic recovery then under way. The 1994 election did not seem to reflect a major realignment of the nation's electorate. Rather it represented a continuation of a long-term trend toward dealignment, or a weakening of party ties. These changes increase the volatility of voters, especially in congressional elections. [21]

The "Contract with America" as an Agenda for Policy Change

One of the most distinctive features of the 1994 election was the drafting of the "Contract with America" as a conservative campaign manifesto. In a widely promoted media event, more than three hundred GOP incumbents and challengers for House seats signed the Contract on the steps of the Capitol on September 27, 1994 (six weeks before the election); eventually a total of 367 candidates endorsed the document. It promised a range of fundamental changes in public policy, among them a rolling back of government regulations and a shrinking of the federal government's role in many policy areas. [22] The Contract reflected the conservatives' determination to finish the uncompleted Reagan Revolution of the 1980s.

Both the Contract provisions and legislative proposals that followed drew heavily from the work of conservative think tanks such as the Heritage Foundation, American Enterprise Institute, Cato Institute, and Competitive Enterprise Institute. For years, in association with conservative intellectuals and talk-radio hosts, they waged a multifaceted campaign to discredit environmentalist thinking and policies and to shift public opinion on these issues. They succeeded to some extent. The Contract also reflected a long-term and carefully developed GOP plan to gain control of Congress to further a conservative political agenda. [23]

Environmental policies were not specifically mentioned in the Contract (actually a very brief document), which was drafted following extensive use of focus groups and surveys to find proposals and language with broad national appeal. Thus, while the GOP's leadership managed to push nine of the ten legislative provisions of the Contract through the House during the first hundred days of the session (a term-limits amendment was the only failure), that achievement did not really signify much. As one committee chair noted, "we deliberately selected issues on which we were virtually unanimous." [24]

Public Support for the Contract?

Did the Republican victory in November imply a public mandate to act on the Contract's provisions related to environmental programs? Little evidence exists to support that contention. For example, according to a CBS News/*New York Times* survey, even by April 1995 nearly two-thirds of the American public said they had never heard or read *anything* about the Contract, and most had no specific knowledge of its provisions. Moreover, studies of voting behavior in the November election found no basis for a voter mandate on the issues. [25] At best, one could read into the election a general preference for less government and less regulation, and a distinct lack of enthusiasm for congressional Democrats. Yet even here the public is ambivalent. Skepticism about government is greater than at any time since the New Deal of the 1930s, but people continue to want the services government provides.

In addition, a large number of surveys, national and regional, indicate that voters make a clear exception for the environment, where they continue to prefer a strong governmental role (see chap. 3). For example, an ABC News/*Washington Post* poll of May 10-14, 1995, asked: "Generally speaking, do you think the federal government has gone too far or not far enough to protect the environment?" Seventy percent of the public said "not far enough," and only 17 percent said "too far"; 11 percent said "about right." These attitudes cut across partisan and ideological lines.[26]

The preponderance of evidence confirms what Republican pollster Linda DiVall concluded in early 1996, that "our party is out of sync with mainstream American opinion" on the environment. Her poll data indicated that 55 percent of Republicans did not trust their own party to protect the environment, and that by a 2-to-1 margin voters had more confidence in the Democrats on environmental issues. These kinds of findings reinforced the efforts of moderate Republicans such as Rep. Sherwood Boehlert (R-N.Y.) to pull their party back from its more extreme positions on the environment.[27]

From Contract to Policy Action

Whatever might be said about the meaning of the 1994 election, the result was clear enough. It put Republicans in charge of the House for the first time in four decades and set the stage for an extraordinary period of legislative action to weaken environmental policy. The "politics stream" shifted abruptly rightward and environmental programs became direct targets.

Important legislative developments in the 104th Congress can be grouped into three categories: regulatory reform initiatives; use of the appropriations process to curtail policy implementation; and legislative reauthorizations for the major programs. The first two preoccupied both the House and Senate in 1995, with little progress made on the third until 1996. Hence I focus here on efforts to alter regulatory decisionmaking and use of the appropriations process.[28]

Regulatory Reform

The most direct effort to alter environmental policy occurred in the House early in 1995. Members were eager, in the words of the Contract, to "free Americans from bureaucratic red tape," which they saw in environmental, health, and safety regulations, and to spur economic growth. In pursuit of those goals, the Contract authors wanted to require "every new regulation to stand a new test: Does it provide benefits worth the costs?" Those ideas found expression in the Job Creation and Wage Enhancement Act of 1995, which mandated extensive cost-benefit analyses and risk assessments in the regulatory processes used by agencies such as the EPA to implement environmental policies.

This act and its counterpart in the Senate, strongly supported by Bob Dole (R-Kan.), then the Senate majority leader, reflected intense lobbying by business groups. These included two broad coalitions, Project Relief and the Alliance for Reasonable Regulation, in addition to the National Association of Manufacturers, trade associations representing diverse industries, and dozens of leading corporations with strong financial stakes in the outcome. Other groups were quick to jump in when they saw an unusual opportunity to curtail federal regulations.[29] The business community's concerns were genuine, yet the approach employed was controversial and unlikely to succeed. Short-term economic relief might be gained, as it was in the Reagan administration, but at the expense of the more important goal of long-term reform of environmental statutes.

The bills the House considered required agencies to follow an elaborate twenty-three-step review process for virtually all federal regulations rather than restricting such analysis to the "big ticket" rules. The EPA estimated it would have to double the staff and triple the paperwork it now devotes to such analysis to comply. In addition, the legislation would supersede existing statutory standards (through a "supermandate") by making economic costs the chief basis for agency decisionmaking even in cases where Congress had chosen to emphasize protection of human health. Extensive legal challenges to agency decisionmaking would also have been allowed, likely throwing many contested decisions into the federal courts. The final legislative package, HR 9, included as well a "takings" provision that would require compensation to landowners when regulations under certain laws reduced property values by as little as 20 percent. In a telling comment about legislative politics in 1995, debate on the bill's provisions appeared to be anchored far more in colorful anecdotes of alleged regulatory abuses and pleas for relief for the business community rather than in scientific or economic facts.[30]

Despite significant misgivings about the bill by economists, scientists, policy analysts, and administration officials who favor *some* economic analysis of environmental proposals, the House overwhelmingly approved the measure (277-141) in March 1995.[31] That action was later ridiculed in the nation's editorial pages and even in cartoonist Garry Trudeau's "Doonesbury" strip.

Regulatory reform bills fared much less well in the Senate. Senator Dole tried three times to bring a companion bill to the Senate floor, but he failed to gain sufficient votes to end a filibuster by those who considered the various bills offered to be too extreme in their effects on public health, safety, and the environment. For instance, John Chafee (R-R.I.), chair of the Senate Environment and Public Works Committee, objected that such bills were "not reforms at all" but "steps backward." As conflict mounted, the Democratic leader, Thomas Daschle (D-S.D.), observed that "no bill is better than a bad bill." President Clinton indicated his strong opposition to the bills, which, along with intense lobbying by a reinvigorated environmental community, effectively derailed regulatory reform for the year.

By early 1996 GOP leaders tried once again to approve regulatory overhauls, now far less ambitious than those considered in 1995. One modest measure was approved in late March, giving Congress greater power to review agency regulations. On other issues, Republicans remained divided and the outlook was uncertain. The business community was also split, although at least some leaders signaled a strategic shift that recognized popular support for environmental protection. Those who worked closely with the President's Council on Sustainable Development announced that modest reforms of existing statutes might be better after all than the drastic changes they sought in 1995.[32]

Appropriation Politics: Riders and Budget Cuts

Perhaps the most striking element of the Republican strategy was the use of a sharp budget axe to institute radical changes in policy rather than trying to do so through legislation. The Reagan administration used a similar budgetary strategy effectively in the 1980s (see chaps. 1 and 5). One of the most avid revolutionaries in the GOP freshman class, Rep. David McIntosh (R-Ind.), explained the logic of this position: "The laws would remain on the books, but there would be no money to carry them out. It's a signal to the agencies to stop wasting time on these regulations." Others were equally blunt. It was, said Billy Tauzin (R-La.), a quicker way to "control the bureaucrats out of control."[33]

Appropriation Riders. The strategy to which these members referred was the unprecedented use of "riders"—legislative stipulations attached to appropriation bills to achieve policy goals such as restricting, remaking, or even eliminating federal programs. More than fifty antienvironmental riders were included in seven different budget bills, largely with the purpose of slowing or halting enforcement of laws by the EPA, the Interior Department, and other agencies until Congress could revise them. One early victory indicated the potential for this strategy. A timber industry-backed "salvage logging" rider attached to the budget rescission bill signed by President Clinton in July 1995 exempted so-called emergency salvage sales from statutory environmental safeguards that restricted logging in national forests. That provision led to extensive logging in old-growth forests and immediate, though unsuccessful, efforts by environmental groups to force its repeal.

In the most notorious case, seventeen riders were appended to the EPA appropriations bill in 1995 in an attempt to prohibit the agency from enforcing certain drinking-water and water quality standards and to keep it from regulating commercial development in wetlands and toxic air emissions from oil and gas refineries, among many other provisions. The EPA was told flatly that it could not spend any money on these activities.[34] Such a strategy is attractive to its proponents because appropriation bills, unlike authorizing legislation, typically move quickly and Congress must enact them each year. Yet use of riders is also widely considered to be an inappropriate way to institute major policy changes. The process does not provide much opportunity to debate the issues openly, and most members have little idea of what such riders will do. In one case, two sentences in "an obscure passage in a vast $80 billion appropriation bill" would have barred the EPA from overseeing protection of wetlands.[35]

The Natural Resources Defense Council successfully characterized the rider strategy as a "stealth attack" on environmental statutes mounted at the behest of corporate polluters, a charge later repeated by both the EPA's Browner and by President Clinton. The environmental groups worked steadily throughout 1995 to "shine a spotlight on the attacks" and gain media coverage that was largely absent in early 1995. They hoped the enhanced visibility of activities on the Hill would help them mobilize an environmentally sympathetic but unaware public. Said one environmentalist: "We're using e-mail, direct mail, faxes and the Internet—anything we can to get people stirred up."[36] The environmentalist campaign against what they termed Congress's "war on the environment" worked. Among other things, the NRDC and other groups gathered more than 1 million signatures on an "environmental bill of rights" delivered to Congress on November 1.

The effect can be seen in votes on the EPA riders. The House first eliminated them on July 28, 1995. Then three days later, in a stunning setback for environmentalists, it reinstated them by a one-vote margin. Eight Democrats who initially voted to strike the provisions failed to vote the second time.[37] Yet after considerable publicity, presidential threats to veto the bill, and further intense lobbying by both sides, the House voted for the third time in three months on the issues and instructed a House-Senate conference committee to remove the riders. Sixty-three "green Republicans" broke with the House leadership to join the moderate forces led by Representative Boehlert, in large part, it seems, because of constituent pressure and media coverage of the issues. Some of these members were, Boehlert suggested, "catching hell back home" over their environmental votes.[38]

Cutting Environmental Budgets. Despite the setback on appropriation riders, GOP leaders tried to capitalize on the momentum of their electoral success by representing the steep reductions in environmental spending as merely part of their larger—and broadly supported—effort to balance the federal budget. However, the depth of the cuts and the way they were targeted on enforcement actions belie the argument. Indeed, House Budget Committee chair John Kasich (R-Ohio), a leading player in the new budget politics, acknowledged as much: "We're going to fund programs that we think are important and not fund the programs that we think are not important."[39]

Initial actions on the budget in the House were nothing short of astonishing in light of public support for environmental programs. Congress had already cut EPA and other agency budgets as part of a rescission bill passed in mid 1995 that reduced the EPA's FY 1995 budget by $1.1 billion (most of it in water quality programs). For FY 1996 House members voted to cut the president's recommended EPA budget by 34 percent overall, proportionately the largest reduction for any major federal agency. Even deeper cuts were proposed for enforcement (50 percent) and in selected program accounts—particularly Superfund and revolving loans to states for wastewater treatment and safe drinking-water projects. The Appropriations subcommittee that recommended the cuts explained why it favored deregulating the environment: "the agency was headed in the wrong direction, for the wrong reasons, and in a manner that can impose unnecessary costs on American industry." [40]

The Senate was less drastic than the House but still harsh on the EPA. A House-Senate conference committee moved closer to the Senate's position. It reduced the EPA's overall budget by 22 percent, safe drinking-water grants to states and localities by 45 percent, and EPA's enforcement programs by 24 percent. As he had threatened, President Clinton vetoed the bill in mid-December 1995, saying the cuts were unacceptably large. Proposed reductions in other environmental agency budgets were generally smaller but nonetheless significant. In some instances, however, budgets were slashed by an even greater amount; funds for international family-planning programs were cut by some 35 percent from 1995 levels.

Irreconcilable differences between budgets that the president and the GOP Congress were willing to accept led to a period of prolonged stalemate in late 1995 and early 1996, and to two governmentwide partial shutdowns as money to operate agencies ran out. The EPA fought back through prominent announcements of forced suspension of pollution monitoring and enforcement activities and cleanup of Superfund sites around the country. Agency officials also suggested that the EPA might have to lay off thousands of its workers in the spring if the budget impasse continued. Similar arguments were advanced by Bruce Babbitt, secretary of the interior, about the "disastrous" budget cuts and their impacts on public lands and natural resources. [41] President Clinton also spoke at length in his January 1996 State of the Union message about the Republican attack on environmental budgets and policies, winning applause and cheers (presumably from Democrats) for his challenge to Congress to "reexamine those policies and to reverse them."

The Republicans received the brunt of the public's wrath for the budget wars, which it saw as yet another illustration of irresponsible gridlock in government. By early 1996 Congress began to backtrack on its fiscal demands. The EPA operated in the first part of 1996 on a series of continuing resolutions, or stopgap funding bills, that limited spending to only about 75 percent of the previous year's level. The White House continued to negotiate with congressional leaders, who were in a more accommodating mood as evidence mounted that the American public had rejected their antienvironmental positions.

By late April 1996 Congress agreed to reinstate many of the earlier cuts in the EPA's budget as part of a broader compromise with the White House on the FY 1996 budget. The EPA's total budget was to be $6.5 billion, or more than $750 million above the level vetoed by President Clinton in December. Nevertheless, the agency, already suffering from insufficient resources, would have to cope with substantially less than it enjoyed in its prerescission FY 1995 budget of $7.0 billion.

Congress also eliminated, or permitted the president to suspend, some of the riders that most concerned environmental groups. These included an extension of the timber salvage measure beyond its September 1996 expiration date and other provisions that would have expanded logging in the Tongass National Forest, prevented EPA oversight of wetlands protection, and prohibited listings of new species under the Endangered Species Act. Clinton used his authority to suspend those riders immediately after signing the appropriations bill.

Despite these compromises, the budget constraints on the EPA, Interior Department, and other agencies are likely to significantly impede their implementation of environmental programs for years to come and to affect the many state programs dependent on federal aid. Continued fiscal austerity does not bode well for future increases in these budgets.

Reauthorizing Environmental Statutes

For most of 1995 Congress was absorbed in regulatory reform battles and cutting government spending, and it made little progress on the legislative front. Severe disagreements among members over the direction of environmental policy contributed to the lack of action. Partisan divisions were especially notable. The League of Conservation voters reported that for 1995 votes on the environment showed the biggest disparity between the two parties ever. House Republicans averaged 15 percent on the league scorecard while Democrats averaged 76 percent. The ratios were similar in the Senate, 11 percent and 89 percent respectively for Republicans and Democrats.[42]

In this political climate only broadly supported measures could be approved. One of those was a bill dealing with so-called unfunded mandates, which Congress approved and the president signed in early 1995. The act would erect new procedural barriers to keep Congress from approving statutes likely to impose unfunded federal mandates of $50 million a year or more on state and local governments. Most observers characterized the new law as weak, and one government study indicated it might exempt as many as two-thirds of major mandates.

Other legislative activity sent important signals about how the GOP Congress would amend the major environmental statutes, although the only other act approved by spring of 1996 was the Farm Bill, which contains significant land conservation provisions. Both parties were anxious to vote on the bill prior to spring planting season; President Clinton signed the measure on April 4. Other actions, however, were far more tentative.

The House passed a revision of the Clean Water Act in May 1995, which the press and environmentalists promptly labeled the "dirty water act" for provisions that significantly weakened protection of wetlands and eased or revoked some of the law's requirements. Sen. John Chafee's Environment Committee chose not to move on similar proposals in the Senate.

Legislative progress on other measures in 1995 and early 1996 was similarly limited as Congress was busy dealing with issues such as welfare, telecommunications, and immigration reform. In October 1995 the House Resources Committee approved a rewrite of the Endangered Species Act (ESA) backed by Rep. Don Young (R-Alaska), the committee's chair, and Rep. Richard W. Pombo (R-Calif.). The Young-Pombo bill would require greater consideration of property owners and economic impacts. Opponents argued that the bill would gut the ESA to appease small landowners and corporate developers, and they vowed to fight it.[43] Neither house approved a final bill as of spring 1996.

Some initial efforts were made as well on revision and renewal of the Superfund hazardous waste program and the Safe Drinking Water Act (SDWA). In November 1995 the Senate approved a rewrite of the SDWA drafted by Senator Chafee's Environment and Public Works Committee, 99-0. Yet partisan disagreements slowed action in the House. Chafee's committee was also making considerable progress on revising Superfund after several weeks of intensive and bipartisan negotiations behind closed doors in April 1996. These and other environmental policies may yet be acted on by the 104th Congress, although significant obstacles remain. Senate Majority Leader Bob Dole, the presumptive Republican presidential nominee, was eager to demonstrate that the Republicans could govern Congress effectively. Thus for several months in early 1996 he tried to facilitate the compromises necessary for enactment.[44] On May 15, however, Dole announced that he would resign his Senate seat in early June to concentrate on his presidential campaign, making environmental policy action in Congress less predictable.

Assessing Environmental Politics in the 104th Congress

Early in the chapter I set out several standards against which to judge the performance of any Congress. These are the extent to which members of Congress demonstrate a capacity and willingness to assess environmental problems accurately, evaluate current programs carefully, and design appropriate policies. For example, there is no shortage of advice on how to reform environmental policies, but any changes that are made ought to improve the effectiveness or efficiency of present programs or ought to be accompanied by compelling arguments for abandoning certain approaches and programs in favor of better alternatives.[45] Revolutionary changes in environmental policy are not inherently undesirable. But they should be evaluated in an open process to determine the extent to which they are likely to achieve what they promise.

Speaker Newt Gingrich would seem to concur with these ideas. In his book *To Renew America* Gingrich took a position on environmental policy reform with which few would disagree:

> Misdesigned programs, questionable science, and rigid bureaucratic enforcement have caused a loss of momentum to our environmental effort. If the current slowdown is seen as an opportunity to reassess and rethink, it will be a good thing. If it becomes an excuse for developers and businesses to undermine a sound environmentalism, it will be a bad thing. The American public will not allow us to turn back on the environment.[46]

Readers can judge for themselves, but key environmental policy decisions of the 104th Congress would seem to fall well short of both these general expectations and the Speaker's standards for reform. Other

Congresses may not be considered sterling successes either. Yet the 104th set new records for hurried consideration of complex policy proposals, insufficient provision for deliberation, neglect of scientific knowledge and administrative experience, and emphasis on ideology over analysis of policy proposals. This Congress also tended to disregard public support for the environmental programs it was eager to curtail and to maintain costly and ecologically damaging natural resource policies environmentalists have long sought to change.

Legitimating Environmental Policy?

Ideally, in a representative legislature like Congress public policies are developed through a process of policy legitimation involving widespread discussion with affected interests. Sufficient opportunities would be provided for debate on alternative proposals and opponents would have the chance to voice their concerns. Major policy changes would be handled through reform of the authorizing statutes, where their impacts would be visible and subject to review by those familiar with program history and operations.

Critics of the 104th Congress point out that it failed to meet such common principles. For example, EPA administrator Carol Browner noted in commenting on the first hundred days that members "acted in haste, did not involve the people on whose behalf they serve and did not do their business in the open."[47] Equity in representation has also been a concern. Among the many objections raised by environmentalists, journalists, and members of Congress themselves was the extraordinary access provided to lobbyists for oil, timber, mining, and chemical and other industries in the drafting of legislation. They rarely had such grand opportunities to affect environmental legislation prior to the 104th Congress.[48]

Other concerns focused on the speed with which legislation moved through the House, and the price paid in poor legislative craftsmanship. The House leadership under Speaker Gingrich and Majority Leader Dick Armey dominated both the standing committees and the appropriation process and sought quick action. The frenetic legislative pace took a toll on policy deliberation as members and their staffs could scarcely keep up with the workload. Rep. Henry Waxman (D-Calif.), the ranking member on the Health and Environment subcommittee, complained about procedures on the full Commerce Committee in 1995: Gingrich, he said, "pushed his committee chairmen, who didn't have time to pay much attention to details. There was a reduction of professionalism of the legislature."[49]

Even if more time had been made available, many members, especially the Republican freshmen, were not inclined to favor a legislative strategy of compromise and consensus building. They viewed such behavior as a sign of capitulation and the abandonment of their ideological convictions. One journalist referred to this behavior as "instinctive dismissal of contrary opinions."

Such beliefs also made the new members far less supportive of the institutional courtesies on Capitol Hill that can help legislators work together on national lawmaking and appreciate divergent perspectives. This freshman class, however, largely inexperienced in the legislative process and lacking in knowledge of environmental policy, was driven by a take-no-prisoners mentality that severely eroded the bipartisanship that had long characterized environmental policymaking. Members of both parties complained often about the new levels of poisonous rhetoric, partisan rancor, and general irascibility and lack of civility in Congress.

At the end of 1995 environmental groups and the Clinton White House were overwhelmingly negative in their appraisals of Congress. Vice President Al Gore captured the sentiment: "The Republican leadership in this Congress is conducting a *jihad* on the environment in the most right-wing agenda we have seen in America this century." The bipartisan League of Conservation Voters took a similar position: "In our 25-year history, the league has never witnessed such an egregious attack on our environmental laws." [50]

Reactions to the Revolution

At least initially, the public and the press did not see this side of the 104th Congress. Outside of several national newspapers and professional news weeklies, coverage of environmental decisionmaking in Congress was so sparse and inadequate that most voters could not hope to learn about what Congress was doing. Coverage focused on the proportion of the Contract that had been acted on and how quickly rather than on the substantive issues. [51]

Despite the inadequate media coverage, opposition to the Republican agenda grew throughout 1995. By the fall Congress found itself censured by a revitalized and politically powerful environmental community, pilloried in the nation's press, and condemned by the Clinton White House. [52] The Clinton administration's senior environmental officials eagerly joined the fray. They painted the Republican majority in Congress as interested solely in fighting a war against government that rewarded corporate interests at the expense of the public's health and environmental quality, and they succeeded in shifting the terms of debate. Speaker Gingrich, referring to the GOP's efforts to curb environmental regulations, acknowledged that "We mishandled the environment all spring and summer" [of 1995]. Tom DeLay (R-Texas), House Majority Whip, was equally candid: "I'll be straight with you—we have lost the debate on the environment." [53]

By late 1995 the counterattack succeeded well enough that some Republican leaders began to signal a partial retreat, worried that the party's antienvironmental image could cause it grievous harm in the 1996 elections. Gingrich announced he would appoint a task force to redefine the party's position on environmental issues. He did so in late March 1996, selecting as cochairs of the sixty-six-member group Representatives Boehlert and Pombo. The task force was asked "to develop and implement a proactive, positive agenda that is both reasonable and reflects a commonsense approach to the environment." [54]

Even the seventy-three House Republican freshmen, the ideological vanguard of the revolution, had what one journalist called an "election-year epiphany." One sign of their new appreciation for electoral politics could be found in their League of Conservation Voters scores. The league gave sixty-one of the seventy-three GOP freshmen scores of zero based on their environmental voting during the first hundred days of the 104th Congress. Yet by the end of 1995 House members with zero ratings for the entire year's votes dropped to thirty-six. Moreover, by that time thirteen of the freshmen consistently supported the league's positions.[55]

The signs of incipient moderation notwithstanding, the rhetoric of revolution continued to echo in the hallways of Capitol Hill, and the voices of resistance persisted in the White House and administrative agencies. Although any outcome is possible in the volatile political climate of the 1990s, policy deadlock may well characterize the near term.

The 104th Congress can be credited with achieving at least some of its goals. It reduced budgets for environmental agencies and programs, and it forced officials to reconsider their regulatory processes and priorities. It succeeded in gaining President Clinton's support for balancing the federal budget within seven years, with long-term implications for environmental policy. It also pushed the Clinton White House to escalate its own efforts at reinventing environmental regulation, which it reported prominently in March 1995. The result was that by 1996 the EPA, Interior Department, Food and Drug Administration, and other agencies had become more sensitive to the costs and burdens of their regulations. They also made adjustments in agency decisionmaking in light of congressional criticism, quietly rolling back some regulations and softening enforcement of others. Many environmental leaders and consumer activists disparaged these political shifts. Conservatives also objected, arguing that the administration was "throwing red meat at its attackers" to "buy off the most vocal critics and head off dramatic reform."[56]

It is also significant that most Americans disapproved of the job the Republican Congress was doing in 1995. Polls in late summer 1995 indicated that the public was just as dissatisfied with Congress as they were with Clinton's performance in the White House. The approval ratings for Congress grew more negative as the year wore on. The same was true for the public's judgment about Speaker Gingrich. He remained generally unpopular with the electorate, with his approval ratings dropping steadily throughout 1995. Even more important—and disturbing—is that such polls describe a public frustration with government and politics that now runs deeper than at any other time in recent memory.[57] As understandable as those attitudes are, they constrain the public's ability to become more engaged with political processes that can help address their concerns at all levels of government.

Conclusions

From many perspectives, environmental policies are at a critical crossroads. They have achieved much, but future gains cannot be assured by relying on conventional regulatory approaches and existing institutional structures. A search for new approaches is imperative. But it requires Congress to rewrite statutory language, not merely to cut budgets and slow the regulatory process (see chap. 17).[58]

The immediate political struggle on Capitol Hill in the 104th Congress, and elsewhere in the nation, has been between two contrasting visions of the path to be taken. One is a revolutionary overhaul of existing environmental and resource policies, particularly as fashioned by conservative think tanks, business groups, and the Wise Use and property rights movements. Another is reform of current policies, as advocated by many policy analysts, and endorsed to some extent by environmental groups, the Clinton White House, and some business leaders. If neither side predominates, we get a third outcome that pleases few: policy gridlock. Gridlock does have the virtue of maintaining the status quo in environmental policy. Yet it also frustrates the development of needed new policies and approaches for the late 1990s and twenty-first century.

The constitutional divisions between the House and the Senate guarantee that newly emergent political forces such as those represented in the House in 1995 and 1996 will have no easy time pushing their legislative agendas. Even if they succeed, they may face a White House, as they did in the Clinton presidency, determined to slow or halt their advance. The 1996 elections may alter the equation. Yet effective policymaking will always require cooperation between the two branches and leadership within both to advance sensible policies and secure public approval for them.

Whatever the short-term outcome, setting new policy directions ultimately requires a greater level of public involvement in environmental politics. This is because such decisions must necessarily address fundamental questions about the role of government, the policies that are most appropriate, the setting of priorities for environmental protection, and the willingness of the American people to bear the costs. Political institutions in a democracy, especially a representative legislature like Congress, are guided by public preferences. Yet the public's political influence depends on its willingness to become more knowledgeable about environmental problems and to participate in the search for effective solutions, from local communities to the national level.

Notes

The epigraph quotes Thomas Bliley, as reported in Bob Benenson, "GOP Sets the 104th Congress on New Regulatory Course," *Congressional Quarterly Weekly Report*, June 17, 1995, 1693. Browner's statement is from John H. Cushman Jr., "Backed by Business, Republicans Take Steps to Overhaul Environmental Regulations," *New York Times*, February 10, 1995, A10.

1. See chap. 1; Henry Kenski and Margaret Corgan Kenski, "Congress against the President: The Struggle over the Environment," in *Environmental Policy in the 1980s*, ed. Norman J. Vig and Michael E. Kraft (Washington, D.C.: CQ Press, 1984); and Michael E. Kraft, "Congress and Environmental Policy," in *Environmental Politics and Policy: Theories and Evidence*, 2d ed., ed. James P. Lester (Durham: Duke University Press, 1995).

2. Ed Gillespie and Bob Schellhas, eds., *Contract with America: The Bold Plan by Rep. Newt Gingrich, Rep. Dick Armey, and the House Republicans to Change the Nation* (New York: Times Books/Random House, 1994); and Bob Benenson, "GOP Sets the 104th Congress on New Regulatory Course," *Congressional Quarterly Weekly Report,* June 17, 1995, 1693-1705.

3. Kraft, "Congress and Environmental Policy"; and Richard A. Cooley and Geoffrey Wandesforde-Smith, eds., *Congress and the Environment* (Seattle: University of Washington Press, 1970).

4. Charles O. Jones, *Separate but Equal Branches: Congress and the Presidency* (Chatham, N.J.: Chatham House, 1995). See also James A. Thurber, ed., *Rivals for Power: Presidential-Congressional Relations* (Washington, D.C.: CQ Press, 1996).

5. Samuel C. Patterson and Gregory A. Caldeira, "Standing Up for Congress: Variations in Public Esteem since the 1960s," *Legislative Studies Quarterly* 15 (1990): 36; and John R. Hibbing and Elizabeth Theiss-Morse, *Congress as Public Enemy: Public Attitudes toward American Political Institutions* (New York: Cambridge University Press, 1995).

6. Richard E. Cohen, *Washington at Work: Back Rooms and Clean Air,* 2d ed. (New York: Macmillan, 1995); and Gary C. Bryner, *Blue Skies, Green Politics: The Clean Air Act of 1990,* 2d ed. (Washington, D.C.: CQ Press, 1996).

7. Gary C. Jacobson, *The Politics of Congressional Elections,* 3d ed. (New York: Harper-Collins, 1992).

8. Jeffrey M. Berry, *The Interest Group Society,* 2d ed. (Glenview, Ill.: Scott, Foresman/Little, Brown, 1989), 16-43; and Kay Lehman Schlozman and John T. Tierney, *Organized Interests and American Democracy* (New York: Harper and Row, 1986), 58-87.

9. David R. Mayhew, *Divided We Govern* (New Haven, Conn.: Yale University Press, 1991); and Jones, *Separate but Equal Branches.*

10. See Paul Portney, "Cartoon Caricatures of Regulatory Reform," *Resources* (Fall 1995): 21-24; and National Academy of Public Administration, *Setting Priorities, Getting Results: A New Direction for EPA* (Washington, D.C.: NAPA, 1995).

11. See William Ophuls and A. Stephen Boyan Jr., *Ecology and the Politics of Scarcity Revisited* (San Francisco: W. H. Freeman, 1992).

12. A useful summary of key legislative actions can be found in the reference work *Congress and the Nation* (Washington, D.C.: Congressional Quarterly Inc., various dates), vol. 3, 1969-1972, 745-849; vol. 4, 1973-1976, 201-320; and vol. 5, 1977-1980, 451-597. On the subgovernment argument, see Christopher J. Bosso, *Pesticides and Politics: The Life Cycle of a Public Issue* (Pittsburgh: University of Pittsburgh Press, 1987), chaps. 6 and 7; and Frank R. Baumgartner and Bryan D. Jones, *Agendas and Instability in American Politics* (Chicago: University of Chicago Press, 1993).

13. Mary Etta Cook and Roger H. Davidson, "Deferral Politics: Congressional Decision Making on Environmental Issues in the 1980s," in *Public Policy and the Natural Environment,* ed. Helen M. Ingram and R. Kenneth Godwin (Greenwich, Conn.: JAI, 1985); and Kenski and Kenski, "Congress against the President."

14. John W. Kingdon, *Agendas, Alternatives, and Public Policies,* 2d ed. (New York: Harper-Collins, 1995).

15. Susan G. Hadden, *A Citizen's Right to Know: Risk Communication and Public Policy* (Boulder: Westview, 1989), esp. chap. 2.

16. Sierra Club, "Scorecard," *Sierra* 72 (January-February 1987): 16-17.

17. Joseph A. Davis, "Environment/Energy," *1988 Congressional Quarterly Almanac* (Washington, D.C.: Congressional Quarterly Inc., 1989), 137.

18. For a fuller discussion of the gridlock over clean air and energy legislation, see Michael E. Kraft, "Environmental Gridlock: Searching for Consensus in Congress," in *Environmental Policy in the 1990s,* 2d ed., ed. Norman J. Vig and Michael E. Kraft (Washington, D.C.: CQ Press, 1994). See also Bryner, *Blue Skies, Green Politics,* and Cohen, *Washington at Work.*

19. Catalina Camia, "Legislators Draw in the Reins on Environmental Rules," *Congressional Quarterly Weekly Report,* April 30, 1994, 1060-1063.

20. Rhodes Cook, "Rare Combination of Forces May Make History of '94," *Congressional Quarterly Weekly Report,* April 15, 1995, 1076-1081.
21. Everett Carll Ladd, "The 1994 Congressional Elections: The Postindustrial Realignment Continues," *Political Science Quarterly* 110 (Spring 1995): 1-23; and Alfred J. Tuchfarber et al., "The Republican Tidal Wave of 1994: Testing Hypotheses about Realignment, Restructuring, and Rebellion," *PS: Political Science and Politics* 28 (December 1995): 689-696.
22. Gillespie and Bob Schellhas, eds., *Contract with America.*
23. Katharine Q. Seelye, "Files Show How Gingrich Laid a Grand G.O.P. Plan," *New York Times,* December 3, 1995, 1, 16.
24. Cited in Adam Clymer, "After Bad Week, Republicans Look to Budget for Rebound," *New York Times,* July 23, 1995, 1, 9.
25. Robin Toner, "G.O.P. Gets Mixed Reviews from Public Wary on Taxes," *New York Times,* April 6, 1995, 1, A12; and Ladd, "1994 Congressional Elections."
26. The poll results are summarized in the Sierra Club's *Planet* 2 (September 1995). For other polling data, see Benenson, "GOP Sets 104th Congress on New Regulatory Course."
27. John H. Cushman Jr., "G.O.P. Backing Off from Tough Stand over Environment," *New York Times,* January 26, 1996, 1, A8; and Margaret Kriz, "The Green Card," *National Journal,* September 19, 1995, 2262-2267.
28. For further details, see Benenson, "GOP Sets 104th Congress on New Regulatory Course"; and reports by the Natural Resources Defense Council: "Breach of Faith: How the Contract's Fine Print Undermines America's Environmental Success," February 1995, and "The Year of Living Dangerously: Congress and the Environment in 1995," December 1995.
29. David S. Cloud, "Industry, Politics Intertwined in Dole's Regulatory Bill," *Congressional Quarterly Weekly Report*, May 6, 1995, 12219-1224.
30. John H. Cushman Jr., "House Passes Bill That Would Limit Many Regulations," *New York Times,* March 4, 1995, 1, 8; Tom Kenworthy, "Letting the Truth Fall Where It May," *Washington Post National Weekly Edition,* March 27-April 2, 1995, 31; and Margaret Kriz, "Risky Business," *National Journal,* February 18, 1995.
31. Paul Portney, "Beware of the Killer Clauses Inside the GOP's 'Contract'," *Washington Post National Weekly Edition,* January 23-29, 1995, 21; and Bob Benenson, "House Easily Passes Bills to Limit Regulations," *Congressional Quarterly Weekly Report,* March 4, 1995, 679-682.
32. John H. Cushman Jr., "House G.O.P. Chiefs Back Off on Stiff Antiregulatory Plan," *New York Times,* March 6, 1996, C20; Cushman, "Businesses Scaling Back Plans to Defang Federal Regulations," *New York Times,* February 3, 1996, 1, 7; and Cushman, "Adversaries Back Pollution Rules Now on the Books," *New York Times,* February 12, 1996, C1-11.
33. Bob Herbert, "Health and Safety Wars," *New York Times,* July 10, 1995, A11.
34. John H. Cushman Jr., "G.O.P.'s Plan for Environment Is Facing a Big Test in Congress," *New York Times,* July 17, 1995, 1, A9.
35. John H. Cushman Jr., "Clause Would End an Agency's Veto on Wetland Plans," *New York Times,* December 12, 1995, 1, 15.
36. See Natural Resources Defense Council, "Stealth Attack: Gutting Environmental Protection through the Budget Process," July 1995; and Gary Lee, "The Green Counterattack," *Washington Post National Weekly Edition,* August 28-September 3, 1995, 15-16. On the poor media coverage in the first half of 1995, see Joe Davis, "The Scoop That Never Was," *Amicus Journal* 17 (Summer 1995): 18-22, and, for a broader review of environmental lobbying strategies, Michael Kraft and Diana L. Wuertz, "Environmental Advocacy in the Corridors of Government," in *The Symbolic Earth: Discourse and Our Creation of the Environment,* ed. James G. Cantrill and Christine Oravec (Lexington: University Press of Kentucky, 1996).
37. Jeffrey L. Katz, "House Revives EPA Restrictions before Passing VA-HUD Bill," *Congressional Quarterly Weekly Report,*" August 5, 1995, 2366-2369.

38. John H. Cushman Jr., "House Rejects Plan to Limit E.P.A.'s Power," *New York Times*, November 3, 1995, 1, A8; and Boehlert interview with *Greenwire*, October 30, 1995.
39. Quoted in Helen Dewar, "House Republicans Have a New Plan," *Washington Post National Weekly Edition*, January 22-28, 1996, 31.
40. Cushman, "G.O.P.'s Plan for Environment."
41. John H. Cushman Jr., "Budget Cuts Leave Environmental Agency Facing a Big Test in Congress," *New York Times*, July 17, 1995, and "Facing Layoffs," *New York Times*, December 24, 1995, 10; Bruce Babbitt, "If All the Trees in the Forest Fall," *Washington Post National Weekly Edition*, October 30-November 5, 1995, 29; and Margaret Kriz, "Land Wars," *National Journal*, September 2, 1995, 2146-2151.
42. League of Conservation Voters, "National Environmental Scorecard, 104th Congress, First Session" (Washington, D.C.: League of Conservation Voters, 1996).
43. Bob Benenson, "House Panel Votes to Restrict Endangered Species Act," *Congressional Quarterly Weekly Report*, October 14, 1995, 3136-3137; and Margaret Kriz, "Caught in the Act," *National Journal*, December 16, 1995, 3090-3094.
44. Margaret Kriz, "The Superfund Saga," *National Journal*, October 21, 1995, 2592-2596; Kriz, "Drinks All Around," *National Journal*, November 18, 1995, 2861-2864; Allan Freedman, "Drinking Water Bill Imperiled by House Delays, Divisions," *Congressional Quarterly Weekly Report*, April 6, 1996, 935-936; and Freedman, "Superfund Negotiators Hope for Bipartisan Compromise," *Congressional Quarterly Weekly Report*, April 20, 1996, 1040-1041.
45. See NAPA, *Setting Priorities;* Michael E. Kraft, *Environmental Policy and Politics* (New York: HarperCollins, 1996); and Gary Bryner, *Reforming the Environmental Laws* (Washington, D.C.: Georgetown University Press, forthcoming).
46. Newt Gingrich, *To Renew America* (New York: HarperCollins, 1995), 197. Gingrich stated the same philosophy in an Earth Day speech in April 1996, where he called for a "new environmentalism" that would achieve higher levels of protection more quickly than under current approaches. See John H. Cushman Jr., "Gingrich Calls for a 'New Environmentalism'," *New York Times*, April 25, 1996.
47. Quoted in *New York Times*, April 9, 1995, 12.
48. See Stephen Engelberg, "Business Leaves the Lobby and Sits at Congress's Table," *New York Times*, March 31, 1995, 1, A10.
49. Quoted in Kirk Victor, "Mr. Smooth," *National Journal*, July 8, 1995, 1758-1762.
50. Gore is quoted in *USA Today*, October 5, 1995, 6A; the league's statement is in its annual report, cited in n. 42.
51. Davis, "Scoop That Never Was."
52. See Margaret Kriz, "Not-So-Silent Spring," *National Journal*, March 9, 1996, 522-526.
53. Gingrich's statement is quoted in *Greenwire*, November 16, 1995, and DeLay's in *Greenwire*, December 18, 1995.
54. See Allan Freedman, "Republicans Concede Missteps in Effort to Rewrite Rules," *Congressional Quarterly Weekly Report*, December 2, 1995, 3645-3647; Freedman, "GOP Trying to Find Balance after Early Stumbles," *Congressional Quarterly Weekly Report*, January 20, 1996, 151-152; and Freedman, "Republicans Strive to Gain Environmental Advantage," *Congressional Quarterly Weekly Report*, May 18, 1996, 1384-1386.
55. Michael Wines, "Freshman Fervor Wanes as Election Time Nears," *New York Times*, March 24, 1996, 1, 15. See also Cushman, "G.O.P. Backing Off."
56. John H. Cushman Jr., "Proposed Changes Simplify Rules on Pollution Control," *New York Times*, March 17, 1995, A8; and John Carey, "The Regulators Rein Themselves In," *Business Week*, August 21, 1995, 61.
57. R. W. Apple Jr., "Polls Shows Disenchantment with Politicians and Politics," *New York Times*, August 12, 1995, 1, 8.
58. NAPA, *Setting Priorities*.

7

The EPA at Risk:
Conflicts over Institutional Reform

Walter A. Rosenbaum

The rate of environmental progress will slacken unless there are profound changes in the legal foundations and management structures of EPA, a continued devolution of responsibility for administering environmental problems, and a serious attempt to integrate programs to combat pollution.

—National Academy of Public Administration, 1995

A former administrator of the Environmental Protection Agency (EPA), asked to comment on the challenges of his job, replied that it was "like beating a train across a grade crossing—if you make it, it's a great rush. If you don't, you're dead."[1] By the mid 1990s, it seemed as if the EPA had finally raced one train too many. In the name of reform, the agency's traditional critics were pressing the most aggressive, potent attack in history on the EPA's existing statutory authority and organizational structure. Moreover, the EPA is vulnerable. Despite significant accomplishments, the agency often appears to regulate in slow motion, to labor unproductively, and to write too many costly and impractical regulations after more than twenty-five years as the nation's most important environmental regulator. Even the EPA's dependable advocates and allies, including the current occupants of the White House, concede that reforms are imperative.

Beyond this, however, acrimony reigns in discussions about the proper reforms and their impact on the agency. The evolving debate, now centered in Congress, appears certain to change the organization and programs of the EPA. The transcendent issue for the agency in the late 1990s is whether these reforms will reinvigorate its environmental programs or subvert them. This chapter examines five of the most significant proposals to emerge from the congressional debate. These proposals seek to require risk-based analysis for all newly proposed environmental regulations; to demand cost-benefit analysis for the same; to allow individuals or organizations to challenge the adequacy of these analyses; to increase the states' authority in implementing EPA regulations; and to gut the agency's operating budget. Both the merits and the liabilities of this agenda receive considerable attention because critics and proponents alike have persuasive arguments regarding such reforms. More important, the analyses illuminate a crucial danger: If applied wisely and selectively, many of these proposals may bring about an urgently needed improvement in the EPA's organization and structure. Adopted indiscriminately, however, such proposals could create an organizational catastrophe.

The Problem of Institutional Capability

The 1994 congressional elections are the proximate cause of the current national debate about the EPA's future. Yet the elections only brought to a boil a conflict that had been simmering for a decade. Ever since its creation in 1970, the EPA has struggled under very difficult circumstances to implement a multitude of complex environmental laws dealing with a daunting array of environmental ills. As early as the mid 1980s, the president's Council on Environmental Quality (CEQ) was already noting that "the Environmental Protection Agency cannot possibly do all the things its various mandates tell it to do."[2] By the early 1990s the National Commission on the Environment, a private sector policy panel including four former EPA administrators, was warning that "comprehensive reform is imperative to refocus the regulatory system on coherent policies that can . . . institute effective incentives for innovation and environmental change."[3] Until the mid 1990s, however, Congress—although increasingly aware of the agency's difficulties—seemed content with limited changes in the EPA's structure and relatively modest reforms in new environmental legislation.

Reform at the EPA was ordinarily cautious and piecemeal because the Democratic majority controlling Congress and its increasingly influential ally, the environmental movement, preferred it that way. Congressional Democrats and environmental organizations, with crucial support from the White House and many congressional Republicans, had promoted most of the major environmental laws enacted during the 1970s and 1980s and enforced by the EPA. Laws like the Clean Air Act and the Clean Water Act quickly became emblematic as "cornerstones" and "foundations" of the new environmental era, which began in the early 1970s. And the EPA itself, deficiencies notwithstanding, appeared to partisans of environmental regulation to be the most compelling bureaucratic symbol and expression of the new national commitment to environmental protection. But the EPA's congressional guardians had created a paradoxical protectorate. In its well-intentioned determination to protect the agency and its programs from unfriendly reform at the hands of the Reagan and Bush administrations, the congressional majority increasingly resorted to legislative strategies that severely diminished the EPA's administrative capability.

A Rising Regulatory Burden

Congressional experience during the Reagan and Bush administrations had convinced the EPA's legislative guardians that a hostile White

House could delay or frustrate the implementation of the law by administrative obstruction. This experience, compounded by historical institutional rivalries, convinced the agency's legislative supporters that administrative obstruction could be frustrated by drastically curtailing opportunities for administrative discretion in implementing environmental laws. Thus, the cordon Congress erected around the EPA was anchored by a multitude of extremely detailed, rigid requirements for implementation written into all new environmental legislation specifically to compel strict and predictable administrative compliance. This legislative micromanagement, concluded the National Academy of Public Administration (NAPA) in a sweeping review of EPA history, left the agency "hobbled by overly prescriptive statutes that pull the agency in too many directions and permit managers too little discretion to make wise decisions."[4] Moreover, Congress continually compounded the EPA's administrative tasks by crafting complex, highly ambitious new regulatory responsibilities for it. Between 1980 and 1994, for example, eight new regulatory programs or major amendments to existing ones were enacted, including Superfund, the Safe Drinking Water Act of 1986, the Superfund Amendments and Reauthorization Act of 1986 (SARA), and the Clean Air Act Amendments of 1990. The 1990 amendments to the Clean Air Act, for instance, required the EPA to hire two hundred new employees and to write fifty-five major new regulations within two years—an impossible task.[5] This continually lengthening list of regulatory tasks also meant an increasing volume of new rules and regulations sure to impose new compliance costs on regulated interests, to incite new litigation, and to incense further the critics of existing regulatory programs. At the same time, the agency's administrative resources seemed increasingly constrained in light of its rapidly mounting regulatory tasks. Between 1980 and 1994, for example, the EPA staff had grown by less than 25 percent and its operating budget in constant dollars by less than 10 percent.[6] This growing disparity between the EPA's responsibilities and its resources made its regulatory goals increasingly problematic.

Disconcerting Results

In chapter 1 we saw that the EPA could still claim some important accomplishments despite its burgeoning regulatory agenda and constrained resources. By the mid 1990s, ambient air levels for the six major pollutants regulated by the Clean Air Act (1970) had decreased significantly, including a dramatic decline by almost 90 percent in airborne lead. Despite the nation's substantial economic growth since the mid 1980s, surface water quality appeared to remain constant and even to improve in some major river basins such as the Potomac and the Ohio. Almost three hundred of the nation's worst toxic waste dumps, the Superfund priority sites, had been cleaned up. Numerous initiatives were under way to achieve the increased waste recycling and materials conservation required by the Resource Conservation and Recovery Act.[7]

But the luster dims when the agency's entire regulatory performance is considered. Ground-level ozone and nitrogen oxide, for example, remain major urban air problems throughout the United States. The source of almost two-thirds of the volume of pollutants in the nation's streams and rivers—nonpoint pollution, including pesticide runoff from crops, contaminants from mining, and landfill leakage—have yet to be substantially controlled. Full restoration work is yet to come for the approximately twelve hundred toxic waste sites on the Superfund Priority List.[8] Few EPA programs dependably produce attractive headlines, and bad news always seems only an official report away. In 1994, for instance, after reviewing the implementation of recent amendments to the Clean Air Act and the decades-old mandates in the Toxic Substances Control Act, the General Accounting Office (GAO) reported bleakly:

> EPA's program for more stringent testing of vehicle emissions, required by the Clean Air Act Amendments of 1990, might not achieve the desired levels because of "uncertainties regarding the diagnosis and repair of failed vehicles and a lack of information on the behavioral consequences of motorists to perceived higher costs and greater inconvenience."[9]

> EPA had been able to issue regulations required by the Toxic Substances Control Act for only nine chemicals in 17 years although thousands of chemicals were eligible for regulation.[10]

> EPA was likely to have difficulty in developing toxic emission standards and implementing the Acid Rain Program in the Clean Air Amendments of 1990 due to budget restrictions.[11]

Additionally, the EPA's programs were becoming increasingly expensive. Authorization for the Superfund program, initially set at about $1.6 billion in 1980, had risen to $15.2 billion in the early 1990s, and EPA estimates suggested an additional $26.4 billion would be necessary for its completion.[12] The EPA's waste treatment grants to the states for improving municipal waste treatment facilities were originally authorized in the early 1970s at $18 billion but had costs in excess of $22 billion by the mid 1990s. Many factors accounted for sharply rising regulatory costs, and many programs were not grossly over budget. Additionally, cost estimates took no account of program benefits. Nonetheless, the EPA's program costs *seemed* to rise relentlessly, and, in politics, appearances often matter as much as realities.

In short, by the mid 1990s the EPA was working in a highly volatile political climate resulting from enormous difficulties inherent in its mission, sluggish adaption in the face of its challenging programs, mounting dissatisfaction with its performance from traditional critics and political allies, and a massively expensive regulatory agenda crowded with mandates to eliminate or ameliorate a host of scientifically, economically, and politically complex environmental problems. And always there was an image problem. The 1994 congressional elections catalyzed these ingredients into a searching and impassioned debate about the EPA's future.

The New Reform Agenda: Agency "Shaking" or Subversion?

The stunning Republican victories in the 1994 elections transformed the political setting of environmental regulation overnight. Republicans, who now controlled both congressional chambers, claimed an electoral mandate for regulatory reform and aimed much of their attack squarely at the EPA. The Republican onslaught threw supporters of existing arrangements on the defensive and gave longtime critics a prime opportunity to advertise the EPA's failures and to suggest their own reforms.

The Republican Agenda

"This is an agency that needs some serious shaking," declared Rep. Jerry R. Lewis (R-Calif.), the new chairman of the House appropriations committee with jurisdiction over the EPA. "Clearly, it is . . . not functioning very well in terms of its responsibilities." The "shaking" Lewis and his Republican colleagues prescribed came in the form of thoroughgoing reform.[13] Those reforms, whose enactment would have fundamentally redesigned the agency's organization and programs, can be gleaned from two specific bills, H.R. 9 and H.R. 1024, and from subsequent Republican budget bills introduced in the 104th Congress. Promoted primarily by Republicans, these initial House proposals were subsequently revised to satisfy the more moderate Republican leadership in the Senate. They remain unapproved in both chambers. Nonetheless, the various legislative versions of the Republican reform agenda commonly include these core proposals:

1. All agencies proposing regulations to protect public health, safety, and the environment would be required to base such regulations on a detailed scientific assessment of how effectively the rules would reduce risks to the public. These risk assessments would also be reviewed by a panel of experts (including industry representatives) and be subject to judicial review as well.
2. Agencies proposing regulations related to health and environmental protection must also perform a cost-benefit analysis on other proposals (including the alternative of not regulating) and certify that the costs of compliance with the proposed regulation were justified by the anticipated benefits. The cost-benefit analysis could, in many cases, supersede existing health-based standards currently required by many laws as the criteria for enacting regulations.
3. Individuals or organizations must have the opportunity to challenge existing regulations and regulatory programs if they did not meet the risk assessment and cost-benefit standards that would be required of all environmental and health regulations under the new standards.
4. State authority to interpret and enforce federal environmental regulations must be strengthened and the EPA's authority to override state interpretations must be reduced. This "devolution" of authority to the states was often accompanied by provisions to greatly reduce

the number of environmental regulations the states are required to enforce at their own expense.

5. The EPA's budget for collecting health, safety and environmental data and for monitoring environmental quality and compliance with environmental regulations should be drastically cut.

Republican congressional leaders predicted enormous benefit from the reform agenda. It would, claimed Senate Majority Leader Robert Dole (R-Kan.), banish "unnecessary and overburdensome regulations."[14] Republican Speaker of the House Newt Gingrich (R-Ga.) asserted that the reforms would rid the EPA of programs and practices that had become "absurdly expensive, creating far more resistance than was necessary and [misallocating] resources on emotional and public relations grounds without regard to either scientific, engineering, or economic rationality."[15]

The Environmentalist Counterattack

Environmentalists and their congressional allies charged that the new agenda amounted to regulatory subversion. The late senator Edmund S. Muskie (D-Maine), a congressional leader in creating the Clean Air Act of 1970, predicted the Republican agenda "would halt twenty-five years of accomplishment and turn the clock back to the days when special interests made the rules and the people absorbed the risks."[16] The Natural Resources Defense Council, an organization representing mainstream environmental groups, asserted that the new proposals would "dismantle the legal structure" supporting current environmental regulation or render "efforts to carry them out exceptionally difficult, if not impossible."[17] EPA administrator Carol Browner warned: "This legislation is not reform, it is a full frontal assault on protecting public health and the environment."[18]

The ensuing debate elicited reform proposals from many points on the political compass besides the Republican party—including the White House—where a conviction existed that reform was imperative. Predictably, Republican proposals were most aggressively supported by many other ideologically conservative social, economic, and political interests long disaffected with the EPA and the laws it administered. However, Vice President Albert Gore, an environmentalist of impeccable credentials, also released in March 1995 the results of a special report on "Reinventing Environmental Regulation," which asserted it was "time to draw upon the lessons we have learned over the last 25 years to reinvent environmental protection in the 21st century." It proposed "a new management system" that "would build upon the strengths of the current system, while overcoming its limitations, . . . [and] reform the system, not undermine it."[19] In August of that year, President Clinton announced a new directive to the EPA and other federal regulatory agencies "to conduct a comprehensive review of . . . rules to identify obsolete and burdensome regulations, then eliminate or revise them." The president's directive conceded some credibility to the EPA's critics:

Without stripping away regulations that protect and improve people's lives, we have shown . . . that it is possible to reform the regulatory system, so that it's less intrusive and more responsive to the American people. . . . By eliminating and streamlining unnecessary, burdensome, and duplicative regulations, the federal government saves money and meddles less in the lives of citizens.[20]

The Republican agenda had in fact targeted genuine, serious problems in the EPA's structure and statutory program even if the GOP's proposed solutions were wildly controversial.

Improving the EPA: Evaluating the Reforms

The most important issue in the EPA debate is which reforms are essential—that is, which address the most compelling problems in a constructive manner—and which (deliberately or not) are no more than an attack on the agency and its programs. The congressional debates vented a torrent of self-serving partisan rhetoric that seldom provided sound analysis. Fortunately, many thoughtful, disinterested studies have provided useful criteria for evaluating the reform proposals and, in the process, have illuminated much about the EPA's style of operation and its history. To begin, any approach to prescribing and evaluating reform implies a standard of judgment: what must the EPA be, and what must it achieve, if it is to be an effective environmental regulator? Five of the most commonly cited standards provide a practical framework for evaluating the proposed reforms. An effective regulatory program should include an explicit and coherent agency mission statement; administrative resources sufficient for the mission; an appropriate organizational structure; feasible programs; and dependable congressional support.

The Need for an Explicit and Coherent Mission Statement

The effective operation of the EPA requires a clear, consistent definition of its purpose and priorities. But the most fundamental reform, a legislative charter, is still the least mentioned in congressional debate. A legislative charter, or an administrative declaration clearly defining its goals and priories, would give the EPA "a well-defined, coherent statutory mission and the flexibility to carry it out." The National Academy of Public Administration in its thorough study of the agency's performance concluded that a statutory mission would provide the EPA with a "clear and consistent direction."[21] Such an institutional definition, common to most other major federal agencies, is a powerful administrative asset for establishing politically and judicially defensible program priorities and for deciding how limited resources must be administratively reallocated. A statutory charter is especially important for administrators in the American political system, dominated by shifting and often highly transient policy coalitions. Shifting legislative and presidential majorities; highly pluralistic, competitive and assertive organized interests; and public institutions acutely sensitive to public opinion all breed a volatile political milieu. Agencies with policy agendas and associated programs unprotected by the stabilizing, conservative influence of charters or other organic laws are especially vulnerable to the disruption of planning, the sudden shifts of political pressure and discontinuity of policy priorities created by short-term changes in public opinion, legislative majorities, or presidential agendas.

Congress has been understandably wary about writing an EPA charter. It would incite a politically nasty bloodletting across the environmental policy spectrum concerning which environmental issues and interests should have priority. It might create opportunities for reconsidering, perhaps for rewriting, long and complex laws originally created only after prolonged, politically costly battles sure to be resurrected by new reforms. In the absence of a mission statement, however, congressional denunciations of the EPA's program mismanagement often seem like Looking-Glass logic that confounds cause and effect, holding the agency responsible for administrative sins arising from congressional failure to define its priorities. Nonetheless, Congress appears powerfully indisposed to forsake its enormous sunk costs in the existing arrangement of the EPA's statutory agenda, however incoherent it may be.

And incoherent it is. The NAPA study, like many others, explains the situation largely in congressional terms:

> The EPA lacks focus, in part, because Congress has passed more than a dozen environmental statutes that drive the agency in a dozen directions, discouraging rational priority-setting or a coherent approach to environmental management. The EPA is sometimes ineffective because, in part, Congress has set impossible deadlines and unrealistic expectations, given the Agency's budget. The EPA can be inefficient, in part, because Congress has attempted to micro-manage the agency through prescriptive legislation, earmarked appropriations, and direct pressure.[22]

As things now stand, the agency is wholly or largely responsible for the implementation of twelve major statutes (see table 7-1) without any guidance on how to establish priorities among major programs or within them when they compete for scarce resources or administrative attention. These statutory activities cover an enormous range of ecological domain, technical or scientific expertise, regulatory activity, and geographic space. Still, the range and diversity of the EPA's competing responsibilities are vastly underestimated in table 7-1 because it does not include major amendments to these statutes. The Clean Air Act Amendments of 1990, for example, consisted of eight hundred pages of fine statutory print (the original act was only fifty pages long) that created more than fifty new programs for the agency. Nor does this list hint at the multitudinous laws administered by other agencies that require EPA participation. The Federal Food, Drug, and Cosmetics Act, for instance, is administered by the Food and Drug Administration (FDA) but authorizes the EPA to establish tolerance levels for pesticide residues on food and food products.

Table 7-1 Major Environmental Laws Administered by the EPA

A dozen major statutes form the legal basis for the programs of the EPA:

The **Pollution Prevention Act** seeks to prevent pollution through reduced generation of pollutants at their point of origin.

The **Clean Air Act** requires the EPA to set mobile-source limits, ambient air quality standards, hazardous air pollutant emission standards, standards for new pollution sources, and significant deterioration requirements and to focus on areas which do not attain standards.

The **Clean Water Act** establishes the sewage treatment construction grants program and a regulatory and enforcement program for discharges of wastes into U.S. waters. Focusing on the regulation of the intentional disposal of materials into ocean waters and authorizing related research is the **Ocean Dumping Act**.

The **Safe Drinking Water Act** establishes primary drinking water standards, regulates underground injection disposal practices, and establishes a groundwater control program.

The **Solid Waste Disposal Act** and the **Resource Conservation and Recovery Act** authorize regulation of solid and hazardous waste, while the **Comprehensive Environmental Response, Compensation, and Liability Act**, known as CERCLA or Superfund, establishes a fee-maintained fund to clean up abandoned hazardous waste sites.

The **Emergency Planning and Community Right-to-Know Act** requires reporting of toxic releases and encourages response for chemical releases.

The **Toxic Substances Control Act** regulates the testing of chemicals and their use, and the **Federal Insecticide, Fungicide, and Rodenticide Act** governs pesticide products and their use.

The **National Environmental Policy Act** requires, in part, the EPA to review environmental impact statements.

Source: Adapted from National Academy of Public Administration, *Setting Priorities, Getting Results* (Washington, D.C.: NAPA, 1995), 182.

In the absence of a statutory charter, the EPA must create priorities according to whatever programs have the largest budgets and most demanding deadlines, or attract the most politically potent constituencies or excite congressional attention.[23] Priorities can suddenly shift when Congress, the White House, or the public respond to a new environmental crisis that seemingly requires immediate attention—the oft-criticized "pollutant of the month" phenomenon. This happened in the latter 1970s, for example, when widely publicized discoveries of abandoned toxic wastes sites across the United States thrust Love Canal into the public vocabulary and convinced Congress to enact the Superfund program that required the EPA to suddenly rearrange its existing programs to accommodate the daunting, hugely complex administrative tasks inherent to the new legislation. Existing programs may be debilitated through budget constraints even though they claim statutory priority, as happened to the chemical testing program mandated by the Toxic Substances Control Act.[24] In the next section we shall consider persuasive arguments that the EPA's regulatory responsibilities could be set by more rational means such as comparative risk assessment, or cost-benefit analysis, or some combination of these. In the absence of a more deliberative approach, however, the EPA's existing priorities now appear to be dictated by tradition, political expediency, or accident.

The Need for Sufficient Administrative Resources

No domain of federal policymaking requires a greater diversity of technical information and professional skills than environmental regulation. Environmental policymaking, in particular, requires a great deal of scientific and administrative support. Among the most crucial scientific resources are technical information and a research and development program that meets the scientific requirements of policymaking. Administrative staff must be adequate in number and professional skills. The administrative budget must be allocated appropriately for the agency's mission. Administrators must have the freedom to be flexible and innovative when carrying out mandated programs. Additionally, monitoring and enforcement are essential if regulatory standards are to be credible.

The Battle of the Budget. No reform on the congressional agenda in the mid 1990s is likely to shake the EPA more severely or perniciously than proposals for massive cutbacks in the agency's budget. Budgets are policies written in decimals and dollar signs. Republican reforms in 1995 frequently proposed cutbacks exceeding 20 percent of the EPA budget, which would almost certainly mean extensive policy retrenchments. These budget eviscerations have been justified by claims that the EPA can do its job better on a much leaner budget, or by assertions that reduced budgets will eliminate "unnecessary" programs. The EPA could greatly improve its internal management practices and thereby produce gains in productivity and some modest administrative cost reduction. But unless Congress means to divest the EPA of its major statutory programs—an unlikely event—the agency cannot withstand budget cuts exceeding 10 percent without a sharp decline in its performance. In this respect, the most damaging budgetary reforms are not so much those that reduce grants to the states for specific activities (such as the Superfund cleanup of toxic waste sites) but those that deplete the basic administrative resources needed for all programs.

And the proposed budget reforms in the 104th Congress do strike hard at resources essential to effective policy implementation across many different programs. The agency's enforcement staff and its support services have been a favorite target, with proposals reaching as high as a 50 percent budget decrease in a single fiscal year.[25] Another popular target has been the technical foundations for regulatory programs: the agency's environmental monitoring, data collection, and data analysis. These programs, barren of political "sex appeal," inconspicuous, and seldom understood, are vulnerable to the budgetary axe because they lack a powerful political constituency. Yet the EPA cannot create or defend risk assessments and sustain enforcement programs and other administrative actions essential to environmental protection without reliable technical data. In the early 1990s, for instance, only three of EPA's twenty-three major programs were appropriately monitored with adequate indicators. Other proposals in 1995 called for a very substantial across-the-board budget decrease for all programs, in some variations approaching 30 percent of the EPA's current budget. Such a budgetary broadaxe would appear insensible to differences in program needs, quality, or performance. Still other proposals targeted the EPA's research and development (R&D) activities through which, among other things, the agency attempts to carry out the research essential to supporting its regulatory programs. Congressional Republicans proposed to reduce the existing R&D budget of $364 million by 10 to 30 percent.

Even an apparently small budget reduction, if placed strategically, can debilitate a major program. For example, in FY 1994 Congress reduced the EPA's overall budget for air quality by a relatively small 6 percent. But this resulted in a 51 percent loss in funds for reducing toxic air emissions and a 31 percent decline in the Acid Rain Program because the agency could not spread the reductions across all air quality programs and was forced, instead, to shrink those programs unprotected by other budgetary mandates. According to the GAO, these reductions "will contribute to the agency's missing some important deadlines established by the Clean Air Act Amendments of 1990" and "have contributed to EPA's postponing the development of some rules mandated by the Clean Air Act." [26] Also, budget reductions of a magnitude exceeding 10 percent will almost certainly mean a significant loss of employees. Even in comparatively good times, Congress has been criticized by many experts for creating "impossible deadlines and unrealistic expectations, given the agency's budget." [27] Major staff reductions unaccompanied by a relaxation of the imperious deadlines and other demanding conditions common to most of the laws the EPA administers is an assurance of continuing failures in program implementation.

If the EPA's budget must be cut, the most desirable reductions would target programs that are excessively expensive. The reforms should also achieve savings without impairing the EPA's ability to enforce needed regulation. The Superfund program and the federal waste treatment grant program together account for more than 60 percent of EPA's total budget. Both programs have been criticized by both friend and foe for excessive cost, waste, and delay in implementation. [28] Significant budget reductions seem possible in both programs without inflicting a costly loss in EPA staff and other administrative resources. Additional transfers to the states of administrative responsibility for other programs would also appear to achieve important savings without severe administrative losses to the agency. In short, if there must be budget reductions, then selective budget cutbacks that avoid indiscriminate cuts in all EPA programs, or refrain from inflicting severe losses in essential administrative services, make sense.

Overcoming Media-Based Organization. Desirable changes in the EPA's media-based organizational structure, like the agency's mission statement, have been virtually ignored by congressional reformers for political reasons. The issues are technical, complex, and unfamiliar to most legislators. No eminent crisis attends the matter. The case for reform is not easily packaged politically or publicly to attract widespread concern. Nonetheless, many informed observers, including many partisans of the EPA and its mission, believe the agency's performance could be significantly improved if its media-based organizational structures were redesigned to encourage more integrated pollution control. [29]

Today, the EPA's most important operational units are, as they have been since the agency's inception, its program offices—often called media offices. These offices are committed to controlling pollution in a specific medium such as air and water, or to dealing with a specific form of pollution such as pesticides or toxics (see fig. 7-1). Each office lives with its own statutory support system: legislatively mandated programs, deadlines, criteria for decisions, and, usually, a steel grip on large portions of its office budget to which it is entitled by the laws it enforces. Thus, the Office of Solid Waste and Emergency Response administers the massive Superfund program, follows the mandated statutory procedures and deadlines of the law, and, in FY 1994, claimed $1.56 billion of the EPA's budget earmarked for toxic waste site cleanup. Each of the offices is populated by a variety of professionals: engineers, scientists, statisticians, economists, professional planners, managers, lawyers, and mathematicians. "Along with their expertise," observes Thomas McGarity, "comes an entire professional [worldview] that incorporates attitudes and biases ranging far beyond the specialized knowledge of particular facts"—viewpoints shaped by the specific mission of their program office and focused on that mission's tasks. [30] This tenacious, media-based design appeals to Congress, environmentalists, pollution control professionals, and many other influential interests, albeit for different reasons. Each media office, in effect, has its own political and professional constituency. Most important, any proposal to change the EPA's organizational design incites apprehension about possible damage to existing programs and raises the specter of a bitter political battle over the alternatives.

Nonetheless, persuasive arguments have been made for a more integrated organizational approach to pollution management. [31] Stated briefly, proponents of reform believe (1) pollution problems are often more efficiently and effectively managed by comprehensive strategies involving coordinate plans across several media; (2) different pollution laws, each entrusted to a separate bureaucracy, often result in inconsistent, even contradictory approaches to managing the same pollutant; (3) different media offices with programs driven by mandated budgets frustrate coordinated pollution management; and (4) integrated pollution management would be more economically efficient. For example, chemical pesticides are currently regulated by different standards depending on where they are found—food, surface water, drinking water, or underground water—and different control technologies are required in each medium. This situation arises because chemical pesticides are regulated under the Food and Drug Act, the Toxic Substances Control Act, the Clean Water Act, the Safe Drinking Water Act, and the Resource Conservation and Recovery Act—each entrusted to a different EPA media office or subunit. An integrated

Figure 7-1 Organizational Chart of the EPA

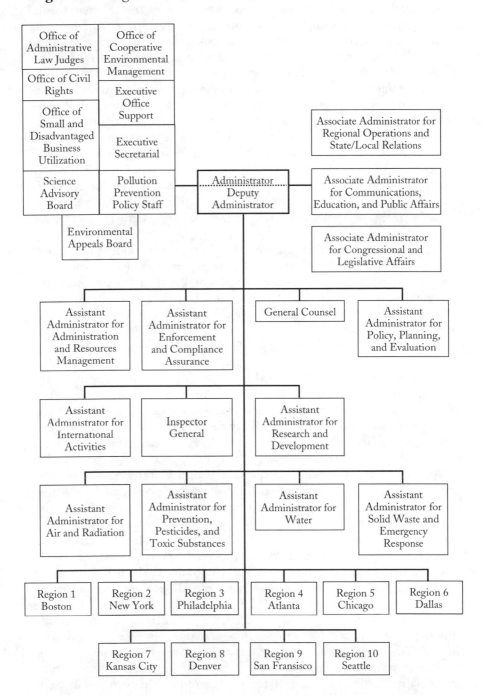

Source: U.S. EPA, Office of Administration and Resources Management; National Academy of Public Administration, *Setting Priorities, Getting Results* (Washington, D.C.: NAPA, 1995), 17.

approach might involve a single standard for regulation in many different media, together with a coordinated approach to control across different media, to be implemented by a single program office. Such an approach might create a greater total reduction in risk of human exposure to a carcinogenic chemical than would be the case if the same chemical were regulated by many different offices according to many different statutory standards.

Achieving more integrated pollution management requires major alterations in many current environmental laws as well as fundamental changes in the EPA's organizational design. Recent EPA administrators have themselves encouraged such reform through initiatives using their own limited authority to make such changes. Thus, administrator Carol Browner, appointed by President Clinton in 1993, attempted to promote collaboration among media offices by organizing senior officials into "leadership teams" to coordinate pollution management between different media programs. Achieving integrated pollution management must necessarily be gradual and somewhat experimental.

Congress could facilitate integrated pollution management by amending the Clean Air and the Clean Water Acts to permit the EPA greater flexibility in coordinating pollution management between its air and water programs and by permitting EPA administrators greater flexibility in budgeting. All these approaches, however, require Congress to educate itself about the importance of such reform and to accept its inevitable political risks and uncertainties. In the mid 1990s Congress appears reluctant to consider such reform.

A Greater Role for the States? Much more attractive to Congress is the devolution of authority to the states in environmental regulation. Almost all federal environmental laws are implemented and enforced through the states after they have demonstrated their ability to carry out these responsibilities. Federal environmental laws require the EPA to delegate considerable responsibility to the states for twenty-four major regulatory programs, but the agency remains responsible for the administrative oversight of these state activities, for issuing rules and guidance to the states concerning how they must administer these programs, and for providing assistance in these activities. This important, and still expanding, role of the states in environmental policy implementation is discussed in considerable detail in chapter 2. Suffice it to note here that the EPA provides on the average about 20 percent of total state funding for such important programs as air quality, drinking water, hazardous waste, and pesticide control. Altogether, these operating program grants to the states exceeded $600 million in FY 1995.[32] Over the past several decades, the states have shown an increased technical and administrative capacity for implementing environmental regulations (see chap. 2). They have also grown more restive under what many consider to be the excessively rigid, numerous, and intrusive EPA rules dictating their interpretation and application of federal environmental regulations. State pressure for greater authority and autonomy in implementing federal environmental law during the early 1980s led to the Reagan administration's unsuccessful proposal for a "new federalism," rejected largely because it seemed a highly partisan, covert effort to subvert major environmental laws. By the mid 1990s proposals to enlarge the state's role in environmental regulation attracted a much broader political constituency because events in the intervening years demonstrated to all sides the need for greater reform in regulatory federalism.

Proposals to increase the states' ability to interpret and to implement federal environmental regulations seem most appropriate when they advance the environmental goals created by federal law. There is little doubt that the EPA's state oversight could be relaxed and the states given more authority in implementing federal laws if the states are provided incentives to achieve mandated environmental goals and if federal program support is not severely reduced to the point where, in effect, the states are asked to do more work for less pay.

The Need for Feasible Policies

Successful environmental regulation requires that those who make policy and those who implement it "must discern and respect the limits of policy choice imposed by the available engineering, scientific, and managerial understanding."[33] In short, policies should be technically, administratively and politically feasible. And policies should be appropriate to the problems or issues to which they are addressed, which means respecting both the strength and limitations of particular policy approaches. By this standard, reform is overdue, particularly because two of the most frequently proposed reforms—risk-based regulation and greater use of cost-benefit analysis—are both familiar and feasible policy approaches when their limitations are respected. Risk analysis and cost-benefit analysis are extensively examined in chapters 9 and 10, respectively. The discussion here will focus primarily upon their specific implications for the EPA.

Needed: Greater Use of Risk Analysis in Policymaking. With the exception of the Clean Air Act and the Federal Food, Drug, and Cosmetic Act, none of the laws currently administered by the EPA permit the agency to base decisions about what to regulate, or how to do it, entirely on the basis of the human health risks posed by a hazard or the risks averted by using a particular control strategy. The agency is usually required to compare, or balance, health risks with such other factors as economic costs and benefits, technological feasibility, time involved in implementation, and much else when deciding its regulatory agenda.[34] Since the mid 1980s numerous studies and many policy experts, including several EPA administrators, have asserted that Congress and the EPA should, whenever feasible, base decisions about regulatory priorities and strategies on some form of "comparative risk assessment." Republican proposals in the 104th Congress, however, routinely *required* that risk assessment be utilized in *all* EPA's regulatory decisionmaking. Generally, proponents of reform—including many environmental organizations and leaders—have made the most persuasive argument for greater, but not mandatory, use of these important policy tools.

Most proposals involving risk assessment, such as the Republican reforms, in reality advocate some form of *comparative* risk assessment. Comparative risk assessment is deceptively simple in principle. The first phase, described by a recent Carnegie Commission report, is "essentially the process of deciding how dangerous a substance is." A series of procedures is undertaken "to identify and qualitatively describe the hazard to be assessed, . . . the level of exposure to the hazardous entity, [and] the response of organisms in question . . . to different dose levels. Finally, the above information is combined to characterize the risk quantitatively." [35] Thus, a hazardous facility (such as an abandoned radioactive waste site) or a substance (such as a chemical) is characterized according to the risk of adverse effects it poses to humans or to the environment. This risk might be expressed, for instance, in terms of increased likelihood of cancer in humans after exposure. "Using risk as a common denominator," asserts former EPA administrator William K. Reilly, "creates a measurement that lets us distinguish the environmental equivalents of heart attacks and indigestion, the broken bones from bruises, . . . thus targeting our limited resources and . . . mobilizing and deploying experience in an efficient and rational way." [36]

Once risk assessments are made for individual hazards, then a *comparative* risk assessment may be created, which ranks different hazards according to their magnitudes of risk. It is this ability to rank that especially appeals to regulatory reformers. It would appear to provide a scientifically defensible, intuitively appealing administrative metric whereby priorities may be assigned to different pollutants according to their estimated risks. It thus aids in deciding how to allocate regulatory budgets, staff, and other scarce resources. Comparative risk assessment might also prove useful in determining which policy best regulates a hazard by suggesting which one achieves the greatest risk reduction. Comparative risk would seem to point a way out of the morass of multiplying health and environmental laws that have piled regulatory burdens on the EPA, as well as state and local governments, without priorities or coherence. "For twenty years we have established goals on a pollutant-by-pollutant basis," argues former EPA administrator William K. Reilly. "Rarely have we evaluated the relative importance of pollutants or environmental media—air, land, and water. . . . We have seldom if ever been directed by law to seek out the best opportunities to reduce risks, in toto." [37] Many experts also believe comparative risk assessment might buffer the EPA against potent, but often misinformed, public preferences about regulatory goals because, as Jonathan Lash, a member of the EPA Science Advisory Board, observes: "public perceptions about the environment are based on a haphazard combination of good and bad information, well-learned fear, outrage, and skepticism, . . . not a proper mindset for setting a rational regulatory agenda." [38]

Unfortunately, comparative risk assessment is also seriously flawed by methodological and data deficiencies widely recognized by risk assessment practitioners, if not always by enthusiasts for risk-based regulation. Thus, many experts believe that while the EPA can use risk assessment widely, it must still be used selectively, as an important but not compulsory component of policymaking.[39]

A more useful approach to enlarging risk assessment in EPA's policy-making appears to be a synthesis of proposals found in legislation proposed by Sen. J. Bennett Johnston (D-La.) in 1993, proposals included in some of the more moderate Republican reform proposals, and ideas offered by the NAPA study. The NAPA study suggested, in particular, two broad changes in EPA's regulatory policymaking:

> Congress should amend EPA's statutes to allow the administrator to consider a wide range of risk-related information when setting standards. . . . Congress should pass legislation establishing a regulatory review process that would ensure that the public has access to EPA's explanation of the risks posed by a problem, the risk-reduction potential of the regulation, and the broadly defined costs and benefits of the approach.[40]

This approach would strongly encourage, but not compel, the EPA to use risk assessment procedures routinely in making its regulatory decisions and to explain publicly the character of the decisions, thus illuminating the kinds of assumptions involved in the assessments, the range of choices, and the variety of information involved. It would also provide Congress with a richer information base about the nature of EPA regulatory decisions and perhaps stimulate more informed debate about the decisions. Perhaps most significantly, it would appear to encourage greater reliance on more rational criteria for making decisions about what to regulate and how to do it—provided Congress permits a reform strategy that liberates the EPA from more draconian, and probably ill-advised, mandates for risk assessment that will ultimately hobble, rather than advance, the regulatory process.

Needed: More Judicious Use of Cost-Benefit Analysis. Arguments for the use of cost-benefit analysis (CBA) in environmental policymaking are discussed in greater detail elsewhere in this volume (see chap. 9). Suffice it to note here that most critics of current environmental laws believe that cost-benefit analysis, in one or more of its many variations, should be used in virtually all decisions concerning what pollutants should be regulated and what management strategies should be adopted. More vigorous use of CBA techniques, argue its proponents, will introduce greater economic rationality into regulatory policies, thereby encouraging more efficiency, cost-effectiveness, and cost savings in regulatory programs. Environmentalists have traditionally opposed the routine use of cost-benefit analysis for environmental policymaking. They recognize that cost-benefit analysis may be attractive in principle, but they believe that in practice it too often distorts economic reality by exaggerating regulatory costs and underestimating or ignoring important environmental benefits—in short, that it is biased against vigorous environmental regulations. This categoric rejection of CBA may be softening as many environmental groups recognize that regulatory cost has become a compelling issue in almost all environmental domains.

Although cost-benefit analysis may be an appealing principle, the particular version promoted by congressional reformers in 1995 would likely have entailed some very undesirable, if not highly disruptive, consequences for the EPA. Reform measures that *require* cost-benefit analysis for all proposed environmental regulations and mandate that adopted regulations demonstrate benefits in excess of costs would drastically alter the use of cost-benefit analysis in federal environmental programs. No statutes currently require the EPA to base regulatory decisions exclusively, or primarily, on cost-benefit analysis. In fact, portions of several major laws, such as the Clean Air Act's provisions for setting ambient air pollution standards, are "cost oblivious" because they require the EPA to ignore costs and to consider only human health effects when setting environmental standards. More often, federal laws instruct the EPA to consider economic costs and benefits together with many other criteria in making decisions—a so-called balancing approach. The Toxics Substances Control Act (TSCA), for instance, requires the EPA to consider a daunting variety of other criteria besides economic factors in deciding whether the risks from exposure to a substance are "unreasonable," including "type of effect (chronic or acute, reversible or irreversible); degree of risk; characteristics and number of humans, plants and animals, or ecosystems at risk; amount of knowledge about effects; available or alternative substances and their expected effects . . . and appropriateness and effectiveness of TSCA as a legal instrument for controlling the risk."[41]

Some laws, such as the Resource Conservation and Recovery Act (RCRA), do not explicitly require regulators to perform any kind of cost-benefit analysis in making their decisions. Both the Reagan and Bush administrations did enforce President Reagan's Executive Order 12291 requiring the EPA, and all other federal agencies, to perform a "regulatory impact analysis" (RIA) on all proposed major regulations in which benefits and costs were compared and to submit the RIAs to review by the White House's Office of Management and Budget (OMB). However, this mandate did not apply to any legislation, like the Clean Air Act, which prohibited the use of CBA. Moreover, agencies were not compelled to use CBA as the sole, or most important, criterion for their regulatory decisions, and agencies often chose to ignore the CBA analysis once it was performed.

Most proponents of CBA, including most economists and even a significant number of environmentalist leaders, would probably agree that cost-benefit analysis can improve EPA policymaking if it were one criterion to be used when writing environmental regulations. But few would endorse its use in all cases or mandate that regulations be promulgated only if they demonstrate net benefits. The reason for this restraint is a realistic appreciation of limitations inherent to all CBA.[42] Cost-benefit analysis often exaggerates regulatory costs and underestimates benefits because it is often impossible to monetize the benefits of many environmental regulations, such as improved public health over many decades or the preservation of pristine air and water in a national park or the protection of an irreplaceable old-growth forest. Some benefits may be incalculable, such as the value of a human life. The credibility of many cost-benefit analyses performed by federal agencies has also been compromised by evidence that data are sometimes very unreliable, or that they have been "cooked" (deliberately misrepresented) by regulators.

EPA officials, like other federal regulators, are often uncomfortable with their own CBA because they suspect their data will not withstand judicial scrutiny. Not surprisingly, some studies suggest that other federal regulatory agencies required to perform CBA under the Reagan and Bush administrations preferred to rely on other criteria for decisions.[43] In recent years, additionally, a growing number of economists have joined environmentalists in asserting that cost-benefit analysis cannot take account of *ecological* costs and benefits involved in regulation.[44] For example, CBA traditionally cannot value a whole ecosystem, or specific flora and fauna, or the habitat of specific species in order to determine not only the benefits of their existence but also the costs implied by their destruction. This growing sensitivity to the importance of environmental valuation has developed alongside rising apprehension among natural scientists about the rate of species and habit destruction among global ecosystems.

Like risk assessment, cost-benefit analysis would seem most valuable to regulatory decisionmaking when used in situations where appropriate data exist to justify its application and when the limitations inherent to the analysis are understood and clearly explained to the relevant public officials. It would seem unwise, however, to *require* the application of CBA to every significant EPA regulatory decision and more reckless to require that regulatory policies be "justified" by cost-benefit analysis. Such requirements would, at the least, frequently compel the EPA to fabricate CBA from dubious data when more credible information is lacking, and to make important regulatory decisions often on the basis of insufficient information. It would also guarantee an avalanche of new litigation, with all the costs and delays involved, as litigants on all sides challenge the reliability of the data. Additionally, environmental policies almost always involve a trade-off between economic efficiency and such other considerations as fairness, public health and safety, or timely response to problems. An attractive CBA ratio cannot be the sole criterion for policy selection, although agencies can strive to make cost reduction a continuing criterion for policy implementation.

A more productive approach, in any case, has already been initiated. In September 1993, President Clinton signed Executive Order 12866, more fully discussed in chapter 5, which encourages but does not require cost-benefit analysis in regulatory decisionmaking, recognizes that benefits and costs may include nontangible considerations, and insists that agencies like the EPA "should" maximize "net benefits" that need not be monetized.[45]

The Need for More Enlightened Congressional Support

From the EPA's inception, its activities have been a matter of intense congressional scrutiny, concern, and criticism. The EPA's programs currently fall under the jurisdiction of six Senate standing committees, seven House standing committees, and thirty-one subcommittees in both chambers. Probably no other federal agency is exposed to so much congressional oversight. So regularly is the EPA a subject of congressional investigation that Congress's own watchdog agency, the General Accounting Office, has a large, permanent branch office at EPA headquarters.

It is readily apparent from the discussion of Congress in chapter 6, and from numerous other descriptions throughout this book of legislative attitudes toward the EPA, that Congress has been in many respects the most politically disruptive presence in EPA's worklife. Congress has treated the agency with almost schizophrenic inconsistency. It has entrusted the EPA with a daunting variety of complex and highly ambitious regulatory programs while hobbling its administrative capabilities through excessive micromanagement and rigid program guidelines. It has been quick to protect the agency's basic structure and programs from emasculation but unwilling to provide realistic and dependable budget support for the programs it has protected. It has been severely critical of the EPA for program failures and contradictions written into the law by Congress itself. And it has been quick to demonize the agency for failure to achieve unrealistic or unrealizable program goals also mandated by Congress. It is understandable that one of the EPA's most legislatively popular administrators, William Ruckelshaus, should still complain that the agency had become Congress's "designated whipping boy." [46]

The many reasons for this adversarial relationship with Congress are explained in chapter 6. Whatever these reasons, the EPA cannot function effectively so long as Congress perpetuates this political polarization and refuses to initiate changes in its own behavior that would improve the EPA's administrative performance. In this respect, Congress could do much. One terse prescription comes from the National Academy of Public Administration: "Congress should refrain from micro-managing the EPA." [47] Congress could also provide the EPA with a realistic budget appropriate to its legislative mandates and reduce the number of committees to which the agency must look for direction and accountability.

Over at the EPA, where *esprit de corps* is always fragile, morale plunged even before the 104th Congress had voted on a single budget proposal or reform initiative affecting the agency. The agency's leadership was already prepared for large-scale Reductions in Force (RIFs). Morbid conjecture abounded concerning who would be RIFed, which offices eliminated. A bunker mentality had settled in; the agency knew which way the reform wind blew.

If the 104th Congress foreshadows the future, the reforms likely to emerge from Congress in the latter 1990s will do the EPA as much harm as good. The Republicans' abrupt acquisition of congressional power in late 1994 created the most promising opportunity in two decades for a searching reappraisal of the EPA's programs and performance and for the enactment of many needed reforms in both. The issues raised by the subsequent congressional debates were, for the most part, timely and significant, bearing directly on critical problems in need of urgent solution. Insofar as the congressional debate has initiated a larger national reexamination of the EPA and the major environmental laws it implements, the debates are useful. However, the congressional reform agenda, if substantially enacted, serves the EPA and its programs poorly and portends grave difficulties for the agency and its programs. Equally important, opportunities to make more constructive changes will have been lost.

Perhaps the most significant aspect of the reform debates in the mid 1990s has been congressional unwillingness to address two of the EPA's most compelling problems: the need for a mission statement and for a more integrated organizational approach to pollution management. Although the reasons for this congressional apathy are understandable—such reforms offer neither attractive political rewards nor public support—they appear to be at the root of many of the EPA's difficulties about which Congress has been increasingly critical. Moreover, Congress has shown little inclination to desist from its habit of writing "hammer clauses," unrealistic program deadlines, inflexible budget mandates, and other micromanagement tools that have compounded the EPA's administrative difficulties. Indeed, more micromanagement in the guise of additional "reform" appears imminent for many of the EPA's major programs such as the Clean Air Act, the Clean Water Act, and Superfund.

Another, more constructive reform lies in proposals that the EPA greatly expand its use of risk-analysis and cost-benefit analysis throughout all its major regulatory programs. Despite problems inherent to each of these policy tools, they can provide the EPA, policymakers, and the public with useful information upon which to make policy decisions and to assign policy priorities when the limits of both strategies are appreciated. Unfortunately, proposals to *require* both procedures for all major regulatory decisions, or to require such decisions to demonstrate a net benefit or significantly increased risk prevention, would further retard the already plodding pace of regulation, add additional administrative costs, and inspire a new outpouring of costly and time-consuming litigation.

Perhaps the most valuable and durable reforms that may issue from the current debate about the EPA and its mission are those that facilitate greater delegation of authority to the states for the implementation of environmental regulations—provided these arrangements are linked to incentives for states to achieve regulatory goals rather than to use their newly acquired powers to delay and subvert regulatory programs. The most problematic aspect of this movement toward a greater state presence in regulatory decisions remains the capacity of the states to provide the necessary financial and administrative resources to support these new responsibilities. Without such resources, increased state responsibility for the EPA's program implementation is likely to mean a de facto weakening of these programs.

By far the most disruptive of all the proposals is a severe cutback in the EPA's operating budget and its many grant programs. It is also the one most likely to be adopted. Even if no other reform proposal were to be enacted in the mid 1990s, the budget cutbacks destined for the agency in the mid 1990s would powerfully inhibit program implementation across practically all the agency's major programs. Further, as the more modest budget cutbacks during the Reagan years demonstrated, the effect of several years' budget shortfalls is magnified through time, even when budget reductions are eliminated in future years. A year or two of budget reductions on the scale proposed for the EPA by the congressional leadership in the mid 1990s will set the agency on a certain course of progressively mounting program failures unless its existing statutory responsibilities are significantly diminished. Proponents of these and other congressional reforms prefer to believe this array will improve the agency's performance—something like administrative shock therapy for a severely incapacitated bureaucracy. Perhaps. But if an administrative risk assessment could be performed for the EPA in the mid 1990s, it would probably suggest that the reforms the agency is likely to experience may be more hazardous than helpful to its future performance.

Notes

1. Quoted in John H. Trattner, *The Prune Book: The 100 Toughest Management and Policy-Making Jobs in Washington* (Lanham, Md.: Madison Books, 1988), 250.
2. Council on Environmental Quality (CEQ), *Environmental Quality, 1985* (Washington, D.C.: GPO, 1986), 14. See also Walter A. Rosenbaum, "The Clenched Fist and the Open Hand: Into the Nineties at EPA," in *Environmental Policy in the 1990s*, 2d ed., ed. Norman J. Vig and Michael E. Kraft (Washington, D.C.: CQ Press, 1994), 121-143.
3. National Commission on the Environment, *Choosing a Sustainable Future* (Washington, D.C.: Island Press, 1993), 8.
4. National Academy of Public Administration, *Setting Priorities, Getting Results: A New Direction for the Environmental Protection Agency* (Washington, D.C.: NAPA, 1995), 1.
5. William K. Reilly, "The New Clean Air Act: An Environmental Milestone," *EPA Journal* 7 (January-February 1991): 3.
6. The EPA's staff and budget levels may be found each year in a report from the U.S. Office of Management and Budget, *The Budget of the United States*. See also appendixes 3 and 4 in this volume.
7. Environmental quality trends may be found in CEQ, *Environmental Quality: 23rd Annual Report of the Council on Environmental Quality* (Washington, D.C.: GPO, 1993), chaps. 1, 2, and 8. See also General Accounting Office (GAO), "Superfund: Cleanups Nearing Completion Indicate Future Challenges," Report no. GAO/RCED 93-88 (September 1993), chap. 1.
8. On the general problem of future Superfund site cleanup, see GAO, "Superfund: Estimates of Number of Future Sites Vary," Report no. GAO/RCED 95-18 (November 1994).
9. GAO, "Clean Air Act Amendments of 1990," Report no. GAO/T-RCED 94-68 (October 29, 1993), 1.
10. GAO, "Toxic Substances Control Act: EPA's Limited Progress in Regulating Toxic Chemicals," Report no. GAO/T-RCED 94-212 (May 17, 1994), 1.
11. GAO, "Air Pollution: Reductions in EPA's 1994 Air Quality Program's Budget," Report no. GAO/RCED 95-31BR (November 1994), 2.
12. GAO, "Superfund: EPA Cost Estimates Are Not Reliable or Timely," Report no. GAO/AFMD 92-40 (July 1992), 1.

13. Representative Lewis is quoted in the *New York Times*, September 23, 1995. On the Republican reform agenda generally, see Bob Benenson, "GOP Sets the 104th Congress on New Regulatory Course," *Congressional Quarterly Weekly Report*, June 17, 1995, 1693-1703; "House Panel Takes Quick Action on Risk Assessment Provisions," *Congressional Quarterly Weekly Report*, February 11, 1995, 450-452; and "Bipartisan Regulatory Rewrite Breezes through Committee," *Congressional Quarterly Weekly Report*, March 25, 1995.

14. *New York Times*, February 22, 1995.

15. Ibid.

16. Quoted in Natural Resources Defense Council, "NRDC Report Documents Sweeping Retreat on Environment," http://www.nrdc.com, February 21, 1995.

17. *New York Times*, February 22, 1995.

18. *New York Times*, February 29, 1995.

19. Al Gore, "Reinventing Environmental Regulation," press release, March 16, 1995.

20. The White House, Press Release, August 3, 1995.

21. NAPA, *Setting Priorities*, 1.

22. Ibid., 8.

23. The implications of this lack of priorities are explored in Marc K. Landy, Marc J. Roberts, and Stephen R. Thomas, *The Environmental Protection Agency: Asking the Wrong Questions*, rev. ed. (New York: Oxford University Press, 1994); Richard N. L. Andrews, "Long-Range Planning in Environmental and Health Regulatory Agencies," *Ecology Law Quarterly* 20, (1993): 515-582; Stephen Cohen and Sheldon Kamieniecki, *Environmental Regulation through Strategic Planning* (Boulder: Westview, 1991), chap. 1; and Edward J. Woodhouse, "External Influences on Productivity: EPA's Implementation of TSCA," *Policy Studies Review* 4 (February 1985): 491-503.

24. On the problems involved in enforcement of the Toxic Substances Control Act, see Kathryn Harrison and George Hoberg, *Risk, Science, and Politics* (Montréal, Canada: McGill-Queen's University Press, 1994); GAO, "Toxic Substances: Status of EPA's Reviews of Chemicals under the Chemical Testing Program," Report no. GAO/RCED 92-31FS (October 1991); and GAO, "Toxic Substances Control Act: Legislative Changes Could Make the Act More Effective," Report no. GAO/RCED 94-103 (September 1994).

25. *New York Times*, November 25, 1995.

26. GAO, "Air Pollution: Reductions in EPA's 1994 Air Quality Program's Budget," 1.

27. NAPA, *Setting Priorities*, 8.

28. On the Superfund problem, see Daniel Mazmanian and David Morell, *Beyond Super-failure: America's Toxics Policy in the 1990s* (Boulder: Westview, 1992); Marc Landy and Mary Hague, "The Coalition for Waste: Private Interests and Superfund," in *Environmental Politics: Public Costs, Private Rewards*, ed. Michael Greve and Fred L. Smith (New York: Praeger, 1992); Charles E. Davis, *The Politics of Hazardous Waste* (Englewood Cliffs, N.J.: Prentice-Hall, 1993); and Roger C. Dover, "Hazardous Wastes," in *Public Policies For Environmental Protection*, ed. Paul R. Portney (Washington, D.C.: Resources for the Future, 1990): 195-242.

29. See Landy, Roberts, and Thomas, *Environmental Protection Agency*; NAPA, *Setting Priorities*, chap. 5; Alfred A. Marcus, "EPA's Organizational Structure," *Law and Contemporary Problems* 54 (Autumn 1991): 5-40; Lakshman Guruswamy, "The Case for Integrated Pollution Control," *Law and Contemporary Problems* 54 (Autumn 1991): 41-56; and the Conservation Foundation, *State of the Environment: An Assessment at Mid-Decade* (Washington, D.C.: The Conservation Foundation, 1984), chap. 6.

30. Thomas O. McGarity, "The Internal Structure of EPA Rulemaking," *Law and Contemporary Problems* 54 (Autumn 1991): 59

31. In addition to sources cited in n. 29 above, see Thomas O. McGarity, *Restoring Rationality* (New York: Cambridge University Press, 1991).

32. NAPA, *Setting Priorities*, 71-77.

33. Landy, Roberts, and Thomas, *Environmental Protection Agency*, 6; see also Ralph A. Luken, "How Efficient Are EPA's Regulations?" *Environmental Law Reporter* 20 (October 1990): 10419-10424; and Evan J. Ringquist, "Evaluating Environmental Policy Outcomes," in *Environmental Politics and Policy*, 2d ed, ed. James P. Lester (Durham: Duke University Press, 1995), 303-327.

34. A useful summary of regulatory risk assessment guidelines followed by the EPA and other federal regulatory agencies is found in John J. Cohrssen and Vincent T. Covello, *Risk Analysis: A Guide to Principles and Methods for Analyzing Health and Environmental Risks* (Washington, D.C.: CEQ, 1989).

35. Carnegie Commission on Science, Technology and Government, *Risk and the Environment: Improving Regulatory Decision Making* (New York: Carnegie Commission, 1993), 76.

36. William K. Reilly, "Why I Propose a National Debate on Risk," *EPA Journal* 17 (March-April): 2.

37. William K. Reilly, "Why I Propose," 3.

38. Jonathan Lash, "Should We Set Priorities Based on Risk Analysis?" *EPA Journal* 17 (March-April): 19.

39. On the problems involved with risk assessment methodologies, see Adam M. Finkel, "Is Risk Assessment Really Too Conservative? Revising the Revisionists," *Columbia Journal of Environmental Law* 14 (1989): 427-467; Robert Formaini, *The Myth of Scientific Public Policy* (New Brunswick, N.J.: Transaction, 1990), chap. 1; Harry Otway and Detlof von Winterfeldt, "Expert Judgment in Risk Analysis and Management: Process, Context, and Pitfalls," *Risk Analysis* 12 (March 1992): 83-93; and Frances M. Lynn, "The Interplay of Science and Values in Assessing and Regulating Environmental Risks," *Science, Technology and Human Values* 11 (Spring 1986): 40-50.

40. NAPA, *Setting Priorities*, 67.

41. CEQ, *Environmental Quality, 1979* (Washington, D.C.: GPO, 1980), 218.

42. Many of the problems with cost-benefit analysis are summarized in Formaini, *Myth of Scientific Public Policy*, chap. 3; see also GAO, "Cost-Benefit Analysis Can Be Useful in Assessing Regulations Despite Its Limitations," Report no. GAO/RCED 84-62 (April 1984); and Richard A. Liroff, "Cost-Benefit Analysis in Federal Environmental Programs," in *Cost-Benefit Analysis and Environmental Regulations: Politics, Ethics, and Methods*, ed. Daniel Swartzman, Richard A. Liroff, and Kevin G. Croke (Washington, D.C.: Conservation Foundation, 1982); and Stephen Kelman, "Cost-Benefit Analysis: An Ethical Critique," *Regulation* (January-February 1981): 33-40.

43. Lester V. Lave, *The Strategy of Social Regulation* (Washington, D.C.: Brookings, 1981), chap. 6; and W. Norton Grubb, Dale Whittington, and Michael Humphries, "The Ambiguities of Cost-Benefit Analysis: An Evaluation of Regulatory Impact Analysis under Executive Order 12,291," in *Environmental Policy under Reagan's Executive Order*, ed. V. Kerry Smith (Chapel Hill: University of North Carolina Press, 1984): 121-166; the review of the CBA's implementation by federal agencies in Kenneth J. Meier, *Regulation: Politics, Bureaucracy, and Economics* (New York: St. Martin's, 1985); and Thomas McGarity, "The Use of Regulatory Analysis in the Decisionmaking Process," *Report to the U.S. Administrative Conference on Regulatory Impact Analysis in Federal Regulatory Agencies* (Washington, D.C.: U.S. Administrative Conference, 1985). For a more recent review, see Cornelius M. Kerwin, *Rulemaking: How Government Agencies Write Law and Make Policy* (Washington, D.C.: CQ Press, 1994), chap. 6.

44. See, for example, Herman E. Daly, *Steady-State Economics* (Washington, D.C.: Island Press, 1991); David Pearce and Dominic Moran, *The Economic Value of Biodiversity* (London: Earthscan, 1994); and Rajaram Krishnan, Jonathan M. Harris, and Neva R. Goodwin, *A Survey of Ecological Economics* (Washington, D.C.: Island Press, 1995).

45. President William J. Clinton, The White House, Executive Order 12866: Regulatory Planning and Review, September 30, 1993, sec. 1a.

46. William Ruckelshaus, "EPA," *EPA Journal* 16 (January-February 1991): 14; see also James J. Florio, "Congress as Reluctant Regulator," *Yale Journal on Regulation* 3 (Spring 1986): 351-382; and Richard J. Lazarus, "The Tragedy of Distrust in the Implementation of Federal Environmental Law," *Law and Contemporary Problems* 54 (Autumn 1992): 311–374.
47. NAPA, *Setting Priorities*, 132.

8

Environmental Policy in the Courts
Lettie McSpadden

*The logical method and form flatter that longing for certainty and
for repose which is in every human mind. But certainty generally is
illusion, and repose is not the destiny of man.*

—Oliver Wendell Holmes

The Role of the Courts in Environmental Policy

In 1803 John Marshall, then chief justice of the United States, established
the power of courts to oversee the constitutionality of actions by other
branches of government when he declared that it is "the duty of the judicial
department to say what the law is." [1] Even before Marshall made this famous
pronouncement, state and federal courts were helping to formulate and
implement public policy through their powers to interpret and enforce laws,
and they continue to do so to this day. Judicial decisions in public policies as
diverse as abortion rights and desegregating public schools have been cele-
brated or deplored by commentators for the last thirty years. Less well publicized, but just as important, has been their participation over the past two
and a half decades in shaping environmental policies from water pollution
control to the preservation of endangered species. Were it not for court
injunctions, even fewer ancient trees would be surviving in the United States.
Were it not for enforcement actions brought by citizen activists, our waters
would be more choked by industrial wastes than they are.

Critics of judicial activism bemoan these developments; yet they are as
much a part of the public policy process as congressional debates and executive management of the budget. Nevertheless, some analysts argue that
judges are singularly unsuited to make policy decisions in technical areas
such as pollution control because they must respond to individual demands
for justice. [2] Other scholars caution against the dominance of technical
experts and urge the continued use of lay judges to counterbalance inequities
that arise when an unrestrained technocracy controls policy. [3] There is a
tension between Americans' desire on the one hand for substantively
"correct" decisions reached by experts and, on the other, for democratic decisions made through public participation and facilitated by the courts' insistence on due process. Like other government institutions, courts are caught
between these two equally important values in the American polity, and they

continue to struggle to reconcile them.

In this chapter I focus on how the federal court system influences environmental policy, how it oversees administrative decisionmaking and triggers new demands made on Congress. In the first section of the chapter I look at how regulatory law has come to involve courts heavily in environmental policy. Next, I consider methods developed by judges to interpret the new laws, how interest groups have tried to use the courts, and the latter's response to these demands. Originally, environmental groups regarded federal courts as sympathetic forums; more recently, business groups have developed their own creativity with the law. I also describe some cases that have been decided in trial and appellate courts. The Supreme Court's orientation toward environmental issues is analyzed, and issues, such as the concept of standing to sue and property rights claims, likely to be discussed into the twenty-first century are considered.

The Common Law: Compensation after Injury

Before environmental legislation exploded in the 1970s, common law concepts such as trespass, personal injury, and liability for damages provided the only legal recourse when people or organizations imposed the costs of their economic activities on others. Parties injured by polluted air, water, toxic wastes, or other hazards may still ask the courts for compensation for the harm imposed on them as a result of a degraded environment. In such cases, however, the burden of proof customarily falls on the plaintiff, who must show that each injury is the fault of a particular polluter. This is difficult to prove, as too many other variables may have contributed to the victims' problems for most judges or juries to assign fault for the injuries.

Relatively few victims successfully prove the culpability of the manufacturer of a product, or the operator of a plant that dumps toxic materials into the air, water, or soil. And they are often dissatisfied by the outcome. From their perspective, the greatest drawback to the judicial remedy of damages is that nothing is done to change the situation whereby the injury occurred. It is often cheaper for the industry to pay damages and continue the harmful behavior. Theoretically, the fear of having to pay damages for injuries done to customers, workers, and innocent bystanders will affect the behavior of firms that manufacture products and dispose of wastes without concern for the consequences. The uncertainty of being sued, however, and the difficulty of establishing proof often diminish the impact of this fear. [4]

The equity suit is an alternative common law remedy to damage judgments. It gives courts the power to issue an injunction forcing the party causing the harm to cease doing so. Judges are loath, however, to order organizations performing essential services for a community, such as operating a hazardous waste landfill, to halt operations. The damage done to third parties is balanced against the economic good that the polluter provides; it is extremely difficult to shut down a business that is providing hundreds of jobs, especially when many different polluters have contributed to a cumulative problem. Just as courts are reluctant to compensate for injuries, so too do they find it difficult to balance interests and restore equity.

Public Law: The Goal of Prevention

The common law of nuisance, trespass, and injury has proved a weak and inconsistent remedy for many problems of environmental degradation. Proponents of resource conservation and pollution control have turned to public law as an alternative. Rather than depending on the fear of a potential lawsuit after harm has been done, statutory law attempts to prevent the harm from occurring. By proscribing certain actions (for example, dumping crude oil into waterways) and prescribing others (for example, treating sewage before release into waterways), lawmakers hope to prevent many injuries to public health and the natural environment. Shifting legal recourse from private law suits between individuals and groups into the realm of public law (with the government as a prominent actor) may redress the imbalance between the two parties in traditional common law cases. Prevention, rather than remediation, is the goal of public law. [5]

The number of statutory environmental laws intended to regulate behavior grew in the 1970s, but this did not reduce the courts' role. Rather, the courts' workload increased greatly, as some of the burden of resolving uncertainty was passed to the courts. The proliferation of new statutory laws not only creates the need for an administrative state to enforce them but also increases the need for courts to interpret them. Regulatory law forces courts to make prospective decisions about the potential for harm rather than retrospective judgments about the causes of demonstrated injuries. It casts judges in entirely new roles as quasi legislators and quasi administrators. [6]

Court Oversight of Administrative Discretion

Federal judges are aware of the new role they are being asked to play in the field of public law and specifically in environmental law. In their traditional role as neutral arbiter of individual disputes, judges have finished their work once a verdict has been rendered; but as makers of public policy, judges must now oversee how well the responsible agency carries out the court's order. In many cases a judge will order an agency to comply with the letter of the law passed by Congress by writing regulations by a certain date, issuing a permit, or even rethinking the grounds for its previous decision. Sometimes a judge must exercise managerial control over the same case for years.

For the period preceding the court's verdict as well, the judge's role has greatly expanded. Judges today often act as intermediaries, bringing opposing parties into their chambers to work out a compromise before the case reaches trial. In so doing, judges' discretion and influence over policy are broadened greatly. The judge's informal role of mediator has meant that the number of cases going to trial has declined. Many cases are settled by the parties and their attorneys, often with judicial encouragement. Indeed, some adversaries in environmental disputes are now able to negotiate their differences without resort to the court system at all through a process called environmental dispute resolution (EDR). This method was pioneered by the Conservation Foundation in the 1980s, and its former president, William Reilly, urged business and environmental groups to use EDR after he was appointed administrator of the Environmental Protection Agency (EPA) by the Bush administration.[7]

Judges have disagreed among themselves about their role in overseeing administrative agency decisions. Judge Harold Leventhal, who in the 1970s sat on the U.S. Court of Appeals for the District of Columbia Circuit, argued that it is the courts' responsibility to guarantee that agencies take a "hard look" at all factors when making their decisions.[8] Judge Leventhal also argued that judges need access to court-appointed scientific experts to help them understand the conflicting testimony of adversarial expert witnesses.

Others have argued that, on these knotty technical issues, the United States needs a "science court" composed of natural scientists to define the common ground among experts over controversies involving scientific phenomena. These panels of expert judges would not be asked to make value judgments but would rule only on the scientific aspects of the policy.[9] Skeptics doubt, however, that these panels would be able to distinguish between scientific fact and value judgments. They also fear that definitive statements from a science court would stifle future debate over the same issues.[10] Judge Leventhal himself was skeptical of separate, specialized courts for environmental cases. He believed the selection of judges for such courts would become a political issue within the administration making the appointments.

One of Judge Leventhal's colleagues on the D.C. Circuit in the 1970s, Judge David Bazelon, was even skeptical of the suggestion that experts be assigned to the courts. Instead, Bazelon proposed that all opinions about an issue be incorporated into the agency's decisionmaking process. Although he did not dispute the complexity of the technical problems facing the courts, Bazelon believed that science and technology are not the exclusive domain of scientists and engineers. Many cases before the courts, he argued, involve major value choices. Although cloaked in technical questions, such cases should nevertheless be open to public scrutiny and participation. Rather than curing the problem with separate, expert advisers for judges, he preferred that all contending groups be able to have their own experts heard before administrative agencies and in court as well.[11]

Interest Groups and the Federal Courts

Judge Bazelon's affinity for a pluralist competition of ideas in the judicial process has been adopted by many interest groups concerned with environmental policy. The same groups that try to influence Congress to pass and modify environmental laws are usually active in tracking the way agencies carry out these laws. Not surprisingly, environmental groups that urged Congress to pass legislation also come before the courts to have the law enforced. Industries and others who were disappointed in the outcomes at either the legislative or executive level also have another chance to influence policy in court. Given the ambiguity of many of the policies made by both legislative and administrative actors, the shift to the courts for further debate is the obvious next step.

Most environmental litigation is initiated by one of three actors. The best known are groups like the National Audubon Society and Sierra Club, which worked to get environmental protection and natural resource legislation passed and reformed in the 1970s. Subsequently, these groups and newer organizations (such as the Natural Resources Defense Council and the Environmental Defense Fund) sued government agencies to carry out their congressional mandates. During the early 1970s they went to the federal courts to get the new laws enforced, where they often succeeded in having their strict interpretations of the laws accepted.

Initially caught off guard by environmental litigation, business and property interests are now responding with increasing confidence and stridency. With their superior legal and economic resources, major corporations and trade associations have asked the courts to reinterpret environmental laws in a more probusiness light. It is common, for example, for both industry and environmental groups to simultaneously sue the EPA over the same regulation; one litigant claims the regulation is too strict, the other that it is too lenient. Often industry and private property owners outstrip environmental groups in the extreme nature of their demands, arguing that the laws themselves should be declared unconstitutional and unenforceable.

Government is the third major actor in environmental law, and it participates on both sides of the issues. When challenged by environmental groups, it often represents an economic or development interest normally associated with major corporations. When challenged by industry, it must defend the law and the environmental point of view. In addition, government agencies have a sizable agenda of their own. After all, their official role is to enforce statutory laws, ensure the conditions of permits, and halt violations of regulations by industry and private property owners.

Originally, government cases were restricted to asking the courts for civil fines. However, in 1981 the EPA established an Office of Criminal Enforcement and began referring cases to the Department of Justice for prosecution. This development met with mixed reviews. Proponents argued that the possibility of incarcerating corporate officials would increase their willingness to comply with environmental laws. Critics complained about the possibility of civil rights violations and claimed that accommodations could be reached without resort to such extreme measures.

Most environmental cases can be classified as one of three modal types—environmental groups vs. government, industry vs. government, and government vs. industry. There is another type of case in which government appeals an environmental victory at the trial level, and these have become more common as the Justice Department has grown more defensive about environmental regulation. There is also a fifth type of case between different agencies and levels of government. In such cases one government body accuses the other of polluting the environment. Reacting against the emphasis in the Reagan and Bush administrations on deregulation, state authorities have increasingly assumed a regulatory stance against such federal agencies as the Department of Defense.

Litigants and Their Changes in Strategy

The traditional approach of environmental groups has been to sue government for regulating too loosely. But in the 1980s these groups began confronting business corporations directly in court in addition to suing the government. Congress facilitated this type of suit by writing into several of the environmental laws provisions for private attorneys general (citizen suits) to enforce them. This power enables a private citizen or group to take legal action against a polluter when a government agency does not.

Disappointed by the EPA's unwillingness to undertake enforcement actions in the 1980s, environmental groups have sued to force individual industries and plants to conform to the limits written into water pollution discharge permits. In this way environmental groups have been able to pursue their disagreements directly with their chief rival, industry, when the responsible agencies are unwilling to play their proenvironmental role.

Calling these cases instances of "judicial activism," conservative critics argue that the litigants do not deserve standing before the courts. Implementation of the laws should be left, they contend, to technical experts in the administrative agencies; environmental groups should not be allowed to involve the courts. This argument has received a sympathetic hearing in some courts, especially the Supreme Court, and is used not only by business defendants but also by government defendants against environmental initiatives.

During the Reagan and Bush administrations, Congress was so convinced of the need for these citizen suits that it continued to add authority for private attorneys general to pollution control laws. In 1990, for example, it amended the Clean Air Act to require permits for plant emissions similar to those issued to industries that discharge wastes into waterways. The reporting system required by permits creates a clear paper trail for private groups to use in court. [12] When the 104th Congress took office after the 1994 elections, however, one element in the "Contract with America" was to change pollution control laws by eliminating private attorney general suits.

In addition to objecting to environmental groups' standing in court, business has found a new theme around which to focus its arguments against government regulation. Developers and other landowners argue that almost any government regulation, federal or state, constitutes an unconstitutional violation of their property rights if it diminishes the value of their land. These litigants use the Fifth Amendment language ("nor shall private property be taken for public use without just compensation") to attack such federal laws as wilderness preservation and endangered species protection; they also cite the Fourteenth Amendment's due process clause to challenge state police powers such as zoning laws. Moreover, in cases where the property owner wins the right to develop, he may also claim compensation from the government for losses suffered in the interim.[13] These arguments have frequently been upheld by the U.S. Court of Claims, which hears suits against the U.S. government for monetary damages, and in many cases by the U.S. Supreme Court (see discussion below in "Patterns in Court Outcomes"). In addition, twenty-six state legislatures passed laws between 1990 and 1995 establishing a right of property owners to be compensated if regulations reduce their property values. This development has sent a chill through federal and state policymakers, who may relax their regulations rather than face large damage judgments.

Developers and other business interests have also developed the strategic lawsuit against public participation (SLAPP suit) to use against public interest groups, such as consumer protection advocates as well as environmentalists. These suits attempt to prevent environmentalists from testifying in public hearings, lobbying zoning boards, and advertising against development projects by arguing that the public interest group has defamed or libeled the developer in opposing the projects. The majority of SLAPP suits are thrown out of court on the ground that they interfere with citizens' right to petition their government for redress of grievance.[14] Because they are filed in various state trial courts, however, they may go unresolved for years, running up legal expenses for the defendants. Under the threat of SLAPP suits many public interest groups may become reluctant to become involved in issues in their communities.

The Types of Issues in Federal Courts

Most federal cases about the environment fall into three categories: (1) National Environmental Policy Act (NEPA) cases, in which public interest groups challenge government projects because of their adverse environmental effects; (2) public health threats, from air and water pollution as well as from toxic materials such as pesticides and hazardous wastes; and (3) natural resource management issues, including disputes over energy development, the use of public lands, and wildlife and wilderness protection.

The Rise and Fall of NEPA

During the "environmental decade" of the 1970s, many cases concerned NEPA, which requires the federal government to write an environmental impact statement (EIS) before undertaking a government-funded or -regulated project, such as highway or dam construction, or permitting the operation of a nuclear reactor. Federal courts initially responded by treating such questions substantively, insisting that agencies should prove that they had indeed taken Judge Leventhal's "hard look" at all aspects of such projects.[15] District and circuit court judges also fashioned stringent procedural requirements for federal agencies to ensure that all interested parties had an opportunity to enter the process, in accordance with Judge Bazelon's desire for complete procedural protection.

By the end of the 1970s, however, the Supreme Court had narrowed the scope of NEPA by overturning many of these cases. In *Vermont Yankee* v. *NRDC* (1978), the Supreme Court reversed two District of Columbia Circuit Court decisions remanding Nuclear Regulatory Commission (NRC) decisions for inadequate treatment of environmental issues, including conservation of energy and disposal of nuclear wastes, before issuing permits for nuclear plants.[16] Writing for a unanimous Supreme Court, Justice William H. Rehnquist chastised the D.C. Circuit for interfering with NRC discretion and substituting its own policy preferences for that of an expert commission. After having their decisions overturned by the Supreme Court repeatedly in the 1970s, the federal courts came to treat the writing of environmental impact statements as a paper exercise. They generally ruled in favor of government projects as long as the EIS requirement had been observed. As a consequence, the number of NEPA cases declined dramatically in the 1980s as environmental groups turned their resources to pollution control and natural resource management issues.

Public Health Threats

Air and water pollution cases have been the most common part of the federal courts' environmental workload. Although air pollution cases constitute a modest percentage of environmental cases, water pollution cases are abundant chiefly because permits are required for every point source, which opens the door to enforcement actions. During the 1980s government enforcement actions dropped off dramatically, but environmental groups replaced many government actions with their own private attorneys general cases. Courts have been receptive to the claim of environmental groups that they are appropriate private attorneys general to enforce pollution control statutes. If the EPA or a state starts a public enforcement action, or if industry reduces its pollution in response to the citizen action, the courts often dismiss environmental groups' cases. Nevertheless, they have achieved their desired end. When pollution continues and enforcement at either the state or federal level is not forthcoming, the courts are willing to give private attorneys general standing and are likely to decide these cases substantively for the environmental groups, even awarding them attorney's fees afterward. With the renewed attack on environmental groups' standing in courts, however, this type of victory may become less common.

New and amended laws treating solid and hazardous waste disposal and cleanup created additional litigation as government, industry, and environmental groups competed to have courts accept their interpretation of the legislation. The 1980 Superfund law provides for recovery of costs from owners and former users of abandoned waste sites, but Congress failed to define liability or explain how to divide it among multiple responsible parties. Consequently, at some Superfund sites, more money has been spent on legal costs discussing how the expense of cleanup will be distributed than in actual cleanup operations.

Trial courts have interpreted Superfund to imply strict liability, which relieves government of the need to prove intent or negligence when demonstrating blame. They have also been willing to assess liability quite broadly on former and present owners, operators, haulers, and users of sites in the 1980s, sometimes holding a few parties responsible for the entire cost when others went bankrupt or could not be located.[17] Congress attempted to relieve innocent parties of liability in the 1986 amendments to Superfund. Amending Superfund to eliminate strict, retroactive, and joint liability was one of the most important items on the 104th Congress's agenda when it came into office in 1995, but thus far gridlock has prevailed. Meanwhile, government and industrial litigants continue to search for additional responsible parties, and courts continue to struggle to assess liability and divide the expenses.

Natural Resources Cases

Energy issues were rarely contested in the courts until the energy crisis in the mid 1970s. Related to energy issues are cases that concern publicly owned land and other natural resources located primarily in the western United States. Although the number of such cases declined somewhat in the early 1980s, energy-public land issues now constitute an important subject for environmental cases. The March 1989 Exxon *Valdez* disaster in Prince William Sound, which spilled 11 million gallons of oil, generated one criminal conviction (which was eventually overturned), and sparked numerous civil actions in both state and federal courts. In September 1994 a federal jury awarded fishermen, native Alaskans, and other residents of the area nearly $300 million in compensatory damages for injuries they suffered and $5 billion in punitive damages designed to punish Exxon for its negligence and ensure against future spills.[18] This award is likely to be reduced substantially on appeal.

Timber and ranching interests are as eager as the oil and gas industry for rapid development of all public lands, and conservation groups are continually seeking to slow this process. One such natural resource conflict that reached the federal courts in the early 1990s was the dispute in the Pacific Northwest over proposals to harvest the last large remaining stands of old-growth timber not protected by wilderness or park status. Conservationists argue that further loss of virgin forests will reduce biodiversity and set a negative example for developing nations that are rapidly depleting their own forests. The timber industry responds that preserving old growth will throw loggers and mill workers out of work during an economic depression in the Northwest. Environmentalists counter that the industry's automation and its trade in raw logs to Japan have eliminated more jobs than conservation ever could. Nevertheless, loggers regard the last stands of ancient forest as a means of staving off the inevitable time when they will become entirely dependent on second-growth trees.

In court the controversy centered around the Endangered Species Act (ESA), which the Fish and Wildlife Service (FWS) interpreted to prohibit anyone from destroying the habitat of endangered or threatened plants and animals. Although the northern spotted owl, which lives in the Northwest forests, had been in decline for years, the Fish and Wildlife Service would not label the species threatened—much less endangered—until a federal judge in Washington State, responding to a suit from the Sierra Club, ordered it to reconsider.[19] Once the FWS had labeled the owl threatened, its interpretation of the ESA's language forced judges to issue injunctions that halted logging in several national forests because of the threat to habitat. At the urging of Washington and Oregon representatives and senators, Congress took the unusual step of stripping the federal courts of jurisdiction over these cases in 1989 and again in 1990. Environmentalists challenged the constitutionality of these acts, but the U.S. Supreme Court upheld the Congress.[20]

After Congress failed to pass similar laws in 1991, trial judges renewed their injunctions against logging areas where the spotted owl lives. The Bush administration argued the law should be amended to accommodate logging, but environmentally oriented members of Congress countered with new bills that would afford protection for old-growth forests for the sake of biodiversity itself rather than relying on finding endangered species that depend on them for habitat. Neither side won the congressional debate before the Clinton administration took office. In 1993 a "timber summit" in Oregon attempted to defuse the situation with a plan to allow some logging and to provide federal funds to retrain out-of-work loggers.

The timber industry began its own press in federal court, and in 1994 the D.C. Circuit reinterpreted the ESA to mean that private landowners do not have to protect endangered species' habitat.[21] This ruling contradicted not only the FWS's original interpretation but also a case decided by the Ninth Circuit, upholding the FWS's interpretation. The Supreme Court accepted the appeal in order to clarify the law and ruled 6-3 in June 1995 that the FWS's interpretation was correct; the word "harm" in the law can be used to protect endangered species' habitat even on private land.[22] This resulted in numerous calls by the Republican majority in the 104th Congress for the immediate and complete rewriting of the ESA.

Patterns in Court Outcomes

There are noticeable trends in the way federal courts interpret environmental laws. Since the 1970s judges in certain regions of the country have tended to reflect the worldviews of the other residents in those areas. Federal courts in the Northeast and Midwest and on the West Coast have tended to favor environmental litigants, whereas judges in the Southeast, Southwest, and Rocky Mountain states have tended to favor development and economic growth.[23] Also, Democratic judges have tended to favor environmental arguments more than Republican judges in all the regions. This became especially evident during the 1980s when the Reagan and Bush administrations carefully screened candidates for the federal bench for their ideological purity, including opposition to governmental regulation. In the early 1990s, when Reagan-Bush appointees dominated the federal circuits, fewer environmental victories were recorded in federal courts.[24]

The Lower Federal Courts

Because courts tend to favor official government actors in all areas of litigation, government agencies win more often than either their industrial or environmental opponents. In fact, the Supreme Court established a precedent that federal courts should defer whenever possible to the expert judgments of administrative agencies.[25] Although environmentalists tended to win more victories in the 1970s than business litigants, in the 1990s the balance shifted. The EPA increased its success rate over environmental groups and lost several significant legal battles to business litigants. In October 1991 the Fifth Circuit in New Orleans overruled the EPA on banning asbestos, a regulation the agency had spent ten years perfecting. The court ruled that the agency had not considered the costs to industry for finding substitutes and that insufficient benefits were to be gained.[26] An extreme example of judicial intervention into administrative decisionmaking, this case contradicts the assertion often made by Presidents Reagan and Bush that they chose federal judges who would uphold agency decisions and refrain from inserting their own values into their opinions. In December 1991 a panel of D.C. Circuit judges—consisting of two Reagan appointees and Clarence Thomas, who was subsequently appointed to the Supreme Court by President Bush—threw out the EPA's twelve-year-old definition of hazardous wastes, which included certain wastes from the petroleum industry.[27]

Divided decisions made by the D.C. Circuit illustrate how volatile the political balance can be in one circuit. In 1988 the EPA promulgated new rules to enforce the amendments to the Resource Conservation and Recovery Act (RCRA), which controls the injection of wastes into wells. The Natural Resources Defense Council claimed that rules controlling migration of hazardous wastes were too lenient, and the chemical disposal industry countersued that they were too severe. The D.C. Circuit Court of Appeals found for the EPA against both litigants. But Judge Patricia Wald, a Carter appointee, objected, arguing that her colleagues were misinterpreting Congress's intention to instruct the EPA to be conservative in deciding what types of wastes could move off site.[28] The NRDC also challenged new EPA-set ambient air quality standards. Judge Wald led another panel of three judges to a compromise decision whereby the EPA was asked to give better justification for its decision not to set a secondary standard to reduce acid rain. One Carter holdover judge argued for remanding more of the standards to the EPA for review, while a new Reagan appointee dissented in favor of supporting the government's revisions completely.[29]

In 1993 the logging industry attacked the Fish and Wildlife Service's reading of the Endangered Species Act in the D.C. Circuit, traditionally a favored forum for environmental litigants. In July 1993 Chief Judge Abner

Mikva, a Carter holdover, ruled against the loggers, agreeing with the FWS that the word "harm" in the ESA meant that private property owners could not destroy the habitat of endangered species. Judge David Sentelle, a Reagan appointee, vigorously dissented, arguing that "harm" means killing the species directly.[30] In March 1994 the third member of the panel, another Reagan appointee, changed his mind on rehearing the case and voted to reinterpret the ESA. This decision flew in the face of the Supreme Court's admonition to lower courts to defer to government agencies when interpreting statute law and was subsequently overturned by the High Court. The decision may signal, however, a new willingness on the part of Reagan and Bush appointees to view agency decisions more critically now that the Democrats are in charge of the executive branch.

In August 1994 the entire D.C. Circuit court voted on whether to hear the case again in order to settle the disagreement within the three-judge panel. The only judges to vote to rehear were Mikva, another Carter holdover, one Reagan appointee, and the newest judge, who was appointed by President Clinton.[31] All six judges voting not to rehear were either Reagan or Bush appointees. After this vote, Judge Mikva left the bench, and President Clinton named his replacement. With two Clinton appointees, one Carter holdover, and seven Reagan-Bush appointees, the D.C. Circuit may soon become as much a magnet for industry litigants as it formerly was for environmentalists.

The U.S. Court of Claims

One forum in which the new property rights movement has received a warm reception is the U.S. Court of Claims, where landowners take their allegations that the government must compensate them for any diminution in the value of their property because of regulations. Two cases involving the filling of wetlands exemplify the court's generosity. In one case the Corps of Engineers, the agency that regulates wetlands, refused to permit a New Jersey developer to build a subdivision on 12.5 acres of wetlands. Although the Corps had authority to deny the permit, the Court of Claims found that the owner had lost all economic use of the wetlands and was entitled to $2.6 million in compensation.[32] The judge accepted the developer's argument that the best use for the land was residential development despite the clear objective of preserving wetlands found in the Clean Water Act. In a second case, the Corps refused a permit to quarry limestone in an area where the aquifer was rapidly becoming polluted by such strip-mining operations. The judge awarded the company $1 million for the loss of all use of its property despite evidence that the land could be sold for about $4,000 an acre.[33]

In both cases the judges rejected the government's argument that the parcels of land were small parts of larger holdings and that their owners had already reaped huge profits from the larger portion of the parcel. The proposed housing development in New Jersey was part of 250 acres, bought for $300,000, most of which had already been developed. The Florida quarry was

98 acres out of 1,560 acres of wetland, most of which had already been mined. The land in both cases had escalated in value, and the court ruled the owners were entitled to the present-day fair market value of the land because they had expected to gain from their initial investment.[34] In both cases the judges also found that the burden on the private property owners outweighed any public benefit from preserving wetlands or preventing groundwater contamination.

In addition to private land use cases, the Court of Claims has been receptive to numerous complaints from timber, mining, and ranching interests, as well as from inholders of private lands inside public parks, that the government's efforts to control uses and to preserve the ecology of public lands interfere with their property rights. These decisions are supported by the property rights philosophy increasingly being espoused by conservative judges and law professors. They have also been supported by recent decisions in the Supreme Court, which has looked favorably on private landowners' claims against state land use regulations.

The Supreme Court and Environmental Issues

Under the leadership of Chief Justice Warren Burger, the Supreme Court in the 1970s and early 1980s was less receptive to environmental claims than were the lower federal courts, overturning almost all proenvironmental cases brought before it. After William Rehnquist became chief justice in 1986, the High Court became even more business oriented as most of the remaining liberal justices were replaced by Reagan and Bush appointees; most environmental litigants stopped taking appeals there. After Reagan appointees in the lower federal courts began upholding industry's property rights arguments, however, government agencies such as the Fish and Wildlife Service felt they had no alternative but to appeal to the High Court when federal and state regulations were attacked.

At the beginning of the 1980s the original Burger court was severely divided, with some holdover liberal justices vigorously opposed to their colleagues' desire to reduce government regulation. At that time, the Court came to opposite conclusions in two similar industry challenges to regulations set by the Occupational Safety and Health Administration (OSHA) to protect workers' health.

The first came from the U.S. Court of Appeals for the Fifth Circuit in New Orleans, known for its probusiness point of view. That court agreed with the American Petroleum Institute that estimated risks to workers from exposure to benzene were not worth the costs to industry to avoid them. In 1980 the Supreme Court upheld this ruling in a 5-4 decision. But in the same year the D.C. Circuit upheld a cotton-dust standard set by OSHA, and the Supreme Court upheld the agency's decision on the grounds that the same law as in the benzene case did not mandate cost-benefit justification.[35] In this case, three of the majority justices in the benzene standard case became dissenters. One changed his position and voted in favor of the cotton-dust standard because the agency had shown that 25 percent of all workers in the industry suffered from a disease caused by inhaling cotton fibers. Five of the justices who made the two OSHA decisions have been replaced, among them the most health-conscious of the original Burger Court: Justices William Brennan and Thurgood Marshall.

Justice Scalia, who leads the most conservative wing of the Court, has responded favorably to business's attacks on the constitutionality of government regulation of property on the grounds that overregulation amounts to taking property without due process. In one case, Justice Scalia, writing for the Court majority, agreed with landowners that the California Coastal Zone Commission attempted to take their property without due process when it tried to force them to provide public access to the ocean in exchange for a permit to rebuild their beachfront house.[36] In another case, Chief Justice Rehnquist addressed an additional question that the Court had avoided until then. Instead of restricting the remedy for any regulatory taking of property to striking down the unconstitutional regulation, he stated that landowners are entitled to be compensated by the state for any loss of value from the property that occurred between the time the regulation was put in place and its invalidation.[37]

In 1992 *Lucas* v. *South Carolina Coastal Council* was decided in favor of a South Carolina landowner who had invested in property before the state passed a law prohibiting developers from building on erodible beach land. Although the Court did not determine whether Lucas had lost all economic use of the land itself, it sent the case back to state court to decide this fact. Justice Scalia's decision said the state's only rationale for justifying its regulation would be through the common law of nuisance, which normally requires proof that harm would be done to adjacent property.[38] This ruling effectively interprets the taking doctrine to mean the state's regulatory powers are restricted to those it would have under the nuisance doctrine in common law. Taken to an extreme, this interpretation could reduce the police powers of the states to prevent property owners from imposing externalities on the larger society only when the state can prove individual harm to specific individuals. The *Lucas* decision eventually forced the state to buy his property at such an inflated figure that it subsequently had to sell the property for development. Following the logic of these property rights cases, in 1994 the Supreme Court ruled that a town in Oregon could not force a commercial property owner to dedicate 10 percent of her land for runoff drainage and to a bicycle and walking path in exchange for doubling the size of the store and paving the parking lot.[39]

Standing to Sue

For environmental litigants, however, another development is more ominous. This stems from several recent Supreme Court decisions that threaten to remove environmentalists' access to all federal courts. In 1972 a far different Supreme Court from the current Rehnquist Court signaled its willingness to look sympathetically on nontraditional litigants who hoped to raise ecological and even esthetic issues in court. Earlier courts had created a barrier for noneconomic grievances through the concept of "standing to sue," which holds that only persons or groups with a particular injury can present their arguments in court. Although the Court did not give the Sierra Club standing in this landmark case, it laid out how this status could be achieved by claiming specific injury to individual club members on the grounds that they used the area in question. [40]

Other environmental groups were quick to take the Court up on this suggestion, and lower federal courts followed precedent by opening their doors to these kinds of suits. This movement quickly reached its peak, however, when a group of law students got into court by alleging they hiked in open space that might be reduced if railroad rates on recycled materials were higher than those on virgin materials. [41] The Burger Court throughout the remainder of the 1970s refused to further open the door to the federal courts. Since then the Rehnquist Court has been gradually narrowing the opening that many on the Court, including Justice Scalia, believe was wrongly left ajar. [42]

This trend was demonstrated in 1990 when the Court refused to allow the National Wildlife Federation to protest a Bureau of Land Management decision to open up some public land to development. Justice Scalia wrote the majority decision that denied standing on the ground that the federation had not demonstrated that it suffered from any specific injury aside from asserting that its members use the public land under consideration for recreation. [43] This case was followed by another in 1992 against the Defenders of Wildlife, who wanted the courts to force the Department of the Interior to challenge overseas projects funded by the State Department that endangered the survival of rare species. Justice Scalia opined again that because the Defenders had suffered no particularized injury (despite language in the Endangered Species Act that permits citizen suits), they had no right to sue. [44]

Both these cases came to the Supreme Court only because the executive branch was willing to make the argument that public interest groups should have no standing to sue. But once the argument about standing was made, the present Supreme Court seemed eager to accept it. This precedent goes beyond those that simply find against the merits of environmental arguments. It implies that the groups with the most effective arguments are not eligible to make them in any federal court. Many critics of the courts agree with Justice Scalia that judges, because of their focus on individual rights, are unsuited to make decisions that can influence broad social policy. They believe technical decisions are better left to administrators with appropriate expertise who can determine priorities for agencies pressed to respond to multiple legislated requirements. [45]

Opponents of this restrictive view of the courts' role argue that executive agencies are no more democratically elected than judges and that Congress would not have provided the mechanism of citizen suits if it trusted administrators to render unerringly correct decisions. Judges admittedly do not have the agencies' concerns for efficient use of resources foremost in mind. But other values, such as individual justice, should outweigh these considerations. Experts do disagree about many technical issues regarding pollution and resource management. Eliminating standing for one group of experts will mean that much information, and even some issues, such as the spotted owl's status as a threatened species, may be precluded from discussion at any level in the federal court system.

Another development that bodes ill for environmental groups is tort litigation reform promised in the "Contract with America." One change passed by the House in the 104th Congress is that losers of lawsuits will be forced to pay the court costs of the winners. This would assist groups hit with SLAPP suits, but it would hurt groups attempting to enforce environmental statutes. If they were to lose, they could be liable for the legal costs of their governmental or industrial opponents. Until now environmental groups have benefited by having cost-recovery written into some of the statute laws, such as the Clean Air and Water Acts, to favor private attorneys general. If all losers were made liable for their opponents' costs, this could dampen environmental groups' enthusiasm for litigation.

Some Projections

The presidential election in November 1992 created an opportunity to begin the slow evolution of the Supreme Court to a more moderate position on the environment. President Clinton's first appointment in 1993 was Ruth Bader Ginsburg, a moderate judge from the D.C. Circuit who had been appointed by Jimmy Carter. She replaced Byron White, the only remaining Democrat on the Court, who resigned soon after Clinton came into office. Although White had been appointed by President John F. Kennedy, he was quite probusiness in his rulings; Justice Ginsburg is therefore likely to push the court in a less prodevelopment direction.

In 1994 Clinton got a second opportunity to appoint a justice when the liberal Justice Harry Blackmun resigned. Although a Republican appointed by Nixon, he had a more proenvironment record than White. His replacement was Stephen Breyer, an appellate judge from the First Circuit known for his expertise in regulatory affairs and administrative law and therefore likely to take an active role in environmental cases. Justice Breyer is especially knowledgeable about comparative risk assessment and cost-benefit analysis and is eager to increase the rationality of agency decisions. [46] He is less likely to accept without economic justification public health arguments, as Justice Blackmun did. Taken together, the two Clinton appointments may stop the Court's drift to the right but leave its rulings on the environment in approximately the same position they have been since Justice Clarence Thomas replaced Justice Thurgood Marshall in 1992.

It takes a long time to change the ideology of the Supreme Court, as its members have life tenure. President Clinton's opportunities will be limited to voluntary resignations and deaths of sitting justices. Except for the two most recent appointees, all remaining justices are Republicans. The 1994 congressional elections, which gave the GOP control of both houses of Congress, raised Republican hopes of recapturing the White House in 1996. The remaining High Court incumbents may want to hold on to their positions until a Republican president can appoint their successors. John Paul Stevens, an independent-thinking appointee of President Gerald R. Ford and the oldest justice, is the most likely candidate to follow the example of Justice Blackmun, but it seems unlikely. Also he is a moderate regarding the environment, and President Clinton will be hard-pressed to get a more liberal appointee through a Republican-dominated Senate. The same logic applies to the lower federal courts, where more than half the judges have been appointed by either President Reagan or President Bush.

Through the remainder of the 1990s it seems likely that most federal courts will scrutinize any regulation of economic behavior whether at the state or federal level. This is likely to take three forms: an increased use of cost-benefit analysis, continued favorable reception to arguments about taking property without due process, and reduced standing for public interest organizations.

The judiciary is likely to be reinforced in the first development by the Congress as it moves to increase the use of cost-benefit and risk-benefit standards in specific pollution control laws, such as the Clean Air Act. In addition, the Clinton administration is also inclined to increase the use of economic calculations in setting environmental standards.

The two other issues are equally supported by the new Congress, although not by the executive branch. If such laws as the Endangered Species Act are amended to provide for compensation for the owners of private property for regulatory "takings," there will be no disagreement between federal law and the Rehnquist Court's interpretation of the Constitution. Instead, conflict will be more likely between the states' attempts to control land uses and the latest interpretation of the due process clause. One principle of the "Contract with America" is to increase state authority at the expense of federal control. However, the Republican majority in the 104th House of Representatives quickly passed a national law to require all levels of government to compensate landowners if regulation diminishes their property value.

Because it is easier to show a specific monetary loss than any other kind, the Supreme Court's standing-to-sue rulings favor economic interests over ecological ones. Industry by definition has a material interest in its cases, and this may mean that only one side of some controversial cases will be fully aired in court. Although the administration could choose not to make standing arguments against allowing environmental interest groups into court, business litigants would still be able to initiate such claims. Congress could decrease or eliminate the citizen suit provisions in some laws, reducing the zone of interest the legislation is designed to protect. Even if environmental groups are unlikely to win the cases they bring, a reduction in their ability to sue is even more important because it prevents them from ever making their arguments.

In addition to the three patterns in Supreme Court decisions, there is a more general societal trend toward negotiated rulemaking and alternative forms of dispute resolution. Many environmental disputes are now settled out of court, with or without judicial supervision. This trend is likely to continue given the high costs of litigation and the increased reluctance of industry and environmental groups to prolong cleanup controversies.

A final complicating factor is the internationalization of environmental disputes. As policies such as protecting the Earth's ozone layer are adopted by international treaties and protocols, the role of U.S. courts in interpreting and administering environmental standards could diminish. Given the lack of enforcement power by international bodies, however, U.S. courts could face an increasing volume of cases brought by foreign parties who seek to challenge U.S. policies that affect their territory. How the courts will respond to such challenges remains to be seen.

Notes

The chapter epigraph quoting Oliver Wendell Holmes is taken from the *Harvard Law Review* 39 (1897).

1. *Marbury* v. *Madison,* 5 U.S. (1 Cranch) 137; 2 L.Ed. 60 (1803).
2. Donald L. Horowitz, *The Courts and Social Policy* (Washington, D.C.: Brookings, 1977); and R. Shep Melnick, *Regulation and the Courts* (Washington, D.C.: Brookings, 1983).
3. Lawrence Tribe, "Policy Science: Analysis or Ideology?" *Philosophy and Public Affairs* 2 (1972): 56; and Joel Yellin, "High Technology and the Courts: Nuclear Power and the Need for Institutional Reform," *Harvard Law Review* 94 (1981): 489.
4. Lettie M. Wenner, *One Environment under Law* (Pacific Palisades, Calif.: Goodyear, 1976), 7-9.
5. James Willard Hurst traced the law's development from common law in the nineteenth century through the development of public laws to regulate individual behavior for the common good. See Hurst, *Law and Social Order in the United States* (Ithaca, N.Y.: Cornell University Press, 1977). Also see Norman Vig and Patrick Bruer, "The Courts and Risk Assessment," *Policy Studies Review* 1 (May 1982): 716-727.
6. Among those who applaud this development are Hurst, *Law and Social Order;* and Abram Chayes, "The Role of Judges in Public Law Litigation," *Harvard Law Review* 89 (1976): 1281-1316. Among those who criticize it are Nathan Glazer, "Toward an Imperial Judiciary?" *Public Interest* 41 (1975): 104-123; and Horowitz, *Courts and Social Policy.*
7. Douglas J. Amy, "Environmental Dispute Resolution: The Promise and the Pitfalls," in *Environmental Policy in the 1990s,* 1st ed., ed. Norman J. Vig and Michael E. Kraft.
8. Harold Leventhal, "Environmental Decisionmaking and the Role of the Courts," *University of Pennsylvania Law Review* 122 (1974): 509-555.
9. The science court's primary spokesperson is Arthur Kantrowitz, chairman of Avco Everett Research. See Arthur Kantrowitz, "Controlling Technology Democratically," *American Scientist* (1975): 505; and Kantrowitz, "Science Court Experiment," *Trial* 13 (March 1977): 48-49.
10. James A. Martin, "The Proposed 'Science Court'," *Michigan Law Review* 75 (April-May 1977): 1058-1091; and A. D. Sofaer, "Science Court: Unscientific and Unsound," *Environmental Law* 9 (Fall 1978): 1-27.
11. David L. Bazelon, "Coping with Technology through the Legal Process," *Cornell Law Review* 62 (1977): 817-832.
12. Pub.L. 101-549, Title V, Section 501, 104 Stat. 2635 28.
13. Richard A. Epstein, *Takings, Private Property, and the Power of Eminent Domain* (Cambridge, Mass.: Harvard University Press, 1985).
14. Penelope Canan, "The SLAPP from a Sociological Perspective," *Pace Environmental Law Review* 7 (1989): 23-32; George W. Pring, "SLAPPs: Strategic Lawsuits against Public Participation," *Pace Environmental Law Review* 7 (1989): 3-21.
15. The high point of the Supreme Court's acceptance of this doctrine came in *Citizens to Preserve Overton Park* v. *Volpe,* 401 U.S. 402 (1971). The Supreme Court in this decision agreed with the lower federal court that the Department of Transportation

had exercised too much discretion in deciding to take a public park in order to build a highway under the Federal Aid Highway Act of 1968.

16. James F. Raymond, "A *Vermont Yankee* in King Burger's Court: Constraints on Judicial Review under NEPA," *Boston College Environmental Affairs Law Review* 7 (1979): 629-664; Richard Stewart, "*Vermont Yankee* and the Evolution of Administrative Procedure," *Harvard Law Review* 91 (1978): 1805-1845; and Katherine B. Edwards, "NRC Regulations," *Texas Law Review* 58 (1980): 355-391.

17. *U.S.* v. *Monsanto Company*, 858 F.2d 160 (4th Circuit, 1988); *U.S.* v. *Maryland Bank & Trust Company*, 632 F. Supp. 573 (D. Md. 1986).

18. *New York Times*, September 17, 1994, 1.

19. *Northern Spotted Owl* v. *Hodel*, 716 F. Supp. 479 (1988).

20. *Robertson* v. *Seattle Audubon*, 112 S. Ct. 1407 SC (1992).

21. *Sweet Home Chapter of Communities for a Great Oregon* v. *Interior Department*, 17 F3d 1463 (1994).

22. *Bruce Babbitt* v. *Sweet Home Chapter of Communities for a Great Oregon*, No. 94-859, 1991 WL 382088 (U.S. Supreme Court, June 29, 1995).

23. Lettie M. Wenner, "Contextual Influences on Judicial Decision Making," *Western Political Quarterly* 41 (March 1988): 115-134.

24. "Courthouse No Longer Environmentalists' Citadel," *New York Times*, March 23, 1992, 1.

25. *Chevron U.S.A., Inc.* v. *Natural Resources Defense Council*, 467 U.S. 837, 104 S.Ct. 2778 (1984).

26. *Corrosion Proof Fittings* v. *EPA*, 33 ERC 1961 (1991).

27. *Shell Oil* v. *EPA*, 34 ERC 1049 (1991).

28. *NRDC* v. *EPA*, 31 ERC 1697 (1990).

29. *NRDC* v. *EPA*, 31 ERC 1233 (1990).

30. *Sweet Home Chapter of Communities for a Great Oregon* v. *Interior Department*, 1 F3d 1 (1993).

31. *Sweet Home Chapter of Communities for a Great Oregon* v. *Interior Department*, 39 ERC 1278 (1994).

32. *Loveladies Harbor* v. *United States*, 21 Cl. Ct. 153 (1990).

33. *Florida Rock Industries* v. *United States*, 21 Cl. Ct. 161 (1990).

34. Lee R. Epstein, "Takings and Wetlands in the Claims Court: *Florida Rock* and *Loveladies Harbor*," *Environmental Law Reporter* 10 (1990): 10517-10521. Thomas Hanley, "A Developer's Dream: The U.S. Claims Court's New Analysis of Section 404 Takings Challenges," *Environmental Affairs* 19 (1991): 317-353.

35. *Industrial Union Department AFL-CIO* v. *American Petroleum Institute*, 100 S.C. 244 (1980); *Textile Manufacturers Institute Inc.* v. *Donovan*, 425 U.S. 490 (1981). See William H. Rodgers Jr., "Judicial Review of Risk Assessments: The Role of Decision Theory in Unscrambling the Benzene Decision," *Environmental Law* 11 (1981): 301-320.

36. *Nollan* v. *California Coastal Zone Commission*, 107 S.C. 3141 (1987).

37. *First English Evangelical Lutheran Church* v. *Los Angeles*, 107 S. Ct. 2378 (1987).

38. *Lucas* v. *South Carolina Coastal Council*, 112 S. Ct. 2886 (1992).

39. *Dolan* v. *City of Tigard*, 114 S. Ct. 2309 (1994).

40. *Sierra Club* v. *Morton*, 405 U.S. 727 (1972).

41. *U.S.* v. *Students Challenging Regulatory Agency Procedures*, 412 U.S. 669 (1973).

42. Antonin Scalia, "The Doctrine of Standing as an Essential Element of the Separation of Powers," *Suffolk University Law Review* 17 (1983): 881-899.

43. *Lujan* v. *National Wildlife Federation*, 110 S. Ct. 3177 (1990).

44. *Lujan* v. *Defenders of Wildlife*, 112 S. Ct. 2130 (1992).

45. In *Sierra Club* v. *Gorsuch*, 18 ERC 1549 (1982), a federal district court in California forced the EPA to set radioactive nuclides standards, which may have taken attention away from other types of priorities the EPA had under the Clean Air Act. See Melnick, *Regulation and the Courts*.

46. Stephen Breyer, *Breaking the Vicious Circle* (Cambridge, Mass.: Harvard University Press, 1993).

PART III. PUBLIC POLICY DILEMMAS

9

Economics, Incentives, and Environmental Regulation

A. Myrick Freeman III

It is helpful to think of the environment as a resource system that contributes to human welfare in a variety of ways. The source of the basic means of life support—clean air and clean water—the environment provides the means for growing food. It is the source of minerals and other raw materials that go into the production of the goods and services that support modern society's standard of living. The environment can be used for a variety of recreational activities such as hiking, fishing, and observing wildlife. It is also the source of amenities and esthetic pleasure, providing scenic beauty and inspiring our awe at the wonder of nature. Finally, and unfortunately in some respects, the environment can be used as a place to deposit the wastes from the production and consumption associated with the modern-day economy. It is this latter use, along with conversion of natural environments to more intensively managed agricultural ecosystems or to residential and commercial development, that gives rise to today's environmental problems.

The environment is a scarce resource. This means that it cannot provide all the desired quantities of all its services at the same time. Greater use of one type of environmental service usually means that less of some other type of service is available. Thus, the use of the environment involves trade-offs. Increasing the life-sustaining or amenity-yielding services it provides may require reducing the use of the environment's waste-receiving capacities or cutting back on development, and vice versa.

Economics is about how to manage the activities of people, including the way they use the environment, to meet their material needs and wants in the face of scarcity. Environmental protection and the control of pollution are costly activities. Society wishes to protect the environment and reduce pollution presumably because the value it places on the environment's life-sustaining and -enhancing services is greater than the value it places on what it must relinquish to achieve environmental improvement.

Devoting more of society's scarce resources of labor, capital, and so forth to controlling pollution necessarily means that fewer of these resources are available to do other things also valued by society. Similarly, the protection of a particular environmental resource to preserve amenities or wildlife habitat typically requires reductions in other uses of that resource, such as mining of minerals and production of forest products.[1] The costs of environmental protection are the values of these alternative uses that are forgone and the labor, capital, materials, and energy that are used up in controlling the flow of wastes to the environment. Because pollution control and environmental protection are costly, it is in society's best interest to be economical in its decisions about environmental protection and improvement.

There are two senses in which this is true. First, society needs to be economical about its objectives for environmental protection. If we are to make the most of our endowment of scarce resources, we should compare what we receive from devoting resources to pollution control and environmental protection with what we give up by taking resources from other uses. We should undertake more pollution control activities only if the results are worth more to us than the values we forgo by diverting resources from other uses such as producing food, shelter, and comfort. This is basically what benefit-cost analysis is about.

Second, whatever pollution control targets are chosen, the means of achieving them should minimize the costs of meeting these targets. It is wasteful to use more resources than is absolutely necessary to achieve pollution control objectives. Yet many environmental protection and pollution control policies are wasteful in just this sense. One of the major contributions of economic analysis to environmental policy is that it reveals when and how these policies can be made more cost-effective.

In the next section of this chapter, I will describe how benefit-cost analysis can be used to decide how far to go in the direction of environmental protection. I also discuss recent applications of benefit-cost analysis to environmental policy decisions and contributions that this economic approach to environmental policymaking might make in the future.

In the third section I will briefly describe the basic approach to achieving pollution control objectives that is embodied in the major federal statutes—the Clean Air Act of 1970 and the Federal Water Pollution Control Act of 1972. The fourth section is devoted to the concept of cost-effectiveness.

Then in the final three sections I describe and evaluate a variety of economics-based incentive devices (such as pollution taxes, deposit-refund systems, and tradable pollution discharge permits) that encourage pollution-control activities by firms and individuals and reduce the overall costs of achieving environmental protection targets. I also discuss the possibility of increasing the use of economic incentives in environmental policy in the 1990s.

Benefit-Cost Analysis and Environmental Policy

Two basic premises underlie benefit-cost analysis. First, the purpose of economic activity is to increase the well-being of the individuals who make up the society. Second, each individual is the best judge of how well off he or she is in a given situation. If society is to make the most of its scarce resources, it should compare what it receives from pollution control and environmental protection activities with what it gives up by taking resources from other uses. It should measure the values of what it gains (the benefits) and what it loses (the costs) in terms of the preferences of those who experience these gains and losses. Society should undertake environmental protection and pollution control only if the results are worth more, in terms of individuals' values, than what is given up by diverting resources from other uses. This is the underlying principle of the economic approach to environmental policy. Benefit-cost analysis is a set of analytical tools designed to measure the net contribution of any public policy to the economic well-being of the members of society.

Although in some respects benefit-cost analysis is nothing more than organized common sense, the term is usually used to describe a more narrowly defined, technical economic calculation that attempts to reduce all benefits and costs to a common monetary measure (that is, dollars). It seeks to determine if the aggregate of the gains that accrue to those made better off is greater than the aggregate of losses to those made worse off by the policy choice. The gains and losses are both measured in dollars and are defined as the sums of each individual's willingness to pay to receive the gain or to prevent the policy-imposed losses. If the gains exceed the losses, the policy should be accepted according to the logic of benefit-cost analysis.

Policies where the aggregate gains outweigh the aggregate costs can be justified on ethical grounds because the gainers could fully compensate the losers with monetary payments and still themselves be better off with the policy. Thus, if the compensation were actually made, there would be no losers, only gainers.[2]

Setting Environmental Standards

Selection of environmental quality standards illustrates some of the issues involved in using benefit-cost analysis for environmental policymaking. An *environmental quality standard* is a legally established minimum level of cleanliness or maximum level of pollution in some part of the environment. Once established, a standard can form the basis for enforcement actions against a polluter whose discharges cause the standard to be violated. Benefit-cost analysis can provide a basis for determining what the standard should be. In general, economic principles require that each good be provided at the level for which the marginal willingness to pay for it (the maximum amount that an individual would be willing to give up to get one more unit of the good) is just equal to the cost of providing one more unit of the good (its marginal cost).

Consider an environment that is badly polluted by industrial activity. Suppose that successive one-step improvements are made in some measure of environmental quality. For the first step, individuals' marginal willingnesses to pay for a small improvement are likely to be high. The cost of the first step is likely to be low. The difference between them is the net benefit of the first step. Further increases in cleanliness bring further net benefits as long as the aggregate marginal willingness to pay is greater than the marginal cost. But as the environment gets cleaner, the willingness to pay for additional units of cleanliness typically decreases, at least beyond some point, while the additional cost of further cleanliness rises. At that point where the marginal willingness to pay equals the marginal cost, the net benefit of further cleanliness is zero, and the total benefits of environmental improvement are at a maximum. This is the point at which the environmental quality standard should be set, if economic reasoning is followed.

The logic of benefit-cost analysis does not require that those who benefit pay for those benefits or that those who ultimately bear the cost of meeting a standard be compensated for those costs. Whether compensation should be paid is considered to be a question of equity. Benefit-cost analysis is concerned exclusively with economic efficiency as represented by the aggregate of benefits and costs. If standards are set to maximize the net benefits, then the gainers could fully compensate the losers and still come out ahead. But when beneficiaries do not compensate losers, there is political asymmetry. Those who benefit call for ever-stricter standards and more cleanup because they obtain the benefits and bear none of the costs, while those who must control pollution call for laxer standards.

An environmental quality standard set according to the benefit-cost rule will almost never call for complete elimination of pollution. Contrast this economic approach to setting standards with what the Clean Air Act says about establishing air quality standards for conventional air pollutants: section 109 requires that primary national ambient air quality standards for these pollutants be set so as to "protect human health" with "an adequate margin of safety." [3] If even the smallest amount of pollution increases the risk of disease or death at least for some sensitive individuals (as may be the case for ozone and fine particulates), a literal reading of the Clean Air Act would require the complete cleanup of these pollutants. But as pollution is reduced below the point where marginal willingness to pay equals marginal cost, the willingness to pay for additional cleanup will decrease while the cost of further cleanup will increase. The extra cost of going from 95 percent cleanup to 100 percent cleanup may be several times larger than the total cost of obtaining the first 95 percent cleanup. Society is rarely willing to pay such costs.

The Uses of Benefit-Cost Analysis

Benefit-cost analysis can be used to evaluate proposed regulations and new environmental policies in the manner just described. Establishing environmental regulations on the basis of benefits and costs is presently authorized by the Toxic Substances Control Act and the Federal Insecticide, Fungicide, and Rodenticide Act. Its use in setting standards is effectively precluded, however, under provisions of the Clean Air Act of 1970 and the

1972 Federal Water Pollution Control Act.[4] Since the mid 1970s, the EPA has been conducting benefit-cost analyses of major regulations even though in many cases they could not base decisions on the results. These analyses are major components of the regulatory impact assessments required under a series of Executive Orders issued by Presidents Jimmy Carter, Ronald Reagan, and Bill Clinton.

In at least one important case, the EPA's careful analysis of the benefits and costs of a regulation led to the adoption of stricter environmental protection. In 1985, the EPA reduced the maximum allowable lead in gasoline from 1.1 grams per gallon to 0.1 grams per gallon. Reducing the lead in gasoline means less lead in the environment. This, in turn, means a reduced incidence of adverse health and cognitive effects in children, a lower incidence of high blood pressure and cardiovascular disease in adults, and lower automotive maintenance expenditures. Not all these benefits can be easily measured in monetary terms. But counting only measurable benefits resulted in a benefit-cost ratio in excess of 10:1, thus justifying the regulation on economic grounds.[5]

Another possible use of benefit-cost analysis is to evaluate existing policies by estimating the benefits actually realized and comparing them with the costs of the policies. In an early effort to evaluate federal legislation on air and water pollution, I found that policies to control air pollution from stationary sources had probably yielded benefits (primarily in the form of improved human health) substantially greater than the economic costs of control, while the opposite was true of the control of automotive air pollution and industrial and municipal sources of water pollution.[6] Where retrospective analysis shows that costs have exceeded benefits, it may be possible to find ways to reduce the costs through adopting more cost-effective policies. But excessive costs may also indicate that the targets or environmental standards need to be reconsidered. For example, the Clean Air Act requirement that air quality standards be set at levels that protect human health without any consideration of costs has led to a standard for ozone (smog) that is undoubtedly too strict from an economic perspective.[7] On the other hand, there is mounting evidence that the standard for airborne particulates is not strict enough and that the benefits of a tighter standard will outweigh its costs.[8] As mandated by Congress in 1990, the EPA is presently conducting a retrospective benefit-cost assessment of the Clean Air Act of 1970. The results of this assessment could lead to a reconsideration of some provisions of the Clean Air Act.

Benefit-Cost Analysis: An Assessment

A major question is whether the state of the art of measurement is sufficiently well developed to provide reliable estimates of benefits and costs. It must be acknowledged that the physical and biological mechanisms by which environmental changes affect human beings are often not well understood. And the economic values people place on environmental changes can seldom be measured with precision. As a consequence, the results of a bene-fit-cost analysis are usually (or at least should be) expressed as most likely values with ranges of uncertainty. For example, the conclusion might be:

> The most likely value for benefits is $50 million with a range of uncer-tainty of plus or minus 50 percent; and the most likely value for costs is $30 million with a range of uncertainty of plus or minus 25 percent.

Even when ranges of uncertainty overlap, as in this example, information of this sort should be useful for decisionmakers who are concerned with how proposed policies would affect people's welfare.

A second question concerns the political context in which analyses of benefits and costs are carried out and used. The typical textbook discussions of the use of benefit-cost analysis implicitly assume a disinterested decision-maker who has access to all the relevant information on the positive and negative effects of a policy and who makes choices based on this information so as to maximize social welfare. The real world, however, seldom corre-sponds to the textbook model. First, as noted above, decisionmakers seldom have perfect information on benefits and costs. But more important, envi-ronmental policy decisions are usually made in a highly politicized setting in which the potential gainers and losers attempt to influence the decision.

Some contend that the benefits of environmental regulation are difficult to quantify and value compared to the costs. They point out that in such a setting the businesses that would bear the costs will be better organized to represent their views. If this is correct, then relying on benefit-cost analysis as the basis for setting environmental standards would appear to justify less environmental protection and pollution control than is really desirable. There are three responses to this argument.

First, this is not so much an argument for rejecting the benefit-cost criterion for decisionmaking as it is for electing and appointing decision-makers who more capable and for trying to achieve greater objectivity and balance of conflicting views. Second, the argument is based on, at best, an oversimplified view of the process. To be sure, proindustry groups will present information that minimizes estimates of benefits and maximizes estimates of costs. However, policy analysts within government seldom accept industry estimates at face value and, for major regulations, often prepare their own estimates of benefits and costs or have them prepared by consultants. At the EPA, most benefit-cost analyses are subject to a rigorous peer review by panels of outside experts established under the guidance of the agency's Science Advisory Board. And there is room in the process for the presentation of alternative estimates and points of view.

Finally, as a factual matter, it is not true that benefit-cost analysis is always biased against environmental protection. For many years decisions on funding for federal water resource development projects were nominally based on benefit-cost analyses. But these analyses used techniques that systematically overstated the benefits of development, understated the economic costs, and ignored the environmental costs of building dams, diverting water for irrigation, and so forth. As a consequence, a number of economically wasteful and environmentally damaging projects were under-taken. Indeed, serious consideration was once given to building a dam in the Grand Canyon.[9] Competent and objective benefit-cost analyses clearly demonstrated that many of these projects were uneconomical even without taking into account their environmental costs. For example, a study showing that economic costs exceeded benefits helped to weaken congressional support for the Dickey-Lincoln School hydroelectric power project on the St. John River in Maine. The Army Corps of Engineers estimated the bene-fit-cost ratio to be about 2.1:1 in 1976, but a more reasonable accounting showed the ratio to be much less favorable—between 0.8 and 0.9:1. This estimate was made without placing a price tag on the cost of destroying a free-flowing wild river.[10] Congress eventually deauthorized this project.

The Future of Benefit-Cost Analysis

The United States has made substantial progress in controlling some forms of pollution over the past twenty years. Examples include emissions of soot and dust from coal-burning power plants and municipal trash incinera-tors and the discharge of sewage and other organic wastes into rivers. In part, this is because these problems were highly visible and the costs of cleaning them up were relatively low. But the pollution problems of the present and future are likely to be much more costly to deal with. Thus, it will be impor-tant to try to estimate what the benefits of cleanup will be.

For example, consider the question of how much further the United States should go in controlling emissions of the substances that form atmos-pheric ozone. This is just the kind of question that benefit-cost analysis is best suited to answer. The authorities in the South Coast Air Basin, of which smog-ridden Los Angeles is a part, recently approved a new air quality management plan to impose additional strict controls on a number of sources of ozone pollution. This plan specifies three tiers of control measures, each tier increasing in stringency. The total cost may exceed $13 billion per year. To put this whopping sum in perspective, consider the cost in 1988 of all federal policies on air pollution control in the United States: about $30 billion per year. Does it make sense to undertake all three tiers of the Los Angeles plan? Paul Portney and his colleagues at Resources for the Future in Washington, D.C., have estimated that the benefits of implementing all three tiers together would be around $4 billion per year.[11] This casts some doubt on the wisdom of going all the way. But undertaking the first and second tiers might be justified. What is required is a comparison of the incre-mental benefits and costs for each tier. Questions of this sort will become increasingly important in the remainder of this decade, and economists will become increasingly busy seeking the information needed to answer them.

For some kinds of problems, analysis of the benefits and costs is made very difficult by the scientific uncertainties concerning the physical and ecological consequences of certain policies. The most important example is the question of preventing or controlling global climate change due to emissions of carbon dioxide (CO_2) and other greenhouse gases. Neverthe-less, some effort to describe and quantify benefits and costs may provide useful information to decisionmakers. For example, William Cline has attempted to estimate the benefits of controlling emissions of CO_2 and to compare them with estimates of the costs of controlling emissions provided by other authors. Although he finds the benefit-cost ratio to be somewhat less than 1, his estimates contain great uncertainties. He concludes that if society is prudent and wishes to avoid unnecessary risks, "it appears sensible on economic grounds to undertake aggressive abatement to sharply curtail the greenhouse effect." [12]

The twin questions of whether to conduct benefit-cost analyses of envi-ronmental policies and how the results should be used by decisionmakers have been brought to center stage in the 104th Congress. During 1995 Congress considered several bills that would substantially change the way that environmental policies are evaluated in this country. These bills would require that all new major regulations be subjected to a benefit-cost analysis and that only those regulations that passed a benefit-cost test could be approved. Some bills would also allow firms to request that existing regula-tions be reviewed and revoked unless their benefits exceeded costs.

Although most economists laud the principles expressed in these proposals, many have serious reservations about some of their specific features. For example, some of the proposals spell out in some detail the methods to be used in conducting the analyses; but the methods are not always state of the art. More important, this legislation would offer affected parties the opportunity to seek judicial review of the analyses. But judicial review is a costly and time-consuming process. Judges without training in economics would be obliged to make decisions about economic theory and method that are outside their areas of expertise. These requirements could bottle up proposed beneficial regulations in court for long periods of time. In fact, the real objective of these proposals may well be to prevent further regu-lation and promote the weakening of existing standards. While Congress is trying to require increased analysis of environmental regulations, it is also attempting to substantially reduce the financial resources available to carry out this work. [13]

Direct Regulation in Federal Environmental Policy

The major provisions of the federal laws controlling air and water pollu-tion embody what is often termed a *direct regulation* (or *command and control*) approach to achieve the established pollution control targets. This direct regulation approach involves placing limits on the allowable discharges of polluting substances from each source, coupled with an administrative and legal system to monitor compliance with these limits and to impose sanc-tions or penalties for violations.

In this approach the pollution control authority must carry out a series of four steps:

1. Determine the rules and regulations for each source that will achieve the given pollution control targets. These regulations might include the installation of certain types of pollution control equipment, restrictions on activities, or control of inputs, such as limiting the sulfur content in fuels. The regulations typically establish maximum allowable discharges of polluting substances from each source.
2. Establish penalties or sanctions for noncompliance.
3. Monitor sources so that incidents of noncompliance can be detected. Alternatively, the authorities might establish a system of self-reporting with periodic checks and audits of performance.
4. Punish violations. If violations of the regulations are detected, the authorities must use the administrative and legal mechanisms spelled out in the relevant laws to impose penalties or to require changes in the behavior of the sources.[14]

Economists have criticized the direct regulation approach on two grounds. First, the regulations require a pattern of pollution control activities that tends to be excessively costly—in other words, not cost-effective. Second, the incentive structure created for firms and individuals is inappropriate. Because compliance is so costly, there is no positive incentive to control pollution, although there is the negative incentive to avoid penalties. Not only is there no incentive to do better than the regulations require, but also the incentives to comply with the regulations themselves may be too weak to overcome the disincentive of bearing the costs of compliance.

Efficiency and Cost-Effectiveness

Even if one objects, for either philosophical or pragmatic reasons, to basing environmental policy on benefit-cost analysis, it still makes good sense to favor cost-effective environmental policies. Cost effectiveness means the stated environmental quality standards are achieved at the lowest possible total cost. The importance of achieving cost-effective pollution control policies should be self-evident: cost savings free resources that can be used to produce other goods and services of value to people.

When several sources of pollution exist in the same area, a pollution control policy must include some mechanism for dividing the responsibility for cleanup among the several sources. The direct regulation form of policy typically does this by requiring all sources to clean up by the same percentage. But such a policy will rarely be cost-effective. A pollution control policy is cost-effective only if it allocates the responsibility for cleanup among sources so that the incremental or marginal cost of achieving a one-unit improvement in environmental quality at any location is the same for all sources of pollution. Differences in the marginal costs of improving environmental quality can arise from differences in the marginal cost of treatment or waste reduction across sources; also, discharges from sources at different locations can have different effects on environmental quality.

Suppose that targets for air pollution control have been established by setting an ambient air quality standard for sulfur dioxide. To illustrate the importance of differences in marginal costs of control, suppose that two adjacent factories are both emitting sulfur dioxide. A one-ton decrease in emissions gives the same incremental benefit to air quality whether it is achieved by factory A or factory B. Now suppose that to achieve the ambient air quality standard, emissions must be reduced by fifty tons per day. One way to achieve the target is to require each factory to clean up twenty-five tons per day. But suppose that with this allocation of cleanup responsibility, factory A's marginal cost of cleanup is $10 per ton per day, while at factory B, the marginal cost is only $5 per ton per day. Allowing factory A to reduce its cleanup by one ton per day saves it $10. If factory B is required to clean up an extra ton, total cleanup is the same and the air quality standard is met. And the total cost of pollution control is reduced by $5 per day. Additional savings are possible by continuing to shift cleanup responsibility to B (raising B's marginal cost) and away from A (reducing A's marginal cost). This should continue until B's rising marginal cost of control is made equal to A's now lower marginal cost. Emissions of a pollutant may have different impacts on air quality depending on the location of the source. This must also be taken into account in finding the least-cost or cost-minimizing pattern of emissions reductions.[15]

Nothing in the logic or the procedures for setting pollution control requirements for sources ensures that the conditions for cost minimization will be satisfied. In setting discharge limits, federal and state agencies usually do not take into account the marginal cost of control, at least in part because of the difficulties they would have in getting the data. Thus, discharge limits are not likely to result in equal marginal costs of reducing discharges across different sources of the same pollutant. One analysis of the marginal cost of removing oxygen-demanding organic material under existing federal water pollution standards found a thirtyfold range of marginal costs within the six industries examined.[16]

Another way to look at the question of cost-effectiveness is to ask how to get the greatest environmental improvement for a given total budget or total expenditure on pollution control. The answer is to spend that money on those pollution control activities with the highest level of pollution control benefit per dollar spent (the biggest "bang for the buck"). For example, if society decides for whatever reason to spend $1 million to control organic forms of water pollution, it should require that the money be spent on industries with the highest pollutant removal per dollar, which is to say, the lowest cost per pound of removal. The study cited in the preceding paragraph shows that spending an extra dollar for controlling organic pollution in a low-cost industry will buy thirty times more pollution removal than spending the same dollar in an industry with high marginal costs.

A number of environmental protection and public health policies are cost-ineffective because of large differences across activities in the marginal costs of control, or in the benefit per dollars spent. For example, a study of the costs of regulating toxic chemicals in the environment and the workplace found that the costs of each life year saved varied widely, both across chemicals and for different regulations on the same chemical. The costs of meeting an exposure standard for benzene varied from $76 thousand per life year saved in rubber and tire factories to $3 million per life year saved in coke and coal chemical factories. And the costs of controlling arsenic emissions varied from $74 thousand per life year saved at copper smelters to $51 million at glass manufacturing plants.[17] These examples clearly show that it would be possible both to lower the compliance cost burden for industry and to increase the number of life years saved by somewhat reducing the requirements imposed on the highest-cost factories and placing stricter requirements on those sources with the lowest cost of compliance.

Probably the greatest opportunities for more cost-effective pollution control are in the realm of the conventional pollutants of air and water. The problem of cost-effectiveness has stimulated many empirical studies comparing the costs of direct regulation policies (under provisions of the Clean Air Act and Federal Water Pollution Control Act) with cost-effective alternatives based on equalizing the marginal costs of meeting environmental quality standards across all sources of pollution. In his review of these studies, Tom Tietenberg found that least-cost pollution control planning could generate cost savings of 30 to 40 percent, and in some cases more than 90 percent.[18] This means that in some instances pollution control costs are *ten times* higher than they need to be.

How can cost savings of this magnitude be realized? Can pollution control policies be made more cost-effective without causing further environmental degradation? The answer lies in changing the incentives that face polluters.

Incentives vs. Direct Regulation

In an unregulated market economy pollution arises because of the way individuals and firms respond to market forces and incentives. Firms find that safe and nonpolluting methods of disposing of wastes are usually more costly than dumping them into the environment, even though such disposal harms others. Because polluters are generally not required to compensate those who are harmed, they have no incentive to alter their waste disposal practices.

Incentives under Direct Regulation

In deciding how to respond to a system of regulations and enforcement, polluters will compare the costs of compliance with the likely costs and penalties associated with noncompliance. The costs of compliance may be substantial, but the costs of noncompliance are likely to be uncertain. Incidents of noncompliance might not be detected. Minor violations, even if detected, might be ignored by the authorities. Rather than commit itself to the uncertain legal processes involved in imposing significant fees and penalties, the overburdened enforcement arm of the pollution control agency might negotiate an agreement with the polluter to obtain compliance at some future date. And even if cases are brought to court, the court might be more lenient than the pollution control agency would wish. All of these problems of monitoring and enforcement of regulations add up to a weak incentive for polluters to comply with the regulations.

One of the consequences of these weak incentives has been high rates of violations of existing standards. For example, for an eighteen-month period in 1981 and 1982, the U.S. General Accounting Office compared the actual discharges of a sample of water polluters with the permissible discharges under the terms of their discharge permits. They found a major noncompliance problem. Eighty-two percent of the sources studied had at least one month of noncompliance during the study period. Twenty-four percent of the sample was in "significant noncompliance," with at least four consecutive months during which discharges exceeded permitted levels by at least 50 percent.[19] It is likely that compliance rates in general have improved since then; but evidence on this point is scarce.

Improving the Incentives

Economists have long argued for an alternative approach to pollution control policy; it is based on the creation of strong positive incentives for firms to control pollution. One form that the incentive could take is a charge, or tax, on each unit of pollution discharged. The tax would be equal to the monetary value of the damage that pollution caused to others. Each discharger wishing to minimize its total cost (cleanup cost plus tax bill) would compare the tax cost of discharging a unit of pollution with the cost of controlling or preventing the discharge. As long as the cost of control was lower than the tax or charge, the firm would want to prevent the discharge. In fact, it would reduce pollution to the point where its marginal cost of control was just equal to the tax and, indirectly, equal to the marginal damage caused by the pollution. The properly set tax would cause the firm to undertake on its own accord the optimum amount of pollution control.

The pollution tax (or charge) strategy has long appealed to economists because it provides a sure and graduated incentive to firms by making pollution itself a cost of production. And it provides an incentive for innovation and technological change in pollution control. Also, because the polluters are not likely to reduce their discharges to zero, the government would collect revenues that could be used to finance government programs, reduce the deficit, or make possible cuts in taxes.

A system of marketable or tradable discharge permits (TDPs) has essentially the same incentive effects as a tax on pollution. The government would issue a limited number of pollution permits or "tickets." Each ticket would entitle its owner to discharge one unit of pollution during a specific time period. The government could either distribute the tickets free of charge to polluters on some basis or auction them off to the highest bidders. Dischargers could also buy and sell permits among themselves. The cost of purchasing a ticket or of forgoing the revenue from selling the ticket to someone else has the same incentive effects as a tax on pollution of the same amount.

Polluters can respond to the higher cost of pollution imposed by a tax or TDP system in a variety of ways. They could install some form of conventional treatment system if the cost of treatment were less than the tax or permit price. But more important technical options also exist. Polluters can consider changing to processes that are inherently less polluting. They can recover and recycle materials that otherwise would remain in the waste stream. They can change to inputs that produce less pollution. For example, a paper mill's response to a tax on dioxin in its effluent might be to stop using chlorine as a bleaching agent. Finally, because the firm would have to pay for whatever pollution it did not bring under control, this cost would result in higher prices for its products and fewer units of its products being purchased by consumers. The effects of higher prices and lower quantities demanded would be to reduce the production level of the firm and, other things being equal, to further reduce the amount of pollution being generated.

A system of pollution taxes or TDPs can make a major contribution to achieving cost-effectiveness. If several sources are discharging into the environment, they will be induced to minimize the total cost of achieving any given reduction in pollution. This is because each discharger will control discharges up to the point where its marginal or incremental cost of control is equated to the tax or permit price. If all dischargers face the same tax or price, their marginal costs of pollution control will be equal. This is the condition for cost-effectiveness. Low-cost sources will control relatively more, thus leading to a cost-effective allocation of cleanup responsibilities. There is no reallocation of responsibilities for reducing discharges that will achieve the same total reduction at a lower total cost.

One difficulty with implementing a pollution-charge system is knowing what the charge should be. In some cases enough is already known about the costs of control for average polluters so that the appropriate charge could be calculated. The charge can be adjusted, too, if experience reveals that it was initially set too high or too low.

One advantage of the TDP system is that the pollution control agency does not have to determine the level of the tax. Once the agency determines the number of permits, the market determines the permit price. Another advantage of a system of TDPs in comparison with effluent charges is that it represents a less radical departure from the existing system. Because all sources are presently required to obtain permits specifying the maximum allowable discharges, it would be relatively easy to rewrite them in a divisible format and to allow sources to buy or sell them. A source with low marginal costs of control should be willing to clean up more and to sell the unused permits as long as the price of a permit were greater than the marginal cost of control. A source with high pollution control costs would find it cheaper to buy permits than to clean up itself.[20]

Recent Developments

A marketable permit program is a key component of the federal program to reduce acid deposition resulting from emissions of sulfur dioxide. The Clean Air Act Amendments of 1990 called for a reduction of sulfur dioxide emissions of 10 million tons per year (to about 50 percent of 1980 levels) by the year 2000. Starting in 1995, major sources of these emissions (primarily coal-burning electric power plants) are receiving permits for emissions (called allowances) equal to a percentage of their historic emissions levels. The numbers of permits will be reduced to the target level in 2000. The cost savings relative to direct regulation are expected to be several billion dollars per year.[21]

In other developments, a TDP system has been implemented by the EPA for emissions of chlorofluorocarbons, the chemicals that cause depletion of stratospheric ozone. And the Air Quality Management District in Los Angeles has set up a TDP system for nitrogen oxides emissions as part of its plan to reduce ozone air pollution (smog). The first set of permits was issued to existing sources of emissions in 1994. Each year for the next ten years, the number of permits will be reduced by between 5 percent and 8 percent. Each source has the choice of reducing emissions in step with the reduced number of permits it receives, reducing emissions by more than the required amount and selling the extra permits, or keeping emissions constant and purchasing additional permits. The choice will be dictated by the marginal costs of reducing emissions relative to the market price of a permit.

Many state and local governments have also been experimenting with various forms of pollution fees in other contexts. Examples include tying the annual fee paid for licenses to operate industrial facilities to the expected quantities of emissions of air and water pollutants, charging households and others "by the bag" for trash collection and disposal, and taxing purchases of automobile tires and motor oil and using the revenues for safe disposal of these products.

More Modest Reforms

The EPA has found several ways to use economic incentives in a more limited way to introduce greater flexibility into the existing legal framework and to foster cost-effectiveness in meeting existing targets. Two of the most interesting of these are the creation of "bubbles" and pollution control "offsets."

Major industrial facilities often have several separate activities or processes, each of which is subject to a different pollution limit or standard. Many of these activities discharge the same substances, yet the incremental costs of pollution control may vary a great deal across activities. The "bubble concept" was so called because it treats a collection of smokestacks or sources within a large factory as if it were encased in a bubble. Pollution control requirements are applied to the aggregate of emissions leaving the bubble rather than to each individual stack or source. The bubble concept allows plant managers, with EPA or state approval, to adjust the levels of control at different activities if they can lower total control costs. But the total amount of a pollutant discharged from the plant must not exceed the aggregate of the emissions limitations for individual processes. Aggregate savings have probably amounted to several billion dollars. Because EPA regulations sometimes require a net reduction in emissions from the "bubble," the net effect on air quality has probably been positive.[22]

The offset policy was created in the mid 1970s to resolve a potential conflict between meeting federal air quality standards and allowing economic growth and development. The Clean Air Act of 1970 prohibited the licensing of new air pollution sources if they would interfere with the attainment of federal air quality standards. Taken literally, this would prohibit any new industrial facilities with air pollution emissions in those parts of the country not in compliance with existing air quality standards. In response to this dilemma, the EPA issued a set of rules that allowed new sources to be licensed in nonattainment areas provided they could show that there would be an offsetting reduction in emissions from existing sources of pollution in the area above and beyond what had already been required— either by installing additional controls on these sources or by shutting them down.

For firms desiring to expand or to enter a region, the offset rules provide an incentive to reduce emissions from existing sources in the region. The offsets need not be limited to reductions at other sources owned by the firm planning a new source investment. Firms are free to seek offsets from other firms as well. Because EPA rules require that offsets be executed on a greater than one-for-one basis, the net impact on air quality has probably been positive.[23] The policy also encourages technological innovation to find means of creating offsets and probably encourages older, dirty facilities to shut down sooner than they otherwise would in order to sell offsets.

Economic Incentives and Environmental Policy in the 1990s

Interest in the use of economic incentives appears to be growing in Congress as well as at the EPA. Evidence of this can be found in two reports released in 1989 and 1991 under the banner of *Project 88*. These reports were cosponsored in the Senate by Tim Wirth (D-Colo.), who is now undersecretary of state for global affairs, and John Heinz (R-Pa.), now deceased. The first report stated that "conventional regulatory policies need to be supplemented by market-based strategies which can foster major improvements in environmental quality by enlisting the innovative capacity of our economy in the development of efficient and equitable solutions."[24] The report urged much greater use of incentive-based systems such as TDPs and pollution taxes. It also suggested how these systems can be applied to many different environmental problems. The second report, *Project 88—Round II,* provided more detailed proposals for using incentive-based policies to deal with global climate change, energy conservation, solid and hazardous waste management, the supposed scarcity of water in the arid West, and the management of our timber and other resources of the National Forest system.[25]

Drawing on these two reports and other sources, I will briefly discuss several possible applications of economic incentive strategies. They include using taxes or tradable permits to reduce carbon dioxide emissions and excessive applications of pesticides, using deposit-refund systems to prevent improper disposal of hazardous wastes, and "getting the prices right" to prevent excessive use of scarce resources.

CO_2 Emissions

If present trends in emissions and atmospheric concentrations of CO_2 continue, average temperatures worldwide could increase by 1.5 to 6 degrees Fahrenheit by the year 2100.[26] If this global warming is to be avoided, or at least retarded, global emissions of CO_2 must be held steady if not substantially reduced. This issue was addressed at the Earth summit in Río de Janeiro in 1992. One result was the Convention on Climate Change, which commits its signatories, including the United States, to stabilize emissions of greenhouse gases at 1990 levels. The United States has not, as yet, established a date for achieving this target.

A major policy question facing all nations is what policy instruments should be adopted to meet this target. One possibility is to implement an economic incentive system such as a tax or TDP program.[27] Given a policy decision to seek a reduction in CO_2 emissions, the case for preferring an incentive-based system over direct regulation is strong. In terms of incentives, enforcement, cost-effectiveness, and administrative ease, both the tax and TDP system come out ahead of direct regulation. One of the important considerations in choosing between a tax and TDP system is the different ways in which the consequences of uncertainty are felt. With a tax, there is uncertainty about the magnitude of the reduction in emissions that will be achieved for any given tax rate. With a TDP system, there is no uncertainty about this because the reduction in emissions is determined by the number of permits the government chooses to issue. But there is uncertainty about the price of permits and the costs that will be incurred in achieving the required reduction in emissions.

Given the commitment to stabilize greenhouse gas emissions, the certainty about the size of the emissions reductions makes a TDP system more attractive than a tax on CO_2 emissions. If such a commitment had not been made, however, there is a stronger case for taxing CO_2 emissions. This is because very little is known about the economic costs of controlling these emissions. Thus, the uncertainty of the costs and economic impact of a TDP system could be a disadvantage. A compromise position would be to start now with a relatively modest tax on CO_2 emissions. The response to the tax would provide information on the relationship between the marginal cost of controlling emissions and the size of the emissions reduction. Many authors have proposed taxes at various rates. Most of the proposals fall in the range of $10-100 per ton of carbon content of the fuel. To put these numbers in perspective, a tax of $75 per ton of carbon is equivalent to an increase in the gasoline tax by about twenty cents per gallon.

Pesticide Use

Heavy use of chemical pesticides in agriculture has resulted in two kinds of environmental problems. First, pesticide residues can adhere to soil particles that erode from the land, causing ecological problems in downstream lakes and rivers. Second, these residues can leach directly into aquifers and contaminate water supplies to households.

The EPA currently has the power to ban specific pesticides entirely or to ban or otherwise regulate applications on particular crops. The degree of erosion and the potential for pesticide residues to leach into groundwater vary widely across different regions of the country. Also the value of pesticide use varies widely by crop and region. Thus, any system of direct regulation is likely to be very cost-ineffective in protecting surface and groundwater quality. The first *Project 88* report suggests placing a tax on the use of certain pesticides both to discourage their use and to encourage the development and utilization of environmentally sound agricultural practices. In the absence of specific knowledge about the costs to farmers of reducing their applications of pesticides, it is difficult to know at what level to set a tax for each pesticide in question.

A better alternative might be a regionally based system of marketable pesticide application permits (PAPs). Local officials could estimate the maximum allowable applications of each pesticide in the region that are consistent with protecting surface and groundwater quality. Farmers could then bid for PAPs in an auction. Some farmers would find that the auction price was greater than the value to them of using the pesticide, so they would seek out other ways to deal with pest problems. Assuming adequate monitoring and enforcement, the maximum safe levels of pesticide application would not be exceeded.

Hazardous Waste Disposal

Federal policy on hazardous wastes focuses on regulating disposal practices. The effectiveness of this policy is highly dependent on the government's ability to monitor and enforce these disposal regulations and to detect and penalize illegal practices. Both industry and government have recognized that the problem of safe disposal can be made more manageable by reducing the quantities of hazardous wastes being generated. The high cost of complying with disposal regulations is itself an incentive for industry to engage in source reduction, but it is also an incentive to violate the regulations on safe disposal, the so-called midnight-dumping problem.

For some types of wastes, a deposit-refund system could provide better incentives to reduce hazardous wastes at their source as well as to dispose of them safely. The system would resemble the deposits on returnable soda and beer cans and bottles established in some states. For example, the manufacturer of a solvent that would become a hazardous waste after it is used could be required to pay the EPA a deposit of so many dollars per gallon of solvent produced. The amount of the deposit would have to be at least as high as the cost of recycling the solvent or disposing of it safely. Because paying the deposit becomes, in effect, part of the cost of producing the solvent, the manufacturer would have to raise its price. This would discourage the use of the solvent and encourage source reduction. The deposit would be refunded to whoever returned one gallon of the solvent to a certified safe disposal facility or recycler. Thus, the user of the solvent would find it more profitable to return the solvent than to dispose of it illegally. In this way private incentives and the search for profit are harnessed to the task of environmental protection.[28] A deposit-refund system has potential applications for a wide variety of products where improper disposal is environmentally damaging but difficult to prevent. Examples include motor oil, car tires, and mercury and lead-acid batteries.

Getting the Prices Right

A surprising number of environmental problems are caused, at least in part, by inappropriate prices for some of the goods and services that people buy and by barriers to the effective functioning of markets. A basic economic principle is that if the price of a good is increased, the quantity purchased decreases, while the quantity that producers are willing to sell increases. Many environmental problems are linked to government policies that keep the prices of some things artificially low. For example, the federal government sells water to farmers in the West at prices that are far below the government's cost of supplying the water. And most states in the arid West either prohibit or place substantial restrictions on the ability of private owners of water rights to sell their water to others who might be able to make better use of it. As a consequence, vast quantities of water are wasted in inefficient irrigation practices while some urban areas face water shortages. This increases the political pressure to build more dams and to divert larger quantities of water from rivers already under ecological stress from inadequate water flows.[29]

The U.S. Forest Service often sells rights to harvest its timber at prices that do not cover the government's own cost of supervising the harvest and constructing access roads. Not only do taxpayers bear the direct financial cost, but there is an indirect cost in that too much forest land is subject to cutting with the attendant loss of wildlife habitat and recreation opportunities.[30]

Free access to public facilities is a special case of a low price. In many urban areas, access to the public highway system is free. Even where tolls are charged, these do not always cover the cost of constructing and maintaining the highways. More important, the tolls do not reflect the costs that each driver imposes on others when he or she enters an already congested highway, slows traffic even further, and increases the emissions of air pollution. If each driver were charged a toll that reflected his or her marginal contribution to congestion, this would reduce the incentives drivers have to use the highway during peak traffic hours. Average speeds would be higher with more efficient use of fuel and less air pollution. This would diminish the pressure to build more roads with their impacts on land use, and so forth.[31]

In some cases, prices are too high. The government supports the prices of some agricultural products at artificially high levels. This gives farmers incentives to plant more of these crops on less productive lands and to apply excessive quantities of pesticides and fertilizers. The result can be excess soil erosion and pollution of streams and rivers in rural areas as runoff carries sediments, pesticides, and nutrients into adjacent waters.

Conclusion

Economic analysis is likely to be increasingly useful in grappling with the environmental problems of the 1990s for at least four reasons. First, as policymakers address the more complex and deeply rooted national and global environmental problems, they are finding that solutions are more and more costly. Thus, it is increasingly important for the public to get its "money's worth" from these policies. This means looking at benefits and comparing them with costs. Therefore, some form of benefit-cost analysis, such as that required by President Clinton's Executive Order 12866, will play a larger role in policy debates and decisions in the future.

Second, the slow progress over the past twenty years in dealing with conventional air and water pollution problems shows the need to use private initiative more effectively through altering the incentive structure. This means placing greater reliance on pollution charges, tradable discharge permits, and deposit-refund systems. I have suggested three possible applications of incentive-based mechanisms to emerging problems, but the list of potential applications is much longer, as is made clear in the *Project 88* reports. The institution of tradable permit programs at the federal level and in Southern California demonstrate the political feasibility of this type of instrument. However, the current political climate appears to be quite hostile to any form of tax increase, even taxes on "bads" such as pollution.

Third, the high aggregate cost of controlling various pollutants and environmental threats makes it imperative to design policies that are cost-effective. Incentive-based mechanisms can play a very important role in achieving pollution control targets at something approaching the minimum possible social cost. Finally, economic analysis can help us to identify those cases where government policies result in prices that send the wrong signals to consumers and producers and fail to provide the right incentives to make wise use of scarce resources and the environment.

Notes

1. There are exceptions to this rule. For example, increasing the rate of timber harvesting can increase the available habitat for white-tailed deer (and their predators). But it reduces the habitat for species that are dependent on old-growth forests.
2. For more discussion of the principles of benefit-cost analysis and applications in the realm of environmental policy, see one of the recent textbooks on environmental economics. Examples include Tom Tietenberg, *Environmental and Natural Resource Economics,* 3d ed. (New York: HarperCollins, 1992); Barry C. Field, *Environmental Economics: An Introduction* (New York: McGraw-Hill, 1994); and James R. Kahn, *An Economic Approach to the Environment and Natural Resources* (New York: Dryden Press, 1995).
3. These so-called criteria pollutants are particulate matter (less than 10 microns in diameter), sulfur dioxide, nitrogen oxides, carbon monoxide, ozone, and lead.
4. Paul R. Portney, ed., *Public Policies for Environmental Protection* (Washington, D.C.: Resources for the Future, 1990), esp. 21.
5. U.S. Environmental Protection Agency, *Costs and Benefits of Reducing Lead in Gasoline: Final Regulatory Impact Analysis* (Washington, D.C.: EPA, 1985).
6. A. Myrick Freeman III, *Air and Water Pollution Control: A Benefit-Cost Assessment* (New York: Wiley, 1982).
7. Paul R. Portney, "Economics and the Clean Air Act," *Journal of Economic Perspectives* 4, no. 4 (1990): 173-181.
8. A. Myrick Freeman III, "The Environmental Cost of Electricity: An Exercise in Pricing the Environment," Bowdoin College Economics Working Paper, 95-116, Brunswick, Maine, p. 31.
9. For a description of how bad economic analysis is used to justify proposals of this sort, see Alan Carlin, "The Grand Canyon Controversy: Or, How Reclamation Justifies the Unjustifiable," in *Pollution, Resources, and the Environment,* ed. Alain C. Enthoven and A. Myrick Freeman III (New York: Norton, 1973).
10. See A. Myrick Freeman III, "The Benefits and Costs of the Dickey-Lincoln Project: A Preliminary Report" (Unpublished paper, Bowdoin College, Brunswick, Maine, 1974); and Freeman, "The Benefits and Costs of the Dickey-Lincoln Project: An Interim Update" (Unpublished paper, Bowdoin College, Brunswick, Maine, 1978).
11. See Paul R. Portney et al., "L.A. Law: Regulating Air Quality in California's South Coast," *Issues in Science and Technology* 13, no. 4 (1989): 68-73.
12. William R. Cline, *The Economics of Global Warming* (Washington, D.C.: Institute for International Economics, 1992), 9. For other perspectives on the economics of global warming, see William D. Nordhaus, "To Slow or Not to Slow," *Economic Journal* 101 (1991): 920-938, and Thomas C. Schelling, "Some Economics of Global Warming," *American Economic Review* 82, no. 1 (1992): 1-15.
13. For more discussion of the proposed legislation and the economic issues involved, see Paul R. Portney, "Cartoon Caricatures of Regulatory Reform," *Resources* 121 (1995): 21-24.
14. For more detailed discussions of the major provisions of federal air and water pollution law, see Paul R. Portney, "Air Pollution Policy," and A. Myrick Freeman III, "Water Pollution Policy," in *Public Policies for Environmental Protection,* ed. Portney.
15. For more detail on this, see any of the texts cited in n. 2 above.
16. Wesley A. Magat, Alan J. Krupnick, and Winston Harrington, *Rules in the Making: A Statistical Analysis of Regulatory Agency Behavior* (Washington, D.C.: Resources for the Future, 1986), table 6-1.

17. Tammy O. Tengs et al., "Five-Hundred Life-Saving Interventions and Their Cost-Effectiveness," *Risk Analysis* 15 (1995): 369-390.

18. T. H. Tietenberg, *Emissions Trading: An Exercise in Reforming Pollution Policy* (Washington, D.C.: Resources for the Future, 1985), 38-47.

19. See U.S. General Accounting Office, *Waste Water Dischargers Are Not Complying with EPA Pollution Control Permits* (Washington, D.C.: U.S. General Accounting Office, 1983). This study and other evidence are discussed by Clifford S. Russell in "Monitoring and Enforcement," in *Public Policies for Environmental Protection*, ed. Portney.

20. A more modest step would be to allow two (or more) sources to propose a reallocation of cleanup requirements between them if they found it to their mutual advantage and if there were no degradation of environmental quality.

21. For a review of the allowance trading program and what has been happening in this market, see Renee Rico, "The U.S. Allowance Trading System for Sulfur Dioxide: An Update on Market Experience," *Environmental and Resource Economics* 5 (1995): 115-129.

22. Robert W. Hahn and Gordon L. Hester, "Marketable Permits: Lessons from Theory and Practice," *Ecology Law Quarterly* 16, no. 2 (1989): 361-406.

23. Ibid.

24. *Project 88, Harnessing Market Forces to Protect Our Environment: Initiatives for the New President,* a public policy study sponsored by Sen. Tim Wirth (D-Colo.) and Sen. John Heinz (R-Pa.) (Washington, D.C.: Project 88, December 1988). See also Bruce A. Ackerman and Richard B. Stewart, "Reforming Environmental Law: The Democratic Case for Market Incentives," *Columbia Journal of Environmental Law* 13 (1988): 171-199; and Richard B. Stewart, "Controlling Environmental Risks through Economic Incentives," *Columbia Journal of Environmental Law* 13 (1988): 153-169.

25. *Project 88—Round II, Incentives for Action: Designing Market-Based Environmental Strategies,* a public policy study sponsored by Sen. Tim Wirth (D-Colo.) and Sen. John Heinz (R-Pa.) (Washington, D.C.: Project 88, May 1991).

26. This is the new consensus forecast of the International Panel on Climate Change as reported in the *New York Times*, September 18, 1995, A1.

27. See Roger C. Dower and Mary Beth Zimmerman, *The Right Climate for Carbon Taxes: Creating Economic Incentives to Protect the Atmosphere* (Washington, D.C.: World Resources Institute, 1992).

28. See *Project 88,* chap. 7; and Clifford S. Russell, "Economic Incentives in the Management of Hazardous Waste," *Columbia Journal of Environmental Law* 13 (1988): 1101-1119.

29. *Project 88—Round II,* chap. 4.

30. Ibid.

31. Kenneth A. Small, Clifford Winston, and Carol A. Evans, *Road Work: A New Highway Pricing and Investment Strategy* (Washington, D.C.: Brookings, 1989); and James J. MacKenzie, Roger C. Dower, and Donald D. T. Chen, *The Going Rate: What It Really Costs to Drive* (Washington, D.C.: World Resources Institute, 1992).

10

Risk-Based Decisionmaking

Richard N. L. Andrews

Environmental regulation in the 1990s is pervaded by the language of risk, and environmental policy analysis by the concepts and methods of quantitative risk assessment (QRA). In 1984 the administrator of the Environmental Protection Agency (EPA), William Ruckelshaus, officially endorsed "risk assessment and risk management" as the primary framework for EPA decisionmaking.[1] In 1987 a major agency report stated flatly that "the fundamental mission of the Environmental Protection Agency is to reduce risks"; and another influential report, issued in 1990, recommended that the EPA "target its environmental protection efforts on the basis of opportunities for the greatest risk reduction."[2] By the end of the 1980s risk-based decisionmaking had become the dominant language for discussing environmental policy in the EPA, and in some other agencies as well.[3]

The adoption of this risk-based framework has important implications for the future of U.S. environmental policy. Originally developed as a technical procedure for evaluating the health risks of toxic chemicals, the risk-based approach has since been promoted as a broader comparative basis for setting priorities across the whole range of EPA's environmental policy mandates—and by other federal agencies, state and local governments, and other countries as well. Risk assessment is now the focus of intensive political debate over trade-offs between environmental concerns and regulatory burdens more generally, and recent legislative proposals to mandate risk-based decisionmaking by statute could either reform or undermine many of the environmental protection statutes of the past quarter-century.

Risk assessment remains controversial, both among scientists and policymakers and in general political debate; even many of its advocates are uneasy that it is often oversold or abused. Risk-based decisionmaking may also be too narrow and too negative to deal adequately with many of the most important policy issues of the present and future. To appraise its significance, one must first understand how it has come to be so widely used, what it is, why it is controversial, and how it is now being applied to the environmental issues of the 1990s.

The Regulatory Legacy

U.S. environmental policy before 1970 included more than seven decades' experience in managing the environment as a natural resource base—lands and forests, minerals, water, fish and wildlife—but pollution control had been left almost exclusively to state and local governments. Beginning in 1970, however, U.S. policy shifted dramatically from managing the environment to regulating it, and from state and local to national primacy. The EPA was created by reorganizing most of the few existing regulatory programs into one agency. Within a decade Congress enacted more than a dozen major new regulatory statutes for federal pollution control, each requiring many individual standards and permits for particular technologies, practices, and substances (see chap. 7).

Risk-Based Regulation

Initially these laws emphasized the use of known technologies to reduce the most obvious problems: urban sewage, automotive air pollution, and the major industrial pollutants of air and water. The Clean Air Act of 1970, for instance, directed the EPA to set national minimum ambient air quality standards for six major pollutants, based on health criteria, and set deliberately "technology-forcing" statutory timetables for reducing emissions from motor vehicles. The Federal Water Pollution Control Act amendments of 1972 required federal permits for all new water pollution sources, again using technology-based standards—that is, "best practicable" and "best available" technologies—to force improved control of wastewater discharges from each industrial process.

As these measures took effect, however, environmental politics became increasingly intertwined with the "war on cancer" and with public fears that pesticides and other manufactured chemicals might be significant causes of cancer.[4] The environmental control agenda was broadened and redirected, therefore, to address the far larger domain of chemical hazards as a whole: toxic air and water pollutants, pesticides, drinking-water contaminants, hazardous wastes, and toxic substances in commerce generally. This domain included thousands of compounds, far too many to address explicitly in statutes. At the time, many of these compounds had not even been well studied, and many of them were not just wastes but had important economic uses.[5]

These substance-by-substance decisions raised serious new problems for environmental protection policy. Asbestos, for instance, clearly appeared to cause cancer in shipyard workers who were continuously exposed to it at high concentrations as they installed it in ships during World War II. But did this mean that asbestos in floor and ceiling tiles was a serious threat to children? Serious enough to require that every school and day care center spend large sums to remove it rather than to improve their educational programs? Similar questions about risk and cost could be raised about many other chemicals the EPA might regulate: industrial chemicals such as polychlorinated biphenyls (PCBs), pesticides such as DDT (dichlorodiphenyltrichloroethane), trace contaminants such as radon in drinking water, and consumer products such as lead in gasoline, pentachlorophenol (PCP, a wood preservative in outdoor paint), and others. Which of these thousands of chemicals should the EPA regulate, and how should it decide? Should it regulate them to eliminate all risk (if that were even possible)? Or to reduce the risk to some minimum level (one in a million, for instance)? Or to some level comparable to other risks people routinely accept voluntarily (driving a car or crossing the street, for instance)? Or to a level justified by economic estimates of the costs and benefits of control? Finally, how much proof of these risks should the agency have to have before regulating?

To control toxic chemicals, Congress enacted "risk based" and "risk balancing" statutes, which required the EPA to assess the risks of each substance it proposed to regulate, and then either to protect the public with "adequate margins of safety" against "unreasonable risks," or to make choices that would balance those risks against economic benefits. In turn, the EPA had to develop methods for *setting risk priorities* among many possible candidates for regulation; for *justifying particular regulatory decisions,* balancing risks against benefits; and for *approving site decisions,* based on an "acceptable risk" for certifying a cleaned-up hazardous waste site or permitting construction of a new facility.[6] A Supreme Court decision in 1980 reinforced these requirements by holding in effect that many proposed environmental health standards for chemicals could be invalidated if the agency did not justify them by quantitative risk assessments.[7]

Risk Assessment and Risk Management

Quantitative risk assessment has been defined as "the process of obtaining quantitative measures of risk levels, where risk refers to the possibility of uncertain, adverse consequences."[8] To the EPA, "risk" normally means "the probability of injury, disease, or death under specific circumstances," and risk assessment means "the characterization of the potential adverse health effects of human exposure to environmental hazards."[9] Note that these definitions combine two separate concepts: hazard (adverse consequence, usually assumed to be a health hazard) and probability (quantitative measures of likelihood or uncertainty). This mixing of two concepts is one cause of the confusion and controversy that surrounds risk assessment.

One fundamental doctrine of this approach was that risk "assessment" should be clearly distinguished from risk "management." Risk assessment, in this view, was a purely scientific activity based on expert analysis of facts. Risk management was the subsequent decision process in which the scientific conclusions were considered along with other elements (such as statutory requirements, costs, public values, and politics).

A National Research Council report endorsed this view in 1983, and it was adopted as the EPA policy by administrator William Ruckelshaus. It remains a basic tenet in the literature on risk assessment, though Ruckelshaus himself later acknowledged the difficulty of maintaining such a clear distinction in practice.[10]

Risk Assessment

Quantitative health risk assessment was rapidly elaborated into a detailed analytical procedure that included four elements:

- *hazard identification,* in which the analyst gathers information on whether a substance may be a health hazard;
- *dose-response assessment,* in which the analyst attempts to describe quantitatively the relationship between the amount of exposure to the substance and the degree of toxic effect;
- *exposure assessment,* in which the analyst estimates how many people may actually be exposed to the substance and under what conditions (how much of it, how often, for how long, from what sources); and
- *risk characterization,* in which the analyst combines information from the previous steps into an assessment of overall health risk: for example, an added risk that one person in a thousand (or a hundred, or a million) will develop cancer after exposure at the expected levels over a lifetime.

Suppose, for instance, that the EPA decides to assess the health risks of an organic solvent used to degrease metal parts: a liquid, moderately volatile, that is somewhat soluble in water and degrades slowly in it.[11] The hazard identification step uncovers several experimental animal studies between 1940 and 1960, all showing lethal toxicity to the liver at high doses but no toxic effects below an identifiable "threshold" dose; cancer was not studied. One more recent study, however, appears to show that lifetime exposure to much lower doses causes significant increases in liver cancers in both mice and rats. The only human data are on exposed workers, too few to draw statistically valid conclusions (two cases of cancer diagnosed in fewer than two hundred workers, when one case might have been expected). From these data the EPA decides that the solvent is a "possible" (as opposed to "probable" or "definite") human carcinogen.

In dose-response assessment, the analyst then uses a mathematical model to predict a plausible "upper-bound" estimate of human cancer risk by extrapolating from the animal studies: from high to low doses, and from laboratory species (rats and mice) to humans. Applying these models to the measured animal data, the EPA estimates a "unit cancer risk" (the risk for an average lifetime exposure to 1 milligram per kilogram [mg/kg] of body weight per day) of about two in one hundred for lung cancer from inhalation, based on studies of male rats, and about five in one hundred for liver cancer from ingestion, based on studies of male mice.

In exposure assessment, the analyst then uses monitoring data and dispersion models to calculate that approximately 80 neighbors may be exposed to about eight ten-thousandths mg/kg of body weight per day, and 150 workers to about one thousandth mg/kg per day; and through gradual groundwater contamination, about 50,000 people may be exposed to one to two thousandths mg/kg per day in their drinking water after about twenty years.

Finally, the risk characterization combines these calculations into numerical upper-bound estimates of excess lifetime human cancer risk. In this hypothetical case, the result might be eight in one hundred thousand of the general population, one in one thousand nearby residents, and three in a thousand workers. Note from the previous paragraph that the actual numbers of neighbors and workers are far smaller, but risk assessments are normally expressed in numbers per thousand for consistency's sake. These estimates are then to be used by the EPA's "risk managers"—that is, the officials responsible for its regulatory decisions—to decide what risks are the highest priority for regulation and what regulatory action (if any) is justified.

Risk Management

In the context of the EPA's statutory authorities, risk management primarily means choosing and justifying regulatory decisions. The EPA administers a complex patchwork of separate statutes, each of which addresses a particular set of problems, establishes its own range of authorized management actions (usually regulations), and specifies its own criteria for making decisions. Some of the laws direct that health risks be minimized regardless of costs; others that the risks be balanced against costs; and still others that the best available technology be used to minimize risks, allowing some judgment about what technologies are economically "available," or that new technologies be developed to meet a standard.[12]

In practice, the EPA and other regulatory agencies appear to apply their own rules of thumb, based on risk and cost, to manage health risks. In one study that examined 132 federal regulatory decisions on environmental carcinogens from 1976 through 1985, two clear patterns emerged. Every chemical with an individual cancer risk greater than four chances in one thousand was regulated; and with only one exception, no action was taken to regulate any chemical with an individual risk less than one chance in one million. In the risk range between these two levels, cost-effectiveness was the primary criterion. That is to say, risks were regulated if the cost per life saved was less than $2 million, but not if the cost was higher.[13]

These findings strongly suggest that risk managers use their own norms to distinguish among *de manifestis* risks (risks so high that agencies will almost always act to reduce them, regardless of cost), *de minimis* risks (risks judged too small to deserve consideration, even though highly exposed or susceptible individuals in the population may be at serious risk), and a gray area in between where judgments of cost-effectiveness are the primary criterion.

Science and Values

Quantitative risk assessment is now used to varying degrees by all the federal environmental and health regulatory agencies. It has also been institutionalized in a professional society (the Society for Risk Analysis), several journals, and a growing professional community of practitioners in government agencies, chemical and other industries, consulting firms, universities and research institutes, and advocacy organizations.

Despite its widespread use, however, serious dispute remains as to how much of risk assessment is really scientific and how much is merely a recasting of value judgments into scientific jargon. The language of risk assessment is less accessible to the general public; does it nonetheless provide a more scientifically objective basis for public policy decisions?

Risk Assessment Policy

Risk assessment in practice is permeated by judgments that cannot be reduced to science. One such judgment governs the selection of substances for risk assessment in the first place. In practice, these judgments are based not only on preliminary evidence of risk but also on publicity, lawsuits, and other political pressures. Another judgment concerns what effects, or "end points," are considered: most focus on cancer, with less attention and usually far less data for other health hazards, species, ecosystems, and environmental consequences.

In conducting each risk assessment, the analysts' own value judgments come into play whenever they must make assumptions or draw inferences in the absence of objective facts. Such judgments are identified collectively as "risk assessment policy." Hazard identification, for example, relies on evidence from epidemiological studies of human effects, from animal bioassays, from short-term laboratory tests (*in vitro*), or simply from comparison of the compound's molecular structure with other known hazards. In practice, these data are usually few and fragmentary, often collected for different purposes, and of varied quality; the analyst must make numerous judgments about their applicability.

For both dose-response and exposure assessment, analysts must routinely use mathematical models to generate risk estimates. Even the best dose-response models, however, are based on simplified biology and fragmentary data. Scientists must interpolate the dose-response relationship between a small number of observations, extrapolate it to lower doses (often far beyond the observed range), and adjust for the many possible differences between species and conditions of exposure.

Similarly, in exposure assessment, analysts must make many assumptions about variability in natural dispersion patterns and population movements, about other sources of exposure, and about the susceptibility of those exposed (for instance, healthy adults compared with children or chemically sensitive persons).

Finally, the analyst must synthesize a characterization of overall risk out of the diverse, uncertain, and sometimes conflicting estimates derived from the previous three steps. Such choices include weighing the quality, persuasiveness, and applicability of differing bodies of evidence; deciding how to estimate and adjust for statistical uncertainties; and even choosing which estimates to present ("best estimate" or "upper bound," for instance, or a range defined by degree of probability).

Given these many unavoidable judgments, the conclusions of health risk assessments are inevitably shaped more by their assumptions than by "facts." The EPA and other agencies therefore developed guidance documents called "inference guidelines," which specify what assumptions and rules of thumb are to be used in calculating risks. Such guidelines cannot be scientifically definitive because the underlying science contains fundamental uncertainties. They are, rather, policy directives, based on a mixture of scientific consensus and political choices about the appropriate level of prudence. These guidelines often have important substantive differences, specifying different assumptions and procedures to be used in producing and presenting risk assessments.[14]

A Conservative Bias?

A major reason for differences among the guidelines was an intense and continuing debate, both scientific and political, over whether the regulatory agencies' risk estimates were systematically biased in favor of excessive caution. If each assumption included some extra "safety factor" favoring health protection, for instance, and especially if those factors were then multiplied (as they often must be), the overall safety factor might be far greater than any of them individually, and sometimes far costlier to achieve. Critics of the regulatory agencies argued that these practices rendered the agency's risk assessments excessively cautious, and that they should be revised to reflect only "best estimates" of risk rather than large margins of safety.[15] Other risk experts argued, however, that many of these assumptions might not be excessively cautious at all. Both human susceptibility and exposure levels can be underestimated as well as overestimated, as can the toxicity of a substance itself and its interaction with other risk factors.

A distinguished risk research group in 1988 identified plausible biological reasons showing that existing risk assessment methods— despite all their "safety factors"—might in fact underestimate some risks of low-level exposure. Given scientific uncertainty, moreover, "best estimate" methods could not themselves avoid value judgments, errors, and biases: they might simply substitute different ones, favoring less prudence toward health protection.[16] Many risk experts therefore argued against using any single "point estimate" of risk as a basis for decisions, and for substituting a range defined by degrees of probability or uncertainty.[17]

Multiple Risks and Risk Management

Value judgments pervade risk assessment even in its simplest forms, such as the risk of a single result (cancer) from a single substance. Most of the "risk management" decisions that the EPA and other agencies must actually make, however, involve far more complex choices among combinations of substances causing several or many kinds of risks to multiple populations.

Imagine, for instance, a relatively common decision issue: the EPA must establish requirements for air and water emissions and hazardous waste storage permits at a new facility for chemical reprocessing and incineration. Many risks must be considered in setting such standards: cancer, respiratory illness, fish mortality, stream eutrophication, crop damage, diminished visibility, and economic hardship to the surrounding community, to list just a few. There may be many beneficial effects as well: reduced damage to health and ecosystems because of improved waste disposal practices, economic benefits to the surrounding community, and others.

In principle, risk assessment can estimate the probability of each of these effects individually. It does not specify, however, which should be considered, nor make them commensurable, nor provide weights specifying their relative importance. In practice, risk assessment has dealt with these issues by simplifying them, focusing on just a few human health effects. This simplification may, however, obscure the more diverse considerations that must be balanced in more complex decisions.

Risk Assessment and Environmental Decisions

By the end of the 1980s risk assessment had become established as the EPA's primary language of analysis and management. The agency's statutes did not contain this consistency of discourse, but most EPA administrative decisions were now couched in terms of how much risk they would reduce: allocating budget priorities among programs, justifying individual regulatory proposals, even framing the EPA's proposed research program for the 1990s. Why?

A Management Tool

From the perspective of senior EPA administrators, such as Ruckelshaus and his successors, formal risk assessment offered an essential management tool. Every head of the EPA faced two nearly intractable problems. One was setting priorities and justifying regulatory decisions for literally thousands of individual chemicals that were candidates for regulation under its several hazardous-substance statutes: hazardous air pollutants, toxic water pollutants, pesticides, drinking-water contaminants, hazardous wastes, and toxic substances generally. Every one of these decisions was likely to be challenged in court, either by industry for regulating too tightly or by environmental groups for failing to protect public health. The second problem was setting priorities across the EPA's many separate programs. The EPA has never had a single overall statutory mission or operating framework: it was created by a presidential reorganization plan, not an act of Congress. Each program was created under a different statute, overseen by different congressional subcommittees, and advocated (and opposed) by powerful constituencies in the glare of the mass media—leaving little discretionary authority for the administrator to set priorities among them.

Risk assessment provided a common denominator—human health risk—by which the administrator could rationalize and defend the administrative decisions he or she ultimately had to make, both among individual chemicals and across the agency's many mandates. Lacking any unified framework or criteria in statutes, the administrator used risk assessment in effect to *create* a more consistent approach, justified by commonsense arguments of reasonableness, consistency, and scientific objectivity. Assistant administrator Milton Russell argued in a 1987 article, for instance, that risk balancing was the only alternative to a much cruder and more fragmented approach, in which priorities were set mainly by historical accident and political influence, and uncoordinated actions might create new risks as great as those they were correcting (for instance, simply moving pollutants from water to land or land to air).[18]

In addition, risk assessment reaffirmed the principle that environmental and health consequences, rather than just the economic costs of compliance, should be the primary criterion for evaluating and justifying the EPA's decisions. During the early 1980s the Reagan administration had greatly expanded the authority of the Office of Management and Budget (OMB) to impose cost-benefit requirements—"regulatory impact assessments"—on environmental regulatory proposals. Risk assessment made risk rather than dollars the focus for justification, permitting the EPA to wrap its decisions in the legitimacy and apparent objectivity of science and in the language of health effects rather than merely economic benefits. Whatever its imperfections, risk assessment redefined the issues in scientific terms, in which the EPA administrator's decisions and staff expertise were normally accorded greater deference than in the broader domains of economics and politics.[19]

Risk Perception and Communication

Although risk assessment strengthened the EPA's hand in dealing with the OMB, it exacerbated conflict between the agency and the general public. First, most controversies over environmental hazards turned on the question of how much evidence was needed before regulating. Public advocacy groups tended to take the position, "If in doubt, regulate to protect health," whereas businesses would reply: "If in doubt, don't regulate until you have proof." Many critics of the EPA used risk assessment to argue *against* aggressive regulation on the grounds that the agency did not have sufficient proof of hazards to justify regulating them.[20] From the perspective of the public, quantitative risk assessment thus tipped such controversies in favor of business, implicitly accepting the view that proof rather than prudence was required to justify regulations and thus imposing costly and time-consuming burdens—analysis, review, and sometimes new research—before any regulatory action.

Second, the professionalization of risk assessment created a new commonality of perspective among risk "experts," who shared a technical view of risks and often disdained the broader concerns of the general public as ignorant, irrational, or self-interested. Many expert risk analysts seemed to believe that their relatively narrow and specialized methods were not just one source of relevant information, but the *only* proper basis for environmental decisions; and these attitudes heightened public distrust of risk analysis.[21] Why were technical estimates of hypothetical cancer risks any more "real," or any more exclusively the proper basis for policy decisions, than public concerns about unanticipated leaks, spills, or plant malfunctions, about risks to their economic well-being, or about harm to their community because of industrial waste disposal? Indeed, what if the estimates made by today's risk analysts turned out to be wrong? Risk analysts reacted by advocating better "risk communication," but many such efforts were essentially one-way attempts—often unsuccessful—to convince the public that the technical understanding of risks was the correct one.[22]

Risk assessment thus remained a controversial procedure, even as it increasingly became the dominant language for justifying regulatory decisions. Beyond a few well-studied substances and health effects, data remained scarce and expensive, basic mechanisms and magnitudes of toxicity remained uncertain, exposure patterns remained vulnerable to many confounding factors, and other important decision considerations could not easily be captured in the language of "risk." Like cost-benefit analysis, therefore, risk assessment became an important tool, but not the ultimate rule, for making environmental decisions.[23]

Comparative Risk Analysis

Quantitative health risk assessment was developed to estimate health risks associated with specific chemicals and exposures, and thus to permit comparisons among the magnitudes of health hazards they posed. It was not originally designed for setting priorities among diverse *kinds* of environmental problems, such as between a chemical threatening health and a development project threatening a wetland. Beginning in the mid 1980s, however, EPA administrators undertook a more ambitious initiative: to use the language of risk as an agencywide framework for setting priorities among all its programs and mandates.

Unfinished Business and Reducing Risk

A pioneering study by the EPA in 1987, entitled *Unfinished Business,* compared the "relative risks" of some thirty-one environmental problems spanning the full range of the agency's responsibilities in relation to four different kinds of risk: cancer, noncancer health risks, ecological effects, and other effects on human welfare. Significantly, this study was *not* a formal quantitative risk assessment, because both data and methodology were lacking for most noncancer risks. Rather, it was based on the consensus of perceptions of relative risk offered by some seventy-five EPA senior managers and on comparisons of those perceptions with opinion-poll data on perceptions held by the general public. These perceived risks were then compared with the amount of effort the agency was devoting to each problem.

The *Unfinished Business* study found that the information available to assess risks for virtually any of these problems was surprisingly poor, and that the agency's actual risk management priorities were more consistent with public opinion than with the problems EPA managers thought most serious. For example, the agency was devoting far more resources to the problem of chemical waste disposal than to indoor air pollution and radon, which appeared to have much greater health risks. The study also found that in most of its programs, the EPA had been far more concerned with public health than with protecting the natural environment itself. Finally, it found that even for public health, localized hazards caused much higher risks to individuals than overall risk estimates revealed.[24]

This study was a remarkably candid step by the EPA to compare its diverse responsibilities and to lay the groundwork for setting priorities among them. In effect, it used the scientifically based language of relative risk to try to build consensus about priorities. By doing so, however, the agency implicitly redefined risk to include not only quantifiable health hazards but also all environmental concerns—making risk assessment a more general language of political debate about environmental priorities. It also implied that such priorities were reducible to a precise technical procedure for risk estimation rather than to a broader process of political choice.

A follow-up study by EPA's Science Advisory Board (SAB) in 1990, entitled *Reducing Risk,* encouraged the EPA to go further with this approach and made substantive recommendations for addressing several high-priority environmental threats. It recommended increased emphasis, for instance, on reducing human destruction of natural habitats and species and on slowing stratospheric ozone depletion and global climate change—and correspondingly less emphasis on more localized concerns such as oil spills and groundwater contamination. Finally, it urged that the EPA use a wider and more flexible range of "market-oriented incentives" to promote cost-effective reduction of environmental risks—pollution charges, tradable emissions permits, emission disclosure requirements, and liability principles, for instance—in place of the more rigid "command-and-control" regulatory requirements that had been its primary policy "tools" so far.[25]

In effect, the *Reducing Risk* report proposed a major reorientation of EPA priorities and tools. More fundamentally, it argued that the agency should *set* priorities and *choose* among policy tools for implementing them rather than mechanically carrying out all the statutory mandates Congress had assigned to it. EPA administrator William Reilly publicly endorsed the report and its recommendations, and made its implementation a personal priority: EPA offices and regions were to use comparative risk studies to justify their annual budget requests, and enforcement priorities were to be based on relative-risk estimates as well.[26]

Despite such strong advocacy from the Science Advisory Board and the administrator, however, the EPA's actual priorities continued to be dominated by its statutes and annual appropriations, which were unusually detailed, prescriptive, and fragmented among separate statutory programs. This rigidity had existed since the EPA's creation and was reinforced by a parallel fragmentation of oversight among separate congressional oversight subcommittees. It was exacerbated in the 1980s by many new restrictions and requirements, which were added to the laws by Congress in response to the Reagan administration's attempts to radically weaken the agency by unilateral administrative actions. These new requirements included rigid statutory deadlines, enforced by "hammer clauses"—serious consequences that would go into effect automatically if the agency missed its deadlines—plus new provisions for citizen suits, court orders, and consent decrees.[27]

The result was that without statutory changes, the EPA administrator had little or no real authority to carry out the SAB's recommendations either to shift priorities or to use more effective policy "tools" to achieve environmental protection.

Technical Comparisons or Public Consensus?

A key unresolved issue for comparative risk assessment was whether it really was a technical procedure to be carried out by experts (as quantitative health risk assessments were claimed to be), or a broader process of assigning value judgments, which should involve public input rather than merely the subjective consensus of technical or administrative elites. Comparative risk assessment modeled on the technocratic procedures of QRA—the "hard" version—implied that risks of different sorts could be reduced to simple measures and that these measures could be compared. Such comparisons, however, required judgments going well beyond science, even for different health risks (cancer versus acute poisoning or developmental disabilities, for instance), let alone for risks to other species and whole ecosystems.[28] Skeptics also criticized narrowly technical comparative risk assessments for forcing false choices by comparing environmental risks too narrowly with one another, a procedure which implicitly biased the comparison by leaving out broader and perhaps more effective policy strategies for reducing risk.[29]

The issue of technical versus political risk comparisons became far more prominent in comparative risk studies sponsored by state governments. In addition to its own initiatives, the EPA promoted comparative risk studies by state and local governments, offering funding for pilot projects and modest increases in state authority to reallocate funds from low-risk to higher-risk problems. By 1994 six states had completed such studies, and others were in progress. Most states used comparative risk assessment as a far more explicitly public process for seeking consensus on environmental risk concerns and priorities. Typically, they would create a technical advisory committee of experts to assemble and assess risk-related data but would then constitute a broader public advisory committee to review this information and propose rankings (often including statewide workshops to invite broader input). A steering committee would then integrate the results. Most states ultimately recommended priorities based on public consensus rather than on technical or administrative judgments alone.

These "soft" versions of comparative risk assessment offered the hope of developing greater political consensus about environmental priorities through an open democratic process. In California, for instance, public involvement produced innovative recommendations for priority attention to high-risk "hot spots" rather than simply listing statewide risk priorities. In most states, however, comparative risk studies have had only marginal impact on actual environmental policies and priorities: overall risk alone was not a sufficient basis for policy decisions, and political commitment—not simply public consensus—was necessary to change entrenched priorities.[30]

Pollution Prevention and Life-Cycle Risks

In 1989, in the midst of its shift toward risk-based priorities, the EPA adopted a new policy statement emphasizing pollution prevention over treatment and safe disposal, establishing the Office of Pollution Prevention to guide its implementation.[31] This policy reflected a growing belief that traditional waste management methods—dilution of wastes in the environment, isolation of materials in shallow landfills, and "end of pipe" waste treatment technologies—were both more costly and less effective than changing the materials and production processes that generated the wastes in the first place. Congress endorsed the new emphasis in the Pollution Prevention Act of 1990 but did not require pollution prevention initiatives. Nor did it supersede the EPA's existing regulatory statutes, many of which—by mandating specific control approaches and investments—remained serious obstacles to prevention incentives.[32]

Pollution prevention provided a valuable step forward in the debate about risks, demonstrating in case after case that preventing environmental risks often costs far less—and provides greater benefits—than building capital-intensive treatment facilities or cleaning up contaminated sites. Two important issues remained, however. One was to assure that pollution prevention initiatives really did reduce pollution and its related risks and did not just introduce different risks that were unregulated. This required a new form of comparative risk study called "life-cycle analysis." This type of analysis would compare products with their substitutes throughout their whole life-cycles— from resource extraction through production, consumption, reuse, and recycling to ultimate disposal. Life-cycle analysis provided valuable new insights into opportunities for pollution prevention and risk reduction. But like other forms of risk assessment, it depended on many assumptions and judgments.

The second important issue was to focus pollution prevention efforts on the most serious risks, rather than just on reducing waste quantities. Up until the 1990s, most pollution prevention initiatives were voluntary. This approach reflected circumstances in which reducing risks served both the polluters' economic self-interest and the social goals of reducing energy and raw materials costs, cutting waste disposal and insurance expenses, and bringing down the sheer cost of regulation, for instance, or of improving companies' public image. But what about reducing risks when it costs the polluter more to do so? In principle, polluters should pay for the full environmental risks of their decisions. But these risks had been difficult or impossible to calculate, and an institutional mechanism had not been created to impose and collect such payments.

The Political Debate over Environmental Risks

From the 1970s to the 1990s, beginning with the pesticide and toxic chemicals statutes, the EPA itself took the lead in promoting risk-based decisionmaking and developing risk assessment procedures to accomplish it. Both the procedures and the resulting decisions remained controversial, however, and by the 1990s the issue of environmental risk became a focal point for a far broader national political battle: about trade-offs between environmental protection and public health on the one hand, and the burdens and costs of regulation on the other.

Questioning Environmental Health Risks

Throughout the 1980s, even as the EPA was committing itself to risk-based decisionmaking, skeptics questioned whether many environmental risks had in fact proved significant. Some of these voices could be viewed as merely self-serving industrial interests or antiregulatory publicists.[33] Others, however, included some respected academic scientists and commentators. British epidemiologists Richard Doll and Richard Peto argued that no clear epidemiological evidence demonstrated increases in most cancers from general public exposure to industrial chemicals. Biochemist Bruce Ames, inventor of the Ames toxicity test, argued that people routinely ingest natural carcinogens far more potent than most exposures to manmade chemicals, without evident ill effects. Philip Abelson, editor of *Science*, repeatedly questioned the assumptions and extrapolations used in the EPA's risk assessments, arguing that they raised needless public fears and wasted money on costly and unnecessary protective measures.[34]

By the 1990s influential critiques had been published that challenged the risks of a number of costly environmental regulations, such as those pertaining to asbestos. Prominent academics and journalists joined the chorus of skeptics. Even some federal officials—including one who played a major role in the decision to evacuate the town of Times Beach, Missouri, following an incident of dioxin contamination—wondered in retrospect if their judgments had been correct.[35] Defenders of the EPA's regulations countered with new evidence suggesting additional risks that had not yet been carefully studied, such as hormonal hazards posed by dioxin to wildlife (and potentially to humans) owing to the toxin's estrogen-mimicking properties. A major review by the National Academy of Sciences also reaffirmed the EPA's risk assessment methods and assumptions.[36] Despite these counterarguments, skeptics gained increasing influence in challenging the EPA's use of scientific risk claims to justify its regulatory decisions.

Regulatory Burdens and Risk Priorities

During the same period, though little noticed by the media and the general public at the time, environmental regulatory mandates were also imposing changing and cumulatively increasing burdens on those who were regulated. The environmental statutes of the 1980s were not only more prescriptive and inflexible than previous ones, but they also imposed far greater burdens on far more targets. Thousands of "small quantity generators" such as dry cleaners must now report their hazardous wastes, and pay high costs for disposal. Thousands of gas stations must dig out and replace their underground storage tanks and pay huge sums for cleanup if they had leaked. Many small manufacturers faced the prospect of MACT standards ("maximum achievable control technology") to reduce toxic air emissions under the 1990 Clean Air Act amendments. The banking and insurance industries, meanwhile, found themselves unexpectedly sharing huge financial liabilities for Superfund sites with their clients.

For local governments, the burden was also becoming far greater. The Clean Water Act required cleanup of municipal wastewater discharges, yet federal wastewater-treatment construction grants were being phased out and replaced by repayable loans. The EPA's landfill standards increased the cost of traditional municipal solid waste management methods by as much as ten times, while its new drinking-water standards required more expensive monitoring and purification efforts. Local governments, too, were required to replace their underground fuel tanks, and many school systems were compelled to remove asbestos from ceilings, floors, and insulation. The 1990 Clean Air Act amendments added costly automatic penalties on cities that failed to achieve new compliance timetables; Superfund liability imposed costs to clean up contaminated municipal landfills, and cities became owners by default of many abandoned industrial sites. Yet local governments had no new revenues to pay for these tasks, and the laws provided no mechanism for setting priorities among them.

In short, while the environmental regulations of the 1970s primarily affected large corporations, those of the 1980s placed much greater burdens on smaller businesses and local governments, whose resources were far more limited and which did not fit the populist image of corporate villain. Local governments themselves, early and important political allies of the EPA, became adversaries. Faced with burgeoning federal mandates, no discretion to set priorities, and disappearing federal subsidies, many cities by the 1990s had joined small businesses and other antiregulatory forces to demand an end to "unfunded federal mandates." The alienation of such an important constituency, particularly at a time when federal budget politics offered no realistic chance of increased funding, posed a serious threat to the EPA.

In fairness to the EPA, the real blame for these regulatory burdens lay not so much with the agency as with the rigid and prescriptive statutes enacted by Congress in the wake of President Reagan's unilateral deregulation initiative. These new laws mandated a vast expansion of federal regulations without funding their implementation and gave the EPA itself no discretion to set priorities or to use more economical tools for their implementation. The result was to fuel a radical backlash against federal environmental regulations that materialized in the 1994 elections and the 104th Congress.

Congress Discovers Risk Analysis

In 1993 and 1994 risk assessment suddenly emerged as a focal point for congressional debate over federal environmental regulation, though the debate was fraught with misunderstandings and hidden agendas. As one knowledgeable observer noted, "no other issue is marked more by confusion and misinformation than the current debate over risk assessment."[37] Some members, such as Sen. Patrick Moynihan (D-N.Y.), proposed bills to make risk assessment a more explicit and visible basis for setting EPA priorities, essentially supporting the agency's own comparative risk initiatives. Others proposed legislation to prescribe changes in risk assessment methodology by statute, such as requiring the EPA to use "best estimates" of risk rather than "upper bounds." Still others sought to make risk assessment a procedural weapon to block environmental regulation, by proposals that would add industry representatives to scientific "peer reviews" and open EPA risk assessments to additional litigation and judicial review.

These proposals were all presented as seemingly reasonable demands for analysis of the risks and costs of regulatory proposals and could easily be confused with one another. Most were unacceptable to EPA supporters, however, out of concern that they would grind the regulatory process to a halt in paperwork and litigation. A coalition of congressional conservatives discovered to their surprise that they could thus block environmental legislation by attaching risk-assessment requirements to proposed bills. A 1993 bill to upgrade the EPA to the status of a cabinet department was derailed by such an amendment, and similar threats ultimately blocked nearly all environmental legislation in the 103d Congress. For regulatory opponents, statutory risk assessment requirements became one of three tactical devices—along with "unfunded mandates" and "takings" bills, collectively labeled the "unholy trinity" by environmental groups—for blocking new environmental laws.[38]

In the Republican-dominated Congress of 1995, even stronger versions of these proposals passed the House of Representatives as elements of Speaker Newt Gingrich's "Contract with America" legislation (see chap. 6). They remained controversial, however, both in the Senate and even among moderate Republicans in the House. By fall 1995 a limited restriction on unfunded mandates had been enacted, but a bipartisan coalition of moderates had stalled both risk assessment and "takings" legislation in the Senate. Opponents of EPA regulation, meanwhile, shifted their tactical emphasis to the appropriations process, seeking radical budget reductions and specific spending restrictions—as well as risk assessment requirements attached to budget bills—to block regulations they opposed. The outcomes of these, too, remained uncertain and contested, particularly in the Senate and under threats of presidential vetoes.

Retrospect and Prospect

Risk-based decisionmaking has become a powerful idea in U.S. environmental policy, yet it is fraught with political agendas and assumptions rather than fulfilling the purely "scientific" role its early proponents claimed for it. Broader questions also remain as to whether the risk-based approach is the most appropriate way to address the far wider range of environmental issues the EPA now faces, let alone the larger global environmental issues that are arguably most important for the future.

The EPA at a Turning Point

The EPA in the mid 1990s stands at a crucial turning point. Its administrative leaders since William Ruckelshaus have fostered the development of systematic procedures for risk-based decisionmaking, initiated comparative risk processes for setting priorities, and advocated market-oriented policy incentives to reduce these risks. Yet the EPA's statutes remain a fragmented patchwork of disparate mandates, most of them dictating specific command-and-control regulatory programs with rigid timetables and little discretion either for establishing priorities or devising solutions; some promote risk reduction more by their regulatory burdens than by purposeful incentives. Some pollutants that appear to pose only remote risks continue to be regulated, while many other important environmental risks remain unaddressed: nonpoint sources of water pollution; losses of natural habitat; global climate change; and archaic subsidies that promote excessive mining, logging, grazing, water use, energy use, auto emissions, and so forth.

The 1994 congressional elections dethroned many of the architects and protectors of the EPA's statutes. While serious statutory reform was now conceivable, the elections also installed far more radical opponents of the agency in Congress. The EPA's programs retain broad public support, but politically they are under siege. In effect, the EPA is now reprising its political battles of the early Reagan years, only this time its opponents are in the Congress and its defenders in the White House.

One possible outcome could be the enactment of useful and moderate reforms. A strong and coherent set of reform recommendations was proposed in a 1995 report of the National Academy of Public Administration (NAPA), commissioned by the congressional appropriations committees. The NAPA report recommended that Congress give the EPA both a coherent statutory mission and the flexibility to carry it out; that the agency continue to set and enforce national standards but allow state and local governments far greater freedom as to how to achieve them ("accountable devolution"); that Congress pass legislation allowing flexibility and market-based incentives to encourage firms to perform better than required ("beyond compliance"); that the EPA improve its own management systems and expand its use of risk analysis and cost-benefit analysis to set priorities and justify decisions; and that the EPA's fragmented environmental statutes and programs be integrated into a single coherent framework.[39]

Leading congressional risk assessment bills, however, appeared more likely to cause ineffectual stalemate than productive reform. These bills would not increase the EPA's authority to set priorities among its mandates, nor its authority to allow more efficient and effective approaches to fulfill them. They would simply require far more paperwork for each regulation, with less funding to produce it and additional opportunities for litigation, thus increasing rather than reducing bureaucratic red tape and hamstringing rather than reforming the regulatory process.

Other proposals, moreover, could cause far more fundamental damage, both to the goal of environmental risk reduction and to the EPA's effectiveness as a regulatory agency. Some amendments initially attached to the House appropriations bill, for instance, would have forbidden the EPA from regulating a whole range of industries and potential environmental hazards, regardless of their risks. If advocates of these proposals were to succeed, the opportunity for needed reforms to *improve* environmental regulation might well be lost once again.

National Environmental Goals

Even if the current congressional debate were to produce meaningful reforms within the EPA, however, risk-based decisionmaking might not produce better decisions for many environmental problems unless it were combined with broader measures to address the fundamental causes of these problems. Better risk-based decisions about regulating individual pesticide compounds, for instance, will probably never be as effective in reducing pesticide hazards as incentives for agricultural businesses to reduce overuse of pesticides in general—yet reducing overall pesticide use may require changes in agricultural policy incentives rather than just in EPA regulations. Similarly, better risk-based decisions about regulating motor vehicle emissions might begin to target enforcement on the worst-polluting vehicles, but without changing more fundamental policies promoting increased auto use, mobile source pollution will continue to increase despite less pollution per car. The EPA's regulatory mandates alone may never effectively reach these causes, even with better risk-based decisionmaking. Similar problems remain unsolved in many sectors, and others will undoubtedly emerge.[40]

Reducing many important environmental risks will thus require changes not just in the EPA's policies, but across all the agencies whose policies create important incentives, such as the Departments of Agriculture, Energy, Transportation, and others. Some other countries are well ahead of the United States in this effort. The Dutch National Environmental Policy Plan, for instance, sets specific targets and timetables for pollution reduction by each ministry and each sector of its economy, updating these each year in its environmental program document. So far the United States has no institutional mechanism for orchestrating such governmentwide risk-reduction initiatives. In 1993 the EPA initiated a "National Environmental Goals Project," which might provide a basis for such a strategy. But, to succeed, this project will require far broader commitment from the president, Congress, and the federal agencies—not to mention the industries and other constituencies that would have to be involved.[41]

From Risk Reduction to Sustainable Development

Beyond the domestic politics of the risk debate lies the larger question of whether risk-based decisionmaking is an adequate approach to the most important environmental issues. Risk assessment in concept seems as self-evidently appropriate to its advocates as common sense: how could reasonable people possibly object to basing environmental decisions on better science, setting priorities based on evidence, or using the most cost-effective actions to reduce the most serious risks? In practice, however, the costs and complexity of such assessments may sometimes outweigh their value: prudence in action is ultimately more important than proof in analysis. The causes are often reasonably clear; the magnitudes and probabilities are imperfectly understood but serious enough to command attention; and the goal need not always be a finely tuned regulation but changes in the directions of very gross trends.

Even more important, the environmental risks that are arguably most serious for the future include international and global issues for which a domestic regulatory approach is inadequate. Examples include transboundary pollution, maintenance of ocean fisheries, stratospheric ozone depletion, global climate change, the environmental impacts of international trade arrangements, and unsustainable pressures of population and economic development on natural processes worldwide. Are these problems amenable to quantitative risk assessment? In principle, perhaps. But in practice these decisions are about far more complex choices than "risk" alone. They are about risks, but they are also about other environmental values—sustainability of natural resources and ecosystems, and esthetics and the appreciation of nature, for instance—and about legitimate nonenvironmental values as well, such as self-determination, fairness, basic human needs, economic welfare, and other considerations just as central to the environmental decisions being made. Calling all these considerations "risks" may simply obscure rather than clarify the issues at stake.

Ultimately, environmental management cannot be *only* a matter of "reducing risks." To sustain human civilizations, we must sustain the environmental conditions and ecosystems that make them possible. As René Dubos has so articulately noted, we humans and our environment constantly shape each other, in beneficial and beautiful ways as well as in damaging and ugly ones.[42] To sustain environmental quality therefore requires positive action and creative vision, not merely control of risks. Where in the language of risk would one find the creative vision of environmental design, or the "City Beautiful"? Or even the stewardship concept of environmental conservation? On a more concrete level, where would one place the idea of rehabilitating degraded ecosystems? The vocabulary of risk-based decisionmaking is a valuable step forward from the patchwork of disparate and sometimes conflicting laws that still defines much of U.S. environmental regulation. But it is ultimately too narrowly focused on justifying the regulation of adverse outcomes to provide an adequate framework for the more complex and creative tasks of environmental management.

These questions require a broader understanding of the interactions between human societies and their environments and a more systematic and positive vision of their future than is provided by the concept of risk. One framework for such a vision was proposed in 1987 by the United Nations' World Commission on Environment and Development in the concept of "sustainable development": meeting the needs of the present in ways that do not compromise the ability of future generations to meet their own needs. This idea was further developed by the U.N. Conference on Environment and Development (the Earth summit) in Brazil in 1992; but as yet it remains more an idealized concept than a specific program. Perhaps the highest-priority task for environmental policy in the 1990s is to spell out its details and work toward its implementation.[43]

Notes

1. William D. Ruckelshaus, "Science, Risk, and Public Policy," *Science* 221 (1983): 1027-1028.
2. Environmental Protection Agency, *Risk Assessment and Risk Management: Framework for Decisionmaking* (Washington, D.C.: EPA, 1984); EPA, *Unfinished Business: A Comparative Assessment of Environmental Problems* (Washington, D.C.: EPA, 1987), 1; EPA, *Reducing Risk: Setting Priorities and Strategies for Environmental Protection* (Washington, D.C.: EPA, 1990), 16.
3. Curtis C. Travis, Samantha A. Richter, Edmund A. C. Crouch, Richard Wilson, and Ernest D. Klema, "Cancer Risk Management: A Review of 132 Federal Regulatory Decisions," *Environmental Science and Technology* 21 (1987): 415-420.
4. Mark E. Rushefsky, *Making Cancer Policy* (Albany: State University of New York Press, 1986), 74-80.

5. Ibid., 59-84.
6. Milton Russell and Michael Gruber, "Risk Assessment in Environmental Policy-Making," *Science* 236 (1987): 286-290.
7. Executive Order No. 12291, February 17, 1981; and *Industrial Union Department, AFL-CIO* v. *American Petroleum Institute,* 448 U.S. 607 (1980). As a legal matter, the extent to which quantitative risk assessment (QRA) is required must be decided on a statute-by-statute basis. Although this decision actually involved a proposed standard by the Occupational Safety and Health Administration for occupational exposure to benzene, it influenced all the regulatory agencies to put increased emphasis on QRA.
8. Vincent Covello and Joshua Menkes, *Risk Assessment and Risk Assessment Methods: The State of the Art* (Washington, D.C.: Division of Policy Research and Analysis, National Science Foundation, 1985), xxiii.
9. ENVIRON Corp., *Elements of Toxicology and Chemical Risk Assessment,* rev. ed. (Washington, D.C.: ENVIRON, July 1988), 9; National Research Council, *Risk Assessment in the Federal Government: Managing the Process* (Washington, D.C.: National Academy Press, 1983), 18.
10. National Research Council, *Risk Assessment in the Federal Government,* 1983; William D. Ruckelshaus, "Science, Risk, and Public Policy"; Ruckelshaus, "Risk in a Free Society," *Risk Analysis* 4 (1984): 157-162.
11. Example adapted from the EPA, "Workshop on Risk and Decision Making" (materials prepared for the EPA by Temple, Barker, and Sloane Inc. and ENVIRON Corp., 1986).
12. For a list see Rushefsky, *Making Cancer Policy,* 68-70.
13. Travis et al., "Cancer Risk Management."
14. Environmental Protection Agency, "Health Risk and Economic Impact Assessments of Suspected Carcinogens: Interim Procedures and Guidelines," *Federal Register* 41, May 25, 1976, 21402-21405; *Federal Register* 51, September 24, 1986, 33992-34054; *Federal Register* 53, June 30, 1988, 24836-24869; Rushefsky, *Making Cancer Policy,* chaps. 3-6.
15. E.g. Philip H. Abelson, "Risk Assessments of Low-Level Exposures," *Science* 265 (1994): 1507.
16. See, for instance, Adam M. Finkel, "Has Risk Assessment Become Too 'Conservative'?" *Resources* (Summer 1989): 11-13; and John C. Bailar III, Edmund A. C. Crouch, Rashid Shaikh, and Donna Speigelman, "One-Hit Models of Carcinogenesis: Conservative or Not?" *Risk Analysis* 8 (1988): 485-497. See also Adam M. Finkel and Dominic Golding, eds., *Worst Things First? The Debate over Risk-Based National Environmental Priorities* (Baltimore: The Johns Hopkins University Press, 1995).
17. National Academy of Public Administration, *Setting Priorities, Getting Results: A New Direction for EPA* (Washington, D.C.: NAPA, 1995), 41-43.
18. Russell and Gruber, "Risk Assessment," 286-290.
19. Terry F. Yosie, "Science and Sociology: The Transition to a Post-Conservative Risk Assessment Era." Plenary address to the 1987 Annual Meeting of the Society for Risk Analysis, Houston, Texas, November 2, 1987. Dr. Yosie was then director of the EPA's Science Advisory Board.
20. Rushefsky, *Making Cancer Policy,* 92-94; see also, e.g., *AIHC Recommended Alternatives to OSHA's Generic Carcinogen Proposal* (Scarsdale, N.Y.: AIHC, 1978).
21. Sheldon Krimsky and Alonzo Plough, *Environmental Hazards: Communicating Risks as a Social Process* (Dover, Mass.: Auburn House, 1989).
22. Ibid.; see also K. S. Shrader-Frechette, *Risk and Rationality: Philosophical Foundations for Populist Reforms* (Berkeley and Los Angeles: University of California Press, 1991).
23. The "tool versus rule" issue has also been discussed in relation to cost-benefit analysis of regulatory proposals: see Richard N. L. Andrews, "Cost-Benefit Analysis as Regulatory Reform," in *Cost-Benefit Analysis and Environmental Regulations: Politics, Ethics, and Methods,* ed. Daniel Swartzman, Richard A. Liroff, and Kevin G. Croke (Washington, D.C.: Conservation Foundation, 1982).

24. EPA, *Unfinished Business.*

25. EPA, *Reducing Risk.*

26. William Reilly, "Aiming Before We Shoot: The Quiet Revolution in Environmental Policy," *Northern Kentucky Law Review* 18 (1991): 159-174.

27. Norman Vig and Michael Kraft, eds., *Environmental Policy in the 1980s* (Washington, D.C.: CQ Press, 1984).

28. Donald T. Hornstein, "Reclaiming Environmental Law: A Normative Critique of Comparative Risk Analysis," *Columbia Law Review* 92 (1992): 562-633.

29. Donald T. Hornstein, "Lessons from Federal Pesticide Regulation on the Paradigms and Politics of Environmental Law Reform," *Yale Journal on Regulation* 10 (1993): 369-446. Some advocates of comparative risk assessment also urged broader risk comparisons, arguing that some nonenvironmental regulations reduced health risks far more cheaply and effectively than many of the EPA's environmental regulations. See, e.g., Stephen Breyer, *Breaking the Vicious Circle* (Cambridge, Mass.: Harvard University Press, 1993); but also Adam Finkel, "A Second Opinion on an Environmental Misdiagnosis: The Risky Prescriptions of *Breaking the Vicious Circle,*" *NYU Environmental Law Journal* 3 (1994): 295-381.

30. Richard Minard Jr., "Comparative Risk Assessment and the States: History, Politics, and Results," in *Comparing Environmental Risks: Tools for Setting Government Priorities,* ed. J. Clarence Davies (Washington, D.C.: Resources for the Future, 1996).

31. EPA, "Pollution Prevention Policy Statement," *Federal Register* 54, January 26, 1989, 3845-3847.

32. Robert Gottlieb, ed., *Reducing Toxics: A New Approach to Policy and Industrial Decision-Making* (Washington, D.C.: Island Press, 1995), 73-83.

33. The American Industrial Health Council (AIHC), for instance, was formed in the 1980s to develop industrywide positions on environmental health risks and risk assessment methods. See, e.g., "Special Edition: Need for Re-Examination of Risk," *AIHC Science Commentary* 5, no. 1 (1994): 1-26. Popular-literature critiques included Edith Efron, *The Apocalyptics: Cancer and the Big Lie* (New York: Simon and Schuster, 1984); and Elizabeth Whelan, *Toxic Terror* (Ottawa, Ill.: Jameson Books, 1985).

34. Richard Doll and Richard Peto, "The Causes of Cancer: Quantitative Estimates of Avoidable Risks of Cancer in the United States Today," *Journal of the National Cancer Institute* 66 (1981): 1191-1285; Bruce Ames, Renac Magaw, and Lois Swirsky Gold, "Ranking Possible Carcinogenic Hazards," *Science* 236 (1987): 271-280; Philip H. Abelson, "Risk Assessments of Low-Level Exposures," *Science* 265 (1994): 1507.

35. See, e.g., Brooke T. Mossman et al., "Asbestos: Scientific Developments and Implications for Public Policy," *Science* 247 (1990): 294; John D. Graham, L. Green, and Marc Roberts, *In Search of Safety: Chemicals and Cancer Risk* (Cambridge, Mass.: Harvard University Press, 1988); Breyer, *Breaking the Vicious Circle;* and Aaron Wildavsky, *But Is It True? A Citizen's Guide to Environmental Health and Safety Issues* (Cambridge, Mass.: Harvard University Press, 1995). In the media, a major change was the replacement of the lead environmental reporters for the *New York Times* and some other influential papers with more skeptical successors: see, e.g., Keith Schneider, "What Price Cleanup?," *New York Times,* March 21-26, 1993.

36. Theodora Colborn, Frederick von Saal, and Ana M. Soto, "Developmental Effects of Endocrine-Disrupting Chemicals in Wildlife and Humans," *Environmental Health Perspectives* 101, no. 5 (1993): 378-384; National Academy of Sciences-National Research Council, *Science and Judgment in Risk Assessment* (Washington, D.C.: National Academy Press, 1994). See also Finkel, "Second Opinion."

37. Terry [J. Clarence] Davies, "Congress Discovers Risk Analysis," *Resources* (Winter 1995): 7.

38. Ibid., 5-8.

39. NAPA, *Setting Priorities.*

40. Hornstein, "Lessons from Federal Pesticide Regulation," 369-446; James J. MacKenzie, Roger C. Dower, and Donald D. T. Chen, *The Going Rate: What It Really Costs to Drive* (Washington, D.C.: World Resources Institute, 1992); Robert Repetto, *Jobs, Competitiveness, and Environmental Regulation: What Are the Real Issues?* (Washington, D.C.: World Resources Institute, 1995).

41. Ministry of Housing, Physical Planning, and Environment, *Highlights of the Dutch National Environmental Policy Plan* (The Hague: Ministry of Housing, Physical Planning, and Environment, 1990); Environmental Protection Agency, *The New Generation of Environmental Protection* (Washington, D.C.: EPA, 1994).

42. René Dubos, *The Wooing of Earth* (New York: Scribner's, 1980).

43. World Commission on Environment and Development, *Our Common Future* (New York: Oxford University Press, 1987); Ismail Serageldin and Andrew Steer, eds., *Making Development Sustainable: From Concepts to Action* (Washington, D.C.: World Bank, 1994). See also chaps. 13 and 15 in this volume.

11

Environmental Justice:
Normative Concerns and Empirical Evidence

Evan J. Ringquist

The context of environmental policy in the mid 1990s is vastly different from the context that existed twenty, or even ten, years ago. Environmentalists are skeptical about many of the new elements of this context, viewing risk assessment, relieving states from federal mandates, "property rights," and some economic approaches to environmental protection as tactics to roll back environmental regulations (see chaps. 2, 9, and 10). One new element of the environmental policy context, however, has the potential to expand efforts in environmental protection: concerns over the unequal distribution of environmental risk, or "environmental justice."

As early as 1971 federal regulators recognized that exposure to environmental pollutants was not distributed equally: minority communities experienced disproportionately high levels of environmental risk.[1] These inequities were largely ignored until the late 1980s, when a number of studies rediscovered that minority neighborhoods generally suffered from worse air quality, worse water quality, more landfills, more sources of toxic pollution, more hazardous waste sites, and weaker enforcement of environmental regulations than did wealthier neighborhoods with smaller minority populations. This evidence has led many activists to charge that environmental protection activities are affected by "environmental racism." But racial discrimination is not the only charge made by environmental justice advocates. These activists claim that the poor and other politically powerless groups are also exposed to higher levels of environmental risk. Charges of racial and class biases in environmental protection have mobilized hundreds of small, grassroots groups into what is generally referred to as the "environmental justice movement." The environmental justice movement has the potential to broaden the base of support for the traditional environmental movement, and it may reinvigorate and refocus the forces of progressive politics behind environmental concerns.[2] In short, it has the potential to change the face of environmental politics and policy.

The discussion of the role played by environmental justice concerns in the policy context will be divided into four sections. First, I will examine instances of "environmental racism" and discuss the development and demands of the environmental justice movement. Second, I will examine the empirical evidence that supports, and sometimes contradicts, the claims of environmental justice advocates. Although the evidence presented in this chapter focuses on toxic chemicals and waste disposal facilities, similar evidence is available regarding the distribution of risk from air and water pollution. Third, I will examine five potential causes of environmental inequity. Finally, I will look at several actions that local, state, and federal officials have taken to remedy environmental inequities, and discuss how appropriate government action in this area depends on how we define the concepts of discrimination and equity.

Environmental Injustice: You'll Know It When You See It

South Chicago, Illinois

One six-by-six-mile area on the South Side of Chicago contains fifty active or closed commercial hazardous waste landfills, one hundred factories (including seven chemical factories), and more than one hundred abandoned toxic waste sites. Near the middle of this toxic wasteland sits the residential development of Altgeld Gardens, a neighborhood of roughly ten thousand residents. In addition to being surrounded by the greatest concentration of hazardous waste sites in the country, Altgeld Gardens itself was built atop the old Pullman Railroad Car company landfill—for decades, an industrial and municipal dumping site.[3] As one might imagine, Altgeld Gardens is not a pleasant place to live. Residents have had a difficult time getting state and federal environmental officials to address the contamination problems in their neighborhood. State officials became more receptive to the residents' complaints, however, when, during an inspection of one particularly noxious toxic waste lagoon, the boat carrying the state environmental inspectors began to disintegrate beneath them.[4] The federal Environmental Protection Agency (EPA), however, has been unwilling to place any of the abandoned hazardous waste sites on the Superfund National Priorities List. Residents do not believe that the many hazardous waste sites in their neighborhood or government officials' reluctance to clean up these facilities are random occurrences. Altgeld Garden's population is 70 percent African American, 11 percent Latino, and suffers a poverty rate nearly double the state's average. Residents believe they are the victims of environmental racism.

Kettleman City, California

In the late 1980s Chemical Waste Management Incorporated (CWM Inc.), one of the nation's largest hazardous waste disposal firms, proposed construction of a large commercial hazardous waste incinerator in Kettleman City, California. The governing board of Kings County approved the facility, and several of the necessary permits were in the process of being issued when the residents of Kettleman City filed a lawsuit to stop construction of the facility. One of the major motivations behind this lawsuit was the belief on the part of the residents that they were the victims of environmental racism. The population of Kettleman City is 95 percent Latino, and a full 40 percent of the residents speak only Spanish. In spite of this, neither the county nor CWM Inc. provided announcements of public meetings, technical reports, or any other official documents in Spanish. Moreover, the county refused to provide residents with a Spanish-language interpreter at the one public meeting held before the county board approved the incinerator. In 1992 a California Superior Court judge ruled that the county government had to translate these environmental review documents into Spanish to ensure meaningful involvement by the residents of Kettleman City. This court case also brought to light the fact that, before approving the incinerator, the Kings County board did not adequately evaluate the effects the facility would have on air quality, local agriculture, or the health of area residents.[5]

St. Regis Reservation, New York

For hundreds of years the Mohawk tribe hunted, fished, and farmed the land that is now the St. Regis reservation. The Mohawks are not the only people, however, who have made productive economic use of the land near the reservation. On the banks of the St. Lawrence River, which is the centerpiece of the St. Regis reservation, sits an abandoned General Motors factory that is now a toxic waste site. Nearby are similar industrial facilities owned by ALCOA, Reynolds Aluminum, and several Canadian companies. Over the past thirty years, pollution from these facilities has destroyed the Mohawk way of life. The St. Lawrence has become so contaminated that tribal members cannot eat fish from the river. The herds of cattle that once roamed the reservation are gone, victims of fluoride poisoning from the nearby GM site. Mohawk families are even advised not to eat the vegetables they grow in their own gardens, for fear of toxic contamination.[6] In short, pollution from the nearby industrial facilities has undermined the entire economic infrastructure of the reservation. With poverty and unemployment at high levels, and with no other viable options for reviving their economy, tribal leaders are being wooed by numerous developers seeking to place everything from solid waste landfills to hazardous waste incinerators on the St. Regis reservation.

This scenario is frequently repeated across the country. Often isolated, reservations have high levels of unemployment and few sources of economic development. This makes them attractive targets for companies seeking to build noxious facilities. A few observers go so far as to claim that the federal Bureau of Indian Affairs is promoting these waste facilities as an economic development strategy for reservations. Because Native American tribes retain some sovereign rights, environmental regulations on reservations are often less strict than those of the states surrounding the reservation, and enforcement of these regulations is often weak (for example, in 1990 only 30 of 280 reservations had offices of environmental protection). For all these reasons, reservations are increasingly viewed as potential dumping grounds, and many Native American leaders claim that reservation residents are being victimized by environmental racism.[7]

The Environmental Justice Movement

Although cases like those described above have been relatively common over the past several decades, the initial prospects for a coalition between the environmental movement and advocates for civil rights, the poor, and minorities looked bleak. Conventional wisdom held that poor and minority individuals were generally unconcerned with pollution and did not share the values of environmentalists. Equally as important, critics of environmentalism claimed that the movement was full of upper-middle-class elites who did not care about the urban environmental problems faced by members of disadvantaged groups. There is some evidence to support these contentions. Mainstream environmental groups often emphasize wilderness preservation and the protection of endangered species over reducing pollution in inner cities. Moreover, the membership lists and leadership positions of these groups are hardly crowded with racial minorities.[8] On the other hand, public opinion polls have repeatedly shown that the poor and members of minority groups are no less concerned about environmental protection than is the general population, and the Congressional Black Caucus routinely has the best environmental voting record of any group in Congress. Finally, many environmental groups do in fact work to improve the quality of the urban environment.[9]

So, contrary to conventional wisdom, the potential for an alliance between environmentalists and social justice advocates has always been present. This alliance began to take shape within small, local grassroots groups protesting the location of hazardous waste facilities. The alliance grew stronger as these grassroots groups developed a permanent presence in local politics, and today the common interests of environmentalists and social justice advocates are articulated and advanced through a multifaceted nationwide network of organizations generally referred to as the environmental justice movement.

The Origins of the Environmental Justice Movement

Nearly all observers agree that the environmental justice movement began in 1982 outside a small town in North Carolina. A hazardous waste management firm, in conjunction with the EPA and the state of North Carolina, proposed construction of a large hazardous waste landfill in Warren County. The residents of Warren County initially received little information about the proposed landfill. When they were finally alerted to the nature of the facility, large demonstrations ensued, where more than five thousand arrests were made. The local residents were not the only ones protesting the landfill. Representatives from the United Church of Christ, the Southern Christian Leadership Conference, and the Congressional

Black Caucus also took part in the demonstrations. Because Warren County was the poorest county in the state, with a population that was 65 percent African American (more than three times the state average), many of the protesters believed this landfill was as much a violation of the residents' civil rights as it was a threat to public health and environmental quality. By linking environmental and civil rights concerns, opponents of the Warren County landfill served as the prototype for the modern environmental justice movement. [10]

Grassroots Opposition to Environmental Injustice

After the Warren County episode, local civil rights and social justice groups across the country began to protest the location of polluting facilities. Soon, these temporary groups that had mobilized around a single facility began to maintain a permanent presence in local politics in order to advance the cause of environmental justice. For example, Concerned Citizens of South Central Los Angeles (CCOSCLA) organized in 1985 to fight a proposed solid waste incinerator. Although the group succeeded in defeating the incinerator proposal, the members of CCOSCLA have since learned that existing facilities in their neighborhood release more toxic chemicals than are released in the entire San Francisco Bay area, making this the most toxic neighborhood in America. CCOSCLA remains a force in Los Angeles politics and now focuses not only on preventing the siting of new polluting facilities but also on reducing pollution from existing ones. Finally, CCOSCLA forges alliances with national environmental groups, such as Greenpeace, when seeking to stop the construction of polluting facilities, and works with other grassroots groups to oppose polluting facilities in neighboring communities. [11]

From Local Grassroots Groups to an Environmental Justice Movement

As the number of local grassroots environmental justice groups grew, and their activities expanded, local activists inevitably came into contact with each other. Through these contacts, environmental justice advocates across the country realized that they shared similar values, faced similar adversaries, employed similar tactics, and faced similar obstacles in pressing for environmental justice. Local groups had initially surmounted these obstacles with the help of national environmental organizations. Although these national organizations still respond each year to several thousand requests for assistance from grassroots environmental groups, local environmental justice groups have banded together into large, regional assistance networks. [12]

The Southwest Network for Environmental and Economic Justice (SNEEJ) is one of the largest and best known of these regional environmental justice networks. It provides local groups with technical assistance and advice on effective organizational management, organizing protests, effective lobbying techniques, and technical analysis. In this capacity, SNEEJ has helped local groups oppose numerous facilities across the Southwest and has even worked with local groups in Mexico to protest hazardous waste incinerators and the waste disposal practices of numerous *maquiladoras* (factories owned by U.S. companies but located just south of the U.S.-Mexican border). SNEEJ also provides a forum within which the environmental justice movement can develop coherent strategies for the pursuit of environmental justice. SNEEJ itself is guided by a twenty-three-member governing council, all of whom are members of minority groups. [13]

The success of SNEEJ has inspired the creation of other large regional environmental justice organizations. In 1990 representatives from several of these groups organized the nation's first conference on race and the incidence of environmental hazards. The final report from this conference was forwarded to the EPA, and several of the coalition's suggestions served as the basis for the agency's efforts to improve environmental equity. In 1991 environmental justice groups from around the country participated in the first People of Color Leadership Summit on the Environment, held in Washington, D.C. The summit drew more than six hundred participants from all fifty states and several foreign countries, and also attracted the participation of the leaders of most of the nation's mainstream environmental groups.

The major product of the summit was a statement of the "principles of environmental justice." These principles serve as criteria for developing and evaluating policies aimed at attaining social and environmental justice. Movement activists view these twin goals as inseparable. Substandard housing, health care, and employment opportunities contribute as much or more to the low quality of life in poor and minority communities as does environmental pollution. Thus, the movement aims to remedy social inequities as it pursues environmental equity. Second, these principles call for guaranteeing the full representation of minority groups and the poor in the policymaking process, particularly through membership in traditional environmental groups. Third, these principles call for increased emphasis on pollution prevention because preventing pollution is the only sure way of reducing environmental risk for all communities. Finally, the principles call for individuals to take part in both government and private decisions that affect the well-being of their communities. They also call for government to provide these groups with the legal and technical advice they need to participate effectively in policy deliberations. The principles also demand that representatives of the local community be allowed to participate in a company's decisions regarding facility location, operation, and waste disposal practices. [14]

Environmental Injustice: A Look at the Evidence

The most serious concern of environmental justice advocates is that inequities in exposure to environmental risks will result in higher rates of disease and death among minorities and the poor. It is extraordinarily difficult to test this concern directly. First, many diseases caused by environmental pollution have other causes as well. Thus, even if we find that poor and minority populations suffer higher levels of these ailments, we can't be sure that these diseases are caused by exposure to pollution. Second, the United States is the only advanced industrial nation that does not gather disease data by income and education, and environmental health data are not routinely collected by race and income.[15]

As a substitute for these data, we can evaluate the evidence that we do have regarding the complex chain of causal relationships that lead to adverse environmental health effects among poor and minority populations. First, I will examine the charge that polluting facilities are located closer to these communities. Second, I will assess the evidence that racial minorities and the poor are exposed to higher levels of pollution. Third, I will look at the evidence on the link between pollution and disease and injury. Finally, I will briefly discuss the rates of disease and injury among the poor and minorities. If proximity to facilities leads to higher levels of pollutant exposure, if exposure leads to disease, and if poor and minority populations experience disproportionately high levels of proximity, exposure, and disease, then we can logically conclude that at least some of this disease is caused by their greater exposure to environmental risk.

The Location of Polluting Facilities

Solid Waste Landfills and Incinerators. The earliest research into environmental racism in facility siting examined the location of solid waste landfills and incinerators. There is no national database on the location of these facilities, so these studies had to examine siting patterns in particular communities. One study found that all the landfills constructed in King and Queen County, Virginia, between 1969 and 1990 were located in communities where a majority of the residents were African American. In another study, sociologist Robert Bullard found that five of six municipal landfills, three of four private landfills, and six of eight municipal incinerators were located in Houston neighborhoods where African Americans made up more than 50 percent of the population. Overall, 82 percent of Houston's waste facilities were located in majority black neighborhoods, though only 28 percent of Houston's population was African American. Bullard claims that the results from the Houston and Virginia studies are not uncommon and that minority communities across the country receive more than their fair share of landfills and incinerators.[16]

Hazardous Waste Treatment, Storage, and Disposal Facilities. More research has focused on the location of hazardous waste treatment, storage, and disposal facilities (TSDFs) than on municipal waste facilities. In 1983 the U.S. General Accounting Office (GAO) examined the location of the four commercial hazardous waste landfills in EPA's region IV (the Southeast). The average minority population of this region was 20 percent, but these hazardous waste landfills were located in four communities where racial minorities made up 38 percent, 52 percent, 66 percent, and 90 percent, respectively, of the local population. Moreover, the average poverty rate in these communities, 26 percent, was significantly higher than for the region as a whole. The GAO concluded that there was enough evidence to be concerned about inequities in the siting of these facilities. Other local community studies have produced similar results. In Baton Rouge, Louisiana, the ten neighborhoods with the highest percentage of white residents contain five TSDFs and 1 percent of the local TSDF capacity, while the ten neighborhoods with the highest percentages of African American residents contain fifteen facilities with 99 percent of the local TSDF capacity. [17] Finally, researchers at the University of Michigan examined the demographics of neighborhoods with hazardous waste TSDFs in Detroit. They discovered that of the people who lived within one mile of these facilities, 48 percent were minorities and 29 percent had incomes below the poverty line. Of the people living more than 1.5 miles from any TSDF, 18 percent were minorities and only 10 percent were poor. [18]

The preeminent study of the location of TSDFs nationwide was undertaken by the United Church of Christ's Commission for Racial Justice (CRJ). The CRJ gathered data on the location of every commercial hazardous waste TSDF in the country and then examined the racial and socioeconomic composition of the ZIP codes within which these facilities were located. The CRJ found that in ZIP codes with no TSDFs, the average minority population was 12 percent. ZIP codes with at least one facility had, on average, a minority population of 24 percent, and ZIP codes with two or more facilities were on average 38 percent minority. The study then created a statistical model to predict the location of commercial TSDFs. This model showed that as the percentage of poor and minority residents of a neighborhood increases, so does the likelihood that the neighborhood has a TSDF. In addition, race was a stronger predictor than poverty. This relationship between race and facility location held even when controlling for region, urbanization, and land value. Commercial facilities make up only about 10 percent of all TSDFs in the country, however. In a study that extended the CRJ's analysis to all TSDFs in the country, I found that race continued to be an important predictor of facility location but that poverty was not (see table 11-1). [19]

Table 11-1 Minorities and the Poor in ZIP Codes with Hazardous Waste TSDFs (in percentages)

No. of TSDFs	African American	Latino	Minority	Poor
None	6.66	4.17	10.93	15.64
1 or more	11.59	6.93	14.76	14.76
At least 5	14.59	9.09	16.34	16.34

Source: Compiled from EPA RCRIS database and U.S. Bureau of the Census 1990 STF 3B.

At least one study calls into question the conclusion that hazardous waste facilities are located in poor and minority communities. A group at the University of Massachusetts compared the demographics of census tracts (areas smaller than ZIP codes) that had commercial TSDFs with nearby census tracts with no facilities and found no relationship between race, poverty, and the location of TSDFs. In essence, these researchers claim there are no biases in the location of these facilities. But this analysis looks only at commercial TSDFs in large cities (ignoring more than 90 percent of all hazardous waste facilities) and does find a relationship between race, poverty, and facility location above the census-tract level.[20]

Exposure to Environmental Pollutants

Just because a person lives close to a polluting facility does not mean he or she is exposed to higher levels of pollution. If regulated facilities are operating properly, if the pollution control equipment on these facilities is working correctly, and if environmental regulations are diligently enforced, the level of exposure near these facilities should be minimal. We must look at the pollution data themselves to determine if pollutant exposure is distributed inequitably.

Toxics Release Inventory Pollutants. The 1986 Superfund Amendment and Reauthorization Act (SARA) requires thousands of factories across the country to report their releases of more than two hundred toxic chemicals. Together, this information makes up the Toxics Release Inventory (TRI). The first TRI in 1987 showed that industry released a total of 5.2 billion pounds of toxic pollutants into the environment. By 1992 this figure had dropped 40 percent to 3.16 billion pounds.[21] These data are relatively new, so few researchers have examined the distribution of these pollutants. We do know, however, that in Los Angeles and Florida those facilities that emit TRI pollutants are concentrated in poor and minority areas; we also know that releases of these pollutants in South Carolina are concentrated in poor areas with racially mixed populations.[22]

In order to examine the distribution of these toxic pollutants more closely, I have aggregated all the TRI data from 1987 to 1991, by ZIP code, and merged these data with information on the race and class composition of all residential ZIP codes in the country (see table 11-2). As seen in table 11-2, as the percentage of all minorities in a neighborhood increases, so does the level of toxic pollution. On the other hand, TRI releases appear to be unrelated to poverty or to the percentage of Latino residents in a neighborhood.

Other Harmful Pollutants. Certain subpopulations of the United States are exposed to exceptionally high levels of certain pollutants; most members of the population are rarely exposed to these chemicals. For example, agricultural workers, especially migrant farm laborers, are exposed to far more pesticides than are other citizens. Researchers estimate that more than three hundred thousand farm workers per year suffer pesticide-related illnesses,

Table 11-2 Toxic Pollutant Emissions in Poor and Minority ZIP Code Areas (in lbs.)

Percentage of the Population	African American	Latino	Minority	Poor
< 5	10,799	14,163	10,133	18,014
5 to 25	25,467	17,017	20,151	12,629
> 25	27,695	11,789	24,315	17,003

Source: Compiled from EPA TRI 1987-1991 and U.S. Bureau of the Census 1990 STF 3B.

attributing from eight hundred to one thousand deaths per year to pesticide exposure. Roughly 90 percent of all migrant farm laborers are African American or Latino.[23] Similarly, African American residents in Detroit, and Native Americans across the country, are exposed to significantly higher levels of PCB and mercury contamination because these subpopulations eat four to five times the amount of fish assumed by EPA models when setting "safe" levels of these pollutants. One study in Wisconsin concluded that the number-one environmental threat faced by Native Americans was the contamination of their food, particularly fish, by toxic pollutants.[24]

Overall Evaluations of Inequities in Exposure to Environmental Risk. Three separate studies have surveyed the research on inequitable exposure to environmental risk and reached generally similar conclusions. In their examination of fifteen studies evaluating the distribution of twenty-one separate environmental hazards, Paul Mohai and Bunyan Bryant find that 94 percent of the relevant studies find racial inequities in the distribution of environmental risk, and 80 percent of the relevant studies find inequalities based on wealth.[25] A 1993 report commissioned by the National Wildlife Federation surveyed sixty-four relevant empirical studies; sixty-three of them found significant environmental disparities by income or race.[26] Finally, in 1995 a group of researchers from Colorado State University scrutinized thirty studies on the distribution of forty-six different environmental risks and found race or class disparities in more than 80 percent of all cases.[27] For all three studies, racial inequalities were more common than income inequalities.

Health Effects of Environmental Pollutants

Evidence that environmental pollution causes adverse health effects in humans comes from two sources: experimental research and epidemiological research. Experimental research, with random assignment of subjects and laboratory controls, provides the best evidence. But the ethical problems of asking human subjects to breathe polluted air or drink water laced with toxic chemicals prevent experimentation. Most of our evidence regarding the health effects of pollutant exposure therefore comes from epidemiological studies, or studies that examine populations of persons accidentally exposed to varying levels of pollution. Epidemiological evidence has its problems as well: the symptoms epidemiologists study are caused by multiple diseases;

the diseases studied have multiple causes; and the subjects of these studies are often exposed to multiple pollutants and other risk factors. In short, epidemiological studies can never conclusively prove that exposure to a particular pollutant caused a particular subject to contract a disease or to die. By ruling out alternative explanations for disease and by producing consistent results across a number of studies, however, epidemiology can provide us with solid evidence of the health effects of pollution.

Toxic Chemicals. Industrial and hazardous waste facilities produce hundreds of toxic pollutants, occurring in literally thousands of possible combinations. It is difficult to find instances where a particular population was exposed to one particular substance. We do, however, have reasonably good evidence regarding the toxicity of certain hazardous chemicals. For example, contamination of the water supply of Woburn, Massachusetts, with chlorinated organics resulted in significantly higher levels of childhood leukemia, birth defects, and perinatal deaths in the population exposed to this water. In addition, after reviewing dozens of studies, Rae Zimmerman finds that exposure to TCDD dioxin increases by 300 percent to 700 percent the risk of developing soft-tissue sarcomas; exposure to formaldehyde significantly increases the risk of nasopharyngeal cancer, but not lung cancer.[28]

Most of the epidemiological research with respect to toxic substances, however, examines the effects of exposure to whole classes of hazardous chemicals. One nationwide study examined all municipalities whose groundwater supplies had been contaminated by toxic chemicals. These researchers found strong relationships between this water contamination and all forms of cancer. Additional research has found that residents downwind from hazardous waste incinerators are 20 to 90 percent more likely to have emphysema, asthma, pneumonia, or allergies. Exposure to these incinerators is also associated with numerous neurological disorders.[29] In one of the most comprehensive studies to date, Sandra Geschwind and her colleagues found that proximity to hazardous waste sites increased the probability of birth defects by 12 to 32 percent and that this risk increased even more if the hazardous wastes had leaked into the surrounding community. Dozens of other studies find that persons living near hazardous waste sites have significantly higher levels of respiratory illnesses, stress, psychological ailments, and immune system disorders than do people who do not live near these facilities.[30]

Inequitable Health Consequences? The evidence is nearly overwhelming that poor citizens and members of minority groups live closer to polluting facilities and are exposed to higher levels of pollution. The evidence also shows that exposure to these pollutants leads to more adverse health effects. We also know that minorities and the poor suffer more illnesses and have shorter life expectancies. Nevertheless, while all of this research provides a mountain of circumstantial evidence, the data limitations described in the introduction to this section prevent us from stating absolutely that environmental pollution disproportionately harms the health of minorities and the poor. Indeed, after surveying much of the same evidence presented here, the

EPA concluded that "although there are clear differences between ethnic groups for disease and death rates, there are virtually no data to document the environmental contribution to these differences."[31]

The one exception to this conclusion is lead poisoning. All Americans have benefited from a remarkable reduction in exposure to lead due to the phaseout of leaded gasoline. A great deal of lead remains in certain localized environments, however. The Centers for Disease Control and Prevention (CDCP) in Atlanta recommends hospitalization when blood lead levels rise to 25 micrograms per deciliter (ug/dl). As part of the second National Health and Nutrition Examination Survey, the CDCP examined blood lead levels in children younger than six years. This study found average blood lead levels of 20 ug/dl for poor children, 21 ug/dl for African American children, and 23 ug/dl for poor African American children living in urban areas—a level nearly as high as the suggested hospitalization guideline. Eighteen percent of these poor, inner-city black children had blood lead levels above 180 ug/dl. A 1988 study by the Agency for Toxic Substances and Disease Registry reached similar conclusions: 60 percent of poor, inner-city black children had elevated levels of lead in their blood.[32]

Causes of Environmental Inequity

The evidence is clear that minorities and the poor face disproportionately high levels of environmental risk, even if the health consequences of this exposure remain unclear. Simply describing this situation, however, is not enough. Social scientists, policymakers, and the citizens who live in these polluted communities are all interested in causation: how and why did this situation arise? Five explanations are generally given for the distribution of polluting facilities, and thus for the distribution of environmental risk: scientific rationality, market rationality, neighborhood transition, political power, and explicit discrimination. The appropriate role for government in assuring environmental equity depends on which causes of environmental injustice are most important.

Scientific Rationality

Engineers, EPA officials, and others are extremely skeptical of the claims of environmental justice advocates. According to these experts, the siting of polluting facilities, especially landfills and hazardous waste TSDFs, is driven by technical criteria. When looking to site a hazardous waste landfill, for example, companies will regard the area's demographics as irrelevant. What matters, they would argue, are the geological characteristics of the site (e.g., does the site sit on top of an important drinking-water aquifer?). If the scientific rationality explanation is correct, then these facilities should be randomly distributed in all types of communities. The reality that polluting facilities are concentrated in poor and minority areas strongly suggests that technical criteria alone do not explain the distribution of these facilities.

Market Rationality

According to proponents of the market rationality explanation, economic factors drive decisions regarding the location of hazardous waste facilities. For companies, the most important economic factors in deciding where to site facilities are cheap land, available labor, access to transportation infrastructure (highways, railroads, ports, etc.), and access to raw materials. Ignoring these factors to target poor and minority communities for polluting facilities would be economically irrational. Although certain economic forces may lead a company to locate a facility in a poor community, this decision is driven by economics rather than discrimination. The evidence supports the notion that economic considerations are important in siting polluting facilities. The CRJ study discussed earlier found that commercial hazardous waste facilities were located in areas with low property values, while the sociologists at the University of Massachusetts concluded that these same facilities were located in areas with large numbers of skilled manufacturing employees. My own research demonstrates that hazardous waste TSDFs are more likely to be located where land is cheap and where raw materials (in this instance, hazardous wastes) are abundant. Much of this same research, however, concludes that the racial and class characteristics of the surrounding area are important even after controlling for these economic factors. In other words, it is unlikely that economic rationality alone explains the distribution of these facilities. [33]

Neighborhood Transition

Any attempt to evaluate the degree of discrimination in siting polluting facilities faces one very large problem: which came first, the facility, or the people in the surrounding neighborhood? Although these facilities may presently be located in poor and minority areas, an argument could be made that when these facilities were first built, the surrounding area was neither minority nor poor. The "neighborhood transition" explanation paints the following scenario. Many polluting facilities originally located in urban, working-class areas for many of the reasons cited by the market rationality explanation. Over time, those residents with the resources to move away from these facilities did so. Because these facilities had reduced the value of the surrounding property, the departing residents were replaced by people who were poor and/or members of minority groups. Thus, although the present-day risks from these facilities may be distributed inequitably, the process of siting these facilities was not discriminatory.

The neighborhood-transition explanation is a plausible argument. Each year between 17 and 20 percent of all households in the United States move, so neighborhoods are constantly changing. Moreover, research by Kerry Smith and others shows that hazardous waste sites and other polluting facilities do drive down the value of surrounding property, and wealthier and more educated residents will pay more to move away from polluting facilities. [34] In short, the middle class is most likely to move away from these facilities, and the housing near these facilities is likely to attract the poor.

Vicki Been has examined the demographics of areas surrounding several hazardous waste landfills and incinerators both before and after these facilities were sited. She found that at the time the siting decisions were made, all four of the hazardous waste landfills in EPA region IV were located in communities where the percentage of African Americans was two to four times the state average. The racial and class characteristics of these areas did not change appreciably after these facilities were built. On the other hand, at the time they were built, only half of all landfills and incinerators in Houston were located in areas that were predominantly African American. By 1990 the neighborhoods surrounding these facilities had changed so that all but one of these facilities were now located in majority African American areas. Poverty levels in the areas surrounding these facilities increased as well. Although these results may not be generalizable to all facilities or neighborhoods, the one study available suggests that neighborhood transition provides only a partial explanation for the inequitable distribution of polluting facilities.[35]

Political Power

The rational political actor will attempt to site polluting facilities where they will face the least amount of political resistance. Although the right to vote is distributed equally, political power is not. Political power is a function of wealth, education, group organizational skills, frequent participation in the political process, and so forth. Certain citizens, particularly members of minority groups and the poor, have fewer of these resources. Hence, political rationality, rather than outright discrimination, appears to best explain the location of polluting facilities.

A report commissioned by the state of California explicitly recommends that the state target areas that "lack social power" when trying to site incinerators. Moreover, when investigating which hazardous waste facilities seek to expand their capacity, James Hamilton of Duke University finds that neither race or class matters much. Instead, facilities are least likely to expand when they are located in neighborhoods where the residents are politically active. Finally, my own research shows that one of the best predictors of whether a permit to operate a hazardous waste TSDF will be approved or denied is not the demographic characteristics of the surrounding neighborhood, but the percentage of neighborhood residents who own their own homes.[36] To sum up, nearly all of the available evidence suggests that when it comes to siting hazardous waste facilities, neighborhood political power matters.

Intentional Discrimination

Many observers, including prominent members of the environmental justice movement like Robert Bullard, claim that minority (and poor) neighborhoods are explicitly targeted to receive polluting facilities, thus proposing that the process of facility siting is driven by environmental racism. Hazardous waste industry officials completely reject this claim. Still, it is difficult to overlook the fact that CWM Inc. has chosen to site all four of its commercial hazardous waste incinerators in communities where African Americans and Latinos constitute the overwhelming majority of the population. CWM Inc.'s largest hazardous waste landfill is also located in a community (Emelle, Alabama) that is 90 percent African American.

EPA officials also reject the contention that government environmental policy decisions intentionally discriminate against poor and minority communities. Yet a 1974 EPA report identifying the most suitable locations for a large hazardous waste landfill selected ten counties where minorities made up 32 percent of the population (the national average is 20 percent).[37] In addition, a 1992 study by reporters at the *National Law Journal* found that average civil penalties for violating environmental laws were higher in white neighborhoods than in minority neighborhoods, and higher in wealthy neighborhoods than in poor neighborhoods. This same study found that cleanup activities at abandoned hazardous waste sites progress more slowly in minority communities.[38]

In many ways, the intentional-discrimination theory is the most difficult to test. Although suggestive, the evidence presented above does not prove discriminatory intent. Moreover, as the other explanations for environmental inequities make plain, discriminatory intent is not necessary to produce discriminatory outcomes. Nevertheless, even though intentional discrimination may not be the most plausible explanation for environmental inequities, we would do well to remember that "harm perpetuated by benign inadvertence is as injurious as harm by purposeful intent."[39]

Remedying Environmental Injustice

In response to the evidence presented above and pressure from environmental justice advocates, private and governmental actors are undertaking a wide variety of activities to remedy environmental inequities.

Policy Changes at the National Level

Presidential Actions. President Bill Clinton has identified environmental justice as a top administrative priority. In February of 1994 the president issued Executive Order (EO) 12898, which requires that "each federal agency shall make achieving environmental justice part of its mission by identifying and addressing, as appropriate, disproportionately high and adverse human health or environmental effects of its programs, policies, and activities on minority populations and low-income populations in the United States and its territories and possessions." In addition, EO 12898 created an interagency workgroup on environmental justice to coordinate the environmental justice plans of all affected federal agencies. Accompanying EO 12898, President Clinton released a Memorandum on Environmental Justice that requires all federal agencies to (a) ensure that all programs or activities receiving federal financial assistance that affect human health or the environment do not discriminate on the basis of race, color, or national origin; (b) analyze the environmental and health effects on poor and minority communities whenever an Environmental Impact Statement is required under the National Environmental Policy Act; and (c) ensure that poor and minority communities have adequate access to public information relating to human health, environmental planning, and environmental regulation. EO 12898 also requires the EPA to fully analyze the environmental effects on poor and minority communities precipitated by the actions of other federal agencies.

Congressional Actions. In 1992 Congress enacted the Residential Lead-Based Paint Reduction Act. This legislation authorizes $375 million for inspection and lead abatement actions in low-income housing, requires the EPA to set up training and certification programs for lead abatement contractors, and provides grants to the states to develop their own lead abatement and training programs. By 1995 the EPA had awarded $11 million in lead abatement program grants to forty-five states and had created five lead abatement training centers. In addition, the Department of Housing and Urban Development distributed more than $275 million in grants to state and local governments for lead abatement in low-income areas. [40]

Congress has been more reluctant to act on other pieces of environmental justice legislation. For example, in 1992 Rep. John Lewis (D-Ga.) and Al Gore, then a Democratic senator from Tennessee, introduced the Environmental Justice Act (EJA). The EJA required the EPA to identify the one hundred areas of the country most polluted by toxic chemicals and designate them as "environmental high-impact areas," or EHIAs. For each EHIA, the act required the EPA to impose a moratorium on siting new sources of toxic pollution in these areas if the agency found evidence of adverse health effects from this pollution. The Environmental Justice Act was reintroduced in 1993 by Representative Lewis and Sen. Max Baucus (D-Mont.). Amendments to the Resource Conservation and Recovery Act proposed by Rep. Bill Clinger (R-Pa.) and Sens. Mike Synar (D-Okla.) and John Glenn (D-Ohio) required private developers and government officials to prepare "community information statements" that would identify the socioeconomic and demographic composition of the areas surrounding any proposed hazardous waste TSDF. Finally, Rep. Cardiss Collins (D-Ill.) proposed the "Environmental Equal Rights Act," which would prevent siting additional hazardous waste TSDFs in poor or minority communities that already have these facilities. None of this proposed legislation was enacted, however, and given the Republican takeover of both houses of Congress following the 1994 elections, it is unlikely that environmental justice legislation will be passed any time soon.

Administrative Actions. The EPA has undertaken a variety of efforts aimed at producing environmental justice. These actions can be grouped into three general categories: agency reorganization, environmental litigation, and research and education. The EPA first responded to the concerns of environmental justice advocates in 1990 by creating an internal environmental equity workgroup to examine evidence regarding the inequitable distribution of environmental risk. The results of the workgroup's research convinced EPA to create a new Office of Environmental Equity (now the Office of Environmental Justice). In addition, the EPA now has an Office of Civil Rights and participates in the National Environmental Justice Advisory Council that helps local communities pursue remedies for instances of environmental discrimination. Finally, each EPA regional office now has an Environmental Justice Coordinator to oversee efforts at improving environmental equity.

One way to reduce inequitable exposures to environmental risk is to sue the actors responsible for producing that risk. In 1993 EPA's Office of Civil Rights began an investigation into the process by which permits were granted to operate polluting facilities in Louisiana's "cancer alley." This investigation bore fruit in 1994, when the EPA sued Borden Chemicals and Plastics for illegally storing and disposing of large quantities of hazardous chemicals that eventually contaminated the groundwater in nearby poor and minority communities. The Borden case is the first in which the EPA has raised the issue of environmental racism.[41]

In several areas, the EPA is going beyond the requirements of EO 12898, embarking on additional research and education activities with respect to environmental justice. For example, in 1990 the EPA began the first survey of pollution on Native American reservations. In 1991 EPA headquarters required all regional offices to complete research on elements of environmental justice that were particularly relevant in their region. In response, the region IX office in San Francisco began testing water quality at migrant labor camps in California, the region V office in Chicago began investigating the extent of lead poisoning among poor children, and the region II office in New York City began a study to see if wealthier neighborhoods received preferential treatment in cleaning up abandoned hazardous waste sites. Each regional office has also begun to collect data on exposure to environmental pollutants by race and income categories.[42]

Finally, in 1992 the EPA created the Minority Academic Institutions Task Force to enhance the interaction between the agency and historically minority academic institutions (MAIs). Responding to the recommendations of this task force, the EPA created the Cooperative Progression Program, with which the EPA recruits promising minority students to pursue careers in the environmental field and eventually work at the agency. In addition, the EPA has either started or expanded research programs at several historically minority academic institutions, and faculty at these MAIs are encouraged to work at the agency through the EPA's faculty fellows program.[43]

Policy Changes at the State Level

Many state governments have struck out on their own to address the issues raised by environmental justice advocates. At least four states

(California, Florida, Texas, and Wisconsin) have created environmental justice commissions, whose job is to evaluate the degree of environmental inequity in their states and propose changes in environmental policy to reduce it. The California legislature has twice passed legislation requiring applicants for toxic facility permits to present data on the demographic and socioeconomic makeup of the area surrounding the proposed facility (i.e., Community Information Statements). Governor Pete Wilson vetoed both bills because they placed an unreasonable burden on business. The Texas Department of Health, however, now requires these data from developers of hazardous waste disposal sites. The state of Arkansas bans waste facilities from being sited within twelve miles of each other, and Alabama now prohibits siting more than one commercial hazardous waste TSDF in any county. [44]

Policy Changes at the Local Level

Most environmental justice advocates are skeptical of the effectiveness of the traditional tools of public policy—legislation and litigation—especially at the national level. Because of this, the environmental justice movement generally targets its political action and pressure at the local level. [45] The contemporary model for local efforts to ensure environmental justice is New York City's "fair share" policy. In 1989 New York adopted a new city charter with two unique provisions ensuring that each borough and neighborhood bears its fair share of (a) locally undesirable land use burdens (prisons, waste facilities, homeless shelters, etc.), and (b) beneficial public services (parks, libraries, health clinics, etc.). The city has developed explicit criteria for determining each borough's "fair share" of these facilities. Each year the mayor produces a list of undesirable facilities that must be built, expanded, or closed. This list must specify the exact location of these facilities in accordance with the "fair share" criteria and also take into account the extent to which the character of the neighborhood will be changed by the concentration of these facilities. Borough presidents and community residents then have at least two years to comment on these plans and to suggest alternative sites for these facilities. [46]

Interest Group Responses to Environmental Justice Concerns

Early in their history, environmental groups sought to keep the environmental movement separate and distinct from general social justice concerns because they feared that an alliance with these concerns might dilute their effectiveness and detract from their ability to attract members. A few national environmental groups, however, have a strong history of minority group involvement and of attending to social justice (Greenpeace, the National Toxics Campaign), and the Earth Island Institute has had an African American president since 1989. Partially in response to criticism from environmental justice advocates, partially in recognition that social justice and the environment are intimately linked, and partially because poor and minority citizens provide an opportunity to increase their membership base, the other mainstream environmental groups have recently become involved in the environmental justice movement. In 1989 the ten largest environmental groups embarked on a minority outreach campaign to increase minority membership and the representation of minorities in group leadership positions. Some of these groups, particularly Greenpeace and the National Wildlife Federation, now actively seek out partnerships with local grassroots groups to combat environmental injustice.

Normative Concerns in Remedying Environmental Injustice

Although government at all levels has acted to promote environmental equity, environmental justice advocates believe much more needs to be done. Their belief leads us to an important question: What *should* government do about observed environmental inequities? To answer this question, we must forge a national consensus regarding, first, what constitutes "discrimination" in environmental protection, and, second, what we mean by "equity."

Defining Discrimination

Does every decisionmaking process that produces discriminatory outcomes deserve the government's attention in order to provide equal protection under the law to all citizens, or are such decisions only legally actionable when there is actual discriminatory intent behind the decision? This is a difficult question, and even our laws apply different definitions of discrimination. For example, violating the fourth amendment's equal protection clause requires discriminatory intent, while violating Title VI of the 1964 Civil Rights Act requires only that an action produce a discriminatory outcome. If we adopt the "discriminatory intent" definition when examining the five causes of environmental inequity presented above, only the fifth cause is clearly an example of discrimination. If we adopt the "discriminatory outcome" definition, however, then any of the causes of environmental inequities presented above require governmental remedy.

Defining Equity in the Distribution of Polluting Facilities

We routinely use the term "equity" as if there were one, universally accepted definition of equity. There are, however, many different definitions. For example, an economist might characterize as equitable a system that requires those who benefit from the production of pollution to also pay its costs. Since wealthy individuals consume more and thus produce more pollution, equity requires that these individuals either live with higher numbers of polluting facilities, or pay others to accept them. A geographic conception of equity, on the other hand, might require that all states, cities or communities have equal numbers of polluting facilities. Still other conceptions might require that polluting facilities be divided proportionately among income classes, racial groups, or even individuals.

One problem with each of these definitions of equity is that a distribution that is equitable at one level often produces inequities at another level. For example, even if polluting facilities were distributed equally between rich and poor, and white and minority neighborhoods, not every neighborhood would receive a facility. Moreover, each of these facilities would not be equally "risky" (e.g., a hazardous waste incinerator is riskier than a garbage dump). Thus, some poor/rich/African American/Latino/Caucasian residents will be exposed to higher levels of environmental risk than others. In short, an equitable distribution of facilities according to group status will produce an inequitable distribution of environmental risk among individuals. Finally, some experts argue that when it comes to disposing of hazardous and radioactive wastes, we should either lock these wastes away from the environment for hundreds of years (for example, in sealed landfills), or ship them to other countries for disposal. But, eventually, all landfills leak, which only transfers the environmental risk across generations, while shipping the wastes to other nations for disposal simply produces environmental inequities on an international scale.

What Definitions of Discrimination and Equity Mean for Public Policy

Defining discrimination and equity is of more than academic interest. How we define these two terms determines in large part the dividing line between acceptable and unacceptable governmental responses to the concerns of environmental justice advocates. If "discrimination" includes only those actions with clear discriminatory intent, and "equity" is defined as communities paying the full costs of the pollution they produce, then government efforts to ensure environmental equity are relatively simple: narrowly enforce antidiscrimination laws, prevent the illegal disposal of wastes, and have rich communities pay poor communities for accepting polluting facilities. In short, government would do few things differently. On the other hand, if we define "discrimination" as any action that produces a discriminatory outcome and "equity" in very broad terms (e.g., equalizing exposure to all environmental risks for all individuals and generations), ensuring environmental equity would require the government to intervene in developer's decisions to build houses and factories, to redistribute income and political power, and to guarantee equal access to medical care, the political process, etc. Regardless of the specific definitions one selects, the point is that until we have clearly defined criteria for what constitutes "discrimination" and "equity," it is impossible to develop practical policies to address the problem of environmental inequity. [47]

We can draw several conclusions from the material presented in this chapter. First, there is solid evidence that minority groups and the poor suffer higher levels of exposure to environmental risk, though the evidence on just what causes this inequitable distribution of risk is less certain. Moreover, there is a strong likelihood that members of these same groups suffer higher levels of environmentally generated disease and death as a result of this elevated risk. Second, national, state, and local governments (and mainstream environmental groups) have all responded to the concerns of environmental justice advocates. Few of these policy responses, however, produce long-lasting changes in the process of allocating environmental risk. President Clinton's Executive Order is in force only as long as he is in office. Congress has refused to act on proposed environmental justice legislation. The EPA's reorganization and research efforts do not actually affect how and where polluting facilities are located. In fact, the only policies that absolutely affect the distribution of environmental risk are the hazardous waste facility siting legislation in Alabama and Arkansas, and New York City's "fair share" program. Third, it is clear that we will have no standards with which to judge either the adequacy or the effectiveness of governmental efforts to ensure environmental equity until we can arrive at some common social understanding of what "discrimination" and "equity" mean in the context of environmental protection. Finally, for the foreseeable future, environmental justice concerns will continue to occupy a place next to risk assessment, federal mandates to the states, property rights, and economic incentives as the major forces reshaping the context of environmental policymaking in the 1990s.

Notes

1. U.S. Council on Environmental Quality, *Environmental Quality* 1971 (Washington, D.C.: GPO, 1971).
2. See Robert Bullard, ed., *Confronting Environmental Racism: Views from the Grassroots* (Boston: South End Press, 1993); and Robert Paehlke, *Environmentalism and the Future of Progressive Politics* (New Haven, Conn.: Yale University Press, 1989).
3. Robert Bullard, "Introduction," in *Unequal Protection: Environmental Justice and Communities of Color*, ed. Robert Bullard (San Francisco: Sierra Club, 1994); and Marianne Lavelle and Marcia Coyle, "Unequal Protection: The Racial Divide in Environmental Law," *National Law Journal*, September 21, 1992.
4. Michael Ervin, "The Toxic Doughnut," *Progressive* 56, no. 1 (1992): 15.
5. Jane Kay, "The Kettleman City Story," *EPA Journal* 18, no. 1 (1992): 47-48.
6. Robert Tomsho, "Indian Tribes Contend with Some of Worst of America's Pollution," *The Wall Street Journal*, November 29, 1990, A1.
7. Ibid.; Jane Kay, "California's Endangered Communities of Color," in *Unequal Protection*, ed. Bullard. For a different view, see Kevin Gover and Jana Walker, "Escaping Environmental Paternalism: One Tribe's Approach to Developing a Commercial Waste Disposal Project in Indian Country," *University of Colorado Law Review* 63 (1992): 933.
8. Philip Shabecoff, "Environmental Groups Told They Are Racist in Hiring," *New York Times*, February 1, 1990, sec. A.
9. Everett Ladd, "Clearing the Air: Public Opinion and Policy on the Environment," *Public Opinion* 5 (1982): 16-20; Paul Mohai, "Black Environmentalism," *Social Science Quarterly* 71 (1990): 744-765; Henry Vance Davis, "The Environmental Voting

Record of the Congressional Black Caucus," in *Race and the Incidence of Environmental Hazards*, ed. Bunyan Bryant and Paul Mohai (Boulder: Westview, 1992).

10. Robert Bullard, "Environmental Justice for All," and Ken Geiser and Gerry Waneck, "PCBs and Warren County," in *Unequal Protection*, ed. Bullard.

11. Cynthia Hamilton, "Concerned Citizens of South Central Los Angeles," and Kay, "California's Endangered Communities of Color," in *Unequal Protection*, ed. Bullard.

12. Andrew Szasz, *Ecopopulism: Toxic Waste and the Movement for Environmental Justice* (Minneapolis: University of Minnesota Press, 1994).

13. L. Pulido, "Restructuring and the Expansion and Contraction of Environmental Rights in the United States," *Environment and Planning* 26 (1994): 915-936; Richard Moore and Louis Head, "Building a Network That Works: SWOP," in *Unequal Protection*, ed. Bullard.

14. Szasz, *Ecopopulism*; Benjamin Chavis, "Foreword," Karl Grossman, "The People of Color Environmental Summit," and Regina Austin and Michael Schill, "Black, Brown, Red, and Poisoned," in *Unequal Protection*, ed. Bullard.

15. Environmental Protection Agency, *Environmental Equity: Reducing Risk for All Communities* (Washington, D.C.: EPA, 1992).

16. Robert Bullard, *Dumping in Dixie: Race, Class, and Environmental Quality* (Boulder: Westview, 1990). See also Bullard, ed., *Confronting Environmental Racism*.

17. General Accounting Office, *Siting of Hazardous Waste Landfills and Their Correlation with Racial and Economic Status of Surrounding Communities* (Washington, D.C.: GPO, 1983); see Bullard, ed., *Confronting Environmental Racism*.

18. Paul Mohai and Bunyan Bryant, "Environmental Racism: Reviewing the Evidence," in *Race and the Incidence of Environmental Hazards*, ed. Bryant and Mohai.

19. Evan Ringquist, "The Sources of Environmental Inequities: Economic Happenstance or Product of the Political System?" (Paper presented at the 1995 Western Political Science Association annual meeting, Portland, Oregon).

20. Douglas Anderton, Andy Anderson, John Michael Oates, and Michael Fraser, "Environmental Equity: The Demographics of Dumping," *Demography* 31 (1994): 229-248.

21. Environmental Protection Agency, *1992 Toxics Release Inventory National Report* (Washington, D.C.: Office of Solid Waste and Emergency Response, 1994).

22. Lauretta Burke, "Race and Environmental Equity: A Geographic Analysis in Los Angeles," *Geo Info Systems* (October 1994): 44-50; Susan Cutter, "The Burdens of Toxic Risks: Are They Fair?" *Business and Economic Review* 40 (1994): 101- 113; Philip Pollock III and M. Elliot Vittas, "Who Bears the Burdens of Environmental Pollution? Race, Ethnicity, and Environmental Equity in Florida," *Social Science Quarterly* 76 (1995): 294-310.

23. Environmental Protection Agency, *Environmental Equity*, vol. 1; Ivette Perfecto and Baldemar Velasquez, "Farm Workers: Among the Least Protected," *EPA Journal* 18, no. 1 (1992): 13-14.

24. Environmental Protection Agency, *Environmental Equity*, vol. 2; Patrick West, "Health Concerns for Fish-Eating Tribes," *EPA Journal* 18, no. 1 (1992): 15-16. See also "Invitation to Poison? Detroit Minorities and Toxic Fish Consumption from the Detroit River," in *Race and the Incidence of Environmental Hazards*, ed. Bryant and Mohai.

25. Mohai and Bryant, "Environmental Racism," in *Race and the Incidence of Environmental Hazards*, ed. Bryant and Mohai.

26. Benjamin Goldman, *Not Just Prosperity: Achieving Sustainability with Environmental Justice* (Washington, D.C.: National Wildlife Federation, 1993).

27. David Allen, James Lester, and Kelly Hill, "Prejudice, Profits, and Power: Assessing the Eco-Racism Thesis at the County Level" (Paper presented at the 1995 Western Political Science Association annual meeting, Portland, Oregon).

28. S. W. Lagatos, B. J. Wessen, and M. Zelen, "An Analysis of Contaminated Well Water and Health Effects in Woburn, Massachusetts," *Journal of the American Statistical Association* 81 (1986): 583-596; Rae Zimmerman, "When Studies Collide: Meta-Analysis

and Rules of Evidence for Environmental Health Policy—Applications to Benzene, Dioxins, and Formaldehyde," *Policy Studies Journal* 23 (1995): 123-240.

29. J. Griffith et al., "Cancer Mortality in United States Counties with Hazardous Waste Sites and Groundwater Pollution," *Archives of Environmental Health* 44 (1989): 69-74; "Hazardous Incinerators," *Science News* 143 (1993): 334.

30. Sandra Geschwind, "Risk of Congenital Malformations Associated with Proximity to Hazardous Waste Sites," *American Journal of Epidemiology* 135 (1993): 1197-1207; D. B. Baker et al., "A Health Study of Two Communities Near the Stringfellow Waste Disposal Site," *Archives of Environmental Health* 43 (1988): 325-334; D. Ozonoff et al., "Health Problems Reported by Residents of a Neighborhood Contaminated by a Hazardous Waste Facility," *American Journal of Industrial Medicine* 11 (1987): 581-597; Dennis Peck, ed., *Psychosocial Effects of Hazardous Toxic Waste Disposal on Communities* (Springfield, Ill.: Charles C. Thomas, 1989); National Research Council, *Environmental Epidemiology: Public Health and Hazardous Wastes* (Washington, D.C.: National Academy Press, 1991).

31. Environmental Protection Agency, *Environmental Equity*, vol. 1, 3.

32. Joel Schwartz and Ronnie Levin, "Lead: An Example of the Job Ahead," *EPA Journal* 18, no. 1 (1992): 42-44; Michael Kraft and Denise Scheberle, "Environmental Justice and the Allocation of Risk: The Case of Lead and Public Health," *Policy Studies Journal* 23 (1995): 113-122.

33. Commission for Racial Justice, *Toxic Wastes and Race*; Anderton et al., "Environmental Equity"; Ringquist, "Sources of Environmental Inequities."

34. V. Kerry Smith, "The Value of Avoiding a LULU: Hazardous Waste Disposal Sites," *Review of Economics and Statistics* 68 (1986): 293; Robert Anderson and Thomas Crocker, "Air Pollution and Property Values: A Reply," *Review of Economics and Statistics* 68 (1972): 293; Gregory Michaels and V. Kerry Smith, "Market Segmentation and Valuing Amenities with Hedonic Models: The Case of Hazardous Waste Sites," *Journal of Urban Economics* 28 (1990): 233; Janet Kolhase, "The Impact of Toxic Waste Sites on Housing Values," *Journal of Urban Economics* 30 (1991): 1-21.

35. Vicki Been, "Locally Undesirable Land Uses in Minority Neighborhoods: Disproportionate Siting or Market Dynamics?" *Yale Law Journal* 103: 1383-1422.

36. Cerrell and Associates Inc., *Political Difficulties Facing Waste-to-Energy Conversion Plant Siting: Report for the California Waste Management Board* (Los Angeles: Cerrell and Associates, 1984); James Hamilton, "Politics and Social Costs: Estimating the Impact of Collective Action on Hazardous Waste Facilities," *Rand Journal of Economics* 24 (1993): 101-125; Hamilton, "Testing for Environmental Racism: Prejudice, Profits, Political Power?" *Journal of Policy Analysis and Management* 95 (1995): 107-132; Ringquist, "Sources of Environmental Inequities."

37. Environmental Protection Agency, *Report to Congress: Disposal of Hazardous Waste* (Washington, D.C.: EPA, 1974).

38. Lavelle and Coyle, "Unequal Protection."

39. Deeohn Ferris, "A Challenge to EPA," *EPA Journal* 18, no. 1 (1992): 28-29.

40. Kraft and Scheberle, "Environmental Justice."

41. "Clinton Actions on Race and the Environment," *National Law Journal*, December 6, 1993, 1; "Agency Watch," *National Law Journal*, December 5, 1994, A16.

42. Environmental Protection Agency, *Environmental Justice Initiatives: 1993* (Washington, D.C.: EPA, 1994).

43. Clarice Gaylord and Robert Knox, "Helping Minorities Help the Environment," *EPA Journal* 18, no.1 (1992): 88-90.

44. Kelly Michelle Colquette and Elizabeth Henry Robertson, "Environmental Racism; The Causes, Consequences, and Commendations," *Tulane Environmental Law Journal* 5 (1991): 153-208; Vicki Been, "What's Fairness Got to Do with It? Environmental Justice and the Siting of Locally Undesirable Land Uses," *Cornell Law Review* 78 (1993): 1001-1085; Deeohn Ferris, "A Call for Justice and Equal Environmental

Protection," in *Unequal Protection*, ed. Bullard; Hamilton, "Testing for Environmental Racism."

45. Bullard, ed., *Confronting Environmental Racism*; Kay, "California's Endangered Communities of Color," in *Unequal Protection*, ed. Bullard; Luke Cole, "Empowerment as the Key to Environmental Protection: The Need for Environmental Poverty Law," *Ecology Law Quarterly* 19 (1993): 619-683.

46. Been, "What's Fairness Got to Do with It?"

47. Ibid.

12

The Greening of Industry: Achievement and Potential

Daniel Press and Daniel A. Mazmanian

Successful environmental policy and pollution reduction are inextricably linked to finding the right mix of negative and positive policy incentives for changing business and industry behavior. Often vilified for its role in causing pollution, industry has been the target of sustained, vigorous command-and-control regulation in the campaign for pollution reduction for close to thirty years. This massive regulatory effort—at $7.24 billion for fiscal year 1995, the EPA has the largest total budget of any federal regulatory agency—has had the effect of substantially reducing the release of pollutants into the environment over what would have been the case in the absence of federal environmental policy. Indeed, in the first quarter-century of the environmental movement, stringent government rules and regulations have strongly correlated with pollution reductions in the United States. [1]

More recently, policymakers have shifted their sights from reduction to pollution prevention by business and industry, and added "incentive-based" and voluntaristic approaches to their arsenal of tools (see chap. 9). Today's most advanced thinking takes this one important step further, exploring methods for "greening" industry: in effect, moving firms away from products and production processes that both require high inputs of virgin raw materials and energy and release high volumes of waste. Such "greening" takes place in ways that internalize the incentives in firms to evolve along this path. This greening strategy is being actively pursued by many companies across the spectrum of U.S. manufacturing sectors through industry initiatives and partnerships that operate well in advance of the formal public policy framework.

Yet, paradoxically, many firms continue to lobby intensely against existing and new environmental policy. These two trends characterize the shallow, short-term events versus the deeper, long-term currents characteristic of environmental politics (see chap. 1). Fearing real or potential costs in the short term, industries seek to curtail, or even roll back, environmental rules and regulations. But corporate leaders and industry associations also recognize the long-term need to dramatically reduce pollution and move to environmentally sustainable production.

This chapter reviews the progress achieved to date in moving industry to pollution control and reduction and discusses some reasons for the discontinuity between the short-term and long-term political goals and activities of U.S. manufacturing firms. We also argue that the most promising way to reconcile these shallow and deep currents—and thereby to achieve greening—is by transforming entire industrial sectors, rather than managing greening by the single-medium (e.g., air, water, land), firm-by-firm command-and-control so much a part of traditional regulation. Why this is so will be discussed along with examples to show how the sectoral approach can be realized. The chapter ends with a look at the contemporary politics of greening, as informed especially by the Republican takeover of Congress in 1995.

From Command-and-Control to Greening: A Cup Half-Full or Half-Empty?

The concept of green industry has many meanings but, essentially, it is analogous to a healthy biological system, where little is wasted and human activity does not significantly undermine species diversity and resource availability. Although it is imperative to gauge progress toward this goal empirically, the process will always be a dynamic one, making attitudes and practices as important as specific indicators. For the transformation to be enduring, industries must change the way they think about their products within the context of their local environments as well as the planet more broadly. There is growing evidence that some of the world's major corporations are in fact greening, accomplishing this by dramatically reducing waste and harmful emissions and restructuring production processes and product lines.[2] As Robert Paehlke suggests in chapter 4, these changes need not always be at the cost of economic growth and expansion. Evidence suggests that no necessary diminution of overall economic growth accompanies even the most stringent environmental regulation, though there are specific industrial winners and losers.[3]

What remains to be seen is the transformation of the vast majority of small and medium-sized businesses throughout industrialized and industrializing nations, and how this can be accomplished rapidly enough to avoid serious ecological collapse. Despite the ecological urgency, industrial sectors are not likely to transform themselves overnight. Tibbs suggests that they will evolve through five steps:[4]

1. compliance with existing environmental laws and partial recycling, including good internal housekeeping of resources and waste;
2. development of management tools that will facilitate green initiatives within and across firms;
3. development of closed-loop recycling processes, using existing ("off the shelf") technologies of waste separation and reuse;
4. significant changes in products and packaging (including "design for disassembly," or DFD); and, finally,
5. development of corporate cultures that fully integrate environmentalism and ecologically beneficial industrial synergies (e.g., wherein one company's waste is another's raw material) of the sort being pioneered by the City of Chattanooga, Tennessee.[5]

The final stage will require significant technological advances in engineering, separation science, and process synthesis.[6] This means that a host of new product life-cycle analyses and designs (assessing environmental impacts from manufacture to disposal), management, accounting, and decisionmaking systems will have to be developed, all of which incorporate direct and indirect environmental costs. Managers will need the flexibility to select the overall mix of products and production processes that is least harmful to the environment and least costly to their firms.[7]

It may be tempting to imagine that this green industrial evolution will take place naturally, in response to the growing scarcity of natural resources and public awareness of the need to change firms as they compete in the global marketplace. But economic and ecological timetables rarely operate in concert. Rather, when left solely to economic considerations and market adjustments, substantial and irreparable harm to biodiversity and the natural environment can occur before patterns of extraction, pollution, and depletion are changed. Hence, the imperative to design the appropriate mix of public policies to stimulate and provide the overarching policy framework for the needed transformation.[8]

Pollution Reduction Programs

In recent years policymakers have begun to redesign policy approaches to foster greening. Many local, state, and federal agencies are exploring different approaches to pollution prevention, multimedia environmental protection, and sustainable development. These state and federal pollution prevention programs are largely voluntary. Agencies and legislators have begun to overlay incentive-based and voluntaristic programs and information-gathering mandates on the old command-and-control structure. At the federal level, five such programs at the leading edge of this new approach are noteworthy for both their successes and limitations. These are the Pollution Prevention Act (PPA) of 1990 and the Green Lights, Energy Star, Toxics Release Inventory (TRI), and 33/50 programs of the federal Environmental Protection Agency (EPA).

The Pollution Prevention Act of 1990. The nation's first federal law aimed at curbing pollution at the source, the PPA of 1990, is designed to expand the level and quality of information available to industry and regulators and is largely voluntary. The law directs the EPA to establish standard methods of measurement and audits for industrial pollution prevention goals. It created the Source Reduction Clearinghouse to help states disseminate information and to provide technical assistance to businesses, and it directed the EPA to form a pollution prevention advisory panel made up of industry, states, and public interest groups. The EPA must recommend federal procurement guidelines for products made through the most environmentally benign manufacturing processes. The act also establishes a new pollution prevention awards program. Finally, the law adds requirements to TRI reports that include a toxic chemical source reduction and recycling report.

How well the act will accomplish its goals remains to be seen. Initial problems begin with measuring pollution prevention. The EPA has found it very difficult to settle on criteria acceptable to both industries and environmentalists. Should it measure overall national progress or local waste discharge; should it measure physical amounts of pollution reduced or reductions in toxicity? And should it measure the efficiency of single plants or efficiency across industry, product, or economic sectors? Similarly, the EPA's pollution prevention goals leave key questions unresolved, such as, should the agency target high-risk products based on their life-cycle, from extraction to production and use? Or should it focus on specific stages of waste generation? Finally, should the agency target particular sectors, industries, or firms that are especially wasteful and hazardous or those where results would come most quickly?[9]

Green Lights. Noting that lighting accounts for 20-25 percent of all electricity sold in the United States and that 80-90 percent of total lighting electricity is consumed by industrial and commercial end users, the EPA launched its Green Lights program in 1991. The program encourages large industrial and commercial facilities to install high-efficiency lighting systems, particularly where these systems will pay for themselves within five years or less. The agency provides technical support (including lighting-upgrade manuals), a database of financial assistance programs and energy service companies, information on specific products, and public recognition for individual companies participating in the program.

In its first three years, nearly seventeen hundred organizations participated in the program. Typical savings in energy bills have been in the range of 20 to 40 percent per year, far above the minimum return of 15 percent suggested by the EPA. In 1994 alone, Green Lights participants reduced their electricity consumption by 1 billion kwh (kilowatt-hour), for a savings of approximately $92 million.[10] And although the program's targets are large industrial and commercial facilities, the EPA reaches out not only to what it calls "partners" (end users of electricity—those who are expected to install efficient equipment) but also to "allies" (utilities, manufacturers, and distributors of lighting equipment) and "endorsers"(trade and professional associations). By defining participants this broadly, the agency has sought not only to save industry money and to reduce energy demand and air pollution, but also to build lasting support and a business infrastructure for energy-efficient lighting products and services.

Energy Star. The EPA launched a similar initiative in 1993, the Energy Star program, which certifies energy-efficient equipment. The most successful part of the program has been with computers. In a few short years, the EPA has signed partnership agreements with 90 percent of all computer, printer, or monitor manufacturers, asking that they install power-down, or "sleep," features in their equipment. Computers now account for 5 percent of all commercial electricity consumption; in the year 2000, that figure could rise to 10 percent. In 1994, 45 percent of all computers and 85 percent of all printers shipped in the United States carried the Energy Star logo.[11]

The Toxics Release Inventory. The Toxics Release Inventory (TRI) was created as a part of Title III of the Superfund Amendments and Reauthorization Act of 1986 (SARA). This amendment, known as the Emergency Planning and Community Right-to-Know Act, requires companies that have ten or more employees and use significant amounts of any of more than three hundred listed chemicals to report their emissions to the EPA annually. The reporting requirements are quite extensive, including the maximum amount of chemicals on site, number of pounds released to different media (air, land, water), and whether discharges are treated, recovered for energy, or recycled.

Like the National Environmental Policy Act of 1970 (NEPA), the TRI requires companies to report their activities but does not mandate that they modify their behavior. To view such policies as "all study and no action," however, would be to miss their contribution to what David Morell calls "regulation by embarrassment." [12] Indeed, environmental groups like Citizens for a Better Environment, INFORM, and Greenpeace have seized on the data released by the EPA to publicize particularly heavy polluters. [13] Moreover, many state environmental agencies are basing their rule making on the TRI reports for industries in their states. Some industries have called for ending the TRI reporting process because of these new regulatory uses.

A little more than 23,000 facilities filed approximately 80,000 TRI forms in 1993, and reported releases of more than 2.8 billion pounds of toxic chemicals, most of these (nearly 60 percent) as air emissions. Although staggering, these figures represent a decrease of 42.7 percent since 1988. [14]

The 33/50 Program. In 1989 the EPA had sufficient TRI data to rank the largest polluters and the chemicals they release. Just nine chemical and petroleum manufacturers were responsible for vast releases of toxics. Rather than call for further regulation of these corporations, William Reilly, then EPA administrator, convened meetings with their senior management, environmental organizations, and agency staff. He emerged with an industry pledge to lead the way in industrywide voluntary reductions.

Thus, in 1991 the EPA launched the 33/50 program, named for its goal of reducing releases of seventeen of the most toxic, high-priority chemicals by 33 percent by 1992 and 50 percent by 1995. As of mid 1994, the agency had identified and contacted more than 8,000 potential participating companies, with 1,242 electing to enroll in the program. [15] Together they represent about a third of the total number of facilities reporting releases of the seventeen program chemicals to the TRI. The EPA reported that the cumulative reduction over the five-year period between 1988 and 1993 by those firms in the 33/50 program totaled 46 percent, or 685,000,000 pounds less than in 1988. This amounted to almost the 50 percent reduction goal set for 1995. [16] In 1993, 33/50 program participants accounted for 98 percent of the 100-million-pound reduction achieved that year. A Resources for the Future (RFF) study of 33/50 program participants determined that the heaviest polluters were most likely to enroll and pledge reductions as a means of

The Business Charter . . .

Adopted in 1990, the Business Charter consists of sixteen principles, which the International Chamber of Commerce (ICC) encourages its members to adopt.

Principles

1. Establish environmental management as a top corporate priority.
2. Incorporate environmentally sound practices into all business functions.
3. Improve corporate policy and practices (toward the environment) continuously and apply them internationally.
4. Educate, train, and motivate employees to follow appropriate practices.
5. Assess environmental impacts before starting new activities or decommissioning a facility.
6. Provide products and services without "undue environmental impact" that can be recycled, reused, or disposed of safely.
7. Inform and educate public about safe operation and disposal of products.
8. Design and operate facilities for sustainable use of natural resources.
9. Conduct research to identify environmental impacts from firm's activities and develop means of minimizing adverse impacts.
10. Modify practices to prevent irreversible degradation.
11. Promote appropriate practices throughout the supply chain.
12. Maintain capabilities to respond effectively to emergencies.
13. Transfer appropriate technologies and management methods throughout industrial and public sectors.

offsetting negative publicity in a highly competitive market, where firms have begun to distinguish themselves on the basis of their company and products' "environmental quality." [17]

Although the EPA considers the 33/50 program a solid success, others are more circumspect. In a 1994 study, the General Accounting Office pointed out that "paper reductions" accounted for 400 million pounds of the reductions achieved between 1988 and 1991—or 27 percent. By the GAO's estimates, many of the reductions in 33/50 program chemicals cannot be directly attributed to the program because 26 percent of the 1988-91 reductions were reported by nonparticipants and 40 percent of the reductions occurred before the program was established. [18] INFORM, the environmental watchdog group, found in a 1995 study that almost a third

. . . for Sustainable Development

14. Contribute to development of public policies and private sector actions to protect the environment.
15. Foster dialogue with employees and the public, and take effective action to address their concerns.
16. Measure environmental performance and provide appropriate information to stakeholders and the public.

In 1992 the Global Environmental Management Initiative (GEMI) created an Environmental Self-Assessment Program (ESAP) to provide practical measurement tools for implementing the ICC Business Charter for Sustainable Development. ESAP focuses on the effectiveness of the management systems in place rather than on the results of specific environmental indicators, such as TRI emissions. ESAP is designed to be conducted by a senior environmental official from within the company. Results of ESAP are intended for internal use by the company. ESAP measures performance on a four-point scale, with 1 the lowest score and 4 the highest.

1. Company responds to laws, requirements, and environmental concerns.
2. Company has systems in place to anticipate problems.
3. Prevention systems are integrated into company functions.
4. Systems are continuously evaluated and improved. Systems exist to solicit, accept, and respond to opportunities for improvement.

Sources. International Chamber of Commerce, *The Business Charter for Sustainable Development: Principles for Environmental Management* (Paris: International Chamber of Commerce, 1991); John T. Willig, ed., *Auditing for Environmental Quality Leadership: Beyond Compliance to Environmental Excellence* (New York: Wiley, 1995).

of the companies pledging reductions did so for amounts they had already reduced by the time the program began in early 1991.[19] This group also pointed out that most reductions probably came from increased end-of-pipe treatment, on-site recycling, and energy recovery rather than from source reduction.

The Transition to Greening

There is ample evidence today that many industry executives and manufacturing associations are beginning to reach beyond specific government programs and to embrace the philosophy of industrial greening as a matter of good business, good public relations, and good corporate citizenship.[20] They are doing so for a number of reasons, including the acceleration of environmental destruction and natural resources consumption over the past half-century; the increasing legal requirements for pollution reduction and environmental protection and associated costs; the unrelenting requirement for more food, clothing, material goods, and employment for the rapidly expanding world population; and the ever-present imperative to operate more efficiently in the global economic marketplace.

Representative of this trend are Canada's environmental roundtables; California's Business Environmental Assistance Center; the Business for Social Responsibility trade association (formed in 1992 with fifty-four members and now nearing seven hundred); firms adopting the CERES principles (formerly the Valdez principles); the Responsible Care Program developed by the Chemical Manufacturers Association (CMA) and now required of all its 175 members; the GEMI (Global Environmental Management Initiative) program, intended to ensure that U.S. corporations stay competitive while going green; and the code of conduct adopted by the International Chamber of Commerce.[21]

Even investment brokers have begun to respond to the greening movement with "socially responsible" environmental investment portfolios, though today they are only a minute part of the investments market. In 1995 about forty mutual funds managing $3 billion offered green investments. Managers of these mutual funds are constantly updating their "social ratings" of industries potentially worthy of investment (though a widely accepted "eco-rating," based, for example, on a company's environmental fines or awards, is not yet available).[22]

These commitments demonstrate that many of the captains of industry do recognize the environmental imperative of greening. Yet if the need is so apparent and the path fairly well laid out, the obvious question is why is the transformation not occurring more quickly? More precisely, why is it not occurring fast enough to satisfy many in business, government, the environmental community, and the general public who are championing it? There are several answers, ranging from lack of awareness and technical know-how to organizational resistance, high production costs, and substantial marketplace constraints. All surely contribute to the failure to move forward aggressively.

Scholars in two fields of research, organizational behavior and economics, are filling in the gaps in our understanding. Scholars of the former examine the business firm for internal motives and changes in organizational design. Researchers have profiled firms at the leading edge of their industry in greening—those that have reached well beyond the legally prescribed activities. They have chronicled how companies have evolved from being heavy polluters to significantly reducing their emissions, better managing their wastes, reformulating their products and production processes in order to use fewer natural resources and energy, and making goods recyclable, more durable, and less toxic.[23]

These leading-edge firms share several characteristics, including visible involvement of corporate leadership in developing and promoting new management philosophies and infiltration of upper management by younger executives and women. To reinforce green strategies, firms have introduced corporate environmental pledges, internal training programs, recycling and conservation programs, and use of "cradle-to-grave" systems of management control, such as full-cost accounting and total quality management (TQM).[24] Of those elements, the two most important appear to be commitment at the top of the corporate hierarchy and a management system designed to track the flow of raw materials, energy, labor, quality, and costs through the operations of the firm.[25] The most frequently identified external factor influencing a change in environmental management is the trauma (e.g., legal liability, consumer backlash) directly experienced by a firm or its industry as a result of some environmental catastrophe.[26]

Economists look at greening from a more theoretical viewpoint, and in doing so they have provided a persuasive case for why the transition to greening is less than many have hoped for. They frame the issues of pollution and greening as a subset of the classic externalities problem (see chap. 9). Firms have little or no incentive to absorb pollution abatement costs or to go green so long as society does not hold them accountable. It makes little sense for them to voluntarily take on the added expenses of pollution abatement or production line reformulation because this could simply place them at a disadvantage with their competitors in the marketplace. The central message of the economic analysis is that greening will not come voluntarily. It will take hold if the problem of acting progressively when others do not—the classic problem of collective action—is solved for the firm.

Moreover, the growing consensus among economists is that while public policy may steer industry toward being more environmentally sensitive, any such shift by industry is far more likely to be affected by the overall level of economic development of a society.[27] This relationship is captured in the so-called Environmental Kuznets Curve, which shows the degree of environmental degradation rising at the early stages of a country's industrialization but eventually declining, in per capita terms, as the economy matures.[28] While this does not imply that greening policy will have no effect, it does recommend placing expectations of policy success within the broad context of a country's level of economic development.

The Environmental Kuznets Curve may present a fair characterization of past firm behavior, but the question remains, "how can we get environmental protection and economic progress at the same time?"[29] On this there is no consensus, though economists are quick to offer a host of policy prescriptions designed to internalize unwanted environmental externalities, most frequently by imposing emissions taxes or fees, or by instituting programs of emissions trading (see chap. 9). For these to be effective, their cost to the businesses involved needs to be substantial. Yet imposing such costs requires strong and effective environmental regulations, monitoring, and enforcement; that is, nothing less than a dedicated, powerful sovereign (a factor ignored by many economists). This is the dilemma of the economists' prescriptions. Though their research is analytically persuasive and their remedies internally consistent, economists offer few remedies for overcoming the political hurdles and business costs of implementing their recommendations. These difficulties make their adoption highly improbable, thus their effectiveness far less than projected, especially on the global scale required.

The Sectoral Approach to Greening and the Problem of Collective Action

Greening may nevertheless be accelerated by public policy aimed at reducing the costs and barriers associated with bringing like firms together to overcome their common managerial, technological, and marketplace barriers to greening. Reducing costs and overcoming barriers are most likely to occur regionally, not at the national level, and within industrial sectors. This suggests that a sectoral-based greening policy will be the most likely to succeed.[30] A "sector" is an industry network consisting of primary producers, a second tier of direct material/energy suppliers, and an outer group of equipment suppliers, associated producers, sales and distribution channels, and end users all related by the production life-cycle.[31]

The important point is that decisions about greening need not be reduced to the conventional economic calculations by individual firms of the total costs and discounted future benefits of a given change or innovation. If the transaction costs of greening[32] can be reduced for a firm through coventuring, cost sharing, and horizontal integration of technical expertise (e.g., across firms and industries), it is much more likely to be in the firm's self-interest to undergo the necessary changes to greening "voluntarily"; that is, not because of government policy so much as a matter of good business practice. Hence, industries are forming sectorwide networks and collaborations to gain sectoral—as opposed to single-firm—advantage in the increasingly competitive global economy. Sectorwide cooperation allows firms to address technical problems arising not just with the primary producer of a product, but also with its raw material (or semimanufactured component) suppliers and consumers, as Cramer and Schot point out: "Since most firms are not themselves involved in all phases of [the product life] cycle, cooperation among firms is necessary. The need for cooperation is not limited to the development of environmentally sound products. Innovation processes of any kind most often do not occur within companies, but between companies."[33]

Market advantage is being won on the basis of flexibility, responsiveness, adaptation, and innovation, which in turn is cultivated and reinforced through sectoral business networks. The chief chronicler of this development, Michael Porter, argues that the firms in these sectoral arrangements are best positioned not only to succeed in business but also to go green and to do so the most quickly.[34] Others have also argued that competitive advantage will become more and more tied to innovations in environmental technologies and management.[35]

From a strategic perspective, sectorwide policy and collaboration offer several advantages to both the participating firms and specific regions of the country as a whole:

- If an entire sector acts, each of its members is far less likely to suffer from fear that others won't change and that they will be left at a comparative disadvantage in the marketplace.
- Informal communications can complement the formal, and this is most likely to occur within a sector.
- Professional organizations already exist and can serve as "change entrepreneurs."
- Governments can and do target sectors, not entire economies; thus, the threat of government intervention is more realistic if focused on sectors.
- Self-policing (providing monitoring and assurance) is more likely within an existing sector (particularly if it is highly networked).
- There is a collective interest of the sector to foster a positive public image.

Evidence of Sectoral Transitions

If public policy and industry efforts move to a sector-based strategy, we should have a way of measuring their progress at reducing environmental impacts and determining if Porter's predictions about environmental innovations are indeed being borne out. The examples of emissions, resource extraction, and pollution control cost that follow thus focus on several industrial sectors.

Major air emission, water effluent, and waste abatement laws have been in place for more than two decades. Monitoring and data gathering since then enable us to examine trends, by sector (measured by standard industrial code classifications). Though the data are not perfect,[36] they provide a reasonably good picture of how industries have responded to the pollution control laws or, to be more accurate, how emissions have followed a downward trend since introduction of the major federal pollution control laws.

A wide variety of industry indicators can be marshaled to provide a reasonable picture of industry's environmental trends. To begin with, emission reductions require the purchase of new equipment, adoption of new management techniques, and recruitment of trained personnel. The best single indicator of these is dollars spent. Abatement expenditures in the public and private sectors have definitely risen, both in terms of total dollars and as a percentage of the gross national product, and with them the costs borne by industry (see fig. 12-1). In 1973 U.S. industries spent about $4.8 billion on pollution abatement, almost equally split between capital and operating costs. By 1993 U.S. industries spent a total of about $26.4 billion

Figure 12-1 Pollution Abatement Costs and Expenditures, Selected Manufacturing Industries, 1973–1993

SIC 26—Paper
SIC 28—Chemicals
SIC 29—Petroleum and coal
SIC 33—Primary metals
SIC 36—Electronics

Source: Department of Commerce, *Pollution Abatement Costs and Expenditures*, MA-200(80)-1 (Washington, D.C.: U.S. Department of Commerce, Bureau of the Census, 1973, 1980, 1985, 1993).

on pollution abatement—$7.5 billion dollars on capital costs and $18.8 billion on operating costs. [37] Almost half of these totals, $12.3 billion, was spent by chemical and petroleum companies.

The results of these effects are captured, again in aggregate terms, in emissions and resource consumption patterns. Nationwide air emissions trends from all manufacturing sources show that most air emissions reached a peak in the early to mid 1970s, declined, then appear to have reached a plateau from the mid 1980s to the present. Manufacturing firms have slowly reduced their annual energy consumption, from 23.97 quads (quadrillion British thermal units, or Btus) in 1970 to 23.85 quads in 1980 to 22.81 quads in 1990. [38] These declines in energy consumption occurred while manufacturing output increased. Taken together, manufacturing industries have decreased their energy intensity (usually measured in Btus per dollar value of shipments and receipts); between 1980 and 1988 energy intensity for all manufacturing groups dropped by 26.7 percent. [39]

The Chemical, Computer Electronics, and Paper Sectors: Brief Overviews

Not all industries are moving at the same pace, and the aggregate industrial indicators mask the significant efforts of individual sectors. Cases from three important manufacturing industries provide a picture of how sectoral efforts at greening are being pursued in practice.

Chemical Manufacturing. Chemical manufacturing facilities are among the largest net polluters in U.S. industry. They release more toxics, by far, than any other single manufacturing sector (total releases and transfers were 1.3 billion pounds in 1993). [40] But the 1993 figures reported by the chemical sector are also vastly smaller—by just over 40 percent—than in 1988. And although chemical companies have increased their total emissions of most conventional air pollutants from approximately 8 percent to 15 percent (depending on the pollutant) between 1985 and 1993, they have done so while increasing production by 15 to 20 percent.

Indeed, pollution prevention has been taken quite seriously in the chemical sector, probably because compliance and liability costs and enforcement fines are so high, chemical company practices undergo tremendous public scrutiny, and most chemical manufacturing firms are large enough to devote considerable resources, in terms of both staff and money, to exploring and implementing environmental management innovations.

Battered by negative publicity, the Chemical Manufacturers Association (CMA) adopted the "Responsible Care" program in 1988. This sector-wide code of conduct is now required of all CMA members and has been adopted in some form by chemical manufacturers in thirty-seven countries. [41] It consists of ten guiding principles and six management practice codes. The guiding principles emphasize responding to community concerns; ensuring safety in all phases of production, transportation, use and disposal; developing safe chemicals and supporting research on health, safety, and environmental effects of products, processes and wastes; and helping to create "responsible" laws and regulations. The management codes are designed to improve each facility's emergency response capabilities; pollution prevention; and safety in production, sales, distribution, and final disposal. The CMA has been adopting quantitative benchmarks to measure its members' progress on each of these codes. [42]

The Responsible Care program is quite self-consciously sectoral. As Porter might predict, CMA members expect the program to succeed with collaborative efforts:

> The Responsible Care program has also spawned an extensive mutual assistance network within the chemical industry, a network that includes very senior management. Companies that are far along in their implementation of the codes are asked to help those companies having difficulty complying. Through its Partnership Program, CMA actively pushes the envelope of Responsible Care beyond the chemical industry. Partners are industries and associations that are not CMA members, but that make, use, formulate, distribute, transport, and/or treat or dispose of chemicals. [43]

It is too early to draw conclusions about the Responsible Care program. Critics point to a large gap between improvements to which CMA members have committed themselves and what companies have actually achieved. Part of the problem is that some of the management codes lack clear performance indicators, and company statistics are not yet independently validated by any third-party observers. [44]

Industrial end users of chemicals are also pulling chemical manufacturers toward environmentally benign practices. Cramer and Schot report that corporate consumers are increasingly reluctant to take delivery of highly toxic chemicals, or compounds "that receive a great deal of negative publicity," such as polyvinyl chloride, cadmium, or chlorofluorocarbons. [45] And to make good on some manufacturers' claims of recyclability, the automobile industry is pressuring chemical companies to use plastics that "have the same chemical structure, which makes it easier to recycle and reuse them." [46] Finally, most firms are seriously concerned about the cost and liability of hazardous waste disposal. Consequently, they are requesting that chemicals be delivered in the exact amounts needed, preferably in returnable containers.

Computer Electronics. Computer manufacturers have also been modifying their environmental impacts substantially over the past decade. In 1988 manufacturers of computer equipment, circuit boards, and semiconductors reported total toxic releases to the environment of 18.3 million pounds. In 1992 this sector reported releases of 13.0 million pounds, a drop of 29 percent. [47] Once thought of as the cleanest of industries, computer manufacturers lost that reputation as the result of stunning groundwater contamination cases (mostly in California) in the 1980s. Circuit board and semiconductor companies had been storing toxic solvents in underground storage tanks that leaked into groundwater supplies, eventually creating twenty-nine Superfund sites in Silicon Valley alone. The government and high-tech firms responded with groundwater remediation programs, but soon afterward the sector faced new evidence of environmental damage from its use of ozone-depleting chlorofluorocarbons (CFCs) and perfluorocarbons (PFCs) for circuit board cleaning.

Although semiconductor manufacturers continue to use 90 percent of the perfluoroethane sold in the United States, chemical and high-tech firms have been rapidly replacing CFCs, PFCs, and solvents with more benign cleaners and developing emissions recovery systems for those applications that still rely on the ozone depleters.[48] For example, Hughes Aircraft invented a citrus-based solvent that saved the company money by reducing its hazardous waste handling costs and by selling access to the material to its competitors.[49] Widespread participation in the EPA's Energy Star program has also helped to reduce this sector's environmental impacts.

Because of the rapid turnover in their products, computer electronics firms face some unusual problems and opportunities in the transition to greening. Frequent innovations make any given model of computer or printer obsolete after about eighteen months, at which time companies usually discontinue a particular model in favor of the next version. Thus, while rapid obsolescence can lead to more wastes, there is also a much higher potential to redesign products with environmental goals in mind. Moreover, most of a computer's costs—and its environmental impacts—are determined by its design, literally before engineers draw up the manufacturing blueprints. So product design changes must be built in to reduce those costs and environmental impacts from the start.[50]

Because of these sector-specific characteristics, computer electronics firms have focused their environmental innovations on product design and recyclability. The Design for Environment initiative, coordinated by the American Electronics Association (AEA), is the most notable. Design for Environment focuses on sharing management and engineering practices concerning the design, production, distribution, and ultimate disposition of computers, printers, copiers, and telecommunications devices. The initiative also promotes mutual aid on regulatory compliance and provides concrete examples of production changes that other firms can implement on the shop floor.[51]

Similarly, industry leaders like Hewlett-Packard and Xerox are beginning to design their products for disassembly (making components easy to take apart), and for recycling (by choosing materials that, once disassembled, yield valuable materials). Some larger firms also take back or remanufacture products or parts of products, using extensive networks of third-party brokers, which provide the critical link in the recycling chain.[52]

Pulp and Paper: A Closer Look. Some segments, though by no means all, of the pulp and paper sector are undergoing an aggressive transition to greening. On the whole, paper companies have been steadily reducing many of their emissions, as well as their energy intensity, on a per ton of product or dollar output basis (see table 12-1).

Table 12-1 The U.S. Pulp and Paper Industry

Indicators	1970s	1980s	1990s
Energy consumption (quads)	1.74 (1972)	2.21 (1985)	2.39 (1993)
Energy intensity (thousand Btus/1987 dollar of value of shipments and receipts)	NA	12.27 (1985)	13.90 (1991)
Toxic releases (lbs.)	NA	276 million (1988)	216 million (1993)
Recycling (percentage recovered wastepaper in pulp)	22.4 percent	26.4 percent	38 percent (1993 est.) 50 percent (2000 est.)
Wastepaper recovered (thousand short tons)	10,530	13,185	20,981
Resource extraction (thousand cords of pulpwood)	67,524	79,703	99,109
Production (paper and paperboard combined, thousand short tons)	52,210	65,834	78,782

Sources: Department of Commerce, *Survey of Current Business,* vol. 52, no. 6; vol. 62, no. 12; vol. 72, no. 11 (Washington, D.C.: U.S. Department of Commerce, Economics and Statistics Administration, Bureau of Economic Analysis, 1972, 1982, and 1992); Environmental Protection Agency, *1993 Toxic Release Inventory Public Data Release Report,* EPA 745-R-95-010 (Washington, D.C.: Office of Pollution Prevention and Toxics, 1995); Department of Energy, *Annual Energy Review* (Washington, D.C.: U.S. Department of Energy, Energy Information Administration, 1994); American Forest and Paper Association, "U.S. Pulp and Paper Industry Energy Efficiency: Calendar Year 1993," unpublished report, November 1994.

The pulp and paper industry used 1.04 billion Btus of fossil fuel and purchased energy in 1992,[53] which accounts for 3.4 percent of U.S. energy consumption from manufacturing in that same year.[54] That figure, however, represents a substantial drop in energy intensity from an industry average of 19.1 million Btus per ton of paper produced in 1972 to 11.7 million Btus per ton of paper produced in 1992.[55]

Between 1985 and 1994 the pulp and paper sector increased its conventional air emissions by approximately 3 to 9 percent, depending on the pollutant.[56] This rise occurred while the industry increased its total output of paper and paperboard from about 52 million tons in 1970 to just under 66 million tons in 1980 and almost 80 million tons in 1990 (see table 12-1). The industry's portion of the gross domestic product in 1985 was $32.9 billion; in 1990 it was $46.2 billion (both figures in 1991 dollars).[57]

The paper sector is still an important polluter in U.S. industry, but it has vastly reduced its emissions, energy demands, and resource usage on a per-unit-produced basis. Without command-and-control, and without pollution prevention and the rising costs of waste management, this sector would impose much greater burdens on the American landscape. There is undeniably tremendous room for improvement as this industry moves toward recycling much more wastepaper, phasing out chlorine and other toxic chemicals in its production process, and reaping further energy efficiency gains.

The paper industry's environmental innovations are being abetted by sectorwide partnerships, communications, and collaboration, many of these occurring with the help of engineering consultants and trade associations.[58] Such collaboration is on the rise, particularly among the less-polluting (greener) recycling segment of the sector and among companies that are expanding or siting new facilities.

Indeed, most paper and pulp companies use engineering consultants because their mills lack the staff necessary to specify all the technical aspects of a new project. Designing a new medium-sized paper mill may require approximately forty thousand man-hours; overseeing mill operations once a project has started can take another twenty thousand hours. In an average engineering firm, sixty employees would be spending substantial amounts of their time over a one- to three-year period on such a project—a personnel commitment well out of reach for all but the largest, most widely integrated firms.[59]

These engineering consultants maintain frequent contacts with equipment vendors, paper mills, scientists, and environmental managers. Their own competitiveness requires them to offer flexible design and management solutions to the paper mills. At times their clients will request a standard, proven set of equipment and design features; in other instances, project sponsors will rely on the consultants to identify marginal improvements in, say, process efficiency or pollution control. In the latter case, engineering consultants play a key role for the sector's competitiveness as well as its eco-industrial transformation.   For example, Loreen D. Ferguson reviewed the topics and authorship of approximately eight hundred paper and pulp technical articles published in conference and symposium proceedings in the United States, Canada, and Germany. She found that 59 percent were written by equipment suppliers or consultants, and that 163 papers out of 800 dealt with recycling and/or deinking.[60]

Equipment manufacturers also play a major role in the greening of the pulp and paper sector by continually improving and testing technologies and disseminating them partly through the consulting firms. If consultants and vendors did not play such proactive roles in innovation and technological development, the costs of networking, new facility expansions, and pollution control innovations would probably be prohibitively high in this sector.

The professional organizations of the pulp and paper industry also play a key role in the sector's collective action efforts. The Technical Association of the Pulp and Paper Industry (TAPPI) is especially effective and attracts literally thousands of members to its major meetings. These meetings offer technical panels on wide-ranging topics, including those with implications for competitiveness as well as for reducing environmental impacts. They also provide some members with substantial leadership opportunities through the association's standing committees. These committees bring together dozens of members to highlight new developments, many of which (e.g., nonwood fiber pulping, recycling) would not have been granted a close hearing if they had been pushed on the industry's agenda "from the outside."

The major lobbying organization for this sector, the American Forest and Paper Association (AFPA), is also viewed as a particularly effective coordinating entity. The AFPA regularly conducts or contracts technical studies and policy analyses of interest to its members. Recently these have included studies of energy intensity in the paper sector (and how firms have steadily reduced their energy intensity) and forecasts of paper recycling potential in the near future. [61]

In sum, sector-based cooperation and networking have become more important to this sector than ever before, and key industry actors have responded by increasing the importance of collaborative mechanisms for innovation and learning. To that end, the technical conferences have proliferated in number, size, and importance with respect to the topics firms need to learn about. More panels and conferences are devoted to recycling, deinking, and alternative bleaching methods (e.g., methods that don't use dangerous elemental chlorine bleaches) than in the past (one national conference, called "Waste Paper," is entirely devoted to paper recovery, deinking, and recycling). Some firms making recycled paper had little involvement in TAPPI conferences until ten years ago because topics of concern to their firms were not well represented. [62]

Leading-edge developments in this sector also tend to involve greener firms, because these are the very ones that must innovate the most; they have fewer years of research and development behind them. As one industry chemist put it:

> The recycling and deinking field is still on the steep part of the learning curve. We cannot afford (literally) to sit on our laurels and feel that the process, chemistry, or equipment we have now will do for the next ten or fifteen years. . . . Deink mills that cannot adapt to the rapid changes will be quickly bypassed by the innovative and creative deinking mills. Equipment and chemistry modifications will not be [made] every ten years but probably every two to three years—maybe even annually. [63]

The whole sector is certainly not greening at the same pace. Many firms still rely on virgin wood fiber and harmful chemicals like chlorine to produce paper. They tend to be located near cheap and plentiful sources of timber and water and thereby hold on to their market shares with very competitive pricing. But the future of greening in the paper sector may depend on replacement of many virgin wood fiber plants with deinking facilities located in the heart of the "urban forest," with its vast sources of multiple grades of recovered wastepaper. [64]

Finally, firms are now less likely to address transaction costs internally. Fifteen years ago there was little perceived need for uniform definitions or standards. Now, however, the industry is demanding a recycled-content standard for paper—or at the very least, a uniform definition—so that individual firms are not faced with varying requirements in all fifty states and the federal government. No firms want to undertake a solo effort to pressure states and regulatory agencies and to offer definitions. Consequently, many work through the AFPA, or the more recent National Office Recycling Project, to change the regulatory and economic environment facing recycled paper manufacturers.

The Backlash against Command-and-Control Environmentalism

The greening of industry in the 1990s has been marked by differential progress; some firms in some sectors are consistently out in front, while others vigorously resist change. Progress toward greening has spread unevenly within and across industrial sectors. And libertarian ideology strongly motivates some corporate leaders to resist not only command-and-control regulation but the nontraditional pollution prevention programs as well.

Thus, despite the good image nurtured by corporate public relations officers, many industry lobbyists today still work assiduously at blocking or rolling back environmental mandates. Indeed, the chemical industry's strong lobbying to weaken existing environmental protection legislation and to prevent new legislation undermines the credibility of its own Responsible Care program.[65] And industry political action committees (PACs) are keeping up a steady stream of campaign contributions to antienvironmental legislators, just as they have done for years.[66] In the spring of 1995 congressional Republicans were sharply criticized for drafting environmental reform bills with the help of industry lobbyists. Democrats and environmentalists accused Republicans of inviting industry to rewrite the Clean Water Act and to vastly complicate the ability of federal agencies to regulate polluters.[67]

The implication for the late 1990s and beyond is that greening will be more of a corporate image than a reality as long as political and corporate leaders struggle with the kind of backlash against command-and-control environmentalism that characterized the mid 1990s and the 104th Congress. But a backlash against command-and-control is not the same as opposition to greening. The challenge for industry and public policy will be to move greening into the shallow political currents now occupied by conflicts over traditional regulatory approaches. The deep and shallow currents of public policy and corporate management need to merge long enough to forge both support for and sustained efforts on behalf of greening.

The Clinton administration has begun to move greening onto the policy agenda by forming the President's Council on Sustainable Development and by launching the Environmental Technology Initiative (ETI). The council, which included twenty-five leaders from government and environmental, labor, and civil rights organizations, was charged with developing a national strategy "to foster economic vitality while protecting our natural and cultural resources." And in his 1993 State of the Union address, President Clinton launched his ETI, designed to stimulate development and use of innovative environmental technologies through technology and process redesign partnerships. The ETI's goals of economic competitiveness are a central feature of this initiative—indeed, the administration frames the ETI as a way of maintaining competitiveness in a rapidly growing economic sector.

The experience of the last twenty-five years demonstrates that manufacturing industries are indeed capable of making tremendous strides toward greening. Some of the firms in today's manufacturing sectors can point to impressive achievements; most have reached a plateau in their pollution reductions. But the potential for greening is now higher than it was in 1970, thanks to innovations in product designs, production processes, and technologies.

In order to realize that potential, public policies must focus not just on individual firms and their products but also on the market demands made by consumers and other producers. By viewing the responsibility for environmental impacts as residing solely with individual firms, we have come to treat environmental protection as an afterthought—a problem that could be fixed with end-of-pipe regulations and equipment. The problem is larger than just one end of the economy. It lies at the intersection of production and consumption. It requires firms, sectors, and individuals at each end to pull manufacturing into the green transition. To effect this transition, public policies must, first, improve our understanding of sectoral networks (and how to change the signals that industrial and end consumers send to producers) and, second, develop policy interventions that motivate sectors to increase their environmental innovations.

Notes

1. Stephen Meyer, "Environmentalism and Economic Prosperity: Testing the Environmental Impact Hypothesis" (Cambridge, Mass.: MIT Project on Environmental Politics and Policy, 1992).
2. Faye Rice, "Who Scores Best on the Environment?" *Fortune* 128 (July 1993): 114-122; and Ted Saunders and Loretta McGovern, *The Bottom Line of Green Is Black: Strategies for Creating Profitable and Environmentally Sound Business* (San Francisco: HarperSanFrancisco, 1993).
3. Robert C. Repetto, *Jobs, Competitiveness, and Environmental Regulation: What Are the Real Issues?* (Washington, D.C.: World Resources Institute, 1995).
4. Hardin Tibbs, "Industrial Ecology—An Agenda for Environmental Management," *Pollution Prevention Review* (Spring 1992): 167-180.
5. Steve Lerner, "Brave New City? Chattanooga, Belle of the 'Sustainable Communities' Ball," *Amicus Journal* 17 (Spring 1995): 22-27.
6. David Allen, "Industrial Pollution Prevention: Critical Review Discussion Paper," *Journal of the Air and Waste Management Association* 42 (September 1992): 1159.
7. Harry Freeman, Teresa Harten, Johnny Springer, Paul Randall, Mary Ann Curran, and Kenneth Stone, "Industrial Pollution Prevention: A Critical Review," *Journal of the Air and Waste Management Association* 42 (May 1992): 618-656; and Gregory Keoleian and Dan Menerey, "Sustainable Development by Design: Review of Life Cycle Design

and Related Approaches," *Journal of the Air and Waste Management Association* 44 (May 1994): 645-668.

8. Michael E. Porter and Claas van der Linde, "Green and Competitive: Ending the Stalemate," *Harvard Business Review* 73, no. 5 (September-October 1995): 120-134.

9. Freeman et al., "Industrial Pollution Prevention."

10. Environmental Protection Agency, *Green Lights—Fourth Annual Report*, EPA-430-R-95-004 (Washington, D.C.: Office of Air and Radiation, 1995).

11. Ibid., 26-27.

12. David Morell, ERM-West Inc., personal communication, June 1994.

13. As with most self-reported data, there are limitations inherent in the TRI and thus in any conclusions drawn with respect to greening. First, companies are seldom, if ever, audited by the EPA, so some reports may not be reliable. Second, companies unfamiliar with the reporting requirements may have made significant errors in the first few years reports were due; indeed, the first year's reports, 1987, are often left out of new TRI analyses. Third, the TRI does not cover a host of other environmental indicators, such as energy and water usage, solid waste (nonhazardous) generation, and most greenhouse gas emissions. Fourth, the EPA does not rank the relative hazards of all releases reported to the TRI; thus, it is difficult to compare the health or ecosystem effects of large or small chemical releases. Fifth, chemical and process substitutions are not accounted for in the TRI data. Thus, if companies reduced their use of one chemical agent, the TRI does not permit one to see whether they substituted that chemical with one of similar or lesser toxicity. Finally, there is no way of identifying "paper reductions"—reductions achieved by changes in the way a company estimates releases, or by decreases in production levels, or by plant closures. Despite these limitations, the TRI is the best, most complete database of industry toxic releases available in the world.

14. Environmental Protection Agency, *1993 Toxics Release Inventory Public Data Release Report*, EPA 745-R-95-010 (Washington, D.C.: Office of Pollution Prevention and Toxics, 1995).

15. INFORM Inc., *Toxics Watch 1995* (New York: INFORM, 1995).

16. Environmental Protection Agency, *1993 Toxics Release Inventory*.

17. Seema Arora and Timothy N. Cason, "An Experiment in Voluntary Environmental Regulation: Participation in EPA's 33/50 Program," Discussion Paper 94-10 (Washington, D.C.: Resources for the Future, 1994).

18. General Accounting Office, *Toxic Substances: Status of EPA's Efforts to Reduce Toxic Releases* (Washington, D.C.: GAO, 1994).

19. INFORM Inc., *Toxics Watch 1995*.

20. Stephen Schmidheiny, *Changing Course: A Global Business Perspective on Development and the Environment* (Cambridge, Mass.: MIT Press, 1992); and Anne T. Lawrence and David Morell, "Leading-Edge Environmental Management: Motivation, Opportunity, Resources, and Processes," in *Special Research Volume of Research in Corporate Social Performance and Policy: Sustaining the Natural Environment: Empirical Studies on the Interface between Nature and Organizations,* ed. Denis Collins and Mark Starik (Greenwich, Conn.: JAI, 1994); and Thomas Gladwin, "The Meaning of Greening: A Plea for Organizational Theory," in *Environmental Strategies for Industry: International Perspectives on Research Needs and Policy Implications,* ed. Kurt Fischer and Johan Schot (Covelo, Calif.: Island Press, 1993).

21. Gladwin, "Meaning of Greening," 48.

22. Ricardo Sandoval, "How Green Are the Green Funds?" *Amicus Journal* 17 (Spring 1995): 29-33.

23. Patricia S. Dillon and Kurt Fischer, *Environmental Management in Corporations: Methods and Motivations* (Medford, Mass.: Center for Environmental Management, Tufts University, 1992); Mark Dorfman, Warren Muir, and Catherine Miller, *Environmental Dividends: Cutting More Chemical Wastes* (New York: INFORM, 1992).

24. John T. Willig, ed., *Environmental TQM*, 2d ed. (New York: McGraw-Hill Executive Enterprises Publications, 1994).
25. Bruce Smart, ed., *Beyond Compliance: A New Industry View of the Environment* (Washington, D.C.: World Resources Institute, 1992); and Schmidheiny, *Changing Course*.
26. See for example Joel Makower, *The E Factor: The Bottom-Line Approach to Environmentally Responsible Business* (New York: Tilden, 1993).
27. Gene Grossman and Alan Krueger, "Economic Growth and the Environment," *Quarterly Journal of Economics* (May 1995): 353-377.
28. World Bank, Dissemination Notes, October 1994.
29. David Gardiner and Paul Portney, "Does Environmental Policy Conflict with Economic Growth?" *Resources* 115 (Spring 1994): 19-23.
30. Michael E. Porter, *The Competitive Advantage of Nations* (New York: Free Press, 1990); and AnnaLee Saxenian, *Regional Advantage: Culture and Competition in Silicon Valley and Route 128* (Cambridge, Mass.: Harvard University Press, 1994); and Kenichi Ohmae, *The End of the Nation-State* (New York: Free Press, 1995).
31. Moving to a sector-based policy has the added advantage of permitting researchers to develop "benchmarks" against which to judge changes that are more meaningful than single firms (where changes can be idiosyncratic) or "all manufacturing" (a level that averages out the achievements of progressive sectors with laggard ones).
32. Transactions costs are those borne by the players when devoting time and energy to bargaining and negotiating over what should be done to provide a collective good, who bears the risks involved in the venture, and through what institutional mechanisms. These costs are associated with nurturing the personal ties that engender trust and build reputations. They result from uncertainties over how other self-seeking, rational players will behave, and the task of devising mechanisms of assurance once an agreement on the production of a good is attained. They are the costs of long-term monitoring and interaction among the players.
33. Jacqueline Cramer and Johan Schot, "Environmental Comakership among Firms as a Cornerstone in the Striving for Sustainable Development," in *Environmental Strategies for Industry: International Perspectives on Research Needs and Policy Implications*, ed. Kurt Fischer and Johan Schot (Covelo, Calif.: Island Press, 1993), 312.
34. Michael E. Porter, "America's Green Strategy," *Scientific American* 264 (April 1991).
35. Joseph M. Petulla, "Environmental Management in Industry," *Journal of Professional Issues in Engineering* 113, no. 2 (1987): 167-183; Johan W. Schot, "Credibility and Markets as Greening Forces for the Chemical Industry," *Business Strategy and the Environment* 1 (1992): 35-44; R. H. Bezdek, "Environment and Economy —What's the Bottom Line?" *Environment* 35 (September 1993); and Cramer and Schot, *Environmental Strategies for Industry*.
36. In practice, there are several problems with available data. Federal reporting requirements have changed over time; earlier data have been found to be inaccurate; and information has been inaccurately reported by some polluters. These problems make trend analysis and comparisons difficult, and the trend analysis must be read accordingly. For example, the EPA and state regulators changed their methodologies for estimating aggregate air emissions from industries in 1985 (from estimating emissions based on economic activity to aggregates of emissions from source reports). Thus, air emissions data from 1970 to 1984 are not comparable with data obtained from 1985 onward.
37. Department of Commerce, *Pollution Abatement Costs and Expenditures*, MA-200(80)-1 (Washington, D.C.: U.S. Department of Commerce, Bureau of the Census, 1980, 1985, 1993).
38. Department of Energy, *Annual Energy Review* (Washington, D.C.: DOE, Energy Information Administration, 1991, 1985, 1980).
39. Department of Energy, *Annual Energy Review*, 1991.
40. Environmental Protection Agency, *Toxics Release Inventory*.

41. Lois R. Ember, "Responsible Care: Chemical Makers Still Counting on It to Improve Image," *Chemical and Engineering News*, May 29, 1995.
42. Ibid., 12.
43. Ibid., 11.
44. Ibid., 13.
45. Cramer and Schot, *Environmental Strategies for Industry*, 319.
46. Ibid.
47. Environmental Protection Agency, *1987-1992 Toxic Release Inventory*, EPA 749/C-94-001 (Washington, D.C.: Office of Pollution Prevention and Toxics, 1994). Figures were compared for firms in SIC codes 3571-3579 and 3672 and 3674.
48. Elisabeth Kirschner, "Praxair Aims to Cool Fluorocarbon Dilemma," *Chemical and Engineering News*, July 24, 1995, 28.
49. Anthony Saponara, "Competitive Advantage and the Environment" (Paper prepared for ERM-West Inc., Walnut Creek, Calif., 1995).
50. Bruce Paton, "Design for Environment: A Management Perspective" in *Industrial Ecology and Global Change*, ed. R. Socolow, C. Andrews, F. Berkhout, and V. Thomas (New York: Cambridge University Press, 1994).
51. Braden R. Allenby and Ann Fullerton, "Design for Environment: A New Strategy for Environmental Management," *Pollution Prevention Review* (Winter 1991-1992): 51-61.
52. Paton, "Design for Environment."
53. American Forest and Paper Association (AFPA), "U.S. Pulp and Paper Industry Energy Efficiency: Calendar Year 1993," unpublished report, November 1994.
54. Department of Energy, *Annual Energy Review* (Washington, D.C.: U.S. DOE, Energy Information Administration, 1994.
55. AFPA, "U.S. Pulp and Paper Industry Energy Efficiency."
56. Sharon Nizich, EPA, personal communication, September 8, 1995.
57. Department of Commerce, *Survey of Current Business*, vol. 73, no. 11 (Washington, D.C.: U.S. Department of Commerce, Economics and Statistics Administration, Bureau of Economic Analysis, 1993).
58. Daniel Press and Daniel A. Mazmanian, "The Greening of Industry as a Problem of Collective Action" (Paper delivered at the annual meeting of the American Political Science Association, New York, September 1-4, 1994).
59. Ibid.
60. Loreen D. Ferguson, "How Long Can We Keep Doing Things the Way We Are Doing Them Now? A Look at the Limits to Current Deinking Technology," in *Proceedings of the 1993 Recycling Symposium of the Technical Association of the Pulp and Paper Industry (TAPPI), New Orleans Convention Center* (New Orleans, Louisiana, February 28-March 4, 1993), 409-416.
61. Franklin Associates Ltd., "The Outlook for Paper Recovery to the Year 2000" (Report prepared for the American Forest and Paper Association by Franklin Associates Ltd., Prairie Village, Kansas, 1993).
62. Press and Mazmanian, "Greening of Industry."
63. Ferguson, "How Long?"
64. Deborah Vaughn Nestor, "Issues in the Design of Recycling Policy: The Case of Old Newspapers," *Journal of Environmental Management* 40 (1994): 245-256.
65. Ember, "Responsible Care," 13.
66. Larry Makinson and Joshua Goldstein, *The Cash Constituents of Congress* (Washington, D.C.: Center for Responsive Politics, 1994).
67. David S. Cloud, "Industry, Politics Intertwined in Dole's Regulatory Bill," *Congressional Quarterly Weekly Report*, May 6, 1995; and Stephen Engelberg, "Wood Products Company Helps Write a Law to Derail an EPA Inquiry," *New York Times*, April 26, 1995.

PART IV. TOWARD GLOBAL ENVIRONMENTAL POLICIES

13

From Stockholm to Río and Beyond: The Evolution of Global Environmental Governance

Marvin S. Soroos

Only three decades ago concern about the deteriorating state of the natural environment was confined largely to the scientific community and groups of environmental activists. Since then the environment has risen rapidly in prominence as a public issue. By the late 1980s it had become a leading policy problem on both national and international agendas.

Two major U.N. conferences held twenty years apart are important landmarks in the emergence and rise of the environment as a global issue, the first being the Conference on the Human Environment in Stockholm in June 1972, the second the Conference on Environment and Development, otherwise known as the Earth summit, or ECO 92, in Río de Janeiro in June 1992.

The Stockholm conference added the environment to the array of global policy problems on the United Nations' agenda. The conference theme, "Only One Earth," conveyed the importance of addressing the myriad threats to the natural environment in a comprehensive and integrated manner in the organs and agencies of the U.N.[1] The most significant outcome of the conference was the creation of the U.N. Environment Programme (UNEP) as part of a broader action plan that was proposed for addressing international environmental problems.

A greater sense of urgency pervaded the 1992 Earth summit, as reflected in its slogan, "Our Last Chance to Save the Earth." A historical landmark as the first global summit conference on environmental problems, the summit illustrates how swiftly the environment has risen to the realm of "high politics"and receives high-level attention from national governments.

The era bounded by the Stockholm and Río conferences saw several significant changes in the environmental situation. First, the ecological crisis deepened significantly as a result of a 40 percent growth in the world population, further industrial development, and a higher material standard of living in much of the world. Air and water pollutants also increased, as did the degradation of agricultural land, the rapid clearing of forests, and the extinction of countless species as a result of habitat loss.[2]

Second, scientific research contributed to a much deeper, but by no means complete, understanding of what has been happening to environmental systems as a result of human activities. These insights have brought new environmental problems to the agendas of international institutions, including those associated with the phrase "global change," a term used by scientists beginning in the 1980s to refer to human impacts on the basic components of the Earth system, in particular on atmospheric processes.[3] At the time of the Stockholm conference, little was known about the problems of ozone depletion and climate change, which by the Río summit had come to the forefront of the global environmental agenda.

Finally, significant changes have taken place since the Stockholm conference in the realm of institutions and policies, both internationally and nationally. UNEP has become the focal point for environmental cooperation throughout the world, and a number of the U.N. specialized agencies and regional organizations, most notably the European Union (EU), have become more active in addressing environmental problems.[4] Numerous international agreements and programs have been adopted to address a broad range of environmental problems. Most states now have environmental ministries and have adopted major bodies of environmental law.

This chapter examines the evolution of global environmental governance from the Stockholm conference to the Río summit and beyond, with an eye to whether it is adequate to address the deepening environmental predicament that humanity faces with the approach of the twenty-first century. The chapter begins with a brief description of the basic foundations of global environmental governance and the roles played by the advanced industrial world, the developing countries, and the countries-in-transition of the former Soviet bloc. The next section contrasts the decisive steps taken by the world community to preserve the ozone layer, with its inability thus far to adopt measures to limit emissions of greenhouse gases that threaten significant climate changes. Finally, the chapter reviews the accomplishments of the Earth summit and follow-up developments, with special attention to whether the Clinton administration has returned the United States to a role of leadership on international environmental policy.

The Foundations of Global Environmental Governance

Governance does not necessarily imply a formally established government with coercive power to enforce its edicts, which is lacking at the global level, but simply the existence of laws and policies that regulate behavior as well as of institutions that facilitate their adoption and implementation.[5] To begin an assessment of global environmental governance, let us consider three principal foundations: world theme conferences, international environmental organizations, and international environmental law and policy.

World Theme Conferences

The Stockholm conference of 1972 ushered in an era of major U.N. theme conferences, otherwise known as "megaconferences" or "global town meetings." These conferences were convened to focus worldwide attention on specific, broadly defined problems and to set forth principles and propose action plans for addressing them. In the environmental realm, conferences were held on population (1974, 1984, and 1994), food (1974), human settlements (1976, 1996), water (1977), desertification (1977), climate (1979, 1990), new and renewable sources of energy (1981), and outer space (1982).[6]

The Stockholm conference became the model for the later conferences, some of which were more successful than others. Scheduling the conference four years in advance permitted an extensive series of preparatory meetings to assemble information and to agree on drafts of documents that could be finalized and adopted at the relatively brief official conference. The actual conference, which lasted less than two weeks, drew delegates from 113 states and representatives from 19 intergovernmental agencies. A number of accredited nongovernmental organizations (NGOs) were also given an opportunity to present their perspectives on the conference agenda. A concurrent event at Stockholm was an informal gathering known as the People's Forum, at which activists and members of NGOs carried on a lively discussion of what they felt were the "real" issues being ignored at the official conference.[7] Informal forums have become a fixture at theme conferences and often attract more press attention than the official meetings.

Most theme conferences adopt two types of nonbinding documents. The first type is a declaration laying out the guiding principles for efforts to address a given problem. The declaration of the Stockholm conference is well known for its Article 21, which proclaimed that states not only "have the sovereign right to exploit their resources in accordance with their policies," but also have the obligation to "insure that activities within their own jurisdiction or control do not cause damage to the environment of other states or areas beyond the limits of national jurisdiction."[8] Most conferences also adopt a plan of action describing specific steps that should be taken to address the problem at hand. The ambitious action plan of the Stockholm conference contained 109 separate recommendations on subjects as diverse as atmospheric testing of nuclear weapons, fisheries, forests, pollution of river systems, and toxic chemicals. Some action plans call for the establishment of new international institutions and the creation of special funds targeted at the needs of poorer countries.

International Environmental Organizations

Numerous international organizations address environmental problems either as their primary function or as part of a broader mandate. By the 1950s environmental issues were on the agendas of several specialized U.N. agencies. Among these were the World Health Organization (WHO), which is concerned with the effects of pollutants on human health; the World Meteorological Organization (WMO), which investigates the consequences of air pollution for climate; the Food and Agricultural Organization (FAO), which monitors the impact of environmental degradation on food production and the overharvesting of ocean fisheries; the International Maritime Organization, which seeks to limit oil pollution from tankers; the U.N. Educational, Scientific, and Cultural Organization (UNESCO), which facilitates scientific research on the environment; and the International Labor Organization (ILO), which addresses environmental threats in the workplace.

Acting on a recommendation of the Stockholm conference, the General Assembly adopted a resolution later in 1972 establishing UNEP. The new organization was designed to stimulate, coordinate, and facilitate environmental efforts by national governments and other international organizations, including the U.N. specialized agencies.

UNEP has had to overcome many obstacles in pursuing its multifaceted mission, not the least of which is its small annual operating budget of less than $40 million and the location of its headquarters in Nairobi, Kenya—far from other centers of U.N. activity. But perhaps UNEP's greatest challenge, as a new international organization with limited resources, has been to gain the respect and cooperation of well-established international agencies, which initially were not receptive to sharing responsibility for addressing environmental problems. With time, however, UNEP has established fruitful partnerships both with other international agencies and with numerous international NGOs, such as the International Council of Scientific Unions, the World Conservation Union, and the World Wildlife Fund.

Many of UNEP's activities involve the collection and dissemination of information about the environment through its Earthwatch Program. The principal component of Earthwatch is the Global Environmental Monitoring System (GEMS), an umbrella organization that coordinates the different monitoring networks, some of which are sponsored by other international agencies. Data are collected regularly on air pollutants, climate, forest cover, water quality, and rare and endangered species. Two other Earthwatch projects that gather and disseminate information are the International Register of Potentially Toxic Chemicals and INFOTERRA, the latter being an international clearinghouse for sharing of a wide range of information on the environment and resource management. [9]

UNEP has also taken an active role as an initiator and manager of international efforts to address various environmental problems. One of its first major management projects was the Regional Seas Programme to facilitate the cleanup of partially enclosed seas, which have become the most heavily polluted parts of the oceans. UNEP supervised negotiations on the so-called Med Plan, through which sixteen nations bordering the Mediterranean Sea committed themselves to reduce the flow of pollutants from ships and from land sources. The plan became the model for similar programs for ten other regional seas, including the Red Sea, the Persian Gulf, the Caribbean Sea, and several coastal seas around Africa and the Pacific Rim. [10] UNEP has also been involved in creating and implementing other major international environmental agreements and programs, including the 1987 Montréal protocol on the problem of ozone depletion and the 1989 Basel convention on the transboundary movements of hazardous wastes. The agency serves as the secretariat for the 1973 Convention on International Trade in Endangered Species and the 1979 Convention on Conservation of Migratory Species. [11]

The World Bank has also been an important international actor in the environmental realm. Beginning in the 1970s, the Bank was sharply criticized for funding large development projects that had devastating impacts on the environment and local populations, such as the Polonoroeste highway project that attracted 400,000 settlers into the Amazonian rain forest of northwest Brazil, the Indonesian transmigration program that relocated 3.5 million people to the nation's less densely populated islands, and India's Sardar Sarovar dam and power project that would force the resettlement of 200,000 people. [12] Since 1987 the Bank has taken steps to reform its record, such as including environmental impacts in its review of proposed projects and instituting a lending program for environmental projects in developing countries, which amounted to $2 billion in 1992. [13] The World Bank, along with UNEP and the U.N. Development Programme, are the implementing agencies for the Global Environment Facility (GEF). Created in 1991 with $1.2 billion in assets, GEF disperses funds to developing countries for projects that will lessen their contributions to global problems such as ozone depletion, climate change, and loss of biodiversity. [14]

Finally, regional and bilateral organizations have a long tradition of addressing environmental problems. For example, several international river commissions facilitate cooperation on matters such as navigation, flood control, hydroelectric projects, and pollution. The commissions for the Rhine and Danube river systems date back to the nineteenth century, while the ones formed for the Plata, Senegal, Niger, Zambezi, and Mekong rivers and Lake Chad were created more recently. The International Joint Commission, set up by Canada and the United States in 1909, deals with threats to the boundary waters between the two countries. The U.N. Economic Commission for Europe has overseen efforts to limit emissions of air pollutants such as sulfur dioxide and nitrogen oxides, which are largely responsible for the serious problem of acidification in the European region. The European Union (formerly the European Community) has taken up the challenge of harmonizing environmental standards and regulations among its member states in conjunction with the creation of a single internal market. Thus far, it has adopted more than 250 environmental controls on subjects such as lead in fuel, sulfur dioxide and suspended particulates, lead in air, emission of pollutants from large power plants, and vehicle exhaust emissions (see chap. 14). [15]

International Environmental Law and Policy

The international agreements UNEP has fostered are only a very small part of an expanding body of international environmental law and policy, a third foundation of global environmental governance. Numerous principles of customary law can be applied to international environmental issues, an example being the liability of states for causing damage to other states. This principle was affirmed by the landmark decision in the Trail Smelter Case (1941) in which a specially convened tribunal ruled that Canada should compensate the United States for damages to orchards in the state of Washington that were caused by air pollutants drifting over the border from a smelter in Trail, British Columbia.[16]

The often vague and ambiguous tenets of customary law, which are susceptible to divergent interpretations, are being gradually supplanted by treaties that spell out specific regulations and responsibilities on a wide variety of environmental matters. A UNEP compendium lists 152 multilateral treaties and other agreements adopted through 1990 that address environmental problems. The rate of adoption of environmental treaties has accelerated during recent decades: only twenty were concluded between 1921 and 1959, twenty-six during the 1960s, forty-nine during the 1970s, and forty-eight during the 1980s.[17] The pace of treaty adoption has continued into the 1990s, including major new agreements on climate change and preserving biodiversity.

Most of these multilateral treaties are responses to specific environmental problems. They do not constitute a comprehensive or integrated body of international environmental law. Some environmental realms are much more thoroughly covered than others. Approximately sixty multilateral agreements deal with the marine environment, such as pollution from oil tankers, dumping of toxic wastes, depletion of fisheries, and pollution of regional seas. By contrast, only a few of the agreements regulate use of the atmosphere as a sink for pollutants; and although the 1982 Convention on the Law of the Sea is quite comprehensive, no negotiations have taken place on a comparable law of the atmosphere. International law has been in place to protect the Antarctic region for more than three decades, but it was not until 1991 that the first multilateral agreement was reached on preserving the Arctic's fragile environment.[18]

The impact of existing international environmental agreements can be questioned on several grounds. Treaties bind only those states that voluntarily agree to comply with them. Thus, they are often lowest-common-denominator agreements designed to maximize the number of states willing to become parties. Even after a treaty is negotiated, many years may pass before there are enough ratifying states for the agreement to come into force. Because international enforcement mechanisms are generally weak, if they exist at all, compliance with treaty obligations depends largely on the good faith of the states being regulated. Despite these intrinsic limitations, some notable successes have occurred in the environmental field: nuclear weapons are not being tested in the atmosphere, oil tankers are discharging less oil, some endangered species are recovering, fewer toxic substances are being dumped in the oceans, and internationally shared river systems are being cleaned up.[19]

In summary, much has been accomplished since the 1972 Stockholm conference in establishing the foundations for global environmental governance. But are these foundations strong enough to provide for effective international environmental management in the face of looming challenges? Can UNEP provide the necessary leadership? Can it coordinate the diverse programs of various environmental agencies that are needed to address complex global problems such as climate change? Will states accept international regulations that impinge on their traditional sovereign prerogatives with regard to population, forests, biodiversity, and other natural resources within their boundaries, or on their use of international commons, such as the oceans, the atmosphere, and outer space?

Differing Perspectives on the Global Environment

Developing the foundations of global environmental governance would be a challenging undertaking even if the world community were of one mind. Unfortunately, the three major contemporary groups of countries—the advanced industrial nations, the developing world, and the former Communist countries—have markedly different perceptions about global environmental problems, who is responsible for them, the priority they should receive relative to other problems, and how the costs of addressing them should be shared.

The Stimulus from Industrialized Nations

The impetus for international efforts to deal with environmental problems as diverse as trade in endangered species, ozone depletion, ocean dumping, deforestation, and threats to the Antarctic has come largely from the advanced industrial countries. These countries have long historical experience with the environmental havoc caused by industrialization and the dangers it poses to human health. Highly publicized episodes, such as London's killer smog in 1952 and the mercury poisoning of the residents of Minamata, Japan, in the 1960s, underscored the need in these countries for much stronger environmental rules and for government agencies created specifically to carry out national environmental policies.[20]

The assertiveness of the advanced industrial countries on international environmental matters can also be attributed to several other factors. Their extensive scientific research programs have brought to light the seriousness of numerous environmental problems, including some that might otherwise have gone unnoticed for decades, such as depletion of the ozone layer. Furthermore, having achieved a relatively high standard of living that satisfies most of the basic material needs of their populations, the industrial countries have had more resources to devote to other priorities—such as a cleaner, healthier environment—which in poorer countries are regarded as unaffordable luxuries. Finally, environmental activism has flourished in their democratic political systems, which allow relatively open access to information on ecological threats and permit interest groups to mobilize public opinion and lobby governments.

The industrial countries are not always of one mind on the gravity of environmental problems or how to address them. For example, as the downwind recipients of acid-forming air pollutants, Sweden, Norway, and Canada have been leading advocates of international rules on transboundary pollution, while persistent opposition has come from upwind countries, in particular the United Kingdom and the United States, which are major net exporters of these air pollutants. Japan, Norway, and Iceland have taken issue with a moratorium imposed on all commercial harvesting of whales, which most other industrial countries support.

Reservations in the Developing World

At the time of the Stockholm conference, policymakers from developing nations approached the environmental issue with both suspicion and a lack of interest. They were indifferent because economic development was a much higher priority for their societies than preserving the environment; some delegates even expressed the view that polluted air over rapidly growing urban areas was a welcome sign of modernization. They were suspicious of the motivations that inspired the first major wave of environmentalism during the late 1960s and early 1970s, concerned that the industrial countries would cite the new burden of funding environmental programs as an excuse for diverting money from development assistance programs. Even worse, warnings that the planet's natural resources were being rapidly depleted, such as the Club of Rome's influential report, *The Limits to Growth*, might encourage the belief that there simply weren't enough natural resources left to permit the industrialization of the Third World (unless, of course, the advanced countries were willing to make deep sacrifices in their life-styles). [21]

Throughout the 1970s, the developing nations, caucusing as the Group of 77, repeatedly used international theme conferences as forums for pressing their demands for economic development. In 1974, Third World delegates to the World Population Conference in Bucharest shunned offers of assistance from the United States and other industrial nations in making contraceptives universally available, while arguing that their population growth rates would decline naturally with economic development. China went so far as to allege that the United States' interest in birth control programs was motivated by a fear that the rapidly growing populations in Third World countries posed a threat to its world dominance. [22]

By the 1980s it was becoming increasingly apparent throughout the developing world that pollution, soil erosion, deforestation, desertification, and population growth were hampering their development. But their new environmental consciousness ran up against harsh economic realities. Referred to as the "lost decade of development," the 1980s were a frustrating period of negative growth and declining standards of living throughout the Third World. Many developing countries were faced with heavy foreign debt, hyperinflation, weak markets, and declining prices for the commodities they exported. Pressured to generate foreign revenues to pay the interest and principal on their burdensome debts and to address the desperate economic needs of their populations, governments of many developing countries saw no choice but to intensively exploit their natural wealth, such as fossil fuels, tropical forests, and cultivable land, regardless of the environmental consequences.

Developing countries continue to be leery of the environmental agenda of the industrial countries, which over the past decade has been dominated by concerns about depletion of the ozone layer, climate change, and loss of biodiversity. They hold the developed countries responsible for the problems of ozone depletion and climate change. This makes them unwilling to accept international limits on their emissions unless the developed countries compensate them for the costs entailed. Why preserve their rich biodiversity, they ask, when the biotechnology firms in industrial nations are the only ones profiting from their raw genetic material? By withholding their acceptance of international environmental rules, developing countries can obtain a great deal of leverage in their dealings with the industrial world. [23]

The Passive Support of the Countries in Transition

For decades the Communist governments of the Soviet bloc espoused Marxist dogma, which suggested that environmental degradation was an inevitable consequence of capitalism, as greedy entrepreneurs shamelessly exploited natural resources and contaminated the environment in their relentless pursuit of profits. Conversely, state managers, who presumably acted on the basis of societal interests, not personal gain, could be expected to strike a better balance between economic growth and preserving the environment. The Communist governments criticized the industrial nations for their environmental excesses, while refusing to admit to their own citizens or to the outside world that their countries had severe ecological problems. [24]

The discrepancy between ideology, laws, and reality in the Communist countries became all too apparent after the veil of official secrecy was lifted in the late 1980s. A single-minded determination to maximize industrial production and enhance military power resulted in severe degradation of the environment in many parts of the region, jeopardizing the health of the people. [25] The Soviet Union had for a long time some of the world's strictest environmental standards, but there was little enforcement. A 1989 Soviet Academy of Sciences report revealed that the environment was seriously degraded in 16 percent of the country's territory. Within these areas were forty-five regions, comprising 3.3 percent of the country, which were categorized as environmental "catastrophes"—the best known being the shrinking of the Aral Sea and the radioactive contamination caused by the 1986 nuclear accident at Chernobyl. [26] Revelations of environmental horrors also came out of eastern Europe, one of the worst being the heavily polluted "black triangle" of Upper Silesia, which straddles present-day Poland, Germany, and the Czech Republic.[27]

Public outrage over the environment contributed to the downfall of the Communist governments and the disintegration of Soviet Union. The environment has not, however, been a priority for the new regimes, which have been preoccupied with severe economic disruptions and political instabilities. Russia's new capitalists appear to be accelerating the assault on the country's natural resources, especially in the vast region of Siberia, while dismantling some of the environmental programs of the previous regime, such as its elaborate system of nature preserves.[28]

The Soviet bloc was generally supportive of international environmental governance so long as it did not require significant sacrifices on its part. It participated actively in the creation of a regime that controls transboundary pollutants that cause acid precipitation in the greater European region.

During the last years of the Soviet Union, President Mikhail S. Gorbachev championed international cooperation on the environment in the U.N.[29] Thus far, the new regimes have been too preoccupied with their formidable domestic economic and political problems to become very involved in international environmental affairs. Furthermore, it remains to be seen whether the new states carved out of the former Soviet Union, Czechoslovakia, and Yugoslavia will honor the commitments made by these former states.

Newly Emergent Threats to the Atmosphere

The differing perspectives of the three major groups of states are apparent in international discussions on how to respond to two atmospheric problems—depletion of the ozone layer and climate change—which suddenly rose to the forefront of the international environmental agenda during the middle to late 1980s. The agreements reached on the ozone layer are arguably the most extraordinary achievement of international environmental diplomacy, while very little has yet been done to address human-induced climate change.

International Policy to Preserve the Ozone Layer

The stratospheric ozone layer shields most of the planet's life forms from harmful ultraviolet radiation. The precarious state of the ozone layer first came to light in 1974, when F. Sherwood Rowland and Mario Molina, scientists at the University of California at Irvine, speculated that chlorofluorocarbons (CFCs), a man-made chemical widely used in industry and consumer products, posed a significant threat to the ozone layer. The two scientists theorized that the CFC molecules would gradually rise through the atmosphere until they encountered intense solar radiation that would break them apart, releasing chlorine molecules, each of which could destroy thousands of ozone molecules in an indefinite series of catalytic reactions.[30]

The Rowland-Molina theory quickly evoked a strong reaction in the U.S. public, which feared a significant rise in the incidence of skin cancer. Consumers turned away in droves from products that contained CFCs as a propellant for aerosol sprays. In 1978 the U.S. Environmental Protection Agency imposed a ban on nonessential uses of CFCs, including aerosol sprays, but only Norway, Sweden, and Canada adopted similar restrictions.[31] Europeans tended to be less persuaded of the threat to the ozone layer, suspecting the United States was seeking to exploit the lead its firms were thought to have in developing CFC substitutes. During the early 1980s lingering scientific uncertainties and declining forecasts of ozone loss detracted from the sense of urgency about the problem and thwarted efforts to negotiate international controls on CFCs. The Vienna Convention for the Protection of the Ozone Layer, which was finally concluded in March 1985, did not mandate any reductions on the use of ozone-depleting substances, but merely called on the parties to take "appropriate measures" to protect the ozone layer.[32]

A new wave of concern about the ozone layer began to build soon after the Vienna Convention was concluded. A British scientific team reported the startling finding that concentrations of ozone over the south polar region during the spring of 1984 were 40 percent less than 1960 levels, a phenomenon that became known as the "Antarctic ozone hole." This was the first evidence of an actual reduction in stratospheric ozone, although it was not yet established that human pollutants were the cause.[33] The next year an international scientific assessment sponsored by UNEP, WMO, and several national agencies projected a 9 percent reduction of the ozone layer by the last half of the twenty-first century.[34] These reports helped the United States to persuade the European countries to accept international regulations on ozone-depleting substances, which were contained in the Montréal protocol, adopted in September 1987. The protocol obliged the parties to reduce the production and use of certain CFCs by 20 percent by 1993 and 50 percent by 1999, using 1986 as the base year. Developing countries were allowed ten additional years to comply.[35]

As bold as the Montréal protocol initially seemed, it soon became apparent that it did not go far enough, as scientists disclosed more bad news about the state of the ozone layer. Definitive evidence showed that the Antarctic ozone hole was caused by human pollutants, and there were also indications of a 2-3 percent loss of ozone over the Northern Hemisphere, which had not been expected until well into the twenty-first century.[36] Du Pont, the leading manufacturer of CFCs, responded to the disturbing reports by announcing it would cease production of CFCs and halons by 1999. The parties to the Montréal protocol, meeting in London in June 1990, adopted revisions to the document that provided for a complete phaseout of CFCs, halons, and carbon tetrachloride by the year 2000, of methyl chloroform by 2010, and of HCFCs (a substitute for CFCs) by 2040. Reluctant developing countries, led by China and India, successfully bargained for ten additional years to comply with the phaseouts as well as a multilateral fund that would assist them in adopting substitutes for the chemicals being phased out.[37]

Reports of even greater amounts of ozone loss, especially over the more heavily populated Northern Hemisphere, prompted a second revision of Montréal protocol at a 1992 meeting of the parties in Copenhagen. The phaseout date for halons was moved up to 1994, for CFCs and methyl chloroform to 1996, and for HCFCs to 2030. Environmentalists were disappointed, however, that the parties could agree on nothing more than a freeze on production of methyl bromide, a chemical widely used as an agricultural fumigant, which had only recently been recognized as a significant ozone depleter.[38]

International Policy to Limit Climate Change

A century ago Swedish scientist Svante Arrhenius speculated on the possibility that human beings might unwittingly be warming up the planet by adding large quantities of CO_2 from the burning of fossil fuels. A monitoring program begun in 1958 has shown a steady rise in the amount of CO_2 in the atmosphere from 312 parts per million (ppm) to 359 ppm in 1994.[39] Analysis of the composition of air bubbles locked deep in the ice sheets of Antarctica and Greenland has revealed that current concentrations of CO_2 are considerably higher than they have been over the past 160,000 years. Scientists further discovered that over this vast sweep of time, fluctuations in temperature between ice ages and interglacial periods correlated with concentrations of CO_2.[40] By the mid 1980s atmospheric scientists were suggesting that human pollutants might have been responsible for a .3 to .6 degree centigrade increase in global temperatures over the past century. Their models also suggested that a doubling of CO_2 concentrations in the atmosphere—which with a continuation of prevailing trends would occur within a century—was likely to cause a global average temperature rise of from 1.5 to 4.5 degrees centigrade.[41]

Public concern about climate change grew in tandem with the rising tide of anxiety about ozone depletion during the remainder of the 1980s. The decade saw an unusual series of the warmest years of the past century coupled with other peculiar weather phenomena, which lent credibility in the public's mind to scientists' warnings about climate change, even though these meteorological phenomena had not been definitively linked to human emissions of greenhouse gases (GHGs). Numerous international meetings were convened to discuss responses to the problem. Negotiations began in 1991 on a convention on climate change, which was to be ready for adoption at the 1992 Earth summit. The negotiations were informed by a 1990 report of the Intergovernmental Panel on Climate Change (IPCC), which was established by WMO and UNEP two years earlier to assess the scientific information available on climate change, its impacts, and possible policy responses.[42]

Conflicting coalitions complicated the task of negotiating the first climate change convention. The advanced industrial countries generally favored an international treaty with specific deadlines for binding limits on CO_2 emissions. By the time negotiations had begun, many of them had unilaterally declared their intentions to freeze or reduce their GHG emissions by either 2000 or 2005. Thus, the United States stood alone among the industrial countries in opposing the binding limits until there was more definitive scientific evidence. The developing countries were drawn into the climate change talks at an earlier stage than in the ozone negotiations, but most were unwilling to limit their use of fossil fuels at the expense of their economic development, especially since the industrial countries were responsible for most of the human additions of CO_2 to the atmosphere. Some of the petroleum-exporting countries, led by Saudi Arabia, also opposed any international rules that would discourage the burning of fossil fuels and thus cut into their exports. Ironically, the most persistent advocates of strong international controls on GHG emissions were another group of developing countries, the thirty-six small island-states, which are especially vulnerable to the rising sea levels and increased frequency of tropical storms likely to accompany global warming.[43]

The Framework Convention on Climate Change (FCCC) adopted at the Earth summit has an ambitious and seemingly unrealistic goal of the "stabilization of greenhouse gas concentrations in the atmosphere at a level that would prevent dangerous anthropogenic interference with the climate system." It is also notable for acknowledging that the developed countries are largely responsible for the buildup of GHGs in the atmosphere and therefore they should "aim" at returning their emissions to 1990 levels by the year 2000, either acting on their own or jointly. At the insistence of the United States, however, none of the parties is *required* to freeze or reduce GHG emissions by a specified date. Moreover, there is no expectation that the developing countries will limit their GHG emissions, even though their share of the global total is expected to rise substantially in coming decades as they undergo industrial development.[44]

Even though the FCCC goes further than other framework treaties, it was a disappointment to many governments and environmental groups that had sought mandated GHG reductions by a specified date. The first conference of the parties, which was convened in Berlin in March 1995, declared that the goal of stabilizing CO_2 emissions at 1990 levels by the year 2000 did not go far enough. It decided that soon after the meeting negotiations would begin on a protocol to be ready by 1997; this protocol would require certain limits or reductions for all GHGs by a specified date.[45] In the meantime, CO_2 emissions are up during the 1990s in both industrial and developing countries, and it appears that few of the former will freeze their emissions at 1990 levels by the end of the decade. The urgency of controlling GHG emissions was underscored by a report of the IPCC released in December 1995. The world's atmospheric scientists, it suggested, agreed that the global warming observed over the past century, and especially during recent years, is likely to have been caused at least in part by human activities.[46]

The Earth Summit and the Politics
of Sustainable Development

The Earth summit of 1992 brought together two major emergent issues of the past quarter-century—the global environment and economic development. Twenty years earlier at Stockholm, the industrial countries were pressured into conceding that the pursuit of environmental goals should not come at the expense of the Third World's aspirations for development. For the next fifteen years the environment and development issues proceeded on largely separate tracks within the U.N. The so-called North-South dialogue on development came to a head in 1974 as the Third World pushed its demands for a "new international economic order" (NIEO). The General Assembly embraced the NIEO by adopting the Charter on the Economic Rights and Duties of States by an overwhelming vote, despite the United States' strong opposition. Negotiations aimed at implementing provisions of the charter floundered during the remainder of the 1970s and were largely discontinued after the Reagan administration took office in 1981, which has been a continuing source of frustration and resentment in the developing world.

The Brundtland Commission

The challenge of reconciling the often divergent perspectives of developed and developing countries on the issues of environment and development was taken up by a special U.N. commission chaired by Norwegian prime minister Gro Harlem Brundtland, which released its influential report entitled *Our Common Future* in 1987. The report elaborated the thesis that poverty and underdevelopment are major causes of environmental degradation and argued that the environment of the developing countries and the former Soviet bloc could not be preserved or repaired without allowing growth and satisfying basic human needs. The report also emphasized the importance of reforming aspects of the international economic order, such as burdensome international debt, that have contributed to the desperate economic plight of so many countries and hamper their efforts to develop.[47]

The commission adopted the concept "sustainable development" to focus on the task of reconciling environmental and economic priorities throughout the world. Defined as "development that meets the needs of the present without compromising the ability of future generations to meet their own needs,"[48] the concept is vague and subject to many and diverse interpretations. Critics argue that sustainable development is an oxymoron that conveniently obscures the profound differences of perspective between the world's rich and poor societies. Nevertheless, the terminology has stimulated a reassessment of the meaning of development in an era fraught with environmental perils, in addition to becoming a conceptual bridge for efforts to forge a critical North-South partnership for addressing the problems of environment and development.

The Earth Summit in Río

The report of the Brundtland Commission provided the stimulus for convening the U.N. Conference on the Environment and Development. The official conference, held June 3-14, 1992, drew representatives from 179 states, including 116 heads of states who participated in the final sessions. The '92 Global Forum, held concurrently with the official conference at a site close to downtown Río, gave representatives of more than seven thousand NGOs, as well as thousands of interested private individuals, a smorgasbord of opportunities to engage in lively discussions on the issues of the summit.[49]

Delegates to the Earth summit focused their efforts on achieving as broad a consensus as possible on several key documents. The nonbinding Río Declaration on Environment and Development set forth twenty-seven guiding principles on strengthening global environmental governance. The eight-hundred-page Agenda 21 presented a detailed, long-term plan of action for implementing the goals of the conference into the next century. The FCCC was one of two binding treaties adopted, the other being the Biodiversity Convention designed to protect endangered species and to ensure that nations with genetic resources would share in the fruits of the biotechnology derived from them. The U.S. led efforts to reach an agreement on a binding treaty to preserve tropical forests, but had to settle for a watered-down Statement on Forest Principles.[50]

Agenda 21 was the principal product of the summit's Preparatory Committee (PrepCom), where it was the subject of often contentious negotiations. Its forty chapters articulate numerous goals and recommendations pertaining to economic and social issues (such as poverty, consumption, health, demographics, and human settlements) and environmental matters (such as threats to the atmosphere, land-use planning, deforestation, desertification, loss of biodiversity, marine pollution, and disposal of toxic chemicals and hazardous and radioactive wastes). The document also calls for a strengthening of the role of various groups (including women, children and youth, indigenous peoples, business and industry, farmers, labor, and nongovernmental organizations). The final part explains what will be needed to implement the plan, such as financial resources, education, international institutions, and legal instruments. Because it is not a treaty, Agenda 21 is not subject to ratification by states and thus not binding on them. It does represent, however, a broad-based agreement on both a vision and a blueprint for a long-term global commitment to sustainable development.[51]

The Earth summit revealed much about the intensity of the international politics of global environmental governance, in particular the contrasting positions of the advanced industrial states and the developing nations.

Representatives from the latter countries repeatedly sought explicit acknowledgment that the blame for global environmental change resides primarily with the highly developed countries, which made extravagant use of the world's resources as they had industrialized and in so doing heavily contaminated the environment with pollutants. These same countries, they argued, should pay the lion's share of the cost of mitigating the world's environmental problems. [52] Agenda 21 called on the advanced industrial countries to provide an additional $125 billion a year to developing countries in financial assistance from 1993 to 2000, but only a small portion of that figure was pledged.

The conference was also remarkable for exposing how isolated the United States had become under the Bush administration on issues of global environmental governance. U.S. opposition to setting targets and deadlines for limiting GHG emissions in the FCCC continued to exasperate leaders from other industrial countries. The United States alone among the developed countries refused to sign the Biodiversity Convention, arguing that the economic and intellectual property rights of the biotechnology industry were not adequately protected. [53] U.S. proposals for a forest convention were strongly opposed by Malaysia and other tropical timber-exporting states, which asserted defiantly that their forests were a national resource subject to their sovereign control. [54]

Beyond the Río Summit

The U.N. created the Commission on Sustainable Development (CSD) to facilitate implementation of Agenda 21 and to monitor follow-up to the Earth summit. This innovative body, which comprises fifty-three elected member states, held its first annual meeting in June 1993. Although it reviews reports on what nations are doing to follow through on their responsibilities, the CSD is not intended to be a watchdog group along the lines of the U.N. Commission on Human Rights. It has taken up numerous environmental and cross-sectoral issues, such as the relationship between trade and the environment, which has come to forefront with the conclusion of the Uruguay Round of trade talks and the creation of the World Trade Organization. [55] Specific issues contained in Agenda 21 were divided into three groups to be taken up during the 1994, 1995, and 1996 sessions of the CSD in preparation for a special session of the General Assembly to be held in 1997.

Issues pertaining to the environment and development have been approached from somewhat different perspectives at a series of major U.N. conferences held since the Río summit. These include the World Conference on Human Rights (Vienna, 1993), the World Conference on Population and Development (Cairo, 1994), the Summit on Social Development (Copenhagen, 1995), and the Fourth World Conference on Women (Beijing, 1995). These conferences are notable for the emphasis on empowering women in the pursuit of economic, social, and environmental goals, which reflected the growth and increased influence of a rapidly growing network of women's nongovernmental organizations.[56]

The Record of the Clinton Administration

Clinton's election in 1992 raised hopes that the United States would once again become a leader in global ecological matters, especially in view of Vice President Al Gore's previous record of environmental activism in Congress and his best-selling book *Earth in the Balance*, which proposed an ambitious global Marshall plan for the environment. Although Clinton has taken some steps to bring the country into line with other industrial nations on environmental issues, the overall performance of his administration has been disappointing to those who expected major policy changes on global issues following the twelve years of the Reagan and Bush administrations.

On climate change, President Clinton promptly embraced the goal of having the United States stabilize its GHG emissions at 1990 levels by 2000. The administration's Climate Action Plan was disparaged, however, for relying too heavily on voluntary restraints by industry. Soon the administration was forced to concede that the United States would not be able to fulfill its commitment to stabilize GHG emissions by the turn of the century. At the Berlin Conference of the Parties to the FCCC in 1995, the United States argued that it was still premature to set a binding timetable for reducing, or even stabilizing, CO_2 emissions, a position reminiscent of the Bush administration's obstructionist role during talks on the original framework agreement.[57] U.S. recalcitrance was especially disappointing to the coalition of island nations, which were urging the industrial countries to agree to a 20 percent reduction in CO_2 emissions by 2005.

Upon taking office, President Clinton promptly reversed the Reagan-Bush policy of withholding U.S. funding to the U.N. Fund for Population Activities, which is discussed by Richard J. Tobin in chapter 15. The U.S. delegation to the 1995 World Conference on Population and Development in Cairo, which was led by Vice President Gore, assumed a leadership role in promoting the conference agenda. But when the press played up the Vatican's opposition to provisions on reproductive rights and health in the draft program (which were strongly favored by women's groups), Vice President Gore sought to soften the language to avoid alienating Catholic voters back home.

President Clinton broke with his predecessors by signing two important international agreements: the Biodiversity treaty and the U.N. Convention on the Law of the Sea, which had been adopted in 1982 despite U.S. opposition to its provisions on seabed mining. The Democratic-controlled Senate failed to ratify the Biodiversity Treaty during its 1993-94 session. Consequently, the United States was relegated to an observer role at the first conference of the parties held in Nassau in 1994. By that time, ninety-two countries had ratified the Biodiversity treaty, including all the industrial countries. Clinton signed the Law of the Sea Convention in 1994 just months before the agreement came into force, one year after the required sixtieth ratification was received. Neither treaty is likely to be ratified soon by the current Republican-controlled Senate, especially while the archconservative Sen. Jesse Helms (R-N.C.) chairs the Foreign Relations Committee.

Looking Ahead

Much has been accomplished in the development of global environmental governance over the past three decades, but does it provide an adequate institutional foundation for coping with the looming ecological challenges of the twenty-first century? The global environment will be under increasing stress due to continued growth in world population, which is projected to rise from 5.7 billion in 1995 to between 7.8 and 12.5 billion by 2050. Even the high estimate assumes a sizable reduction in global fertility rates.[58] Climate change is likely to be the other dominant environmental threat, which will require an accommodation between North and South in which the former agrees to cut back substantially on its profligate use of natural resources and the latter to compromise on its plans to modernize using large amounts of fossil fuels.

The concept "sustainable development" inspires hope that humanity can escape its ecological predicament while meeting the material needs of current and future generations. Agenda 21 provides a blueprint of a strategy for achieving sustainability in the next century, but thus far there are discouragingly few signs that either North or South is committed to making the revolutionary changes in life-styles, energy use, industry, transportation, and agriculture that are necessary to turn this bold plan into a reality. The contrasting roles the United States played in the decisive international response to the ozone-depletion problem, and the failure thus far to come to grips with climate change, point to the critical importance of U.S. leadership in the future development of global environmental governance. For the time being, however, the Republican-controlled Congress will make it difficult for the Clinton administration to make substantial commitments to implement Agenda 21 and the other agreements adopted at the Earth summit.

Notes

1. See the study commissioned for the conference by Barbara Ward and René Dubos, *Only One Earth: The Care and Maintenance of a Small Planet* (New York: Norton, 1972).
2. See Constance Mungall and Digby J. McLaren, eds., *Planet under Stress: The Challenge of Global Change* (New York: Oxford University Press, 1990).
3. See Martin F. Price, "Global Change: Defining the Ill-Defined," *Environment* 31 (October 1989): 18-20, 42-44.
4. See Robert V. Bartlett, Priya A. Kurian, and Madhu Malik, eds., *International Organizations and Environmental Policy* (Westport, Conn.: Greenwood, 1995).

5. For a discussion of the concept "international governance," see Oran Young, *International Governance: Protecting the Environment in a Stateless Society* (Ithaca: Cornell University Press, 1994), 12-32.

6. For a discussion of the role and dynamics of world conferences, see A. LeRoy Bennett, *International Organizations: Principles and Issues,* 3d ed. (Englewood Cliffs, N.J.: Prentice-Hall, 1984), 293-323.

7. For a description and analysis of the political dynamics of the Stockholm conference, see John R. Handelman, Howard B. Shapiro, and John A. Vasquez, *Introductory Case Studies for International Relations: Vietnam/Middle East/the Environmental Crisis* (Chicago: Rand McNally, 1974), 60-83.

8. United Nations, *Report of the United Nations Conference on the Human Environment,* UN Doc. A/Conf. 48/14, 1972.

9. For a description and assessment of UNEP's early projects, see Lynton K. Caldwell, *International Environmental Policy: Emergence and Dimensions,* 2d ed. (Durham, N.C.: Duke University Press, 1990), 71-88. See also *Annual Report of the Executive Director 1990* (Nairobi: UNEP, 1991).

10. See Peter M. Haas, *Saving the Mediterranean: The Politics of International Environmental Cooperation* (New York: Columbia University Press, 1990).

11. See Carol A. Petsonk, "The Role of the United Nations Environment Programme (UNEP) in the Development of International Environmental Law," *American University Journal of International Law and Policy* 5 (Winter 1990): 362-367.

12. See Bruce Rich, *Mortgaging the Earth: The World Bank, Environmental Impoverishment, and the Crisis of Development* (Boston: Beacon, 1994).

13. For a critique of the environmental reforms of the World Bank, see Philippe G. Le Prestre, "Environmental Learning at the World Bank," in *International Organizations and Environmental Policy*, ed. Bartlett, Kurian, and Malik, 83-102.

14. Andrew Jordan, "Paying the Incremental Costs of Global Environmental Protection: The Evolving Role of GEF," *Environment* 36 (July-August 1994): 12-20, 31-36.

15. John McCormick, "Environmental Policy and the European Union," in *International Organizations and Environmental Policy*, ed. Bartlett, Kurian, and Malik, 41.

16. See James Barros and Douglas M. Johnston, *The International Law of Pollution* (New York: Free Press, 1974), 177-195.

17. Tabulated from *Register of International Treaties and Other Agreements in the Field of the Environment* (Nairobi: UNEP, 1991), UNEP/GC.16/Inf.4. See also Peter M. Haas and Jan Sungren, "Evolving International Environmental Law: Changing Practices of National Sovereignty," in *Global Accord: Environmental Challenges and International Responses,* ed. Nazli Choucri (Cambridge, Mass.: MIT Press, 1993), 401-430.

18. See Marvin S. Soroos, "The Odyssey of Arctic Haze: Toward a Global Atmospheric Regime," *Environment* 34 (December 1992): 6-11, 25-27.

19. For a discussion of achievements and limitations of international treaty making on the environment, see Lawrence E. Susskind, *Environmental Diplomacy: Negotiating More Effective Global Agreements* (New York: Oxford University Press, 1994).

20. For a description of the London smog, see Peter Brimblecombe, *The Big Smoke: A History of Air Pollution in London since Medieval Times* (London: Methuen, 1987), 165-169. For background on the Minamata mercury poisonings and subsequent court cases, see Donald R. Kelley, Kenneth R. Stunkel, and Richard R. Wescott, *The Economic Superpowers and the Environment: The United States, the Soviet Union, and Japan* (San Francisco: W.H. Freeman, 1976), 192-194.

21. Donella H. Meadows, Dennis L. Meadows, Jorgen Randers, and William W. Behrens III, *The Limits to Growth* (New York: Universe Books, 1972).

22. See Marcus F. Franda, "The World Population Conference: An International Extravaganza," *Fieldstaff Reports: South East Asia Series* 21 (September 1974).

23. For a discussion of the positions of developing countries on these and other issues, see Marian A. L. Miller, *The Third World in Global Environmental Politics* (Boulder: Lynne Rienner, 1995).

24. See Charles E. Zeigler, *Environmental Policy in the Soviet Union* (Amherst: University of Massachusetts Press, 1987).
25. See Murray Feshbach and Alfred Friendly Jr., *Ecocide in the USSR: Health and Nature under Siege* (New York: Basic Books, 1992).
26. D. J. Peterson, *Troubled Lands: The Legacy of Soviet Environmental Destruction* (Boulder: Westview, 1993), 7-11.
27. See Hilary F. French, "Restoring the East European and Soviet Environments," in *State of the World 1991*, ed. Lester Brown (New York: Norton, 1991), 93-112; and Jon Thompson, "East Europe's Dark Dawn: The Iron Curtain Rises to Reveal a Land Tarnished by Pollution," *National Geographic* 179 (June 1991): 36-69.
28. Natalia Mirovitskaya and Marvin S. Soroos, "Socialism and the Tragedy of the Commons: Reflections on Environmental Practice in the Soviet Union and Russia," *Journal of Environment and Development* 4 (Winter 1995): 97-102.
29. Mikhail Gorbachev, "Our Grandchildren Will Never Forgive Us," *Vetsnik* (March 1990): 41-43.
30. Mario Molina and F. Sherwood Stewart, "Stratospheric Sink for Chlorofluorocarbons: Chlorine Atom-catalyzed Destruction of Ozone," *Nature* 249 (1974): 810-812.
31. Sharon L. Roan, *Ozone Crisis: The 15-Year Evolution of a Sudden Global Emergency* (New York: Wiley, 1989), 71-86.
32. Richard E. Benedick, *Ozone Diplomacy: New Directions in Safeguarding the Planet* (Cambridge, Mass.: Harvard University Press, 1991), 40-50.
33. Roan, *Ozone Crisis*, 125-141.
34. World Meteorological Organization et al., *Atmospheric Ozone 1985*, 3 vols. (Geneva: WMO, 1986).
35. See Karen T. Litfin, *Ozone Discourses: Science and Politics in Global Environmental Cooperation* (New York: Columbia University Press, 1994), 78-116.
36. Robert T. Watson, Sherwood Rowland, and John Gille, "Ozone Trends Panel Executive Summary" (Washington, D.C.: NASA, 1988).
37. For an analysis of the negotiations leading up to the London revisions, see Benedick, *Ozone Diplomacy*, 129-198.
38. Litfin, *Ozone Discourses*, 156-176.
39. Lester R. Brown, Nicholas Lenssen, and Hal Kane, *Vital Trends 1995: The Trends That Are Shaping Our Lives* (New York: Norton, 1995), 66-67.
40. See Stephen H. Schneider, *Global Warming: Are We Entering the Greenhouse Century?* (New York: Vintage, 1989).
41. United Nations Environment Programme, World Meteorological Organization, and International Council of Scientific Unions, *An Assessment of the Role of Carbon Dioxide and of Other Greenhouse Gases in Climate Variations and Associated Impact* (Geneva: WMO, 1985).
42. Intergovernmental Panel on Climate Change, "Policy Makers' Summary of the Scientific Assessment of Climate Change" (Report prepared by Working Group I, June 1990), 1.
43. For an overview of the negotiations on climate change, see Matthew Paterson and Michael Grubb, "The International Politics of Climate Change," *International Affairs* 68 (1992): 293-310.
44. For a detailed analysis of the FCCC, see Daniel Bodansky, "The United Nations Framework Convention on Climate Change: a Commentary," *Yale Journal of International Law* 18 (1993): 451-558.
45. Christopher Flavin and Odil Tunali, "Getting Warmer: Looking for a Way Out of the Climate Impasse," *World Watch* 8 (March-April 1995): 10-19.
46. William K. Stevens, "Experts Confirm Human Role in Global Warming," *New York Times*, September 10, 1995, 1, 6.
47. World Commission on Environment and Development, *Our Common Future* (New York: Oxford University Press, 1987), 67-91.
48. Ibid., 43.

49. Brad Knickerbocker, "Alternative Earth Summit Gives Voice to Grass Roots," *Christian Science Monitor*, June 8, 1992, 3.

50. See Peter M. Haas, Marc A. Levy, and Edward A. Parson, "Appraising the Earth Summit: How Should We Judge UNCED's Success?" *Environment* 34 (October 1992): 6-11, 26-33; *The Global Partnership for Environment and Development: A Guide to Agenda 21, Post-Río Edition* (New York: United Nations, 1993).

51. *Agenda 21: Programme of Action for Sustainable Development* (New York: United Nations, 1992).

52. See Anil Agarwal and Sunita Narain, "We Can No Longer Subsidize the North," *Development Forum* 20 (May-June 1992): 15.

53. Paul E. Lewis, "U.S. at the Earth Summit: Isolated and Challenged," *New York Times*, June 10, 1992, 8.

54. William K. Stevens, "Bush Plan to Save Forests Is Blocked by Poor Countries," *New York Times*, January 9, 1992, 1, 8.

55. Jared Blumenfeld, "Institutions: The United Nations Commission on Sustainable Development," *Environment* 34 (December 1994): 2-5, 33.

56. See Dick Kirschten, "Woman's Day," *National Journal*, April 30, 1994, 1016-1019.

57. Margaret Kriz, "Lukewarm," *National Journal*, July 18, 1993, 2028-2032; Christopher Flavin, "Climate Policy: Showdown in Berlin," *World Watch* 8 (July-August 1995): 8-9.

58. Craig Lasher, "Population," in *A Global Agenda: Issues before the 49th General Assembly of the United Nations*, ed. John Tessitore and Susan Woolfson (New York: University Press of America, 1994), 184.

14

Environmental Policy and Management in the European Union

Regina S. Axelrod

The building of the European Union (EU) has transformed western Europe. The objective of establishing a common internal economic market has contributed to the openness of national borders and the harmonization of many policies once in the exclusive domain of individual member states. The EU has also established some of the strongest and most innovative environmental protection measures in the world and has increasingly taken the lead on international environmental issues such as global warming. In principle, environmental protection now enjoys equal weight with economic development in EU policymaking.

Political will and public support have been the key to EU success in approaching the environment from an integrated perspective. First, the legal foundations have been firmly established so that the Union has an unchallenged right to protect the environment. Second, all states recognize that without common environmental policies, barriers to free trade will emerge. Common environmental policies thus strengthen the prospects for creation of a single economic market. Third, political, economic, and geographic diversity has challenged policymakers to develop innovative strategies for overcoming differences and sharing burdens equitably. The EU is moving into the forefront in such areas as stabilization of carbon dioxide emissions, waste reduction, environmental auditing, and "ecolabeling."

The European Union is thus an important model to study, both as the most advanced regional organization of states and as an experiment in sustainable environmental development, or "green capitalism." If it succeeds in strengthening environmental protection while liberalizing trade, the EU may provide a model for other regions of the world such as North America and East Asia.

The Political Origins of the EU

The quest for political and economic union in Europe had its origins in the 1920s and 1930s, when it was recognized that some kind of supranational organization was needed to avoid brutal competition, protectionism, and war. But it was the experience of World War II that convinced statesmen to seek a new type of unity. U.S. economic assistance under the postwar Marshall Plan also called for regional cooperation.

The first step toward building a more integrated Europe was the formation of the European Coal and Steel Community (ECSC). The idea of French economic planner Jean Monnet and French foreign minister Robert Schumann, it was created by the Treaty of Paris on April 18, 1951. The original ECSC members were Belgium, France, Germany, Italy, Luxembourg, and the Netherlands. Its economic goal was to pool the production of coal and steel for the benefit of all six countries. Its other purpose was to lock Germany politically and economically into a stable partnership with western Europe.

Other cooperative activities were slow to develop, but in June 1955 the six ECSC members decided to move toward closer economic integration. They saw a European free trade area or "common market" as a means to increase industrial and agricultural exports, to redistribute resources to economically depressed areas, and to encourage travel among countries. The result was the 1957 Treaty of Rome, which established the European Economic Community (EEC) and the European Atomic Energy Authority (Euratom). In the 1970s the United Kingdom, Ireland, and Denmark joined the EEC, and Spain, Portugal, and Greece followed suit by 1986. Austria, Finland, and Sweden became full members in 1995, bringing the current membership to fifteen. [1]

There were no explicit provisions for protection of the environment in the original Treaty of Rome. Community policy for the environment dates instead from the 1972 Paris summit of the heads of state and government of the EEC, which proposed that an Environmental Action Programme be established under Article 235, which permits legislation in new areas if consistent with Community objectives. In effect, an environmental agenda was added to the Treaty of Rome. [2]

The Single European Act (SEA) of 1986 was the next milestone in the development of the treaties. This act accelerated the integration process by calling for establishment of a single internal economic market by the end of 1992. It set out more precise goals for harmonizing economic policies and eliminating border controls and other barriers to the free movement of goods, services, labor, and capital across Europe. Equally important, the SEA added a new section to the Treaty of Rome (Articles 130r, 130s, 130t) that formally defined the goals and procedures of EC environmental policies and called for "balanced growth" by integrating environmental policy into all other areas of Community decision-making.

The Maastricht treaty (also called the Treaty of European Union), which entered into force in 1993, called for closer political and monetary union—including development of a common European currency—by the end of the decade. It broadened the structure of the community and renamed it the European Union, while also further strengthening environmental policymaking authority and procedures. Insofar as the momentum toward closer integration continues, environmental policy is likely to be determined increasingly in Brussels.

The EU as an Ecological and
Socioeconomic Bioregion

To fully comprehend the environmental issues associated with EU integration, it is important to recognize that the fifteen member states differ from each other not only in population distribution, culture, and socioeconomic characteristics, but also in climate, topography, hydrology, and natural resources. The 370 million people in the EU live in a land area that reaches from Finland in the north to Spain and Italy in the south, and from Ireland and Portugal in the west to Greece in the east (approximately 3,235 square kilometers). The accession of Finland, Sweden, and Austria increased the population of the EU by 6.2 percent and the land area by 37 percent. The population density varies from 15 per square km in Finland to 368 in the Netherlands.[3] Climate varies from the cool maritime areas of the North Sea to the sunny, dry regions of the Mediterranean. The terrain ranges from mountainous Alpine regions in France, Austria, and Italy to areas below sea level in the Netherlands. There are 300 soil types, 200 kinds of vegetation, more than 600 species of birds, 130 species of mammals, and 60 fish species, with great local diversity.[4]

Environmental problems in Europe are quite similar to those in the United States (see box, p. 302). Economic growth and industrial development have taken a similar toll. Many species are threatened with extinction. Air and water pollution is most severe in the more industrialized north, but the Mediterranean region is now severely threatened as well. In the late 1980s CO_2 emissions ranged from 8 million tons in Ireland and 11 million tons in Portugal, to 166 million for the United Kingdom and 201 million for Germany.[5] Acid precipitation is estimated to cost 300 million ECU a year,[6] and has killed or damaged large areas of forests (what the Germans call *Waldsterben*). Industrial regions have high concentrations of toxic and hazardous wastes. Agricultural areas have been subject to intensive farming for centuries, leaving soils depleted and threatened by waste accumulations. Lost agricultural production is estimated at 1 billion ECU per year.[7] Pollution emissions and discharges easily cross national frontiers in the air or rivers (many of which flow through several countries).

The energy sector demonstrates some of the most important differences among states and highlights the complexities of achieving common environmental policies. Differences in basic fuel sources lead to different policy orientations toward allowable emissions and risks. Germany subsidizes its coal industry and France does the same for nuclear power. Because 75 percent of France's electricity is nuclear-generated, it is less concerned about fluctuations in oil prices. France actually generates a surplus of electric power that it would like to sell to other countries. But the Germans prefer to utilize their extensive coal resources by developing cleaner coal-burning technologies. The Dutch have no interest in either nuclear power or coal but have some of the largest fields of natural gas in Europe, which they would like to market as a less-polluting fuel. Fossil fuels (coal, oil, gas) predominate in the

Major Environmental Threats in the European Union

Air. "Air quality . . . continues to give cause for concern in most towns and cities due to the increasing emissions of the principal pollutants into the air from motor vehicles. . . . Simulations for the year 2000 suggest there will be some improvement, but at the same time further deterioration in urban and industrial growth areas."

Water. "Despite the investments made over the last 20 years or so, on the whole there has been no improvement in the state of the Community's water resources. There have been more cases of deterioration in quality than of improvement. With demand rising as it is at present, the impending depletion of freshwater resources in certain regions may create major problems in the future, particularly in the Mediterranean countries."

Soil. "Physical degradation of the soil is widespread throughout the Community. The soil was long thought to have unlimited absorptive capacity, but now it is becoming increasingly difficult for it to perform its many vital functions, as a source of biomass in the form of crops and timber, as a habitat and as an ecosystem stabilizer. An increase in the pollution content has been observed at many sites. Pollution . . . by heavy metals and organic products is increasing not only . . . around industrial centres . . . but also in some rural areas, as a result of the combination of air pollution and farming."

Waste. "The volume of waste generated is increasing at a far greater rate than treatment and disposal capacity. A major effort to set up . . . household refuse collection networks has ensured that virtually all the urban waste in the Community is actually collected. Nevertheless, landfill remains the commonest disposal method. Processes such as composting or recycling are gaining ground but remain too limited to alleviate the growing landfill problem."

The quality of life. "Urban population growth will continue at a rapid rate in the cities of southern Europe, particularly along the coast, putting further pressure on the population's quality of life. Without rigorous measures to protect the rural environment in places where desertification is becoming acute, the countryside will continue to deteriorate."

High-risk activities. "As man learned to protect himself from natural risks, he also began to apply more and more high-risk techniques. Not only the workers employed in these activities are at risk but also the local population as well. The nuclear power industry, the chemical industry, the transport of hazardous substances and, more recently, the genetic engineering industry all pose new risks."

Source: Fifth Programme on the Environment of the European Commission, 1992.

United Kingdom, but this country tends to lag in pollution control technologies. Italy relies on imported oil for electricity generation and also imports natural gas from Algeria and the former Soviet Union. It faces a serious problem because electricity consumption has risen faster than supplies. Belgium relies on nuclear power for nearly half its electricity, while Denmark has no nuclear plants and is a leader in developing renewable energy sources such as wind power. These national differences in resource endowments, government subsidies, employment patterns, and vested economic interests make it difficult to legislate common EU policies for mitigating the environmental impacts of energy production and consumption.

Other political differences also complicate the Union environmental agenda. The northern, more industrialized states have a history of stringent environmental legislation and a high level of public awareness on environmental issues. They oppose policies that would compromise their level of environmental protection. Germany is particularly concerned about the effects of acid rain on its forests and the dangers of nuclear waste. Not coincidentally, it has the largest Green party and perhaps the most respected national environmental ministry. The Netherlands, a "low country," has a special interest in the potential sea-level rise from global warming and has developed the most comprehensive national environmental plan for addressing this issue. Denmark also has high environmental standards in part because of close ties to its Scandinavian neighbors.

The southern tier of states and Ireland tend to place greater emphasis on economic development than on the environment. Rural areas in these countries have different environmental problems from those of the urban areas to the north, although large cities in Spain, Italy, and Greece also have major pollution problems. These states argue that they cannot meet the same environmental standards as more wealthy states. Spain, for example, has been undergoing rapid industrialization and claims it will need to increase its CO_2 emissions for some time. Spain, Portugal, Greece, and Ireland all benefit from special EU funds to help them improve their environmental infrastructures. The entire Mediterranean Basin is threatened by soil erosion, water pollution, and toxic waste accumulations that will require massive cleanup efforts and strain Union resources.

Public Opinion and the Green Movement

Public opinion polls indicate that Europeans are deeply concerned about the environment and becoming more so. A *Eurobarometer* opinion survey conducted in the summer of 1989 asked respondents in EU countries to rank the twelve most important national and international issues facing them; an astounding 94 percent ranked environmental policy very important, second only to unemployment. The difference among countries was slight, ranging from 98 percent among Germans to 91 percent for the

Portuguese and Irish. [8] A study completed for the European Commission in the spring of 1992 indicates that the percentage of Europeans who consider the environment "an immediate and urgent problem" has risen dramatically since 1988 to a high of 85 percent (see table 14-1). Concern is greatest in France, eastern Germany, Greece, the Netherlands, and the United Kingdom. [9] On specific issues, the Italians and Spaniards are worried most about water pollution, while air pollution concerns are greatest among the Germans, Dutch, Greeks, and Italians. Industrial waste disposal is the problem of most general concern throughout the EU. [10]

But does this mean that Europeans are willing to give up national control over environmental policy to the European Union? In most countries, yes, according to another recent survey: 64 percent said environmental policy should be an EU responsibility (31 percent disagreed). Support for joint decisionmaking ranged from 81 percent in the Netherlands to 45 percent in Denmark (see table 14-2).

The Union's northern countries have the strongest ecological and conservation movements. Green parties have won representation in the national parliaments of Belgium, Germany, Greece, Ireland, Italy, Luxembourg, the Netherlands, Portugal, and several other European countries. [11] They have also done fairly well in elections to the European Parliament, electing a total of twenty-two members in 1994. Although this was six less than in the outgoing parliament, mainly due to the loss of nine French delegates, two more countries (Ireland and Luxembourg) elected Green delegates to join those from Germany (twelve), Italy (three), Belgium (two), Denmark, and the Netherlands (one each). [12] But the green movement has had a larger impact through its influence on other political parties and on European public opinion generally. [13] This was manifest during the summer of 1995 in widespread public protests against the proposed disposal of the Brent Spar oil platform in the North Sea and against the resumption of French nuclear weapons testing in the South Pacific.

Table 14-1 European Opinion on the Urgency of Environmental Problems, 1986–1992

Perceived Urgency of the Environmental Problem	1986	1988	1992
An immediate and urgent problem	72%	74%	85%
More a problem for the future	22	20	11
Not really a problem	3	3	2
Don't know/no answer	3	3	2

Source: Eurobarometer 37 (June 1992).

Note: The question asked was: "Many people are concerned about protecting the environment and fighting pollution. In your opinion, is this . . . ?"

Table 14-2 Support for the EU's Environmental Decisionmaking

Nation	Support for Joint Decisionmaking
The Netherlands	81%
Germany	71
France	68
Belgium	62
Italy	62
Greece	58
Spain	58
Luxembourg	55
Portugal	53
Ireland	49
Denmark	45

Source: Commission of the European Communities, *Eurobarometer* 41 (July 1994), A34-35.

Note: The question asked was whether environmental policy should be decided jointly within the European Union or by national governments.

EU Institutions and Policymaking Processes

European Union Institutions

The primary institutions of the EU are the council, the commission, the parliament, and the European Court of Justice. The EU Council in Brussels consists of representatives from the governments of each of the member states. When the heads of state meet, it is known as the "European Council," but normally council meetings involve the fifteen ministers responsible for the topic under discussion. The council is the most important EU body because it must approve all legislation. Its "directives" must be adopted by the individual member states and incorporated into national law within a specified period of time (usually two years). EU "regulations" that automatically apply to the states can also be enacted, but they are less common. In general, the council's actions reflect the national interests of the states. Under the Single European Act, many decisions can now be taken by a "qualified majority" of the council, that is, by a special voting procedure that gives greater weight to larger states than smaller ones but does not require unanimity.

The EU Commission is a body of twenty commissioners (and their staffs) who head twenty-two directorates-general (DGs). DG XI is responsible for the environment, nuclear safety, and civil protection. The commission's task is to initiate EU legislation and to oversee its implementation by member states. Its president, currently Jacques Santer, is sometimes referred to as the "European president." A multinational bureaucracy of some 13,000 serves the commission and its directorates in Brussels.

The 626-member European Parliament (EP), by contrast, is elected directly by people from constituencies in each country and tends to reflect the diverse interests of political parties and groupings across Europe. The parliament has a moving seat. It holds plenary sessions in Strasbourg, France, much of its staff is in Luxembourg, and it holds most of its committee meetings in Brussels. Draft legislation from the commission is submitted to the EP, which can either accept the draft as is or propose amendments. The parliament must also approve the commission budget and EU treaties; it also votes on the appointment of the president and commissioners.

Parliament is not regarded as a true legislature because it cannot initiate legislation. However, the Maastricht treaty allows a majority of members (MEPs) to request that the commission develop a proposal if it concerns implementation of the treaty, and EP committees can also informally influence policy formation in other ways. In areas of law where the council votes by qualified majority, a unanimous vote is required to adopt a proposal if the EP rejects the council position. In addition to this "cooperation" procedure, the Maastricht treaty further increased parliament's leverage by introducing a new "co-decision" procedure covering fourteen areas, including environmental action programs. In this case, if the EP does not agree with the council position after a second reading, a conciliation committee is formed to resolve differences. If agreement still cannot be reached, the EP can reject the proposal by majority vote, giving it a de facto veto. The new procedure could increase the EP's role in policymaking, make decisionmaking more transparent, and reduce the "democratic deficit" until parliament receives full legislative powers.[14]

The relative weakness of the European Parliament is nevertheless unfortunate because it has the strongest environmental orientation among the EU institutions. After the 1989 election the Greens were the fourth-largest grouping in parliament. Besides providing an omnipresent environmental constituency, they have been successful in the "greening" of the more traditional parties and in lobbying the commission and council to keep environmental issues on the EU agenda. Other parties also play an influential role on the Committee on Environment, Public Health, and Consumer Protection, which handles some 40 percent of all parliamentary business. But committee members of all shades tend to support environmental legislation, and this tendency is expected to grow with the addition of new member states.

The European Court of Justice, located in Luxembourg, considers cases brought before it by the commission, the council, member states, or citizens concerning the application of EU treaties. Its decisions are binding on member states, though there is no mechanism for directly enforcing them (national courts are relied on to carry out decisions). The court is frequently asked for advisory opinions on legal disputes between the EU and the states as well. Some of the court's decisions have played an important role in defining the rights of member states to enact environmental legislation under Article 100a that may violate EU treaty provisions prohibiting restraints on trade. For example, in the 1988 "Danish bottle case," the court upheld Denmark's law requiring the use of returnable bottles for beer and soft drinks on grounds that its environmental benefits were sufficient to justify a minor restraint on trade. (However, the Court rejected the requirement that bottles be approved by the Danish government.[15] Like courts in the United States, the European Court is emerging as an important policymaker in balancing economic and environmental interests) (see chap. 8).

The Policy Process

Policymaking within the EU is more "political" than a formal review of the institutions might suggest.[16] Because the EU is a fluid and developing institution, policymaking is complicated by uncertainty over roles, powers, and decision rules. As we have seen, the council, commission, and parliament perform different functions from those of the three branches of U.S. government.

The commission and parliament can be viewed as supranational bodies, whereas the council remains essentially intergovernmental. Under their terms of appointment, the commissioners and their staffs are international civil servants who are not supposed to serve any national interest. Thus the commission's proposed legislation tends to favor greater "harmonization" of Europewide policies. Parliament also tends to favor stronger EU policies, especially in such fields as environmental and consumer protection that are popular at home. The council, by way of contrast, is usually more cautious because of its sensitivity to national political interests and the costs of implementing EU policies (which largely devolve on national governments). The council is more likely to invoke the principle of subsidiarity, under which actions are to be taken at the Union level only if they cannot be carried out more efficiently at the national or local level.

Conflicts of interest among the states are evident in the council. A fluid coalition of Germany, Denmark, and the Netherlands has pushed the hardest for environmental protection. These countries often have higher standards than the EU to start with and they would like other states to adopt their norms. In some cases they have succeeded. For example, Germany was influential in proposing tough air pollution controls on large combustion plants, while the Netherlands convinced the council to essentially adopt its high standards for small car and truck emissions (see discussion below).[17] By contrast, the poorer countries of southern Europe, occasionally with the United Kingdom and Ireland, have been more reluctant to support such measures. In the future, the accession of Sweden, Finland, and Austria is likely to strengthen the proenvironmental coalition.

Lobbying by private interests is also omnipresent in the EU. Industry is very concerned about the impact of new environmental legislation on business and maintains an army of lawyers in Brussels. Both the commission directorates and parliamentary committees regularly consult such interests, which tend to represent the largest companies and trade associations. Environmental, consumer, and other public interest groups also have representation. An umbrella organization in Brussels, the European Environmental Bureau, represents some 120 national groups. It closely monitors DG XI and tries to influence proposed legislation.[18] Other international environmental organizations such as the World Wildlife Fund and Greenpeace also lobby intensely.

Environmental policy is closely related to other issues such as economic competition, taxation, research and development, energy, and transportation. Effective policymaking thus requires interaction and cooperation among many EU directorates and parliamentary committees. Formal and informal working groups and task forces try to work out mutually compatible strategies. For example, the development of efficiency standards for electrical appliances involved a working group of members from DG XI and the energy directorate (DG XVII). The divergent perspectives of these directorates often lead to different policy preferences, as do those of the agriculture, transportation, trade, and other "economic" directorates. In the absence of formal mechanisms for resolving differences, the leadership skills of the individual commissioners and the president of the commission are often critical in achieving agreement.

Final policy resolution by the commission and council usually involves extensive political compromise. Sometimes this takes the form of "side payments." For example, in an effort to gain approval for a tax to reduce CO_2 emissions, a burden-sharing plan was worked out under which some states agreed to exceed EU norms so that other states could proceed more slowly in meeting the targets. Such arrangements are creating what is often referred to as a "multispeed" Europe.

The Harmonization of Environmental Standards

The rationale for creating common EU policies and "harmonizing" standards is to level the economic playing field. The danger is always that the lowest common denominator will prevail. In the case of environmental standards, this could result in EU norms that are considerably weaker than those of the leading states.

Article 130r of the Treaty of Rome states that the EU will take action to preserve, protect, and improve the quality of the environment and that "[Union] policy on the environment shall aim at a high level of protection." This implies a minimum standard that is not the lowest and that all areas should be brought up to an acceptable level. Article 130s allows the council to decide (with some exceptions) which environmental matters can be taken by "qualified majority." Article 130t further specifies that "measures taken by the EU do not prevent any Member State from maintaining or introducing more stringent protective measures, provided that these are compatible with the treaty."[19]

The lead states such as Germany can thus retain higher environmental standards than other countries so long as the European Court does not find them in violation of other sections of the treaty. Naturally they would rather bring the EU norms up to their level so they are not at a competitive economic disadvantage. But they have often moved ahead of the EU. For example, Denmark, the Netherlands, and Germany require high levels of materials recycled. Denmark regulates the content of gasoline more strictly, while the Netherlands has a variety of taxes and charges on energy consumption and automobile pollution emissions.

Such policies have met a good deal of opposition from the slower states. In one case, Italy, Greece, and France claimed that German standards for use of the chemical pentachlorophenol (PCP) were more stringent than required under a 1989 directive (91/73/EEC), and therefore represented a barrier to trade (PCP is used on leather imported into Germany). The commission upheld the German standard on grounds that it applied equally to German and non-German companies.[20] In the case of the Dutch tax on "dirty" cars, France threatened legal action but later dropped it when it became evident that public opinion favored stricter auto emission standards for the EU as a whole.[21]

Despite these difficulties, the EU has made considerable progress toward accommodating national differences on the environment. As mentioned above, a "multispeed" Europe is already emerging in which some countries move faster than others, but all are moving in the direction of higher environmental standards. One method for achieving this is to set high EC standards with two "tracks" for achieving them. Some states will adopt the mandatory standards (based on currently available technology), while others may adopt even higher standards based on the latest advances in science and technology. Another approach is for the less-developed states to be given additional time to meet the EU standard; but all states must eventually achieve it. Political realities and considerations of equity cannot be ignored in pursuit of the elusive level playing field.

A large area of uncertainty remains over the compatibility of individual national actions with the elimination of barriers to trade under Article 100a of the treaty. The Danish bottle case described earlier suggests that the European Court will allow strict national standards to stand if they do not present barriers to trade or contribute to arbitrary discrimination and if there is a sufficiently clear environmental basis for them. These decisions are made on a case-by-case basis, however, and the criteria will continue to evolve.

Another area of uncertainty is which environmental decisions can be made by qualified majority in the council. The Maastricht treaty places most environmental decisions in this category (whereas previously unanimity was normally required). At the same time, the treaty places greater emphasis on the principle of subsidiarity, under which actions should be taken by the member states unless the objectives can be better achieved through EU actions. Maastricht's ambiguity and uncertain status leave the application of these principles unclear. These and other issues should be discussed at the EU Intergovernmental Conference (IGC), which began an eighteen-month process in Turin, Italy, in the spring of 1996 to review the treaty.

The European Environment Agency

A proposal to create a European Environment Agency (EEA) was introduced in the European Parliament by Jacques Delors, then president of the European Community, in January 1989. The limited resources of DG XI to gather environmental data, improve enforcement of environmental directives, and achieve harmonization of legislation seemed to justify a stronger institutional capacity. After vigorous debate and more than two years of negotiations, a compromise regulation was adopted on May 7, 1990 (90/1210/EEC). The new agency was to be governed by a management board with representation from the states and the commission as well as scientists designated by parliament. The resolution provided for review of EEA's functions after two years, with the possibility of expanding them at that time.

Unfortunately, establishment of the EEA was held up because agreement could not be reached on a site. The EEA became a hostage to a larger controversy within the EU over the future location of Union institutions. In particular, there was a widespread desire to move the seat of parliament from Strasbourg to Brussels, where most of its actual work is done. France consequently blocked the siting of the EEA in order to bring pressure on other states to maintain the parliament in Strasbourg. In the interim, a task force made up of a shadow group of experts (acting as consultants to DG XI) planned a work program for EEA, collected information, and began drafting a "state of the environment" report for all of Europe.[22]

In 1994 the EEA was finally situated in Copenhagen, Denmark, with Domingo Jimenez-Beltran as its first executive director. The regional focus of the EEA has expanded to include non-EU states from central and eastern Europe that share its aims.

The first task of the EEA is to develop an information and observation network that will be used for environmental assessments and to promote the integration of data and the development of analytical models to improve environmental policy. Integrated approaches that identify common causes of related environmental problems and help to reduce costs are emphasized. Among the policy areas EEA will focus on are air quality, marine and coastal environments, inland water quality, conservation of natural resources, and soil and forest management. Further goals include informing the public about the state of the environment; offering technical assistance on environmental policy implementation; and serving as an information resource for EU institutions, member states, nongovernmental organizations, the academic community, and the media. Although the EEA has no enforcement powers, it is preparing (in conjunction with DG XI) a review of the Fifth Action Programme for the commission.

The Fifth Action Programme

Since 1972 the commission has developed an agenda to guide its activities for a five-year period, called action programmes. The guiding principle of the Fifth Programme, adopted in 1992, is "sustainability."[23] This principle, derived from the 1987 Report of the World Commission on Environment and Development, *Our Common Future*, goes beyond the concept of balanced growth espoused by the Single European Act. It attempts to operationalize the report's definition of sustainability: "development which meets the needs of the present without compromising the ability of future generations to meet their own needs."[24] This principle is seen as especially critical if Europe is to reconcile its push for economic growth under the "1992" single market with preservation of the environment.

The new program calls for "integration of environment considerations in the formulation and implementation of economic and sectoral policies, in the decisions of public authorities, in the conduct and development of production processes, and in individual behavior and choice."[25] All EU policies are said to be dependent on achieving sustainable practices. New strategies are suggested for dealing with such problems as cross-media pollution, pollution prevention at the source, and alternatives to command-and-control regulation. The program goes beyond environmental cleanup and pollution mitigation in calling for more fundamental behavioral changes. The key sectors targeted are industry, energy, transportation, agriculture, and tourism.

A significant management innovation of the Fifth Programme is the establishment of several new environmental committees to encourage such changes. A new consultative forum brings together actors from industry, business, government, trade unions, public interest groups, and the appropriate directorate-general of the commission. It provides opportunities for sharing responsibility in developing and implementing policy with the individuals and groups that will be most critical to its success. A second committee tracks the application of EU environmental law in the states and works directly with the responsible parties to improve state implementation—an approach that involves information exchange and assistance on how to achieve better compliance. (This may raise questions in the future about the EU's legal competence to advise states on the application of EU law.) A third committee is a forum for exchange of views on more general issues to improve mutual understanding. There are also officials within each directorate-general who are assigned to work closely with DG XI to ensure integration of their policies with environmental legislation. All of these initiatives represent efforts to improve follow-up of EU actions in the states and to make the policy process more open and transparent.

Current Legislation

The EU has approximately two hundred environmental laws in force. The following section describes some of the most important concerns now being addressed.

Reduction of Carbon Dioxide. Concern over global climate change due to the accumulation of CO_2 and other greenhouse gases in the atmosphere has been particularly strong in Europe. It is widely perceived that continued burning of fossil fuels could produce major disruptions in weather patterns and cause rising sea levels that could imperil such countries as the Netherlands. Recognizing that industrial nations are largely responsible for the problem, a June 1990 summit meeting of the European Council (heads of state) in Dublin called for a Union strategy to reduce greenhouse emissions.

The Dublin summit was followed by a council meeting of environment and energy ministers in October 1990, at which it was agreed that CO_2 emissions should be stabilized at 1990 levels by the year 2000 in the Union as a whole. The council asked the commission to develop a strategy to meet this target, including fiscal and economic instruments to promote energy efficiency.

The most exciting and politically controversial proposal is for the use of economic instruments such as a carbon tax to reduce fuel consumption and pollution, improve energy efficiency, and encourage development of alternative energy sources. The commission proposed a Unionwide tax on oil beginning at $3 a barrel in 1993 and rising $1 per year up to $10 a barrel in 2000.[26] Other fuels, including coal and nuclear, would be taxed at rates according to their energy and carbon content. Because the EU does not have the authority to levy taxes directly, the tax would have to be adopted by individual states and harmonized like the value added tax (VAT) to avoid competitive disadvantages.[27]

Carlo Ripa di Meana, the former environment commissioner, was a strong supporter of this concept and hoped to be able to take a Union agreement on the carbon tax to the Earth summit in Río de Janeiro in June 1992. The council anticipated approval of the text by May.[28] Because of further disagreements among member states, however, the council was unable to act on the proposal in time. With nothing to show for his efforts, and the United States blocking a global climate treaty with targets for CO_2 reduction, Ripa di Meana ultimately refused to attend the summit. It has been difficult for Europe to move ahead on the tax without willingness by the United States and other industrial nations to take similar actions. It is estimated that without further actions, CO_2 levels in Europe will rise 5.2 percent between 1990 and 2000 and 16 percent by 2015.[29]

Although the council failed to produce an agreement on a CO_2 tax, the idea is not dead. Some states have already adopted their own version of the tax. The commission has thus suggested a modified proposal that would allow member states to keep or introduce national taxes (with an option to exclude energy intensive industries) until 2000; after that, a harmonized structure could be introduced. Environmental commissioner Ritt Bjerregaard has declared her commitment to environmental taxes as a means to realize sustainable development.

The EU is pursuing other means of improving energy efficiency, even though Europeans utilize only half as much energy per capita as Americans. It is supporting a variety of research and development (R&D) programs such as the Joule program for nonnuclear energy research and the Thermie program for bringing renewable energy, conservation, and clean fossil fuel technologies to the marketplace. Also, interest in least-cost planning would create incentives for electric power utilities to save energy by reducing customer demand. The Special Actions for Vigorous Energy Efficiency (SAVE) program was launched in October 1991 to encourage energy savings through consumer information, new energy efficiency standards, environmental audits, and least-cost planning.

Transportation presents other problems. Although the EU has passed legislation to reduce automobile air pollution, the full impact of the new standards will not be felt for several years. It is predicted that auto ownership will continue to increase rapidly (by 45 percent between 1987 and 2010), thereby offsetting even these gains. There is thus interest in expanding rail and other public transportation. The commission is developing a strategy for "sustainable mobility," which includes such things as standards for the sulfur content of fuels, state aid for combined inland water/rail transportation, and taxes and charges on dirty fuels and vehicles.[30]

Transfer of Hazardous Wastes. The creation of the internal market poses some interesting questions about hazardous waste management. Although hazardous waste is only about 20 percent of the total waste stream, it is already routinely shipped across borders in Europe. France and the United Kingdom are net importers, while Germany and the Netherlands are exporters. It was predicted that the volume of such waste would increase with higher rates of economic growth after 1992, raising "the specter of large quantities of dangerous waste moving freely across Europe in search of the cheapest and least regulated outlets."[31] The elimination of border checks could make it more difficult to monitor this movement.

The European Union adopted Regulation 259/93/EEC in February 1993, which requires prior authorization of transfrontier waste shipments within the EU whether they are hazardous or not. National authorities can refuse to accept waste. The enabling legislation promotes self-sufficiency within each state and encourages local waste disposal. The commission is considering legislation that would require permits, registration, and management plans for the handling of all hazardous waste. A ban on the transfer of hazardous waste to developing countries for recycling was proposed by the commission and adopted by the council in June 1995.

Packaging. Another component of the commission's comprehensive waste management plan is the reduction of solid waste through changes in packaging standards and increased reliance on recycling and reuse of materials. Packaging is a large contributor to the waste stream, accounting for 50 million tons a year in the EU, of which only 18 percent was recycled in 1991.[32]

Some of the northern countries have already begun to enact stringent packaging and recycling laws, which could pose barriers to trade. Germany has the most ambitious program, requiring manufacturers and/or store owners to take back packaging for reuse or recycling. Industries are allowed to establish their own collection sites alongside government recycling centers. By 1995 industry was required to collect and recycle 80 percent of its packaging. There are similar standards for glass, tin, and aluminum. The Flemish region of Belgium and the Netherlands already have packaging reduction programs.

On July 15, 1992, the EU commission approved a draft packaging directive that would have established a recovery target of 90 percent by weight, which states would meet through their own programs. Within ten years, 60 percent of all recovered waste would have had to be recycled, 30 percent incinerated with energy recovery, with the remainder receiving final disposal (e.g., in landfills). [33]

The directive was finally agreed to by the council after a lengthy negotiating process. Germany, Denmark, and the Netherlands opposed the legislation because it was too weak. The conciliation procedure had to be used because Belgium objected to an EP amendment on the use of economic instruments. Directive 94/62/EC has a recovery target of between 50 and 60 percent by weight of the packaging and between 25 and 45 percent by volume of the packaging to be recycled. The directive must be transposed into national legislation within five years (the normal time is two years). Greece, Ireland, and Portugal have lower targets but must meet the EU standard by 2005. It allows states to go beyond the targets if there is no restriction on trade.

The final legislation is weaker than earlier drafts and represents considerable compromise. The targets are lower than the parliament wanted, but the council did modify its position on a number of issues raised by the EP. It was the most heavily lobbied EU legislation in recent history.

Ecolabeling. Consistent with the principles of green capitalism and of encouraging consumers to adopt sound environmental policies, the EU Council adopted a regulation (880/92) on "ecolabeling" on March 23, 1992. The purpose is to identify products that are environmentally "friendly" with special labels. The criteria for rating products stress eliminating pollution at the source and minimizing environmental impacts throughout the life-cycle of the product, including disposal costs. The impacts on the health and safety of workers, the use of best available technologies in manufacturing, and use of recyclable and recycled materials are also weighed in the labeling process.

Implementation of the regulation has been slow and cumbersome. The process requires commission approval of the criteria for each product. Industrial, consumer, and environmental groups lobby whichever country takes the lead in formulating the criteria for a product. To date criteria have been established for only five products: dishwashers, washing machines, paper towels, toilet paper, laundry detergents, and soil improvers. There is some discussion that implementation should be turned over to the EEA before disillusionment turns to abandonment.

Eco-Audit and Management Scheme. Regulation 1836/93/EEC was adopted in June 1993 after a five-year period of negotiations. [34] Green auditing and eco-auditing employ a new approach emanating from the Fifth Action Programme to encourage industry to voluntarily meet environmental sustainability goals and to enable consumers to choose "green companies." It allows companies to use an EU eco-audit logo if they meet certain requirements: they must have an environmental policy and a plan for implementing environmental performance goals; they must assess their environmental performance every three years; and they must communicate the results to the public. Since some states already had such schemes (e.g., Denmark and the

Netherlands), there was a need to harmonize such legislation. Industry likes the flexibility of the voluntary approach. The EP is concerned, however, that industry has adopted its position because a voluntary scheme is less binding than legislation.

Integrated Pollution Prevention and Control. One problem in Europe, as in the United States, is that most efforts to control industrial pollution have focused on end-of-the-pipe controls rather than on prevention. Another common issue is that each type and medium of pollution has been regulated separately (e.g., air, surface water, groundwater, hazardous waste, etc.), often requiring industries to obtain multiple permits to address each specific source. There has thus been a movement to integrate and simplify the permit process and to shift the emphasis to source reduction and pollution prevention.

After more than two years of vigorous debate, the European Council reached a common position on a new Integrated Pollution Prevention and Control (IPPC) directive in June 1995. The directive, which if approved by parliament would go into effect for new plants in 1998 and for existing installations by 2008, would allow industries to obtain a single permit providing for the best overall combination of techniques for achieving environmental protection. Compromises were made in drafting the policy to allow southern countries (Italy, Spain, Portugal, and Greece) more flexibility in meeting Best Available Technology (BAT) standards. As in other areas, it appears that a "two-speed Europe" is developing.[35]

Implementation

The success of the Union's commitment to environmental protection will depend on the extent to which states actually take the actions required by EU legislation. States must enact EU law into national law (transposition of law), but this is not always accomplished within the prescribed time periods. They are also responsible for applying and enforcing the law. A great many political and administrative forces within the states affect the outcomes. The greener states with a tradition of national environmental regulation generally have the best record of EU environmental enforcement. They have more sophisticated administrative infrastructures for putting EU mandates into operation. The extent to which regions within states (and their citizens) comply with EU law also varies. Thus, as one scholar puts it, "achieving compliance with the directive once it is transformed into national law is far more complex and problematic than simply incorporating Community directives into national legal codes."[36]

The EU does have enforcement mechanisms at its disposal. Article 169 of the treaty allows citizens, local authorities, businesses, or interest groups to lodge complaints on the inadequate application or transposition of EU law directly before the commission. Once a complaint is brought, efforts are made to mediate the dispute or to informally persuade the national government to take appropriate action. If a party is found to be in violation of EU law, the commission can issue a formal notice to the state. If all else fails, a case can be brought before the European Court of Justice to force compliance. However, resolution can take many years. Article 171 of the Maastricht treaty now allows the European Court to levy financial penalties, but the Court has been reluctant to utilize this power.

In 1984, in the environment and consumer protection sector, there were 65 cases in which formal notice was given to a state; 2 cases were referred to the European Court. In 1993 this had increased to 98 formal notices and 7 court referrals. Enforcement of EU law varies widely among individual states. For example, for all policy sectors (agriculture, transportation, internal market, and so forth) in 1993, 125 formal notices were given to Portugal and Greece, respectively, 119 to Germany, 108 to Italy, 106 to France, and 98 to the United Kingdom. The overall rate for transposition of environmental legislation was less than for other sectors; it varied from 98 percent transposed for Denmark to 81 percent for Italy.[37]

Some of the variation in compliance is related to differences in levels of citizen and interest group awareness. Some states may have proportionately more complaints lodged because their citizens are more alert, informed, and able to bring matters to the attention of the EU. But differential enforcement is also the result of variations in the budgets and other resources of governments to carry out EU mandates. Because states choose their own means of compliance, differences are inevitable in the instruments used and in the severity of penalties levied against violators.

Some examples may help to illustrate these problems. A 1985 directive (85/337/EEC) requires member states to conduct environmental impact assessments (EIAs) on public and private projects. Some states have incorporated this requirement into existing national law, while others passed new laws. But the legal requirements for EIAs, the level and competence of the administering authorities, the extent of public participation, the role of judicial review, and the quality of resulting assessments vary greatly across countries.[38] Because this directive has the greatest number of infringements of all environmental laws, the commission has proposed amendments that would more precisely define its application to projects and the type of information and assessment required (OJ C130 1994).

The United Kingdom and the European Commission disagreed over the need for an EIA for the proposed high-speed rail link between London and the Eurotunnel being constructed under the English Channel. The commission initiated proceedings against the United Kingdom in October 1991, arguing that an assessment should have been done in this case as well as in a number of others. The British government countered that it was grandfathered in because the EU law had not been transposed at the time of the siting decision. Although disagreement persisted over the date for implementing the law, the case was not taken to the European Court for fear that it could affect British ratification of the Maastricht treaty.[39] Nevertheless, in November 1992 the court condemned the United Kingdom for failing to implement a 1980 directive on water quality. It was the first time the United Kingdom was condemned for a breach of environmental standards.[40]

In perhaps a more typical case, the court found Italy guilty of noncompliance with an EU directive on protection of wild birds (79/409/EEC). Because Italy had not limited bird hunting nor incorporated an amendment (86/411/EEC) to the original directive into Italian law, it was ordered to pay legal costs. In another case, France was censured by the court for failing to comply with EU directives on air pollution. As a consequence, in October 1991 France incorporated the directives directly into French law.[41]

Conclusion

This review of environmental policy does not cover all the issues addressed by the European Union. One can nevertheless conclude that the EU is committed to protecting its environment during the process of economic and political integration. Environmental concerns are to be integrated into all EU policy at the earliest stages of planning. DG XI has made institutional reforms to deal with new problems and has taken seriously its mandate to improve compliance and enforcement. There is greater consultation with industry, other EU institutions, and environmental and consumer groups. The latter, which are not as well organized or funded as in the United States, have increasing access to the commission and its staff.

The EU recognizes that environmental problems are serious and that managing them effectively is vital to the success of the entire common market project. Most EU civil servants and parliamentarians see the European Union as better suited to dealing with transboundary pollution problems and other issues than the individual countries. They share an optimism that accommodations, although difficult, can be made to ensure progress toward solving environmental problems in all of the states. It is doubtful that this could be achieved by countries acting individually. However, some states interpret the principle of subsidiarity in order to promote national solutions, thereby thwarting the effectiveness of EU policy.

To be successful in the long run, the European Union must increase its popular support. The recent economic recession and dissension over monetary union, agricultural subsidies, border controls, and ratification of the Maastricht treaty itself suggest that popular representation through the European Parliament must be strengthened if EU institutions are to gain further legitimacy and effectiveness. The addition of new member states will compound this problem.

The enlargement of the EU, with the likelihood of further expansion to most of the central and eastern European countries after 2000, presents major new challenges for environmental policy. Enlargement may require significant adjustments in pollution standards to accommodate new states, as well as more fundamental changes in voting procedures, implementation processes, and relationships among EU institutions.[42] Despite political problems, the gradual disappearance of national frontiers with the anticipation of monetary union and political integration coincide with the promotion of environmental objectives. Several greener states, especially the recent members, will push the European Union toward higher standards. The prospect of the EU continuing to promote sustainable development reconciling economic growth with environmental protection will be strongly influenced by the results of the Intergovernmental Conference discussions in 1996, as well as by the strength of general support for the concept of European integration.

Notes

1. On the general history and development of the EC/EU see, e.g., Desmond Dinan, *Ever Closer Union?* (Boulder: Lynne Rienner, 1994); and William Nicoll and Trevor C. Salmon, *Understanding the European Communities* (Savage, Md.: Barnes and Noble, 1990).
2. For a summary of the first four plans and a general description of EC environmental legislation, see Stanley P. Johnson and Guy Corcelle, *The Environmental Policy of the European Communities* (London: Graham and Trotman, 1989). An overview of EC policies is also given in *Environmental Policy in the European Community*, 4th ed. (Luxembourg: Office for Official Publications of the European Communities, 1990). A more comprehensive analysis is offered in Ludwig Krämer, *E.C. Treaty and Environmental Law* (London: Sweet and Maxwell, 1995).
3. *Eurostat,* "Rapid Reports: Economy and Finance," 8/12/94; and *The Enlargement of the European Union* (Luxembourg: Office of Publications of the European Union, 1994). See also *Environmental Indicators* (Paris: Organization for Economic Cooperation and Development, 1991).
4. *"1992" The Environmental Dimension,* Task Force Report on the Environment and the Internal Market, at the request of the Commission of the European Communities (Bonn: Economica, 1990), 44-45. See also European Environmental Agency, *Europe's Environment: The Dobris Assessment* (Luxembourg: Office of Publications of the European Communities, 1995).
5. *Environmental Indicators,* 19.
6. The ECU, or "European Currency Unit," is a monetary unit based on all of the national European currencies. At exchange rates prevailing in mid 1996, one ECU equaled approximately $1.20.
7. *Environmental Policy in the European Community,* 13.
8. Ibid., 34.
9. *Europe Environment* (Brussels: Europe Information Service), N. 389, June 19, 1992, I, 7.
10. *A Social Portrait of Europe* (Luxembourg: Office for Official Publications of the European Community, 1991), 106-107.
11. Extensive documentation on all the European Green parties, including those in the European Parliament, can be found in Mike Feinstein, *Sixteen Weeks with European Greens* (San Pedro, Calif.: R and E Miles, 1992). See also Sara Parkin, *Green Parties: An International Guide* (London: Heretic, 1989).
12. Neil Carter, "The Greens in the 1994 Parliamentary Elections," *Environmental Politics* 3 (1994): 495-502.
13. Ferdinand Muller-Rommel, ed., *New Politics in Western Europe: The Rise and Success of Green Parties and Alternative Lists* (Boulder: Westview, 1989); and Dick Richardson and Chris Rootes, eds., *The Green Challenge: the Development of Green Parties in Europe* (London: Routledge, 1995).
14. Ken Collins, "Plans and Prospects for the European Parliament in Shaping Future Environmental Policy," *European Environmental Law Review* (March 1995): 74-77; and David Judge, David Earnshaw, and Ngaire Cowan, "Ripples or Waves: the European Parliament in the European Community Policy Process," *Journal of European Public Policy* 1 (June 1994): 27-52. See in general Francis Jacobs and Richard Corbett,

The European Parliament, 3d ed. (Boulder: Westview, 1995); and Martin Westlake, *A Modern Guide to the European Parliament* (London: Pinter, 1994).

15. "Commission of the European Communities v. Kingdom of Denmark—Case 302/86," *Report of Cases Before the Court,* vol. 8 (Luxembourg: Office for Official Publications of the European Communities, 1988). On the role of the court generally, see L. Neville Brown and Tom Kennedy, *The Court of Justice of the European Communities,* 4th ed. (London: Sweet and Maxwell, 1994).

16. See, e.g., Stephen George, *Politics and Policy in the European Community,* 2d ed. (New York: Oxford University Press, 1991); and Alberta M. Sbragia, ed., *Euro-Politics* (Washington, D.C.: Brookings, 1992).

17. Nigel Haigh, "New Tools for European Air Pollution," *International Environmental Affairs* 1, no. 1 (Winter 1989): 33; and Charlotte Kim, "The Cats and Mice: The Politics of Setting EC Car Emission Standards," CEPS Standards Programme: Paper No. 2 (Brussels: Centre for European Policy Studies, May 1992), 19.

18. See "European Federation of Environmental NGOs" (Brussels: European Environmental Bureau, n.d.); and Christian Hey and Jutta Jahns-Bohm, *Ecology and the Single Market* (Brussels: European Environmental Bureau, 1989).

19. Johnson and Corcelle, *Environmental Policy,* 344; and Krämer, *E.C. Treaty and Environmental Law,* 65-66, 71-86, 99-106.

20. *Europe Environment* (Brussels: Europe Information Service), N. 389, June 19, 1992, I, 9.

21. For excellent analyses of this case, see Kim, "Cats and Mice"; and Henning Arp, "Interest Groups in EC Legislation: The Case of Car Emission Standards" (Paper presented at a workshop held at the University of Sussex, March 22-28, 1991).

22. See EEA, *Europe's Environment: The Dobris Assessment.*

23. Commission of the European Communities, *Toward Sustainability: A European Community Programme of Policy and Action in Relation to the Environment and Sustainable Development,* I,1, COM(92)23 final (Brussels, March 27, 1992), 3, 18.

24. World Commission on Environment and Development, *Our Common Future* (New York: Oxford University Press, 1987).

25. Commission of the European Communities, *Toward Sustainability,* 3.

26. Paul L. Montgomery, "Heavy Energy Tax Is Proposed to Curb Emissions in Europe," *New York Times,* September 26, 1991; "A Community strategy to limit carbon dioxide emissions and to improve energy efficiency," Communication from the Commission to the Council, SEC(91)1744 final, Brussels, October 14, 1991.

27. *Europe Environment,* N. 387, "Dossier on CO_2 Tax," May 19, 1992, V.3.

28. "A Community strategy to limit carbon dioxide emissions and to improve energy efficiency," Council Conclusions, SN/283/91, Brussels, December 13, 1991, 3-4.

29. *European Trends* (Third Quarter 1994): 43.

30. "Green Paper on the Impact of Transportation on the Environment: A Community Strategy for Sustainable Mobility," Communication from the Commission, COM(92)46 final, Brussels, February 20, 1992, 37, 44.

31. *Environmental Policy in the European Community,* 35.

32. "Draft Proposal for a Council Directive on packaging and packaging waste," DG XI-A4, XI/369/91, 21/2/92, final draft, 2.

33. Ibid., 6.

34. Pamela Barnes, "The Environmental Audit Scheme," *European Trends* (Third Quarter 1994): 80-86.

35. "Environment Council Makes Breakthrough on IPPC, Ambient Air, Seveso Directive Update," *International Environment Reporter,* June 28, 1995, 491-492.

36. Alberta Sbragia, "Environmental Policy in the European Community: The Problem of Implementation in Comparative Perspective," in *Towards a Transatlantic Environmental Policy* (Washington, D.C.: European Institute, 1991), 52.

37. See *Eleventh Annual Report on Monitoring the Application of Community Law (1993),* Commission of the European Communities, COM (94)500 final, Brussels, 29.03.94, 70, 83, 104.

38. R. Coenen and J. Jorissen, "Environmental Impact Assessment in the Member Countries of the European Community" (Karlsruhe, Germany: Kernforschungszentrum Karlsruhe), 1989; and W. R. Sheate, "Amending the EC Directive (85/337/EEC) on Environmental Impact Assessment," *European Environmental Law Review* (March 1995): 77-82.

39. *Europe Environment,* N. 393, September 8, 1992, I, 6; and press release, "United Kingdom Infringement, Environment, Termination/Reasoned Opinion," Brussels, July 31, 1992.

40. Ibid., N. 399, December 1, 1992, I, 10.

41. *Europe Energy,* N. 367, November 15, 1991, I, 7.

42. Pamela Barnes, "The European Union and the 1996 IGC: Crisis or Opportunity?," Environmental Policy Centre for European Union Studies, University of Hull, England, 1995.

15

Environment, Population, and the Developing World
Richard J. Tobin

Environmental problems occasionally make life in the United States unpleasant and inconvenient, but most Americans tolerate this unpleasantness in exchange for the benefits and comforts associated with a developed, industrial economy. Most Europeans, Japanese, and Australians share similar life-styles, so it is not unexpected that they too typically take modern amenities for granted.

When life-styles are viewed from a broader perspective, however, much changes. Consider, for example, what life is like in much of the world. The U.S. gross national product (GNP) per capita was almost $25,000, or about $475 per week in 1993, but millions of people live in countries where weekly incomes are less than 5 percent of this amount, even when adjusted for differences in prices and purchasing power. In Mozambique, the world's most impoverished country, real per capita incomes are about one-fiftieth of those in the United States. Throughout sub-Saharan Africa about half the population survives on less than a dollar a day. In much of Latin America, there has been no progress in reducing poverty over the past twenty-five years, and extreme poverty is widespread.[1]

Low incomes are not the only problem facing many of the world's inhabitants. In some developing countries, women, often illiterate with no formal education, will marry as young as age thirteen or fourteen. During their childbearing years, these women will deliver as many as six or seven babies, most without the benefit of trained medical personnel. This absence is not without consequences. The chance of a woman dying due to complications associated with pregnancy, childbirth, or an unsafe abortion is hundreds of times higher in many poor countries than it is in Europe or the United States.[2]

Many of the world's children are also at risk. Only one out of a hundred American children die before the age of five; in many Asian and African countries as many as 20 to 25 percent do. *Every day* nearly forty thousand children under five die in developing countries from diseases that rarely kill Americans. Most of the deaths are caused by one or more of the following diseases: tetanus, measles, malaria, diarrhea, whooping cough, or acute respiratory infections, most of which are easily and cheaply prevented or cured.[3]

Of the children from these poor countries that do survive their earliest years, millions will suffer brain damage because their pregnant mothers had no iodine in their diets; others will lose their sight and die because they lack vitamin A. Many will face a life of poverty, never to taste clean water, enter a classroom, visit a doctor, have access to even the cheapest medicines, or eat nutritious food regularly. To the extent that shelter is available, it is rudimentary, rarely with electricity or proper sanitary facilities. When a poor child in Jakarta wants to bathe, as an example, he might lower himself into the open sewer that flows through his family's squatter settlement. Because their surroundings have been abused or poorly managed, millions of those in the developing world will also become victims of floods, famine, desertification, water-borne diseases, infestation of pests and rodents, and exceedingly noxious levels of air and water pollution.

As these children grow older, many will find that their governments do not have or cannot provide the resources to ensure them a reasonable standard of living. Yet all around them are countries with living standards well beyond their comprehension. The average American uses about thirty-three times more energy and consumes about 50 percent more calories per day—far in excess of minimum daily requirements—than does the typical Indian. The Indian might wonder why Americans consume a disproportionate share of the world's resources when she has a malnourished child she cannot afford to clothe or educate.

In short, life in much of Asia, Africa, and Latin America provides a different array of problems than those encountered in developed nations, which are responding to the benefits and consequences of development. The residents of poor countries, in contrast, must cope with widespread poverty and a lack of economic development. Yet both developed and developing nations often undergo environmental degradation. Those without property, for example, may be tempted to denude tropical forests for land to farm. Alternatively, pressures for development often force people to overexploit their base of environmental resources.

These issues lead to the key question addressed in this chapter: can the poorest countries, with the overwhelming majority of the world's population, improve their lot through sustainable development? According to the World Commission on Environment and Development, sustainable development meets the essential needs of the present generation for food, clothing, shelter, jobs, and health without "compromising the ability of future generations to meet their own needs." To achieve this goal, the commission emphasized the need to stimulate higher levels of economic development without inflicting irreparable damage on the environment.[4]

Whose responsibility is it to achieve sustainable development? One view is that richer nations have a moral obligation to assist less fortunate ones. If the former do not meet this obligation, not only will hundreds of millions of people in developing countries suffer but the consequences will be felt in the developed countries as well. Others argue that poorer nations must accept responsibility for their own fate; outside efforts to help them only worsen the problem and lead to an unhealthy dependence. As an illustration, biologist Garrett Hardin insists that it is wrong to provide food to famine-stricken nations because they have exceeded their environment's carrying capacity. In Hardin's words, "if you give food and save lives and thus increase the number of people, you increase suffering and ultimately increase the loss of life."[5]

The richer nations, whichever position they take, cannot avoid affecting what happens in the developing world. It is thus useful to consider how U.S. actions influence the quest for sustainable development. At least two related factors affect this quest. The first is a country's population; the second is a country's capacity to support its population.

Population Growth: Cure or Culprit?

Population growth is one of the more controversial elements in the journey toward sustainable development. Depending on the perspective used, the world is either vastly overpopulated or capable of supporting as many as thirty times its current population (slightly more than 5.7 billion in mid 1995 and increasing at an annual rate of about 1.5 percent).[6] Many of the developing nations are growing faster than the industrial nations (table 15-1), and nearly 80 percent of the world's population lives outside the developed regions. If current growth rates continue, the proportion of those in developing countries will increase even more. Between 1995 and 2025 more than 95 percent of the world's population increase will occur in the latter regions, exactly where the people and the environment can least afford such a surge.

Table 15-1 Estimated Populations and Projected Growth Rates

Region or Country	Estimated Population (millions) 1995	2010	2025	Annual Net Percentage Increase	Number of Years to Double Population Size
World total	5,702	7,024	8,312	1.5	45
Developed countries	1,169	1,232	1,271	0.2	432
United States	263	300	333	0.7	105
Japan	125	130	126	0.3	277
Canada	30	34	37	0.7	102
Developing regions	4,533	5,791	7,041	1.9	36
China	1,219	1,385	1,523	1.1	62
India	931	1,183	1,385	1.9	36
Bangladesh	119	161	194	2.4	29
Sub-Saharan Africa	586	892	1,290	3.0	23
Cote d'Ivoire	14	23	37	3.5	20
Uganda	21	32	48	3.3	21
Mexico	94	118	137	2.2	34
Brazil	158	194	225	1.7	41

Source: Population Reference Bureau, *1995 World Population Data Sheet* (Washington, D.C.: Population Reference Bureau, 1995).

Africa is particularly prone to high rates of population growth. Populations in Côte d'Ivoire, Kenya, Liberia, Niger, Togo, and Uganda were growing by at least 3.3 percent per year in the mid 1990s. This may not seem to be much until we realize that such rates will double the countries' populations in about twenty-two years. The continent has another dozen countries that are expected to increase their populations by 3 percent or more per year. Of the fourteen countries with crude birth rates of at least forty-five per thousand in 1993, all but one is in Africa. Fertility rates measure the number of children an average woman has during her lifetime. Eighteen of the twenty-three countries with fertility rates at six or above are in Africa. By comparison, the birth rate in the United States was sixteen per thousand in 1993, and its fertility rate slightly above two.

High rates of population growth are not necessarily undesirable, and criticisms of high rates often bring rebuke. In the 1970s, for example, when the United States and other industrial nations urged developing countries to stem their growth, many responded with hostility. To pleas that it initiate family-planning programs, China complained that they represented capitalist efforts to subjugate the world's poorer nations. China viewed a rapidly growing population as highly desirable because it contributed to increases in domestic production and "accelerated social and economic development."[7]

African delegates to a conference on population in 1973 reported that many of their countries prize high levels of fertility and resent foreigners lecturing them about population growth. Pointing to Africa's vast natural resources and low population density, the delegates insisted that their continent could accommodate a much larger population and that Africa's anticipated economic development would easily satisfy the needs of a growing population. The Africans also offered an alternative view of the world situation that criticized the West's profligate waste of scarce resources. Developed nations, the delegates believed, wanted to resolve shortages of world resources, not by restricting their own use or reducing their own populations, but by restricting growth in poor countries.[8]

By the late 1970s and early 1980s, however, many developing countries no longer viewed high population growth as desirable. They found themselves with many young, dependent children, increasing rates of unemployment, a cancerous and unchecked growth of urban areas, and a general inability to provide for the social and economic demands of ever-larger populations. Many developing countries also realized that if their living standards are to improve, their economic growth must exceed their rate of population increase.

Although many countries altered their attitudes about population growth, they soon realized the immensity of the task. The prevailing theory of demographic transition suggests that societies go through three stages. In the first stage, in premodern societies, birth and death rates are high, so populations remain stable or increase at low rates. In the second stage, death rates decline and populations grow more rapidly because of vaccines, better health care, and more nutritious foods. As countries begin to reap the benefits of economic development, they enter the third stage. Infant mortality declines, but so does the desire or need to have large families. Population growth slows considerably.

This model explains events in the United States and many European countries. As standards of living increased, birth rates declined. The model's weakness is that it assumes economic growth; in the absence of such growth, many nations are caught in a "demographic trap."[9] They get stuck in the second stage. This is the predicament of many developing countries today. In some of these countries the situation is even worse. Their populations are growing faster than their economies, and living standards are declining. According to the U.N. Children's Fund, average incomes dropped by as much as 10 to 25 percent in much of Africa and Latin America in the 1980s. These declines create a cruel paradox. Larger populations produce increased demands for health and educational services; stagnant economies make it difficult to respond.

The opportunity to lower death rates can also make it difficult to slow population growth. In a dozen Asian and African countries the average life expectancy at birth is less than fifty years (compared with seventy-six in the United States and eighty in Japan). If these Asians and Africans had access to the medicines, vitamins, and nutritious foods readily available in the developed nations, then death rates would drop substantially. Life expectancies could be extended by twenty years or more.

There is good reason to expect death rates to decline. Over the past twenty-five years the United Nations and other development agencies have attempted to reduce infant mortality by immunizing children against potentially fatal illnesses and by providing inexpensive cures for diarrhea and other illnesses. These programs have met with enormous success, and more is anticipated. The World Health Organization indicates that it is possible to reduce mortality among children under age five by as much as 20 percent between 1993 and 2000 and to prevent most deaths due to tetanus and measles. These two diseases now kill more than 1.7 million children per year.[10] Reduced mortality rates among children should also reduce fertility rates, but the change will be gradual, and millions of children will be born in the meantime. Most of the first-time mothers of the next twenty years have already been born.

Given these problems, the success that Cuba, Kenya, Sri Lanka, South Korea, Thailand, and Zimbabwe have had in lowering their population growth rates is remarkable. Thailand cut its growth rate by half in fifteen years by using both humor and showmanship. A private association distributes condoms at movie theaters and traffic jams, sponsors condom-blowing contests, and organizes a special cops-and-rubbers program each New Year's Eve. The association also offers free vasectomies on the king's birthday; for those who cannot wait, the normal charge is $20.[11]

Kenya, which once had the one of the world's highest population growth rates, will have reduced its total fertility rate by more than half between 1970 and 2000 because of its increased emphases on elementary and secondary education, government-sponsored family-planning campaigns, and reducing child mortality. Zimbabwe has met with similar success through its government's funding of "community-based distributors" of advice and free contraceptives—eight hundred women on bicycles—plus efforts to persuade men of the virtues of limiting the size of their families. To gain men's attention, the government once sponsored a soccer match—the Family Planning Challenge Match—in which actors dressed as giant condoms and injectable contraceptives danced around a couple to encourage their use of family planning. [12]

Perhaps the best known but most controversial population programs are in India and China. India's family-planning program started in the early 1950s as a low-key educational effort that achieved only modest success. The program changed from volunteerism to compulsion in the mid 1970s. The minimum age for marriage was increased, and India's states were encouraged to select their own methods to reduce growth.

Several states chose coercion. Parents with two or more children were expected to have themselves sterilized. To ensure compliance, states threatened to withhold salaries or to dismiss government workers from their jobs. Public officials were likewise threatened with sanctions if they did not provide enough candidates for sterilization. One result was a massive program of forced sterilization that caused considerable political turmoil. [13] Although the program was eventually relaxed, India was able to cut its fertility rate by more than 30 percent between 1970 and 1993. This is remarkable progress, but cultural resistance may stifle further gains. India currently adds another 17.5 million inhabitants each year. If such growth continues, India could become the world's most populous country within the next half-century.

Whether India becomes the world's most populous nation depends on what happens in China. Sharply reversing its earlier position in the late 1970s, the Chinese government conceded that too-rapid population growth was leading to shortages of jobs, housing, and consumer goods, further frustrating efforts to modernize its economy. [14] To reduce the country's population growth rate, the government now discourages early marriages. It also adopted a one-child-per-family policy in 1979, and the policy is stringently applied in most urban areas. The government gives one-child families monthly subsidies, educational benefits for their child, preference for housing and health care, and higher pensions at retirement. Families that had previously agreed to have only one child but then had another are deprived of these benefits and penalized financially.

The most controversial elements of the program involve the government's monitoring of women's menstrual cycles; instances of forced abortions and sterilizations, some occurring in the last trimester; and even female infanticide in rural areas. Chinese officials admit that abortions have been forced on some unwilling women. These officials quickly add, however, that such practices represent aberrations, not accepted guidelines, and that they violate the government's policies.

China's initial efforts lowered annual rates of population growth considerably. Total fertility rates declined from 5.8 in 1970 to 2.0 in 1990. Perhaps because of this success, the program began to encounter extensive resistance and, in some areas, outright disregard. Consequently, the government relaxed its restrictions and exempted certain families, particularly in rural areas, from the one-child policy. These policy changes led to a 20 percent increase in the birth rate between 1985 and 1987, and China soon announced that it had abandoned its goal of a population of 1.2 billion by 2000. [15] Abandoning this goal does not mean that China has forsaken its population goals. Renewed concern about population growth in the late 1980s caused the Chinese government to reassess the effectiveness of its programs and to reinforce its efforts to limit births. If these programs fail and birth rates increase, China's population could approach 2 billion by the middle of the twenty-first century.

The U.S. government's position toward China's population policies has been inconsistent. For many years the U.S. government viewed rapidly growing populations as a threat to economic development. The United States backed its rhetoric with money; it was the single largest donor to international population programs. The official U.S. position changed dramatically during the Reagan administration in the 1980s. Due to its opposition to abortion, the administration said the United States would no longer contribute to the U.N. Population Fund because it subsidized some of China's population programs. None of the fund's resources are used to provide abortions, but the U.S. ban on contributions nonetheless continued during the Bush administration.

Within a day of taking office, President Bill Clinton announced his intention to alter these policies, to provide financial support to the fund, and to finance international population programs that rely on abortions. The U.N. International Conference on Population and Development in Cairo, Egypt, in September 1994, provided an opportunity for the Clinton administration to advocate its preferences before an international audience. A draft Program of Action acknowledged an interdependence among population, economics, environmental quality, and human rights. The program also advocated increased reliance on family planning, which became a hotly contested issue at the conference. Delegates from the United States promoted the universal availability of reproductive health services. Without urging abortion, these delegates argued that women should have access to safe abortion services.

Not all discussion focused on abortion, and a majority of the countries represented in Cairo were able to agree on many common ideas. Perhaps the most important of these gave "prominence to reproductive health and the empowerment of women while downplaying the demographic rationale for population policy." [16] In adopting this perspective, the Cairo conference reflected a major victory for the United States, which was widely perceived as one of the conference's most effective participants.

In tandem with this achievement, the Clinton administration dramatically increased financial support for family planning in developing countries even in the face of cuts in the overall U.S. budget for foreign assistance. With the Republicans gaining control of the Congress in 1995, however, much of this momentum was soon reversed. In the federal budget for FY 1996, for example, Congress cut U.S. foreign assistance for population and family planning programs in developing countries by 35 percent. The United States is the world's largest contributor to such programs. As a result of the cuts, the head of the U.N. Population Fund estimated that 17 to 18 million unwanted pregnancies would occur.

Concerns about abortion are not the only reason that many people have qualms about efforts to affect population increases. Their view is that large populations are a problem only when they are not used productively to enhance development. The solution to the lack of such development is not government intervention, they argue, but rather individual initiatives and the spread of capitalist, free-market economies. Advocates of this position also believe that larger populations can be advantageous because they enhance political power, contribute to economic development, encourage technological innovation, and stimulate agricultural production.[17] Other critics of population control programs also ask if it is appropriate for developed countries to impose their preferences on others. As one scholar has asked: "Isn't it time wealthy white people stopped telling Third World peasants who aspire to a better life how many children and what kind of economy to have?"[18]

Another issue that has been much debated involves the increased access to abortions, and who chooses to have them. For example, the consequences of efforts to limit population growth are not always gender neutral. In parts of Asia male children are highly prized as sources of future financial security whereas females are viewed as liabilities. In years past the sex of newborns was known only at birth, and in most countries newborn males slightly outnumber newborn females. With the advent of amniocentesis and ultrasound, however, the sex of a fetus is easily ascertained. This knowledge is often the basis of a decision to abort female fetuses. Research on male-female birth rates has found that Chinese and Korean parents are typically open-minded in their preferences for their first-born child. If the first-born child is female, however, then the ratio of male-to-female births for subsequent children increases dramatically in the two countries. Among second-born children in Korea, males outnumber females by a six-to-five ratio; among third-born children, males outnumber females by a nine-to-five ratio. In India, where the marriage of a female often obligates her parents to provide a dowry, many couples opt for inexpensive abortions of female fetuses to avoid the financial hardship of a dowry. In an assessment of eight thousand abortions in Bombay that followed the determination of the fetuses' sex, all but one fetus was female.[19]

In sum, the appropriateness of different population sizes is debatable. There is no clear answer to whether growth by itself is good or bad. The important issue is a country's carrying capacity. Can it ensure its population a reasonable standard of living?

Providing Food and Fuel for Growing Populations

Sustainable development requires that environmental resources not be overtaxed so that they are available for future generations. As Lester Brown points out, however, when populations exceed sustainable yields of their forests, aquifers, and croplands, "they begin directly or indirectly to consume the resource base itself," gradually destroying it.[20] The eventual result is an irreversible collapse of biological and environmental support systems. Is there any evidence that these systems are now being strained or will be in the near future?

The first place to look is in the area of food production. Nations can grow their own food, import it, or, as most nations do, rely on both options. The Earth is richly endowed with agricultural potential and production. Millions of acres of arable land remain to be cultivated, and farmers now produce enough food to satisfy the daily caloric and protein needs of a world population exceeding 12 billion, far more than are already alive.[21] These data suggest the ready availability of food as well as a potential for even higher levels of production. This good news must be balanced with the sobering realization that nearly a billion people in the developing world today barely have enough food to survive.

As with economic development, the amount of food available in a country must increase at least as fast as the rate of population growth; otherwise, per capita consumption will decline. If existing levels of caloric intake are already inadequate, then food production (and imports) must increase faster than population growth in order to meet minimum caloric needs. Assisted by the expanded use of irrigation, pesticides, and fertilizers, many developing countries, particularly in Asia, dramatically increased their food production over the past two or three decades. Asia's three largest countries—China, India, and Indonesia—are no longer heavily dependent on imports. Between 1983 and 1994, China and Indonesia were able to increase their agricultural production per capita by more than 25 percent.[22] The average citizen in both countries now consumes more calories than the minimum daily requirement, which is about 2,350 calories per day.

Despite these and a few other notable successes, much of the developing world is in the midst of a long-term agricultural crisis. Of the fifty poorest countries (thirty of which are in Africa), thirty produced less food per person in early 1990s than they had fifteen years earlier. Not surprisingly, daily caloric consumption decreased in many of these countries. In thirteen of these fifty countries, average annual agricultural production increased between 1979 and 1993, but at a rate slower than that of the countries' rate of population increase. Ghana's population grew at an annual rate eleven times higher than its rate of agricultural production. In many developing countries the average daily caloric consumption, already below subsistence levels in the early 1980s, declined still further by the mid 1990s as agricultural productivity per capita plunged by as much as 20 to 30 percent in some places (table 15-2). Many nations consequently face severe problems with food security.

Some people consume more and others less than the average daily caloric intake in each country. The result is that in many countries that exceed average caloric requirements, many people are on the brink of starvation. In India, Indonesia, Laos, Nepal, Pakistan, and the Philippines, the average resident consumes more than the required number of calories each day, but more than a third of the children under five in these countries are malnourished. [23]

Low levels of production can be attributed to inefficient farming practices: lack of irrigation, fertilizers, appropriate strategies for managing pests, and in some instances corruption or incompetence. Zaire exemplifies several

Table 15-2 Changes in Agricultural Production and Daily Caloric Intake

Country	Index of Food Production Per Capita (1979–1981 = 100) Year 1994	Daily Caloric Supply Per Capita Years 1980	Daily Caloric Supply Per Capita Years 1992	Aggregate Household Food Security Index[a] Years 1990–1992	Aggregate Household Food Security Index[a] Years 2010
Liberia	54.6	2,398	1,640	60.6	75.6
Angola	64.6	2,184	1,839	67.5	76.5
Zambia	86.6	2,196	1,931	72.0	72.0
Kenya	88.2	2,161	2,075	69.6	72.8
Mozambique	76.4	1,953	1,680	45.2	68.9
Haiti	66.1	2,067	1,706	20.5	78.7
Nicaragua	64.7	2,293	2,293	79.7	81.7
United States	105.2	3,333	3,732	—	—
Canada	108.8	3,041	3,094	—	—
India	126.1	1,959	2,395	83.0	86.8
China	154.3	2,332	2,727	87.9	93.4

Sources: U.N. Food and Agriculture Organization (FAO), *FAO Yearbook: Production 1994* (Rome: FAO, 1995), 49-50 and 233-234; FAO, Committee on World Food Security, Twentieth Session, *Assessment of the Current World Food Security Situation and Medium Term Review* (Rome: FAO, February 1995), 12-13.

[a] The Aggregate Household Food Security Index (AHFSI) "calculates the food-gap between the undernourished and average national requirements, the instability of the annual food supply and the proportion of undernourishment in the total population." See FAO News Release PR 94/6, "32 African Nations Face Food Security Problems" (March 27, 1994). Scores range from 0 (total famine) to 100 (complete, risk-free food security). Scores above 85 indicate high food security; scores from 76 to 85 indicate medium food security; scores between 65 and 75 represent low food security; scores below 65 indicate a critical food security situation. The FAO computes the AHFSI only for low-income, food-deficit countries.

of these problems. According to the Food and Agriculture Organization (FAO), Zaire is "land abundant." With few agricultural inputs (that is, with traditional farming practices), Zaire was capable of producing almost twelve times as much food as it needed in 1975, according to FAO calculations. With a higher level of inputs, the country could feed all Africans several times over. Despite its potential, Zaire's increase in food production per capita between 1984 and 1994 lagged behind its population growth.

If current agricultural practices are continued, more than half of the 117 developing countries studied by the FAO will not be able to provide minimum levels of nutrition by the turn of the century. If, however, their agricultural practices are improved significantly to include complete mechanization and other high-technology approaches, then ninety-eight of the countries could feed themselves by 2000.[24]

It is possible to increase agricultural outputs, as the FAO found, but its calculations did not incorporate practical limitations. No consideration was given to whether money would be available to purchase the higher level of inputs.[25] The calculations also assumed that all land that could be cultivated would be cultivated; no cropland would be lost to degradation or soil erosion; no livestock would be allowed to graze on land that had the potential to grow food; and no nonfood crops, such as tea, coffee, or cotton, would be grown! The study also assumed that only minimum nutrition levels would be satisfied and that production could be distributed appropriately. In short, the current-practice scenario is likely to offer a better indication of the state of agricultural production over the near term.

This scenario is discouraging. In many countries there is not enough arable land to support existing populations, and some developing countries have already reached or exceeded the sustainable limits of production. Up to 80 percent of the land in sub-Saharan Africa is threatened by degradation, and millions of acres of forested areas are destroyed on the continent each year.[26] Kenya had the agricultural potential to support less than 30 percent of its population in 1975. With its anticipated growth, Kenya will be able to provide for an even smaller share of its population, at least with continued low levels of agricultural inputs. Many other Asian and African countries face similar predicaments. Their populations are already overexploiting the environment's carrying capacity. These people are thus using their land beyond its capacity to sustain agricultural production. One estimate suggests, as an illustration, that farmers in India, Pakistan, Bangladesh, and West Africa are already farming virtually all the land suitable for agriculture.[27] Unless changes are made soon, production will eventually decline and millions of acres of land will become barren.

Increased use of fertilizers can boost agricultural production, but increases in production rarely match (and often lag) increases in the use of fertilizer. Pakistan's use of fertilizer increased by more than 90 percent between 1979 and 1993, but this produced only a 1.2 percent annual increase in agricultural production. Bangladesh more than doubled its use of fertilizer over the same time period, but this was not enough to prevent a decline in agricultural production per capita.

It is important to appreciate as well that the nature of diets changes as nations urbanize. Irrespective of differences in prices and incomes, according to the International Food Policy Research Institute, "urban dwellers consume less grain and demand more meat, milk products, and fish than their rural counterparts."[28] This preference leads to increased requirements for grain to feed animals, more space for forage, greater demands for water, and increased pollution from animal waste. China provides one of the best examples of this phenomenon. Its consumption of red meat is increasing at about 10 percent per year, and the number of cattle in China increased by almost 60 percent between 1980 and the early 1990s. Changes in the composition of diets can be anticipated in many other countries. In fact, in virtually every low-income country, urbanization is increasing faster than overall population growth (in many instances, three to four times faster).

Food imports offer a possible solution to deficiencies in domestic production, but here, too, many developing countries encounter problems. In order to finance imports, countries need foreign exchange, usually acquired through their own exports or from loans. Few developing countries have industrial products or professional services to export, so they must rely on minerals, natural resources (such as timber or petroleum), or cash crops (such as tea, sugar, coffee, cocoa, and rubber). Advances in biotechnology can also affect the developing countries' ability to find export markets for their crops. Scientists can produce artificial vanilla in laboratories. If they can do so on a large scale, Madagascar will lose opportunities to export one of its largest sources of foreign exchange.

Economic recessions and declining demand in the developed world cause prices for many of these commodities to fluctuate widely. The prices that exporting nations received for tea and sugar were lower in 1994 than in 1990. The drop in the value of exported commodities cost African nations more than $50 billion between 1986 and 1990. To cope with declining prices for export crops, farmers are forced to intensify production, which implies increased reliance on fertilizers and pesticides, or to expand the area under cultivation in order to increase production. Unfortunately, these seemingly rational reactions are likely to depress prices even further as supply outpaces demand. As the area used for export crops expands, less attention is given to production for domestic consumption.

There are opportunities to increase exports, but economic policies in the developed world can discourage expanded activity in the developing countries. Farmers in developed countries—especially Japan, Europe, and the United States—received more than $175 *billion* in subsidies from their governments in 1994, often resulting in overproduction and surpluses. These surpluses discourage imports from developing countries, reduce prices further, and remove incentives to expand production. Subsidies and protectionist trade policies in the developed nations also prevent access to many markets. The United Nations estimated in 1992 that subsidies and trade barriers cost developing countries about $500 billion a year in lost income,[29] about ten times as much as they received in foreign assistance. There is obvious irony in these figures. Without access to export markets, developing countries are denied their best opportunity for economic development, which, historically, has provided the best cure for rapid population growth and poverty.

Developing countries could once depend on loans from private banks or foreign governments to help finance imports. Now, however, many developing countries are burdened with massive debts, which exceeded $1.75 trillion in 1994—seventeen times larger than in 1970. This debt often cannot be repaid because of faltering economies. Failures to make interest payments are common, and banks are increasingly hesitant to lend more money.

Developing countries that attempt to repay their debts find that interest payments alone take a large share of their earnings from exports. In the late 1970s about $40 billion in net aid per year was transferred to the developing countries. The flow of resources was reversed in the 1980s. Poor countries' payments of principal and interest were higher than the value of new loans and foreign aid received from rich countries, and this situation persisted until 1993.[30] Many developing countries have asked that their repayments be rescheduled or their debts forgiven. Many banks have been forced to accept the former; most have rejected the latter. In sum, at a time when many countries are not growing enough food, they also find that they cannot afford to import the shortfall, particularly when droughts and poor harvests in exporting countries cause prices to rise.

Shortages in developing countries are not limited to food. Rather than rely on electricity or natural gas, as is common in developed countries, more than 3 billion people in these countries depend on wood or other traditional fuels for heating and cooking. In much of the world, however, fuelwood is in short supply, and efforts to acquire it are time-consuming and environmentally destructive. A typical household in some parts of East Africa spends as many as three hundred days per year searching for and collecting wood. Despite such efforts, the FAO believes that about 100 million people, half in Africa, are unable to meet their daily minimum needs for fuelwood. Another 1 billion, mostly in Asia, are able to satisfy their needs, but only through unsustainable exploitation of existing resources.

The Destruction of Tropical Forests

Shortages of fuelwood point to a much larger and potentially catastrophic problem—the destruction of tropical forests. The rain forests of Africa, South America, and Southeast Asia are treasure chests of incomparable biological diversity. These forests provide irreplaceable habitats for as much as 80 percent of the world's species of plants and animals, most of which remain to be discovered and described scientifically. Among the species already investigated, many contribute to human well-being. More than one-quarter of the prescription drugs used in the United States have their origins in tropical plants. Viable forests also stabilize soils, reduce the impact and incidence of floods, and regulate local climates, watersheds, and river systems.[31] In addition, increasing concern about the effect of excessive levels of carbon dioxide in the atmosphere (the greenhouse effect) under-scores the global importance of tropical forests. Through photosynthesis, trees and other plants remove carbon dioxide from the atmosphere and convert it into oxygen. The functions that tropical forests perform are so ecologically priceless that some people argue that these forests should be protected as inviolable sanctuaries. However desirable such protection might be, what often occurs is exactly the opposite. Tropical rain forests, contend Paul and Anne Ehrlich, "are the major ecosystems now under the most determined assault by humanity." [32]

At the beginning of this century, tropical forests covered approximately 10 percent of the Earth's surface, or about 5.8 million square miles. The deforestation of recent decades has diminished this area by about one-third. Estimates of current rates of deforestation vary, but some experts believe that the pace of destruction is accelerating, with a total loss of about 2 percent of all tropical forests each year—an area about the size of Florida. In some areas the pace is much quicker, as nations seemingly rush to destroy their biological heritage and the planet's life-support systems. If current rates of deforestation continue unabated, only a few areas of forest will remain untouched. Humans will have destroyed a natural palliative for the greenhouse effect and condemned to extinction perhaps half of all species.

Causes and Solutions

Solutions to the problem of tropical deforestation depend on the root cause. One view blames poverty and the pressures associated with growing populations and shifting cultivators.

Landless peasants, so the argument goes, invade tropical forests and denude them for fuelwood, grazing, or to grow crops with which to survive. Frequent clearing of new areas is necessary because tropical soils are often thin, relatively infertile, and lack sufficient nutrients. Such areas are illsuited for sustained agricultural production.

In spite of this knowledge, some governments have actively encouraged resettlement schemes that require extensive deforestation. In Brazil, which has about 30 percent of the world's tropical forests, the government opened the Amazon region in the name of land reform. The results were spectacular. After the government built several highways into the interior and offered free land to attract settlers, the population of some Amazonian states soared by as much as a hundredfold between the mid 1960s and the late 1980s. Thousands of square miles of forest were cleared each year to accommodate the new arrivals and to provide them with permanent settlements.

Indonesia's transmigration program moves people from the densely populated island of Java to sparsely populated, but heavily forested, outer islands. Other forested land is being cleared to increase the acreage allotted to cocoa, rubber, palm oil, and other cash crops intended for export.

Another explanation for deforestation places primary blame on commercial logging intended to satisfy demands for tropical hardwoods in developed countries. Whether strapped for foreign exchange, required to repay loans from foreign banks, or subjected to domestic pressure to develop their economies, governments in the developing world frequently regard the resources of tropical forests as sources of ready income. Exports of wood now produce about $15 billion in annual revenues for developing countries, and some countries impose few limits in their rush to the bank. In the mid 1990s Southeast Asia contained about 25 percent of all tropical forests, but the region produces more than three-quarters of the value of all exports of tropical hardwoods.

If tropical forests were managed in an environmentally sustainable manner, the flow of income and benefits to local populations could continue indefinitely. Unfortunately, few tropical forests are so managed, and many countries are now becoming victims of past greed and too-rapid exploitation. About three-dozen countries were net exporters of tropical hardwoods in the late 1980s, but fewer than ten of these countries will have enough wood to export at the end of the 1990s.

Recognizing the causes and consequences of deforestation is not enough to bring about a solution. Commercial logging is profitable, and few governments in developing countries are equipped to manage their forests properly. These governments often let logging companies harvest trees in designated areas under certain conditions. All too frequently, however, the conditions are inadequate or not well enforced because there are too few forest guards. Paltry wages for guards also create opportunities for corruption.

Although penalties can be imposed on those who violate the conditions, violators are rarely apprehended. When they are, the fine is often less than the profits that accrue from the violation. Some countries require companies with concessions to post bonds, which are returned once the companies complete mandatory reforestation projects. Here again, however, the amounts involved are often so low that many companies forfeit their bonds rather than reforest. Moreover, concessions are typically granted for brief periods that discourage reforestation. When a logging company receives a twenty-year concession, granting it a right to cut for twenty years, no incentive exists to replant trees for someone else's benefit when many trees take forty to fifty years to reach maturity. For every one hundred acres of tropical forests that are cleared, only about one acre is reforested and managed in an environmentally sound manner. [33]

An Alternative View of the Problem

As the pace of tropical deforestation has quickened, so have international pressures on developing countries to halt or mitigate it. In response, leaders of developing countries quickly emphasize how ironic it is that developed countries, whose increasing consumption creates the demand for tropical woods, are simultaneously calling for a reduction of logging and shifting cultivation in developing countries.

In addition, the developing countries correctly note Europe's destruction of its forests during the industrial revolution and the widespread cutting in the United States in the nineteenth century. Why then should developing countries be held to a different standard than the developed ones? Just as Europeans and Americans decided how and when to extract their resources, developing countries insist that they too should be allowed to determine their own patterns of consumption. One observer, examining the situation in Indonesia, cast the problem in economic terms. He wondered how bureaucracies in poor countries can overcome domestic pressures for economic development. He raised this question after hearing the views of an Indonesian involved with logging. As the Indonesian businessman declared, "We are a profit-oriented company, and if that means destroying the environment within the legal limit, then we will do it." [34]

Such views are not universally shared, and change is in evidence in many developing countries. Thailand imposed a nationwide ban on logging in 1989, despite projections that the ban would cause thousands of people to lose their jobs. Ghana, Côte d'Ivoire, and the Philippines similarly announced restrictions on logging in the late 1980s. These are well-intentioned efforts, but in each instance the restrictions were imposed well after they could do much good. Moreover, such restrictions can be counterproductive. Without an assured stream of revenue from timber sales, incentives for sustainable management decline. [35]

International collaboration between wood-producing and wood-consuming nations offers one hope in the battle against deforestation. To date, however, such collaboration has only a modest record. The International Tropical Timber Organization (ITTO), formed in 1985, was on the brink of collapse just a few years later. [36] Several importing nations had refused to pay their full dues, Japanese importers boycotted ITTO's meetings, and the organization could claim few accomplishments other than its tenuous survival. The ITTO issued best-practice guidelines for the management of tropical forests in 1990; it has asked all countries to adhere to these guidelines by 2000 and to ensure that all exports of tropical timbers after that date are from sustainably managed forests.

Will tropical forests survive? Solutions abound. What is lacking, however, is a consensus about which of these solutions will best meet the essential needs of the poor, the reasonable objectives of timber-exporting and timber-importing nations, and the inflexible imperatives of ecological stability.

Fortunately, there is a growing realization that much can be done to stem the loss of tropical forests. For example, nearly ninety countries had developed tropical forest "action plans" by 1994. These plans describe the status of tropical forests in each country as well as strategies to preserve them for future generations. Unfortunately, implementation of these plans does not always parallel the good intentions associated with them. Likewise, rather than seeing forests solely as a source of wood or additional agricultural land, many countries are now examining the export potential of forest products other than wood. The expectation is that the sale of these products—such as cork, rattan, oils, resins, and medicinal plants—will provide economic incentives to maintain rather than destroy forests.

Other proposed options to maintain tropical forests include programs to certify that timber exports are from forests that are managed sustainably. Importers and potential consumers would presumably avoid timber products without such certification. For such programs to be successful, however, exporters would have to accept the certification process and there would have to be widespread agreement about what sustainable management means. No country would want to subject itself to the process only to be told that its timber exports do not meet the requirements for certification.

A second approach would impose taxes on timber exports (or imports). The highest taxes would be imposed on logging that causes the greatest ecological costs; timber from sustainable operations would face the lowest taxes.[37] Yet another option would increase reliance on community-based management of forest resources. Rather than allowing logging companies with no long-term interest in a forest to harvest trees, community-based management would place responsibility for decisions about logging (and other uses) with the people who live in or adjacent to forests. These people have the strongest incentives to manage forest resources wisely, particularly if they reap the long-term benefits of their management strategies.

Debt-for-nature swaps provide still another means to protect fragile environments. These swaps allow countries to reduce their foreign debts, which are usually denominated in dollars, in exchange for agreements to increase expenditures of local currencies on environmental activities. Sustained concern about tropical forests suggests that many other imaginative ways to protect these forests will soon emerge. Having noted these causes for optimism, it is important to emphasize that much remains to be done if tropical forests are to be preserved.

Conflicting Signals from the Industrial Nations

Improvements in the policies of many developing countries are surely necessary if sustainable development is to be achieved. As already noted, however, industrial countries sometimes cause or contribute to environmental problems there.

Patterns of consumption provide an example. Although the United States and other industrial nations can boast about their own low rates of population growth, developing nations reply that patterns of consumption, not population increases, are the real culprits. This view suggests that negative impacts on the environment are a function of population growth plus consumption and technology.

Applying this formula places major responsibility for environmental problems on rich nations, despite their relatively small numbers of global inhabitants. The inhabitants of these nations consume far more of the Earth's resources than their numbers justify. Consider that the richest one-fifth of the world's nations control about 85 percent of the world's income and consume about 60 percent of its food and more than three-quarters of its energy, chemicals, timber, and iron and steel. These nations similarly generate more than 90 percent of all hazardous and industrial wastes, and the United States leads the world in per capita production of trash. Consider as well that these relatively few rich nations are likewise responsible for releasing more than two-thirds of all greenhouse gases and more than 90 percent of all ozone-depleting chlorofluorocarbons into the atmosphere.[38]

More specifically, much of the responsibility for this situation can be placed on Americans. They represent less than 5 percent of the Earth's inhabitants, yet they consume almost 30 percent of the world's commercial energy. Much of this energy is used to fuel Americans' love for the automobile, one of the most environmentally harmful technologies known to humans. While Americans increased their numbers by about 20 percent in the 1970s and 1980s, the total number of automobiles in use in the United States grew by more than 50 percent. Moreover, American drivers encounter some of the world's lowest prices for gasoline. Adjusted for inflation, the cost of gasoline in the Untied States was lower in the mid 1990s than at any time in the previous thirty years and half of what it had been in the early 1980s. Low prices encourage consumption rather than conservation, and rates of growth in consumption of gasoline exceed U.S. rates of population growth.

Although the United States made sizable gains in fuel efficiency in the 1970s and 1980s, many of these gains are being eroded in the 1990s as Americans drive faster and farther, and as they increasingly rely on vans and sport utility vehicles rather than cars.[39] The typical American still uses about two and one-half times more gasoline per year than does the typical German. Americans' profligacy with fossil fuels provides part of the explanation for U.S. production of almost one-fifth of the emissions that contribute to global warming.

As environmental scholar Paul Harrison has noted, because of such inequalities in consumption, continued population growth in rich countries is a greater threat to the global environment than it is in the developing world. He adds that if relative consumption and levels of waste output remain unchanged, the 57 million extra inhabitants likely to be born in rich countries in the 1990s will pollute the globe more than the extra 900 million born elsewhere. Other experts suggest that if Americans want to maintain their present standard of living and levels of energy consumption, then the ideal population for the United States is between 40 million and 100 million.[40]

Causes for Optimism?

Although there is cause for concern about the prospects for sustainable development among developing countries, the situation is neither entirely bleak nor beyond hope. The populations of Malaysia, Thailand, Korea, Tunisia, Botswana, and Syria are the beneficiaries of considerable social and economic development over the past two decades. Similarly, the number of chronically malnourished people in developing countries declined by more than 150 million between 1970 and 1990, and the number of families in developing countries with access to clean water surged in the 1980s. Small-pox, a killer of millions of people every year in the 1950s, has been eradi-cated. Between 1970 and 1993, infant mortality rates declined in nearly all developing countries—in many by significant amounts. [41] The infant mortal-ity rate in Tunisia was 127 per 1,000 live births in 1970; the rate was only 42 per 1,000 live births in 1993. Over the same time period, China's rate declined from 69 to 30, Iran's from 131 to 35, and Costa Rica's from 59 per 1,000 to only 14. These and other dramatic improvements prompted the World Bank to conclude that "health conditions around the world have improved more in the past forty years than in all previous human history." [42]

However dire the current food situation may be in much of sub-Saha-ran Africa, there is hope for progress there as well. Agricultural experts believe that, after years of decline, "the region has achieved many if not all of the preconditions for sustained growth in agricultural production," and such changes can increase growth in agricultural production by at least 4 percent per year. [43] Such growth would allow daily caloric consumption to increase. More generally, human ingenuity and technological advances have allowed increases in food production to exceed increases in populations over the past forty-five years. Even without further innovations, agricultural intensifica-tion has the potential to feed millions of additional people yet to be born.

The international community is also demonstrating a new recognition of the Earth's ecological interconnectedness. At the request of the U.N. General Assembly, the World Commission on Environment and Develop-ment was established in 1983 and charged with formulating long-term envi-ronmental strategies for achieving sustainable development. In its report, *Our Common Future*, the commission forcefully emphasized that although environmental degradation is an issue of survival for developing nations, fail-ure to address the degradation satisfactorily will guarantee unparalleled and undesirable global consequences from which no nation will escape. [44] This report's release in 1987 prompted increased international attention to envi-ronmental issues in the late 1980s and early 1990s.

This attention manifested itself most noticeably in the U.N. Confer-ence on Environment and Development in Río de Janeiro in 1992 (see chap. 13), which, in turn, led to the creation of the U.N. Commission on Sustain-able Development. The commission reviews nations' efforts to implement international environmental agreements and their progress in achieving sustainable development. The World Summit for Social Development, held in Copenhagen in March 1995, marked another effort to focus attention on the plight of the world's poor.

Most of the developing nations at these international forums recognize their obligations to protect their environments as well as the global commons. At the same time, however, these nations argue that success requires techni-cal and financial assistance from their wealthy colleagues. However desirable the protection of tropical forests and biological diversity and the prevention of global warming and a depleted ozone layer, the poor nations cannot afford to address these problems in the absence of cooperation from richer nations.

The prospects for achieving such cooperation are uncertain. On the one hand, for example, developing nations like China and India want to provide refrigerators to as many of their inhabitants as possible. These hundreds of millions of refrigerators will require extraordinary amounts of chlorofluorocarbons (CFCs) unless companies in developed nations are willing to share or give away the scientific secrets associated with substitutes for the CFCs. These companies are reluctant to do so, arguing that they are in business to make money, not to give away valuable trade secrets.

This reluctance has important consequences. China's economic growth over the past decade boosted its share of the world's CFC emissions from 3 percent in 1986 to nearly 20 percent in 1995. China's emissions of gases that contribute to global warming can also be expected to increase rapidly as it industrializes. China has vast reserves of coal, which are burned to produce electricity, albeit without the pollution control devices typically installed on power plants elsewhere. Moreover, the Chinese are among the least efficient users of energy in the world. They require more energy to produce a given level of economic output than all but a few countries.

On the other hand, providing assistance to the developing nations requires leadership and a willingness to compromise national interests for global ones. The nations at the Earth summit approved international agreements covering biological diversity, the protection of tropical forests, and reductions in emissions that contribute to global warming. The Bush administration initially refused to sign the first, irritated advocates of the second, and worked vigorously to weaken the third. Without support and cooperation from the United States, the prospects for successful implementation of these agreements is diminished.

Delegates at the Río conference also approved Agenda 21, a plan for enhancing global environmental quality. The price tag for the recommended actions is huge—an estimated $600 billion per year for seven years, of which developed nations would be expected to provide at least $125 billion per year, or about twice as much as they now devote to all foreign assistance each year. Rich nations could afford to provide this amount if they donated as little as .70 percent (*not* 7 percent, but seven-tenths of 1 percent) of their total economic output to the developing world each year. Only Norway, Sweden, Denmark, and the Netherlands exceeded this target in the mid 1990s. The Japanese pledged to move toward the recommended target, but U.S. foreign assistance as a percentage of its GNP declined steadily between the 1960s and 1995. At .15 percent of GNP in 1994, U.S. assistance to developing nations was well below the target level and the lowest among twenty-one advanced industrial countries.

The prospects for increasing U.S. assistance to address environmental problems in developing countries are not good. Most Americans believe that Asians and Africans should solve their own environmental problems. According to an opinion survey conducted in early 1995, most Americans also believe that the U.S. government provides far more assistance than it actually does to poor countries. The survey found that the average respondent thinks that about 18 percent of the U.S. federal budget is devoted to foreign assistance, but that 8 percent would be an appropriate amount. The actual amount is about 1 percent. Other surveys have found that Americans are also opposed to providing additional money and technology to foreign countries if they will be used to improve environmental conditions.[45] Whatever the American public's perspective, the Republican-controlled 104th Congress severely curtailed U.S. foreign assistance in the latter half of the 1990s.

Despite Americans' seeming reluctance to share their wealth, other nations have demonstrated an increased willingness to address globally shared environmental problems. Within the past few years many international environmental agreements have been signed, and many more are likely in the future (see chap. 13). Most of the world's industrial nations have agreed to eliminate the use of key CFCs, the international community is beginning to make some headway in protecting endangered species of plants and animals that find themselves in international trade. This same international community now operates a Global Environment Facility (GEF), a multibillion-dollar effort to finance environmental projects in developing countries. The World Bank, the U.N. Development Programme, and the U.N. Environment Programme implement the GEF and distribute funds to address four priority areas: global warming, loss of biological diversity, pollution of international waters, and depletion of the ozone layer.

These institutional changes and agreements will not be sufficient to protect the environment without concerted and effective international action. The economic, population, and environmental problems of the developing world dwarf those of the industrial nations and are not amenable to immediate resolution, but immediate action is imperative. Millions of people are steadily destroying their biological and environmental support systems at unprecedented rates in order to meet their daily needs for food, fuel, and fiber. Driven by poverty and the need to survive, they have become ravenous souls on a planet approaching the limits of its tolerance and resilience. Whether this situation will change depends on the ability of residents in the developing countries not only to reap the benefits of sustained economic development but also to meet the demands of current populations while using their natural resources in a way that accommodates the needs of future generations. Unless the developing nations are able to do so soon, their future will determine ours as well. It is both naive and unreasonable to assume that the consequences of population growth, environmental degradation, and abysmal poverty in developing countries will remain within their arbitrary political boundaries.[46]

Notes

1. World Bank, *World Development Report 1995* (New York: Oxford University Press, 1995), 220-221. Due to differences in the costs of goods and services from one country to another, gross national product per capita does not provide comparable measures of economic well-being. To address this problem, economists have developed a measure that reflects purchasing-power parity (PPP). Such a measure attempts to

equalize the prices of identical goods and services across all countries, with the United States as the base economy. For a humorous but helpful explanation and application of the PPP concept, see "McCurrencies: Where's the Beef?," *Economist,* April 27, 1996, 82, which compares the price of a MacDonald's Big Mac hamburger in thirty-three countries. For the status of economies in Latin America, see International Food Policy Research Institute (IFPRI), *A 2020 Vision for Food, Agriculture, and the Environment in Latin America: A Synthesis* (Washington, D.C.: IFPRI, 1995).

2. Population Action International (PAI), *Reproductive Risk: A Worldwide Assessment of Women's Sexual and Maternal Health* (Washington, D.C.: PAI, 1995).

3. U.N. Children's Fund (UNICEF), *State of the World's Children 1989* (New York: Oxford University Press, 1989), 37. UNICEF's annual report on this subject is an excellent source of information about the status of children in developing countries.

4. World Commission on Environment and Development, *Our Common Future* (London: Oxford University Press, 1987), 8, 43.

5. John N. Wilford, "A Tough-Minded Ecologist Comes to Defense of Malthus," *New York Times,* June 30, 1987, C3.

6. Population Reference Bureau, Inc., *1995 World Population Data Sheet* (Washington, D.C.: Population Reference Bureau, 1995). Colin Clark, *Population Growth and Land Use,* 2d ed. (London: Macmillan, 1977), 153 ("the world's potential agricultural and forest land could supply the needs of 157 billion people"); Paul Ehrlich and Anne Ehrlich, *Extinction* (New York: Random House, 1981), 243 (starting a gradual decline of the human population is "obviously essential"). For an excellent discussion of the world's carrying capacity, see Vaclav Smil, "How Many People Can the Earth Feed?" *Population and Development Review* 2 (June 1994): 255-292.

7. Richard Bernstein, "World's Surging Birthrate Tops the Mexico City Agenda," *New York Times,* July 29, 1984, sec. 4, 3; "Speech by the Head of the Delegation of the People's Republic of China at the World Population Conference," Bucharest, August, 1974," in *Population and Development Review* 2 (June 1994): 452.

8. National Academy of Sciences (NAS), "African Seminar on Population Policy," in *In Search of Population Policy: Views from the Developing World,* ed. NAS (Washington, D.C.: NAS, 1974), 57-60; and U.N. Food and Agriculture Organization (FAO), *The State of Food and Agriculture 1983* (Rome: FAO, 1984), 66.

9. Lester R. Brown, "Analyzing the Demographic Trap," in *State of the World, 1987,* ed. Lester R. Brown (New York: Norton, 1987), 20.

10. World Health Organization (WHO), *Executive Summary of the World Health Report 1995: Bridging the Gaps* (Geneva: WHO, 1995), 13.

11. "The Good News: Thailand Controls a Baby Boom," *Time,* Asian international ed., January 2, 1989, 37.

12. Nancy Chege, "Kenya's Plans for Its Children," *World Watch* 8 (January-February 1995): 20-22; "Zimbabwe: Shrinking Families," *Economist,* July 30, 1994, 37; "Reaching Goals in Zimbabwe," *Open Files,* June 1995, 6.

13. K. Srinivasan, "Population Policy and Programme," in U.N. Economic and Social Commission for Asia and the Pacific, *Population of India* (New York: United Nations, 1982), 161. For a discussion of India's family planning programs, see Sharon L. Camp and Shanti R. Conly, *India's Family Planning Challenge: From Rhetoric to Action* (Washington, D.C.: Population Crisis Committee, 1992).

14. U.N. Department of International Economic and Social Affairs, *World Population Policies,* vol. 1 (New York: United Nations, 1987), 127-129.

15. Marshall Green, "Is China Easing Up on Birth Control?" *New York Times,* April 23, 1986, A25; "The Mewling That They'll Miss," *Economist,* August 13, 1988, 27. For an analysis of the application of China's population policies, see Susan Greenhalgh, Zhu Chuzhu, and Li Nan, "Restraining Population Growth in Three Chinese Villages, 1988-93," *Population and Development Review* 20 (June 1994): 365-395.

16. C. Alison McIntosh and Jason L. Finkle, "The Cairo Conference on Population and Development: A New Paradigm?" *Population and Development Review* 21 (June 1995): 223.

17. Chief among these advocates is Julian Simon. See his book, *The Ultimate Resource* (Princeton, N.J.: Princeton University Press, 1981). See also Ester Boserup, *The Conditions of Agricultural Growth* (London: Allen and Unwin, 1965).

18. Sheldon L. Richman, letter to the editor, *New York Times*, June 30, 1992, A22.

19. Chai Bin Park and Nam-Hoon Cho, "Consequences of Son Preference in a Low-Fertility Society: Imbalance of the Sex Ratio in Korea," *Population and Development Review* 21 (March 1995): 59-84; R. K. Sachar et al., "Sex Selective Fertility Control—An Outrage," *Journal of Family Welfare* (1990): 30-35.

20. Brown, *State of the World*, 21.

21. Per Pinstrup-Anderson, the director-general of the International Food Policy Research Institute, believes the world can easily feed 12 billion people one hundred years from now. See "Will the World Starve?" *Economist*, June 10, 1995, 39.

22. FAO, *FAO Yearbook: Production, 1994* (Rome: FAO, 1995), 49-50.

23. Bread for the World Institute, *Hunger 1995: Causes of Hunger* (Silver Spring, Md.: Bread for the World Institute, 1994), 109-111; World Bank, *World Development Report 1995*, 214.

24. FAO, *Potential Population-Supporting Capacities of Lands in the Developing World* (Rome: FAO, 1982).

25. Brown, *State of the World*, 24. The criticisms of the study are from Brown's analysis of the FAO report.

26. Ousmane Badiane and Christopher L. Delgado, eds., *A 2020 Vision for Food, Agriculture, and the Environment in Sub-Saharan Africa* (Washington, D.C.: IFPRI, 1995), 7.

27. Paul Harrison, *The Third Revolution: Environment, Population and a Sustainable World* (New York: I. B. Taurus, 1992), 45; IFPRI, *A 2020 Vision for Food, Agriculture and the Environment in South Asia: A Synthesis* (Washington, D.C.: IFPRI, 1995), 2.

28. Jikun Huang, Scott Rozelle, and Mark Rosegrant, "China and the Future Global Food Situation," IFPRI, 1995.

29. "Farming," *Economist*, June 3, 1995, 97; U.N. Development Programme, *Human Development Report 1992* (New York: Oxford University Press, 1992), 67.

30. Organization for Economic Co-operation and Development (OECD), Development Assistance Committee, *Development Cooperation 1994* (Paris: OECD, 1994), 58-59, 62-63.

31. NAS, *Population Growth and Economic Development: Policy Questions* (Washington, D.C.: NAS, 1986), 31; FAO, Committee on Food Development in the Tropics, *Tropical Forest Action Plan* (Rome: FAO, 1985), 2, 47.

32. Ehrlich and Ehrlich, *Extinction*, 160.

33. Michael Richardson, "Indonesia Wonders If Timber Boom Will Backfire," *International Herald Tribune*, September 5, 1988, 1; Alan Thein Durning, "Redesigning the Forest Economy," in *State of the World 1994*, ed. Lester R. Brown (New York: Norton, 1994), 31.

34. Michael Vatikiotis, "Tug-of-War over Trees," *Far Eastern Economic Review*, January 12, 1989, 41.

35. FAO, *World Agriculture: Towards 2010* (New York: Wiley, 1994), 223.

36. Margaret Scott, "Unequal to the Task," *Far Eastern Economic Review*, January 12, 1989, 38; Marcus Colchester, "The International Tropical Timber Organization: Kill or Cure for the Rainforest?" *Ecologist* (September-October 1990).

37. Edward B. Barbier, Joanne C. Burgess, Joshua Bishop, and Bruce Aylward, *The Economics of the Tropical Timber Trade* (London: Earthscan, 1994); Durning, "Redesigning the Forest Economy."

38. UNICEF, *The State of the World's Children, 1994* (New York: Oxford University Press, 1994), 23-24.

39. Agis Salpukas, "What Next, Tail Fins? Fast Speeds and Big Cars Send Gas Consumption Up," *New York Times*, February 15, 1996, D1.

40. Harrison, *Third Revolution*, 256-257; David Pimintel and Marcia Pimentel, "Land, Energy and Water: The Constraints Governing Ideal U.S. Population Size," *NPG Forum*, January 1990, 5.

41. Marc J. Cohen and Don Reeves, "Causes of Hunger," in *A 2020 Vision for . . . Latin America*; World Bank, *World Development Report 1995*, 214. By way of comparison, the infant mortality rate in the United States decreased from twenty to nine deaths per one thousand live births between 1970 and 1993.

42. World Bank, *World Development Report 1993* (New York: Oxford University Press, 1993), 21.

43. Badiane and Delgado, ed., *A 2020 Vision for Food, Agriculture, and the Environment in Sub-Saharan Africa*, 6.

44. World Commission on Environment and Development, *Our Common Future*.

45. Marcy E. Mullins, "How Three Nations View the Future," *USA Today*, June 1, 1992, 8A; Rae Tyson, "Poll: Environment Tops Agenda," *USA Today*, June 1, 1992, 1A. Both articles report the results of public opinion surveys conducted in May 1992 by the Gordon S. Black Corp. The surveys questioned approximately one thousand adults. *USA Today* provided additional information on the surveys to the author. The University of Maryland's Program on International Policy Attitudes surveyed 801 adults in January 1995 about their perceptions of U.S. foreign assistance. See *USA Today*, May 23, 1995, 6A.

46. Moni Nag, "Overpopulation Becomes Our Problem Too," *New York Times*, May 21, 1992, A28.

16

International Trade and Environmental Regulation
David Vogel

This chapter explores the increasingly important and contentious relationship between international trade and environmental regulation. It begins by explaining why these two policy areas have recently become more closely linked, and then reviews environmentalists' criticisms of trade liberalization. The next two sections explore controversies surrounding the environmental impact of the General Agreement on Tariffs and Trade (GATT) and the North American Free Trade Agreement (NAFTA) and also examine their specific environmental provisions. The concluding section of the chapter assesses the likely impact of trade liberalization on environmental standards.

The Growth of Policy Linkages

Debates over the possible environmental consequences of the GATT and NAFTA reveal the extent to which the formerly distinct policy areas of trade and regulation have become increasingly linked.[1] The growth of policy linkages between these two issue-areas is in turn related to the convergence of two critical postwar trends: an increase in both the volume of world trade and the amount and scope of environmental regulation.

Thanks to the GATT at a global level, and to other treaties and agreements at a regional level, such as those associated with the European Union (EU), tariff levels have declined steadily throughout the postwar period. As a consequence, trade negotiations have begun to pay greater attention to nontariff barriers (NTBs)—government policies, designed to protect domestic producers, that discriminate against imports through means other than tariffs. Examples of NTBs now restricted by both the GATT and the EU include quotas, procurement policies favoring domestic producers, and subsidies. Another important category of NTBs consists of government regulations and, more specific to the topic of this chapter, environmental standards. Many of these regulations, often inadvertently, but sometimes intentionally, restrict trade by imposing greater burdens on foreign producers than on domestic ones.

Reducing the role of government regulations as obstacles to trade has become an important priority of both regional and international trade negotiations and agreements. In the second half of the 1980s, for example, the EU's precursor, the European Community (EC), chose to harmonize many environmental and consumer regulations to prevent them from being used to

345

restrict trade among member states. EC law also required its member states to admit any product approved for use in another member state. Likewise, a major result of the Uruguay Round GATT negotiations, which created the World Trade Organization (WTO), was to strengthen the Standards Code, originally established in 1979 to prevent national standards from serving as "technical barriers to trade." NAFTA also includes a number of provisions that seek to restrict its members (Canada, Mexico, and the United States) from using NTBs to undermine regional economic integration.

Economic integration has thus subjected an increasing number of public policies that were formally the exclusive purview of national governments to both regional and international scrutiny. Trade liberalization has made the politics of environmental protection more global: it means that governments, in formulating their environmental policies, must now take into account their impact not only on national producers but on their foreign competitors as well. At the same time—as the tuna-dolphin dispute discussed below will illustrate—trade agreements also provide foreign producers with a legal vehicle for challenging the domestic regulations of their trading partners, if those regulations appear to unfairly discriminate against their exports. Consequently, agreements to expand trade are gradually undermining national regulatory sovereignty.

The second trend fostering increased policy linkages between trade and regulation has been the steady expansion of environmental regulation. The past three decades have witnessed a significant increase in the number of government regulations that directly affect traded goods. These include automobile emission standards; rules governing the content and disposal of packaging; chemical safety regulations; regulations for the processing, composition, and labeling of food; and rules to protect wildlife and natural resources. The steady growth of protective regulation has forced exporters to cope with an increasingly diverse and complex array of national standards, many of which have made trade more difficult. Because nations generally want to maintain their own standards in spite of—or sometimes because of—the burdens they impose on imports, the continual growth of national environmental regulations represents a growing source of trade conflict.

The scope of environmental policy also grew steadily during the second half of the 1980s. Many environmental issues have taken on a global dimension that requires the coordination of national regulatory policies. These include saving endangered species located in foreign lands or international waters, protecting the ozone layer, safeguarding the shipment and disposal of hazardous wastes, and preserving tropical forests in developing countries. This coordination often means trade restrictions, however, either as a means to prevent "free riding" or because the harm itself is trade related.

As a result of the expansion of both trade and regulation, the debate between supporters of environmental regulation and advocates of free trade has become both more visible and more contentious. Free trade advocates want to limit the use of regulations as barriers to trade, while environmentalists and consumer advocates want to prevent trade agreements from serving as barriers to regulation. The trade community worries about an upsurge of "eco-protectionism"—the justification of trade barriers on environmental grounds. For their part, consumer and environmental organizations fear that trade liberalization will serve to weaken both their own country's regulatory standards as well as those of its trading partners.

Environmentalists and Free Trade

Many environmental groups have become increasingly critical of treaties and trade agreements that promote liberalization. As one activist put it, "When they call me protectionist, I respond, 'Well, if protecting the earth, if protecting the air, if protecting the water, and indeed human life is protectionist, then I have to admit I am protectionist'."[2] Although their views are by no means uniform, the environmental community does share a number of criticisms of free trade.

A primary concern of environmentalists is that growing international competition will weaken national regulatory standards. Although there is a broad global trend toward stricter and more comprehensive environmental policies, national regulations and their enforcement continue to vary significantly. Indeed, if anything, the variance has increased in recent years as the world's "greener" nations such as the United States, Germany, Austria, the Netherlands, and the Scandinavian countries have significantly tightened their regulatory requirements on industry. Even more important, although many developing countries have recently begun to strengthen their regulatory standards, the disparity between their regulations and of those of developed nations remains substantial in many cases.

As tariffs and other trade barriers between developed and developing nations fall, producers in the developed nations are increasingly forced to compete with goods produced in nations with laxer standards. Environmentalists fear that producers in industrial nations will demand the relaxation of their country's regulatory standards in order to remain competitive; alternatively, they may relocate their production to "pollution havens," thus giving developing nations a still greater incentive to keep their standards lax or even to lower them further. Hence, trade liberalization is likely to result in a regulatory "race to the bottom" as nations compete with one another by weakening their environmental standards.

Environmentalists also worry that trade liberalization directly harms environmental quality. Trade liberalization increases the level of global economic activity; indeed, that is among its major purposes. But the Earth's ability to sustain current levels of economic growth is limited. By increasing the rate at which the Earth's scarce natural resources such as forests, fossil fuels, and fisheries are consumed, free trade undermines sustainable development. Liberal trade policies also indirectly contribute to the greenhouse effect by stimulating an increase in the use of fossil fuels, thus endangering the welfare of the entire planet. Finally, environmentalists worry that accelerating the rate at which goods and raw materials are transported around the world increases not only energy use but also the likelihood of accidents, such as oil or chemical spills in international waters.

Environmentalists argue that trade liberalization is especially damaging to the environment in developing countries. As these countries become more integrated into the global economy, their economic policies are likely to become more environmentally destructive. Agricultural production shifts to export crops, thus encouraging the destruction of forests and increasing the use of pesticides; fisheries, forests, and other natural resources are exploited at a greater rate; and fossil fuels, increasingly used in the production of export crops, exacerbate local air pollution. At the same time, a significant share of exports to developing nations consists of "toxic trade," or hazardous substances, which can have adverse environmental consequences.

The GATT

GATT Rules and Decisions

Environmentalists have expressed not only their general concerns about the impact of free trade on regulatory standards and environmental quality. But they have also criticized a number of the GAAT's specific provisions. The primary international organizational vehicle for promoting trade liberalization, the GATT has attempted to discourage national subsidies to industry in order to create a more level playing field among producers in different countries. But these domestic subsidies may provide important incentives for firms to install pollution abatement equipment or to finance other improvements in environmental quality. Similarly, the GATT explicitly prohibits a country from imposing countervailing duties on imports produced under lower environmental standards than its own. This restriction makes it impossible for "greener" countries to protect more environmentally responsible producers from having to compete with less responsible foreign ones. The GATT also limits the ability of countries to impose export bans on the grounds that these bans treat foreign and domestic producers differently. But such bans can often be critical to a nation's ability to protect its own forests, fisheries, or wildlife from excessive exploitation.

Environmentalists have been particularly critical of GATT rules that limit a signatory nation's ability to use trade measures to influence the environmental policies of its trading partners. This was a central issue in the tuna-dolphin case, the most visible and controversial trade-dispute panel decision in the GATT's nearly fifty-year history. Indeed, environmental opposition to the Uruguay Round GATT agreement was mobilized largely in reaction to the 1991 decision that declared sections of the Marine Mammal Protection Act to be in violation of U.S. obligations under the GATT.

In the eastern tropical Pacific, where approximately one-quarter of tuna are harvested, dolphins commonly swim above schools of tuna. As a result, the large purse-seine nets used to catch tuna also kill large numbers of dolphins. By the late 1960s dolphin fatalities had reached roughly 500,000 per year. In order to protect dolphins, the United States imposed limits on the number of dolphins that could be killed annually by U.S. commercial tuna-fishing vessels.

By the late 1980s, thanks to the tightening of U.S. regulatory standards, along with various improvements in fishing technology, incidental dolphin mortality by U.S.-registered vessels had declined by more than 90 percent. Foreign fishing fleets, however, continued to kill dolphins at a higher rate than their American counterparts. A major portion of these tuna were then exported to the U.S. market, which accounts for approximately half of global tuna consumption. Following a 1990 federal court decision, the United States prohibited imports of tuna from Mexico, Venezuela, and the Pacific islands of Vanuatu. This embargo affected approximately $30 million worth of tuna imports annually.

Mexico challenged the U.S. embargo on the grounds that GATT rules prohibit a nation from using trade policies to affect regulatory policies outside its legal jurisdiction. The GATT disputes panel ruled in favor of Mexico. According to the panel, GATT rules permit signatory nations to issue regulations to protect their own citizens or land. Thus, a nation can impose whatever restrictions it wishes on products consumed within its borders—provided they do not discriminate between foreign and domestic products—as well as on the production of goods or natural resources within its borders. The panel also ruled, however, that a nation cannot regulate how foreign nationals produce goods or raw materials outside its legal jurisdiction. Accordingly, the United States cannot dictate to Mexico how it can harvest tuna: it cannot make access to its domestic market contingent on Mexico adopting dolphin protection practices similar to its own.

This decision outraged American environmentalists. As an article in the magazine of the Sierra Club put it, "Meeting in a closed room in Geneva . . . three unelected trade experts . . . conspired to kill Flipper."[3] An environmental activist predicted: "in the 1990s, free trade and efforts to protect the environment are on a collision course."[4] Lori Wallach, a spokeperson for Congress Watch, a public interest lobbying group founded by Ralph Nader, proclaimed: "This case is the smoking gun. We have seen GATT actually declaring that a U.S. environmental law must go. These [trade] agreements must be modified to allow for legitimate consumer and environmental protections."[5] Many American environmental and consumer groups subsequently announced their opposition to a new GATT agreement, claiming it threatened the ability of the United States to establish and enforce its own regulatory standards.

Environmentalists specifically argued that the GATT dispute panel ruling rested on an artificial and outdated distinction between domestic and extrajurisdictional environmental regulations. They claimed that because all mankind shares a common biosphere, the U.S. environment is adversely affected by the killing of dolphins by Mexican fishing fleets, even if this takes place in international waters. As two environmental lawyers argued, "The panel's domestic limitation is nonsensical because it fails to take into account the fact that domestic environmental harms are now, increasingly, being traced to actions occurring beyond a nation's borders. Limiting the reach of a nation's environmental laws to domestic activities substantially undercuts its ability to protect itself from adverse extraterritorial activities."[6] Moreover, "the GATT's focus on 'products' makes it virtually incapable of capturing the environmental costs of externalities related to methods of production."[7]

Even more disturbing to many environmentalists, the ruling appeared to threaten the legality of the provision of a number of international treaties that rely on trade restrictions to protect the global commons. For example, the Montréal protocol permits nations to restrict the imports of products produced by chemicals that endanger the ozone layer, and the Convention on International Trade in Endangered Species (CITES) relies entirely on trade restrictions to protect endangered plant and animal species. And if the world's nations were ever able to agree on an international treaty limiting emissions of greenhouse gases, it too might run afoul of the GATT if its enforcement provisions permitted nations to restrict imports from noncomplying nations.

Greening the GATT

The response by environmentalists to these challenges has been mixed. A few groups have strongly opposed trade liberalization agreements of any kind. Other groups have adopted a more moderate stance, opting to influence treaty negotiations so that their concerns are addressed. Even before the GATT panel had issued its ruling on the tuna-dolphin case, a number of environmental organizations had begun to urge that the GATT be amended to take into account the growing linkages between trade and environmental regulation. A discussion paper published by the World Wildlife Fund (WWF) two months before the tuna decision was handed down noted that the original 1947 GATT agreement was "negotiated without any express references to the environment," adding that, "on the occasions when the GATT has been amended and strengthened, it has also been without reference to environmental concerns."[8] Not surprisingly, GATT dispute panels have developed expertise and been interested "only in the objective of liberalizing trade," ignoring the implications of their rulings on environmental protection.[9]

The tuna-dolphin decision clearly made the case for reforming the GATT even more compelling. "If a 19-year-old conservation law not generally perceived to be protectionist in intent could be viewed by a GATT panel as a fundamental violation of world trade rules," writes Steve Charnowitz, "then it became easy to explain to the public why such rules were in need of reform."[10] At demonstrations in front of the U.S. Capitol, environmentalists carried posters depicting a monstrous "GATT-zilla," with a dolphin in one arm and a canister dripping DDT in the other, chanting the GATT's new slogan: "Guaranteeing a Toxic Tomorrow."[11] Friends of the Earth argued that the GATT is "fundamentally at odds with environmental protection" and urged that it either be suspended or dramatically modified. [12] The Earth Island Institute claimed that "without substantial overhaul, GATT will pose a grave threat to environmental protection laws throughout the world." [13]

A number of environmental organizations proposed a new GATT article to guarantee "environmental conditionality—the idea that countries should not be penalized for taking measures that conflict with GATT rules, if their main purpose is to protect the environment." [14] They also urged that the WTO be instructed to give "high and formal priority to environmental concerns," in particular to sustainable development. [15] In addition, they have demanded that GATT dispute-settlement procedures be reformed to make them more open and to permit the introduction of evidence about the impact of trade rules on environmental regulations and standards.

The Terms of the Uruguay Round Agreement

The Uruguay Round agreement, which concluded in 1994 and was ratified by the U.S. Congress the following year, did not address any of the specific issues raised by the tuna-dolphin dispute, let alone the broader questions concerning the future relationship between trade and the environment. But largely as a response to the criticisms of the GATT made by environmentalists, it did explicitly acknowledge one formerly tacit principle. The preamble to the Standards Agreement, now incorporated into the provisions of the WTO, marks the first mention of the word "environment" in the GATT itself. It states that each country "may maintain standards and technical regulations for the protection of human, animal, and plant life and health and of the *environment*." [16] It also notes that a country should not be prevented from setting technical standards (which include environmental regulations) "at the levels it considers appropriate," a phrase meant to discourage nations from harmonizing standards in a downward direction. [17] In addition, the Agreement on Subsidies and Countervailing Measures permits governments to subsidize up to 20 percent of one-time capital investments to meet new environmental requirements, provided that its subsidies are directly linked and proportional to environmental improvements. This provision makes the granting of environmental subsidies somewhat easier.

At the same time, in an effort to reduce the use of national consumer and environmental regulations as nontariff barriers, the Uruguay Round agreement also requires that national standards or "technical barriers to trade" "not be more trade-restrictive than necessary to fulfill a legitimate objective, taking into account the risks nonfulfillment would create." [18] An earlier draft would have imposed a stricter test of technical barriers to trade by requiring that standards be the "least trade-restrictive available." But this was modified at the insistence of the United States, once again reflecting the influence of the American environmental movement on U.S. trade policy. [19]

GATT and the Environment

Revising the GATT's rules to better reconcile free trade and environmental protection will be high on the agenda of the post Uruguay Round of trade negotiations. Indeed, this process has already begun. In 1991, acting on the suggestion of the members of the European Free Trade Association (EFTA), the GATT agreed to convene its Working Group on Environmental Measures and International Trade, which had been established in 1971 but had never met. EFTA members stated that they wanted "a rule-based analytical discussion on the interrelationship between trade and environment . . . to ensure that the GATT system was well equipped to meet the challenge of environmental issues and to prevent disputes by . . . interpret[ing] or amend[ing] . . . certain provisions of the General Agreement." [20] At the GATT's April 1994 ministerial meeting during which the Uruguay Round agreement was formally ratified, a resolution was approved committing the soon-to-be-established WTO to undertake a systematic review of "trade policies and those trade-related aspects of environmental policies which may result in significant trade effects for its members." [21]

The convening of the GATT working group was initially opposed by some developing countries that had misgivings about having the GATT examine environmental issues. They feared GATT rules would be weakened to permit advanced industrial nations wider latitude in restricting imports from developing nations on environmental grounds. There was a strong consensus, however, among most GATT signatory nations that the GATT should address the increasingly important linkages between trade and regulatory policies. Indeed, the turnout of delegations for an informal meeting of this working group appeared to set a record.

Among the most important tasks of the WTO's Trade and Environment Committee, the successor body to the GATT working group, will be to examine the consistency of the seventeen international environmental agreements that provided for enforcement through trade restrictions. For as the GATT's annual report conceded, the General Agreement's principles needed to be carefully reexamined "to make certain that they do not hinder multilateral efforts to deal with environmental problems." [22]

The North American Free Trade Agreement (NAFTA)

The Emergence of Controversy

Consumer and environmental organizations in the United States have expressed concern about the environmental impact of NAFTA, the free trade agreement negotiated among the United States, Mexico, and Canada. Throughout the negotiations, groups opposing the agreement focused on the environmental impact of northern Mexico's nearly two thousand *maquiladoras*. Due to the lax enforcement of Mexico's environmental laws, these plants, producing and assembling goods that are permitted to enter the United

States duty-free, were found to be generating substantial amounts of pollution, much of it toxic. The National Wildlife Federation characterized "the border pollution issue as its highest priority in U.S.-Mexican environmental relations." [23] The National Toxics Campaign reported that many *maquiladoras* were disposing their hazardous wastes illegally, contaminating rivers and streams. [24] Finally, environmentalists pointed out that contamination levels in the Rio Grande were many times greater than those considered safe for recreational use. [25]

The effects of this pollution were not confined to Mexico; consumer and environmental groups pointed out that the border regions of the United States were also affected. Raw sewage dumped into the New River in northern Mexico was being carried across the border to California, while Tijuana's inadequate waste-disposal system was polluting beaches in San Diego. In San Elizario, Texas, where a shared aquifer was found to be contaminated, "35 per cent of the children contract hepatitis A by age eight, and 90 percent of adults have it by the age of 35." [26] A public health official from El Paso, Texas, already faced with rates of hepatitis, dysentery, and tuberculosis substantially above the U.S. average, warned that "unless the government marries free trade and the environment, we will be totally burnt. We cannot cope with more growth." [27] An American environmental writer predicted that "if Bush gets his version of free trade between the United States and Mexico, this systematic poisoning of an entire region . . . could prove impossible to stop." [28]

Environmental groups focused on a second, related issue regarding the environmental impact of a general increase in U.S. investment in Mexico. Many environmentalists expressed the fear that NAFTA would encourage American firms to take advantage of Mexico's laxer enforcement of its pollution laws to relocate their production throughout all of Mexico. This would further exacerbate Mexico's pollution problems and, at the same time, cost American jobs. Craig Merrilees, the San Francisco codirector of a grassroots organization opposed to NAFTA, stated: "We think the experience across the border is the best predictor of what will happen under a broader agreement. It's a Wild-West, dump-and-run kind of situation that has turned the 2,000-mile border into one big Love Canal." [29]

A third concern revolved around the trade agreement's impact on U.S. regulatory standards. Many public interest groups feared that a free trade agreement with Mexico would result in downward harmonization of consumer health and safety standards because the United States' stricter product standards could be challenged by Mexico as nontariff barriers. Mexico is the largest supplier of produce to the United States, and many pesticides prohibited or suspended by the Environmental Protection Agency (EPA) are used by Mexican farmers. "Fruit and vegetables imported from Mexico have DDT and other pesticide residues that have been banned in the United States. If a free trade agreement further liberalizes agricultural commerce, years of U.S. environmental reform could be undone." [30]

The Debate over NAFTA

In July 1990 Friends of the Earth became one of the first American environmental groups to issue a statement on NAFTA. In a document submitted to the International Trade Commission, the organization contended that the negative environmental impact of the Free Trade Agreement (FTA) indicated the need to extend the scope of U.S.-Mexico negotiations to include environmental issues. Three months later a series of meetings were held among representatives of various Mexican social movements and their U.S. and Canadian counterparts. Subsequently, twenty-four Canadian, Mexican and U.S. environmental groups issued a declaration calling for the inclusion of environmental issues in the negotiations over NAFTA.[31]

Four months later, representatives of seventeen American labor, environmental, agricultural, consumer, and religious organizations held a press conference in Washington to demand that Congress not extend fast-track negotiating authority for NAFTA.[32] Their position was supported by produce growers from Florida, who urged that their fruit and vegetables be excluded from the agreement because they faced unfair competition due to lower wages and weaker environmental regulations in Mexico. Subsequently, Congress added pressure to broaden the scope of NAFTA. On March 7, 1991, two influential legislators, Rep. Dan Rostenkowski (D-Ill.), House Ways and Means Committee chair, and Sen. Lloyd Bentsen (D-Texas), Senate Finance Committee chair, wrote a letter to President George Bush warning him that fast-track approval was in danger unless the administration indicated its willingness to address the treaty's environmental and social impacts. They urged that parallel negotiations be held on the environment and workers' rights.

For American environmental groups, often frustrated by their inability to have a greater impact on environmental policy outside the United States, the political opportunity offered by NAFTA was unprecedented: the debate over the treaty in the United States provided them a vehicle for influencing the environmental policies of a developing country. As Stewart Hudson of the International Program Division of the National Wildlife Federation put it, "We have to take a stand here and set a correct model."[33] For their part, Mexican environmentalists also saw NAFTA as a unique opportunity: working with their counterparts in the United States to shape the treaty's terms could enable them to dramatically increase their hitherto limited leverage over Mexican environmental policy.

The participation of environmental groups in the anti-fast-track coalition helped to legitimize congressional opposition to extending the president's fast-track negotiating authority. "Opposing fast-track on environmental grounds," writes Roberto Suro, "was easier than arguing the concerns of labor with the attendant risk of being accused of being in the pocket of 'special interests'."[34] The environmental issue quickly became a "lightning rod for legislators who have many reasons to be obstreperous on free trade."[35] Thus House Majority Leader Richard Gephardt (D-Mo.), long a prominent opponent of trade liberalization, stated in a public letter to President Bush that his willingness to support NAFTA depended not only on the treaty being rewritten to protect American jobs but also on the inclusion of strict environmental safeguards. He argued that "neither Mexico nor Canada nor America is benefitted by a system that benignly looks upon massive air pollution, poisonous pesticides and child labor as 'comparative advantages'."[36]

As the debate over NAFTA heated up in the spring of 1991, both the Mexican and the U.S. governments began to recognize that the environmental critique of NAFTA threatened the trade agreement's approval in the U.S. Congress. To demonstrate his commitment to environmental protection to the United States, Mexican president Carlos Salinas dramatically closed Mexico City's largest oil refinery, a major source of air pollution. Two months later, the United States Trade Representative (USTR) agreed to appoint five representatives from environmental nongovernmental organizations (NGOs) to its top-level NAFTA advisory committees, and the White House pledged to conduct parallel negotiations to develop a border environmental plan with Mexico.

Following these preliminary concessions on the part of the Bush administration, the Natural Resources Defense Council (NRDC) and the National Wildlife Federation (NWF) agreed to support an extension of fast-track authorization. Although many environmental organizations and consumer groups continued to oppose fast-track, the president had succeeded in splitting the environmental movement. The support of the NRDC and the NWF played a critical role in securing congressional approval of the administration's request for an extension of fast-track negotiating authority for both the GATT and NAFTA. However, the administration's victory was a close one: fast-track passed the House by only thirty-nine votes.

Two months after fast-track passed the U.S. Congress, the United States and Mexico released a draft plan committing both countries to cooperate on improving environmental quality along their common border.[37] EPA administrator William Reilly stated that the plan was intended to "reassure those who have concerns about the environmental consequences of free trade."[38] It called for additional investment in wastewater treatment plants, increased restrictions on cross-border shipments of hazardous wastes, and the hiring of more officials to enforce environmental laws in Mexico. The following month, U.S. Trade Representative Carla Hills assured environmentalists that NAFTA would not be rushed through until proper safeguards were in place. She promised that the United States was "not going to bend environmental and safety commitments," adding that "we've no intention of letting pesticides come in from Mexico as we wouldn't from Italy or France."[39]

Sergio Reyes Lujan, Mexico's undersecretary of ecology, promised that his country would not become a haven for polluters. He stated: "there should be no doubt that any factory rejected by the United States will not be acceptable in Mexico." [40] Mexican officials claimed that NAFTA would help to improve the quality of Mexico's environment both by making Mexico richer and by removing the incentive for firms to locate along the border rather than in the less-crowded interior.

EPA head William Reilly argued that the Mexican president "has made it clear that his country has never been more committed to its environmental responsibilities." But while promising that "the U.S. will continue to work with Mexico to achieve the environmental safeguards both countries seek," he also urged Americans to "be realistic and sensitive to Mexican concerns." [41] American environmentalists countered with their own "green language" treaty, which called for the establishment of a commission to ensure that environmental standards—and enforcement—would be identical in all three countries. [42] A broad coalition of anti-NAFTA organizations also warned that unless the treaty contained provisions for cross-border enforcement, Mexico would not carry out its promise to tighten environmental enforcement.

NAFTA was officially signed by the heads of state of all three nations shortly after the 1992 American presidential election. Upon assuming office, however, the Clinton administration declined to submit the trade agreement to Congress. Instead, it began to negotiate a number of changes in the agreement, including the addition of a supplementary environmental agreement. The changes were announced in the summer of 1993, when the administration submitted the treaty along with the side agreement to Congress.

The subsequent debate over NAFTA sharply divided the environmental community, as it did the business community. A number of NGOs, including Friends of the Earth, Public Citizen, and the Sierra Club, continued to strongly oppose NAFTA. They viewed the agreement as both too weak and too powerful: they feared the environmental side agreement would be ineffective in making Mexico enforce its environmental laws and highly effective in making the United States lower its regulatory standards. But equally significant, six major national environmental organizations, including the NRDC, the Audubon Society, the Environmental Defense Fund, and the WWF, endorsed the agreement. They concluded that the provisions of the supplementary environmental agreement on which they had insisted and which they helped the Clinton administration negotiate offered adequate regulatory safeguards. They were disappointed, however, that it did not include any specific procedure for raising environmental standards or their enforcement to the highest common denominator. [43]

The Terms of NAFTA

NAFTA seeks to prevent its signatory nations from using environmental regulations to gain a comparative advantage either by making them too strict or too lax. The agreement both prohibits any country from lowering its environmental standards to attract investment and permits its signatories to impose stringent environmental standards on new investments, provided they apply equally to foreign and domestic investors. It also requires all three countries to cooperate on improving the level of environmental protection and encourages, but does not require, the upward harmonization of regulatory standards.

As the direct response to the concerns of environmentalists over the implications of the GATT decision in the tuna-dolphin case, the agreement specifically states that the provisions of several international environmental agreements—including the Montréal protocol, the Basel convention on hazardous wastes, and CITES—take precedence over NAFTA. In some cases, it also allows each nation to continue to enforce "generally agreed upon international environmental or conservation rules or standards," provided they are "the least trade-restrictive necessary for securing the protection required."[44] At the same time, while "NAFTA in no way attempts to reduce national standards to a lowest common denominator ... it does seek to limit the ability of signatories to use such regulations as surreptitious protectionist devices."[45] A Committee on Standards-Related Measures will attempt to develop common criteria for assessing the environmental hazards of products as well as methodologies for risk assessment.

The agreement's most innovative feature is its supplemental agreement on the environment, though this is not part of NAFTA itself. It was negotiated by the Clinton administration with considerable input from American environmental organizations. The supplemental agreement established the Commission for Environmental Cooperation, headed by a secretariat and council composed of senior environmental officials from each country and advised by representatives of environmental organizations. Addressing some of the criticisms of GATT dispute procedures made by environmental groups following the tuna-dolphin decision, it extends to citizens the right to make submissions to the commission on any environmental issue, requires the secretariat to report its response to these submissions and, under certain circumstances, permits its reports to be made public. In fact, these provisions provide more opportunities for nonbusiness participation than current U.S. law, which permits only aggrieved producers to file complaints with or to sue the International Trade Commission, the body responsible for enforcing U.S. trade laws.

In addition, the commission was given the authority to consider the environmental implications of both processes and production methods, or, in its words, the "environmental implications of products throughout their life-cycles," thus in effect dissenting from the position of the GATT tuna-dolphin dispute panel.[46] Although the side agreement does not require any of the three signatories to enact new environmental laws, it does authorize the use of fines as well as trade sanctions for the nonenforcement of new or existing ones, though only the former can be applied against Canada. Although the commission is empowered to address any environmental or natural resource issue, the range of issues subject to dispute settlement panels is limited to the enforcement of those environmental laws that are related to trade or competition among the parties.

NAFTA and the Environment

The debate over NAFTA marked a new level of environmentalist participation in the making of U.S. trade policies. Previously, debates over trade agreements negotiated by the United States had been dominated by interest groups whose primary concern was their economic impact. With NAFTA, the regulatory dimensions of a trade agreement became politically salient. "The principal legacy of the NAFTA process," writes Stephen Mumme, "is the mobilization of environmental groups in the trade policy arena. For the first time environmentalist groups have made a serious run at shaping international trade policy." [47]

In addition, U.S. NGOs had a major impact on the terms of the agreement and specifically on the inclusion of an environmental side agreement. [48] Unlike labor unions, a number of environmental organizations were willing to support free trade with Mexico in exchange for specific provisions in the side agreement. This, in part, explains why the powers granted to the Commission for Environmental Cooperation exceeded those granted to its counterpart on labor standards. Literally hundreds of meetings took place between executives of large environmental groups and administration officials. The support of environmentalists was, in fact, critical to the passage of the agreement in Congress. As a result of the input and influence of American environmental organizations, NAFTA is the "greenest" trade agreement ever entered into by the United States.

Moreover, the debate over NAFTA and the environment had an important spillover effect on Mexican environmental policies. Thus, in the midst of the debate, the U.S. and Mexican governments announced an integrated plan to clean up their common border. They agreed to spend approximately $1 billion over three years—about two-thirds of which would come from Mexico—to construct water treatment plants, better roads, and solid waste disposal sites along the border. This plan represented the first large-scale attempt to integrate the planning and environmental strategies of the two governments and was an explicit recognition of the linkages between natural resources and trade. It included funds to construct a $200 million plant to end the water pollution from Tijuana that had closed San Diego beaches and $19 million for a new sewage treatment facility in Nuevo Laredo, Mexico. The plan also contained a $50 million World Bank loan to improve environmental enforcement and a $200 million loan to reduce air pollution in Mexico City. To address the latter problem, Mexico enacted legislation requiring that all new vehicles be equipped with catalytic converters.

To emphasize its own commitment to environmental regulation, and at the same time to diffuse environmental opposition to the trade agreement, the Mexican government also began a crackdown on polluters, doubling the number of its inspectors along the border, and temporarily closing hundreds of *maquiladoras* for failing to comply with Mexican environmental regulations. It also passed legislation requiring all new industries to submit environmental impact reports.[49]

Moreover, the Mexican government, which rarely inspected its industrial plants prior to the debate over NAFTA, conducted more than eleven thousand such inspections in 1992 and 1993, resulting in the partial or full closure of several hundred facilities, including seventy in Mexico City. It also established an environmental attorney general's office to prosecute both domestic and foreign industries. The budget of the Mexican Secretariat of Social Development (SEDESOL), the agency responsible for formulating and implementing Mexican development policy, increased from $4.3 million in 1988 to $88.4 million in 1992; and annual government spending on environmental protection grew tenfold between 1988 and 1991.[50] Mexico also significantly tightened its automobile emission standards, bringing them into closer alignment with those of the United States. And, notwithstanding its victory in the GATT against the United States, Mexico instituted a number of changes in fishing fleet practices that have significantly reduced dolphin mortality.

It is difficult to assess the actual impact of NAFTA on Mexican environmental standards and their enforcement, largely because the environmental dimensions of the agreement were overshadowed by Mexico's 1995 financial crisis. However, as the Mexican economy resumes its growth and its industry becomes more closely integrated with that of the United States, Mexico's environmental quality will steadily improve. This, however, will be a long-term process. In this context it is worth noting that it took the European Community nearly a generation to begin a serious effort to improve the environmental standards of its southern, less "green" member states. It may well, therefore, be several years before NAFTA has a significant impact on Mexican environmental standards.

The Environmental Impact of Trade Liberalization

What is likely to be the overall impact of more liberal trade policies on environmental protection? To a significant extent, any assessment of the environmental impact of trade liberalization depends in large measure on one's analysis of the relationship between environmental quality and economic development. If the two are viewed as incompatible, then clearly trade liberalization will, by definition, have adverse environmental consequences, especially for developing countries. Alternatively, if economic development is understood as making possible an improvement in environmental quality, then trade liberalization can have a positive environmental impact.

The evidence suggests that for relatively poor countries, increased economic growth and economic interdependence generally does result in a deterioration of domestic environmental quality: pollution levels increase and natural resources are depleted at an accelerating rate. But environmental quality tends to improve as per capita income increases because nations are in a better position to devote resources to conservation and pollution control. Thus, in the long run, economic development may actually contribute to the strengthening of environmental standards.

Nor is it the case that trade liberalization necessarily results in more environmentally irresponsible economic practices. On the contrary, the experiences of Latin America and the formerly Communist nations of eastern and central Europe indicate that the polluting and energy-inefficient firms are also likely to be economically inefficient. By exposing these firms to global competition, trade liberalization improves local environmental conditions. [51] In agriculture, the lowering of barriers to trade tends to transfer production from developed to developing nations. Because farming in developing countries tends to be less capital intensive, overall environmental quality improves. Simultaneously, land is freed up in the developed nations for conservation and other purposes. [52]

As the recent changes in Mexican environmental policies suggest, increased economic interdependence has not resulted in a regulatory "race to the bottom." With the exception of a handful of industries, it seems that the costs of compliance with environmental standards are relatively modest. Accordingly, firms seem to have little incentive to migrate to "pollution havens" to lower their production costs, even with the removal of barriers to trade. In fact, there is no evidence that nations have lowered their environmental standards in order to retain or attract investment. [53]

Indeed, in many cases, stricter domestic regulatory standards represent a source of competitive *advantage* because it is often easier for domestic firms to comply with them. For example, recycling requirements almost invariably work to the advantage of those firms that produce close to their customers, thus providing domestic firms with an important incentive for supporting them. Moreover, the lure of access to green export markets has played a critical role in encouraging firms to support stricter domestic product standards. For example, in the early 1970s Japan modeled its automobile emission standards on those of the United States—its major export market—while an important factor underlying the support of German auto firms for stricter EC emissions standards during the 1980s was the fact that the vehicles they were producing for sale in California were already meeting the world's stricter emission standards. Likewise, according to a recent study conducted by the U.S. General Accounting Office, countries that export significant quantities of agricultural products to the United States frequently take U.S. standards into account in establishing their domestic pesticide regulations. [54] Moreover, as Michael Porter has argued, stricter regulatory standards can also encourage domestic firms to develop improved pollution control technologies, which they can then export as the regulatory standards of their trading partners become stronger. [55] Thus, in a number of cases, increased economic interdependence has led to the strengthening rather than the weakening of environmental standards—a "race to the top" that has been characterized as "the California effect." [56]

It is also important to note that many of the environmental abuses attributable to trade liberalization have more to do with domestic politics than international economics. Trade liberalization does not dictate the rate at which a nation allows its natural resources to be exploited or the value it accords to hardwood forests, jungles, or endangered wildlife. These are essentially set by national governments. Developed nations have made enormous progress in protecting their domestic environments; there is nothing in the terms of international trade agreements that prevents developing nations from doing likewise. Moreover, if the developed nations are dissatisfied with the environmental practices of developing nations, they have no shortage of vehicles with which to improve them. Trade restrictions are rarely the most effective or efficient mechanism.

What about the role of trade agreements and treaties such as the GATT and NAFTA in preventing nations from adopting stricter regulatory standards on the grounds that these constitute nontariff barriers? This is a complex and important issue: it is often difficult to distinguish between environmental standards that may inadvertently discriminate against imports and those that do so intentionally. Environmentalism can easily become an excuse for straightforward economic protectionism. Yet nations that wish to maintain stricter regulatory standards must be permitted to do so—even if those standards complicate access to their domestic markets.

The tension between trade liberalization and environmental regulation should not be exaggerated. Only a handful of national regulations has been held to be inconsistent with trade agreements, and these have tended to be blatantly discriminatory. Both the GATT and NAFTA explicitly protect the right of nations to establish whatever regulatory standard they deem appropriate, provided they can be scientifically justified and are as "least trade-restrictive" as possible. Even more important, these agreements have not prevented a steady increase in the number and scope of regional and international environmental agreements. In fact, notwithstanding the fears of environmentalists, it is highly unlikely that the GATT (now the WTO) would uphold a challenge to the use of trade restrictions to enforce an international environmental agreement. Significantly, an important reason why the GATT dispute panel ruled against the United States in the tuna-dolphin case was that no international environmental treaty protected dolphins. The United States violated the GATT in part because it had acted unilaterally.

Clearly, environmentalists, and the protectionist producers with whom they have often formed alliances, have been unable to prevent the enactment of more liberal trade policies: in November 1993 Congress approved NAFTA, and fourteen months later it ratified the Uruguay Round GATT agreement. Nevertheless, this chapter has shown that environmentalists did have an important impact on the terms of both trade agreements. This impact was constructive: the NAFTA supplementary agreement includes a number of provisions that will help to better reconcile trade liberalization with environmental protection, while the very participation of environmental organizations in the debate over NAFTA pressured Mexico into tightening its regulatory standards and strengthening their enforcement. Although the impact of environmentalists on the GATT/WTO has been less dramatic, here too they have succeeded in placing the impact of the provisions of international trade agreements on environmental standards in both the United States and its trading partners firmly on both the domestic and international trade policy agenda. As a result of their criticisms, the WTO too is likely to be slowly "greened," albeit at a slower pace than many environmentalists prefer.

Tensions between both national and international environmental policies and trade liberalization will continue to persist. Yet, on balance, the postwar period has witnessed both a strengthening of environmental standards and an increase in trade liberalization. There is no reason to expect that this relationship will change significantly in the future. However, there is every reason to expect that the debate over trade and the environment will remain highly controversial and that the environmental movement will continue to play a critical role in shaping trade agreements in the future.

Notes

1. This is the central theme in David Vogel, *Trading Up: Consumer and Environmental Regulation in a Global Economy* (Cambridge, Mass.: Harvard University Press, 1995).
2. Quoted in Stewart Hudson, "Coming to Terms with Trade," *Environmental Action* (Summer 1992): 33.
3. Paul Rauber, "Trading Away the Environment," *Sierra* (January-February 1992).
4. James Brooke, "America—Environmental Dictator?" *New York Times*, May 3, 1992, 7.
5. Stuart Auerbach, "Endangering Laws Protecting the Endangered," *Washington Post National Weekly Edition*, October 7-13, 1991, 22.
6. Robert Housman and Durwood Zaelke, "The Collusion of the Environment and Trade: The GATT Tuna-Dolphin Decision," *Environmental Law Reporter* (April 1992): 10271.
7. Matthew Hurlock, "The GATT, U.S. Law, and the Environment: A Proposal to Amend the GATT in Light of the Tuna-Dolphin Decision," *Columbia Law Review* 92 (1992): 2100.
8. Charles Arden-Clarke, "The General Agreement on Tariffs and Trade: Environmental Protection and Sustainable Development," World Wildlife Fund Discussion Paper (June 1991), 91.
9. Ibid.
10. Steve Charnowitz, "Environmental and Labor Standards in Trade," *World Economy* 15, no. 3 (May 1992): 336.
11. Ibid.
12. William Lash III, "Green Gang's GATT Holdup," *Journal of Commerce*, December 10, 1993.
13. Ibid.
14. "Can GATT Go Green?" *New Scientist*, November 10, 1990, 11.
15. Ibid.
16. Richard Steinberg, "The Uruguay Round: A Legal Analysis of the Final Act," *International Quarterly* 6, no. 2 (April 1994): 35.
17. Ibid.
18. Daniel Esty, *Greening the GATT* (Washington, D.C.: Institute for International Economics, 1994), 170.
19. Ibid., 50.

20. "Several Countries Urge Quick Start to GATT Environmental Work," *Focus: The GATT Newsletter* 80 (April 1991): 9.
21. "Decisions Adopted by Ministers in Marrakesh," *Focus: The GATT Newsletter* (May 1994): 9.
22. "Several Countries," 23.
23. Robert Pastor, "NAFTA as the Center of an Integration Process: the Non-Trade Issues," in *Assessing the Impact of North American Free Trade*, ed. Nora Lustig et al. (Washington, D.C.: Brookings, 1992), 182.
24. Eva Regnier, "Trade Policy and the Environment: U.S.-Mexico Free Trade," *Journal of the IES* 35, no. 2 (March-April 1992): 83.
25. Pastor, "NAFTA," 182.
26. Ibid.
27. Damian Fraser, "Environment Hit by Too Much Free Trade," *Financial Times*, July 2, 1992, 4.
28. William Burke, "The Toxic Price of Free Trade in Mexico," *In These Times*, May 22-28, 1991, 2.
29. Jonathan Marshall, "How Ecology Is Tied to Mexico Trade Pact," *San Francisco Chronicle*, February 25, 1992, A8.
30. Richard Rothstein, "Exporting Jobs and Pollution to Mexico," *New Perspectives Quarterly* 8, no. 1 (Winter 1991): 23.
31. Ibid., 20.
32. Ibid., 18-19.
33. Roberto Suro, "In Search of a Trade Pact with the Environment in Mind," *New York Times*, April 14, 1991, E4.
34. Ibid., 20.
35. Ibid., 4.
36. Rep. Richard Gephardt, "Letter to President George Bush," March 27, 1991.
37. Keith Bradsher, "U.S. and Mexico Draft Plan to Fight Border Pollution," *New York Times*, April 2, 1991, C1, C6.
38. Ibid., C6.
39. Jane Kay, "Environmentalists Urge Tough Mexico Trade Law," *San Francisco Examiner*, September 9, 1991.
40. Ibid.
41. William Reilly, "Mexico's Environment Will Improve with Free Trade," *The Wall Street Journal*, April 19, 1991, A15.
42. Damian Fraser, "Mexicans Yearn for a Mañana That Brings the American Dream," *Financial Times*, March 20, 1991, 6.
43. For criticisms of the environmental provisions of both NAFTA and the side agreement, see Gary Hufbauer and Jeffrey Scott, *NAFTA: An Assessment*, rev. ed. (Washington, D.C.: Institute for International Economics, 1993), 92-97.
44. Michelle Swenarchuk, "NAFTA and the Environment," *Canadian Forum* 71 (January-February 1993): 13.
45. Roberto Salinas-Leon, "Green Herrings," *Regulation* (Winter 1993): 31.
46. Quoted in James Sheehan, "NAFTA—Free Trade in Name Only," *The Wall Street Journal*, September 9, 1993, A21.
47. Stephen Mumme, "Environmentalists, NAFTA, and North American Environmental Management," *Journal of Environment and Development* 2, no. 1 (Winter 1993): 215.
48. Keith Bradsher, "Side Agreements to Trade Accord Vary in Ambition," *New York Times*, September 19, 1993, 1, 15.
49. Diana Solis, "Mexico Cracks Down on Pollution, Spurred in Part by Trade Talks," *The Wall Street Journal*, February 10, 1992, A10.
50. William H. Lash III, *NAFTA and the Greening of International Trade Policy* (St. Louis, Mo.: Center for the Study of American Business, Washington University in St. Louis, 1993), 11.
51. See for example, Nancy Birdsall and David Wheeler, "Trade Policy and Industrial Pollution in Latin America: Where Are the Pollution Havens?" in *International Trade*

and the Environment, ed. Patrick Low (Washington, D.C.: World Bank, 1992), 159-168.

52. For a comprehensive analysis of the impact of trade liberalization on both economic efficiency and environmental quality, see *The Greening of World Trade Issues,* ed. Kym Anderson and Richard Blackhurst (Ann Arbor: University of Michigan Press, 1992).

53. There is an extensive literature of the relations among economic regulation and trade patterns, international competitiveness, and corporate location decisions. See, for example, Richard Stewart, "Environmental Regulation and International Competitiveness," *Yale Law Journal* 102, no. 8 (June 1993): 2077-2079; and Judith Dean, "Trade and the Environment: A Survey of the Literature," in *International Trade and the Environment,* ed. Low, 16-20.

54. Quoted in Charles Pearson, "Trade and Environment: The United States Experience" (New York: U.N. Conference on Trade and Development, January 1994), 52.

55. See Michael Porter, *The Competitive Advantage of Nations* (New York: Free Press, 1990), 685-688; and also Curtis Moore and Alan Miller, *Green Gold* (Boston: Beacon Press, 1994).

56. See Vogel, *Trading Up,* chap. 8.

PART V. CONCLUSION

17

The New Environmental Agenda

Norman J. Vig and Michael E. Kraft

Our vision is of a life-sustaining Earth. We are committed to the achievement of a dignified, peaceful, and equitable existence. A sustainable United States will have a growing economy that provides equitable opportunities for satisfying livelihoods and a safe, healthy, high quality of life for current and future generations. Our nation will protect its environment, its natural resource base, and the functions and viability of natural systems on which all life depends.

—President's Council on Sustainable Development
February 1996

The pace of change in our world is speeding up, accelerating to the point where it threatens to overwhelm the management capacity of political leaders. This acceleration of history comes not only from advancing technology, but also from unprecedented world population growth, even faster economic growth, and the increasingly frequent collisions between expanding human demands and the limits of the earth's natural systems.

—Lester R. Brown
1996

As the twentieth century comes to an end, environmental quality has come to occupy a central place in the public policy of the United States and other advanced industrial countries. There is an emerging consensus that all nations must move rapidly toward new forms of "sustainable development" in the next century if future generations are to survive and prosper. Indeed, it is no longer possible to think about economic growth and development without considering the ecological impacts of virtually all human activities. Yet, as Lester Brown suggests above, it is by no means certain that the human race will succeed in managing the planetary balance.

The concept of sustainable development was first defined and popularized by the World Commission on Environment and Development in its 1987 report, *Our Common Future*,[1] and was further elaborated at the 1992 U.N. Conference on Environment and Development (see chap. 13). In the United States the National Commission on the Environment, a prestigious group of private individuals including four former heads of the Environmental Protection Agency (EPA), also called for rethinking environmental policies in terms of this concept:

> U.S. leadership should be based on the concept of *sustainable development.* By the close of the twentieth century, economic development and environmental protection must come together in a new synthesis: broad-based economic progress accomplished in a manner that protects and restores the quality of the natural environment, improves the quality of life for individuals, and broadens the prospects for future generations. This merging of economic and environmental goals in the concept of sustainable development can and should constitute a central guiding principle for national environmental and economic policymaking.[2]

The President's Commission on Environmental Quality, a committee of corporate, foundation, and environmental group executives set up by President George Bush, issued a report in early 1993 that called for establishing a national council on sustainable development.[3] Bill Clinton took up the challenge by appointing a new President's Council on Sustainable Development. The council, consisting of twenty-five leaders from industry, government and the environmental community, was charged with formulating a sustainable development plan for the United States. The council's report, issued in February 1996, called for a new generation of flexible, consensual environmental policies that would maximize economic welfare while achieving more effective and efficient environmental protection. It concluded that "in order to meet the needs of the present while ensuring that future generations have the same opportunities, the United States must change by moving from conflict to collaboration and adopting stewardship and individual responsibility as tenets by which to live."[4]

To recognize environmental sustainability as a guiding principle will not, however, solve the problem of making difficult policy choices that involve other important social values. Although many of these choices may no longer be regarded as zero-sum trade-offs, they will often require financial sacrifices and changes in social behavior. This means that environmental policies will continue to generate strong political resistance from established economic and bureaucratic interests. Political opposition is also likely to grow among antienvironmental and property rights organizations (see chap. 3). And as environmental protection deepens, success in policy implementation will increasingly depend on public understanding and acceptance of the need for social and behavioral change.

The current impasse over environmental regulation in the U.S. Congress illustrates the difficulties ahead. The Republican majority elected in 1994 has thus far shown little awareness or acceptance of the concept of sustainable development. Indeed, the emphasis of the "Contract with America" has been almost entirely on reducing regulatory costs and government spending (see chap. 6). The concept of international collaboration to ensure resource sustainability and to prevent global climate change and other ecological disasters appears repugnant to this new brand of conservatism. Environmentalists, for their part, have largely adopted a defensive strategy of blocking most congressional initiatives in the hope of preserving the statutory foundations of environmental policies built up over the past quarter century.[5]

The overwhelming evidence presented in this book and other recent studies suggests, however, that neither the current policy structure nor dreams of a major regulatory rollback and withdrawal from global environmental obligations will provide satisfactory answers in the future. Environmental policy success will require, as the National Commission on the Environment, the President's Council on Sustainable Development, and the National Academy of Public Administration all suggest, much more innovative strategies and tools than have characterized past regulation.[6] Many chapters in this book have emphasized the need for new policy approaches, including greater use of economic incentives, comparative risk assessment, voluntary partnerships, informal dispute resolution, and community involvement.

The remainder of this chapter discusses the need for better integration of environmental values into national policymaking and identifies seven of the most pressing environmental issues on the national agenda. It also outlines seven innovative approaches to environmental management and concludes with some general reflections on the need to rethink political strategies and the long-term choices that must be made if we are to maintain the health of the planet.

Integrating Environmental Policies

Perhaps the greatest obstacle to more rational and effective environmental policymaking at present is the absence of any mechanism for integrating and coordinating policy actions on the basis of an overall strategy or set of priorities. As pointed out in chapter 7, the EPA lacks both a statutory charter defining its priorities and authority over most matters involving natural resources and land use. Even within its own areas of competence, it is driven by separate legal mandates that make it difficult to set priorities based on comparative risk assessment or some other common standard. Efforts in both the Bush and Clinton administrations to elevate the EPA to a cabinet-level department ended in failure (see chap. 5). Other agencies, such as the Council on Environmental Quality (CEQ), have lacked the legal and political stature to coordinate the policies of cabinet departments and other executive agencies, while efforts to control agency policies through budgetary and regulatory oversight or special bodies such as the Quayle Council on Competitiveness have focused too narrowly on reducing administrative and regulatory costs.

To remedy these weaknesses, President Clinton created a new White House Office of Environmental Policy (OEP) shortly after taking office. It was given the formidable task of coordinating environmental initiatives throughout government and ensuring consideration of environmental factors in other areas of policy formulation. Its director, Kathleen McGinty, was to attend meetings of the cabinet and other top-level bodies such as the Domestic Policy Council and National Security Council to ensure the integration of environmental values. Although OEP played an active role in many areas of policy development, often with the support and aid of Vice President Gore, it was merged into the CEQ in late 1994 when McGinty assumed the vacant chair of the latter body. Given its small staff and low profile, the revamped council may have little more than marginal impacts on policy coordination.

The need to institutionalize policy coordination will increase as domestic and international policymaking converge in many fields. This will certainly be the case if environmental considerations are to become integral to defense planning, trade negotiations, and foreign policy generally. Agencies such as the Defense Department, the State Department, and the Office of Trade Representative will need to strengthen their environmental policy capabilities and build much stronger institutional links with the EPA and other environmental agencies. Scientific agencies like the White House Office of Science and Technology Policy (OSTP), the National Oceanic and Atmospheric Administration (NOAA), and the National Aeronautics and Space Administration (NASA) have taken on major environmental research responsibilities and must be incorporated more fully into the policymaking process.

In addition to interagency communication and coordination, environmental policy integration requires changing the institutional cultures within traditional resource departments and agencies. The Department of the Interior contains several major subcultures ranging from the consumption orientation of the Minerals Management Service and the Bureau of Land Management to the more preservationist values of the Fish and Wildlife Service. Secretary Bruce Babbitt is pushing the department toward a more balanced conservation ethic. Employees within the Agriculture Department's Forest Service are forcing a shift in that agency as well to more ecologically sensitive management practices. Under Hazel O'Leary, the Department of Energy is also developing a more transparent and accountable institutional culture, yet the department remains wedded to conventional assumptions about rising energy demand and supply.

The potential for greater coordination and coherence in environmental policymaking will depend heavily on the White House in the foreseeable future. While pressure is mounting for enactment of a new comprehensive environmental statute, it is unlikely that Congress will be able to agree on a single approach. It may be more useful, therefore, to focus on the most important policy issues and a variety of alternatives for improving policy effectiveness.

Key Policy Issues

Although strengthening the institutional capabilities of government is clearly necessary for improved environmental policymaking, this will not obviate the need to make difficult political choices on many contentious issues at both ends of Pennsylvania Avenue. Some of these issues involve environmental problems that have long been discussed but not seriously addressed; others involve problems that have only recently been recognized. The following is an overview of substantive issues likely to occupy Congress and the president in the future.

Energy Consumption and Climate Change

In the mid 1990s energy supplies in the United States were plentiful and real fuel prices were at historically low levels. Partly for this reason, there was little concern for energy conservation or development of alternative energy supplies. The Energy Policy Act of 1992 had provided modest support for alternative fuels and more energy efficient appliances, buildings and industrial equipment, but its principal thrust was toward increasing domestic production of coal, oil, and nuclear power. During his election campaign Bill Clinton expressed strong interest in moving energy policy in a more sustainable direction (see chap. 5). Congress has shown no interest, however, in energy policy issues, and the Clinton administration has largely retreated from its promises. Following a spurt in fuel prices in April 1996, Senate Majority Leader Bob Dole (R-Kan.) called for the repeal of the 4.3-cent-a-gallon gasoline tax Congress approved in 1993, and President Clinton tried to ease prices through release of federally owned oil. Neither focused on the need to reduce the nation's appetite for oil.

There are several reasons to be concerned. First, petroleum imports have risen dramatically in the past decade and now exceed half of total U.S. oil consumption. Under current policies, reliance on imports will continue to increase, reaching 60 percent by early in the twenty-first century. Oil accounts for up to half of our current foreign trade deficit and threatens our national security by maintaining our dependence on Middle East producers. Second, our inefficient use of energy is a threat to our future international economic competitiveness. Other nations such as Japan and Germany have already taken the lead in developing many energy-efficient technologies. Third, and perhaps most important, fossil fuel burning is the principal source of greenhouse gas emissions that may cause disastrous climate changes. The threat of global warming is likely to require a transition to noncarbon fuel sources such as solar and wind power and biomass in the next century.

New scientific evidence underscores the threat of global climate change. Temperature measurements from several sources indicate that global warming resumed in 1994 after a two-year dip attributed to volcanic eruptions and that 1995 may have been the hottest year on record.[7] The Intergovernmental Panel on Climate Change, a U.N.-sponsored group of 2,500 scientists from around the world, issued a report late in 1995 warning that "the balance of evidence suggests that there is a discernible human influence on global climate" and that global warming is likely to set off massive ecological and social disruptions in coming decades if fossil fuel consumption is not greatly reduced.[8]

President Clinton reversed the position of the Bush administration by promising to reduce emissions of greenhouse gases to 1990 levels by the year 2000, thus committing the United States to the goal of the Framework Convention on Climate Change (FCCC), signed at the 1992 Río Conference on Environment and Development.[9] He also promised to establish a specific timetable to meet this target. The "Btu" tax proposed in his first budget was to become the centerpiece of his new strategy, but this proposal was roundly defeated in Congress (see chap. 5). Thereafter Clinton retreated, leaving Vice President Gore to cobble together a makeshift "climate action plan" to meet the requirements of the FCCC. This plan, based largely on voluntary industrial efforts to conserve energy, falls considerably short of achieving the CO_2 goals for the year 2000, as even the administration concedes.[10] There appears to be little if any support for even these measures among congressional Republicans, who have targeted the climate change program for significant budget reductions.

Although the Clinton administration has increased funding for energy conservation and renewable energy technologies, it has not been willing to confront the oil or auto industries. While it launched a partnership with automobile manufacturers to develop a "clean car" that would get three times the mileage of current cars, negotiations with the automakers have failed to achieve consensus on future mileage goals. Rapid growth in sales of trucks and sport utility vehicles, which are subject to a lower mileage standard, have offset past gains.[11] Yet Clinton is unwilling to pursue higher corporate average fuel economy (CAFE) standards, despite campaign promises to the contrary.

As in the Bush administration, the United States is once again in the embarrassing position of dragging its feet on new treaty obligations to reduce CO_2 emissions. At the Berlin conference of parties to the FCCC in March 1995, the American delegation argued for weaker targets and "joint implementation" that would "allow countries to offset their own emissions by investing in clean energy projects or planting trees elsewhere."[12] The final agreement, known as the Berlin mandate, calls for a protocol to be signed at the next major conference in Kyoto, Japan, in 1997 that will set quantified targets and specific timetables for further reductions in greenhouse emissions after 2000.[13] Bill Clinton, or his successor, will thus face a critical test of commitment to global environmental protection early in the next administration.

Biodiversity and Endangered Species

Loss of biodiversity ranks with climate change as the greatest long-term threat to the global environment. Scientists estimate that about 5 percent of all plant and animal species become extinct each decade, which is hundreds of times the historical, or "normal," rate.[14] As in the case of global warming, we are only beginning to understand the complexities of natural ecosystems and their relationships to species preservation. Yet we know that many of the natural systems that support the greatest diversity of species—such as tropical rain forests and coastal estuaries—are under severe development pressure. For this reason, biodiversity was a central focus of the Río conference and resulted in a new international treaty that was signed by all major nations except the United States (see chaps. 5 and 13).

To his credit, President Clinton promptly signed the biodiversity treaty and has sought to develop a national policy for preservation of critical ecosystems. His secretary of interior, Bruce Babbitt, established a National Biological Service to survey the remaining biological resources of the United States. His department has pursued a wide range of new strategies to identify and protect important natural areas before individual species are threatened. The Clinton administration has actively sought to promote compromises over such controversies as preservation of the northern spotted owl in old-growth forests of the Pacific Northwest, restoration of the Florida Everglades, and protection of the California gnatcatcher in coastal sage habitats. In the case of the spotted owl, Clinton convened a forest "summit" and worked out a policy (known as "option 9") that protected most of the disputed old-growth forest while allowing logging in other, less critical, areas.[15]

The spotted owl case is particularly important because it forced a test of the Endangered Species Act (ESA). When the Bush administration attempted to circumvent the law by allowing logging in the owl's habitat after the bird had been designated a threatened species, environmental groups won a federal court order that prohibited all logging in the area (see chap. 8). Other interests, including the Sweet Home Chapter of Communities for a Great Oregon, a pro-logging group, then challenged the ESA in court, claiming that Congress had not intended to prohibit harm to habitats but only the intentional "taking" of the actual species in question. Although a circuit court upheld this interpretation, it was rejected by the U.S. Supreme Court in a landmark decision in 1995.[16]

Despite this victory for environmentalists, the *Sweet Home* case indicated widespread opposition to the ESA by property rights groups and the "Wise Use" movement, backed by timber, mining, and development interests. They launched a major effort in the new Republican Congress in 1995 to rewrite the ESA, which is up for reauthorization.[17] Legislation introduced by Sen. Slade Gorton (R-Wash.) and Rep. Richard Pombo (R-Calif.) would virtually end implementation of the law by requiring prohibitive economic justifications before listing species and compensation of private landowners for loss of development rights.[18] These issues are likely to become increasingly contentious in the future.

Most environmentalists agree that efforts to preserve individual species are likely to fail unless large tracts of habitat are set aside. The urgency of stabilizing habitats to ensure survival of species has also been underscored by a panel of the National Academy of Sciences.[19] There is an emerging consensus in the Clinton administration that whole ecosystems must be protected through a wide variety of collaborative arrangements (see below). Congress should revise the Endangered Species Act to provide incentives for such multiparty voluntary agreements as an alternative to individual species listing when feasible rather than seeking to weaken the goals of the law.

Clean Water and Wetlands

The Clean Water Act (CWA), last amended in 1987, is also up for reauthorization.[20] As in the case of the ESA, the new Republican Congress has worked closely with business and industry lobbyists to rewrite key provisions of the law. A bill that passed the House of Representatives in May 1995 was criticized by environmentalists and the press because it would ease restrictions on discharges of a wide variety of industrial pollutants, halt progress toward control of urban and agricultural water runoff, delay efforts to clean up the Great Lakes, eliminate federal protection of up to 80 percent of all wetlands, and require compensation for regulatory "takings."[21]

Although such draconian revisions are not likely to be enacted, the CWA raises several difficult issues for the future. One is how to control "nonpoint" pollution from farm fields, construction sites, mining, forestry, and urban runoff, which together account for as much as two-thirds of all surface water pollution. Solutions may require tighter regulation of pesticide and fertilizer use as well as new land use controls to protect watersheds. Under the 1987 CWA revisions, states are required to develop plans for nonpoint source controls, but they are not mandatory and Congress has provided little funding for this purpose.

Congress is also phasing out federal wastewater treatment grants to states and, as part of a budget rescission in 1995, eliminated most funding for implementation of the Safe Drinking Water Act (SDWA). Contamination of wells and other drinking-water supplies is a growing problem in the United States as well as in developing nations. Implementation of the SDWA has become highly controversial because its requirements for testing and removal of a long list of possible contaminants pose costs that many small communities cannot afford. Congress will have to decide whether all of the federal controls are necessary to protect public health or whether greater responsibility can be returned to state and local governments. In a rare display of bipartisanship, in early 1996 Congress appeared close to agreement on legislation that would devolve much greater authority to the states.[22]

The most explosive issue in the clean water reauthorization concerns sec. 404, which regulates the dredging and filling of wetlands. After promising a policy of "no net loss" of wetlands during the 1988 campaign, President Bush found himself mired in controversy when members of his staff rejected a proposed revision of the government wetlands manual by the agencies charged with wetlands protection. The new manual redefined various types of wetlands according to scientific criteria such as vegetation and soil chemistry rather than using traditional measurements of standing water. Responding to opposition from a coalition of land developers, farmers, and energy interests, the White House quickly stepped in to block the more restrictive definitions. The Quayle Council proposed language that would have removed more than half of existing wetlands from the definition (see chap. 5). Although this effort failed, Republicans in the 104th Congress are attempting to write new definitions into the Clean Water Act that would allow classification of wetlands according to ecological value but eliminate requirements for preserving all but the most important ones. This approach was rejected by a study of the National Academy of Sciences released just before passage of the House bill in May 1995 on grounds that not enough is known about the ecological functions of wetlands to release most of them from protection. [23]

President Clinton promised a "real no net loss policy" for wetlands during his election campaign and has threatened to veto any legislation weakening the Clean Water Act. However, his administration has bowed to growing criticism from state and local governments as well as from a wide array of property rights groups and development interests by easing enforcement of some wetlands restrictions, especially for small property owners (under five acres). EPA administrator Carol Browner has tried to reduce confrontation by working out voluntary agreements among land developers, farmers, and environmentalists to preserve or restore certain wetlands in exchange for releasing others. But it remains to be seen how effective these restoration projects are and whether pressure will mount to pay compensation to landowners affected by regulatory "takings" (see chap. 8). Wetlands are likely to remain a hot item on the congressional agenda.

Hazardous and Nuclear Waste

The storage, treatment, and disposal of hazardous and toxic wastes present another series of intractable problems in our industrial society. Despite growing efforts by manufacturers to reduce the use of hazardous and toxic materials (see chap. 12), the volume of dangerous waste continues to accumulate rapidly. Many solid and hazardous waste facilities have been closed, while others, such as incinerators, are meeting increasing public opposition. Nuclear power plants built in the 1960s and 1970s are also running out of space for storing spent fuel long before a permanent repository for high-level radioactive wastes is available. It remains uncertain whether the site for such a facility now under study at Yucca Mountain, Nevada, will ever be found acceptable. Interim solutions such as temporary storage in above-ground casks arouse public fears and NIMBY (not in my backyard) resistance. [24] The cleanup of highly contaminated military weapons plants and other federal energy and defense facilities also presents a massive task, while the federal Superfund program for cleaning up abandoned toxic waste sites has fallen far behind schedule (as of early 1996 only about three hundred and fifty of more than twelve hundred sites on the national priority list had been restored). According to one study, cleanup of all military and civilian sites could cost $750 billion or more over the next thirty years.[25]

A major overhaul of our national hazardous and toxic waste laws is considered necessary by many.[26] There is broad agreement in both parties that the Comprehensive Environmental Response, Compensation and Liability ("Superfund") Act must be rewritten. The Superfund program is excessively costly owing to the extensive litigation involved in determining responsibility for cleanups, wasteful spending on elaborate remediation plans, and long delays in implementation. States and local governments have little influence on cleanup goals, often making them victims of unwanted federal actions. During the waning days of the 103d Congress, the Clinton administration came close to brokering a bipartisan compromise for Superfund revision supported by industry, insurance companies, environmentalists, and federal and state officials.[27]

Rather than building on these efforts, the new leaders of the 104th Congress announced their intention to start over in redrafting the Superfund law. Republican lawmakers have put forward proposals that would fundamentally alter its principles and procedures. These include total or partial repeal of retroactive liability for pollution (the "polluter pays" principle); exemption of many potentially responsible parties such as small businesses, banks, and municipalities from liability; and provision of economic incentives for voluntary cleanups or partial rebate of expenditures to those required to pay. Other proposals would freeze the listing of Superfund sites, give states control of cleanup goals, and eliminate supervision of projects by EPA regional offices. Meanwhile, the collection of taxes from oil and chemical companies, which finances the Superfund, was allowed to expire at the end of 1995, requiring shutdown of more than half of current cleanup sites.[28]

This situation cannot be allowed to continue, making it imperative that more moderate leaders such as Sen. John Chafee (R-R.I.), chair of the Senate Environment and Public Works Committee, be allowed to work out a new bipartisan compromise. It is likely that any solution will include greater flexibility in setting site-specific cleanup standards, new dispute resolution procedures for reducing or eliminating litigation, and greater involvement by states and communities in managing projects. EPA administrator Carol Browner has already encouraged such changes in promoting voluntary agreements to clean up less-contaminated land in urban areas known as "brownfields" that can be restored sufficiently for industrial development.

Environmental Justice

Although dating from the same era, the civil rights and environmental movements have had little in common until recently. It is increasingly recognized, however, that low-income and minority groups are disproportionately exposed to environmental hazards such as lead poisoning, industrial air pollution, and toxic waste sites. This is particularly true in poor urban neighborhoods and in the South, but research indicates that it holds for the nation as a whole when factors such as socioeconomic status are controlled (see chap. 11). African Americans, Hispanics, Asians, and Native Americans have formed hundreds of new grassroots organizations to fight pollution in their communities, and mainstream environmental groups have become more sensitive to such inequities. Beginning in the Bush administration and accelerating under Clinton, the EPA and other federal agencies have begun to document unequal patterns of pollution exposure and investigate their causes.

The Clinton administration also established a new Office of Environmental Justice (OEJ) within the EPA to coordinate agency efforts to reduce impacts on minority and low-income populations and to assist communities in environmental cleanup activities. In February 1994 President Clinton issued Executive Order 12898, which called for all federal agencies to develop strategies for achieving environmental justice. The political climate in 1996 was less encouraging for such initiatives, but the problems remain, and both the White House and Congress need to give more attention to environmental inequities and ways to reduce them. This applies to global inequities as well. Striking economic and environmental inequities exist between poor and rich nations (see chap. 15). They can be addressed in part through implementation of Agenda 21, the plan for global sustainable development in the twenty-first century approved at the 1992 Earth summit. These human dimensions of environmental policy and administration are likely to require increasing attention in the future.[29]

International Aid and Cooperation

International cooperation to prevent global climate change, protect the stratospheric ozone layer, and preserve biodiversity is becoming an increasingly important part of the national environmental agenda. Other areas requiring greater collaboration include transboundary pollution, preservation of ocean fisheries, international hazardous waste shipment, export and use of agricultural pesticides and chemicals, and a host of issues relating to nuclear fuel reprocessing, destruction of nuclear weapons, and weapons proliferation. Many of these issues are beginning to be perceived as critical foreign policy and national security concerns. For example, it is recognized that environmental degradation is increasingly a source of local and regional conflict that produces large numbers of "environmental refugees." The potential impacts on the world economy are also staggering.[30]

The Clinton administration has taken a more aggressive stance on most of these issues than its predecessors and has upgraded our institutional capacities for environmental diplomacy.[31] Former senator Timothy Wirth was appointed to a new position as undersecretary of state for global affairs; he has played a leading role at a number of international conferences such as the U.N. Conference on Population and Development held in Cairo in 1994. In a memorandum issued in February 1996, Secretary of State Warren Christopher ordered all State Department divisions to make environmental concerns a top priority in promoting U.S. interests, noting that "environmental initiatives can be important low-cost, high-impact tools in promoting our national interests."[32]

One of the most contentious issues for international environmental policy is support for U.N. and other multilateral family planning and population programs. The Reagan and Bush administrations cut off aid for such programs due to concern that funds could be used to promote abortions. President Clinton restored funding for population programs and increased financial support for other international bodies such as the Global Environment Facility, a fund operated by the World Bank to support environmental projects in developing countries. Unfortunately, the Republican Congress severely cut the budget for these and other foreign assistance programs in 1996.[33] There appears to be little support in Congress for any programs that address the problems of developing nations discussed by Richard Tobin in chapter 15. Indeed, the current majority appears hostile to all international environmental treaties and commitments, raising profound doubts about our ability to lead in the future.[34]

Trade and the Environment

The newest issue on the national agenda is the relationship between international trade and environmental protection. Until recently environmental problems were considered outside the scope of trade negotiations. But passage of the North American Free Trade Agreement (NAFTA) in 1993 and completion of the Uruguay Round of the General Agreement on Tariffs and Trade (GATT) in 1994 raised serious concerns about the potential impacts of free trade on national environmental restrictions. President Clinton refused to sign NAFTA until a side agreement on environmental and labor safeguards was added, but the GATT treaty left such issues to be resolved by the new World Trade Organization (WTO). The experience of the European Union suggests that freer markets and environmental protection need not be incompatible, a point also underscored by David Vogel (see chaps. 14 and 16). The implementation of the new agreements will, however, have to be monitored closely to ensure that they do not undermine existing national environmental protection standards and conservation efforts.[35]

At the same time, global markets for pollution control equipment and energy efficient and environmentally friendly products are expanding rapidly; indeed, the "green technology" market is estimated to be $400 billion annually.[36] During the 1992 campaign Clinton and Gore frequently warned that the United States was falling behind nations such as Germany and Japan in taking advantage of these opportunities. Their administration has subsequently supported a wide range of initiatives to promote environmental technologies and sales abroad (see below). But congressional attempts to curtail these programs and to abolish the commerce and energy departments raise doubts about the future of these policies as well.

New Strategies and Methods

The need to "reinvent government" to encourage innovation and experimentation was a prominent theme during the 1992 elections. Environmental regulation has been singled out as a leading candidate for such experimentation for some time, but relatively few departures have yet been made from the traditional standards-and-enforcement approach adopted in the 1970s. In most areas the EPA is still charged with writing detailed regulations requiring individual polluters to install specific technologies to mitigate emissions or discharges at "the end of the pipe." Such "command and control" regulation of major pollution sources has had some success in improving environmental quality (see chap. 1) and will continue to be needed to protect public health and environmental resources against many immediate threats. But a broad consensus has now developed among economists, business leaders, government officials, and environmental professionals that more efficient and cost-effective methods are necessary if we are to address the expanding environmental agenda of the 1990s and beyond. The following section lists seven areas in which new policy approaches are receiving wide discussion.

Pollution Prevention

Perhaps no idea has received more widespread general support than the wisdom of preventing pollution before it occurs rather than trying to clean it up later. Prevention is often far less expensive for companies and eliminates potential liability. It spares people from harmful exposure to wastes. It is the only way to halt deterioration of the environment in the long run. Yet only a tiny fraction of the EPA's resources is devoted to *prevention,* while the remainder is directed to end-of-the-pipe cleanups (see chap. 7). The reason is that most of the environmental statutes (see app. 1) require after-the-fact controls. They are based on the assumption that environmental problems can be managed without significant changes in existing production technologies and consumption patterns. This assumption can no longer be sustained.[37]

The Bush administration deserves credit for passage of the Pollution Prevention Act of 1990, which established prevention as an EPA priority for the first time and authorized cooperative programs with industry to install energy-efficient lighting and to encourage source reduction of toxic wastes. Hundreds of companies voluntarily participate in these programs mainly because pollution prevention reduces costs. Companies are also becoming more sensitive to their environmental image. The resulting "greening of business" is perhaps the most hopeful sign of current environmental progress (see chap. 12).

Pollution prevention can be extended to all sectors, including energy, transportation, agriculture, and defense. In many cases relatively simple process changes or materials substitution can produce dramatic results at low cost. It is also the most effective strategy for reducing pollution from many small, decentralized sources such as garages and dry cleaners that are difficult to regulate directly. The Clinton administration has extended a number of EPA industrial partnership programs begun during the Bush administration and has required pollution reduction planning throughout the federal government. Reauthorization of laws such as the Resource Conservation and Recovery Act and Clean Water Act provide further opportunities for incorporating incentives for waste reduction and prevention.

Comparative Risk Assessment

Comparative risk assessment is discussed in chapters 7 and 10. The logic of this approach lies in the variable magnitude of risk to public and ecosystem health posed by environmental threats ranging from the deterioration of the ozone layer to urban smog. Environmental policies attempt to reduce these risks, but they do so with wildly different efficiency. Hence a great deal of money can be spent by governments and private parties without an appreciable return in risk reduction, that is, in improved public health and environmental quality.

Comparative risk assessment is intended to facilitate the setting of priorities for action by the EPA and other agencies and thus to increase the rationality of environmental policy. The case for such an approach has been made by the EPA since 1987, and it became a major policy objective under William Reilly in the early 1990s. The agency's Science Advisory Board strongly endorsed comparative risk assessment in its widely read 1990 report *Reducing Risk,* in which it urged the agency to target its environmental protection efforts based on opportunities for the greatest reduction in risk. Since then, the EPA has supported risk assessment projects in each of its regions and in a number of states and communities. The EPA still lacks statutory authority, however, to allocate resources based on such assessments.[38]

More extensive use of risk assessment for setting priorities depends on improved methodologies for measuring risk. As Richard Andrews notes in chapter 10, present methods are subject to significant limitations, which have led to uncertainty about the actual risks posed and thus about the need for corrective action. The uncertainty fuels controversy over the use of these methods to set public policy, for example, over the level of pesticide residues permitted in the nation's food supply or allowable concentrations of chemicals in drinking water. Another major challenge is the need to reconcile public and expert perceptions of risks. The two are often sharply at odds. In some cases the public is more concerned about environmental and health risks (for example, from hazardous wastes and oil spills) than are the experts. In other cases (such as indoor air pollution, drinking-water quality, and loss of biological diversity), the experts are more worried than is the public. More often than not, congressional policies have reflected the public's view of risk. The result is that the EPA is often mandated to devote time and resources to relatively low-priority risks while ignoring greater ones.

Congress should give the EPA more discretion to set priorities based on comparative risk analysis in the years ahead. However, as discussed in chapter 6, the regulatory reform bills stemming from the "Contract with America" were widely criticized as inappropriate and unworkable.[39] Congress must be careful not to politicize risk assessment if it is to become a more useful tool for environmental management. It should avoid mandating specific risk assessment methodologies and procedures and encourage the EPA to utilize a broad range of risk evaluation techniques to focus its efforts where they will do the most good.[40]

Environmental Taxes, Incentives, and Markets

Economists have long espoused the concept of internalizing environmental costs by taxation or other means of pricing "externalities." As A. Myrick Freeman points out in chapter 9, use of such devices as environmental taxes or fees and tradable pollution allowances can often achieve environmental goals more efficiently than command-and-control regulation. In an era of scarce public resources, it makes sense to maximize environmental quality benefits from pollution control expenditures. The idea of utilizing market incentives to encourage behaviors that prevent pollution and conserve resources now has broad support among environmentalists as well as in the business community.[41] Indeed, many believe that if environmental damage were fully accounted for (through "full cost pricing") the level of environmental protection would be much higher than at present.

Energy taxes have been among the most widely discussed market-oriented approaches, and the Btu tax proposed by Clinton was designed to motivate changes in both consumer preferences and industrial production. In the absence of higher fuel prices, energy will continue to be wasted as indicated by a recent surge in sales of light trucks and utility vehicles which get considerably lower gas mileage than cars. Taxes or fees could be designed to discourage use of such gas guzzlers, to reduce use of toxic chemicals and virgin materials, and to discourage generation of solid and hazardous waste. Conversely, tax credits could be offered for a wide range of "green" business practices, and rebates could be given for the purchase of environmentally benign products. European nations are experimenting with a variety of such taxes and incentives.[42]

A more direct way to utilize the marketplace is to encourage the design, manufacture, and sale of "green" consumer products. Many products are already being marketed as environmentally safe because they contain no toxic substances, are energy efficient to operate, or contain recycled materials or are themselves recyclable. Evidence suggests that many consumers prefer buying such products and will often pay at least a modest premium for them, and several green consumer guides have been published. One problem is that environmental advertising is often misleading. Several proposals have been made for federal legislation to regulate environmental claims and to establish a national environmental labeling system comparable to those in European nations (see chap. 14). Ideally, such ecolabels should advise consumers of the environmental costs of products over their entire life-cycle from materials processing and manufacturing to ultimate disposal.

Finally, government subsidies to environmentally destructive activities like timber harvesting on public lands and cheap water supply to western farmers should be eliminated. Secretary of the Interior Bruce Babbitt announced in early 1993 sweeping plans to raise grazing, timber, mining, and water use fees to market levels, reversing a "century of practices that have promoted development of the West at government expense." Although these initiatives have thus far been stymied by western senators and representatives, there is mounting pressure from free-market conservatives and taxpayer groups as well as from environmental liberals to eliminate these forms of corporate welfare. A "Green Scissors" coalition representing such disparate interests has identified potential savings of $39 billion over the next ten to fifteen years from such cuts.[43]

Devolution to States and Communities

One of the most common criticisms of current environmental policy is that it is too heavily centered in Washington. The "Contract with America" and other conservative proposals have called for wholesale return of federal powers to the states. Much of this argument derives from general ideological antipathy toward the federal government and, especially, toward its regulatory authority. However, the argument is not solely ideological. State and local officials have become increasingly critical of the EPA's bureaucratic procedures and have demanded greater flexibility in implementing federal programs. For their part, many environmentalists see demands for devolution as conspiracies to weaken the federal system of regulation built up since 1970 and rightly warn of a "race to the bottom" if states are allowed to set their own standards.

States do vary greatly in their commitment to environmental protection and in their capacity to effectively implement policies. However, as pointed out by Barry Rabe in chapter 2, they have greatly improved their capabilities over the past quarter-century and in many cases are now far more innovative than the federal government. In this light, the National Academy of Public Administration has proposed selective devolution of functions to the states so that the EPA can concentrate its attention on problems of genuinely regional, national, and international significance. For example, the states could be given much greater authority to set cleanup requirements for local Superfund sites and drinking-water protection, while the EPA would maintain surveillance over transboundary problems such as air and water pollution. The agency could practice "differential oversight" in these areas as well, allowing states with good performance records in implementing federal pollution laws greater flexibility than states that have not met federal standards.[44]

Individual companies and communities might also negotiate comprehensive compliance agreements with the EPA that allow them to develop their own methods for meeting pollution prevention and reduction goals. For example, under EPA's "beyond compliance" program currently being tested in some states, companies that exceed federal and state pollution standards are allowed almost complete freedom to devise their own control strategies. In sum, a shift is needed toward national performance standards that allow considerable flexibility in devising strategies for meeting goals at all levels of government.

Collaborative Planning

Within the federal-state structure, there are enormous opportunities for improving environmental performance through new collaborative planning and decisionmaking processes. Collaborative planning involves a search for voluntary, consensual solutions to environmental problems through joint participation by federal, state, and local agencies; business and industry; environmental groups; other interested nongovernmental organizations; and citizens. Such processes can be used to address a wide range of problems such as preservation of wetlands, wildlife habitat, and other natural resources; development of area-wide pollution prevention strategies; and siting of facilities to promote social and racial justice. Such collaborations will require both development of many new intergovernmental partnerships and much greater involvement of local communities in place-specific decisions. [45]

One increasingly popular form of collaborative planning is the development of habitat conservation plans that protect endangered species while permitting some development in surrounding areas. [46] The Clinton administration has encouraged such agreements as an alternative to invoking laws such as the Endangered Species Act, which typically produce extended litigation and conflict. By intervening before an ecosystem becomes so degraded that few options are left, this approach facilitates carefully planned trade-offs between environmental protection and economic growth and thus supports the goal of sustainable development. In the case of large-scale projects such as restoring water flow in the Florida Everglades and cleaning up the Great Lakes, it will be necessary to involve a host of government actors and private parties if the plans are to succeed.

Another form of collaboration involves government-industry or industry-environmental group partnerships to reduce toxic waste, save energy, and prevent other forms of "pollution (several of these programs are discussed in chapter 12). The Clinton administration has launched a number of new programs such as the Common Sense Initiative (to encourage waste reduction in individual industrial sectors) and Project XL (which recognizes companies for exceptional leadership in pollution reduction). Environmental organizations have also collaborated with major corporations in designing pollution prevention programs. For example, the Natural Resources Defense Council is currently working with Amoco Petroleum, Dow Chemical, Monsanto, Rayonier, and the New Jersey Department of Environmental Protection on a Pollution Prevention Pilot Project (4P) that will cut both production and environmental compliance costs while reducing pollution at chemical manufacturing plants.[47]

In the future there will be increasing emphasis on collaboration to promote "sustainable communities." The President's Council on Sustainable Development describes such communities as follows:

> Sustainable communities are cities and towns that prosper because people work together to produce a high quality of life that they want to sustain and constantly improve. . . . In sustainable communities, people are engaged in building a community together. They make decisions for the long term that benefit future generations as well as themselves. They understand that successful long-term solutions require partnerships and a process that allows for representatives of a community's diverse sectors to be involved in discussions, planning, and decisions that respond directly to local needs. They also recognize that some problems cannot be solved within the confines of their community and that working in partnership with others in the region is necessary to deal with them.[48]

In the mid 1990s communities all across the United States—large and small and urban and rural—were beginning to develop their own plans for sustainability. Collaborative planning and decisionmaking could be found in virtually all of these efforts.

Environmental Research and Technology Development

Increased support for environmental science and policy research is essential if we are to deal effectively with the growing list of domestic and global environmental problems demanding attention. More precise and systematic knowledge is needed in many areas of science if we are to set environmental priorities on the basis of relative risks and benefits. Although support for environmental research has recovered from its low point in the Reagan administration, it remains a small fraction of the $71 billion federal R&D budget. Total federal environmental research runs to about $5 billion a year, of which roughly 10 percent finds its way to the EPA. The rest is divided among twenty other federal agencies. Even with the higher levels of support over the past few years, the scientific community argues persuasively for increasing environmental research dollars.[49]

The largest spending increase in recent years was for global climate research, which rose fivefold to more than $1 billion in the early 1990s. Yet by FY 1996 53 percent of federal R&D was still devoted to military purposes despite the demise of the Soviet Union and the end of the cold war. Moreover, the 104th Congress showed little enthusiasm for investment of public funds in science and technology. Global change research was a special target of congressional Republicans, who expressed great skepticism about the seriousness of the problems faced. Overall environmental research programs were initially slated for an 18 percent budget cut, with many programs suffering cuts of 50 percent or more.[50] The Clinton administration proposed significant increases for environmental R&D in its FY 1997 budget, but Congress may well reduce those amounts significantly.[51]

Despite the less than positive political climate, we now have an opportunity to redirect R&D in many of the government's seven hundred research laboratories toward environmental and energy problems. In another promising initiative, in 1994 the Clinton administration proposed a "green industrial policy" to promote the development and adoption of environmental technologies. Among other actions, the administration hoped to assist in the commercialization of new products and help promote sales of green technologies overseas. Congress has been distinctly cool to the idea of governmental promotion of environmental technologies. Where the program received $139 million in FY 1995 and Clinton favored raising it to $192 million in 1996, Congress chose to appropriate only $46 million.[52] Nevertheless, these kinds of proposals illustrate what could be done through governmental sponsorship of applied environmental research.

One area in which more R&D could pay the greatest dividends is in developing highly energy-efficient technologies and renewable energy sources. A 1991 report by four major environmental and energy organizations concluded that the United States could reduce its energy consumption by 30 percent to 50 percent and cut CO_2 emissions by as much as 71 percent over the next forty years if it developed renewable energy technologies. Moreover, such a sustainable energy transition would result in at least *$1.8 trillion* in savings to the economy.[53] Energy conservation and renewable energy production are relatively labor-intensive compared with current practices, so such a transition could create substantial employment. One study calculates that a major effort in this direction could lead to a net increase of 1 million jobs by 2010.[54] Such findings should be rapidly assessed and exploited by government laboratories in cooperation with private industry.

Environmental Accounting

Many of our difficulties in utilizing economic efficiency criteria to guide environmental policy stem from the inaccuracy of our accounting systems in measuring environmental costs and benefits. The national indexes of output, gross national product (GNP) or gross domestic product (GDP), have come under increasing criticism. Although widely used as primary indicators of the state of our economy and national welfare, they count all expenditures for pollution control and cleanup as part of our output of goods and services but do not subtract the economic value of losses caused by environmental degradation and depletion of nonrenewable resources.[55] Increased pollution thus counts positively rather than negatively, while depreciation of environmental capital is ignored. As Vice President Gore put it, "For all practical purposes, GNP treats the rapid and reckless destruction of the environment as a good thing!"[56]

A number of economists and international agencies, including the World Bank, have been developing alternative measures of welfare that more accurately value environmental goods and services and overall quality of life. The United States does considerably less well on some of these scales than on conventional economic indexes. The Commerce Department has begun to use "satellite accounts" for assessing the depletion of natural and environmental resources in order to develop more accurate measures of net domestic product. Until we begin to think differently about basic economic indicators, we are unlikely to make genuine progress toward sustainable development.

Rethinking Environmental Politics

Broadening the definition of environmental policy to include economic sustainability and social justice presents great challenges and opportunities for political action. The monumental scope of the ecological problems now recognized is mind-boggling and calls for action on nearly every front. Insofar as the fundamental problems are long term and global, they are likely to command an increasing share of intellectual and financial resources for decades to come. The concept of sustainable development touches every aspect of human life, from individual life-styles and tastes to the corporate strategies of multinationals. We are still in the early stages of conceptualizing many of the implications, but they undoubtedly carry far beyond our preoccupations of the past two decades with national regulation of specific types of pollutants or preservation of individual species and landscapes.

Environmental policy itself thus has to be rethought in "ecological" terms; that is, reconsidered in relation to the larger social, economic, political, and moral systems within which it is embedded. To be successful, environmentalists will be challenged to develop new skills and broaden their understanding of other human values. As Robert Paehlke suggests in chapter 4, there is great potential for integrating and balancing the "three Es"— environment, economy, and ethics. But alliances with civil rights, social justice, and community development groups may require greater tolerance of differences and, in many cases, more flexibility and modesty in advocating particular solutions.[57] A willingness to try less intrusive and centralized approaches such as market incentives and local education and consensus building might often lead to superior results. At the same time, we need to become much more aware of our responsibilities to the global ecological system.

A strong case can be made, as Christopher Bosso does in chapter 3, that an environmental "movement" no longer exists. Instead, thousands of independent local community organizations and protest groups are proliferating alongside the two dozen or so large and well-established national conservation and environmental organizations in Washington, D.C. Although the latter are often effective in lobbying on national policy, pressure from the grassroots organizations may be even more important in mobilizing public opinion and effecting change. States and local communities will play a larger role in fashioning environmental solutions in the future. In any case, the remainder of the 1990s will likely bring increased pluralism and fragmentation among environmental groups working at different levels on different issues.

Offsetting this trend, environmentalists at all levels should benefit from rapid expansion of the Internet. Electronic access to vast quantities of environmental information is now easily available to anyone with a computer and modem. World Wide Web sites dealing with environmental issues extend from government agencies such as the EPA to the Natural Resources Defense Council, and the development of green software, databases, networks, and bulletin boards has been growing rapidly. Although the full effects of using these technologies and databases remain unclear, there are enormous opportunities for citizens to communicate with each other and to circulate reports and data across computer networks.

Governing the Future

It has been said that for the first time in evolutionary history human beings have achieved a greater measure of influence over the future of their planet than evolution itself. If this is so, we have no alternative but to decide what kind of future we want. One possibility is to continue on our present course of human development. A growing world consensus holds, however, that this course cannot be sustained without triggering catastrophic changes in the Earth's natural systems. A 1992 report of the U.S. National Academy of Sciences and the Royal Society of London opened with a dire warning: "If current predictions of population growth prove accurate and patterns of human activity on the planet remain unchanged, science and technology may not be able to prevent either irreversible degradation of the environment or continued poverty for much of the world."[58] We do not know whether changes in the planetary life support system, such as deterioration of the atmospheric ozone layer, are irreversible. Yet most environmental experts believe we have time to preserve our essential life support systems if we act with sufficient foresight in the next few decades.

Doing so will demand far more international cooperation and "governance" than we now have.[59] The challenges we face are ultimately human and political: meeting basic human needs, limiting population growth, restricting consumption of nonrenewable resources, building a sense of world community, and negotiating mutually beneficial agreements among nations. These problems can be resolved only with a much longer time horizon than we are accustomed to in democratic societies. Political leadership is therefore essential. Democracies have proved capable of sustaining national and international efforts to defeat enemies in war and to contain them for decades in peacetime. But our success in defeating communism hardly means "the end of history," as Francis Fukuyama has suggested.[60] Rather, the coming decades will bring even more pressing challenges if we are to stabilize life on the planet for ourselves and for the generations to come.

Notes

The chapter epigraph quotes the "Vision Statement" from the report of the President's Council on Sustainable Development, *Sustainable America: A New Consensus for Prosperity, Opportunity, and a Healthy Environment for the Future* (Washington, D.C.: GPO, 1996), iv; and Lester R. Brown, "The Acceleration of History," in *State of the World 1996*, ed. Lester Brown et al. (Washington, D.C.: Worldwatch Institute, 1996), 3.

1. World Commission on Environment and Development, *Our Common Future* (New York: Oxford University Press, 1987).
2. *Choosing a Sustainable Future: The Report of the National Commission on the Environment* (Washington, D.C.: Island Press, 1993), xi.
3. *Partnerships to Progress: The Report of the President's Commission on Environmental Quality* (Washington, D.C.: President's Commission on Environmental Quality, January 1993). See also Business Council for Sustainable Development, Stephen Schmidheiney, chair, *Changing Course: A Global Business Perspective on Development and Environment* (Cambridge, Mass.: MIT Press, 1992).
4. President's Council on Sustainable Development, *Sustainable America*, 1.
5. For overviews of the Republican agenda, see Margaret Kriz, "A New Shade of Green," *National Journal*, March 18, 1995, 661-665; Kriz, "Out of the Wilderness," *National Journal*, April 8, 1995, 864-869; and Bob Benenson, "GOP Sets the 104th Congress on New Regulatory Course," *Congressional Quarterly Weekly Report*, June 17, 1995, 1693-1701.
6. National Academy of Public Administration, *Setting Priorities, Getting Results: A New Direction for EPA* (Washington, D.C.: NAPA, 1995).
7. William K. Stevens, "A Global Warming Resumed in 1994, Climate Data Show," *New York Times*, January 27, 1995; Stevens, "'95 the Hottest Year on Record as the Global Trend Keeps Up," *New York Times*, January 4, 1996.
8. Stevens, "Experts Confirm Human Role in Global Warming," *New York Times*, September 10, 1995; Stevens, "Scientists Say Earth's Warming Could Set Off Wide Disruptions," *New York Times*, September 18, 1995; Stevens, "In Rain and Temperature Data, New Signs of Global Warming," *New York Times*, September 26, 1995.
9. Richard L. Berke, "Clinton Supports Two Major Steps for Environment," *New York Times*, April 22, 1993.
10. President William J. Clinton and Vice President Albert Gore Jr., *The Climate Change Action Plan* (Washington, D.C.: White House, October 1993); William K. Stevens, "With Energy Tug of War, U.S. Is Missing Its Goals," *New York Times*, November 28, 1995.
11. James Bennet, "Truck's Popularity Undermining Gains in U.S. Fuel Savings," *New York Times*, September 5, 1995; Agis Salpukas, "What's Next, Tail Fins?" *New York Times*, February 15, 1996.
12. Christopher Flavin, "Facing Up to the Risks of Climate Change," *State of the World 1996*, ed. Brown et al., 36.
13. Michael Grubb and Dean Anderson, eds., *The Emerging International Regime for Climate Change: Structures and Options after Berlin* (London: Royal Institute of International Affairs, 1995).
14. Michael L. McKinney and Robert M. Schoch, *Environmental Science: Systems and Solutions* (St. Paul: West Publishing, 1996), 317. Estimates range from 1 to 11 percent, with 5 percent being about the average. At this rate, "as many as half the world's species could be extinct sometime in the twenty-first century."
15. For an excellent analysis of Clinton's timber policies, see Margaret Kriz, "Timber!," *National Journal*, February 3, 1996, 252-257.
16. John H. Cushman Jr., "Environmentalists Win Victory, but Action by Congress May Interrupt the Celebration," *New York Times*, June 30, 1995.
17. Bob Benenson, "Endangered Species Act Comes under the Gun," *Congressional Quarterly Weekly Report*, March 18, 1995; Kriz, "Out of the Wilderness"; Timothy Egan, "Industry Reshapes Endangered Species Act," *New York Times*, April 13, 1995.

18. William K. Stevens, "Future of Endangered Species Act in Doubt as Law Is Debated," *New York Times*, May 16, 1995; "Conservatives Tug at Endangered Species Act," *New York Times*, May 28, 1995; and Margaret Kriz, "Caught in the Act," *National Journal*, December 16, 1995, 3090-3094.

19. National Academy of Sciences, National Research Council, *Science and the Endangered Species Act* (Washington, D.C.: National Academy Press, 1995); John H. Cushman Jr., "Quick Action on Protection of Habitats Is Urged," *New York Times*, May 25, 1995.

20. For an excellent overview of the issues, see Debra S. Knopman and Richard A. Smith, "Twenty Years of the Clean Water Act," *Environment* 35 (January-February 1993): 17-20, 34-41.

21. John H. Cushman Jr., "Lobbyists Helped the G.O.P. in Revising Clean Water Act," *New York Times*, March 22, 1995; Cushman, "House Panel Backs Easier Water Standards," *New York Times*, March 30, 1995; and Bob Benenson, "Water Bill Wins House Passage, May Not Survive in Senate," *Congressional Quarterly Weekly Report*, May 20, 1995, 1413.

22. Margaret Kriz, "Drinks All Around," *National Journal*, November 18, 1995, 2861-2864; and Allan Freedman, "Drinking Water Bill Imperiled by House Delays, Divisions," *Congressional Quarterly Weekly Report*, April 6, 1996, 935-936.

23. John H. Cushman Jr., "Scientists Reject Criteria for Wetlands Bill," *New York Times*, May 10, 1995. On the Quayle Council's role, see Joseph Alper, "War over the Wetlands: Ecologists v. the White House," *Science* 257 (August 21, 1992): 1043-1044.

24. William J. Broad, "Deadly Nuclear Waste Piles Up with No Clear Solution at Hand," *New York Times*, March 14, 1995. See also James Flynn et al., *One Hundred Centuries of Solitude: Redirecting America's High-level Nuclear Waste Policy* (Boulder: Westview, 1995).

25. Milton Russell, E. William Colglazier, and Bruce E. Tonn, "The U.S. Hazardous Waste Legacy," *Environment* 34 (July-August 1992): 12-14, 34-39.

26. See especially Daniel Mazmanian and David Morell, *Beyond Superfailure: America's Toxics Policy for the 1990s* (Boulder: Westview, 1992); and Donald Munton, ed., *Siting by Choice: Waste Facilities, NIMBY, and Volunteer Communities* (Washington, D.C.: Georgetown University Press, 1996).

27. John H. Cushman Jr., "Administration Plans Revision to Ease Toxic Cleanup Criteria," *New York Times*, January 31, 1994; and Margaret Kriz, "How the Twain Met," *National Journal*, June 4, 1994.

28. Allan Freedman, "Superfund Negotiators Hope for Bipartisan Compromise," *Congressional Quarterly Weekly Report*, April 20, 1996, 1040-1041; John H. Cushman Jr., "Program to Clean Toxic Waste Sites Is Left in Turmoil," *New York Times*, January 15, 1996.

29. See chap. 11 and Aaron Sachs, "Upholding Human Rights and Environmental Justice," in *State of the World 1996*, ed. Brown et al., 133-151.

30. Norman Myers, *Ultimate Security* (New York: Norton, 1993); Hal Kane, "Leaving Home," in *State of the World 1995*, ed. Brown et al., 132-149.

31. Steven Greenhouse, "The Greening of American Diplomacy," *New York Times*, October 9, 1995.

32. Quoted in *Greenwire*, February 20, 1996.

33. Robin Toner, "Clinton Orders Reversal of Abortion Restrictions Left by Reagan and Bush," *New York Times*, January 23, 1993; and Barbara Crossette, "U.S. Aid Cutbacks Endangering Population Programs, U.N. Agencies Say," *New York Times*, February 16, 1996.

34. See, e.g., William K. Stevens, "G.O.P. Seeks to Delay Ban on Chemical Harming Ozone," *New York Times*, September 21, 1995.

35. See Hilary F. French, *Costly Tradeoffs: Reconciling Trade and the Environment*, Worldwatch Paper 113 (March 1993); and U.S. Congress, Office of Technology Assessment, *Trade and the Environment: Conflicts and Opportunities* (Washington, D.C.: GPO, May 1992).

36. *Greenwire*, February 20, 1996. See also Curtis Moore and Alan Miller, *Green Gold: Japan, Germany, the United States, and the Race for Environmental Technology* (Boston: Beacon, 1994).

37. See Joel S. Hirschhorn and Kirsten U. Oldenburg, *Prosperity without Pollution* (New York: Van Nostrand Reinhold, 1991); Richard Andrews, "Heading Off Potential Problems," *EPA Journal* 18 (May-June 1992): 41-45; and Business Council for Sustainable Development, *Changing Course.*

38. See NAPA, *Setting Priorities*, chap. 5.

39. John H. Cushman Jr., "Republicans Clear-Cut Regulatory Timberland," *New York Times*, March 5, 1995.

40. See NAPA, *Setting Priorities*, chap. 3; and J. Clarence Davies, ed., *Comparing Environmental Risks: Tools for Setting Government Priorities* (Washington, D.C.: Resources for the Future, 1996).

41. See, e.g., David Malin Roodman, "Harnessing the Market for the Environment," in *State of the World 1996*, ed. Brown et al., 168-187; Robert Repetto, Roger C. Dower, Robin Jenkins, and Jacqueline Geoghegan, *Green Fees: How a Tax Shift Can Work for the Environment and the Economy* (Washington, D.C.: World Resources Institute, 1992).

42. Organisation for Economic Co-operation and Development, *Environmental Taxes in OECD Countries* (Paris: OECD, 1995).

43. Jill Lancelot and Ralph De Gennaro, "'Green Scissors' Snip $33 Billion," *New York Times*, January 31, 1995.

44. NAPA, *Setting Priorities*, chap. 4.

45. President's Council on Sustainable Development, *Sustainable America*, chap. 4, "Strengthening Communities." See also DeWitt John, *Civic Environmentalism: Alternatives to Regulation in States and Communities* (Washington, D.C.: CQ Press, 1994).

46. See Timothy Beatley, *Habitat Conservation Planning: Endangered Species and Urban Growth* (Austin: University of Texas Press, 1994); and Reed F. Noss and Allen Y. Cooperrider, *Saving Nature's Legacy: Protecting and Restoring Biodiversity* (Washington, D.C.: Island Press, 1994).

47. President's Council on Sustainable Development, *Sustainable America*, 30.

48. Ibid., 85-86.

49. Carnegie Commission on Science, Technology, and Government, *Environmental Research and Development: Strengthening the Federal Infrastructure* (New York: Carnegie Commission, December 1992).

50. Linda E. Greer and Christopher P. van Loben Sels with Gerard Piel, "Formula for Failure: Consequences of Proposed Federal Science Funding Cuts" (Washington, D.C.: Natural Resources Defense Council, September 1995).

51. Andrew Lawler and Jeffrey Mervis, "Battle Lines Drawn for 1997 R&D Budget," *Science* 271 (March 22, 1996): 1658; and Colin Norman, "House Puts Its Stamp on the Budget," *Science* 269 (August 11, 1995): 748-749.

52. See Al Gore, "Environmental Technologies for a Sustainable Future," *EPA Journal* 20 (Fall 1994): 6-8. The report was "Technology for a Sustainable Future" (1994). On the budget decisions, see Paul Blustein, "Pulling the Rug on High-Tech Industrial Policy," *Washington Post National Weekly Edition*, December 25-31, 1995.

53. Alliance to Save Energy, American Council for an Energy-Efficient Economy, Natural Resources Defense Council, and Union for Concerned Scientists (UCS), *America's Energy Choices* (Cambridge: UCS, 1991).

54. Howard Geller, John DeCicco, and Skip Laitner, *Energy Efficiency and Job Creation* (Washington, D.C.: American Council for an Energy-Efficient Economy, 1992); and Joseph J. Romm and Charles B. Curtis, "Mideast Oil Forever?" *Atlantic Monthly* 277 (April 1996): 57-74.

55. See Robert Repetto, "Earth in the Balance Sheet: Incorporating Natural Resources in National Income Accounts," *Environment* 34 (September 1992): 12-20, 43-45; Herman E. Daly and John B. Cobb Jr., *For the Common Good* (Boston: Beacon, 1989),

62-84; and Clifford Cobb, Ted Halstead, and Jonathan Rowe, "If the Economy Is Up, Why Is America Down?" *Atlantic Monthly* 276 (October 1995): 59-78.

56. Gore, *Earth in the Balance,* 185.

57. See, for example, Martin Lewis, *Green Delusions: An Environmentalist Critique of Radical Environmentalism* (Durham, N.C.: Duke University Press, 1992); and Robert C. Paehlke, *Environmentalism and the Future of Progressive Politics* (New Haven: Yale University Press, 1989).

58. Quoted in Lester Brown, "A New Era Unfolds," *State of the World 1993,* ed. Lester Brown et al. (New York: Norton, 1993), 3.

59. See Lamont C. Hempel, *Environmental Governance: The Global Challenge* (Washington, D.C. Island Press, 1996).

60. Francis Fukuyama, *The End of History and the Last Man* (New York: Free Press, 1992).

Appendix 1 Major Laws on the Environment, 1969–1996

Legislation	Implementing Agency	Key Provisions
		Nixon Administration
National Environmental Policy Act of 1969, PL 91-190	All federal agencies	Declared a national policy to "encourage productive and enjoyable harmony between man and his environment"; required environmental impact statements; created Council on Environmental Quality (CEQ).
Resources Recovery Act of 1970, PL 91-512	Health, Education and Welfare Department (later Environmental Protection Agency)	Set up a program of demonstration and construction grants for innovative solid waste management systems; provided technical and financial assistance to state and local agencies in developing resource recovery and waste disposal systems.
Clean Air Act Amendments of 1970, PL 91-604	Environmental Protection Agency (EPA)	Required administrator to set national primary and secondary air quality standards and certain emission limits; required states to develop implementation plans by specific dates; required reductions in automobile emissions.
Federal Water Pollution Control Act (Clean Water Act) Amendments of 1972, PL 92-500	EPA	Set national water quality goals; established pollutant discharge permit system; increased federal grants to states to construct waste treatment plants.
Federal Environmental Pesticides Control Act of 1972 (amended the Federal Insecticide, Fungicide, and Rodenticide Act of 1947), PL 92-516	EPA	Required registration of all pesticides in U.S. commerce; allowed administrator to cancel or suspend registration under specified circumstances.
Marine Protection Act of 1972, PL 92-532	EPA	Regulated dumping of waste materials into the oceans and coastal waters.

(Continued on next page)

Appendix 1 *(Continued)*

Legislation	Implementing Agency	Key Provisions
Coastal Zone Management Act of 1972, PL 92-583	Office of Coastal Zone Management, Commerce Department	Authorized federal grants to the states to develop coastal zone management plans under federal guidelines.
Endangered Species Act of 1973, PL 93-205	Fish and Wildlife Service, Interior Department	Broadened federal authority to protect all "threatened" as well as "endangered" species; authorized federal grants to assist state programs; required coordination among all federal agencies.
		Ford Administration
Safe Drinking Water Act of 1974, PL 93-523	EPA	Authorized federal government to set standards to safeguard the quality of public drinking water supplies and to regulate state programs for protecting underground water sources.
Toxic Substances Control Act of 1976, PL 94-469	EPA	Authorized premarket testing of chemical substances; allowed EPA to ban or regulate the manufacture, sale, or use of any chemical presenting an "unreasonable risk of injury to health or environment"; prohibited most uses of PCBs.
Federal Land Policy and Management Act of 1976, PL 94-579	Bureau of Land Management, Interior Department	Gave Bureau of Land Management authority to manage public lands for long-term benefits; officially ended policy of conveying public lands into private ownership.
Resource Conservation and Recovery Act of 1976, PL 94-580	EPA	Required EPA to set regulations for hazardous waste treatment, storage, transportation, and disposal; provided assistance for state hazardous waste programs under federal guidelines.
National Forest Management Act of 1976, PL 94-588	U.S. Forest Service, Agriculture Department	Gave statutory permanence to national forest lands and set new standards for their management; restricted timber harvesting to protect soil and watersheds; limited clearcutting.

Surface Mining Control and Reclamation Act of 1977, PL 95-87	Interior Department	Established environmental controls over strip mining, limited mining on farmland, alluvial valleys, and slopes; required restoration of land to original contours.
Clean Air Act Amendments of 1977, PL 95-95	EPA	Amended and extended Clean Air Act; postponed deadlines for compliance with auto emission and air quality standards; set new standards for "prevention of significant deterioration" in clean air areas.
Clean Water Act Amendments of 1977, PL 95-217	EPA	Extended deadlines for industry and cities to meet treatment standards; set national standards for industrial pretreatment of wastes; increased funding for sewage treatment construction grants and gave states flexibility in determining priorities.
Public Utility Regulatory Policies Act of 1978, PL 95-617	Energy Department, states	Provided for Energy Department and Federal Energy Regulatory Commission regulation of electric and natural gas utilities and crude oil transportation systems in order to promote energy conservation and efficiency; allowed small cogeneration and renewable energy projects to sell power to utilities.
Alaska National Interest Lands Conservation Act of 1980, PL 96-487	Interior Department, Agriculture Department	Protected 102 million acres of Alaskan land as national wilderness, wildlife refuges, and parks.
Comprehensive Environmental Response, Compensation, and Liability Act of 1980 (CERCLA), PL 96-510	EPA	Authorized federal government to respond to hazardous waste emergencies and to clean up chemical dump sites; created $1.6 billion "Superfund"; established liability for cleanup costs.

Reagan Administration

Nuclear Waste Policy Act of 1982, PL 97-425; Nuclear Waste Policy Amendments Act of 1987, PL 100-203	Energy Department	Established a national plan for the permanent disposal of high-level nuclear waste and authorized the Energy Department to site, obtain a license for, construct, and operate geologic repositories for spent fuel from commercial nuclear power plants. Amendments in 1987 specified Yucca Mountain, Nevada, as the sole national site to be studied.

(*Continued on next page*)

Appendix 1 *(Continued)*

Legislation	Implementing Agency	Key Provisions
Resource Conservation and Recovery Act Amendments of 1984, PL 98-616	EPA	Revised and strengthened EPA procedures for regulating hazardous waste facilities; authorized grants to states for solid and hazardous waste management; prohibited land disposal of certain hazardous liquid wastes; required states to consider recycling in comprehensive solid waste plans.
Food Security Act of 1985 (the Farm Bill), PL 99-198	Agriculture Department	Limited federal program benefits for producers of commodities on highly erodible land or converted wetlands; established a conservation reserve program; authorized Agriculture Department technical assistance for subsurface water quality preservation; revised and extended the Soil and Water Conservation Act (1977) programs through the year 2008.
Safe Drinking Water Act of 1986, PL 99-339	EPA	Reauthorized the Safe Drinking Water Act of 1974 and revised EPA safe drinking water programs, including grants to states for drinking water standards enforcement and groundwater protection programs; accelerated EPA schedule for setting standards for maximum contaminant levels of eighty-three toxic pollutants.
Superfund Amendments and Reauthorization Act of 1986 (SARA), PL 99-499	EPA	Provided $8.5 billion through 1991 to clean up the nation's most dangerous abandoned chemical waste dumps; set strict standards and timetables for cleaning up such sites; required that industry provide local communities with information on hazardous chemicals used or emitted.
Clean Water Act Amendments of 1987, PL 100-4	EPA	Amended the Federal Water Pollution Control Act of 1972 and extended and revised EPA water pollution control programs, including grants to states for construction of wastewater treatment facilities and implementation of mandated nonpoint-source pollution management plans; expanded EPA enforcement authority; established a national estuary program.

Global Climate Protection Act of 1987, PL 100–204	State Department	Authorized the State Department to develop an approach to the problems of global climate change; created an intergovernmental task force to develop U.S. strategy for dealing with the threat posed by global warming.
Ocean Dumping Act of 1988, PL 100–688	EPA	Amended the Marine Protection, Research, and Sanctuaries Act of 1972 to end all ocean disposal of sewage sludge and industrial waste by December 31, 1991; revised EPA regulation of ocean dumping by establishing dumping fees, permit requirements, and civil penalties for violations.

Bush Administration

Oil Pollution Prevention, Response, Liability, and Compensation Act of 1990, PL 101–380	Transportation Department, Commerce Department	Sharply increased liability limits for oil spill cleanup costs and damages; required double hulls on oil tankers and barges by 2015; required federal government to direct cleanups of major spills; required increased contingency planning and preparedness for spills; preserved states' rights to adopt more stringent liability laws and state oil spill compensation funds.
Pollution Prevention Act of 1990, PL 101–508	EPA	Established Office of Pollution Prevention in EPA to coordinate agency efforts at source reduction; created voluntary program to improve lighting efficiency; stated waste minimization was to be primary means of hazardous waste management; promoted voluntary industry reduction of hazardous waste; mandated source reduction and recycling report to accompany annual toxics release inventory under SARA (see above).
Clean Air Act Amendments of 1990, PL 101–549	EPA	Amended the Clean Air Act of 1970 by setting new requirements and deadlines of three to twenty years for major urban areas to meet federal clean air standards; imposed new, stricter emissions standards for motor vehicles and mandated cleaner fuels; required reduction in emission of sulfur dioxide and nitrogen oxides by power plants to limit acid deposition and created a market system of emission allowances; required regulation to set emission limits for all major sources of toxic or hazardous air pollutants and listed 189 chemicals to be regulated; prohibited the use of chlorofluorocarbons (CFCs) by the year 2000 and set phaseout of other ozone-depleting chemicals.

(Continued on next page)

Legislation	Implementing Agency	Key Provisions
Intermodal Surface Transportation Efficiency Act of 1991 (ISTEA), PL 102-240	Transportation Department	Authorized $151 billion over six years for transportation, including $31 billion for mass transit; required statewide and metropolitan long-term transportation planning; authorized states and communities to use transportation funds for public transit that reduces air pollution and energy use consistent with Clean Air Act of 1990; required community planners to analyze land use and energy implications of transportation projects they review.
Energy Policy Act of 1992, PL 102-486	Energy Department	Comprehensive energy act designed to reduce U.S. dependency on imported oil. Mandated restructuring of the electric utility industry to promote competition; encouraged energy conservation and efficiency; promoted renewable energy and alternative fuels for cars; eased licensing requirements for nuclear power plants; authorized extensive energy research and development.
The Omnibus Water Act of 1992, PL 102-575	Interior Department	Authorized completion of major water projects in the West; revised the Central Valley Project in California to allow transfer of water rights to urban areas and to encourage conservation through a tiered pricing system that allocates water more flexibly and efficiently; mandated extensive wildlife and environmental protection, mitigation, and restoration programs.

Clinton Administration

In the first two years of the Clinton administration, the 103d Congress (1993-1994) failed to enact any new major environmental policies, although in 1994 it approved the California Desert Protection Act. That act set aside some 7.5 million acres of protected wilderness, or about one-third of California's desert terrain. At the time this book was going to press, political stalemate between the Congress and the Clinton White House had prevented final action on renewal of any of the major environmental statutes, most of which were up for reauthorization in 1995 or 1996. These included the Endangered Species Act, Clean Water Act, Safe Drinking Water Act, and CERCLA, among others (see chap. 6). Of these the Safe Drinking Water Act had the best prospects for approval in 1996. Readers who would like a brief description of any legislation that the 104th Congress eventually enacts, or statutes approved by succeeding Congresses, should consult *Congressional Quarterly Weekly Report* or Congressional Quarterly's annual *Almanac*.

Appendix 2 Federal Spending on Natural Resources and the Environment, Selected Fiscal Years, 1980–1996 (in billions of dollars)

Budget item	1980	1984	1988	1992	1994	1995	1996 (Est.)
Water resources	4.085 (7.273)	3.781 (5.405)	4.295 (5.528)	4.768 (5.176)	5.340 (5.340)	4.212 (4.109)	4.048 (3.855)
Conservation and land management	1.302 (2.318)	1.389 (1.985)	2.650 (3.411)	4.652 (5.050)	5.190 (5.190)	5.392 (5.260)	4.659 (4.437)
Recreational resources	1.642 (2.923)	1.453 (2.077)	1.647 (2.120)	2.690 (2.920)	2.792 (2.792)	2.734 (2.667)	2.503 (2.384)
Pollution control and abatement	4.672 (8.318)	4.037 (5.770)	4.932 (6.347)	6.605 (7.171)	6.595 (6.595)	5.880 (5.737)	6.638 (6.322)
Other natural resources	1.395 (2.484)	1.622 (2.318)	1.852 (2.384)	2.575 (2.796)	2.770 (2.770)	2.831 (2.762)	2.821 (2.687)
Total	13.096 (23.315)	12.282 (17.556)	15.376 (19.789)	21.290 (23.114)	22.687 (22.687)	21.049 (20.535)	20.669 (19.685)

Sources: Office of Management and Budget, *Historical Tables, Budget of the United States Government Fiscal Year 1996* (Washington, D.C.: GPO, 1995); and *Analytical Perspectives, Budget of the United States Government Fiscal Year 1997* (Washington, D.C.: GPO, 1996).

Note: The upper figure represents budget authority in nominal dollars. Actual budget outlays usually differ only slightly from these amounts. Figures for 1980 are provided to indicate pre-Reagan administration spending bases. The lower figure in parentheses represents budget authority in constant 1994 dollars. Figures for 1995 and 1996 are deflated using an estimate of 2.5 percent a year. Amounts are adjusted to 1994 dollars using implicit price deflators for federal government purchases of nondefense goods and services as calculated by the Bureau of Economic Analysis, Department of Commerce.

[a] FY 1995 amounts reflect mid 1995 rescissions and are final budget authority for 1995. Figures for FY 1996 estimates are taken from the Clinton administration's FY 1997 budget submitted to Congress in early 1996. They are close to the amounts agreed to by the White House and Congress in late April 1996 after extended negotiation.

Appendix 3   Budgets of Selected Environmental and Natural Resource Agencies (in billions of dollars)

Agency	1975	1980	1985	1990	1994	1995[a]	1996[a] (Est.)
Environmental Protection Agency operating budget[b]	0.850 (2.167)	1.269 (2.259)	1.340 (1.827)	1.901 (2.215)	2.484 (2.484)	2.471 (2.411)	2.413 (2.298)
Interior Department total budget	3.818 (9.732)	4.678 (8.328)	5.016 (6.840)	6.690 (7.795)	7.460 (7.460)	7.542 (7.358)	6.856 (6.530)
Selected Agencies:							
Bureau of Land Management	0.400 (1.019)	0.919 (1.636)	0.800 (1.090)	1.226 (1.429)	1.166 (1.166)	1.180 (1.151)	1.137 (1.083)
Fish and Wildlife Service	0.207 (0.528)	0.435 (0.775)	0.586 (0.798)	1.133 (1.320)	1.207 (1.207)	1.278 (1.247)	1.223 (1.165)
National Park Service	0.416 (1.060)	0.531 (0.946)	1.005 (1.371)	1.275 (1.485)	1.532 (1.532)	1.453 (1.418)	1.479 (1.409)
Office of Surface Mining	NA	0.180 (0.320)	0.377 (0.515)	0.295 (0.344)	0.308 (0.308)	0.293 (0.286)	0.314 (0.299)
Forest Service	0.956 (2.436)	2.250 (4.005)	2.116 (2.886)	3.473 (4.047)	3.555 (3.555)	3.613 (3.525)	3.083 (2.936)
Army Corps of Engineers (civilian)	1.449 (3.694)	3.234 (5.757)	2.883 (3.931)	3.164 (3.687)	3.925 (3.925)	3.344 (3.262)	3.249 (3.094)

Sources: Office of Management and Budget, *Budget of the United States Government*, fiscal years 1977, 1982, 1987, 1992, 1996, 1997 (Washington, D.C.: GPO, 1976, 1981, 1986, 1991, 1995, and 1996).

Note: The upper figure represents budget authority in nominal dollars. Actual budget outlays differ only slightly from these amounts. The lower figure in parentheses represents budget authority in constant 1994 dollars. Figures for 1995 and 1996 are deflated using an estimate of 2.5 percent a year. Amounts are adjusted to 1994 dollars using implicit price deflators for federal government purchases of nondefense goods and services as calculated by the Bureau of Economic Analysis, Department of Commerce.

[a] FY 1996 estimates are taken from the Clinton administration's FY 1997 budget submitted to Congress in early 1996. The figures for 1995 reflect a sharp decrease in spending imposed by Congress in a mid 1995 budget rescission act. The FY 1996 estimates as they appear in the 1997 budget are close to the amounts the White House and Congress agreed to in late April 1996 for the FY 1996 budget that began the previous October.

[b] The EPA operating budget is the most meaningful figure. The other two major elements of the total EPA budget historically have been sewage treatment construction grants (now called water infrastructure) and Superfund allocations. Both are subtracted from the total to calculate the operating budget. Water infrastructure authority (not adjusted for inflation) totaled $7.7 billion in 1975, $3.4 billion in 1980, $2.4 billion in 1985, and $1.9 billion in 1990. Spending for 1995 was $2.9 billion and for 1996 is estimated to be $2.8 billion. Superfund authority in 1985 (there was no program in 1975 and 1980) was $0.69 billion, and $1.5 billion in 1990. Spending for Superfund was about $1.4 billion in 1995 and is estimated to be $1.3 billion for 1996. The total EPA budget was $6.4 billion for FY 1994, $5.7 billion for FY 1995 following a congressionally imposed rescission, and an estimated $6.5 billion for FY 1996. For consistency, all figures are taken from the president's budgets for the respective years.

Appendix 4   Employees in Selected Federal Agencies and Departments, 1980, 1990, 1995

Agency/department	1980	1990	1995 (Est.)
Environmental Protection Agency	13,867	16,013	18,900
excluding Superfund-related employees[a]	NA	12,685	15,176
Bureau of Land Management	9,655	8,753	7,699
Fish and Wildlife Service	7,672	7,124	6,823
National Park Service	13,934	17,781	19,503
Office of Surface Mining	1,014	1,145	988
Forest Service	40,606	40,991	34,849
Army Corps of Engineers	32,757	28,272	25,550

Sources: U.S. Senate Committee on Governmental Affairs, "Organization of Federal Executive Departments and Agencies," January 1, 1990, and earlier years. Figures for the Environmental Protection Agency are taken from U.S. Office of Personnel Management, Federal Civilian Workforce, Office of Management and Budget, Budget of the United States Government, fiscal years 1982, 1993, and 1996. All numbers for 1995, except EPA totals, are measured in workyears (full time, direct). Staff totals were generally lower by the end of 1995 as a result of budget cuts.

[a] The Superfund program was created only in late 1980.

Index